MASS POLITICS

MASS POLITICS

Studies in Political Sociology

EDITED BY

Erik Allardt AND *Stein Rokkan*

WITH A FOREWORD BY *Seymour M. Lipset*

The Free Press NEW YORK
Collier-Macmillan Limited LONDON

$\boxed{Fp}$

THE FREE PRESS
A Division of The Macmillan Company
866 Third Avenue, New York, New York 10022

COLLIER-MACMILLAN CANADA LTD., Toronto, Ontario

Library of Congress Catalog Card Number: 77-78608

printing number
1 2 3 4 5 6 7 8 9 10

CONTENTS

Contributors   vii

Foreword   ix
SEYMOUR MARTIN LIPSET

Preface   xi

Introduction: International Cooperation in Political Sociology   1
STEIN ROKKAN

I. *Cleavage Systems and Mass Politics*

1. Political Cleavages in "Developed" and "Emerging" Polities   23
   SEYMOUR MARTIN LIPSET

2. Types of Protest and Alienation   45
   ERIK ALLARDT

3. Depoliticization and Political Involvement: A Theoretical and
   Empirical Approach   64
   ULF HIMMELSTRAND

4. The Trend Toward Political Consensus: The Case of Norway   93
   ULF TORGERSEN

II. *Geography, Class, and Voting Behavior*

5. Aggregate Election Data and British Party Alignments,
   1885–1910   107
   JAMES CORNFORD

6. Geography, Social Contexts, and Voting Behavior in Wales, 1861–1951   117

   KEVIN R. COX

7. Aspects of Electoral Behavior in English Constituencies, 1832–1868   160

   T. J. NOSSITER

8. Regional Contrasts in Norwegian Politics   190

   STEIN ROKKAN and HENRY VALEN

III. *The Party and the Polity*

9. An Authoritarian Regime: Spain   251

   JUAN J. LINZ

10. Majority Rule and the Representative System of Government   284

   WARREN E. MILLER

11. The Hegemonic Party System in Poland   312

   JERZY J. WIATR

12. The Typology of Party Systems—Proposals for Improvement   322

   GIOVANNI SARTORI

Notes   353

Index   389

CONTRIBUTORS

ERIK ALLARDT, University of Helsinki

JAMES CORNFORD, University of Edinburgh

KEVIN R. COX, Ohio State University

ULF HIMMELSTRAND, Uppsala University

JUAN LINZ, Yale University

SEYMOUR M. LIPSET, Harvard University

WARREN E. MILLER, Inter-University Consortium for Political Research, Ann Arbor

T. J. NOSSITER, University of Leeds

STEIN ROKKAN, University of Bergen

GIOVANNI SARTORI, University of Florence

ULF TORGERSEN, University of Oslo

HENRY VALEN, University of Oslo

JERZY WIATR, Polish Academy of Sciences

FOREWORD

THE COMMITTEE on Political Sociology was created by the International Sociological Association in September 1959. Operating under the rules of the I.S.A. it was at first limited to 18 members, no more than two of whom might come from one country. The Committee took as its main task the bringing together of scholars from various countries to discuss their research. Thanks largely to funds made available by UNESCO and local host institutions, we have met about once every two years since our formation. These meetings have generally included many younger scholars not formally affiliated with the Committee.

The most evident output of the C.P.S. has been the various publications discussed in the Allardt-Rokkan preface. More important than these works, however, has been the emergence of a common theoretical and methodological perspective among a group with diverse cultural and intellectual backgrounds. The late Peter Nettl commented after attending our Cambridge meeting in 1965 that he was astonished at the parallelism of outlook among those associated with the Committee. It would be personally invidious to point to specific ways in which changes have occurred in the orientations and research procedures of our associates, but the evidence is plain for any one who has followed our work.

The Committee is about to enter a new stage. Although it has always included political scientists and sociologists in its ranks, its formal discipline identity was with sociology. Beginning in 1970, the Committee will be jointly affiliated with the International Sociological Association and with the International Political Science Association. The limitations on the size of membership will also be lifted in 1970. Hence we expect to expand our membership and areas of inquiry. This change, which the existing committee has worked for, may reduce its efficacy as a source of close cooperation and exchange among a limited number of people. Conversely, however, the gain resulting from the inclusion of many more scholars and from the possibility of treating on a variety of topics should outweigh this loss.

Given the change in operation of the C.P.S., Stein Rokkan and I decided that we should make way for a new set of officers. The two of us have served since 1959 as Secretary and President of the Committee. We look forward to continued collaboration with the new officers of the expanded committee who will be chosen in 1970.

I am especially glad that this volume, which includes samples of much of what we have done during the past ten years, will appear at this transition point in our work. I expect that the next ten years will be even more productive than the first decade.

Seymour Martin Lipset

Cambridge, Massachusetts

PREFACE

THIS VOLUME brings together papers and reports from four conferences organized under the auspices of the Committee on Political Sociology, a body of collaborating scholars from many countries initially sponsored by the International Sociological Association, and now also by the International Political Science Association: the first conference took place in Bergen in 1961, the second in Tampere in 1963, the third in Cambridge in 1964, and the fourth at Brussels in 1967.

The papers from two of these conferences were originally published in separate collections, but these are now unavailable: the volume edited by Stein Rokkan on the basis of the Conference on Political Participation held in Bergen in 1961[1] and the volume edited by Erik Allardt and Yrjö Littunen after the First International Conference on Comparative Political Sociology held in Tampere in 1963.[2] For a variety of reasons only one third of the chapters in the first volume and about one fourth of those in the second are reprinted in this volume. Several of the remaining chapters of the Bergen volume are currently printed in another collection issued by the Committee on Political Sociology: a volume by Stein Rokkan and his associates on *Citizens, Elections, Parties.*[3] In the majority of cases the papers originally presented in these two early collections have been thoroughly revised and updated for this new volume. This, of course, does not mean that they give detailed accounts of developments in the different countries up to the most recent elections or surveys: they are included in this collection because they exemplify new methodological approaches and original analytical perspectives rather than because of the recency of the development described.

The other papers have been added from later meetings organized by the Committee to add further depth and variety to the thematics of this joint volume. The important paper by Giovanni Sartori grew directly out of the discussions at Tampere and first served as a position paper at an administrative meeting of the Committee during the Sixth World Congress of Political Science in Geneva in September, 1964; it was later presented for fuller

Notes to the Preface are on page 353.

discussion at the Second International Conference at Cambridge in December, 1965, but will later, after still further revision, find a central place in Sartori's long-awaited treatise on *Parties and Party Systems*. We have incorporated it in this volume not only because of its powerful analysis of fundamental distinctions in the study of party systems but also because it marks an important phase in the development of our Committee.

The further papers by Cornford, Cox, and Nossiter were all originally presented at the sessions on Electoral Research organized by the Committee within the framework of the Seventh World Congress of Political Science at Brussels in 1967: these help to add further depth to the *historical* dimension of analysis brought out with such vigor in many of the contributions at the early conferences of the Committee. If there is one common core of consensus in the collective deliberations of the Committee it is on the crucial importance of developmental sequence for the structuring of contemporary mass politics: party systems and voter alignments must be studied diachronically and cannot be adequately understood through analyses at any one cross-section. This is the central thrust of the argument in another of the Committee's publications: the volume on *Party Systems and Voter Alignments* edited by Seymour Martin Lipset and Stein Rokkan.[4] The sessions on Electoral Research at the Brussels Congress served to develop this theme further; it is hoped that the papers on long-term time series presented in this collection will add further stimulus to the work in historical political sociology and possibly generate new organizational initiatives in the not too distant future.

To acquaint those still outside the Committee's circle with its work and its policies we have added as an introduction to this volume an extensive report on the first decade of cooperative efforts in the field of political sociology. We hope that this account will be of some help for those who are ready to organize similar work in other areas of the social sciences.

This volume would not have seen the light of day without the active help and encouragement by the members of the Committee, quite particularly the President, Seymour Martin Lipset. We are also very much indebted to a number of research institutions for material help in the realization of this project: the Institutes of Sociology in Bergen and Helsinki, the Michelsen Institute and the Center for Advanced Study in the Behavioral Sciences. We are also very grateful for the excellent technical help we have enjoyed at the Free Press.

ERIK ALLARDT
STEIN ROKKAN

Helsinki and Bergen

MASS
POLITICS

INTRODUCTION

INTERNATIONAL COOPERATION IN POLITICAL SOCIOLOGY:
Current Efforts and Future Possibilities

STEIN ROKKAN

The Background

The sociology of politics grew out of cross-national comparisons. The early pioneers were great travelers and correspondents: they acquired intimate knowledge of the social structures and the cultural conditions of several nation-states and they sifted and analyzed this information in an effort to account systematically for differences in the style and organization of politics and government. Tocqueville traveled in Britain and the United States and compared what he found in the two societies with that he knew about France. Marx and Engels were intimately familiar with conditions in Germany, in France and in England and established a vast network of correspondents to keep them informed of developments in each country. The pioneering students of party organizations and electioneering practices, Ostrogorski and Michels, were widely traveled and knew from inside many of the mass movements emerging in country after country with the extension of the suffrage to the lower classes. The great systematizer Max Weber did not travel quite so much but processed enormous quantities of documentary data in his efforts to develop a consistent conceptual framework for the comparison of societies and political systems. Detailed knowledge of variations in social structure, in cultural norms and in political arrangements was a *conditio sine qua non* for the development of any systematic theory. A sociology of politics could not possibly be built on data from one single national community, however large and however varied in its structure: to build up a systematic discipline, data

Notes to this section are on pp. 353–354.

from a variety of societies and polities would have to be assembled, evaluated and compared.

This belief in the need for systematic comparisons was a basic premise in the work of the earlier pioneers. It was one thing, however, to state this need and to be inspired by this ideal, quite another to carry out the detailed and painstaking empirical research required to give substance to these vast programs. In fact, the easy optimism of the early pioneers was soon to be countered by a wave of hard-headed empiricism: the "data-gathering revolution" in the social sciences,[1] the emphasis on rigorous accountability in the collection of information, the establishment of stricter criteria of representativity and clearer canons of inference, brought about a narrowing of perspectives, a concentration on the concrete, the local and the national, a rejection of universal comparisons. The social sciences had to establish their methodological status and to win recognition in the academies of each nation and in this very struggle had to abandon the initial comparative perspective: the result was a long succession of local and national studies, often at a high level of methodological sophistication, but with only incidental bearing on the central problems of a comparative sociology of politics. Through a curious process of Hegelian dialectics, this stage of "national empiricism" is gradually giving way to a third stage in the development of systematic political sociology: a return to the early concerns with universal comparisons but at a higher level of methodological rigor. The "data revolution" has brought forth in country after country vast bodies of data on social conditions, cultural configurations and political processes, and the possibilities of assembling and collating such data for evaluation and comparison have increased with the development of mechanical and electronic devices for the handling of information. The early pioneers had to pick their way in each country and assemble on their own such data as they needed. The contemporary political sociologist is in a very different position, at least when he wants to compare the economically and educationally developed countries of the world: there is not only a plethora of journalistic descriptions in each country but there is also a wealth of data from systematic counts and surveys, local studies, case studies, content analyses and other research undertakings. This does not mean that the data can be rigorously compared, but at least they are there and can be used in evaluating possibilities of stricter comparisons and in interpreting similarities and differences with other systems. At least when studying the developed countries the political sociologist can no longer "go it alone": he cannot make do with his own observations and his own perusal of documents but must cooperate with colleagues in many countries, get to know their studies and their data, cooperate with them in confrontations of findings and meet with them to discuss the implications of comparisons and the possibilities of stricter tests of similarities or differences between countries. Comparative research has become a collective enterprise, it is no longer a matter of individual information-gathering and synthesis.

The Organization of an International Network of Political Sociologists

The International Sociological Association has throughout its existence given high priority to the encouragement of comparative research. It pioneered a series of comparative studies of stratification and mobility and it set up a remarkably dynamic committee of experts from a wide range of countries to develop a basic study design, to encourage teams in each country to carry out the studies, and to assemble and evaluate the results as they became available.[2] The success of this enterprise encouraged the Association to create a series of further Research Committees during the 1950's: one for industrial sociology, another for urban sociology, a third for the sociology of the family, further ones for religion, education, leisure, mass media, medicine, psychiatry and law. Not all of these have proved as active and as successful as the one on stratification and mobility: much has depended, clearly, on the amount of international communication and exchange already established in the given field and on the availability of resources for joint action.

The Committee on Political Sociology was a latecomer within this program of the International Association. The establishment of such a committee was first proposed at the Fourth World Congress of Sociology in Stresa in September 1959: the sponsors of the proposal were Shmuel Eisenstadt, Morris Janowitz, Seymour Martin Lipset and Stein Rokkan. The Executive Committee of the ISA resolved to establish the proposed Committee in 1960 and the first newsletters to the members were circulated from the Secretariat at the Chr. Michelsen Institute in Bergen in the autumn of that year.

The initial membership of the Committee consisted of 17 sociologists from 13 countries:

TABLE 1-1

Country	Member	Institution
Argentina	Gino Germani	University of Buenos Aires (now at Harvard University)
Finland	Erik Allardt	University of Helsinki
France	Raymond Aron	Sorbonne
	Mattei Dogan	Centre d'Etudes Sociologiques, CNRS
German F. R.	Otto Stammer	Freie Universität, Berlin
Israel	S. N. Eisenstadt	Hebrew University
Italy	Giovanni Sartori	University of Florence
Norway	Stein Rokkan	Chr. Michelsen Institute, Bergen (now at the University of Bergen)
Poland	Julian Hochfeld	University of Warsaw and Department of Social Sciences, UNESCO, Paris
	Jerzy Wiatr	University of Cracow (now at the Polish Academy of Sciences, Warsaw)
Spain	Juan Linz	Columbia University (now at Yale)

TABLE 1–1 (*continued*)

Country	Member	Institution
Switzerland	Roger Girod	University of Geneva
United Kingdom	Mark Abrams	Research Services, Ltd., London
	R. T. McKenzie	London School of Economics and Political Science
United States	Morris Janowitz	University of Chicago
	S. M. Lipset	University of California, Berkeley (now at Harvard University)
Yugoslavia	R. Lukic	University of Belgrade

The ISA Executive designated as President of the new Committee Seymour Martin Lipset and as Secretary Stein Rokkan.

Early Action

It took some time before the Committee could establish a program of action of its own. Several of the members were already engaged in cooperative activities and were able to move ahead with joint enterprises under the general sponsorship of the Committee, but these activities did not form an explicit part of the Committee's own program. The first of these joint undertakings was the UNESCO Seminar on Citizen Participation in Social and Political Life, organized at the Chr. Michelsen Institute in Bergen in June 1961. A number of Committee members took part in the Seminar and presented papers there: some of these were published in a volume issued by the Chr. Michelsen Institute, others were printed separately.[3] The Seminar highlighted a number of convergencies in the methodology and the conceptual orientation of current research in the sociology of politics and set a pattern for further activities under the auspices of the Committee.

The Committee held its first administrative meeting in September 1961, on the occasion of the International Congress of Political Science. The discussion focused on action to be taken in the development of a distinct program of exchange, research and publication.

Three courses of action seemed to be open to the Committee in the initial phase of growth:

it could decide to limit itself to the organization, whether within the World Congresses or between them, of *symposia on chosen topics* in its field;

it could set itself up as a *sponsor* of joint enterprises of comparative research, whether initiated among its own members or from outside;

and it could finally aim at the development and execution of a *long-term program of its own*, possibly along the lines of the ISA Committee on Stratification and Mobility.

The first course of action was already open to the Committee, and the members agreed to concentrate on the organization of meetings and symposia before developing a distinct program of cross-national research under the Committee's own auspices.

The first task entrusted to the Committee was the organization of a series of sessions within the general programme set up for the Fifth World Congress of Sociology, to be held in Washington, D.C., in September 1962. The Committee decided to concentrate these sessions on two major themes in the sociology of politics: *Citizenship and Political Authority* and *The Social and Cultural Bases of Political Cleavage.*

The first set of sessions were part of the general discussion of the central theme of the Congress: The Sociology of Development. Papers were commissioned on three clusters of problems in the study of processes of political change under the impact of economic growth: the *entry of new groups* into the political arena of each national community, the *modernization of the governmental apparatus,* and the *strains toward monolithic ideologies* in the early phases of development.

The sessions were organized as follows:

The Entry of New Groups into Politics
    Chairman: RAYMOND ARON
    Rapporteur: ERWIN SCHEUCH

    Papers:

REINHARD BENDIX and STEIN ROKKAN	The extension of political citizenship to the lower classes: a comparative perspective.
PERRY HOWARD	New groups in Louisiana politics.
ROBERT T. MCKENZIE and ALLAN SILVER	Conservatism, industrialism and the working-class Tory.
V. A. SHTEYNBERG	The process of democratization in a Soviet Republic.

    Discussants:
        T. H. MARSHALL
        DANIEL LERNER
        WILLIAM KORNHAUSER
        JUAN LINZ
        Y. A. ZAMOSHKIN

Problems of Political Modernization in Developing Countries
    Chairman: S. N. EISENSTADT
    Rapporteur: ERIC DE DAMPIERRE

    Papers:

LUCIAN PYE	The processes of political modernization.
GEORGE BLANKSTEN	Revolution and modernization: Mexico vs. Cuba.

FRANCIS X. SUTTON   Fitness for self-government and de-
                                     velopment in Modern Africa.

Discussants:
A. BEKOMBO
REINHARD BENDIX
TORCUATO DITELLA
DWAINE MARVICK
K. BUSIA

Monolithic vs. Competitive Politics in the Early Phases of Growth
Chairman: SEYMOUR MARTIN LIPSET
Rapporteur: ERIK ALLARDT

Papers:
TORCUATO DITELLA   Monolithic ideologies in comparative
                                     party systems: the Latin American
                                     case.

MORRIS JANOWITZ   The military in the political develop-
                                     ment of New Nations: a comparative
                                     analysis.

ROBERT SCOTT   The political culture of Mexico.

Discussants:
RAYMOND ARON
DANIEL BELL
G. E. C. CATLIN
S. N. EISENSTADT
GINO GERMANI
JERZY WIATR

Reports on these discussions and a small selection of the papers have since
been printed in the *Transactions of the Fifth World Congress of Sociology.*[4]
    The second set of sessions was organized on a theme of the Committee's
own choice. A great number of Committee members had carried out studies of
the socioeconomic, cultural and ideological bases of the party systems and
the voter decisions in their own countries and were concerned to compare
their findings and to discuss their implications. The two sessions devoted to
this theme were organized as follows:

The Social and Cultural Bases of Political Cleavages: First session
Chairman: SEYMOUR MARTIN LIPSET
Rapporteur: JUAN LINZ

Papers:
ROBERT ALFORD   Class voting in the Anglo-American
                                     political systems.

| ERIK ALLARDT | Factors explaining variations in strength of political radicalism. |
| JERZY WIATR | Electoral systems and elements of pluralism in a one-party state: Poland. |

Discussants:
HEINZ EULAU
ROBERT T. MCKENZIE
ADAM ULAM

Second Session
  Chairman: ROBERT T. MCKENZIE acting for OTTO STAMMER
  Rapporteur: STEIN ROKKAN

Papers:

MARK ABRAMS	The political division of the British middle class.
MATTEI DOGAN	*Les bases sociales des partis politiques en France et en Italie.*
JUAN LINZ	The cleavage structure of W. German politics.

Discussants:
RENATE MAYNTZ
ALESSANDRO PIZZORNO
JULIUS GOULD
ALAIN TOURAINE

Brief reports on the discussions have appeared in the *Transactions* of the Congress. Most of the papers were subsequently reworked and expanded for printing in a publication prepared under the sponsorship of the Committee: a volume edited by the President and the Secretary on *Party Systems and Voter Alignments.*[5]

The First International Conference on Comparative Political Sociology: Tampere 1963

The World Congress at Washington also made it possible for the Committee to assemble for its second administrative meeting. Two topics dominated the discussion: the possibilities of developing a long-term program of joint activities and the organization of a first symposium under the explicit auspices of the Committee in 1963.

Raymond Aron developed a proposal for a series of coordinated studies of party structure and party systems and asked other members to contribute further plans for detailed comparative inquiries on specific points within this broad scheme. Several such papers were commissioned for further discussion at the meeting planned for 1963.

This International Conference on Comparative Political Sociology was made possible through a generous grant by UNESCO to the Finnish National Commission and through further support from the Finnish Government and the School of Social Sciences at Tampere. The Committee at its Washington meeting drew up the general lines of the program of the Conference and a detailed statement on the themes, papers and discussions was later prepared by Erik Allardt, Seymour Martin Lipset and Stein Rokkan.

The central theme of the Conference was to be: *Parties and party systems in the process of economic growth: changes in structure, functioning and political importance.*

It was proposed that the Conference be organized around four sets of papers within the general framework suggested by Aron:

1. Papers on the development of parties and party constellations in the *early phases of development.*
2. Papers on *differences within nations between economically advanced and economically underdeveloped areas:* differences in party organization, the character of membership, in the extent of party division in local politics, etc.
3. Papers on the role of *parties vs. interest organizations in decision-making process:* the extent of tie-ins between parties and interest organizations and the current tendencies toward a decline in partisanship and development of new channels of organizational influence on policy formation.
4. Papers on changes in national cleavage structure under the *impact of efforts of supranational organization*: mainly on changes in party alignments under the impact of the developing European institutions.

No specific papers could be commissioned in the fourth group: very little research has as yet been done on the impact of European integration on domestic party alignments.[6]

For the other three groups altogether twenty-two papers were commissioned and prepared. The original division in three groups proved difficult to maintain, however: several papers cut across the clusters of problems singled out in the original plan while others opened up new lines of inquiry and could not be fitted into the scheme devised by the planners. This is only to be expected in a field at the crossroads of so many disciplines and so many intellectual traditions.

Summaries of the papers and the discussions can be found in a report prepared for UNESCO by Yrjö Littunen and Erik Allardt.[7]

The Tampere Conference offered opportunities for detailed discussions of the future work of the Committee. Two sessions were devoted to the consideration of the alternatives before the Committee. Raymond Aron, regrettably unable to take part in the Conference in person, had prepared a planning paper calling for a series of comparative analysis of the social and cultural bases for different party systems. The Berlin group headed by Otto Stammer had also worked out plans for comparative studies: as set out by Kurt Shell, these plans centered on the collection and evaluation of dated data on the structures and functions of each party and called for the development of joint designs for such studies.

There was general agreement on the desirability of a long-term program, but no consensus on priorities within such a program. A variety of topics were suggested for future symposia and a number of concrete possibilities of comparative data-gathering and analyses were aired. It was clear to all the participants in the discussion that it would not be possible to draw up one single project of comparative research for all members to join in: there was no single, manageable set of problems they all were free and willing to study within a common framework in each of their countries. On this point the Committee on Political Sociology clearly would have to deviate from the pattern of operation established by the first of the ISA Committees, the one on Stratification and Mobility. Instead, the Committee would have to organize its work around a few teams of members and others concerned to advance their preferred lines of data-gathering and analysis.

The Second International Conference: Cambridge 1965

These divisions over program priorities were reflected in subsequent meetings during 1964 and 1965. In 1964, the Committee organized a first set of sessions on Electoral Research within the framework of the World Congress of Political Science in Geneva. These sessions helped to bring together sociologists, political scientists, and historians interested in quantitative analysis of electoral processes and proved very useful to the Committee in its attempts to establish contacts with graduate students and junior research workers interested in cooperating in comparative projects. The International Political Science Association has proved a useful ally in these efforts and has encouraged the organization of regular sessions of this type at its World Congresses: a second set of sessions on Electoral Research was in fact also organized at the Seventh Congress in Brussels in 1967.

The administrative meeting organized at Geneva in September 1964, drew up plans for a Second International Conference. This was organized by Philip Abrams at the University of Cambridge in December 1965, and focused on three themes:

The Contributions of the Classics
    Papers by
        S. M. LIPSET   on OSTROGORSKI
        J. LINZ   on MICHELS
        E. ALLARDT   on DURKHEIM
        PHILIP ABRAMS   on NEUMANN and DUVERGER
The Growth and Decline of the Mass Party
    Papers by
        J. CORNFORD and U. TORGERSEN   on early party developments
                                       in Britain and Norway;

R. T. McKENZIE and H. VALEN   on oligarchy vs. pluralism in
the organization of parties;
MARK ABRAMS and RICHARD ROSE   on changes in techniques of
mass participation.
The Development and Transformation of Party Systems
Papers by
JEAN BLONDEL
PETER NETTL
STEIN ROKKAN
GIOVANNI SARTORI
and ERWIN SCHEUCH

At an administrative meeting held after the Conference a number of proposals for a cooperative international research were set forward. One of these, by Richard Rose, later of the Department of Politics of the University of Strathclyde, was expanded into an application to the Nuffield Foundation in 1966: this was a proposal to assemble, for ten to fifteen competitive democracies, the available data on social, economic and cultural determinants of electoral behavior and to organize joint analysis sessions on such data. The project was offered some initial funding in 1967 and was discussed in some detail at the Third International Conference organized by the Committee: this took place in Berlin in January 1968.

Political Sociology at the Sixth World Congress

The Research Committee played a major role at the first "mass" congress of sociologists at the international level: the one at Evian on Lake Geneva in September 1966. The Committee did not only take a prominent part in the organization of the plenary Round Table on Cross-National Comparative Research[8]: it also staged the four public Committee sessions with heaviest attendance during the entire Congress. The President and the Secretary also took on heavy responsibility for the organization of a joint meeting of all the officers of Research Committee: the outcome of this meeting will be detailed in a separate section below.

The Committee organized its own sessions at Evian around four major themes of comparative political sociology:

I. *Approaches to the Comparative Politics*
This session was chaired by SHMUEL EISENSTADT and featured papers by
REINHARD BENDIX
STÉPHANE BERNARD
PETER NETTL
TALCOTT PARSONS
GÜNTHER ROTH
and ADAM PRZYWORSKI and JERZY WIATR
II. *Dimensions of Party Systems*
This session was chaired by SEYMOUR MARTIN LIPSET and focused on some

of the issues raised in the Introduction to the Committee volume on *Party Systems and Voter Alignments*.

There were papers by

> KOYA AZUMI
> R. EBBIGHAUSEN
> GITA IONESCU
> MORRIS JANOWITZ with KLAUS LIEPELT and DAVID SEGAL
> JUAN LINZ[9]

III. *Comparative Elite Studies*

This session was presided over by MATTEI DOGAN and offered an opportunity for the discussion of papers by:

> NERMIN ABADAN
> ERICH GRUNER
> DIETRICH HERZOG
> HARRY M. MAKLER
> DWAINE MARVICK
> and ULF TORGERSEN

IV. *Parties and Movements in Developing Nations*

This final session was organized by GINO GERMANI. There were papers by

> A. AKIWOWO
> DARIO CANTON
> SZYMON CHODAK
> OSCAR CORNBLIT *et al.*

Some of these papers have been published in the *Transactions* of the Congress, others have been revised and printed in scholarly journals and collections. The Committee did not find it necessary to arrange for a separate publication of its Congress papers: the administrative meeting held during the Congress decided that the Committee should concentrate its publication program on the papers and proceedings of the Conferences and working groups it could get under way *between* Congresses.

The Third International Conference: Berlin 1968

The administrative meeting held during the Sixth Congress also agreed on the themes of the Third International Conference on Comparative Political Sociology; this was to be held at University of Berlin in January 1968. The German member of the Committee, Otto Stammer, had generously offered to take charge of the organization of the Conference and had enlisted several members of the staff of the *Institut für politische Wissenschaft* in the preparatory work. The German group was able to find funds to cover some of the Conference costs from the Federal Ministry of Science, and the United States National Science Foundation contributed some travel funds. A grant was also made from the central funds of the International Sociological Association.

This proved to be the largest of the Conferences held under the auspices of the Committee: there were thirty participants from ten different countries. The Conference was organized around three themes:

I. THE SOCIOLOGY OF THE MASS PARTY

The sessions on this theme were organized by Dietrich Herzog and featured papers by

> Robert Alford
> Nils Diederich
> M. Dittberner
> Richard Hamilton
> Dietrich Herzog
> Juan Linz
> Peter Christian Ludz
> Armin Meyer
> Richard Rose
> Erwin Scheuch
> and Rudolf Wildenmann

II. STUDENT POLITICS

These sessions were organized by Seymour Martin Lipset and attracted a great deal of attention. A number of student leaders and younger research workers from the Free University took part in an animated discussion of the conditions triggering student revolts against academic, administrative and political authorities. Only two papers were presented, one by Lipset, the other by the Berlin political theorist Jürgen Fijalkowski, but a great variety of research undertakings were reported on in the discussion.

III. SOCIAL STRUCTURE, PARTY SYSTEMS AND VOTING

This section of the Conference offered a first opportunity for a detailed discussion of the design of the project launched under the auspices of the Committee by Richard Rose. One session was devoted to a critical discussion of the model for the discussion of party systems presented in the Introduction to *Party Systems and Voter Alignments*: Erik Allardt and Giovanni Sartori offered critiques of the new approach and Stein Rokkan presented an extended model for the analysis of variations among European party systems and discussed possibilities of linking up his model for the mobilization processes through the 1920's with a set of hypotheses about the "unfreezing" of party systems in the 1960's. In the subsequent sessions the comparative analysis project was presented and discussed in considerable detail. Richard Rose offered a check list of the variables to be considered in the analysis of the sociocultural influence on voting and presented a "model paper" for Britain. Philip Converse considered the priorities among such variables and a number of electoral experts presented examples of analytical procedures for their countries:

> Hans Daudt for the Netherlands
> Mattei Dogan for France

KLAUS LIEPELT and HENRY VALEN for Austria, Germany and
Norway
BO SÄRLVIK for Sweden

VITTORIO CAPECCHI was unfortunately unable to attend to present the
findings of his extensive analysis of the educational and the economic factors
accounting for the strength of the Left in Italy.[10]

The papers of the Berlin Conference were subsequently collected in an
offset volume for circulation by the Institut für politische Wissenschaft: Otto
Stammer, ed., *Party Systems, Party Organizations and the Politics of New
Masses.*[11]

The Future of the Committee: Reorganization and Reorientation

To the responsible officers of the International Sociological Association,
the mushrooming of Research Committees constituted a challenge and a
risk: there was general agreement on the need for decentralized activities
between the World Congress but there were concomitant dangers of fragmentation and duplication of efforts. The Association originally set up a
number of strict rules for the Committees:

no Committee should have more than *eighteen members*
no sociologists should be a member of *more than two* Committees
there should not be more than two members from *any one country* on one
Committee
each Committee should meet *at least once* between World Congress

The most active of the Research Committees soon found these rules too
rigid and decided to explore the possibilities of establishing an alternative
constitutional structure for the Association. At the initiative of the President
and Secretary for Political Sociology a meeting of all officers of Research
Committees was called immediately before the Sixth Congress at Evian:

COMMITTEE	COMMITTEE OFFICERS			
	President	Vice-President	Secretary	Other Members
Family	R. Hill		J. Mogey	
Knowledge	K. H. Wolf			
Law	R. Treves	A. Podgorecki	W. M. Evan	
Leisure	J. Dumazedier			
Mass. Comm.			E. Morin	
Medicine	G. Reader	E. Freidson		
Political	S. M. Lipset		S. Rokkan	
Psychiatric	A. Rose			
Religion			N. Birnbaum	H. Desroches
Science	R. K. Merton		J. Ben-David	
Stratification				R. Dahrendorf
Urban	R. Glass		J. Westergaard	
Work and Organization	W. H. Scott			

The discussion focused on questions of organizational structure: at first on the structure of the Research Committees themselves, later on the possibilities of a radical reorganization of the entire International Association.

This did not mean that functions and activities were lost sight of: on the contrary, the discussion of the great diversity of functions taken on by the Committees quite naturally led to a consideration of the limitations and rigidities imposed on them through the current structural regulations.

The "eighteen-member rule" laid down in the circular issued by the ISA Executive in February 1963, had clearly proved unworkable: all the Committees which had been able to mount programs of some size had been forced to get around this rule through a variety of *ad hoc* arrangements and the Committees which had so far found it difficult to develop their activities had felt constrained though the need to keep up a number of "paper" members for reasons of diplomatic representation. There was general agreement that cross-national research could not be effectively advanced through Committees of this structure: such research required a flexible setup for the establishment of efficient working groups for limited periods of time and would only be hampered through the insistence on the participation of entire Committees. A number of speakers pointed to the difficulties of reconciling within the current structure two very different functions: (*a*) the organization of specific projects of cross-national research, (*b*) the development of an international professional milieu within the given subfield of sociology.

To enable the Committees to fulfil their international research functions, it was generally agreed that the eighteen-member rule had to be dropped. What was required instead was a small nucleus of active organizers and a number of working parties set up to develop specific projects of collaboration, whether stock-taking jobs, secondary analyses or fresh data-gathering.

It proved much more difficult to reach agreement on the structural requirements of the *second* Committee function: the development of an international professional milieu in the given subfield. Seymour Martin Lipset proposed that the Statutes of the ISA be changed to allow the establishment of *sections*. This would gradually change the character of the Association and make it a body of individual professionals as well as a federation of regional and national associations and institutes. A clear majority of the Committee officers felt that this possibility ought to be explored. Not all Committees would be ready to transform themselves into membership sections within the next decade, but this was an option they ought to be given through a change in the Statutes of the Association. Only one Committee, the Committee on Urban Sociology, took issue with this proposal; it was argued that it would prove extremely difficult to reach agreement on membership criteria and that the development of such sections of individual members would threaten the cohesion of the Association and strengthen the interests of the developed countries to the detriment of the emerging nations. The representatives of the other Committees agreed that the continued trend toward further specialization endangered the unity of sociology but felt convinced that decentralization through the development of sections was the best strategy against potential splinter movements. It was known that at least one of the Committees had worked on plans for the establishment of a separate International Association within its field: such tendencies toward fission might be met through the establishment of open sections field by field and through the strengthening of the machinery for cross-field collaboration.

All officers agreed that no amount of organizational restructuring would help unless ways could be found to improve the finances of the Committees. The present level of UNESCO financing was pitifully inadequate but might be improved through regular arrangements for contracts for specific activities. The opening up of sections might help to finance secretarial activities through direct membership levies, but this clearly would not go very far. The officers urged the Association to step up negotiations with national and regional bodies to ensure support for the work of the Committees beyond the levels possible under the present arrangements with UNESCO.

After extensive discussion of these issues, the officers finally agreed to submit, with the reservation on the "sections" proposal already noted, the following Recommendations to the Council and the Executive of the ISA:

1. The Officers of the Research Committees at their meeting on September 3-4 at Evian gave detailed consideration to the regulations issued by the ISA Executive Committee on 18 January 1963 (A.I.S./1963/2) and came to the conclusion that the recommended maximal size of eighteen members is both too large and too small: too large for efficient functioning, too narrow to allow active encouragement of new developments in a range of countries.

2. These limitations emerged with great force from a review of the current and projected activities of the Research Committees, the emerging ones as well as the established. The Committees have taken on a wide range of functions: not just the organization of international conferences in their chosen fields, but also the encouragement and sponsorship of specific research projects, the advancement of training seminars in the methods appropriate in the given field, the fostering of new institutions (such as the Scientific Commission of the International Union of Family Organization by the Committee on Family Research), the organization and publication of journals, bibliographies and censuses of research in progress, and so forth.

3. In the face of such diversity, the meeting recognized that specific proposals could not cover every functional field and concentrated its attention on recommending an organizational framework that would be sufficiently flexible to ensure effective coordination. The meeting recognized the need to prepare its suggestions in such a way that future developments in international sociology could be accommodated within them.

4. The meeting foresaw that three distinct developmental stages had to be provided for in its proposals:

First, the appointment of new committees in emerging fields of international interests,

Second, the reorganization of existing committees to increase flexibility and efficiency,

Third, the recognition that some committees are ready to be transformed into sections: into organizationally delimited bodies of scholars specialized in distinct fields of the discipline. Membership in such sections would be both by individuals and by specialized organizations or centers. The meeting was of the opinion that while sections may prove divisive in individual membership organizations, in federations of organizations such as the ISA, individual membership by sections might serve a cohesive function and add to the strength of the total structure.

5. The meeting further emphasized the need to encourage active membership. Inactive members should be removed from the list of membership in research committees through the establishment of limited terms of office and periodic elections.

6. Concretely, the meeting agreed to propose these regulations:
  6.1. *The establishment of new committees.*
    6.11. The Executive Committee of the ISA may establish new committees whenever, in its judgment, there is a sufficient amount of international interest in the given field and there are possibilities of significant advances through cooperation.
    6.12. Once the decision has been reached to set up a new committee, the Executive Committee of the ISA shall appoint a President, a Secretary, and on occasion a Vice-President, and empower these officers to co-opt further members of a Board up to a total membership of no more than *six*.

  6.2. *The reorganization of existing committees.*
    6.21. For existing committees, the Executive Committee of the ISA shall at each Congress appoint a President, a Secretary, and on occasion a Vice-President, and empower these officers to co-opt additional members of a Board of not more than six members in all.
    6.22. The Board shall have the power to establish working groups for specific purposes, e.g. research projects, censuses of research, or regional activities.

  6.3. *The establishment of sections.*
    6.31. Once a Board believes that there is a broad enough international body of practitioners in its special field, it may present a request to the Executive Committee of the ISA for recognition as a *section*.
    6.32. Criteria for membership in a section shall be drawn up by the given Board and communicated for ratification to the ISA.
    6.33. The Board of a section shall be elected by its membership at each Congress but their appointment to office shall be subject to ratification by the Executive Committee of the ISA. The Boards of sections shall have the same powers as the corresponding units of Research Committees, but shall, in addition, be allowed to levy section dues on their membership.

7. It is recommended that the officers of the committees and the sections be given opportunities to meet regularly with each other, and that, to ensure efficient coordination of the activities of all these bodies, the ISA secretariat delegate one full-time staff member to carry out the necessary services for these several bodies.

8. One important function of this full-time staff member would be to receive and coordinate budget proposals from the Research Committees and the sections between Congresses. The ISA in turn should be prepared to allocate part of its resources to the activities of its Research Committees and sections and to sponsor applications for funds from other sources. Without such concerted efforts to

strengthen the financial basis of their work, the recommended changes in the structure of the Research Committee and the suggested move toward the establishment of membership sections will not bring about any of the hoped-for improvements in the machinery for international cooperation among sociologists.

The recommendations were subsequently presented to the ISA Council at its regular meeting during the Sixth World Congress. The Council unanimously agreed to adopt the proposed reorganization of the existing Research Committees (sect. 6.2. above) and asked the Executive Committee to set up a commission to study, in due time before the Seventh World Congress, a possible restructuring of the Association along the lines suggested and to draw up a proposal for a new set of Statutes.

The Constitutional Commission met in December 1966, and agreed to recommend a change in the Statutes and to propose a new set of regulations for the Committees. The Commission did not find it possible to recommend the establishment of *sections* but suggested that this question be made the subject of detailed discussion at the Seventh World Congress scheduled for September 1970. The Executive Committee at its meeting in Geneva in May 1969, adopted the recommendations of the Commission and agreed to submit the proposed Amendments to the Statutes for ratification by the Council of national representatives. A formal decision on the statutory changes cannot be taken before the plenary session of the Council in 1970.

Meanwhile the Research Committees have been asked to proceed to reorganize their structure and to establish Boards and working groups as required.

The Committee on Political Sociology has not yet established a firm structure of working groups. At the administrative meeting in Berlin in 1968 it was decided that the Committee should welcome the establishment of project groups as plans for cooperative research are developed and get funded. It was found impossible to set up strict rules for the admission of such working groups: the main criterion would be efficiency in bringing together research workers from more than a minimum of countries. As of July 1968 five working groups can be said have been definitely established under the Committee:

I. The group on *Comparative Electoral Behavior* under Richard Rose. This group met under the auspices of the Committee at Loch Lomond in July 1968.

II. The group on *Comparative Student Politics* under Seymour Martin Lipset. This group is generating a variety of projects and clearly will have its hands full in the years to come.

III. A group on *Comparative Nation-Building* under Shmuel Eisenstadt and Stein Rokkan. This group is barely under way but will cooperate with UNESCO and the International Social Science Council in developing specific projects.

IV. A working group on *Armed Forces and Society* under Morris Janowitz.

This group held major conferences in 1966 and 1967[12] and has drawn up plans for three projects:

1. Social recruitment, prestige and socialization of military professionals.
2. The performance of military regimes.
3. United Nations Peacekeeping activities.

Given the marked increase in the scope of the activities under this group, the President and the Secretary of the Committee have proposed a change in its status at the Seventh World Congress. If this proposal is accepted a separate Research Committee on Armed Forces and Society will be launched at the time of the Congress and will be given a distinct role in the program.

V. A fifth working group has been established under the leadership of Terry Clark. This is centered on *Comparative Community Studies* and has already applied for separate status under the Association; a decision on this question will be taken at the World Congress in 1970.[13]

A number of further working groups may get established during the next few years if funds can be found for the planning and execution of projects. A group on comparative political elites under Mattei Dogan and Dietrich Herzog will be established in the near future. Another group on fascism has been proposed by Gino Germani and may be launched in 1970. Given the very limited resources available to the Association and to the Research Committee, the only possible strategy is to encourage such local and national initiatives and to establish facilities for the linking up of opposite numbers once a project has been launched in one country. It has become more and more clear that the Committee cannot possibly organize research on its own; it must rely on active national teams and must concentrate its efforts on the establishment of channels for the multiplication of contacts and the linking of initiatives.

To this end, the Committee has become increasingly concerned to establish some regularity in its publications. Two of the early volumes of papers prepared under the auspices of the Committee have been out of print for some time: the volume edited by Stein Rokkan on the basis of the Bergen Conference in 1961 and the volume on the Tampere Conference in 1963 edited by Erik Allardt and Yrjö Littunen. To remedy this, a selection of papers from the two Conferences have been brought together in the present volume. To these have been added four closely related papers from later meetings held under the auspices of the Committee. This collection should not only help to make available a number of important papers frequently cited in the literature of comparative political sociology but will also help to make the work of the Committee and its many offshoots better known to younger sociologists and political orientists interested in joining the international network of cooperating scholars. Further publications under the Committee are in preparation or under discussion. It is hoped that in the future it will be possible for the Committee to command sufficient funds from royalties to defray the cost of preparing for regular publication selections of papers from all Conferences held under its auspices.[14]

Political sociology is a hybrid, a discipline without a clearcut identity. This is a weakness, but it is also a source of strength and innovation. Political sociologists are drawn in many different directions but they may still exert a unifying influence on the development of macro-approaches in sociology and of system approaches in political science.

Neither the Committee as a body nor its members as individual scholars can make progress toward the completion of the many tasks confronting the disciplines in isolation from other efforts in the social sciences. Political sociologists depend heavily on the data and the findings of other social scientists; they want to study the impact of social, economic and cultural conditions on political structures and processes and to get anywhere in such studies, whether within the single nation or across several nations, they will have to rely on the results and the insights reached by students of such conditions. The work of the Committee on Political Sociology must be fitted in to a broader framework of efforts to advance comparative cross-national research in the social sciences. UNESCO and the International Social Science Council have taken steps in recent years to launch a program of this kind. They have called attention to the need for an *international network of data archives* for comparative analysis,[15] and they have tried to encourage international discussions of *alternative methods of quantitative cross-national comparison.*[16] The ISA Committee on Political Sociology has taken an active role in these developments and will no doubt be given opportunities to add further contributions in the future. Among the concrete tasks to be tackled in these efforts to internationalize the social sciences, these are perhaps most likely to appeal to members of the Committee: the preparation of *Guides to Data for Comparative Research* and the development of a network of archives of basic data for analysis. One of the first initiatives sponsored by the Committees is already nearing fruition: the first volume of the *International Guide to Electoral Statistics* was published in 1969, and another volume is already in preparation. Similar volumes for data on parties, voluntary associations, interest groups and the mass media are under discussion and members of the Committee on Political Sociology will no doubt again play an important part in the implementation. Work on the preparation of inventories of the contents of important political polls and surveys country by country is also far advanced and will prove of great importance for some of the working groups under the Committee. Archives for ecological data by small administrative units such as communes have been established in a number of countries often on the basis of initiatives by members of the Committee, and will provide important resources for the organization of comparative research on processes of political development.[17] Whether the Committee will ever be able to move on from such catalogues of past data to the organization of fresh gathering is still an open question. At least at the current stage of flux and uncertainty it appears more important that the Committee serve as a forum for the exchange of research ideas and the confrontation of independently produced findings. Such exchanges and confrontations are bound to stimulate further work and may in a few cases lead to the organization of international research teams for specific tasks of comparative data-gathering and analysis.

What is essential at this stage is the maintenance of a framework for regular encounters of data-gatherers and theoreticians. Political sociology developed its methodological characteristics and its theoretical orientations during the quiet years of consolidation and deideologization from 1945 to 1965. These were years of solid methodological achievements, of unhurried attempts at theoretical systematization: the slow pace of political development, at least in the advanced countries of the West, made it possible and justifiable to proceed with such elaborate precision in the conduct of research and in the interpretation of findings. Most of the papers in this collection reflect the conditions of this period of political calm, the best, if not the most challenging, period in the history of the discipline. This does not mean that the papers are out of date: far from it. These papers from a calmer period in the development of reflection and research on processes of mass politics set a series of challenges for the new generation of scholars. How far could the current waves of protest and disruption have been predicted from the data for the earlier phases in the democratization process? How far are the explanatory models worked out for the period through the early 1960's still valid, and how can they be rebuilt and extended to be of any use in the next decade? How will it be possible to maintain the high level of professional craftsmanship reached in the earlier period in the conduct of research on the disturbing developments of the present? These questions will stay at the top of the agenda of the Committee on Political Sociology for years to come. The current waves of revolt and violence have set a great challenge to the discipline and may produce deep splits between the cooler observers and the more passionate activists, but the need for an effective machinery for international exchanges and confrontations will remain as great as ever. The years ahead may prove some of the richest and most productive in the life of our international Committee on Political Sociology.

ONE

Cleavage Systems and
Mass Politics

1
POLITICAL CLEAVAGES IN "DEVELOPED" AND "EMERGING" POLITIES

SEYMOUR MARTIN LIPSET

ALTHOUGH many discussions of the possibilities for democratic politics in the emerging nations of the "third world" are posed in terms of whether or not these nations can successfully absorb political models established in the developed countries, it is not really possible to speak of a "western" political system. A variety of factors have contributed to the vast array of party systems existing in the developed nations.[1] These include the different ways in which mass suffrage parties first emerged, the various conditions under which lower-class parties formed their basic ideologies, whether a polity derives its authority from historic legitimacy or from post-revolutionary populism, the extent to which different nations have resolved the tensions flowing from the key power cleavages common to the history of western industrial societies, such as the place of religion, universal suffrage, the distribution of national income and resources, and the variations in electoral systems. Clearly much of the existing differences reflect the institutionalization of past bases of opinion cleavage; once formalized in political parties these cleavages have survived the decline or disappearance of the original social conflicts which gave rise to party divisions. Parties, like all other

Reprinted from *Cleavages, Ideologies and Party Systems*, edited by Erik Allardt and Yrjö Littunen (Helsinki: The Westermarck Society, 1964). This paper was written as part of the program of the Research and Training Group on Comparative Development of the Institutes of International Studies and Industrial Relations of the University of California at Berkeley.

Notes to this chapter are on pp. 354–360.

institutions, tend to foster self-maintaining mechanisms. They necessarily seek bases of support and new issues to perpetuate themselves. And as Ostrogorski well noted, loyalty to parties is often comparable to identification with a religious denomination.[2] Each party retains a body of loyal adherents who see their party allegiance as an important part of their identity.

Variations in national party systems are linked to historical factors but this does not prevent the formation of broad generalizations about the development of party systems in democracies of the developed world for the purpose of comparison with the polities of the "third world." This paper will deal briefly with some of the varying historical conditions which have affected Western party systems, particularly in their formative periods, in order to point up some major differences in the bases of cleavage in the existing and emerging democracies.

The Development of Western Party Divisions

The modern political party is in large measure the resultant of the democratic electoral system. Before the establishment of the suffrage there were, of course, controversies about the policies of government. In the absolutist state, such disagreements were resolved at the level of the monarchy. As the upper social strata, such as the landed nobility, sought to restrict the powers of the king, parliaments of various kinds emerged and shared some of the state's power. In these parliaments, men with common interests, values, or backgrounds joined together into loose factions which some historians have called parties. These groups, however, had no common program, little or no organization, and little discipline. They did not seek to gain power through elections, but did so by breaking off support from other factions, or by winning the backing of the king. Where an electorate existed, it was usually quite small and under the control of the local nobility, as in Great Britain.

As forms of electoral democracy advanced in nineteenth-century Europe, a contest developed in most countries between two elements, generally labeled liberals and conservatives. The Liberals tended to favor democratic reforms and some further extension of the initially quite limited suffrage, to oppose an established church and religious control of education, and to attract to their ranks men who favored a variety of social and economic reforms. The Conservatives tended initially to oppose extension of the suffrage (though they changed to support it in some countries, seeing the possibility of drawing support from "deferential" lower strata who responded to *conservative* efforts to improve their circumstances on the basis of *noblesse oblige*), to support the privileges of the traditional church, and to have the backing of the more traditionalist elements in society such as the old dominant landed class and the nobility. Given a very restricted electorate, these parties lacked cohesion. Local notables controlled their constituencies regardless of how they voted in Parliament and despite the consequences of government policies. The two parties were subdivided into various factions and new combinations kept reforming within them.[3]

The introduction of the working class as a political force, however, soon changed this picture. As the workers organized into trade unions and legal or semi-legal political groupings, the upper classes gradually made concessions to the demand for adult suffrage. Sometimes these concessions were a result of the fear of revolution; at other times they were due to fulfillment of the democratic ideology of a victorious liberal group; and often they resulted from the efforts of one or another party to increase its base of electoral support. Conservatives felt they could rely on the votes of the religious and tradition-minded peasantry in many countries.[4]

The inauguration of manhood suffrage, however, whatever the reason for its adoption, changed the nature of politics. The techniques necessary to win votes in a mass electorate required, as Ostrogorski indicated, the creation of the party organization. Thus the first formal party organizations emerged in American cities. Tammany Hall and its brethren were necessary for the mobilization of the voters. Considerable funds were required for campaigning and professional politics developed in response to a felt need.

In Europe, as Max Weber pointed out, the Socialist parties were the first to successfully adapt to the new situation and create bureaucratic parties dominated by professional politicians.[5] These parties had an elaborate formal structure, dues-paying members, and branches which held regular meetings. They established party newspapers and created a network of groups tied to the party such as social clubs, women's associations, and youth organizations. They also formulated the concept of rigid party discipline, that the elected representatives were responsible to the party and must act according to party demands.

The emergence of the socialists as a political force within the context of manhood suffrage changed the structure of much of European politics. Mass based religious and agrarian parties developed in a number of countries, and tended to adopt many of the organizational procedures of the socialists. The Conservatives and Liberals were also forced to react to the logic of dealing with a mass electorate by adopting organizational procedures in many ways similar to those of the American or Socialist parties. On the whole, however, those parties which are lineal descendants of nineteenth-century liberal and conservative parties, led by notables, have never been as successful in creating large-scale membership parties as parties stemming from mass organizations such as the Marxist and religious ones.

Class Tensions and Politics in the Formative Period of Western Polities

The modern ideological conflicts affecting industrial society originated in the problem of locating old pre-industrial upper classes, the church, the mass citizenry, and the working class within the polity. In the United States the place of the old upper class, religion, and suffrage were determined before the working class became a significant force. Thus, the workers did not have to fight their way into the electorate; the right of universal suffrage existed before the class existed. In much of Europe, on the other hand, these issues remained to be fought out together. In Germany, Austria-Hungary, Sweden, and Belgium, universal suffrage for males was not granted until shortly before or during World War I.[6] The aristocracy and even the monarchy retained important areas of power and privilege. And the established church continued to fight to retain or regain ancient privileges. In the Latin countries, particularly France and Italy, the Catholic Church rejected—almost until World War I—any cooperation between Catholics and the state which had denied the Church privileges it demanded on moral grounds. The working class left, therefore, was often at war with the old right, with organized religion, and with the bourgeoisie.

The prolonged intensity of class conflict in many continental nations was due to the overlap of economic class conflict with "moral" issues of religion, aristocracy and status. Because moral issues involve basic concepts of right and wrong, they are much more likely than economic matters to result in civil war or at least sharp class cleavage. To work out compromises over wages and hours or tax policy is easy. To compromise with what is held to be heresy or a basic threat to the right way of life is much more difficult.

When accounting for the variations in class consciousness and class conflict among different industrial societies, we must examine the differences in the dynamics of their status systems. In general, the more rigid the status demarcation lines in a country, the more likely the emergence of explicit class-oriented parties. This variation in structure and its consequences may be illustrated by contrasting the political histories of the United States and Europe. Because the United States did not inherit a fixed pattern of distinct status groups from a feudal past, the development of working-class political consciousness required an act of intellectual imagination. American workers had to be "taught" that they were members of a common "class" and that they should cooperate against other classes. In Europe, however, workers were placed in a common class by the value system of the total society. In a real sense, workers absorbed a "consciousness of kind" from the social structure. Socialists did not have to teach them that they were in a different class; the society and the upper classes did it for them.

Nevertheless, there is considerable variation in the political behavior of different classes among European countries. The British have had a strong Labor party for nearly half a century, but it has always been less "radical" than most of the socialist parties on the continent. Never having had a Marxist phase and always friendly to religion, it adopted socialism as a goal only towards the end of World War I. Moreover, the Labor Party does not oppose the monarchy, and its leaders accept aristocratic and other honorific titles from the crown. The comparative moderation of British class conflict and politics has been related to several factors: its aristocracy assimilated the leaders of new classes, first the bourgeoisie and later labor; its period of rapid industrialization occurred before the emergence of socialist movements; and the rights of citizenship—universal male suffrage and the freedom to form unions—were granted prior to the formation of large-scale political and economic organizations by labor. Thus the emphasis on status classes in Britain facilitated the forming of class political groups which could operate from their beginning to obtain "more" for their members and supporters without having to fight for their place in the polity.

Some analysts of German politics have contended that the great stress on *Stände*, estate or status groupings, accounts for the close ties of status group and party support in pre-Hitler Germany. "Probably in no other country would the analysis of the social composition of party organizations show it to be so homogeneous as do the results of sociological studies of the electorate."[7] The great emphasis on status differences in Germany accounted for the large number of middle- and upper-class parties, each representing a distinct status group and having a distinct ideology.

Similarly, the cleavage between the Socialists and Communists within the German working class reflected status concerns. Communist support came disproportionately from the less skilled "*lumpen*" elements among the workers. To this lower stratum the German socialist movement exhibited a hostility not found elsewhere.[8]

The greater propensity for political extremism of both left and right in German history is related to the strong desire to preserve *Stände* rights. On the one hand, the Prussian aristocracy sought to retain their control over the major institutions of the polity, even to the extent of denying the middle classes access to most leading positions. Like the English aristocracy they sought to win the support of the masses against the bourgeoisie by passing many welfare measures. But unlike the English they did not allow workers' organizations and leaders to have full citizenship rights. From 1878 to 1891, the Socialists were outlawed as a party and Prussia, the main state of the Reich, did not have equal suffrage until Germany was defeated in World War I.[9] This refusal to allow the workers' leaders a share in political power forced the Socialist movement to maintain a revolutionary posture in its ideology.

German middle-class support of the Nazis may also be linked to the strong status emphasis in the culture. Studies of this phenomenon have assumed they were motivated by a desire to maintain their privileges, threatened by the universalistic values incorporated in the Weimar republic and fostered by the Social Democrats, and undermined by the economic catastrophe of the thirties. And the Nazis appealed strongly to this aspect of German middle-class values.

Note that in southern and western Germany, where status lines were less rigid, the conservative classes had been willing—even before World War I— to admit the workers' political movement into the body politic by enacting universal suffrage. And conversely, the workers' movement demonstrated that it did not want to destroy the state, but to be admitted to it. As contrasted with Prussia, the Socialist parties in these states developed a moderate and pragmatic ideology, gave considerable support to Bernstein revisionism, and even backed "bourgeois" cabinets. Conversely, the most reactionary elements in German society had their primary base in the most feudal region of the country, Prussia-beyond-the-Elbe. In the 1912 Reichstag, only four of the

Conservative party members were elected from non-Prussian constituencies, and of the fifty-one Prussian conservatives forty-five were aristocrats who came from these eastern regions characterized by the predominance of large landowners.[10]

The same regions heavily supported enemies of the Weimar Republic. The Conservatives, remaining hostile to the Republic, secured their strength basically in the same non-modern areas as they did before the war. And while the aristocratic supporters of conservatism, on the whole, did not join the Nazis before 1933, the various analyses of electoral statistics during the early thirties in Germany reveal that the support of Nazism came disproportionately from those strata least involved in modern industrial society. According to the Census of 1933, a large majority of Germans lived in rural areas or communities with less than 25,000 population, and these sections gave the Nazis far greater support than did the more urbanized and industrialized larger cities. Similarly, the larger the proportion of the labor force employed in small business establishments, the higher the Nazi vote. "The ideal-typical Nazi voter in 1932 was a middle-class self-employed Protestant who lived either on a farm or in a small community, and who had previously voted for a centrist or regionalist political party strongly opposed to the power and influence of big business and big labor."[11]

The presence in the same country of large working-class extremist movements (e.g., anarchist and Communist) and ultra-reactionary political tendencies among the middle and upper classes has been explained by many political analysts as a consequence of certain unique elements in social structure. Schumpeter, for instance, has argued that the persistence of the power and social influence of a nobility until quite late in the capitalist period in Britain and Germany, unlike the situation in the three Latin countries (France, Italy, and Spain), played an important role in reducing the working-classes' antagonism to the state. His thesis is that the aristocracy served as "protective strata" for the workers, helping to enact various social reforms, and thus giving them a sense that the state might be an effective instrument of social improvement. In countries where status differences remained strong, but which lacked a still powerful aristocracy that could foster a variant of anti-bourgeois "Tory socialism," as in the southern Latin nations, the workers became alienated from state and society as they developed conscious political and economic aims.[12]

A related hypothesis suggests that the peculiarly unstable politics of these nations has been related to the cultural factors which inhibited economic growth and led their business classes to follow the logic of pre-capitalist and mercantilist society. As Mario Einaudi once put it:

[I]n those countries where the development of the middle classes has been stunted and limited so that their twentieth century bourgeoisie bears a striking resemblance to the bourgeoisie of the days of Louis Phillipe, there will be a continuing strong assertion of political views which have disappeared in those countries in which "everybody" belongs to the middle class.[13]

The Latin business classes preserved far longer than their counterparts in northern Europe a semi-feudal stratum with strong emphasis on family property and stability. To a greater extent than in the more mature industrial nations, family-owned concerns continued to play a dominant economic role and to follow pre-capitalist emphases on maintaining intact the family fortune and status; this limited their willingness to take economic risks or to enter into competition. The politics of the bourgeoisie were oriented towards maintaining the stability of existing business, i.e., protecting marginal producers.[14]

Management in these countries retained ideologies of authority over workers that emerged during early industrialization, but which were inappropriate to class relations in a mature industrial society. They continued to expect particularistic loyalties from their employees, to think it proper to deny them the right to collective bargaining. In the relatively small family-owned businesses, the processes of bureaucratization and rationalization— stable definition of rights and duties, systematic universalistic ordering of authority relationships, publicity of decisions, division of labor with the appearance of personnel experts or specialists in labor relations, and the like—did not emerge. Any threat to limit the rights of the business classes either by state or trade-union action was bitterly resented and opposed on moral grounds as an effort to undermine the very fabric of the social order, private family property.

The working class in these "halfway" industrialized countries found it difficult to develop legitimate, stable trade-unions, and their political parties were unable to secure major structural improvements. As a result, the more politicized or class-conscious elements within the class continued to maintain the attitudes of alienation from the body politic characteristic of workers during the period of early rapid industrialization.[15] The emphasis within the society on status differentiation facilitated the emergence of strong class-conscious groupings. And to a much greater extent than elsewhere, these movements adhered to revolutionary anti-societal doctrines, first those of anarchosyndicalism and later of communism. This was the response of the Latin working class to being "in the society, but not of it."[16] And the revolutionary ideology of the working-class groups reinforced the fears and hostility of the middle and upper classes to any proposal that might give these groups increased access to power within industry or the state.

As in Germany, those sections of France and Italy resembling other industrialized capitalist nations (e.g., in having large-scale bureaucratized industries) were the ones in which the business classes demonstrated a greater willingness to accept trade-unionism as a legitimate and permanent part of the industrial system and in which anarcho-syndicalism was weakest. Before 1914 in France and Italy, the Socialists were most powerful in the areas of large industry; the anarcho-syndicalist unions were strongest in the areas where the particularistic values of small business were dominant. A similar pattern in Communist and Socialist support was found in France between World War I and World War II. The Communists in general inherited the centers of syndicalist strength. Since World War II, however, the Communists have replaced the Socialists as the dominant working-class party and are disproportionately strong within large industry, a point which I have elaborated elsewhere.[17]

Variations in the working-class politics of the three major Scandinavian nations have been accounted for by the social consequences of the historic timing and pace of early industrialization, factors alluded to here in discussing other countries. The Danish labor movement has always been among the most moderate in Europe; the Swedish one underwent a period of considerable radicalization in the first decade of this century; while the Norwegian leftists exhibited their most revolutionary phase during and shortly after World War I. The Norwegian historian Edvard Bull has developed the most widely accepted explanation for the variations among these countries:

> He focussed on one central "macro" variable: *the suddenness of the changes brought about by industrialization.* He developed a general proposition . . . : the *slower* the growth of industry and the more of its labour force that can be recruited from already established urban committees, the less leftist the reactions of the workers and the less radical their party; the *more sudden* the growth of industry and the more of its labour force has to be recruited from agriculture and fisheries, the more leftist the workers and the more revolutionary their party.[18]

The history of these nations would seem to validate Bull's proposition. Denmark experienced gradual economic and urban growth; Swedish industry developed very rapidly from 1900–1914; while Norway had the highest rate of growth of all three between 1905 and 1920, and experienced the greatest radicalization. Further evidence may be adduced from many other nations to show that periods of large-scale dislocations of population occasioned by rapid industrialization and urbanization have often led to the expression of deep class conflict.[19] However, such tensions usually decline, as Friedrich Engels put it, wherever "the transition to large-scale industry is more or less completed . . . . [and] the conditions in which the proletariat is placed become stable."[20]

The factors underlying the emergence of a moderate labor and socialist movement in Belgium before World War I further illustrate the syndrome determining the variations in intensity of European politics.[21] Belgium and Britain were the first two nations to industrialize in Europe; hence the worst of the social strains occasioned by rapid industrialization and urbanization occurred before the rise of the modern labor movement. As Val Lorwin puts it, in explaining the differences between the Belgian and the French and German movements: "Belgium's industrialization began earlier, and it became more urbanized than France."[22] Such factors, however, do not explain why the Belgian conservatives showed a propensity to compromise with labor militancy, thereby preventing the development of the vicious circle appearing elsewhere, in which the aggressiveness of one class occasioned similar reactions from the other. In his comprehensive comparative study of European socialism, Carl Landauer suggests that the conflict was moderate in

Belgium because historically it had been less of a *Standestaat* than any of its neighbors, and that industrialization and capitalism flourished where feudal values had been weakest:

> Belgium is a business country, with a weak feudal tradition—much weaker than in Germany, France, or Britain ... In Belgium, fewer upper-class people than elsewhere think that they owe it to their pride to resist the aspiration of the under-privileged ... [E]ven less than in Britain or France and certainly less than in Germany was exploitation motivated by the idea that the humble must be kept in their places; in Belgium, more than anywhere else, was the desire to force the worker to accept small pay, long hours, and otherwise unfavourable conditions of employ-ment a pure dollar-and-cent proposition. The argument that a prolonged strike, even if it leads to defeat of the workers, would be extremely hard on business had more of an echo and met with weaker counteracting tendencies in bourgeoisie and government than in several other industrial countries.[23]

The situation in Finland illustrates yet another dimension in the variables which affected the political process in pre-World War I Europe. In some ways, the factors which affected the ideological tensions in the Finnish party system resemble those operative in some of the emerging nations of the contem-porary "third world" which are discussed below. In the nineteenth century, Finland was a Duchy under the Czar of Russia. A small Swedish-speaking minority was heavily represented among the privileged classes. Universal suffrage and trade-union rights did not exist. A Socialist party, formed at the end of the nineteenth century, appealed to the class discontents of the newly emerging working-class and the much larger farm tenant population. In effect, however, as was to occur later in many colonial countries of Asia and Africa, the Socialists addressed themselves to the interrelated issues of class, cultural and linguistic needs, democratic rights, and national independence. This meant that, though the movement necessarily had to be revolutionary in its ideology, it could successfully appeal for support to strata far removed from the relatively small working class. And the winning of universal suffrage in 1906 (following on the General Strike throughout the Czarist empire in 1905), resulted in the Socialists securing 40 per cent of the seats in Parliament, more than such parties won in any other nation in Europe. Their parliamentary support grew to 43 per cent in 1910 and 45 per cent in 1913. In 1916, the Socialists still fighting the class, cultural, and national battle, actually secured a parliamentary majority. The subsequent strength of Finnish Com-munism in large measure stems from the commitment to radical Marxian concepts fostered by the Finnish Socialists during the period of Czarist rule.[24]

Although the political expression of class tensions was to change con-siderably between the pre-1914 and the post-1945 situations, structural hypotheses similar to those used to account for variations in the earlier period would seem to be relevant for the latter. The values and behavior patterns inherent in the status system, the pace of industrial development and urbaniza-tion, the pattern of management-labor relations linked to the bureaucratization of enterprises, and the degree to which diverse sources of political cleavage overlap, all remain as key sources of variation in class politics.[25]

Typologies of Western Party Systems

It is impossible to locate the determinants of the varying party systems in the democratic developed nations by a simple analytic framework. The number of parties which exist is a function of the complexity and intensity of the social cleavages which seek political representation, and of the nature of the electoral system. Nations such as France, where the strains derivative from conflicts over the place of the church, the relations among diverse status groups, economic interest struggles, and orientations toward political authority have persisted for over a century, have a complex cleavage structure difficult to resolve within a two- or three-party system. Conversely, it is difficult to see any reason why the divisions among Swedes, Norwegians, or Danes could not be handled within a two-party system, other than the fact that their system of proportional representation encourages the continuation of a number of separate parties with historic roots. This issue of the number of parties has been discussed in detail elsewhere and need not be repeated here.[26]

Similarly, the factors which affect the degree of ideological intensity, and the extent to which the democratic rules of the game are accepted by all important actors in the polity, are also too complex to be dealt with in detail in a discussion such as this. To a considerable extent, the intensity of cleavage and the character of attitudes toward the democratic system are associated with the severity of strains experienced by significant strata. Those strata which experience the tensions of rapid industrialization and urbanization tend to be much more radical than those inured to being part of an urban industrial society; nations in which democratic rights (full suffrage and trade-unions) for all have been institutionalized prior to the emergence of a mass working class tend to have more moderate and legitimate opposition politics than those in which suffrage or trade-union rights were resisted deep into the present century; those nations which are relatively well-to-do and which have a high per capita income reveal less significant strain between the classes and consequently less ideological politics; those countries which allocated citizenship rights to new classes, the bourgeoisie and later the workers, without requiring revolutionary overthrow of the symbolic source of traditional authority, the monarchy, also tend as a group to have more stable and less virulent politics than others.

If we turn now to an examination of the sources of party cleavage in contemporary democratic countries, it is clear that the role relationships which have proved most likely to generate stable lines of party support are largely aspects of stratification, as between higher and lower orders in status, income and power, or aspects of cultural differences, as between specific groups which vary widely in their views of the nature and values of the good society. The prototype of the first cleavage is class parties, of the second, religious parties. Differences rooted in stratification are likely to be most preponderant in economically developed stable polities in which much domestic political controversy may be described as the "politics of collective bargaining," a fight over the division of the total economic pie, over the extent of the welfare and planning state, and the like. Cultural or deeply rooted value conflicts are much more characteristic of the politics of developing countries with unstable polities. In such nations, in addition to conflicts rooted in class controversy, there is a division based on the differences in outlook related to institutions which originated in the pre-modern era, and to those which foster or are endemic to social and economic development. Examples of cultural conflicts include the confrontation of those who seek to maintain the traditional position of historic religion, the status and privileges of higher social strata such as the nobility, or social relationships within families and other institutions which represent a way of life characteristic of a relatively static rural society, against those who seek to change these patterns of behaviour toward a more universalistic social system. And many of the variables associated with positions in a *kulturkampf* are not linked to stratification, but to involvement in traditional or modern institutions and to generational experiences. For example, poor religious peasants may be conservatives, while well-to-do young professionals may be radical; the young and better educated may oppose the older and the less educated. Sex, too, may provide a basis for diversity where cultural issues are significant. The woman's role in most societies requires her to be more involved in religious institutions and less in modern economic ones, to be less educated on the average than men, and consequently to be more supportive of traditionalist parties than of modernizing ones.

If we consider the developed countries first, it is clear that in all of them there is a correlation between the generally accepted degree of leftism or conservatism of political parties and their support in terms of stratification variables. The more liberal or left-wing parties are disproportionately supported by those with low income, by workers, by poorer farmers, by the less educated, by members of religious groups defined as low status and by those invidiously identified in racial or ethnic terms.[27]

This pattern comes out most clearly in the five predominantly English-speaking democracies. In all of these countries the factors of lower-class status, Catholic religion, and recent immigrant background are associated with support for the Democrats or with Labor and Liberal politics. The size of the correlation varies among these nations and other factors enter as well, but it seems clear that stratification as rooted in occupation, income, religion and ethnicity, perceived as status defining variables, accounts for much of the variation in party support.[28]

The picture is somewhat more complicated in the various multi-party systems of continental Europe. In some of them, cleavages rooted in the pre-industrial society of the late eighteenth and much of the nineteenth century continue to influence the nature of party division. Perhaps the most striking example of this is the name of the party which represents the views of the

Dutch orthodox Calvinists, the Anti-Revolutionary party. The Revolution which this party is against is the French Revolution of 1789.

In spite of the variations among them, these countries do have a number of elements in common. First, the historic cleavage between liberal and conservative, or religious parties, which arose in the nineteenth century before the rise of socialism as a significant force, has been maintained in most of them. In Scandinavia this cleavage is represented by the continuation of strong Liberal and Conservative parties, in Catholic Europe and Germany by the existence of Christian Democratic parties and liberal or other anti-clerical bourgeois parties. All of these countries have strong working-class oriented parties. Here, however, they differ greatly as to whether there is one dominant Social-Democratic party opposed by a small Communist party, or whether there is a mass Communist party which is larger than the Socialists, as in France, Italy, and Finland. A number of these countries, particularly the Scandinavian, also have agrarian or peasant parties.

In spite of the great diversity in the continental multi-party systems, class and religion would seem to be the preponderant sources of difference among the parties. Lower income and status are associated with voting for the working-class oriented parties. On the whole, where there are large Communist and Socialist parties, the latter derive greater support from the more skilled and better educated workers, although there are important exceptions, particularly in the case of Finland. Communists also tend to draw support among the socially uprooted in rapidly changing areas, and among those who have been unemployed in the past. The religious parties draw their backing from the centers of religious strength, regardless of class, and thus gain support from both rich and poor, although they are disproportionately strong among farm people and among women. The urban religious manual workers seem to have many of the same economic interests and policy orientations as the Social Democratic workers, and they usually adhere to Christian trade-unions which work closely with socialist unions. The Liberal parties on the whole, parts of Scandinavia excepted, tend to be relatively small, 7–15 per cent, and to be based on the anti-clerical bourgeois and professional groups. Scandinavian Liberalism is somewhat different. It resembles the Old English Liberal party and though backed by irreligious bourgeois and professional groups, also draws support from the quite religious Scandinavian equivalents of the English non-conformists, who oppose the Conservatives as supporters of the traditional Lutheran Church Establishment. The Scandinavian Conservatives, in turn, seem to be the party of the more well-to-do, both rural and urban, and of those involved in the traditional church.

As mentioned above, the pluralistic party structure of Scandinavia appears to be due largely to a system of proportional representation which helps preserve diverse non-socialist parties. These could just as easily represent their constituents within the more conservative party of a two-party system, were the system to facilitate this. The picture is somewhat different in Catholic and Southern Europe. There, a lower level of economic development, failure to develop legitimate political institutions, and the superimposition of the various conflicts of the nineteenth century over the status of the old privileged classes, the position of the church, and the economic class struggle, have resulted in a cleavage structure which cannot be readily fitted into a broad two-party coalition structure. Broadly speaking, the "normal" division in these nations is a three-party one consisting of a large multi-class Catholic party, based disproportionately on the rural population, opposed by a large Socialist party rooted in the urban working class, with a much smaller middle-class oriented anti-clerical Liberal party, which holds the balance of power. This pattern is found in Belgium, Luxembourg, Germany, and Austria. In Holland, the problem is complicated further by the presence of three conflicting religions, each of which has its own party, but if the religious parties are considered as one force, the Dutch pattern resembles the above four nations. In France and Italy, however, the strains are clearly more intense, and both the clerical and anti-clerical sectors of the nation have been greatly divided, so that each has a six-party structure.

The Parties of the Third World

In the first flush of democratic enthusiasm after World War II, many believed that the newly independent states of Africa and Asia, as well as the "old" nations of Latin America would support democratic polities strongly resembling those of Western Europe and the overseas English-speaking democracies. Currently, with the emergence of military and one-party regimes in many of these nations, an almost total pessimism concerning the democratic potential of these countries has replaced the early hopes. Scholars, journalists, and politicians from the stable democracies now conclude that they erred in anticipating democratic institutions in nations whose economy and culture were not yet ready to sustain the tensions of party conflict. Although it is much too early to make definitive conclusions about the polities of the "third" world, it is clear that neither extreme of optimism or pessimism concerning the future of democracy is justified. In fact, outside of the Communist nations, the majority of the peoples of Asia and South America live in democratic polities, in which the press is free and opposition parties operate openly within and outside of parliament. Only in Africa can one say that one-party and military regimes predominate, and even there the most populous state, Nigeria, with a population not much smaller than that of all the other former French and English Sub-Saharan African ruled states combined, has more than one party as do the Congo, Uganda, Somalia, and Sierra Leone.[29] In South America, opposition politics exist in Argentina, Chile, Uruguay, Brazil, Venezuela, Colombia, Bolivia, Mexico, and Peru. Some of these nations would hardly be considered models of democratic polities, particularly since the military has intervened in the recent past to limit the possible results of elections in Peru, Argentina and Brazil. But it is clear that the vast majority of South Americans do not live under dictatorships. The same conclusion holds for non-Communist Asia. There, states containing the bulk of the population are clearly democratic—India, Ceylon, Israel, Lebanon, Turkey, Malaysia, the Philippines, and Japan. Unfortunately, the same can not be said for Burma, and the remaining Moslem states of the Asian continent, but these, while possessing many votes in the United Nations, contain considerably fewer people than the democratic Asian polities.

The considerably greater cultural and historical diversity of the "third" world than that of the developed nations complicates the search for a single set of factors associated with the propensity to sustain competitive party systems among the less developed nations. Evidence for the association between level of economic development, literacy, and the existence of a stable democratic polity is one step in this search.[30] More fruitful, perhaps, in the long run, are the attempts to locate, and even measure, the consequences for political development of varying rates of social mobilization, of the process by which diverse strata are "integrated" into the larger modernizing sector of society.[31] Such changes, however, may result in a breakdown in national solidarity and early efforts at a democratic polity, since rapid social change, with its consequent high rates of mobility, initially results in considerable social displacement, incongruencies of status, and makes for considerable discontent with existing institutions. Many have pointed out that such processes produce people who are "disposable," available for new, often authoritarian or irresponsible political movements. As European history well demonstrates, modernization involves "a succession of what might be called crises of access . . . . . [periods involving] a social and political adjustment to new claimants to power, prestige, status."[32] Thus the very tendencies which enhance the conditions necessary to sustain an integrated and democratic polity may destroy embryonic efforts at such developments. Gino Germani has, in fact, suggested that a condition for increasing the probability that the processes of mobilization and modernization will support rather than undermine the chances for democracy "consists in the possibility of these social processes occurring in successive stages. In other words a nation requires sufficient time and opportunity between stages of mobilization [incorporation of additional segments of the population] to integrate each given stratum. This is what occurred in the West both with respect to political integration and other forms of participation."[33] The hypotheses which have been proposed concerning variations in extent or rate of economic development, modernization, and mobilization, or integration of populations, and the special characteristics of the polities of the "third" world are yet to be tested by rigorous comparative research.[34] There are few efforts to differentiate among the types of party systems which exist within these countries, as has been attempted for the western democracies. To do so at this early stage of the comparative studies of these nations would be rash, considering the scarcity of intensive studies of their political parties.[35] The following part of this discussion will seek to bring out some additional patterns of political cleavage and of political development in the emerging nations, without attempting to arrive at any definitive statement on the factors involved and their interrelationships.

The political pattern of Latin America is closer to those of Europe than are those in the other areas of the developing world. Nineteenth- and early twentieth-century party conflicts resemble those of Latin Europe, from which Latin America derived much of its culture, religion, and earlier political ideologies.[36] The first cleavages were largely between pro-clerical, rural upper-class dominated Conservative parties and anti-clerical, bourgeois controlled Liberal parties. Socialist and anarcho-syndicalist movements arose on the working-class left before World War I in a number of countries, but secured relatively little strength.[37] During the inter-war period, and since World War II, however, political movements have emerged which are comparable to many in Africa and Asia. These movements express various forms of nationalist, anti-imperialist doctrine, oppose foreign domination of the economy, and seek through state control or ownership of the economy to foster rapid economic development. The ideological content of such parties has varied greatly. Between the late 1930's and the end of World War II, some, such as the movements of Perón in Argentina, Vargas in Brazil, and the M.N.R. in Bolivia, took over many of the trappings of Fascism or Nazism. They differed, however, from European fascist movements in being genuinely based on the working-class or poor rural population. Since the war each adopted conventional left-wing ideologies, and has cooperated with various Communist movements (Trotskyist in Bolivia, orthodox in the other two). Others have been aligned continually with the Communists, explicitly or in a fellow-traveling fashion. Communist parties have been particularly strong in Chile and Brazil. Still other movements such as the Aprismo of Haya de la Torre in Peru, the Acción Democrática of Rómulo Betancourt in Venezuela, and the National Liberation Movement of José Figueres in Costa Rica, may best be described as nationalist Social Democrats, comparable to the Indian Congress party. Most recently, Christian Democratic parties have arisen in many of the Latin American nations, as in Chile and Venezuela, tending on the whole to be relatively leftist supporters of land reform, economic planning, and of state intervention to foster economic development. And the various leftist movements have drawn considerable support from university students and intellectuals, a social category which includes a considerable segment of the university graduates in underdeveloped states.[38] The Castro movement is an example of a successful effort based initially on youthful members of the modernizing elites.[39]

A special pattern of "elitist" leftism which has appeared in many parts of the "third" world is military support for radical social reforms, i.e., for economic development and modernization. The military in a number of countries such as Turkey, parts of the Arab world, and some in South and South-East Asia have helped place leftist politicians or officers in power. The basis for military "leftism" would seem to be the concern of many officers to enhance national strength and prestige in a world in which these positions are seemingly a function of the degree of national economic development. While there is no necessary common interest shared by the nationalist leftist elites and the military in underdeveloped areas, governments based on such alliances have operated in many countries such as Burma, Pakistan, Egypt, Mexico, and Indonesia. In countries dominated by traditional minded oligarchies, the military has often represented the only well-educated, western oriented, nationalist group favorable to modernization and capable of taking and holding power.[40] On the other hand, in various parts of Latin America mass-based reformist politicians have been overthrown by military juntas with links to traditional oligarchies. It should be noted, moreover, that the pessimistic conclusions of Morris Janowitz concerning the inability of the military leaders to successfully engender the processes necessary for economic and social development *when they take power in their own right* would seem to be warranted.[41]

The predominant pattern of political cleavage characteristic of those emerging nations which retain some version of democratic politics is a division between modernizing and traditionalist elements, which overlaps with, and to a considerable extent supersedes, the traditional left-right stratification-based conflict of the older and more stable polities. To an important degree, socialism and communism are strong because they are symbolically associated with the ideology of independence, rapid economic development, social modernization, and ultimate equality. Capitalism is perceived as being linked to foreign influences, traditionalism, and slow growth. Hence leftist movements secure considerable backing from the better educated who favor modernization. In many nations in Asia, Latin America, and Africa, the better educated who are also more well-to-do are often the most significant backers of the more aggressively leftist tendencies.[42] There is ample evidence for this in the support of conservative parties by both impoverished religious peasants and the landholding elite, while backing for the left is drawn heavily from the better educated members of the urban white-collar and professional classes, with the urban proletariat and peasants only entering as a force on the left after the modernizing elite groups have turned to them for support.[43] This pattern is brought out clearly in Japan. That nation, though more developed than any other country outside of Europe or the English-speaking countries, has resembled the other emerging nations in its politics. In the 1920's, leftist groups were most successful among the students and other sections of the elite.[44] Public opinion surveys completed in recent years reveal that since World War II, education is more highly correlated than class position with modernism and leftism. University students and graduates disproportionately back variants of socialism. On the other hand, less educated poor peasants and workers who are still tied to traditional social structures (e.g. workers in the highly paternalistic, numerous small factories and shops), support the conservative party.[45]

Tendencies similar to those in pre- and post-war Japan are evident in many other less developed emerging nations among university students and occupations requiring higher levels of education.[46] Data from surveys of student attitudes in various countries reveal a tendency for those taking the more modern fields to be more leftist, while fields which train for the older professions, such as law, tend to be more traditionalistic. The findings from the student surveys are not as clear-cut as one might anticipate, in part, perhaps, because of the differential utilization of graduates from different fields. Those studying "modern" subjects are more likely to find lucrative employment after graduation than are those who major in the more classic humanistic disciplines. The discrepancy between the needs of developing societies for technicians and scientists and the disproportionate preference of students in some of them for the more traditional fields of law and the humanities, often means that the latter are found disproportionately in the ranks of the "educated unemployed," or underpaid.[47] The inappropriateness of their university study for a subsequent career may thus contribute to the enhanced leftism of the university educated. In the larger sense, however, it may be argued, as John Kautsky has done, that the university trained, as a class, constitute a socially dislocated group in underdeveloped states:

> The key role of the intellectuals in the politics of underdeveloped countries is largely due to their paradoxical position of being a product of modernization before modernization has reached or become widespread in their own country. In the universities, the intellectuals absorb the professional knowledge and skills needed by an industrial civilization; they become students of the humanities and social sciences qualified to teach in universities, and they become lawyers and doctors, administrators and journalists, and increasingly also scientists and engineers. When they return from the universities, whether abroad or not, the intellectuals find, all too often for their taste, that in their societies their newly acquired skills and knowledge are out of place . . . .
>
> During their studies, the intellectuals are likely to acquire more than new knowledge. They also absorb the values of an industrial civilization . . . . On their return, they find that these values, too, are inappropriate to the old society . . . .
>
> To the extent, then, that a native intellectual has substituted for the values of his traditional society those of an industrial one—a process which need by no means be complete in each case—he becomes an alien, a displaced person, in his own society. What could be more natural for him than to want to change that society to accord with his new needs and values, in short, to industrialize and modernize it?[48]

The politics of developing nations must be seen, then, in the words of the Japanese sociologist Joji Watanuki, as reflecting the cleavages of "cultural politics." By this is meant "the politics where the cleavage caused by differences in value systems have more effect on the nature of political conflict than the cleavages based on economic or status factors." While Watanuki does not deny "the working of economic interest or status interest," he does argue that in countries oriented toward rapid development such as Japan, one finds "the relative dominance of cultural or value cleavages, the superimposition of this cleavage on others . . . ."[49] Similarly, two students of comparative Latin American politics, Kalman Silvert and Frank Bonilla, have postulated the hypothesis that in the early phases of modernization or development of the "third" world, one should expect to find "very broad ideological alliances—all those in the innovating camp opposed to all those aligned against it."[50] As Watanuki notes, "cultural politics" are usually presented in *weltanschau-*

ungen, total ideological terms, in which all issues are "easily universalized as aspects of general principles, and are reacted to in highly emotional terms . . . . sometimes suggesting the existence of a more deep-rooted basis for interest conflicts than actually exists."

It should be stressed that none of those who have commented on the politics of developing nations as reflecting value cleavages suggest the absence of class-linked political conflict.[51] They all note that *mass-based* leftist parties necessarily draw support from the workers or impoverished sectors of the rural population. Even the Castro movement, which originated among University graduates and drew much of its support from relatively well-to-do middle- and upper-class advocates of modernization was able to secure heavy backing from the poor and uneducated after seizing power.[52]

These differences within the emerging nations, of course, have a parallel in the past, and to some extent the present, of the developed countries in the form of the *kulturkampf* over the place of religion, discussed earlier. Many of the educated, well-to-do bourgeois groups backed leftist anti-clerical parties in nineteenth century Europe. The Liberal parties stem from this source. The modern scientific professions, such as medicine, tended to back the left, while the professions rooted in tradition, such as the law, were heavily conservative. Teachers and professors in secular schools tended to be on the anti-clerical left. And even today these differences influence political behavior in nations such as France and Italy. Leftist parties, while primarily based on the lower strata, do draw some support from the historically anti-clerical (modernized) sectors of the middle class.[53]

But if the modernizing-traditional division contributes strongly to the support which the radical left draws from privileged elite groups in the emerging nations, it is also true that the conditions under which democratic politics are attempted in these states produce heavy support for the left from the lower strata as well, thus making it very difficult for conservative parties to find significant bases of support. This is, in part, because the large mass of the population in such nations live in impoverished conditions. But poverty alone does not breed discontent. In much of nineteenth century Europe, conservative parties led by members of the privileged classes, secured heavy backing from the urban and rural poor. They had the weight of traditional legitimacy and identification with the summits of an established status system on their side. Poor persons, like all others, had been reared to accept the old institutional order. Generally speaking, people are unlikely to change opinions or allegiances which they have held for a long time, Hence leftist groups, modernizing factions, and others favoring large scale change in the nineteenth century, found that significant segments of the lower strata refused to support them. And conservatives, such as Bismarck and Disraeli, consciously sought to keep such support for conservative politics by following a deliberate policy of *noblesse oblige,* of favoring various welfare measures which would enhance the circumstances under which the poorer classes lived. Under such conditions, leftist or innovating parties became serious contenders for political office only after a long and arduous struggle for support.

Those mechanisms inherent in all stratified societies which serve to secure lower-class acceptance of the values of the system thus help to balance the relative strength of conservative and leftist parties. The leftists appeal to the interests of the more numerous lower strata, but the "deference vote" provides the conservatives with a large segment of the votes of the under-privileged. (Japan, Thailand, Iran, and Ethopia, monarchies which were never colonies, seemingly still retain a large deferential population.)

In many of the new and emerging nations, however, the assumption that the lower classes enter the polity still showing deference to traditional institutions, values, and privileged classes does not hold.[54] Many high status positions are associated with hated foreign imperialisms, and with social institutions regarded by large sections of the modernizing elites as contributing to the perpetuation of national inferiority. Thus conservative parties backed by businessmen and/or the rural elite face the difficulty that they do not have the weight of traditional legitimacy or a significant "deference vote" on their side.[55] Leftism and nationalism are often identified with the nation and the modernizing elite. The lower strata, in so far as they are politically conscious, may be won to the side of a radical leftism identified with symbols of national independence.

In such a contest, in which one large section of the elite supports leftist ideological goals, and in which the large majority of the population lives in poverty, the chances are small for the existence of conservative parties representing the traditional elite, or stressing the need for gradual rather than rapid change, as viable electoral alternatives. But as I have noted elsewhere:

> Although conservative groups in most new nations are deprived of the link with historic national values which they have in old states, there is at least one traditional institution with which they may identify and whose popular strength they may seek to employ: religion. The leftist national revolutionaries, in their desire to remake their society, often perceive traditional religion as one of the great obstacles; attitudes and values which are dysfunctional to efforts to modernize various institutions are usually associated with ancient religious beliefs and habits. And the efforts by the leaders of new states to challenge these beliefs and habits serve to bring them into conflict with the religious authorities.
>
> A look at the politics of contemporary new nations indicates that in many of them religion has formed the basis for conservative parties. . . .[56]

In Latin America, for example, religion-linked traditionalism furnishes a large base of support for conservative parties, particularly in relatively unchanging rural areas.[57] In a number of Moslem countries such as Turkey, Morocco, Pakistan, Malaysia, and Indonesia, religious-linked parties have been able to win considerable support when contesting elections. Similarly, in India, the Hindu religion currently provides a base around which a conservative party, the Jana Sangh, may win support. With very few exceptions, however, religious linked traditionalism does not appear strong enough to provide conservative opposition parties with a sufficient mass appeal to form a significant alternative to modernizing radical movements.

Conclusions

The differences in the bases of party and ideological cleavage between the developed and underdeveloped world are of more than academic interest to the student of comparative politics. Clearly, the fact that a considerable section of the embryonic (student) and actual elites of the "third world" adhere to seemingly extreme versions of leftist ideologies, while the bulk of the university-educated elites of the developed countries espouse conservative or moderate reform doctrines, makes mutual understanding and communication difficult. In developed western societies, parties are increasingly agencies of "collective bargaining," representing the conflicting demands of diverse groups and strata. In the emerging nations, parties, particularly left-wing or nationalist ones, and in many of these nations all parties fit this category, see themselves not as representatives of particular groups which seek "more" of the total national pie, but rather as the bearers of programs and ideologies most likely to successfully mobilize society for a massive effort at economic development. In the developed nations, Marxism and Socialism are primarily the ideologies of the less well-to-do, and are naturally opposed by the privileged sectors. In the underdeveloped nations these ideologies serve as slogans to legitimate the efforts of certain elite strata to become or remain the ruling class, and to exact sacrifice from and impose hardships upon the poor for the sake of achieving the attributes of an economically powerful state.[58]

It should be clear that efforts to generalize about the relation of given statuses and roles to political behavior, seen in terms of the historic left and right categories set in nineteenth- and twentieth-century Europe, prove inadequate when applied to most of the "third" world of Asia, Africa, and Latin America. This paper has attempted to introduce a discussion of comparative party systems by pointing out some of the historical and other factors which account for diversity in bases of political cleavages. A comprehensive theory of politics which accounts for the behaviour of all organizations calling themselves "parties," whether operating in the stable democracies, new states, or totalitarian regimes, is yet to be developed.[59] Meanwhile, we may conclude that exporting models of party systems and ideologies which "work" in advanced industrialized areas to less advantaged ones is not only bad social science, but much worse, may result in disastrous politics, as when ideologies of the western underprivileged serve to justify intensive exploitation by the new ruling classes of the capital-accumulating Communist and "third" worlds. Rather than serving to articulate and justify the demands of the working class, as in the western industrialized nations, the ideologies of the left as often applied by elites in the developing countries serve to mask a basic cleavage of interest between rulers and ruled, and to legitimate the political myth of a monolithic identity of elites and masses. In nineteenth- and twentieth-century Europe, Marxism and socialism have called to the attention of the workers and the poor generally that there is a basic continuing conflict over economic returns between themselves and those who control the means of production; in the contemporary Communist and the authoritarian states of the underdeveloped world, Marxism and socialism are defined to mean that the interests of both the controllers of the economy and the impoverished workers and peasantry are the same.[60] In nineteenth-century Europe, Marxism justified a struggle for the creation of free trade-unions which exercised the right to strike, and for the rights of free speech, press, assembly, and competitive representative parties; in the contemporary Communist and many "third world" countries, Marxism is used by the ruling strata to supply arguments denying all of these rights.

This use of Marxism as the ideology of the aspiring elites of pre-industrial societies was, of course, never anticipated by Marx and Engels. Rather, they conceived of socialist doctrines as helping to fulfill the aspirations of the working class in highly developed capitalist industrial societies. Socialist movements would only come to power in nations which had reached as high a level of industrialization as was possible under capitalism.[61] Socialism was never seen as an approach to rapid industrialization, rather it involved an effort to create a society with a higher state of genuine freedom in which workers and others would be liberated from the authoritarian restrictions inherent in bureaucratic industrial organization. Hence, the very concept of socialism as used by Marx and Engels had no meaning except in a post-capitalist, post-industrial society in which machines liberated humanity from tedious work. Many Marxists, such as Rosa Luxemburg and Julian Martov, consequently, were horrified by the Bolshevik seizure of power in Russia in 1917, because they believed that it was sociologically premature, that it could only result in a severe distortion of socialism and hold back efforts to create the type of society, libertarian socialism, envisaged by Marx and Engels. And, in fact, Marxism and socialism in the Soviet Union have served to justify the most intensive form of exploitation of human labor to secure "surplus value" for capital accumulation that the ruling class of any industrializing nation has ever attempted since the beginning of the Industrial Revolution.

The possibilities for the establishment and institutionalization of democratic procedures in the nations which now lack them are in large part dependent on the emergence of political cleavages rooted in interest and value differences that do not give any one political force predominant strength. A doctrine which denies sociological validity and political legitimacy to such differences once the party of the "workers" or the "people" is in power is a major obstacle to the formation of democratic polities. In this respect, Marxist doctrines as postulated in the underdeveloped world are profoundly different from those which justified the eighteenth- and nineteenth-century bourgeois revolutions in the West. The latter, though also organized under universalistic ideologies of equality which served to justify the aspirations of the new bourgeois elite to replace the old aristocratic one, nevertheless assumed the validity of interest differences, that the poor and the rich, the landed and the commercial classes, had separate interests. Democracy requires a recognition of the legitimacy of conflict and interest representation among the diverse groups in society, regardless of the form of economic organization. The breakdown of communication between western and non-western socialists is a result of the tremendous gap which exists between them given the considerably divergent connotations and social functions which socialism has taken on in different parts of the world. The possibility that socialism may regain in the "third" and Communist worlds its historic role as the ideology sustaining the lower strata's aspirations for more power, status, and income, can not be ruled out. Endemic in its definition is an anti-elitist, egalitarian view of society. And as recent events in some of the Communist countries suggest, some do use the ideology of socialism to justify efforts to bring the accepted social myth and reality into harmony, much as in the United States, men have used the American Creed to press for social equality.[62] The very concepts around which the members of the "new class" defend their right to exclusive possession of power may yet serve to undermine the autocratic systems which they have erected.

TYPES OF PROTESTS AND ALIENATION

ERIK ALLARDT

A Basic Paradigm

TWO BASIC characteristics of any collectivity, society or group, are (1) that there is some degree of pressure toward uniformity, and (2) that there is some division of labor in the collectivity. Throughout the history of sociology a core theoretical problem has been to analyze how these two variables explain solidarity and conflict. It has, however, been pointed out that there are considerable difficulties in combining theories about pressure toward uniformity with theories about division of labor.[1] The same has been said about solidarity and conflict. It has been contended that there are difficulties in developing theories that would render good explanations of both solidarity and conflict.[2] A major point of departure here is that this position is too pessimistic.

There is, to be sure, also conflicting empirical evidence regarding in particular the relationship between pressure toward uniformity and solidarity and conflict. Notably within the field of small group research it has often been shown how group solidarity and pressure toward uniformity are positively related. On the other hand, political sociologists dealing with large-scale and highly industrialized societies have been apt to stress an almost contrary result: they have emphasized crisscrossing cleavages and the variety of interests as conditions for solidarity.[3]

The results stressing the positive relationship between pressure toward uniformity and solidarity have been summarized and formalized in Festinger's theory on social comparison processes. In small group research the term solidarity is usually replaced by the term cohesion, and cohesion is usually

---

Notes to this chapter are on pp. 360–361.

defined in terms of the attraction of members to the group. The wish to stay or leave the group is often used as a good indicator of this attraction. In any case, Festinger's central notion is that the individual strives to compare himself with others as regards his abilities and opinions; therefore, situations in which comparisons are possible are attracitve. The more uniform the individuals are in their opinions and abilities, the greater the possibility of comparisons. Consequently, the more uniformity in the group, the more attractive it is, and, accordingly, when cohesion is defined through attraction, the more uniformity, the more cohesion in a social group.[4]

An examination of the empirical evidence Festinger cites for his theory indicates that he almost always refers to groups which are very undifferentiated. His theory is not verified in groups requiring a high degree of differentiation such as work groups with a clearcut division of labor. On the contrary, dissimilarity seems to increase cohesion.[5] This is even more evident when studying total and differentiated societies; in them strong pressures toward uniformity seems to make for a decrease in solidarity.

Of course, cohesion in small groups and solidarity in large-scale societies have to be defined somewhat differently. The wish to stay or leave the group, used as an indicator for attraction is hardly useful in the study of solidarity in total society. A citizen cannot withdraw from his society in the same way as he can withdraw from a small group or from an association. Solidarity with a society may be defined through the concept of legitimacy. Solidarity prevails as long as people believe that the sociopolitical system of their society is legitimate, or do not act in order to change the system through noninstitutionalized means. If solidarity is defined in this fashion then, of course, legitimacy conflicts are simply the obverse of solidarity. The relation between solidarity and conflicts other than those related to legitimacy has to be studied empirically, and such conflicts may very well increase solidarity.

In any case, it seems that Festinger has derived his propositions by excluding one important form of social processes, namely the phenomenon Homans labels *human exchange*. The activities or goods exchanged can, of course, be of many kinds. One can exchange love, respect, protection, as well as material goods. Of crucial importance here are such exchange relations in which the goods or items exchanged are of many different kinds. There are certainly many situations in which individuals explicitly or implicitly compare themselves with dissimilar persons. In such a situation the question phrased by Homans is apt to arise: does a person's reward for the exchange correspond to his costs and investments? Two persons may help each other precisely because they have strongly dissimilar skills. In such a situation the comparison may focus on the question of whether the Other is able to give as much in exchange as Person gives, but the point is that their behavior may be far from similar or uniform.[6] It is only as regards the result, the ability to match the other in rewards given, that they have to be similar. The exchange of dissimilar items is what we usually call a situation of division of labor. In fact, it seems as if Festinger's main proposition can be applied only to situations where there is no or very little exchange or differentiation within the group. We may, therefore, reformulate Festinger's proposition: when there is a small amount of exchange or division of labor, then the more the uniformity, the stronger the cohesion (or solidarity).

When exchange relations dominate and rewards are principally obtained through exchange of dissimilar activities and goods, the situation is entirely different. Apparently what really counts in an exchange relation is the outcome, the fact that the rewards exchanged between two persons roughly correspond to each other. The question is, what other kinds of behavior are likely to be educed from groups in which there is a great amount of exchange. Since the outcome is what counts, and this can be obtained through an exchange of dissimilar things and goods, some tolerance towards dissimilarity has to be developed. Exchange relations can hardly persist unless people are willing to grant each other great personal freedom. Tolerance toward deviance has to be developed. Therefore, pressures toward uniformity are likely to result in a decrease in the attraction to a situation or a group. We may conclude: the greater the amount of exchange in a group and the less the uniformity, the stronger the cohesion (or solidarity).

The distinction between solidarity through uniformity and solidarity through variety leads to Emile Durkheim's theory on the division of labor.[7] Durkheim's basic idea is that mechanical solidarity rests on what he calls likeness, whereas organic solidarity is due to the division of labor. A society with mechanical solidarity is held together mainly through normative coercion; deviants are severely punished, and penal, repressive law is important. With increasing division of labor, restitutive law regulating relations of exchange comes into the foreground. The necessity to punish deviants diminishes, and as a consequence, men are willing to grant each other more freedom and equality.

Durkheim's analysis can be seen as resting on the association between three major variables: the degree of solidarity, the degree of pressure towards uniformity and the degree of division of labor. A slight reformulation of Durkheim is, of course, needed. Instead of saying, as Durkheim does, that mechanical solidarity is based on similarity and organic solidarity is based on the division of labour, we can assume that they are two separate variables that can be used together to explain both types of solidarity. Durkheim speaks of uniformity or similarity, but the crucial variable seems to be pressure towards uniformity, as is also indicated by his stress on penal law and punishments. The two independent variables, pressure toward uniformity and division of labor, are theoretical terms and need, of course, a specification when used in empirical studies. As a preliminary and theoretical definition, we may state that division of labor is defined in terms of the number of dissimilar items for exchange: the higher the number of items for exchange, the greater the division of labor. Strong pressure towards uniformity may be defined as having two necessary conditions: (*a*) existing social norms are specific and related to strong sanctions that are applied with great consistency, and (*b*) there are no or very few conflicts between norms.

Durkheim not only speaks of the conditions that increase solidarity, but he also mentions situations in which solidarity is weak or lacking. It is perhaps significant for Durkheim that he deals with exceptions as if they were mainly exceptions to organic solidarity. As long as one treats pressure toward uniformity and division of labor as separate variables, it is logical to think of two types of low or weak solidarity, as indicated in the typology of Fig. 2–1.

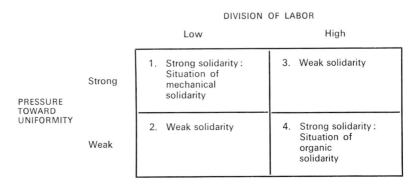

Figure 2–1

Since solidarity is defined as the observe of legitimacy conflicts, we may reformulate the contents of the table in the following propositions:

1. The less developed the division of labor and the stronger the pressure toward uniformity, the less the likelihood of legitimacy conflicts.
2. The less developed the division of labor and the weaker the pressure toward uniformity, the greater the likelihood of legitimacy conflicts.
3. The more developed the division of labor and the stronger the pressure toward uniformity, the greater the likelihood of legitimacy conflicts.
4. The more developed the division of labor and the weaker the pressure toward uniformity, the less the likelihood of legitimacy conflicts.

By presenting this crude typology it is by no means maintained that the degree of solidarity is influenced only by our independent variables. The expansion of the typology can be pursued in two major ways. One alternative is to introduce new variables into the typology, whereby the number of major types would greatly increase. Another way is to show that a number of specific situations are really special cases of the major types. Partly due to the empirical data available, the latter alternative is here judged to be more fruitful.

The two independent variables are of course not very easy to operationalize. In studies of total societies the degree of division of labor can be measured in a number of ways. For gross comparisons between societies and communities, the degree of industrialization or indices of economic development may be taken as sufficiently precise indicators.

Pressure toward uniformity is a more difficult concept to operationalize, and it seems also difficult to find an overall indicator useful in different social systems.[8] It is however, possible to indicate types of societies and communities in which the pressure toward uniformity may be regarded as particularly strong:

1. Tribal societies. Many, if not all, tribal societies can be characterized as having strictly enforced and severe social norms. There are nonspecialized and diffuse pressures directed toward large, rather vaguely defined categories of ascriptive statuses.[9]

2. Brutal dictatorships.

3. Societies strongly stratified according social class or social rank. In such societies lower-class individuals are hindered by class barriers to indulge in social exchange. Inequalities of an economic nature, thus, are subsumed under factors, which make for a strong pressure toward uniformity. Economic factors relate to our model in two ways. The overall economic output is one aspect of the division of labor whereas the distributive process is accounted for the pressure toward uniformity.

4. Societies in which constraints are particularly imposed on groups that earlier have had a good social position. There may be, for instance, middle-class groups that are loosing in status and rank because other groups have become more powerful. They are likely to experience constraints imposed on them, and they will tend to develop aggressive political attitudes. As in case 3, however, the pressure toward uniformity is strong only for a part of the population.

An Empirical Illustration: Industrial and Backwoods Radicalism

Finnish political life, and particularly the strength of the Communist movement in Finland, provides a good case for testing the propositions derived from the basic paradigm. The Finnish Communist movement has had a rather heavy mass support. During the period after World War II, the Communists have received between 20.0 and 23.5 per cent of the total vote in national elections. Furthermore the Finnish working-class vote has been almost equally divided between the Communists and the Social Democrats.

Although caution is necessary, it is reasonable to say that the Communist vote during the 1950's more strongly indicated a protest against the system than the votes for other parties. It is, however, hardly so that the Finnish Communist voters regard the whole Finnish sociopolitical system as illegitimate.[10] Rather they are apt to accept the political system, whereas some aspects of the economic system as well as certain administrative bodies are foci of protest and discontent. Survey studies indicate that a much greater proportion of the Communists than, for instance, the Social Democrats express discontent of an economic nature. Likewise, a greater proportion of the Communists than of the Social Democratic voters also express discontent with the administrative leadership in Finnish society, with the courts, with the Armed Forces, and so forth. This is particularly true for 1950's, the period covered by the findings used in this paper.[11] In any case, the Communist vote reflects a certain type of protest, which may be formulated so that the Communist voters more often than others are questioning the legitimacy of the Finnish sociopolitical system. When studying conditions of societal solidarity it is therefore fruitful to study the social sources of Communist support and to compare it with the support of other parties having a large lower-class vote.

In popular Finnish political terminology, Communist support is often described in terms that are clearly related to one of our independent variables, namely to division of labor. The communism in the southern and western parts of Finland is often labeled *Industrial Communism* whereas the communism in the north and the east is known as *Backwoods Communism.*" As the names suggest, Industrial Communism exists in regions which are industrialized and developed whereas Backwoods Communism is concentrated in less developed, rural regions. The problem here is to specify under what conditions Industrial and Backwoods Communism are strong. Their background is, of course, different as regards the degree of industrialization in the communities in which these two forms of communism exist but the question is whether there are also other differences.

The social background of these two kinds of radicalism have been studied both through survey studies and ecological research. The data units in the ecological analyses have been the 550 communes in the country. The communes, both the rural and urban ones, are the smallest administrative units in Finland, and they have a certain amount of self-government. Primarily because of the long historical tradition of local self-government, the communes form natural areas in the sense that the communes are important for people's identification of themselves. The communes are also the territorial units for which statistical data are easiest to obtain. In the analyses a file of seventy quantitative ecological variables referring to conditions in communes in the 1950's were used as a starting point.[12]

In analyzing the data, factor analysis was used primarily, although the correlation matrices reveal from the start many consistent patterns. Because a single factor analysis is not always interesting—it gives just a structure or a conceptual framework—the communes were divided into five groups. For each of the five groups of communes (called communities) in what follows, separate correlational and factor analyses were done. Of the five groups, three represented the more developed regions in southern and western Finland, and two the more backward regions in northern and eastern Finland:

Groups of developed communities
1. Cities and towns
2. Rural communities with a Swedish speaking population along the Southern and Western Coast of Finland
3. Rural communities in Southern and Western Finland

Groups of less developed communities
4. Rural communes in Eastern Finland
5. Rural communes in Northern Finland

The intention of making separate analyses for the five different regions was to inquire whether Communist voting strength is explained by different or similar background factors in different regions.[13]

The comparisons of the findings for the five regions reveal some quite consistent patterns. The background factors of Communist strength in the three developed regions are very similar, and so are the background factors in the two less developed regions. However, the background factors in Communist strength in the developed regions, on the one hand, and in the backward regions, on the other, seem to be very different.

In the developed regions the Communists are strong in communities in which

1. *political traditions* are strong. This is indicated mainly by the fact that the Communists tend to get a heavy vote in those communities in which there are stable voting patterns.

2. *economic change* is comparatively slow. This is mainly indicated by the fact that communities with a strong Communist support have had a rather slow rise in per capita income during the 1950's. These communities were modernized and industrialized in an earlier period.

3. *social security* is comparatively high. The communities with a heavy Communist vote are those in which there is no or very little unemployment and those in which the standard of housing is high.

4. *migration both into and out of the communities is small.* The communities with a heavy Communist vote have a very stable population.

The foregoing are the conditions prevailing in those developed communities in which the Communists get a heavy vote. When focusing on the background factors of Communist strength in the less developed and more backward communities, a very different pattern is revealed. In the more backward communities the Communist vote is heavy when:

1. *traditional values* such as the religious ones, have recently declined in importance.

2. *economic change is rapid.* In the backward regions the Communists are strong in those communities which have had a considerable rise in the per capita income during the 1950's and weak in those communities in which the income rise has been small.

3. *social insecurity prevails.* Communities with Communist strength are those in which unemployment has been common. It may be said that unemployment in Finland is mainly a question of agrarian underemployment. Unemployment strikes those who are both small farmers and lumberjacks.

4. *migration is heavy.* There is a heavy migration both into and out of the communities.

While Communist strength in the developed regions, the so-called Industrial Communism, seems to be associated with background factors reflecting stability, almost the contrary is true for Backwoods Communism. It is strong under conditions of instability and change.

Observations of particular strongholds in the developed and in the backward communities strongly support the results of the statistical analysis. The strongest Communist centers in the developed regions are towns that industrialized comparatively early. They are often towns in which one or a few shops completely dominate the community. Some of the communities voting most heavily Communist in rural Finland are located in Finland's northernmost province of Lapland. These communities are usually those in which there are many indications of a rapid modernization process.

In order to correctly assess the social background of Industrial and Backwoods Communism, it is important to observe also the background factors of the voting strength of the main competitors of the Communists. The Social Democrats are the competitors for the working-class vote in the more developed regions in southern and western Finland. In the backwoods of the north and the east, however, the Agrarians are the ones who compete with the Communists for the lower class vote. The data and the findings clearly indicate that the Social Democrats in the south and in the west, on the one hand, and that the Agrarians in the north and the east, are strong in clearly different communities than the Communists. In the developed regions the Social Democrats are strong in towns and industrial centers undergoing rapid change and having a high amount of migration. In fact, workers who move from the countryside to the cities much more often vote Social Democratic than Communist. As has been shown, the Communists have their strength in communities with little migration. In the backward regions the Agrarians are strong in the most stable, the most traditional and the most backward communities. There are strong indications that a Communist vote in the more

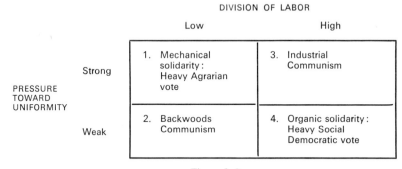

Figure 2–2

backward regions is a symptom of modernization. A switch of the vote from the Agrarians to the Communists is also a switch from traditional, particularistic loyalties to a more universalistic form of political thinking. In northern and eastern Finland the breakdown of regional barriers and loyalties is clearly associated with a tendency to vote Communist.

The results can be summarized in terms of our simple theoretical model. The conditions associated with Communist support in the developed regions reflect hindrances of movement, strong group ties and strong social pressures. Most of the crucial conditions related to Industrial Communism reflect, directly or indirectly, some kind of hindrances to people in using their resources and abilities. Strong political traditions, slow economic change, and a small amount of migration can all be taken as indicators for strong pressures toward uniformity. In the backward regions the contrary is true. Radicalism is strong in those communities in which the social constraints are weak. The decline in traditional values, rapid economic change, social insecurity and a high amount of migration can all be interpreted as indicators of a low pressure toward uniformity. Accordingly, the findings fit very well into the fourfold table earlier presented (see Fig. 2–2).

Protests and Reference Groups: Institutionalized and Diffuse Deprivation

The theoretical model presented can be used for further explorations of the different kinds of protest displayed by Industrial and Backwoods Communism. According to the model, cells 2 and 3 describe situations in which people are apt to feel discontent and deprivation. There is also a likelihood for legitimacy conflicts in these situations. The political effects of the discontent will presumably depend very much on who the discontented compare themselves with. This leads to a consideration of the concept of reference group—a tricky concept because as we know, it has many denotations. Of these denotations, however, two seem to be crucial. On the one hand, a person's reference group is the group with which he identifies himself and from which he obtains his social norms and standards for social perception: this is his *normative reference group*. On the other hand, the term also refers to a group with which a person compares himself when he evaluates his status and his rewards: this is his *comparison reference group*. These two kinds of reference groups cannot always be empirically separated because the group for identification and the group for comparison often seem to be the same. In Festinger's theory of social comparisons it is assumed, for instance, that the two kinds of reference groups usually coincide because a person tries to be similar to those to whom he is comparing himself. It is obvious, however, that these two kinds of reference groups do not always coincide, and that we need a specification of the conditions under which the group for identification and the group for comparison are the same, different or altogether absent.

It goes without saying that there are many kinds of groups that may function as foci for identification and comparison. The groups relevant here are those related to a person's social status and the evaluation of his rewards. In modern industrialized societies social classes or strata are presumably most often used when a person either tries to justify the rewards he gets or tries to evaluate whether his rewards are just or unjust. In any case, when speaking here of normative and comparison reference groups they denote groups identifiable in a total society, such as classes or strata.

It will be argued that the two major kinds of reference groups tend to coincide in situations of mechanical and organic solidarity, whereas this is not the case in the two situations or weak solidarity.

In a society of mechanical solidarity the satisfaction of individuals and their ability to predict the behavior of others is mainly produced through similarity and strong attachment to specific social norms. Outgroups and, accordingly also, alternative comparison groups are simply not available. As a result the group for identification and for comparison tend to be the same. We may summarize:

> 5. The less developed the division of labor and the stronger the pressure toward uniformity (mechanical solidarity), the more the normative and the comparison reference groups tend to be the same.

In a society of organic solidarity, individual satisfaction and also ability to predict how other people behave is obtained mainly through intensive social exchange of items of many different kinds. People will be satisfied if they are hindered as little as possible in exchanging rewards. They compare their rewards and inputs with those with whom they are in exchange, and they tend to regard their exchange partners as norm-senders. In a summary form:

> 6. The more developed the division of labor and the weaker the pressure toward uniformity (organic solidarity), the more the normative and the comparison reference groups tend to be the same.

In a situation of high division of labor and strong pressure toward uniformity, there exists a rather high amount of social exchange but it is inhibited in many ways. The potentialities for a free exchange are hindered for instance by class and race barriers. Usually there will exist a very clear demarcation line between the rulers and the ruled. This is also the situation, described by Marx, in which the proletariat develops class-consciousness and clearly realizes its special position. Intraclass communication becomes strong, whereas interclass communication declines. In more general terms, people will tend to feel closely tied to their own group, whereas they compare themselves to members from other groups in evaluating their rewards. In summary form:

> 7. The more developed the division of labor and the stronger the pressure toward uniformity, the more people will tend to have distinct normative and comparison reference groups, and the more the normative and comparison reference groups will tend to be different.

If the situation described by proposition 7 prevails for a longer period of time, the deprivation felt because the rewards received are experienced as unjust will become institutionalized. Groups with a history of being deprived will tend to socialize their younger members to experience relative deprivation. The result can be labeled *institutionalized relative deprivation*.

The situation of low division of labor and weak pressure toward uniformity (cell 2) also leads to deprivation but of an entirely different kind. The division of labor is undifferentiated, and the individuals have few opportunities for the social exchange of rewards of different kinds. At the same time the social constraints are weak, and the individuals will experience difficulties in predicting the behavior of others. They have, so to speak, neither social norms nor the wishes of exchange-partners to rely on. The result is that groups both for identification and comparison tend to be lacking. In this situation the individual feels deprived because he cannot find relevant reference groups. The result can be labeled *diffuse deprivation*. As a summary:

8. The less developed the division of labor and the weaker the pressure toward uniformity, the less the likelihood that people have relevant normative and comparison reference groups.

Some specific behavior patterns are likely to be found in situations of institutionalized relative deprivation as well as in situations of diffuse deprivation. In situations of institutionalized relative deprivation, one can expect a high amount of social participation and organizational activities. The individuals are strongly tied to their communities and social classes but are isolated from the total national community. Social participation tends to be planned and instrumental.

In situations of diffuse deprivation, one may expect a low level of organizational activity. Political participation, if high, can be expected to be expressive and momentary. The individuals are isolated not only from the national community but also as individuals.

Backwoods and Industrial Radicalism as Illustrations of Diffuse and Institutionalized Deprivation

The relationship between the two forms of radicalism and the two types of deprivation can be substantiated by at least three independent observations of the Finnish Communist movement:

1. The Communists in the developed communities in the southern and western parts of the country have an efficient organizational network. According to the studies of some particular cities in the more developed parts of Finland, it appears that there is a network of Communist organizations that corresponds to the national network of all associations and voluntary organizations. The Communist network performs for its members the same social functions as the national network for citizens in general. There are women's clubs, sports associations, children's clubs, and so on. The situation is on this count very different in the north and the east. It is true that the population in the northern and eastern parts of the country has become politically alerted since World War II. This increase in the political consciousness is mainly displayed only during elections. It has not displayed itself as a

general increase in social and intellectual participation. The Communist support in the north and the east is concentrated in groups in which the opportunities for social and intellectual participation is slight. A nation-wide study of youth activities shows that the young Communist voters in the north and the east belong to the most passive in the country as far as general social participation is concerned.[14]

2. Many observations of the Communist centers in the developed regions of the South and the West show how the Communist alternative in the elections is the conventional and respectable one. The Communist voters in these communities are well integrated in their communities and stable in their jobs. The population, and notably the Communist voters, in backward regions in the northern and eastern parts of Finland are in an entirely different position. This is already clear from the settlement patterns in the north and the east compared to the south and the west. Whereas life in the latter region has been always much more village-centered, the houses and farms in the north and the east have always been more isolated. Many of the Communist voters are small farmers who have to work as forestry workers in the winter. Unemployment in Finland has mainly the character of agrarian underemployment and this seasonal unemployment is particularly strong in those northern and eastern communities in which the Communists receive a heavy support. Today work for the unemployed is provided by the Government but it means that the unemployed have to leave their homes and communities for longer periods. In any case, whereas the Communist voters in the developed regions are strongly tied to their communities, the Communist supporters in the north and the east are much more migratory. This observation is also supported by the results from factor analysis in which a great amount of migration was characteristic for communities with a heavy Communist vote.

3. According to survey findings, the Communist voters in the more developed regions are the first to decide how to vote during election campaigns. Among the Communist voters in the north and the east, however, there is a very high proportion of voters who make their decision at the last minute. According to a national survey in 1958, as many as 82 per cent of the Communist voters in the south and the west have made their voting decisions at least two months before the elections while only 56 per cent of the Communist voters in the north and the east made their decision at that early moment. The latter was the lowest percentage in all groups established on the basis of party and geographical area.

The difference between Backwoods and Industrial Radicalism can be now summarized.

Backwoods Radicalism	*Industrial Radicalism*
Exists in communities of low division of labor and weak pressure toward uniformity	Exists in communities of high division of labor and strong pressure toward uniformity
Diffuse deprivation	Institutionalized deprivation
Low organizational and social participation	High organizational and social participation

Backwoods Radicalism	*Industrial Radicalism*
High expressive political participation	High instrumental political participation
Loosely integrated into their communities	Strongly integrated into their local communities
Isolated as individuals from groups	Strongly tied to their social class but isolated from the total national community

Descriptions of the social background of radical movements on the Left resemble closely those given here as related to Backwoods Radicalism. In particular, this seems to be true for those findings and propositions usually subsumed under the label of the theory of mass society. According to this theory, the supporters of radical movements are usually described as uprooted and without ties to secondary groups which in turn would bind the individuals to the community or society at large.[15] This description goes for Backwoods Radicalism, but it does not offer an explanation of Industrial Radicalism. Traditional Marxist theory, on the other hand, seems to render a good explanation of Industrial Radicalism. As stated before, Industrial Radicalism is characteristic for situations in which the proletariat already has developed a clear class-consciousness and in which intraclass communication is high but interclass communication low. The communities in which Industrial Radicalism is strong have polarized class conflicts, and very much of a two-class situation, as is assumed in traditional Marxist theory.[16]

Attitudes to Modernization and Social Change: Observations in the Australian New Guinea

In testing the model here presented it is worthwhile to look also at other data than those related to Finnish communism. The model should give some help in explaining protests in different settings. Of particular interest are developing societies. In them, however, it does not seem to be relevant to study legitimacy conflicts in the same manner as in studying already established societies. What can be done, however, is to inquire whether reactions to social and political change in developing societies can be described in terms of our structural variables, division of labor and pressure toward uniformity. The observations presented here are chosen from Australian New Guinea. The choice of New Guinea has, it has to be admitted, personal reasons.[17] The author knows New Guinea better than other developing societies. It is, however, not difficult to present a rationale why examples from New Guinea are particularly fruitful here. New Guinea, and particularly the Australian territories, provide today an example of a society in which there is both a nonindigenous administration and an extremely rapid modernization process. Few areas provide such a wide range of both individuals and behavior patterns on the dimension of modernization.

We have discussed societies as social systems without paying much attention to the multitude of subsystems within a society. A more important problem, however, is that developing societies often contain several almost independent political and social systems that do not constitute subsystems of each other. In colonial and developing societies we may thus talk about *the traditional, the colonial* and *the future system.* As such, these systems are, of course, abstract types. Some individuals may be committed to and even try to define their identity in terms of all the systems. The crucial point, however, is that division into the three systems provides a qualitative variable by which differences between individuals can be described. A discussion about solidarity and attraction to the society and its political system is hardly possible without distinguishing between these three types. In developing societies the main question is perhaps not the degree of solidarity but rather to which system attraction is directed.

The question is: how will our structural variables determine the attachment to these different systems? A tentative answer, based on observations in New Guinea, is given in the typology of Fig. 2–3.

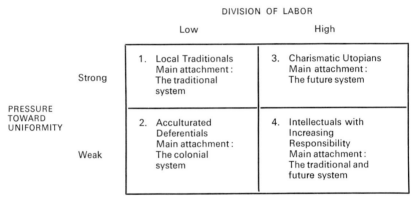

Figure 2–3

A short description of these types and their commitments is called for. In Australian New Guinea, as probably elsewhere, the most distinctive representatives of the various types are found among leaders and individuals with some kind of influence. The types refer mainly to such individuals.

1. Local Traditionals have few items for exchange, and their behavior is strongly regulated by traditional norms and values. The most outstanding representatives of this type are to be found among leaders of tribes and villages that have remained largely untouched by the modernization process. Their main reaction to change consists of explicit resistance.

2. Acculturated Deferentials have few items for exchange and are rather free from norms and values of the traditional village of tribal society. They have to observe rules in their interaction with whites and administration officials; but when no superiors are in sight they tend to lack rules for behavior altogether. They perceive themselves as having a small number of items for exchange, particularly when compared with Charismatic Utopians. Representatives of this type are particularly found among indigenous in-

dividuals who have served the colonial administration for a long time. They may possess a deep-seated aggression toward whites, but it is unlikely that this would be expressed in overt behavior. Their main attitude is that of deference and anxiety about showing enough loyalty to the administration. They may be characterized as definitely uninterested in social change.

3. Charismatic Utopians feel that they have many items for exchange but the exchange process is hindered by rules, inequality, color bars, and so forth. The most outstanding representatives are leaders of local politico-economic movements. Some of these leaders, such as Paliau, who operated in Southern Manus,[18] and Tommy Kabu in the Purari Delta,[19] have been described in anthropological literature. As leaders they rely on their charismatic qualities, but in their action programs they stress the technical, the rational and the economic. They want to get rid of the Australians and the Europeans but at the same time they try to copy the methods and techniques of the Australians and the Europeans. In today's New Guinea they are the only ones who are really concerned about technical advancement and instrumental adaptation to modernization, but they also tend to overstress it. They are overtly hostile to everything traditional. They are, accordingly, strongly committed to social change and their world is the new society.

4. The Intellectuals with Increasing Responsibility are today mainly found among young teachers, doctors, journalists, government clerks, and so on. In New Guinea, they are still few in number. Individuals who have spent a part of their life in European and international centers of learning and culture, as in the case with intellectuals in the new Asian and African countries, are still lacking. What is crucial, however, is that the type of intellectual who has strongly dominated the political scene in new states is clearly coming into prominence in New Guinea also.

In fact, the Intellectuals with Increasing Responsibility are much more attached to the traditional pattern of life than both the Acculturated Deferentials and the Charismatic Utopians. Even in Australian New Guinea it seems to be quite clear that these usually young educated individuals, who represent the intellectual in developing states, have greater interest in the traditional ways of life than the older deferent clerks and low-status officials within the administration. The young intellectuals also seem to be much more respected among the indigenous population than those who are strictly committed to serving the Australian administration. The intellectuals have a two-fold attachment. They consider both the traditional and the new society legitimate. They are interested in social change but feel that cultural revival ought to be combined with it.

On the basis of the discussion the following hypotheses can be formulated:

9. Individuals living under conditions of low division of labor and strong pressure toward uniformity are apt to resist and to be hostile to social change.
10. Individuals living under conditions of low division of labor and weak pressure toward uniformity are apt to be indifferent to social change. If hostile reactions occur, they will take the character of wish-fulfillment beliefs.

11. Individuals living under conditions of high division of labor and strong pressure toward uniformity are apt to have favorable attitudes toward social change and hostile attitudes to those who are conceived of as resisting social change.
12. Individuals living under conditions of high division of labor and weak pressure toward uniformity are apt to have favorable attitudes toward both social change and the existing social system.

These hypotheses deal with individual attitudes toward change under different structural conditions. Our point of departure was the degree and kind of legitimacy conflicts in different societies of different social structures. It is apparent that what is called organic solidarity and organically solidary societies presuppose social change. In the case of colonial or developing societies this is also obvious. With increasing division of labor, change initiated to eliminate inequalities tends to increase solidarity to the new developing system and decrease the likelihood for hostile outbursts and movements. This is certainly true for differentiated and industrialized societies also. In societies with a high degree of division of labor, exchange relations will easily become institutionalized in such a fashion that some individuals will be excluded from exchange unless social change is often initiated. Social change is an extremely general concept, and change can take many directions. We cannot simply say that social change is a prerequisite for organic solidarity. We may, however, say that in societies with high division of labor, social changes that decrease existing inequalities tend to increase solidarity. This may be seen as a continuous process, as the institutionalization of exchange relations easily leads to the establishment of obstacles in exchange.

Types of Alienation

Both the findings about Finnish communism and the observations on the attitudes among the indigenous elite toward modernization in the Australian New Guinea suggest two distinctive types of alienation. In the situation of relatively high division of labor and strong pressure toward uniformity, the ones hindered from obtaining rewards from social change will experience *powerlessness*. Powerlessness is a state in which the individual feels that he does not have any control over the rewards he receives. If we want to apply Marxist terminology, we may say that powerlessness is a state of feeling separated from the means of production. If powerlessness leads to political reactions, it will result in fairly systematic and instrumental activities. This is true for both Industrial Radicalism and for some of the strongly organized New Guinean movements led by such men as Paliau. The individuals will feel that they lack power and influence, and when they react politically they aim at changing the whole power structure.

In the situation of low division of labor and weak pressure toward uniformity, the kind of alienation displayed is best described by the term *uprootedness* or simply *uncertainty*. Uprootedness is a feeling state in which the individual does not clearly know what to believe, what rules to follow, what his position or motives are, how the situation is structured. Uprooted people, too, can easily become mobilized, but it is apparent that political activities of uprooted people are strongly expressive and unsystematic. The political reactions consist less of systematic attempts to change the power structure than of a search for normative and comparison reference groups.

Alienation is, of course, a term that varies in meaning, but the structural model here applied can at least be used for suggesting how some of the different meanings of alienation relate to each other. In an often-quoted paper, Melvin Seeman distinguishes between five major forms of feelings of alienation: powerlessness, meaninglessness, normlessness, self-estrangement, and isolation.[20] As Seeman does, it is assumed here that alienation is a kind of feeling state. The conditions for the emergence of alienation have to be clearly separated from alienation itself. Among such conditions one could list factual isolation, factual separation from the means of production, and so forth. Seeman's five forms are obtained through an analysis of the literature, but Seeman does not offer a systematic typology in which the types are logically related to each other. One distinction is already mentioned here, and it seems also in Seeman's list reasonable to distinguish powerlessness from the rest. Powerlessness belongs in our typology in cell 3, whereas all the other forms can be subsumed under the concept of uprootedness or uncertainty and belong in cell 2, characterized by diffuse deprivation.

By elaborating the concept of pressure toward uniformity, it seems possible to suggest a certain relationship between the different forms of uprootedness and uncertainty. Pressure toward uniformity can manifest itself in a number of ways. We may say that social values, social norms, role-expectations can educe and contain demands for uniform behavior. All of them can restrict social exchange. In addition to values, norms and role-expectations, lack of situational facilities may constitute hindrances for exchange. In his work on collective behavior, Neil Smelser assumes that these four factors form a hierarchical and cumulative order in such a fashion that values determine norms, roles and situational facilities, whereas, for instance, norms do not determine values but strongly influence both role-expectations and situational facilities. Lowest in the hierarchy we have the situational facilities. Smelser's typology of collective movements follows the same pattern. Value-oriented movements that are focusing on the change or restoration of social values influence not only the values in society but also the norms, roles and situational facilities. Collective movements focusing on situational facilities such as the panic and the craze, on the other hand, do not influence values, norms and roles.[21] In the same fashion it seems possible to arrange the forms of alienation in a cumulative pattern. Uncertainty concerning values (or goals, purposes, and so forth) may be labeled as meaninglessness, uncertainty regarding norms (or institutionalized means) as anomic alienation, uncertainty regarding roles (or motives, and so forth) as self-alienation, and uncertainty regarding situational facilities as situational alienation. Their relationships can be described by the following cumulative pattern:

Table 2–1

Forms of Alienation	UNCERTAINTY REGARDING			
	Values	Norms	Roles	Situations
Meaninglessness	+	+	+	+
Anomic alienation	−	+	+	+
Self-alienation	−	−	+	+
Situational alienation	−	−	−	+
No alienation	−	−	−	−

All these forms may educe political reactions which very much will follow the pattern described by Smelser. If mobilized, the alienated who feel meaninglessness will be apt to join value-oriented movements. Anomic people will be particularly easy to mobilize into norm-oriented collective movements, whereas self-alienated people are easy to mobilize into sudden collective outbursts of hostility. People who feel themselves lost in a situation will easily panic or join a craze. There are no possibilities to test the hypotheses of the

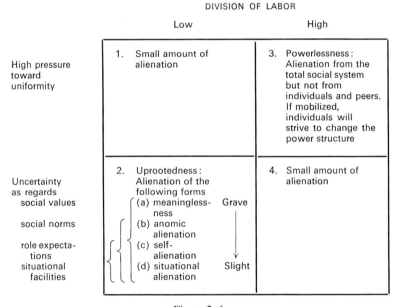

Figure 2–4

cumulative nature of alienation here because the political phenomena analyzed either have to be classified as powerlessness or meaninglessness. It seems reasonable, however, to state that many movements of the Radical Right are norm-oriented movements. They occur in particular when new forms and rules have been introduced, and when it is felt that traditional political rules have been violated. Such norm-oriented movements do not aim at changing the values of society; they aim at restoring traditional rules and forms of behavior. Many supporters of the Radical Right definitely aim at the upholding of prevailing values although they strongly detest, for instance, the behavior of the present politicians.

One objection against the assumption of the cumulative pattern of alienation is that it is possible to point out cases in which individuals seem to be alien to some prevailing values although they almost slavishly stick to the norms or to their roles. They may be called ritualists, in accordance with Merton's famous paradigm of modes of adaptation.[22] They are not included among the alienated here as it seems reasonable to assume that they cannot be described as uprooted or torn by feelings of uncertainty. As long as feeling states and not the consequences for the system is used as the criterion for alienation, it seems difficult to classify the ritualists among the alienated. They are usually strongly committed to the system to which they belong in spite of the fact that their behavior may have dysfunctional consequences for the system they are serving. Ritualists are presumably not easily mobilized, and in this sense ritualism does not result in political reactions.

In terms of the structural variables in the model, the discussion of the types of alienation can now be summarized in the four-fold scheme of Fig. 2–4.

The distinction between powerlessness and uprootedness is fairly well substantiated by the empirical evidence presented. The assumption of the cumulative nature of the forms of uprootedness is a hypothesis advanced on purely conceptual grounds.

DEPOLITICIZATION AND POLITICAL INVOLVEMENT:
A Theoretical and Empirical Approach

ULF HIMMELSTRAND

The Concept of Depoliticization: The End of Ideology?

SEYMOUR M. LIPSET reports that a Swedish newspaper editor once told him that politics in Sweden is boring. "The only issues are whether the metal workers should get a nickel more an hour, the price of milk should be raised, or old-age pensions extended." Lipset goes on to say: These are important matters, the very stuff of the internal struggle within stable democracies, but they are hardly matters to excite intellectuals or stimulate young people who seek in politics a way to express their dreams.[1]

It is possible that there was less of an *explicit* emphasis on high-powered ideological themes in Swedish politics at the time when Lipset's remarks were published than, say, thirty years earlier. This notwithstanding, the description of Swedish politics which Lipset seems to accept without reservations is a very poor description—poor even as a caricature. This is not a context in which to belabor this point further, however.[2] But we must concede that politics in Sweden, as in many other countries, up till quite recently, seemed to have been transformed from vivid clashes over ideology to what *some* people consider a dull technical discussion about means for promoting goals questioned by none. This process is often referred to as "the end of ideology" or as a depoliticization of politics.[3]

This is a somewhat revised version of the original paper which appeared in *Acta Sociologica*, vol. 6 (1962), pp. 83–110. I am grateful to the Center for Advanced Study in the Behavioral Sciences for offering me the opportunity and facilities needed to carry out the revision.

Notes to this chapter are on pp. 361–365.

In this paper we will raise two points. First, we will question the meaning of the term "depoliticization" itself, and, secondly, we will try to specify what kind of people are bored, or perhaps excited, about the new style of politics that is emerging. We do believe that there are *some* people who find great interest in factual and even technical discussions about political issues, and we wish to explore the psychology of involvement versus noninvolvement in that context. In doing this we will try to distinguish political involvement and political participation, the latter concept referring to action and the first-mentioned concept referring to more attitudinal and emotional variables.

Our first concern is to explore the dimensions of the term "depoliticization."

Depoliticization seems to imply a transformation of political *ideologies* into a set of more or less distinct administrative *technologies* based on a widespread consensus as to what kind of goals one should try to attain. Even if ideological differences are not wiped out altogether, ideological differences are de-emphasized in a depoliticized political community.

If we want to find out whether some depoliticization in this sense has taken place in a given political system, we should take a closer look at the political debate, in the parliament, in the newspapers, and so on. When issues with purely factual, technical or economical implications became more frequent at the cost of references to values and themes prominent in traditional political ideologies, we might speak of an increasing degree of depoliticization.

Herbert Tingsten has exposed this trend toward depoliticization to comment and criticism both as an eminent political scientist[4] and as the chief-editor between 1946 and 1960 of *Dagens Nyheter*, a daily Stockholm newspaper. His picture of Swedish political life has been criticized, however. It has been maintained that even though the fundamental values of the various political parties in Sweden may be overlapping to a considerable extent, priorities within sets of such values are allocated in distinctly different ways. The ways such priorities are defined probably are expressions of the ideological bent of each political party. On issues of old-age pensions, support to families with children in the growing ages, the organization of the educational system, economic and fiscal policies, and more generally on issues relating to the balance between productive and redistributive concerns, between private and public control and investment, and so forth, different ways of defining priorities may be found in the different parties. Those critical of Tingsten's views have been anxious to point out that these differences are not purely a matter of political technology, but differences with regard to interpretations of such classical concepts of political theory as equality, liberty, and brotherhood.

Any disagreement about the level of depoliticization of politics in a given country or political community poses a question of definition as well as a question of fact. To determine whether ideological consensus prevails and whether political ideologies are actually left at the roadside on the way to political decisions, one must have a clearcut notion of ideology. This becomes particularly important since somewhat different types of criteria are claimed to indicate the existence and impact of ideologies.

In this particular paper we are more concerned with the structure and function of political ideologies than with their actual content. But it seems impossible to define ideology, in a generally acceptable way, without some general reference to the *kind* of content to be found in an ideology.[5]

As a first approximation to a useful definition of ideology, we suggest the following rather lengthy formulation from which we hope to carve out a more condensed definition later on.

An ideology consists of an assortment of interrelated sets of statements that satisfy the following criteria:

1. they all concern the same category of societal or interpersonal relationships;
2. some of them indicate desirable values to be realized in these relationships (the core values of the ideology);
3. some of them seek to diagnose deficiencies (injustice, suffering, and so forth) in these relationships as seen from the vantage point of such values (the diagnostic component of ideologies);
4. some of them seek to explain how these deficiencies have come about (the explanatory component of ideologies);
5. some of them offer cures or policies supposed to eliminate or reduce the deficiencies (the policy component of ideologies);
6. some of them consist of appeals to people to believe the diagnoses, and explanations, to apply the policy or take the action necessary (the agitational or propagandistic component of ideologies);
7. some of them describe an ideal state of affairs that supposedly can be arrived at as a result of the cure or the action, and which represents a realization of the core values of the ideology (the kiliastic or utopian component of ideologies).[6]

By stating that an ideology consists of an *assorted* set of statements, we have made it clear that an ideology may be indicated also when several of the various types of statements mentioned are missing. In order to preserve or build a sufficiently precise core meaning of the term "ideology," we must mention, however, which types of statements are *necessary* and which are *optional* components of an "ideology." It seems to us that the only criterion which is necessary for defining an ideology is the presence of *either* (2), that is, statements expressing the core values of the ideology, *or* (7), statements expressing an ideal state of affairs to be attained. The simultaneous presence of both types of statements is not necessary. Some ideologies have a very explicit kiliastic component; others do not. However, we do not claim that this is the only reasonable way to define ideology. For instance, when Marxism is classified as an ideology rather than as a scientific theory, this may seem to imply a definition of the term ideology which subsumes diagnostic and, perhaps, explanatory statements as necessary elements under that term. Marxism is made up largely of diagnostic and explanatory assumptions about the impoverishment of the working classes, the concentration of capital, and so on. Marx has given a lot of attention to the deficiencies of feudal and bourgeois and imperialist regimes. Since any diagnosis is based on certain values or ideals, at least by implication, we could decide to make either one of components (2), (3) or (7) a necessary and sufficient criterion of an ideology, and the other components optional. It makes little, if any, difference to our following argument whether we decide to incorporate or exclude component (3), that is, the diagnostic component as a necessary criterion in our definition of ideology. The important point to make here is that unless there is a specification of values or of an ideal state of affairs, the other types of statements mentioned in our preliminary definition of ideology will stand quite unrelated to each other except by reference to one and the same subject matter in terms of the societal or interpersonal relationships involved. It should be noted that our preliminary definition requires some kind of relationships to exist between the various types of statements indicated in the definition.

By avoiding to state in more detail what kind of interrelations exist between the different sets of statements making up an ideology (according to our preliminary definition), we have left it open to question whether these sets of statements are related to each other by some kind of deontic logic, psycho-logic,[7] or by culturally conditioned or prescribed patterning of verbal response, or by mixtures of these.

A set of valuational, diagnostic and explanatory statements that emerge as justifications or rationalizations of political or economic action in which an individual or group is already indulging, perhaps for other reasons, con-stitutes as much of an ideology, according to our definition, as a set of such statements springing from a predominant concern over the realization of certain core values or ideal states of affairs.

In applying the rather complex kind of definition of ideology suggested above with its necessary, or necessary and sufficient, and optional criteria, we confront both difficulties and challenges. One challenge is to explore and interpret, and perhaps reduce, the various types of ideology that emerge from considering all the theoretically possible combinations of absence or presence of the optional kinds of statements referred to in the definition. In this paper, however, we will only argue about some of these combinations that seem particularly interesting from the point of view of depoliticization.

A difficulty that is more pertinent to our main theme in this paper is how to use the suggested definition of ideology as a guide in attempting to define derived variables such as "the significance of an ideology in politics." Will a greater significance of an ideology in politics be indicated wherever the necessary and perhaps sufficient components—that is, (2) or (3) or (7) in the definition—are seen to be more salient or frequent in political debates, speeches and editorials? Not necessarily. Criteria which are necessary and sufficient in defining a phenomenon in a way that makes it easy to distinguish it clearly from other members of its *genus proximum* in a *classificatory* context, do not necessarily concern those components of the phenomenon that are particularly vital and significant in an *actron* context. As a matter of fact it is quite easy to conceive of realistic cases where the significance of ideology in politics can be proved to be rather small in spite of quite numerous references to core ideological themes, whereas in other cases ideology can be found to be important despite a minimum number of references to core values of the given ideology. Tingsten has made some remarks that suggest such a possibility. He has pointed out the disconnected way in which symbols referring to core values of political ideologies may be used in depoliticized politics. These symbols have tended to become "mere honorifics, useful in connection with elections and political festivities."[8] They do not seem to effectively guide practical politics in periods between elections. The fact that references to ideological core values or ideals are rather numerous at times does not necessarily prove the significance of ideology, then. In contrast, we might think of politicians who consider ideology mainly a guide for political deliberation and action, and are not particularly concerned with the use of core symbols of ideology as elements in a political *ritual of intensification*. We may find only scanty references to values and ideals of political ideology among these kinds of politicians. But ideology may still be a crucially important element in their policy-making endeavors.

Obviously it is the fact that ideologically flavored value statements can be used for other purposes than to guide political analyses, decision making and action that causes us to be a bit suspicious about a simple frequency count of such statements as an indicator of the significance of ideology in practical politics. But what other indicators do we have? On what grounds do we conclude that politicians who make only scanty references to ideological core values still are guided largely by ideological considerations in their policy making?

If we find in a larger set of diagnoses of societal and interpersonal relationships, *and* in policy proposals, votes, decisions *and* in action, a consistent pattern which seems to derive from some more general evaluative principle, then it may seem justified to start believing that this is indicative of an ideology significant also in the context of political action. However, such a pattern of consistency is far from sufficient proof that there really is a significant ideology lurking in the background. Modern statistical techniques like factor analysis and latent structure analysis have enabled us to trace underlying evaluative structures from sets of manifest choices; but evidently not every latent structure that seems to derive from some overriding value can be identified as an ideology, if significant departure from the common usage of the term "ideology" is to be avoided. Any idiosyncrasy, for instance, is reflected in some consistency of choice within a more or less broad set of choices. Now, it may very well be that some ideologies most adequately can be described as rationalizations of idiosyncrasies; but ideologies are not idiosyncrasies.[9] Obviously, then, something more than a fairly consistent pattern of social diagnosis, policy proposals, votes, and so forth, is needed to substantiate a conclusion that asserts the existence of an ideology that significantly contributes to guiding political action. In principle, the problem is very much the same as that encountered in interpreting and naming "factors" in factor analysis. But evidently the problem is much more general.

We suggest that the following perhaps somewhat vague—but for our discussion, sufficiently precise—criterion be introduced. If at least *some* of the more powerful or highly "loaded" indicators of an underlying latent structure or factor consist of explicit references to either core values, ideals, or diagnoses known to belong in a particular line of ideological argument, then we are willing to conclude that a consistent pattern of indicators which can be traced back to underlying "latent structures" or "factors" is indicative of an "ideology at work."

Our previous argument seems to invite a definition of ideology as a structured assortment of explicit or implicit beliefs and appeals concerning deficiencies, and/or causes, and/or policies and action, and/or ideals relating to some delimited kind of societal or interpersonal relationships, and to some minimum set of *explicitly* held values applying to these relationships.

By stating that beliefs and appeals may be *implicit* or unstated, we are inviting studies of ideology as latent as well as manifest structures.

By requiring the observation of "explicitly held values," we have indicated the necessity to put certain limits to what can be *implied* from studies of latent structure as being an ideology.

By stating that only a *minimum* set of explicitly held values are needed as indicators of an ideology, we wish to indicate that fairly infrequent references to values relating to societal and interpersonal relationships does not necessarily invalidate the existence of an ideology as long as these references do not fall below a certain minimum. In our discussion we have likewise suggested that a frequent reiteration of evaluative ideological statements does not necessarily indicate a strong concern for the content of the given ideology, as such a reiteration of ideological statements can be made for other reasons, for instance as part of some political ritual of intensification in a context far removed from any serious political action or policy making.

Some Various Meanings of the Term "Depoliticization"

Far from simplifying our discussion of depoliticization as "the end of ideology," we have made it more complicated by introducing the definition of ideology suggested above. As a matter of fact we will not be able to spell out all the possible implications for the term "depoliticization" of our previous discussion concerning the meaning of the term "ideology." Still, it would seem to be of some advantage in our following argument to have a fairly explicit definition of ideology as a point of departure.

That the term "depoliticization of politics" is a broad and rather ambiguous concept seems quite obvious from our preceding discussion. It seems that the term may imply at least three different things:

First, it may mean simply the *development of ideological consensus*. This was suggested in the very first paragraphs of this paper. It seems rather reasonable to assert that there is less of ideological dissensus now than it was fifty years ago. It seems equally safe to propose that complete ideological consensus is far from achieved in Sweden. As a matter of fact it is quite obvious to anyone familiar with Swedish politics that the latter part of the sixties has seen a renewed emphasis and a sharper articulation of ideological differences between the political parties on the left and on the right. We will pay more attention to these recent developments in our concluding section.

Second, depoliticization may imply that the *impact of ideology* in practical politics is becoming weaker. Even if there is considerable ideological dissensus left at the level of manifest ideological statements, there may be much less dissensus on the level of specific political decisions. This might indicate that ideology has little influence over practical politics. Here belongs also Tingsten's observation that ideological symbols often are removed from the arena of practical politics to serve as elements of ritual in particular kinds of situations like elections and political festivities. For some purposes it is useful to distinguish this latter aspect of ideological impact from the previously mentioned aspect which rather deals with the discrepancy in content between manifest ideological statements and specific political decisions. We will call this new aspect the *separation of functions of ideological statements and of practical politics.*

Third, the term depoliticization has been used in the sense of a decreasing *saliency of manifest ideological statements.* This refers directly to the number of explicit references in the political debate to values and themes prominent in traditional political ideologies, as opposed to the number of references dealing with purely factual, technical and economical issues of political relevance. As a shorthand for this variable we will sometime use the term *ideological saliency.* Logically, this term is not quite correct from the point of view of our defining ideology as a latent structure which finds expression also in other symptoms than manifest ideological statements. With the full understanding of the reader that only saliency of *manifest ideological statements* is meant, this shorthand might still be used.

Analytically, the four aspects of depoliticization mentioned above— ideological consensus, impact of ideology, separation of functions of ideological statements and of practical politics, and saliency of manifest ideology— are quite independent for the most part. This can be demonstrated quite easily by constructing quantitative indexes to express these variables.[10] Empirically some of these variables may to some extent be intercorrelated— at least under certain conditions. Most evident is the likelihood that a pronounced separation of functions of ideological statements and practical politics is associated with a weak impact of ideology in practical politics. But even this relationship is conditional—as we will have an opportunity to indicate later on (*see* p. 76).

Depoliticization, then, is not a single unitary variable but rather a sensitizing concept referring to a property space with at least four dimensions.[11] In a later section of this paper, another aspect of depoliticization will be suggested, not because complication is itself desirable but because there are some troublesome facts about differential "depoliticization" of different political parties which must be faced up to. In order to prepare ourselves for confronting this new complication we will now try to reduce the present property space to more manageable proportions.

However important the variable of *manifest ideological dissensus-consensus* might be for comparative purposes, we find this variable less important in a short-range analysis of democratic political systems which still are characterized by quite noticeable ideological dissensus. This variable, then, will simply be left out of consideration here, or rather taken as a given factor.

The *impact of ideology* as measured by the degree of discrepancy between manifest ideological structure and specific policy decisions is probably negatively correlated with *separation of functions of ideology and politics*—at least in democratic multiparty systems.[12] For theoretical reasons which will be apparent later on we prefer to focus attention here on the latter variable.

The remaining property space is two-dimensional—separation of functions of ideology and politics and ideological saliency constituting the two different properties of this space.

The property space represented in Table 3–1 can be reduced in the way

TABLE 3–1

		Saliency of Manifest Ideology:	
		Lo	Medium · Hi
Separation of functions of ideology and practical politics:		"Pragmatic" concern for ideology	
	Lo	Spurious depoliticization	No depoliticization
	Hi	Genuine depoliticization	"Expressive" concern for ideology concealed depoliticization

indicated by the labels in the different cells of the table. To some extent these labels only summarize our previous discussion. By the term "spurious depoliticization" we wish to indicate that political ideologies may be quite effective in spite of the low saliency of manifest ideological statements, as long as the frequency of ideological statements exceed the minimum required by our definition of ideology and no separation of functions of ideology and policy has taken place. *Concealed depoliticization* is the term we have chosen to label a state of affairs characterized by a medium or above medium saliency of manifest ideology but a high degree of separation of functions of ideology and practical politics, ideology in this case probably having the function of expressing the identity of a particular political party, the loyalty to the party, and so forth, rather than the pragmatic function to guide political action.

Several assumptions are built into this somewhat reduced property space.

In this paper only one such assumption will be made explicit. We assume that a low saliency of manifest ideology has different implications depending on whether there is a low or a high functional dissociation of ideology and practical politics. Where very few ideological statements are being made (low saliency of manifest ideology), and where the few ideological statements that still occur are made mostly in expressive contexts far removed from practical politics, only a weak impact of ideology on political decisions can be expected. The resulting state of affairs rightfully deserves the label *genuine depoliticization*. An equally low saliency of manifest ideology is less clearly indicative of a weak ideological impact when no significant separation of functions of ideology and practical politics is in evidence. The frequency of ideological statements as contrasted to the number of statements with factual, technical or economical implications is a particularly ambiguous index of depoliticization when the dominant ideological style is "pragmatic" rather than "expressive." It is easy to see why. People representing the "pragmatic" ideological style do not feel a dominant need to reiterate, to paraphrase or to be expressive about their ideology. This, of course, will reduce substantially the number of times ideological references are made. Still, ideology may be at work—both as a largely latent structure, which can be discovered either by modern statistical techniques, or by the kind of careful, qualitative and structural scrutiny of political editorializing, political speeches, parliamentary debates, and political decisions exemplified in Leif Lewin's excellent study of the theme of social and economic planning in Swedish politics,[13] and in a phenomenological sense, as experienced by the political actors themselves.

Functions of Political Ideology

If we want to know more about conditions favoring the development of different types and degrees of depoliticization in given political systems, the functions of political ideologies should occupy much of our attention. We have already mentioned the pragmatic versus the expressive function of ideologies. In this section we will elaborate this distinction a little further.

The *pragmatic* function of ideology is the function of picking goals for political action. The *expressive* function is determined by the need to indicate the legitimacy of the party elite or to express symbolically the identity and unity of the party, the loyalties to the party, and so forth. The adequacy of this terminology can be questioned, I suppose. Talcott Parsons, for instance, has pointed out that the term *expressive* contains concealed ambiguities.[14] The same is certainly true about the term *pragmatic* or the term *instrumental* which is also used as a contrast to *expressive*.[15] As no standardized terminology exists in this area, and no better alternatives are known to me than the terms "expressive" and "pragmatic", these terms will be used here provisionally in the sense indicated above. More precisely a pragmatic function of ideology is indicated when the intended and recognized consequences of using the given ideology consist in action geared to approaching (or attaining) goals specified by this ideology.

By an expressive function of ideology is meant that the intended and recognized consequences consist in emotional gratification, arousal of positive sentiment, loyalty or devotion with regard to the given ideology, in a group or movement supporting or vindicating that ideology.[16]

The late President Kennedy, in a commencement speech at Yale on June 11, 1962, made some interesting remarks illustrating the contrast between expressive and pragmatic styles with regard to certain myths of the national economy (big-bad-government, the virtue of a balanced budget, and so forth):

As every past generation has had to disenthrall itself from an inheritance of truisms and stereotypes, so in our time we must move on from the reassuring repetition of stale phrases to a new, difficult but essential confrontation with reality . . . . Too often we hold fast to clichés of our forebears. We enjoy the comfort of opinion without the discomfort of thought.

A person with a pragmatic political style may have to face the "discomforts of thought" and of "confrontation with reality" whereas an expressive political style protects the individual against such straining experiences and instead provides him with reassurance and emotional gratification.

In understanding the term "pragmatic" function of ideology as used in this paper one should thus take precaution not to subsume under this term those cases where "pragmatically" inclined politicians use an expressive reiteration of ideological symbols as an *instrument* to mold party members and potential voters to greater loyalty with the party.[17] This, according to our terminology, still is an illustration of the expressive function of ideology since the likely and intended consequences of ideological exhortation in this case is the arousal of sentiments of loyalty or devotion. The pragmatic function of ideology is indicated only when ideology is actually used as a guide to political decisions by all those concerned with decision making.

Goals for political action are selected, in the pragmatic case, on the basis of what one assumes to be the fact about chosen goals once they are attained, as well as on the basis of ethical standards inherent in the given ideology. Improved knowledge about facts as well as factual observations indicating actual or expected societal changes may thus lead to a rational reshuffling or to replacements in the hierachy of political goals and subgoals. The technical nature of the factual explorations preceding such a formulation of goals, should not make us believe that technology here has taken precedence over ideology. Factual exploration may provide a better or more up-to-date map of the goal area; but within this area specific points and paths cannot be selected to constitute goals and subgoals without utilizing some value standards. If these standards are made explicit in a sufficient number of cases the impact of ideology is clearly indicated.

Moreover, where a pragmatic ideological style is prevailing, the selection of means or piecemeal subgoals of practical politics is always made with an eye on what is feasible. Best things should never be allowed to kill good things, according to the pragmatic style. This also makes for less emphasis on political rhetoric.

I am not trying here to suggest that pragmatic ideologists always behave consistently according to some model of rational decision making. I want to point out, simply, that leading politicians with a pragmatic concern for ideology will *try* deliberately to use standards inherent in their ideology in a rational way when specifying the ends and means, or the alternatives and consequences relevant to a particular policy proposal,[18] while leading politicians with an expressive concern for ideology will tend to use ideology for expressive purposes rather than for specifying the details of policy proposals. *Since these details will have to be specified anyhow, a politician with an expressive political concern must specify them on the basis of more or less coincidental values derived from any interests, pressures and traditional ways which happen to make themselves felt at the moment.* In this case such values most likely do not get thoroughly clarified and evaluated from an ideological point of view in the context of the given policy problem. This may result in haphazard, incongruent and internally disruptive patterns of policy. The extent of this disruption depends on the degree of diversity, conflict or integration of those interests, pressures and traditions which are elements of the given social structure. The more diverse, incongruous and disintegrated the given sets of structural elements are, the more disruptive will a dominantly expressive political style probably be for effective policy formation. One specific prediction which can be derived from this hypothetical generalization is that a predominantly expressive political style would be less detrimental to coordinated policy formation in a fairly well-integrated and homogeneous country like Sweden than it would be for instance, in the U.S.A.

Our last remarks have suggested some dysfunctions, in a larger context, of political ideologies having expressive rather than pragmatic functions. It is interesting to note on this point that an expressive ideological style not only permits further disruption of a social structure which already happens to be somewhat fragmented but that this expressive style may get reinforced by the very disruption it helps to create. It is well acknowledged that unifying expressive symbolism often springs from a need to overcome or rather to cover up growing disintegration.[19] We can visualize a circular process here, expressive ideology resulting in more disintegration, and disintegration resulting in more expressive ideological symbolism. This is not the place to spell out in any detail the assumptions which can be made about the forces which accelerate or retard this circular process. Only one question which is relevant in this context will be singled out for consideration, the question about the origin of expressive ideological symbolism. This question will be dealt with only in the specific context of Swedish party politics, however. Some theoretical assumptions with a more general applicability will, of course, be involved in our analysis of this particular case. As a matter of fact our analysis of the case necessarily must be rather speculative for the simple reason that systematically collected data are notoriously lacking in this area.

On the Functions of Ideology Among Political Parties in Sweden

The following interpretation of the role of ideology in Swedish party politics deserves at best to be called another piece of informed but yet not sufficiently supported opinion. These opinions are stated here as hypotheses for future research but also to highlight some generalizations about the role of ideology in the various processes which have been classified under the term depoliticization.

My hypothesis is that those Swedish political parties which have occupied the opposition for more than thirty years (except for a short period during the Second World War when all parties joined hands for reasons of national unity), and particularly the Liberal Party, have been more depoliticized than the Social Democratic Party in the sense that they have more clearly dissociated ideology and practical politics. This is done by retaining ideological emblems such as "individual freedom," "private initiative," "free enterprise," "state coercion," "stupefying collectivism," and so forth, for occasions of unifying, ritual activity, while at the same time carrying on practical politics very much on the merits of each single issue with only casual concern for ideology. What is conceived as the "merits of each issue" seems to have been determined largely by economic interests (the taxation issue) and probably also by considerations of what might constitute efficient propagandistic and traditionalistic appeals.

Using the labels introduced in our property space (Table 3–1) the hypothesis suggested above—and it is only a hypothesis—may be stated like this. I believe that the bourgeois opposition for some time has been in a stage of *concealed depoliticization* which, in periods of greater political calm, seemingly has bordered on *genuine depoliticization*. A larger number of rows in Table 3–1 would of course have permitted a more precise statement of this hypothesis. I do not believe that the separation of functions of manifest ideology and practical politics is extreme among the opposition parties, only that it is significantly more marked than in the Social Democratic Party.

From the point of view of sociological theory it would not be unexpected if the opposition parties in Sweden actually dissociate ideology and practical politics the way I have assumed they do. Having been out of power for a very long period of time and finding that votes are gained and lost in a rather unexpected manner these parties have not been able to rely on *political effectiveness* as a source of unity and legitimacy in relation to its own party members and sympathizers. Of course, "political effectiveness" might be specified according to several quite different criteria. Here a general understanding of what is meant by this term is quite sufficient.[20] The capacity to gain votes in elections, to promote reforms which are soon accepted even by some of its previous adversaries, etc. are some criteria of political effectiveness. Not being able to rely on political effectiveness in this sense, "quasi-permanent" opposition parties have to seek other sources of identity and unity. Ideological faithfulness expressed under suitable circumstances is another source of party identity and unity. Political effectiveness cannot be sacrificed altogether, however. It is necessary for the party always to have a place in the train of progress. Being caught between the horns of this dilemma, ideological faithfulness and political effectiveness both being sought for, a dissociative solution of the type I have indicated is ready at hand to a "quasi-permanent" opposition party.

The Social Democratic Party, on the other hand, has been in power for a long time. The other parties certainly have contributed to the social reforms carried out during this period, the achievements of Swedish industry have made it economically feasible to carry out these reforms, and the willingness of the powerful trade-union and cooperative movements to act in a socially responsible way have provided the stability necessary both for Swedish economic growth and for long-term reforms. But still, of course, Social Democrats look upon Swedish Welfare as being produced mainly under the enlightened leadership of the Social Democratic Party.[21] Such a point of view could be held without depreciating the roles of other political parties, organizations and industry.

Political effectiveness, then, ought to be a main source of unity and legitimacy within the Social Democratic Party. In this kind of situation there is less need to cling to unifying ideological symbolism as a source of identity. Ideology can be used in the pragmatic style, that is as a ground for creative transformation of values into action and of social and economical discoveries into values rather than as a refuge for pickled and preserved symbols of the past. This pragmatic function of ideology does not presuppose the loud reiteration of high-level ideological abstractions or glittering generalities.

My hypothesis about the different degrees of separation of functions of ideology and political decision-making in Swedish political parties should not be misconstrued to give the impression that I have altogether absolved the Social Democratic Party from exhibiting any such "dissociative" tendency. I have spoken only about the *relative* magnitude of the degree of separation of functions of ideology and practical politics. Moreover, I want to emphasize that if the Swedish Social Democratic Party had been in a more or less permanent opposition as long as the Liberal Party, "dissociative" tendencies might have been as evident in the Social Democratic Party as I think they now are among the Liberals.[22]

If I am correct in my description of the somewhat different roles played by ideology in the Social Democratic Party and the opposition parties we should not be surprised to find different people giving different estimates of the size of the dissensus between these parties. Such varying estimates may result not only from the personal biasses of particular observers but also from the fact that these observations are made at different points in time. Between elections when practical politics is in focus, party differences undoubtedly look smaller than they do at elections or in campaign speeches where expressive ideological symbolism becomes more salient. My hypothesis states that this broadening gap around election time depends mainly on an increased emphasis on dissociated ideological themes in the opposition parties. In my opinion such a dissociative shifting of gears from practical to expressive concerns, and back again when election is over, is less evident in the Social Democratic Party.[23]

A Propositional Summary on the Origins of Diverse Ideological Styles, and on Ideological Functions and Dysfunctions

1. A political ideology which predominantly serves as a source of individual emotional gratification or as a source of legitimacy and unification in a collective context is said to have an expressive function or style. We speak of an instrumental function or style of an ideology when it serves predominantly as a guide to the formulation and implementation of concrete political proposals and policies.

There are both personal and structural sources of a predominantly expressive ideological style. It seems that an individual exhibiting the psychodynamic syndrome of the "authoritarian personality" is more likely to take up an expressive ideological style.[24] However, in this paper we are only interested in the structural sources of variations in ideological style.

2. A given political ideology will tend to be used mainly as a source of legitimacy and unification under structural conditions which on the one hand seem to undermine or threaten the legitimacy of political actors (persons, parties, and so on) involved, and which on the other hand tend to cut off these political actors from most or all alternative sources of legitimacy —such as charisma, tradition, constitutional legality, widespread popular support, political and economic efficiency, and so forth.[25]

3. A political ideology can be used as a source of legitimacy only if it is removed from contexts where it is seen as relevant to the fluctuating exigencies of everyday political policy making, and "frozen" into a sacred constant form; ideological revisions and changes motivated by changing circumstances give an impression of arbitrariness, opportunism and manipulation which offer little in the way of legitimacy.

4. A political ideology which is removed from contexts where it is seen as relevant to everyday political policy making no longer benefits from the feedback of information from the making and implementation of political policy, and will thus become an increasingly outdated and irrelevant source of guidelines for political decision makers, particularly in times of rapid social change and diversification.

The outmoded and irrelevant character of ideologies that are maintained in the expressive rather than the pragmatic or instrumental style may seem to be of little consequence since such ideologies are removed from contexts where they are seen as relevant to policy making and where they might influence policies. There are two ways, however, in which such outmoded and irrelevant ideologies still might significantly influence the course of political policy making. First, we can conceive of situations where the competition for power in a given political system is so close and so critical that legitimization through ideological faithfulness alone, or through attacks on revisionists, becomes insufficient, and where some kind of transformation of high-level, high-pitched ideological themes into *political action* is seen as necessary by some of the participants in the race to outdo some of their main contenders for power. We will not discuss this case further, but in the following propositions, wish to draw attention to certain conditions under which political ideologies, while still having mainly an expressive function, *indirectly* can influence the context and the structure of political decisions.

5. The more pronounced the expressive style with which politicians or parties hold their ideological convictions, the more likely it is that they will be left without relevant and up-to-date ideological guidelines for policy formation and decision making, and left therefore to specify policies on the basis of any interests, pressures or prejudices that happen to make themselves felt at the moment, which may result in haphazard and internally disruptive patterns of policy.

6. A predominantly expressive ideological style of politics will have less disruptive consequences in societies which, because of a high degree of cultural homogeneity, and because of fairly efficient redistributive social welfare and equalization mechanisms, have little potential for disruptive conflict; but the higher the potential for disruptive conflict, the more likely it is that an expressive ideological style will contribute to speeding up the disruption, while more pragmatic ideological convictions more probably would have allowed registering the threat of disruption in time for necessary preventive or reconstructive activity to be taken.

7. Within the framework set by the "rules of the game" which are actually practiced in a given political context, we will find that the more expressive the predominant ideological style in, say, a political party or any other relevant organizational political unit, the more likely it is that emerging conflict *within* the unit is dealt with in terms of exclusion or neglect of the weaker, less powerful subunit in the name of ideological unity or consensus.

The Impact of Depoliticization on Political Involvement in the Electorate

In the previous sections we have dealt with some aspects of so-called depoliticization on the level of party organizations and party leadership. In this section we will turn our attention to the electorate. Depoliticization, whether spurious or genuine, is sometimes supposed to cause a significant decline in political involvement and participation among the citizens. This supposition, however, is not in full accordance with data. Voting turnout has been increasing in Sweden for a long time. Since 1928 and up to 1960 voting has increased from 67 per cent to 85 per cent. Among young voters, who have been assumed to be particularly frustrated by not being able to "express their dreams" in political behavior, there has been an increase of more than 10 per cent in voting turnout since the beginning of the forties.

Even though these data seem to contradict the hypothesis that *political participation* declines as depoliticization proceeds, the hypothesis that *political involvement* declines with depoliticization can still be held. Thanks to well-organized systems for mass communication and for facilitating attendance at the ballot box it is quite possible to obtain in modern democracies as well as in totalitarian states, an extremely high degree of participation in elections while at the same time having a fairly low or only a medium degree of personal involvement in political matters among the voting masses.

The distinction made between *political participation* and *personal involvement in politics* (or *political involvement* which will be our short-hand term) is a distinction between behavior on the one hand and subjective emotional state or feeling of arousal on the other. Behavior may take place without having any subjective feeling tone attached. Subjective emotional states may exist without being expressed in behavior.

Having these basic distinctions in mind we can formulate three fundamental questions about depoliticization, political involvement and political participation. In order to make our questions more precise we prefer to center our attention here on one and only one of the dimensions underlying the sensitizing concept of depoliticization, the dimension of *ideological saliency*. This dimension is the one which seems most relevant at the level of the electorate. Ideological saliency is less complex than the other dimensions of depoliticization and consequently more likely to be perceived by the average citizen.

These are our questions about the idological saliency of a given political community, and the political involvement and participation of its citizens:

1. Is a decline in political involvement among citizens a necessary effect of a declining ideological saliency? If not, under what circumstances will ideological saliency decline without a consequent weakening of political involvement?

2. Given various degrees of ideological saliency in a political community, what are the conditions promoting a balanced development of participation and involvement in politics, and what are the conditions creating an unbalanced state of affairs, participation being much higher than involvement, or *vice versa*?

3. Given various combinations of participation and involvement levels in a democracy, what are the consequences for the functioning of the democratic system of these various combinations?

In this paper I will deal mainly with the first question. However, a few remarks about the two other questions will be made in the concluding part of this paper.

SOME BASIC ASSUMPTIONS AND DERIVATIONS ABOUT THE DYNAMICS OF POLITICAL INVOLVEMENT

Basic to our approach in the following is the assumption that to a large extent the political involvement of the ordinary citizen depends on the *goodness-of-fit* or *affinity* between the politically relevant predispositions of the individual and political aspects of his environment. If there is such a fit, an exchange is likely to occur between the individual and his environment, the individual being emotionally gratified in the process. Next time he encounters this particular aspect of his environment he will anticipate emotional gratification; he will feel involved. According to these assumptions the *amount* of exchange taking place is as important as the goodness-of-fit between environment and individual predispositions. If there is a good fit but no lively exchange with the relevant parts of the environment ego will not feel particularly involved.

It goes without saying that there are other factors than the goodness-of-fit between political environment and relevant individual predispositions which determine the degree of political involvement of a given individual. Degree of education and exposure to political stimuli generally, the position of the individual in the social structure, the individual's perception of the possibilities for influencing the political process (cf. Sidney Verba on political participation in *Acta Sociologica* 6:1-2), and many other sociologically important factors could be mentioned as codetermining the degree of political involvement of an individual. In this paper, however, we are not concerned with repeating all these wellknown and rather well substantiated results.[26] The applicability of the goodness-of-fit hypothesis in describing some of the dynamics of political involvement on the level of the mass electorate has not been made the object of much theorizing or empirical research however.[27] This seems to be a sufficient reason for pursuing research along these lines.

Goodness-of-fit between individuals and their political environments has been specified for the most part in terms of so-called *cross-pressures* or *counter-pressures* which can be defined as consisting of a less good fit between the political allegiance of individuals and the political loyalties prevailing in their environments. No reference has to be made here to all the wellknown research showing that cross-pressures makes for a lower turnout of voting. However, my own research has indicated that while certain young people with an instrumental or pragmatic outlook on politics are more likely to react to cross-pressures by not voting than are those with an expressive concern for politics, these young "pragmatist" non-voters are as involved, as interested and as knowledgeable in politics as voters with an expressive concern, or even more so.[28] Cross-pressures and counter-pressures defined in terms of the *content* of the political allegiance of an individual and of relevant parts of his environment, then, do not seem to be related to *political involvement* the way they are to *electoral participation*. In dealing with political involvement, I have turned in my own research to the goodness-of-fit of political "style" rather than to the content of individual and environmental political allegiance. My basic assumption on this point states that a decreasing ideological saliency in a given political environment need not result in a declining political involvement among people in that environment as long as there is a "good fit" between the environmental political style and the political style of the individual citizens concerned.

The basic elements of our argument thus far are the terms "political environment," "politically relevant individual predispositions," "political style" which refers both to individuals and environments, and "goodness-of-fit" which here concerns the relationship between individual and environmental political styles. Before any more precise empirical hypotheses can be derived these terms must be further specified.

We can specify the term political environment first by indicating the two main types of communication channels which serve to expose the citizens to political stimuli. One channel is the word-of-mouth, the transmission line passing through relatives, friends and workmates who act as informal opinion leaders or mediators. The second channel is provided by mass media, particularly by television.[29] The receiving ends of these two channels define two types of meeting grounds, partly overlapping to be sure, for environmental and individual political styles. Because the data soon to be presented were gathered in 1955 and 1956, that is before TV had made its breakthrough in Sweden, we will focus our attention here mainly on that part of the environment which comes to the individual by way of word-of-mouth. A few remarks will be made later on about the new dimension introduced in election campaigns by TV, however. To distinguish these two components of environment we will use the term *immediate* environment for relatives, friends, workmates, acquaintances, and so forth, and the term *mediate* environment for the content of mass media.

Two dimensions of political style will be distinguished in the immediate environment of citizens: (a) degree of ideological saliency, and (b) the predominance of people with an expressive or a pragmatic concern with political ideology in the given environment.

Similarly, politically relevant individual predispositions will be specified along two dimensions: (c) strength of concern for political ideology, and (d) type of concern for political ideology, be it expressive or pragmatic or something in between.

From the point of view of testing hypotheses relevant to our original interest in the effects of so-called depoliticization on the political involvement of ordinary citizens, variables (a) and (c) above seem to be the most adequate. Goodness-of-fit in the relationship between (a) and (d) might also help to define some important conditions for different effects of depoliticization on political involvement. In the data available to us no observations of environmental ideological saliency, that is of variable (a), are included, however. The only kind of hypothesis we can test empirically with available data is a hypothesis stating the effects of various combinations of variables (b) and (d) on political involvement.

H:1.1 When individuals with an expressive concern for political ideology find that in their immediate environment most other people also have an expressive type of concern with political ideology, and when individuals with a pragmatic concern for ideology also find an agreement of ideological style between themselves and their immediate environment, we have a good fit between environmental and individual ideological styles and a resulting higher level of political involvement among the individuals concerned, other things being equal. Less political involvement will result in cases where less agreement can be found between individual ideological styles and the ideological style prevailing in the immediate environment of the given individuals.

Even though this is not strictly a hypothesis about the effects on political involvement of various degrees of ideological saliency, an empirical test of H:1.1 may be considered an indirect test of a hypothesis dealing with ideological saliency and political involvement. In H:1.1 the environmental variable is the proportion of people with an expressive or a pragmatic concern for political ideology in a given immediate environment. This aggregated variable may be taken as a predictive indicator of environmental ideological saliency if the following assumption holds true:

A:1   In the immediate environment of a person, ideological saliency will be high if the proportion of persons with an expressive concern for ideology in that environment is much higher than the proportion of persons with a pragmatic concern for ideology; and the ideological saliency will be low if these proportions are reversed.

Our first empirical hypothesis was numbered H:1.1 rather than H:1 because I think there is place for some qualifications of this hypothesis. These qualifications will be introduced later on under H:1.2. The nature of the qualifications can be indicated by making clear that the goodness-of-fit assumption on which H:1.1 is based probably holds true only for certain kinds of people. Some other people do not seem to depend to such an extent on a good fit between their own political style and the style prevailing in their immediate environment in order to develop and to sustain a strong political involvement. There are some assumptions we can make about what kind of people are dependent on such a good fit and what people are not so dependent.

I assume that on the level of the mass electorate people with an expressive concern for ideology will be more dependent on a good fit between their own ideological style and the prevailing style in their immediate environment than will people with a pragmatic concern for ideology. There are fairly good theoretical reasons for this assumption.

On the level of the mass electorate an expressive concern for ideology means that one is oriented toward symbolic gratifications in the area of a given ideology. Consummatory symbol acts like listening to glittering ideological generalities or voicing one's opinion with the aid of honorific symbols of ideology are criteria of an expressive concern for ideology.[30] Such consummatory symbol acts give rise to a significant emotional feedback if they are performed in a congenial or fitting social context. But if this congenial context is removed, the emotional feedback will cease. Symbol acts by themselves cannot produce stimuli which provide a refill of emotional involvement. Apart from some cases where deep-seated personal anxieties provide the superstructure of political ideology with continuous emotional reinforcement, the repetition of consummatory symbol acts in a context which is not congenial to expressive symbolism will in the long run probably end in the wearing out or the "extinction" of these symbol acts. Renewed contact with a congenial environment may, however, produce a revival or a "spontaneous recovery" of such "extinguished" symbol acts.[31] This is why we have assumed those with an expressive concern for political ideology to be particularly dependent on a good fit between their own type of ideological concern and the type prevailing in their social environment, for the maintenance of their political involvement.

Those with a pragmatic concern for political ideology I assume to be less dependent on the opportunity to interact with their psychological equals, for the following reason. The type of concern for politics which characterizes this kind of people will most likely bring them in touch with fairly specific factual and technical issues rather than with diffuse and emotive political symbols. It seems that such issues rather often are productive of a kind of strain, which creates a need for digging deeper and for expanding one's factual and technical knowledge in political matters even further, at least among people with a concern for matters like this. This process may to a certain extent be self-perpetuating, new facts creating new problems, and new problems creating a need for new facts, and so forth.[32] Furthermore this process can be assumed to be less dependent on the existence of an emotionally congenial environment than the process assumed to maintain political involvement among "expressive" subjects. Some dependence on being among psychological equals probably remains among those with a pragmatic concern for political ideology, however. Other "pragmatists" will be most capable to furnish the kind of questions and arguments about factual, technical and economical matters that feed the process resulting in the maintenance and development of political involvement in this case.

A person who has a taste for ideological argument but who is at the same time very much concerned with problems of practical application of ideology, and of transforming ideology to take account of new developments in the given problem area, ought to be particularly independent of having a good fit between his own ideological style and the style prevailing in his environment in order to maintain his political involvement. In a sense he would fit in everywhere. He would be at home with deeply concerned ideologists but equally congenial among those who center most of their attention on salient factual, technical and economical issues of politics. He could be disturbed by the separation of functions of ideology and practical politics which he may have noticed in his environment, but since he is equally involved in ideological argument and practical application of ideology it seems likely that he will react to this disturbing dissociation as a challenge to meet rather than as a repulsive phenomenon to which he is justified to turn his back.

The ideological style outlined in the preceding paragraph is a pragmatic style. It is quite clear, however, that we have lumped together undiscriminatingly, up till now, under the label of a "pragmatic concern for ideology" some rather different types of "pragmatic concern." Speaking of a pragmatic concern with ideological issues we may put our emphasis on the word "pragmatic" or on the term "concern." By putting our emphasis on the word "pragmatic" we may want to indicate that questions about factual, technical and economical matters are at the forefront of interest of this kind of person, ideology being only a neat way to summarize certain given value preferences —but nothing more. By putting more emphasis on the word "concern" we may want to indicate that this kind of person attaches real importance to ideology. To a person whose concern for ideology is pragmatic, ideology is important mainly by functioning as a vehicle for creative transformation of values into social and political action, and of social and economical dis-coveries into values, as I have mentioned previously. This function of ideology distinguishes those with a pragmatic concern not only from those who use ideology as an expressive platform but also suggests differences of degree within the group which we have lumped together as having a pragmatic concern for ideology. Between the "ideological realism" of those with an expressive concern for ideology and the "ideological nominalism" of those who are mainly concerned with the pragmatic aspects of ideological issues, and who only consider ideology a neat and fairly general summary of favored political decisions, we can find those who are convinced both that the explication of ideological concepts is helpful in formulating policies, and that the empirical analysis of political processes, social and economical change, and so on, is helpful in improving ideological concepts. This kind of people are definitely pragmatic rather than expressive in their concern with ideology but they are pragmatic in a somewhat more sophisticated way than those who exhibit what we have merely suggested by the term "ideological nominalism."[33]

It seems well advised, then, to split in two separate types what we have previously lumped together simply as people with a pragmatic concern for political ideology. Here these two types will be called *pure pragmatists* and *pragmatic ideologists*, the latter type representing the somewhat more sophisticated way of being pragmatic about a political ideology. In addition to these two types we have, of course, the *expressive ideologists*, those having an expressive concern with political ideology. After having arrived now at these three different types of ideological style it is time to summarize our previous discussion about the kind of people who are most and least depend-ent on a good fit between their own ideological style and the style prevailing in their immediate environment in order to develop and to maintain their political involvement. I have suggested that expressive ideologists are most dependent, pure pragmatists less dependent and pragmatic ideologists not at all dependent on such a good fit between individual and environmental ideological styles.[34]

This assumption leads logically to the following supplement to our first empirical hypothesis H:1.1.

H:1.2   The dependence of an individual's political involvement on the degree of similarity between individual and environmental ideological styles—a dependence predicted by H.1.1—holds most clearly for expressive ideologists, while this relationship becomes less strong among so-called pure pragmatists and completely vanishes among pragmatic ideologists since they are entirely independent of the degree of similarity between individual and environmental ideological styles for the maintenance of their political involvement, other things being equal.

It is important to keep in mind that this hypothesis is stated as valid only on the level of the mass electorate. On higher levels of political participation other factors than goodness-of-fit of ideological styles are probably much more prepotent in determining the degree of involvement felt by the people concerned. When speaking of "ideologists" in H:1.2 we are thus using this term in a very diluted sense to fit the range of concern for ideology to be found at the level of the mass electorate.

SOME EMPIRICAL DATA ABOUT POLITICAL INVOLVEMENT AS DEPENDENT ON INDIVIDUAL AND ENVIRONMENTAL IDEOLOGICAL STYLES

To simplify empirical as well as theoretical treatment of the type of concern with political ideology just mentioned I have reduced that typology of expressive ideologists, pragmatic ideologists, and pure pragmatists to one single, presumably continuous variable: *the degree of affective loading of ideological symbols and symbol acts as opposed to the affective loadings of symbol-referents and referent acts.*[35] Everyday experience shows that persons who express positive valuations with respect to a certain object or event sometimes attribute more importance to the opportunity of expressing these valuations verbally than to dealing with the concrete referents of all these appreciative words in the way of learning to know them, manipulating them, and/or consuming them. In this case the affective loadings of ideological *symbols* as opposed to their *referents* cause the individual to use these symbols as gratifying in themselves, irrespective of their concrete referents. This is what we have called the *expressive* type of concern for ideology. The case of the *pragmatic* type of concern for political matters is characterized by another distribution of affective loadings, most of the weight being laid on the importance of locating and dealing with the concrete referents of the valuative statements of the ideology. In this case gratification will be attained more readily by dealing with the concrete referents of the ideology than with the symbols of ideology.

A series of Guttman-scales have been constructed for various attitude areas to measure the degree of affective loading of the symbols and symbol acts as opposed to the symbol-referents and referent acts in these areas.[36] The items of these scales elicit opinions about how important it is to discuss in a factual way one's opinions in a given attitude area, to stick to them whatever the facts, to consider them matters of principle, to rely on "men of principle" rather than on men with a practical or scientific know-how in the relevant area, "to enjoy the comfort of opinion without the discomfort of thought," and so forth.

For reasons having to do with the use of the term "affective *loadings*" these scales have previously been called *L*-scales. In order to avoid continued confusion of our *L*-scale with the Minnesota Multiphasic Personality Inventory *L*-scale (the so-called *lie*-scale), we have rebaptized our *L*-scale, and now call it the KEY-scale. KEY-scales order respondents from a *high*-KEY, presumably characterized by an expressive-consummatory use of verbal symbols (= expressive ideologists) to a *low*-KEY assumed to tap the pragmatic-instrumental attitudinal style (= pure pragmatists). At the *zero point* of these Guttman-scales, as determined, for instance, by intensity analysis, we can define a *medium*-KEY, or rather a *mixed*-KEY position. *Mixed*-KEY subjects, presumably, do not favor symbolic gratification to the neglect of attaining, on the referential level, the values which are prescribed on the symbolic level. We assume that *mixed* or *medium*-KEY subjects have a better understanding than either *high*-KEY or *low*-KEY subjects of the two-way communication that may exist between symbolic activity on the one hand, and activities dealing with the symbol-referents on the other, symbolic activities guiding the search for goals and for information, and activities dealing with symbol-referents providing information, gratification or disappointment, which reinforces or modifies the structure of values and of factual assumptions existing on the symbolic level.[37] *Medium*-KEY subjects, then, correspond fairly well to what we have called pragmatic ideologists.

From what we have just said about the KEY-scale, one can argue that its name is justified not only from a heuristic point of view but also on theoretical grounds. Obviously the terms "high key" and "low key" as used in ordinary English in characterizing, say, different styles of political oratory do relate meaningfully to the "highs" and "lows" indicated on our KEY-scale. But we can also say on more theoretical grounds that the variable of "affective loading of ideological symbols as opposed to the affective loading of symbol-referents" which presumably is being measured by our KEY-scale is a *key* variable determining the extent of fusion or separation of feedback and directive processes between the levels of symbolic and referent activities in given areas of ideological concern.

Turning our attention to the operationalization of *environmental* ideological styles we can still use the KEY-scale. The proportion of, say, *high*-KEY "expressive ideologists" in a given environment can be used as an indicator of the prevailing ideological style in that environment.[38] To *high*-KEY subjects there will be a better fit between their expressive ideological style and the style prevailing in their environment, the larger the proportion of *high*-KEY subjects in that environment. There will be a less good fit between the "pure pragmatism" characteristic of *low*-KEY subjects and the ideological style of their environment, the larger the proportions of *high*-KEY subjects in that environment. *Medium*-KEY subjects are a special case: their assumed independence of environmental ideological styles makes the concept of fit less relevant on this point.

Our hypothesis H:1.1-2 can now be made operational by rewriting it in terms of the KEY-scale.

H(op):1.1–2 Among "pragmatic ideologists" (*medium*-KEY subjects) no correlation will be found between degree of political involvement and the proportions of political styles in their social environments; among "expressive ideologists" (*high*-KEY subjects) a positive correlation will be found between their political involvement and the proportion of other *high*-KEY subjects in their particular environments; and among "pure pragmatists" (*low*-KEY subjects) there will be a negative correlation

between their political involvement and the proportion of *high*-KEY persons in their environment.
The regression coefficient for the negative correlation among *low*-KEY subjects will be smaller than the regression coefficient for the positive correlation among *high*-KEY subjects.

   The first part of the prediction given in H(op):1.2 is clearly substantiated as can be seen from the diagram (Fig. 3–1). There is no correlation between

Figure 3–1

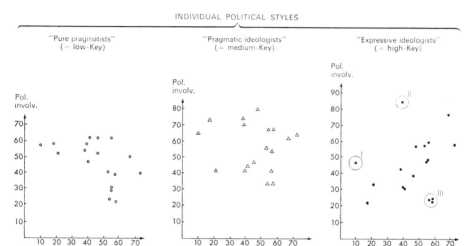

INDIVIDUAL POLITICAL STYLES

Environmental
Political Styles

Note: This diagram is adapted from Himmelstrand, *op. cit.*, p. 352. The proportions of *high*-KEY and *low*-KEY subjects which define the different environmental ideological styles refer to a set of environmental obtained by subclassifying a national sample of 1,523 young men between 20 and 30 years in 18 environmental classes on the basis of three variables: (1) the rural-urban variable, (2) education plus exposure to political information, and (3) degree of verbal exchange about political issues. Cf. *ibid.*, pp. 341–344 and 348–350. The scale of political involvement used is described and its validity discussed in *ibid.*, pp. 220–224 and 344–347.

the political involvement of *medium*-KEY subjects and the political style prevailing in their environment, while there is a positive and a negative correlation, respectively, for *high*-KEY and *low*-KEY subjects. Visual inspection of the diagrams seems to lend support also to the second part of the prediction. However, the regression coefficients for the positive and negative correlations seen in the diagrams, are not according to our expectations. The regression coefficient for the positive correlation among *high*-KEY subjects is only $+.28$, while the negative correlation among *low*-KEY subjects exhibits a regression coefficient equal to $-.42$. This partial reversal of our prediction can be seen to depend on a few deviant cases which are encircled in the diagram. A closer look at these cases suggests the following interpretation: Self-ratings of involvement, which are basic to our scale of political involvement, depend not only on motivational factors of the type mentioned in our previous discussion, but also on comparisons with others, or with one's own activities in other fields than politics. The deviant cases are on the average characterized by either a very high or a very low degree of political activity.[39] Removing these extreme cases among low-KEY as well as high-KEY subjects, and thereby presumably eliminating the influence of comparative judgments on the scores of our involvement scale, the regression coefficients turn out the way we predicted: $-.12$ for low-KEY and $+.76$ for high-KEY subjects, low-KEY subjects thus being less dependent on the ideological style of their environment than high-KEY subjects.[40]

The empirical results here presented derive from a study which was made before television became important in Swedish election campaigns (see p. 81). I believe that somewhat different results would have been obtained if TV had been as important at the time of that study as it is now. The average level of political involvement would probably have been higher. The question remains whether this higher average level of political involvement would have implied only a changed value of the parameter representing the height of the regression lines in our diagram or whether also the gradients of these lines would have been changed. It is possible that factual, technical and economical themes appear very much more stimulating to an expressive ideologist when they are transmitted through the "hot" medium of television than they are when coming from the mouths of pragmatically inclined acquaintances—at least if such themes are conveyed in a way that exploits the visual and dramatic potentialities of TV. Citizens with an expressive attitudinal style who otherwise have little interest in the more factual aspects of political messages are thus mobilized to become somewhat involved in politics, even in an environment which on the whole does not fit their political style. If this is so, it may imply that the regression line representing the covariation of political involvement with goodness of fit between individual and environmental ideological styles will be less steep among expressive ideologists than predicted by H(op): 1.1–2. Whether the inclination of the regression line for low-KEY pragmatists will become less steep as a result of exposure to politics over TV is difficult to say without more specified knowledge about the characteristics of such TV messages.

In a different perspective one can describe the entry of TV into the political communication network as a new opening for charismatic appeals—charisma here taken in a broad sense pertaining to political parties as well as to political personalities. What Charles Osgood has described as the *dynamism* factor in the "semantic space" of political symbols probably becomes even more important with TV.[41] Anyone or any party who projects an image of action and vigor—a type of projection for which the TV medium is eminently suitable—will thereby be able to mobilize significant segments of a "mass-society" as well as dropouts from a dissolving "plural society."[42] This kind of mobilization which implies reinforcement and elaboration of already existing expressive and consummatory orientations to political and ideological symbols in the mass audience depends not so much on *what* record of political accomplishments, and *what* perspective on future political developments are presented through TV, but on *how* it is done. Content becomes less important than style. Or, more precisely: a given content can become significant to important segments of prospective voters only by being exhibited in a style which has "dynamism."

Conclusions

A decreasing ideological saliency is an important aspect of so-called depoliticization. Depoliticization in this sense is often supposed to cause a decline of subjective involvement in political affairs. However, our theoretical analysis as well as our empirical data suggest a somewhat different idea. Subjective involvement in political affairs will probably not be reduced *throughout the citizenry* when ideological saliency becomes less manifest. Much will depend on the ideological style of individual citizens and of their immediate environments, and on the "goodness of fit" of individual and environmental ideological styles. Only if there is a less good fit between individual and environmental ideological styles do we suspect a decline of political involvement. The dimension of ideological style which has been the main focus of my research, can be indicated by labels such as the "pure pragmatist," the "pragmatic ideologist," and the "expressive ideologist." A Guttman scale—the so-called KEY-scale—was used to measure the dimension presumably underlying these labels.

The goodness-of-fit assumption, when elaborated, leads to the more specified conclusion that depoliticization in the sense of a decreasing ideological saliency will cause a decline of political involvement only if expressive ideologists dominate the citizenry. A low saliency of manifest ideological themes will not fit the expressive ideologists. On the other hand pure pragmatists may get even more involved in political matters if there is some degree of such depoliticization. Pragmatic ideologists who are characterized by their ability to integrate ideological and pragmatic considerations, seem to be able to maintain their political involvement regardless of the ideological style prevailing in their political environment.

Ultimately these conclusions will have to be tested by comparative research in political communities exhibiting various degrees of ideological saliency, or at different times in one and the same community. Experimental studies comparing artificially created "political communities" with various degrees of ideological saliency are also possible.

Political involvement rather than political participation has been the main dependent variable in this paper. However, the interplay of individual and environmental ideological styles which I have mentioned seems to be an important determinant also of the structure if not the degree of political participation. Data not presented here suggest that people with an expressive concern for the symbols of ideology generally are less active in situations which require and promote knowledge about the realities with which these symbols are dealing.[43] It seems as if people with an expressive concern for ideology would tend to distribute their participation in a different way than the pure pragmatists or the pragmatic ideologists. A more "intensive" participation structure seems to be the rule among "expressive ideologists," their memberships being restricted to one association, or a few very similar ones, and their activities to a small set of partisan symbol acts. We might characterize this particular kind of structure by saying that it exhibits a high degree of *membership crystallization*. Quite another picture with a more "extensive" structure of participation and activity seems to dominate among those with more of a pragmatic orientation to ideological issues. Here we might talk of a low degree of membership crystallization, since memberships are distributed among several different kinds of associations and organizations rather than crystallized around one particular type.[44]

It is interesting to note, as we have done, that expressive ideologists not only seem to be particularly dependent on environmental support to maintain their political involvement but also tend to crystallize their group memberships in a way which maximizes exposure to congenial and supporting ideological styles only. But even if degree of membership crystallization is determined partly by individual style, other determining factors of a collective or societal nature most likely are equally or more important. Extent of geographical and social mobility in the population at large, rate of urbanization, range and efficiency of mass communications, all these factors have their part in determining whether or not individuals with an expressive ideological style are successful in crystallizing their memberships so as to insulate themselves against people with contrasting ideological styles.

The likelihood of exposure to contrasting ideological styles is also dependent on the *distribution* of ideological styles within the citizenry, and between the citizenry and the polity, of course. Gabriel Almond's concept of a "cultural dualism" in political systems, polity and citizenry being characterized by contrasting ideological styles, seems relevant here.[45] In the final analysis, the extent of such a dualism of political culture in conjunction with the other collective and structural factors previously mentioned will have to be considered to account for the prevalence of various degrees of fit between individual and environmental ideological styles, and to explain variations of political involvement among the citizens.

We do not deny the importance of even other factors, like education and perceived possibilities of influencing political decisions, in determining the degree of subjective involvement in political affairs; but in this paper ideological saliency, ideological style and the goodness-of-fit of such styles have been singled out for particular consideration.

The theory and data presented in this paper suggest some problems for democracy. If depoliticization gathers momentum in the political bodies while at the same time large or crucially important part of the public retain much of an expressive concern for political matters, this kind of dualism of political culture may give rise to wavering and irrationally unstabilizing changes of political involvement. Between elections when the factual, technical and economical issues of depoliticized politics are most prominent, politics may seem very dull indeed to the expressive ideologists in the public. In this period reforms and legislation, however, may be accepted as we accept most of the helpful gadgets which become part of our lives. But when election time comes, and the honorific symbols of ideology once again are in the air, all this can be drastically changed. Politics becomes important—but in a way disconnected from life between elections. Reforms and legislation recently accepted in a matter-of-fact way now may be perceived as sinister manipulations with the freedom or with the welfare of the individual, or lost out of sight completely in the glaring light of party symbolism.

But we can also conceive of another type of shift of political "tuning" from interelection to election time which mostly operates in the opposite direction. Between elections some citizens whose personal orientation to politics is expressive may be caught up in a cobweb of honorific terms from bourgeois political culture, like "individual freedom," "private initiative," "free enterprise," "big-bad-government," and so forth. Concepts of bourgeois political language seem to be a potent aspect of the political culture outside of organized party activities and electioneering, even in a country like Sweden. But when election time comes and the campaign starts rolling, political allegiance may become less of a personal affair to these citizens and more a question of loyalty to one's peers and workmates, and their political allegiance might be Social Democratic. An involvement with certain bourgeois political symbols between elections thus turns out to have little connection with the political behavior mobilized in election time.[46]

From a democratic point of view this particular kind of transformation of interelection political apathy or low involvement into high involvement at election time does seem to be a bit problematic for the simple reason that it is hard to know what "phase" of the transformation best represents the individual citizen. If one's normative theory of democracy insists on, or at least favors, representation of fairly reflected opinions with rather clearcut practical and concrete reference, the problem does not become less difficult to solve since it would seem less than feasible to construct a machinery that would tap public opinion only when each individual citizen in his phase-movement is optimizing his own rationality and practicality. However, if changes of ideological saliency in the political propaganda is accompanied by a gradual and consonant development of ideological style in the electorate, seems to be a probable development in Sweden, a wavering and disconnected change in the public mood is less likely to occur and the problem of representation just indicated becomes less pressing. If the ideological style of individual citizens acquires a better fit with the pragmatic ideological style of what we have called a spuriously depoliticized political system so as to minimize the dualism of style in political culture, ideology may become a ground for creative transformation of values into action, and of social and economic discoveries and innovations into values rather than a refuge for pickled and preserved notions of the past.

Finally a few words about the limitations of this paper as seen in the light of some more recent political developments in Sweden (and elsewhere) after 1966.

Having emphasized mainly structural and functional aspects of ideological impact in political affairs, the *content* of political ideology, and the degree of dissensus with regard to ideological content deliberately have been passed over very superficially in this paper. But the ideological resurgence which can be sensed in many countries where very recently the "end of ideology" was supposed to be immanent cannot be completely understood in the usual functional terms, but must be traced back to emerging or rediscovered structural strains in these societies, and perhaps also in some cases to the absence of structures which could completely absorb, tackle or transform these structural strains within the old framework. When, for instance, the Swedish Social Democratic government and the Swedish trade unions, largely because of their own efforts to strengthen the economy by removing "market imperfections," increasingly have been confronted with a strong, powerful and demanding private sector, and have been trying to balance this development by increasing the economic power of the government, this has forcefully reintroduced the old ideological issue of the public versus the private interest which, in Sweden, for some time had been forgotten, or at least swallowed up in the realities and rhetoric of collaboration. The resurgence of such ideological issues in response to structural change is a phenomenon which cannot be studied properly with the theoretical notions presented in this paper. However, once such an ideological resurgence has taken place, or introduced as a given fact, the conceptualization of diverse ideological styles that we have suggested would still seem to offer fruitful avenues of sociological analysis.

THE TREND TOWARD POLITICAL CONSENSUS:
The Case of Norway

ULF TORGERSEN

THIS PAPER takes its point of departure in the current concern within political science and political sociology with a phenomenon, or rather a cluster of related phenomena, which has been very noticeable in many post-World War II western political systems. This is the trend toward decreasing political conflict and increasing political consensus. This trend has been given various names. Words like "the end of ideology," "*fin de l'âge idéologique*" and "*Entideologizierung*" have been applied, but there is little doubt that the problems referred to are essentially similar. I think that within this overall cluster of problems one can further make a distinction between four analytically separate, though empirically intertwined problems:

First, there is the problem of the decreasing-differences between the platforms and programs of the various parties. This is a problem concerning the major alternatives of political choice existing within a political system;[1]

Second there is the question of the character of the intellectual and academic discussion in the various countries, of the extent to which new aspects of politics, or new perspectives on politics have tended to change its focus and character;[2]

Third, there is the problem of mass activity, of the extent to which the disappearance of a "hot" political climate has had the consequence of

Reprinted from *Acta Sociologica*, vol. 6 (1962), pp. 159–172.

Notes to this chapter are on pp. 365–366.

sapping the strength of the parties, and leaving them as pretty empty organizational shells, since what they offer is just the difference between "tweedledee" and "tweedledum," in a society where other and more exciting ways of spending one's leisure time have emerged;[3]

Fourth, there is the problem of the possible restructuring of the channels of political influence; there have been cases in which the parties in a country (a very good case in point is Austria) have established elaborate agreements between themselves in order to share power. A related problem concerns the extent to which the parties appear to the various groups which want to influence the decisions of the central authorities to be the appropriate channels of pressure.[4]

In this paper I want to make a brief excursion into all these four related topics with reference to one country, Norway. To this I will add a few comments, on the whole speculative, on the possible preconditions of the current state of affairs.

Decreasing Differences Between the Parties

If in one short word one wants to characterize the political situation in present-day Norway, *depoliticization* seems to be the one that fits best.

The trend in this direction is not exclusively a postwar phenomenon. But it is in the postwar period that the tendencies towards a decline of the previously strong political tensions and the bitter conflicts between the left and the right, really have gained momentum. Without doubt the war had a noticeable effect in establishing cross-party ties, stemming from loyalties from the underground activities. The period immediately after the war was characterized by a minimum of political conflict, and it was supposed that this was something that had come to stay. This was not exactly what happened. The election in 1949 showed a rather marked increase in political conflict between the parties, but I think that rather than interpreting this event as an indicator of anything else it should be seen as an event necessary for displaying to the electorate the distinctiveness of the parties. The events that have followed the 1949 election have rather emphasized this interpretation. The development has been more and more in the direction of decreasing political conflict. This had led to the situation that many areas of decisions have been "taken out of politics"— such as foreign politics and defence politics—and it has led the parties to compete for a position in the center of the battle, and to try to move away from any position that might be interpreted as *extreme*. The parties have differed somewhat in their strategies for reaching this highly desired goal: each of the parties have their own special groups that must not be forgotten in the general concern for getting the vote of the "marginal voter." This means that the character of this endeavor and the internal problems that stem from this, vary from party to party, but the essential problem is the same.

The *Labour party* was before the war a party inclined toward a Marxian interpretation of society and politics. The new program adopted in 1949 showed how far the party had moved in the direction of a broad "people's party" covering all social groups. The party has largely dropped its plans for nationalization. This development may have been facilitated by the fact that nationalization was in the more revolutionary period described as "state capitalism," an especially wicked variety of capitalism. The party thus had had no important history of socialization plans: its very "revolutionary" past eased the transformation to a purely pragmatic orientation. The party still maintains that the goal is "socialism," a noun usually defined in a rather loose way, but that there are many means of achieving it, and that nationalization is not among the best, as a committee on that question expressed it some years ago. It is also highly indicative of the present temper within the Norwegian Labour party that when a member of the opposition urged the Labour government to throw away old-fashioned ideas just as the British Labour party was in the process of doing, the Prime Minister replied that this really had been done years ago by the Scandinavian socialist parties.[5] The party has not been able to transform itself without some internal conflicts. In 1957 a small splinter party seceded, but stayed a minute sect, and in 1961 another splinter party, this time with a lot more backing, was established, mainly as a result of the ambiguous stand taken by the Labour party on the question of nuclear weapons in Norway. Generally the Labour leadership has shown great flexibility in adapting to the various strains of the geographically and socially highly heterogeneous party.

The *Conservative party* has also traveled toward the center, but from the opposite direction. In 1949 the party fought the election battle under the slogan "Let us change the system," but the lack of success forced the party to take up other lines of propaganda. More deep-seated forces were at work, too. The Conservative party has since the war been going through some rather crucial changes: besides the business element the element of white collar workers has become increasingly more important. The attempt to win over this rapidly growing social class to conservative policies has forced the party to softpedal the liberalist and all-out business orientation, and to stress the essentially reformist and welfare state-accepting character of the party. It has grown more "me-too-ist" in the more recent political campaigns, and has more or less said that "anything you have done I'd have done better." This change of strategy has meant a certain alienation from the business elements in the party, and a very hostile attitude between "Libertas," essentially a business-financed fund for anti-socialist information, and the Conservative headquarters. This has partly been tackled through attempts to consolidate the organization and to bureaucratize the party, in order to make it more independent of business sources of financing, but the issue is not quite solved.

A similar problem exists within the *Agrarian party*. For quite a long time after the war the Agrarian Party was close to an activist line of policy, and took a rather conservative stand on many issues. Gradually, however, this line has been abandoned and the leadership within the party has shifted to men who have been more conciliatory in their attitudes to other parties and perspectives. The party has changed its name to the *Center party*, and has recently been involved in negotiations with the other "parties of the center," in order to see what could possibly be done in order to solidify themselves as a "third force" in Norwegian politics. So far very little has come of it.

The *Liberal party* is one of these parties, and it has all the time emphasized its middle-of-the-road character. But this party is exactly the party which has suffered the greatest losses in the more recent elections. Torn between the various demands from the city liberals, the farm interests and the fundamentalist antialcohol section of the party it has been able to please no one completely, and its political importance has declined. The other of these parties is the *Christian People's party*, which represents the more fundamentalist sections of the population. It made some headway just after the war, but seems to have been on the decline recently.

The *Communist party* has been declining gradually since the war, and thus testifies to the reduction of the extreme positions in political life.

This development towards the political center has not gone on unnoticed by the politicians themselves. The parliamentary records and the newspapers abound in statements to the effect that the postwar period has eliminated really fierce political fights. "The area of political disagreement has been greatly reduced," said one of the Conservative leaders. "The most important feature is that we have been able to work out certain norms that are accepted by everybody."[6] One of the leaders of the Liberal party expressed the notion that the party programs "were essentially similar." The Labour Prime Minister said in 1957 that there were many areas "where there is no deep disagreements between the parties," and recently stated this even more emphatically: "When it really comes to brass tacks, it appears as if we don't have very much to fight about, really. Quite obviously none of the parties are very excited about being too different from the others."[7] A clearer and more explicit description of the present absence of political conflict would be hard to find.

Politics and the Academic Debate

Let us now turn away from the debate going on in the political arena to the, presumably, more reflective and at any rate more detached orientations of men with primarily intellectual concerns. Again we find the same general pattern of decline of excitement about what is usually called the "old" issues of politics; if there is any great concern with political issues, these are likely to be rather different from the "old" ones. Just to emphasize the lack of concern with the old questions: in a recently published jubilee-book of graduates from the University of Oslo, the graduates were asked about the present applicability of the distinction "bourgeois"—"socialist." Only about 10 per cent answered, but among those who did answer there was almost complete unanimity about the outdated character of the distinction, which was supposed to have mainly historical interests.[8]

As I mentioned, this reduced concern for the traditional lines of political cleavage may have different results, and it may be hard to say which one is the most common. Partly the result is reduced concern for politics. The content of the leading Norwegian periodical *Samtiden* has since the war gradually shifted from social problems to highly personal and philosophical problems, in a way similar to the change following the decline of interest in political questions among intellectuals in Norway at the turn of the century.[9]

In part, interests among academics have turned in new directions. If one looks at the Conservative Student Association at the University of Oslo, it is quite evident that there has been a very clear change of emphasis and leadership. While in the period up to well past 1950 the organization was mainly interested in the "old" questions, and mainly run by students from the Law School, which is the traditional Conservative stronghold at the University of Oslo, the interest has since gradually changed to other fields, and the activities of the Conservative students are now much more literary and philosophical. This change, which has meant that students of liberal arts have become more important within the association, is a change which is partly associated with the decline of interest in politics *proper*, but it also ties in with the more general development within the Conservative party. The Conservative groups that fight the business elements within the Conservative party through appeals to Burke, and who have had considerable success, have had close connections with this student association. One might question the logical connection between Burke and a switch to white-collar appeals, but as a fact it cannot be doubted.

The Socialist student organizations exhibit somewhat different features. One of them is independent of the Labour party: it was expelled some years ago. It is essentially Socialist on the questions of domestic politics and usually demands more nationalization, but the most important issues are foreign policy issues. The other organization belongs to the Labour party and follows very much the same policy as the party.

The Channels of Influence

The decreasing difference in the actual program of the parties has led to none of the consequences that have occurred in Austria. The cooperation of the parties has not been formally established, but there is hardly any reason to assume that this is of any real importance; for all practical purposes the co-operation between the party leaders has been as effective as it could possibly be.

This means that even if there is no "charter of interparty cooperation" there is just as much "waning of opposition" as in the cases described by Kirchheimer. This is in a way a direct consequence of the ideological similarity: the standard argument of the Labour party against the Conservative opposition is now not that they have hatched wicked plots and sinister schemes, but that they in fact do not have any other program at all, and the standard retort is that this is because the Labour party has improved in a Conservative direction. Leaving aside the question of the amount of truth in these statements, it is pretty evident that this makes for rather amiable parliamentary conditions.

Indeed, cross-party friendships in Parliament have become much more frequent in the recent years than they were immediately after the war, and it has made for rather smooth between-party cooperation. This has also had another effect: it now happens very rarely that a Cabinet minister stakes his position on one particular piece of legislation or other measure that has to be accepted by Parliament. This has happened in *one* case after the war, apart from the cases in which the whole government threatened to go, and caused general surprise and a reaction which heralded the resigning minister as particularly brave and principled.

It is probably part of a relatively stable and conflictless democracy that the different party elites feel as loyal to each other as to their own followers: such cross-party loyalties help to check their inclination to exploit situations for short-term gains for their own party. Some sociologists have in this seen the outstanding characteristic of what they call "pluralistic politics" as against "ideological politics."[10] We do not disagree in principle in this conclusion but we must ask ourselves exactly how much a society can have of such cross-party loyalties before it saps the sources of a vital political system: the activity of the citizens in political organizations. We shall look a little closer into this problem in the next section of this paper.

Mass Mobilization for Political Purposes

We have so far described some trends within the strata of the population closest to politics, among the people most likely to express their conception of how it really works, but we have said next to nothing about corresponding trends in the broader activities of the rank-and-file voters. The questions most central in this respect are the following:

To what extent has the decreasing political tension brought about a decrease in *electoral turnout*?

To what extent has the decreasing political tension tended to reduce people's involvement in the *organized party activity*?

To what extent has the decreasing political tension worked to limit people's *participation in the electoral contest*, e.g. their attendance at meetings, their turnout at rallies and so forth?

We shall try to give a brief overview of the trends visible within these areas. The evidence presented will in some respects be incomplete, and in other ways quite circumstantial; nevertheless we think it gives at least some credence to the conclusions that we will suggest.

Table 4–1 summarizes the trends in electoral turnout from 1945 to 1959. For a variety of reasons, turnout was generally low throughout the country at the first postwar elections in 1945. There was a steep increase from 1947 onwards, then a culmination in 1949 and 1951, and since that time either stagnation or some decline. There are important differences, however, between the largest cities and the rest of the country.

In the case of *parliamentary* elections voting reached a peak in 1949 and has

TABLE 4–1

Electoral Turnout 1945–1959

		PARLIAMENTARY ELECTIONS				MUNICIPAL ELECTIONS				
		1945	1949	1953	1957	1945	1947	1951	1955	1959
All cities	Men	82.0	87.8	84.9	83.1	73.8	80.9	81.0	77.4	77.7
	Women	79.5	85.2	83.2	81.9	67.2	77.5	79.5	77.0	76.8
Oslo	Men	87.3	88.5	85.0	83.7	73.4	83.5	83.2	79.7	79.0
	Women	83.5	86.1	84.0	82.7	66.1	79.3	81.7	79.9	78.3
Bergen	Men	81.8	86.3	82.0	79.9	72.9	78.7	77.4	72.9	74.2
	Women	86.8	84.5	81.7	79.1	65.7	76.3	77.1	72.1	72.9
Trondheim	Men	81.0	86.7	82.6	80.9	69.2	75.4	78.6	75.0	75.3
	Women	78.8	83.3	80.8	79.8	59.8	69.5	76.8	74.7	74.2
Stavanger	Men	86.0	87.6	89.2	81.5	75.5	78.4	80.9	74.2	77.6
	Women	80.6	83.2	80.1	82.1	70.3	77.4	80.1	74.8	76.6
Rural	Men	77.2	83.5	80.7	79.2	70.3	73.0	73.1	71.8	73.3
communes	Women	68.0	74.8	72.8	73.2	56.7	62.1	64.4	65.2	68.0

since dropped back several percentage points. This drop is most marked in the largest cities: in Oslo 4.8 for men and 3.4 for women, in Bergen 6.4 and 5.4, in Trondheim 5.8 and 3.5, in Stavanger 6.1 and 1.1. The decline was less marked in the smaller cities and in the countryside. This difference comes out very clearly in the *local* elections. For these the peak year was 1951. The decline from 1951 to 1959 was for Oslo 4.2 and 3.4, for Bergen 3.2 and 4.2 for Trondheim 3.3 and 2.6, for Stavanger 3.3 and 3.4. By contrast there was a slight *increase for the men and quite a marked one for the women in the rural communes*. We may interpret this as evidence that there are two opposite movements at work in the system: in the center there is increasing *de-politicization* and some slight decline in the level of mass mobilization while in the periphery there is still at work a process of *increasing politicization* through further party efforts. For further details on turnout levels in the rural communes the reader is referred to the paper by Rokkan and Valen.[11]

Is this same trend discernible in the fluctuations in party membership?

There is no indication of a general trend: the situation differs from party to party. For the *Labour party* the records indicate (*Table 4–2*) a gradual decline in membership figures since roughly 1949. That year the membership reached an all-time high; never before and never since has the party had so many members. From that year on we have witnessed a pretty regular decline; the figures for 1959 indicate 162,093 members, and this is most likely to be some-what inflated, particularly because of multiple affiliations. The sources do not allow assessments of how much of the decline has been in collective member-ship and how much in individually affiliated members. Data from the Oslo branch of the party indicate a stronger decline in individual membership than in collective membership. The decline in absolute membership figures implies an even more distinct drop in the percentage of the Labour voters who are party members (see *Table 4–2*). This is less marked for Oslo, where, however,

Table 4–2

Reported Membership in the Labour Party 1946–1959

	THE WHOLE COUNTRY			OSLO		
	Total Individual and Collective Members	Total Labour Votes	Members %	Total Individual and Collective Members	Total Labour Votes	Members %
1946	197638			46934		
1947 (municipal el.)	202043	550477	36.7	55618	91065	61.1
1948	203094			59426		
1949 (parliamentary el.)	204055	803471	25.4	61948	119741	51.7
1950	200501			65504		
1951 (municipal el.)	179361	659290	27.2	62710	107249	58.5
1952	178102			62915		
1953 (parliamentary el.)	178004	830448	21.4	62499	119784	52.2
1954	174575			61272		
1955 (municipal el.)	174080	696411	25.0	60892	110266	55.2
1956	170823			59195		
1957 (parliamentary el.)	163991	865675	18.9	57339	129456	44.3
1958	165455			57267		
1959 (municipal el.)	162093	729503	12.2	x	118849	48.2

s o u r c e s : Figures for the whole country are from the annual reports of the Norwegian Labour party, issued under the title Det norske arbeiderparti: *Beretning*, for the years in question. The figures for Oslo were obtained from the annual reports from the Oslo Labour party, issued under the title Oslo Arbeiderparti: *Beretning*. For both figures members of youth organizations are included. Computations of the member-voter ratios therefore are not *quite* exact, as the membership figures include individuals below voting age. For 1959 the computation for Oslo is based on the 1958 figures.

the same general trend appears to be present. The relative decline is even more marked in the percentage of individual members: in 1949 there were about 7,300 out of 119,000, or about 6 per cent in 1957 5,700 out of 129,000, or less than 4 per cent. It is well known that the Labour party looks with considerable worry on this trend. The drop in membership does not, however, seem to be associated with any marked turn away from Labour at the polls: on the contrary, despite this decline in membership, the Labour party has since the end of the war almost invariably solidified its position in the electorate, both in the capital and in the country as a whole.[12]

The lack of relationship between this decline of party activity and the results at the polls is brought out very clearly in the case of the Labour youth organization. There is very little reason to believe that the Labour party has any particularly weak positions among the young voters. And still it is the youth branch of the party that has suffered the most drastic decline. In Oslo, the number of youth members dropped from 1,800 in 1949 to 500 in 1957, and similar tendencies have prevailed in many other areas of the country.

If we turn to the *Conservative party*, we find a different picture. According to the figures reported by various agencies within the Conservative organization, the party has had an extraordinary growth during the first decade of the postwar period. This growth is supposed to have increased the figures for the Conservative party proper (here Women's Conservative Associations and Young Conservatives are not counted) from 39,655 in 1949 to 66,385 at the end of 1952, to 72,905 in 1958 and 71,343 in 1960. Added to this growth comes the membership for the Conservative Youth organization; it claims to have reached the figure 20,000 members in 1950 and has stuck to that figure ever since, the latest record known to the author being for 1958. For the Oslo branch of the Young Conservatives a similar stagnation seems to have occurred: in 1951 they claimed to have 16 locals in Oslo, with a total membership of about 3,200, in 1954 they reported 3,000 members in 12 locals, in 1957 2,800 and in 1959 3,000 members. These figures certainly are higher than those reported by the Labour Youth Organization, though there may be reason to assume that the concept of membership here may be somewhat more elusive. Without arguing about this, we will, however, call the attention to the stagnation in the figures. For many years the Conservative organization has kept as their official figure a total of 100,000 for all categories of members and used this to indicate their strong position among the voters. The party has also recently given figures for the total number of members of voting age: in 1956 93,000, in 1957 95,976, in 1958 96,931, and in 1960 97,509. This is a slight increase, which roughly matches the increase in votes. On the whole, I think that there is fairly good reason to assume that there has been a stagnation in absolute figures, and probably a loss in relative terms in the last five years.

For the *Communist party* there has most certainly been a marked decrease since 1949, but to buttress this with exact figures is extremely complicated, due to the high level of secrecy of internal party affairs.

For the other parties, the Christian People's party, the Liberal party, and the Agrarian party, we have not been able to get hold of membership over any length of time.[13] On the whole, there is reason to believe that the proportion of the members relative to the voters is likely to have declined somewhat during recent years. The absolute figures reported by the parties are either declining or stagnant, while the number of voters have increased for both of the parties we have evidence for.

Very much the same factors that seem to reduce people's willingness to *join* parties seem to be present when it comes to attending the campaigns put up by the different parties before the elections. This is of course partly a two-way causation as the decrease in the organizational strength reduces the capacity for arranging meetings, organizing rallies and so forth. As a consequence, the number of meetings arranged by the parties before the elections have tended to decline pretty clearly since the 1949 election campaign.

The data supporting this assumption are somewhat scanty, and some of the evidence is rather circumstantial. But there is a remarkable similarity in the conclusions which can be drawn.

The Labour party arranged during the 1949 campaign roughly 5,000 meetings throughout the country. In 1953 there were only 3,200 meetings and in 1957 (the King died so the plans were not actually carried out) the plans included some 2,000 meetings. Indeed, the reduction is even more marked, since among these meetings are also counted "discussion" meetings, where more than one party is present. Such meetings hardly ever occurred before 1953, when they were used occasionally, but with fairly great success, as it meant more of a show for the audience, and there were plans for quite a number in 1957. This means that an increasing proportion of the meetings we have given figures for cannot be classified as purely Labour meetings.

The Agrarian party arranged about 2,000 meetings in 1949, and had planned roughly 1,000 meetings for 1957.

That this decline in meetings had started in 1953 is also indicated by some other data: The Conservative party in the province of Rogaland arranged 54 meetings in 1949, 50 in 1953, while the corresponding figures for the Labour party are 168 and 130. The Conservative party in the province of Buskerud had more than 50 meetings in 1949, in 1953 less than 30; the figures for the Labour party were 160 and 100 respectively.

Concluding Remarks: The Consensus and Its Preconditions

We have given a somewhat perfunctory analysis of the political conditions in postwar Norway, but we have not touched on the question of the origin of these conditions or the likelihood that they will remain stable. It goes without saying that our treatment of that subject will be even more cursory: what we can do is primarily to offer some comments on the theories presented in accounting for similar phenomena in other western political systems. The essence of my criticism, so far as Norway is concerned, is that too much emphasis has been placed on the purely social and economic aspects of the historical development and too little on the character of the political institutions.

The starting point for my considerations along these lines is a dissatisfaction with the tendency to look at modern western history as if it is approaching some absolute zero. In the case of Norway, this perspective is simply grossly misleading. The normal state of affairs in this country during the last 150 years has not been a high-pitched ideological crisis; on the contrary, this situation has been rather unusual, more unusual, maybe, than in most other countries. Consensus rather than dissensus has been the prevailing condition. Just to give a brief summary: political consensus was the rule almost until 1880. With the exception of the period following 1814 and the short rupture of political peace resulting from labour unrest in 1848, there was substantial agreement on most questions until well into the 1870's. Then there was a tense period until 1884, followed by a cooling-off period that ended sometime before 1905. This was followed by a relatively peaceful period until the end of World War I, when the labour movement was radicalized, and finally joined the Comintern in 1920. 1884 and 1919–1920 were probably the tensest moments during the last 150 years; here I leave aside the exogenous conflict with Germany. The situation of the twenties changed very soon, however. The radicalization of the Norwegian Labour party is very well known to most political sociologists, but what they invariably fail to notice is the extremely speedy deradicalization that brought the party from membership in Comintern to the Cabinet in the course of four years. Any analysis which limits itself to the strictly social variables, such as "speed of industrialization," will rightly assess the basis for the radical upsurge, but such an approach will fail to come to grips with the problems contained in the limited level of revolutionary activity displayed (concrete plans for revolutionary activity, such as real preparation for armed conflict hardly existed) and in the rapid decline of the revolutionary wave.[14]

In this respect it is helpful to look back at the other event just mentioned, the crisis in 1884. At this time, the political system was changed from one dominated by civil servants to a parliamentary system, but without leaving any unresolved deep conflicts, and without essentially threatening the legitimacy of the system. In a sense there is a basic similarity between these two events: in both cases the tension was reduced after a reasonably short time. The political system was in both cases able to incorporate new movements and new elites in an extremely rapid fashion.

These remarks are meant as a reminder that too much attention to the social basis of new political movements is in a way to ignore "politics," because it tends to divert the attention from the fact that a social movement is not just an expressive act by some social collectivity, it is just as much an organized effort to get something, and the chances that groups will get these things depend upon the character of the political action of those whose cooperation is needed if they are to be able to get it in a relatively peaceful fashion. To try to explain social movements by leaving out the policy of the "established elites" and the political institutions is like trying to explain the moves of one of the two players of a game of chess, while closing one's eyes to what the other player is up to, and to the rules of the gmae.

The implication of this is that it helps little to study social movements, comparatively or otherwise, if this is not done in the sense of a study of their interaction with the established social institutions or elites. In the Norwegian case this has mainly this relevance to the problems just stated: because of the weakness of ascriptive values in the Norwegian civil servant upper class, and later in the business upper class, their ability to withstand the pressures from below and their tendency to co-opt the new elements have been rather marked traits of their political strategy, and their relatively unmilitary orientation— due to the absence of military traditions and of a strong army—has reinforced this tendency to appease rather than to fight back. Only when such considerations are included in the reflections about the causes of depoliticization can we hope to come to grips with the question. And the consequence of such an analysis must be a deep concern not only with the character of the new social movements, but with the broader capacity—if so metaphysically tinged phrases can be accepted—of the political system to weed out the sources of conflict by appropriate "action."

It will be seen that one of the explanations that arise from this is that Norway is relatively free of internal political tension because it has been that way all the time. If this is to push the problem one step back, the answer is that this is the nature of historical explanation. I have not here given any really sufficient account of the possible sources of this peaceful state of affairs. Rather I have sketched some of the possibilities that should be looked into because the usual explanations are seen to be deficient. They may describe the potential social movements, and they may throw light on qualities pertaining to the early phase of such movements. But a broader and in a sense more "political" orientation is needed in order to account for their future fate, as in the case of the Norwegian trend towards political consensus.

TWO

Geography, Class, and Voting Behavior

5

AGGREGATE ELECTION DATA AND BRITISH PARTY ALIGNMENTS, 1885–1910

JAMES CORNFORD

Introduction

ALTHOUGH both the volume and the sophistication of work on the historical study of British electoral politics have increased greatly over the last few years, the tendency has been to concentrate either on the politics of particular regions over time or on particular general elections in imitation of the contemporary Nuffield election studies.[1] There is much to be said for these tactics, but it may also be useful to combine the two dimensions to get a national picture over time. This paper is a modest attempt to follow the example of W. Dean Burnham[2] by examining aggregate election data for what they can be made to reveal about "the British Political Universe" in the first period of its modern electoral system, in which eight general elections were contested with the same franchise qualifications and constituency boundaries. The aim is threefold: to provide an overall picture of electoral stability and change, and hence of party fortunes; to trace different patterns in different regions and types of constituency; and to examine the variations in the impact of the main political developments of the period.

The British Electoral Scene, 1885–1910[3]

Between 1885 and 1910 the British electoral system combined marked regional differences in the basic division of the vote (or party strength) and considerable national homogeneity in short-term fluctuations. The technicalities of the system yield none of the ingenious devices Burnham found for measuring political behavior in the United States, but they do create difficulties in comparing constituency with constituency or election with election, and make it more than usually hazardous to argue from the aggregate to individual behavior.[4]

A paper prepared for the World Congress of I.P.S.A., Brussels, Sept., 1967.

Notes to this chapter are on pp. 366–367.

REGIONAL VARIATIONS IN PARTY STRENGTH

The simplest means of demonstrating regional differences in party strength over time is to fall back from margins of victory to security of tenure: Table 5–1 gives the distribution of seats in the different regions by the number of times they were won by the Conservatives (and their allies the Liberal Unionists after 1886) and demonstrates conveniently the well-recognized fact of Liberal strength in Scotland, Wales and the North as against the Unionist predominance in the South and Home counties.

TABLE 5–1

Regional Differences in Party Strength

REGION	NUMBER OF SINGLE MEMBER CONSTITUENCIES WON BY UNIONISTS IN GENERAL ELECTIONS, 1885–1910			
	0–2 Times	3–5 Times	6–8 Times	Total
Scotland	39	19	10	68
Wales	27	4	1	32
North	17	6	5	28
Yorkshire	31	5	12	48
Lancashire	15	18	27	60
Midlands	22	16	28	66
East	7	12	9	28
West	3	8	16	27
South West	8	9	11	28
London	12	17	31	60
South	1	5	20	26
Home Counties	0	3	40	43
Britain	182	122	210	514

This impression is confirmed if we look at the ninety-eight seats that were never won by Unionists at general elections between 1885 and 1910, seventy-seven of which were in Scotland, Wales, Yorkshire and the North. The eighty-one seats always won by the Unionists were more evenly distributed about the country, with concentrations in the Home Counties (19), London (15), and Lancashire and Cheshire (11). The social character of the safe Unionists constituencies[5] raises the question of whether the geographical divisions used here are relevant. Scotland and Wales are quite clearly distinct entities with their own traditions and consciousness, but even here internal social, economic and cultural differences were reflected in political differences. This is more true of say London, whose politics are quite clearly divided on social lines, and it would be a mistake to make too much of regional differences, especially in the somewhat arbitrary divisions I have used for England, until an analysis is undertaken which holds social and economic factors constant. Nevertheless it is clear that different areas of the country did have different political traditions, and that the same party label often means different things in different places.

Table 5–1 shows the balance in the single member constituencies for the whole period.[6] But, while there were marked fluctuations of party strength in all regions between 1885 and 1910, some had returned to the division of 1885 and 1910 and others had changed significantly.

Table 5–2 prompts two observations which I shall examine more closely after looking at short-term fluctuations: first, that with the exception of the

TABLE 5–2

Party Division of Single-Member Constituencies at the General Elections of 1885 and December 1910

		Con.	Lib. Unionist	Liberal	Other*
Scotland	1885	8	—	55	5 (Crofters)
	Dec. 1910	6	3	57	2
North	1885	7	—	20	1
	Dec. 1910	5	2	18	3
Yorkshire	1885	16	—	32	—
	Dec. 1910	11	—	32	5
Lancashire and	1885	36	—	23	1 (Irish Nat.)
Cheshire	Dec. 1910	28	1	23	8 (1 Irish Nat.)
Midlands	1885	16	1	49	—
	Dec. 1910	26	10	24	6
West	1885	9	—	19	—
	Dec. 1910	14	4	9	—
Wales	1885	4	—	27	1
	Dec. 1910	3	—	25	4
South	1885	16	—	10	—
	Dec. 1910	20	1	5	—
South-West	1885	8	—	19	1 (Radical)
	Dec. 1910	11	5	12	—
East	1885	11	—	17	—
	Dec. 1910	13	1	14	—
Home Counties	1885	39	—	4	—
	Dec. 1910	37	—	5	1 (Ind. Cons.)
London	1885	35	—	25	—
	Dec. 1910	26	3	27	4

*Lib–Lab or Labour unless otherwise indicated.

South, any marked Unionist improvement is associated with Liberal Unionist success (Midlands, South-West, West); second, that any marked Unionist decline is accompanied by the appearance of successful Labour and Lib-Lab candidates.

SHORT–TERM FLUCTUATIONS

The measurement of voting changes from election to election is complicated by two factors: the changing numbers of uncontested constituencies and the great variation among constituencies in sizes of electorate. Both make it difficult to compare aggregate votes meaningfully. As Lloyd has shown,[7] uncontested constituencies can be used as an independent measure both of local party strength and morale and of the changing significance of elections. The Liberals' failure to contest Conservative strongholds in the general elections of 1886, 1895 and 1900 reflected an accurate if dispirited estimate of their chances, while the Conservative practice after 1880 of contesting even hopeless constituencies reflects the development of elections from local tests of influence into national contests between the parties. The number of seats left uncontested does correlate with other measures of party fortunes, but to aggregate the votes in the remaining constituencies means comparing different sets of constituencies from election to election and raises the problem of size: given the different sizes of electorate, votes were not equal, and as the constituency was the unit in which voting took place, it ought to be retained in any analysis of changes of party support. The relative advantages of the parties in the distribution of their support among constituencies is another question. For this reason Tables 5–3 and 5–4, showing fluctuations in the party division of the vote, are based on comparisons of the mean Unionist percentage in seats contested in both of any pair of elections.

TABLE 5–3

Mean Unionist Percentages at Adjacent Elections, 1885–1910

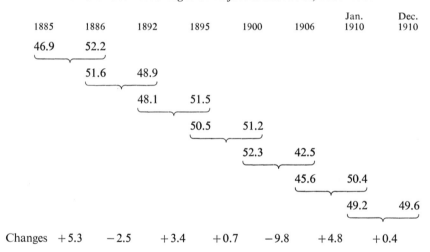

1885	1886	1892	1895	1900	1906	Jan. 1910	Dec. 1910
46.9	52.2						
	51.6	48.9					
		48.1	51.5				
			50.5	51.2			
				52.3	42.5		
					45.6	50.4	
						49.2	49.6

Changes   +5.3   −2.5   +3.4   +0.7   −9.8   +4.8   +0.4

These tables suggest that although there was a swing back to the Liberals in 1892 it was not enough to offset their losses in 1886, and that the election of 1906 was the only one which saw an improvement on the Liberal position of 1885; this was lost at the subsequent elections and the mean Unionist gain 1885 to 1910 Dec. was 2 per cent. Overall it might be said that the Liberals had reasserted themselves, but how far was the election of 1906 a return to the situation of 1885? One means, tentatively offered, for judging the similarity of election patterns is to look at the correlations of party percentages (Table 5–5).

TABLE 5-4

Mean Unionist Percentages Seats Contested at General Election of 1885 and Each Other

Seats Contested in Common	1885	1886	1892	1895	1900	1906	Jan. 1910	Dec. 1910
334	46.9	52.2						
417	47.7		50.8					
336	45.9			52.2				
306	45.5				52.1			
372	48.4					46.0		
390	48.2						50.1	
355	47.9							49.9
Change from 1885		+5.3	+3.1	+6.3	+6.6	−2.4	+1.9	+2.0

TABLE 5-5

Correlation of Unionist Percentages at Adjacent Election, 1885–1910

1885/1886	0.663
1886/1892	0.771
1892/1895	0.849
1895/1900	0.751
1900/1906	0.611
1906/1910 Jan.	0.892
1910 Jan./1910 Dec.	0.964

The two low correlations coincide with the large swings of 1886 and 1906, but if the swing in 1906 had restored the status quo of 1885 one would expect a high correlation between 1885 and 1906, whereas the correlation is only 0.562. This suggests that the composition of party support had changed, as was indicated by the regional changes in the distribution of seats (Table 5–2).

Regional Changes and the Impact of Home Rule

Table 5–6 shows the mean Unionist percentage of the vote in the seats contested in each region in the elections of 1885 and Dec. 1910.

A number of points can be made here. First with the exception of Wales and Lancashire and Cheshire, all regions had moved towards the Unionists. Again with the exception of Wales, London, and Home Counties and the South, all had moved toward a more equal division of the vote. The overall effect of this movement can be better shown by comparing the distribution of Unionist percentages in 1885 and Dec. 1910 (Table 5–7).

Column 3 constitutes seats likely to change hands—the numbers of seats in this column increased overall, but not in Lancashire and the South where they remained the same, or in the Home Counties where safe Unionist seats, and Wales where safe Liberal seats increased, or in London which became increasingly polarized between the parties.

Table 5-6

	MEAN UNIONIST PERCENTAGE OF THE VOTE		CHANGE	DIFFERENCE FROM NATIONAL MEAN CHANGE
	1885	1910 Dec.		
Scotland	41.2	45.2	+4	+2
North	45.1	47.1	+2	0
Yorkshire	48.2	49.2	+1	−1
Lancashire and Cheshire	51.8	50.3	−1.5	−3.5
Midlands	45.4	50.5	+5.1	+3.1
West	46.6	49.1	+2.5	+0.5
Wales	46.8	41.9	−4.9	−6.9
South	49.4	53.6	+4.2	+2.3
South-West	47.0	51.3	+4.3	+2.3
East	46.8	48.8	+2	0
Home Counties	55.8	56.5	+0.7	−1.3
London	52.0	53.5	+1.5	−0.5

Table 5-7

Distribution of Unionist Percentages, 1885 and 1910 December

	(1) Less than 35	(2) 36–45	(3) 46–55	(4) 56–65	(5) More than 65
1885	26	115	165	42	7
1910 Dec.	13	81	196	54	11

The regional differences in 1885 could only be explained by reference to their social and economic structures and political histories, and these would in turn account for the different impact of political events between 1885 and 1910. In Table 5–2 we observed that Unionist gains over the period were associated with the presence of Liberal Unionists. The election of 1886 saw a general swing to the Unionists which was recorded in all but a handful of seats. But the issue appears to have had a lasting impact on the division of the vote in those places where the Liberal party actually split. At least the swing to the Unionists is higher than the national average between 1885 and 1910 in five regions, and four of these—Scotland, the Midlands, the West and the South-West—had substantially more Liberal Unionists as members than the national average (Table 5–8).

The relationship becomes stronger in the cases of Scotland and the Midlands by breaking down the regional totals (Table 5–9).

Aggregate figures are only a plausible guide to what may be happening to the individual, and the examination of constituencies in Scotland and the Midlands shows a great variety of individual patterns. Liberal Unionist intervention more often brings a permanent Unionist gain, although there are seats in which the Conservatives make gains in 1886 and hold them—these tend to be stable in population and electorate—and there are also places where the Liberals recover despite it.

TABLE 5–8

Liberal Unionism and Unionist Gains

	Difference from national mean % change 1885–1910 Dec.	Difference from national % of seats held at some time by Lib. Unionists
Scotland	+2	+15
North	0	− 3.5
Yorkshire	−1	− 9
Lancashire and Cheshire	− 3.5	+ 1
Midlands	+3.1	+10.5
West	+0.5	+20.5
Wales	− 6.9	− 4
South	+2.2	+ 1.7
South-West	+2.3	+27.5
East	0	− 3.5
Home Counties	− 1.3	−18
London	−0.5	− 7

TABLE 5–9

	Difference from national mean % change 1885–1910 Dec.	Difference from national % of seats held by Liberal Unionists
North Scotland	− 7.1	+ 8
South Scotland	+ 2.6	+19
Staffordshire	+ 3.4	+21
Warwickshire	+ 15.3	+30
Rest of Midlands	+ 0.6	− 3.5

Turnout

For the sake of comparability, turnout has been calculated in the same way as party percentage, that is, as a mean for all seats contested at pairs of elections as shown in Table 5–10.

When these changes are compared with those for mean Unionist percentages (Graph 5–1), it is clear that until 1906 Unionist success was inversely correlated with turnout, but that this relationship was reversed in 1910, when turnout was higher than ever before. This relationship can be more precisely measured by correlating changes in Unionist percentage with changes in turnout at adjacent elections (Table 5–11).

The Unionists were clearly helped by the fall in turnout in 1886 and by the rise in 1910, and the Liberals benefited by the rise of 1906. The political factors in 1886 and 1906 are clear enough: Home Rule split the Liberals in 1886, and Unionist policy on tariffs, education and South Africa knit them together in 1906.[8] Likewise the factors making for the Unionist resurgence in 1910 can probably first be found in the policies of the Liberal government. Together with the low number of uncontested seats, the turnout figure for Jan. 1910 shows that the electorate was more fully mobilized behind the

TABLE 5–10

Mean Turnout at Adjacent Elections, 1885–1910

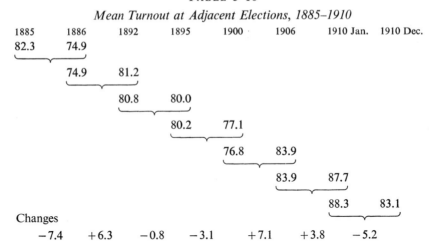

1885	1886	1892	1895	1900	1906	1910 Jan.	1910 Dec.
82.3	74.9						
	74.9	81.2					
		80.8	80.0				
			80.2	77.1			
				76.8	83.9		
					83.9	87.7	
						88.3	83.1

Changes

−7.4	+6.3	−0.8	−3.1	+7.1	+3.8	−5.2

TABLE 5–11

Correlations of Changes in Unionist Percentage and Turnout, 1885–1910

1885/1886	−0.361
1886/1892	−0.086
1892/1895	−0.033
1895/1900	−0.083
1900/1906	−0.223
1906/1910 Jan.	+0.394
1910 Jan./1910 Dec.	+0.074

GRAPH 5–1

Mean Turnout and Unionist Percentage Changes at Adjacent Elections,
1885–1910

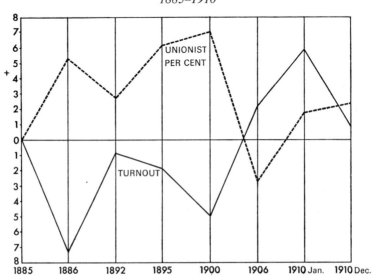

parties than at any election since 1885. But again the national effect of changes in turnout is most valuable as an indication of what is worth looking for in electoral histories of individual constituencies.

Individual Constituencies

The attempt to produce a national picture inevitably leads to the elimination of variety, and, because of the necessities of comparison, the exclusion of some interesting political developments which upset the pattern of two-party competition, such as the intervention of third-party candidates. In returning from the aggregate to the individual constituency, I have found it particularly useful to add a third dimension to those of party vote and turnout, and that is the growth of the electorate. I have done this by calculating for each constituency the party votes and the nonvoters for the election of 1885 as percentages of the electorate, and the figures, including the electorate, for all subsequent elections on the same base. I have not reduced this mass of data to any formal order, but I can give a few indications of some of the more important points that emerge from a rapid preliminary survey.

GROWTH OF THE ELECTORATE

There were, as one would expect, marked differences in the rates of growth between constituencies. Some central city and rural constituencies lost population and their electorates fell as much as ten points. On the other hand suburban and industrial county constituencies had increases of up to 300 per cent. There was not, however, a constant relation between the growth of the population and the electorate. In some places the electorate fell in the nineties and then spurted forward between 1900 and 1906, despite what appears to be a fairly continuous increase in the population. The size of the electorate was to some extent politically controlled,[9] and this is further evidence of the decline and revival in Liberal morale.

GROWTH OF ELECTORATE AND PARTY SUCCESS

There was no straight relationship here: in the suburbs of Liverpool and London, constituencies with very large increases of electorate remained politically stable and Unionist strongholds. But through most of the country with variations and exceptions, the Liberals appear to have benefited from the rapid growth of the electorate after 1900. The typical pattern in constituencies with stable electorates—central city, rural and small town constituencies and mostly Unionist—was to move with the general swing from election to election, with the Unionist vote reaching a peak in 1895–1900 but without any major realignment thereafter. In the constituencies with rapid growth—most marked between 1900 and 1906—there is also a dramatic increase in the size of the Liberal vote between 1900 and 1906, though this is not always great enough to resist a similar increase in the Unionist vote in Jan. 1910. This is not a matter of increased percentages, but increases in the real numbers of voters, which were in many cases greater than the growth of the population. This emphasizes the mobilization of Jan. 1910 noted in the discussion of turnout: not only did a larger proportion of the electorate turn out, the electorate itself was a larger proportion of the population. The trends in electoral growth were not uniform across the country however, and in some areas, notably the Northern towns, the Liberal revival and electoral growth were already evident in 1900.

Labour

Examination of the individual constituencies also enables us to look at what may be considered in the long term the most important political development of the period—the emergence of the Labour party. This has of course been carefully chronicled,[10] and the constituency histories confirm the political differences evident in the founding of the Labour Representation Committee. Three patterns of Labour takeover emerge: one, where Labour replaces an ineffective Liberal party in working-class urban constituencies previously won by Conservatives and clearly gets out a much better vote than the Liberals had done: this is the pattern in parts of Lancashire and London.[11] The second is where Labour stands in two-member seats in alliance with a Liberal: it is not clear that in these constituencies Labour could have been successful by itself and certainly where Labour candidates stood against two Liberals they were not successful, and in Portsmouth in Jan. 1910 the "left" vote was split and the seats won by Unionists. The third pattern was for Labour simply to replace the Liberals in what had previously been safe or winnable seats, partly as a result of the Macdonald-Gladstone electoral pact. This pattern is found in Wales, Yorkshire, Durham and the Midlands and is closely connected with the politics of the miners. In some cases the change of party did not entail a change of candidate, as local unions affiliated to the Miners Federation became officially Labour despite a predominantly Liberal tradition.[12] The voting patterns in these constituencies tend to confirm the gradualness of the change from Liberal to Lib–Lab to Labour. They differ very little from constituencies with comparable rates of growth and previous party history, which remained Liberal.

6

GEOGRAPHY, SOCIAL CONTEXTS, AND VOTING BEHAVIOR IN WALES, 1861–1951

KEVIN R. COX

IN A RECENT review paper, a plea was made for "more detailed analyses of ranges of variation within countries," and it was added that "only through such efforts of massive data-gathering and analysis can we avoid the Scylla of hasty overgeneralization and the Charybdis of myopic attention to local and national peculiarities."[1] Of Britain this is particularly so: there are a number of studies of politics at the national level[2] and a few studies of political behavior in selected urban communities[3] but very little of what could be called cross-locality or intranational comparison. Recent attempts by Cornford[4] and Lee[5] stand as signposts to the road ahead and exemplify the possibilities of working with data for large ecological units which undergo rapid and frequent changes of boundaries but they do not indicate a large body of similar ecological literature.

While such work suggests an extensive laboratory for intranational comparative work, it would be a mistake to employ as a theoretical model in such analyses the theoretical framework employed by André Siegfried in his *géographie électorale*[6] and manifest in much of the ecological work that has followed: the ecological fallacies, the frequent satisfaction with prediction rather than explanation, and the interest in regional idiosyncrasy rather than in the development of theory are all too evident in much ecological analysis. In this paper, an attempt is made to obviate these difficulties by treating the ecological data as descriptions of the social structural environment affecting individual voting decisions.

This paper was originally prepared for delivery and discussion at the World Congress of the International Political Science Association, Brussels, September 1967.

Notes to this chapter are on pp. 367–371.

The specific aims of this paper are largely substantive: the paper concentrates on Welsh voting behavior over the period 1861 to 1951 and attempts to identify the social structural factors accounting for variations in voting behavior between different parts of Wales and to identify the sources of the apparent high degree of class voting in Wales. This region is a fruitful area for ecological study in Britain: not only is there a good deal of internal political variation ranging from the high Labour majorities of the South Wales coalfield to the British Liberal strongholds in rural Wales, but there is also a relatively large historical and sociological literature oriented towards the social and political evolution of late nineteenth- and twentieth-century Wales. Moreover, vis-à-vis other areas of Britain, Wales reveals very high levels of left-wing radical voting in different social classes. In terms of survey data, Blondel has shown that in Wales, the strength of the Labour party among the lower class is above average whereas the strength of the Conservative party in the middle class is below average.[7] Further, an analysis using aggregate data has shown that levels of left-wing voting in Wales—defining left wing as including the Liberal party and the Communists—are highly underpredicted when regressed on social class measures.[8] It is from considerations such as these that the second substantive aim of this study stems.

Methodological Orientation

The data resources available for this study consist of large amounts of ecological data and qualitative observations made in newspapers, and historical and social studies together with a very limited amount of survey data for 1960–1961. In the study of voting behavior, moreover, two sets of independent variables have been postulated. The first set of variables refers to the individual characteristics of the voter—his age, sex, social class, and so forth; the second set of variables refers to the characteristics of the community or community context in which he lives and works—the suburban context, the small town as opposed to the large town, agricultural areas as opposed to manufacturing areas. Observed patterns of voting behavior result from the interaction of individual characteristics and contextual characteristics. Here, given a large amount of ecological and historical data and very limited survey data, an attempt is made to evaluate the effect in Wales of some contextual variables defining regional milieux. Such an approach to behavior has been dubbed contextual analysis by James S. Coleman.[9] Ideally, in order to obtain a comprehensive evaluation of the role of different regional contexts in voting behavior, it would be desirable to incorporate data on individuals; such data are only available for 1960–1961 and they will be incorporated into the current analysis via the testing of predictions made on the basis of the contextual analysis.

Operationally, contextual analysis calls for at least two steps—the identification of the areal bounds of a study universe and the identification of the social structural dimensions of the context. With reference to the drawing of areal boundaries for study universes, Alker has drawn attention to the so-called universal fallacy: the notion that one can make reliable inferences regarding interrelationships of variables at the regional level from associations established at the level of some larger universe.[10] There are few guidelines in the literature for the identification of behaviorally meaningful study universes. It seems likely, however, that the confinement of a study universe to an area exhibiting homogeneous social organization in terms of language, religion, and so forth, is likely to provide more meaningful relationships than universes which cut across such regions. Certainly, such attributes as a common language and a common religion provide a basis for the rapid diffusion of social and political values. A study of Belgian voting behavior by Smet and Evalenko, for example, has identified an interesting and behaviorally significant contrast in relationships between left-wing voting and social class for the Flemish-speaking areas and Walloon-speaking areas respectively.[11] Another study of peasant rioting in Czarist Russia found that the distribution of rioting could only be explained when the total study universe was divided into a more urbanized section and a less urbanized section.[12] It is on the basis of these considerations that Wales, with its distinctive Nonconformist culture and its legacy of a large Welsh-speaking population, is considered here independently of the United Kingdom as a whole.

Given a study universe, the investigator must also define social and political structural contexts with which to describe the social structural variation present within the study area. Here the investigator is faced with two problems: (a) a number of theoretical concepts which, though able to describe social structural variations or political variations, overlap in their meanings; (b) a large array of possible indicators with which to operationalize these theoretical constructs. The technique of factor analysis provides a way out of this impasse. Alker has described factor analysis as "a tool for empirically oriented concept formation: the reduction of a large variety of empirical indicators to a small number of conceptual variables."[13] Selvin and Hagstrom have also commended the utility of factor analysis for its ability to reduce a large number of variables to a much smaller number of dimensions of variation; they stress its use for providing social structural dimensions for contextual analyses using survey data.[14]

In contextual studies of voting behavior, factor analyses have been used in at least two ways: (a) identification of factors to be later used as explanatory variables with some political behavioral variable as the dependent variable: the dependent variable can be either aggregate in nature or obtained from survey data also providing social characteristics and attitudes of respondents.[15] (b) A second use of factor analysis in contextual studies is to include aggregate measures of political behavior in the input variables and then examine the factor loadings of those behavioral variables in order to identify those factors with which they are most closely associated.[16] This has the advantage that the factors can be used with survey data as sociopolitical contexts; it is the approach adopted in this paper.

Given a factor analysis defining the social contexts within which individuals act, available survey data may be examined within categories defined by factor score intervals. If the factor analysis is of the latter kind, in which political behavioral variables measured in aggregates are included in the factor analysis, then the quantitative ecological analysis may yield hypotheses about the behavior of individuals which can be tested further using the survey data. In this paper an attempt is made to test some predictions of individual behavior from the factor analytical and historical evidence.

The Socio-Political Milieux of Wales

Twenty-nine social and political variables from Censal and other sources have been selected as input variables for the factor analysis and these are indicated in Table 6–1. All political variables are measured by mean values for

TABLE 6–1
The Variables

Variable Name	Amplified Description of the Variable
Unemp.	Per cent of Occupied Males, Unemployed
Soc. class III	Per cent of Occupied Males Aged Fifteen and Over in Social Class III
Divers. occ.	Index of Diversification of Occupations
Wk. on own	Per cent of Occupied Males Working on Own Account
Early sch. lve.	Per cent of Occupied Males Leaving School Before Age 15
Liberal	Mean Percentage of Total Vote Gained by Liberal Party, 1950–51
Labour	Mean Percentage of Total Vote Gained by Labour Party, 1950–51
Participation	Mean Percentage of Total Electorate Voting, 1950–51
Polarization	Class Polarization
Sex ratio	Sex Ratio
65 over	Per cent of the Population Aged Sixty-five and Over
Pers. p. rm.	Persons per Room
Soc. class I.II.	Per cent of Occupied Males Aged Fifteen and Over in Social Classes I and II
Soc. class IV.V.	Per cent of Occupied Males Aged Fifteen and Over in Social Classes IV and V
Occ. sex ratio	Occupational Sex Ratio
Agriculture	Per cent of Occupied Males in Agriculture
Mining	Per cent of Occupied Males in Mining
Services	Per cent of Occupied Males in Services
Manufacturing	Per cent of Occupied Males in Manufacturing
Roman Catholic	Roman Catholic Masses per 1000 Population
Nonconformist	Per cent of Population, Nonconformist
Pop. density	Population Density
Labour party	Per cent of Electorate in Labour Party
Jewish	Synagogues per 100 Population
Pop. cha.	Percentage Population Change, 1931–51
Methodist	Per cent of Population, Methodist
Mean residual	Mean Residuality, 1950–51
Welsh only	Per cent of Population Speaking Welsh Only
Welsh. Engl.	Per cent of Population Speaking Welsh and English

the General Elections of 1950 and 1951 and all social and economic variables are defined for the Census year of 1951.

With reference to the list of variables in Table 6–1 specific attention should be paid to the following. First, many of the variables have been chosen on the basis of the criterion that they can tell us something about the characteristics of communications networks in terms, for example, of the degree to which interpersonal communication is facilitated. The proportion speaking Welsh, the proportion belonging to Nonconformist chapels and population density are of this nature. Second, certain variables have been selected as measures of social structure to provide surrogates for social values. The proportion belonging to the different social class groups are of this nature, with the Census designation Social Class I and II signifying upper-class and upper-middle-class groups and Social Class IV and V signifying lower-class groups. Third, among the political variables, the per cent voting Labour also includes the Communist vote. The variable entitled mean residuality 1950–1951 refers to the magnitude of the residual from the regression of left-wing voting behavior on occupational and social class variables for England and Wales as a whole. Its distribution in Wales is shown in Figure 6–1. This regional study is a part of a much larger study aimed at identifying the sources of behavioral variation in areas over- and under-predicted by occupation and social class variables.[17] The term left wing includes the vote for the Labour party, Liberal party and the Communists. Reversing signs, therefore, the residuals could be interpreted as residuals from the regression of the per cent Conservative vote on the same independent variables. Finally, certain difficulties were experienced in locating data for certain of the variables deemed important. This was particularly so for measures of Jewish and Roman Catholic populations and the eventual indicators used—population per synagogue and population per Roman Catholic mass—are recognized as far from ideal.

The intercorrelations of the variables were computed and the intercorrelation matrix subjected to a principal axis factor analysis.[18] The factor loadings were rotated to Kaiser's varimax criterion and the rotated values—facilitating empirical interpretation—can be observed in Table 6–2. Table 6–3 presents loadings greater than +.40 or less than −.40 and is intended to present a simplified picture of Table 6–2. The loadings may be interpreted as simple correlations between the original variables and the factors.

TABLE 6–2

Factor Loadings for Wales

	I	II	III	IV	V
Unemp.	.1018	.0515	.8305	−.0623	.0102
Soc. class III	−.8257	.0305	.2440	.2127	−.2369
Divers. occ.	.2819	−.7571	.2708	−.0376	.1591
Wk. on own	.8828	−.0180	−.3123	−.2771	.1312
Early sch. lve.	−.3847	−.7369	.2371	.1696	−.2291

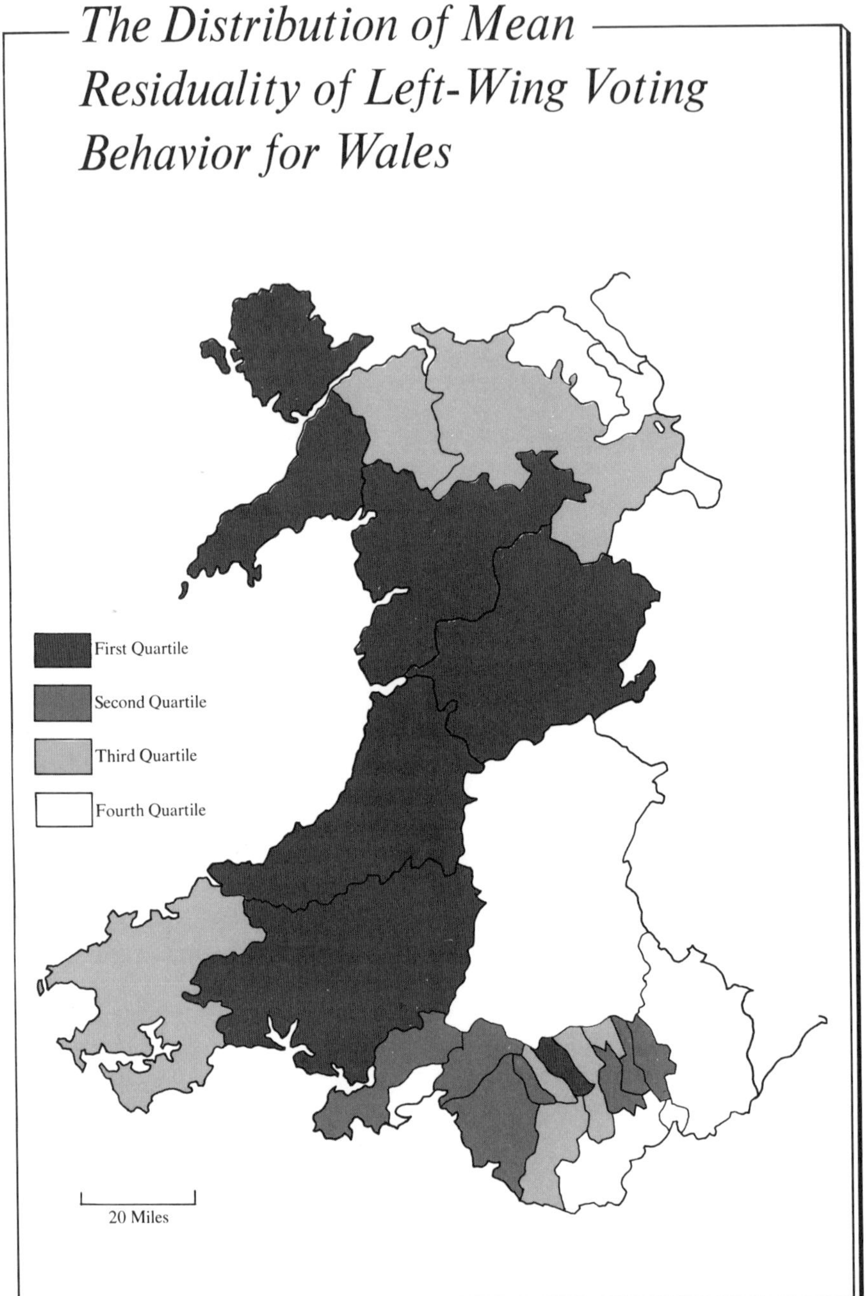

The Distribution of Mean Residuality of Left-Wing Voting Behavior for Wales

First Quartile

Second Quartile

Third Quartile

Fourth Quartile

20 Miles

Figure 6–1

TABLE 6–2 (*continued*)

	I	II	III	IV	V
Liberal	.8380	.0276	−.3194	−.0916	−.0283
Labour	−.3824	−.5113	.6890	.1928	−.1809
Participation	−.5406	−.2091	.0758	.1642	.5308
Polarization	−.3391	−.5365	.5984	.3656	−.0087
Sex ratio	.2484	.8645	−.0029	.0635	.0140
65. over	.8290	.2030	.0815	−.1364	.3254
Pers. p. rm.	−.7490	.3367	−.3938	−.0722	−.2785
Soc. class I.II.	.6707	.3402	−.5358	−.3321	.0275
Soc. class IV.V.	−.0956	−.5938	.5838	.2865	.2420
Occ. sex ratio	−.1547	.8964	−.2511	.1018	−.0404
Agriculture	.7770	−.0473	−.4146	−.4094	.0962
Mining	−.1824	−.4948	.8035	−.1446	.0478
Services	−.1637	.7552	−.5161	−.0079	−.0074
Manufacturing	−.5236	.0279	−.1348	.7126	−.1780
Roman Catholic	−.1341	−.4563	.5334	−.0277	−.1523
Nonconformist	.8000	—.0504	.1768	—.0612	−.2655
Pop. density	−.2456	.0007	.0436	.7989	.0959
Labour party	−.0074	−.1545	−.5949	.0222	.5651
Jewish	−.1737	.7243	.1452	−.0609	.1088
Pop. change	−.2142	.3054	−.7021	−.0687	.2883
Methodist	.3325	.2932	−.1926	−.0877	.6865
Welsh only	.8277	.0683	−.0107	−.1333	.0989
Welsh. Engl.	.8668	˙.0765	.1862	−.0814	−.0991
Mean residual	.8343	−.3337	.1282	−.0330	−.2203

TABLE 6–3

Factor Loadings Greater than 0.4 for Wales

	I	II	III	IV	V
Per cent of male occupied labor force, unemployed			+		
Per cent of occupied males[a] in Social Class III	−				
Diversification of occupations	−				
Per cent of male occupied labor force working on own account	+				
Per cent of male occupied labour force leaving school before age 15	−				
Mean percentage Liberal vote, 1950–51	+				
Mean Labour vote, 1950–51		−	+		
Mean percentage participation, 1950–51	−				+
Status polarization		−	+		
Sex ratio		+			
Per cent of population aged 65 and over	+				
Persons per room	−				
Per cent of occupied males[a] in Social Classes I and II	+		−		
Per cent of occupied males[a] in Social Classes IV and V		−	+		
Occupational sex ratio		+			

TABLE 6–3 (*continued*)

	I	II	III	IV	V
Per cent of male occupied labor force in agriculture	+		−	−	
Per cent of male occupied labor force in mining		−	+		
Per cent of male occupied labor force in service industries		+	−		
Per cent of male occupied labor force in manufacturing industries		−		+	
Population per Roman Catholic Mass		+	+		
Per cent of population, Nonconformist	+				
Density of population				+	
Per cent of electorate in Labour party			−		+
Population per synagogue		+			
Percentage population change, 1931–51			−		
Per cent of population, Methodist					
Per cent of population speaking Welsh only	+				
Per cent of population speaking Welsh and English	+				
Mean residuality, 1950–51	+	−			

aAged fifteen and over.

In this study, factors one and two will form the raw data for the definition of sociopolitical contexts. Although it is true that the present Labour vote loads relatively heavily on factor three, the variable "Mean Residuality" identified those areas that are atypical from the point of view of class structural effects on voting in England and Wales as a whole, and it is explaining these anomalies that in large part concerns us here. Factor one, it will be noted, explains 69.9 per cent of the variance of mean residuality and factor two explains 11.1 per cent of that variance.

The geographical distribution of the factor scores on factors one and two can be observed in Figures 6–2 and 6–3 respectively. Examination of the two maps shows that there are considerable identities between them. Although factor one has relatively high values in Northwest Wales, so does factor two. Again, both reach their low points in the South Wales coalfield area. In actuality, factor scores on the two factors are linearly associated to a high degree, and it is possible to draw a two-factor map by aggregating into regions on a nearest neighbor basis from the points on a scatter diagram. The map of factors one and two combined formed in such a manner would be exactly equivalent to the map displayed in Figure 6–3. It seems, therefore, that the geographical units employed in this study can be arranged into a continuum on the two dimensions of factors one and two. Inferring from the content of factors one and two in terms of the loadings of specific variables, at one end of the continuum are areas with heavy Welsh speaking, Nonconformist, old and agricultural populations in which there is very little polarization of status, a large proportion of women, relatively high occupational sex ratios and a lower proportion in the lower class. At the other end of the continuum

Distribution of Factor Scores on Factor One for Wales: 1950-51

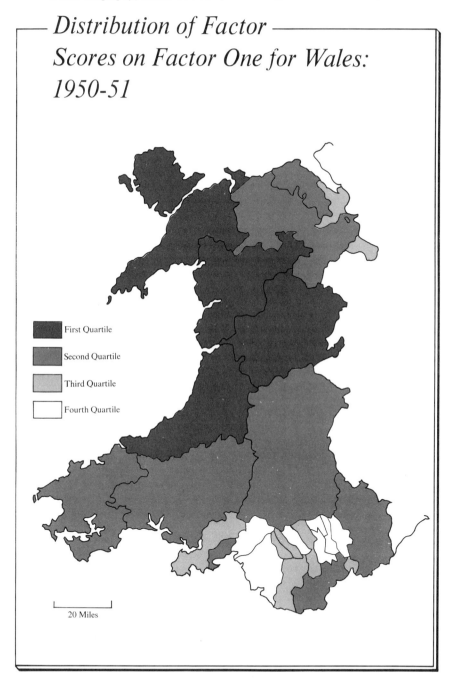

First Quartile

Second Quartile

Third Quartile

Fourth Quartile

20 Miles

Figure 6–2

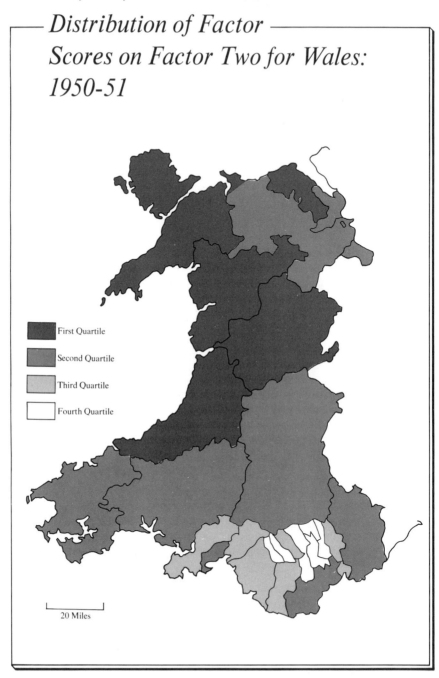

Distribution of Factor Scores on Factor Two for Wales: 1950-51

First Quartile

Second Quartile

Third Quartile

Fourth Quartile

20 Miles

Figure 6–3

are located those geographical units characterized by English-speaking populations in which Nonconformity has lost its hold: young, nonagricultural populations in which there is a great deal of status polarization, a relatively low proportion of women, low occupational sex ratios, high proportions of miners in the labor force and a high proportion of people in the lower social class.

The political significance of the continuum resides in the fact that geographical units with high scores on both factors are associated with high percentage Liberal votes and low percentage Labour votes; geographical units with low scores on both factors are associated with high percentage Labour votes and low percentage Liberal votes. The magnitude of residuality is relatively high at both ends of the continuum in such areas as Northwest Wales and the South Wales coalfield respectively and is relatively low in such South Wales coastal cities as Cardiff, Swansea and Newport.

The continuum suggests a twofold regional typology of agricultural, Welsh-speaking, Nonconformist areas on the one hand and mining, English-speaking, non-Nonconformist areas on the other hand. This bipolarity allows one to define sociopolitical milieux in terms of which the current voting behaviour anomalies and relationships observed in the factor analysis can be analyzed.

In referring to specific geographic portions of these two contexts common place names will be used. For this purpose urban Wales may be considered as consisting of the counties of Glamorgan and Monmouth together with the towns of Cardiff, Swansea, Newport and Merthyr Tydfil. Rural Wales consists of the counties of Anglesey, Brecon, Cardigan, Caernarvon, Carmarthen, Denbigh, Flint, Merioneth, Montgomery, Pembroke, and Radnor. The places to which these names refer are shown on Figure 6–4.

The Social Milieux in 1861

THE SOCIAL MILIEUX OF RURAL WALES

Between about 1870 and the end of the nineteenth century, rural Wales experienced the rise of a political Liberalism that was to endure in that area almost to the present day. The aim of the following section is to provide some insight into the social structural sources of Liberalism by examining social organization as it existed immediately prior to the emergence of the Liberals as a political force in rural Wales.

Briefly, the social structure of rural Wales in the mid-nineteenth century can be typified as one of economic dependence between tenantry and aristocracy but with sharp religious and social cleavages between the two occupational categories. Just as agrarian societies in the Baltic areas of Finland and Russia were similarly stratified, so in Wales an Anglican, English-speaking and thoroughly anglicized aristocracy faced a Welsh-speaking, Nonconformist tenantry with a considerable disparity in economic and political power existing between them. Here the tenantry and the landlords will be discussed

The Welsh Study Area

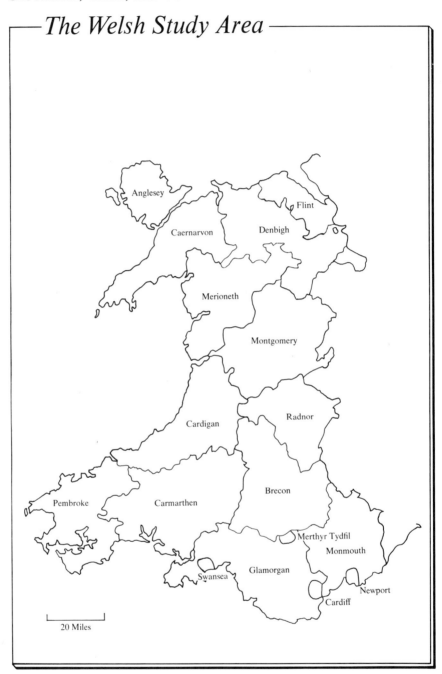

Figure 6–4

in turn; we will then examine the external links which these groups had with other areas, the possibility of an impending political change, and internal geographical differentiation of the milieux.

Rural Wales and the Welsh Tenantry. In 1861, rural Wales was a land of farmers: nearly half of the occupied population was engaged in farming. It is clear from later reports that modesty rather than magnitude characterized the size of their farms. The Royal Commission on Land reported at the end of the nineteenth century upon "the marked and peculiar feature of rural economy in Wales; viz., the prevalence of a large number of small separate farms of what may be described as the peasant and family type."[19] Such small farms were leased from large landowners in a tenancy-at-will form on a year-to-year basis; tenants were experiencing at this time, however, decreasing security of tenure with little protection against eviction or rent increase.[20]

The size of farm had an important effect upon agrarian structure. Most of the farms were so small that the employment of additional help was at a minimum. Data extracted from the 1861 Census by the Royal Commission on Land exemplify this characteristic: Whereas in the eastern counties of England there was an average of ten farm workers per farmer, and five per farmer in the English Midlands, in Wales the figure was less than two per farmer. The ratio of family relatives working on farms to farmers was also particularly high in Wales.[21]

Moreover, rural Wales was hardly cosmopolitan. Most of the inhabitants had been born in Wales; in all rural counties, at least 87 per cent of the population was indigenous to Wales, while in the urban areas of the southeast, nearly 20 per cent of the population had been born outside of Wales.

The dominating institutions of Welsh life were the Nonconformist chapels —the chapels of the Baptists, Methodists and Congregationalists:

All of the most noteworthy flowerings of Welsh culture in modern times owe a great deal to this religious impetus. The development of a distinctive kind of radicalism in politics to which we shall return later, the zest for education, and indeed, the versatility, the "culture" of the common people ... none of these things can be understood except as extensions of the interest originally aroused by religion to new but related fields of thought and activity.[22]

Figure 6–5 attempts to show the distribution of Nonconformists in Wales in 1851. The percentages refer to the Nonconformist share of the number of persons attending the most numerously attended services, by counties, on a Sunday in 1851. In only one Welsh county—Radnor—was the Nonconformist percentage less than seventy per cent and in the northwestern portion of Wales, the chapel was dominant to a much greater extent—a pre-eminence which, as will be seen, this area was to retain.

The chapel was central as a source of social action in rural Wales; the Nonconformists had both a source of discontent and a network through which to transmit information. Discontent stemmed from the civil disabilities imposed on Nonconformists at this time: such disabilities included exclusion from government office and from the universities of Oxford and Cambridge.

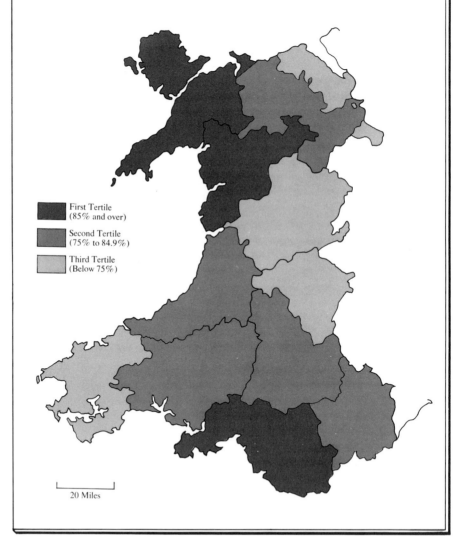

Distribution of the Nonconformist Proportion of the Number of Persons Attending the Most Numerously Attended Services, by Counties on a Sunday in 1851

First Tertile
(85% and over)

Second Tertile
(75% to 84.9%)

Third Tertile
(Below 75%)

20 Miles

Figure 6–5

As far as agencies of organization are concerned, the holders of power within the Welsh tenant society were the deacons of the chapels. As the gentry withdrew from national life, the Nonconformist ministers became indisputable popular leaders, dominating press and pulpit.[23] As J. E. Vincent wrote: "the ministers of Nonconformity, amongst whom are to be found to this day, the most active Radical politicians and journalists in Wales. Their political influence in Wales, especially in the agricultural districts, is not at all inferior to that of the Roman Catholic priests in Ireland; they are the makers of M.Ps."[24] Indeed, for such social relationships formed the vital context for the rise of Welsh Liberalism, which is examined below.

Linguistically, much of rural Wales was Welsh speaking. Figures are not available for any date earlier than 1891, but the data for the latter reveal a high incidence of Welsh-speaking people in the rural counties of Anglesey (88.8 per cent), Caernarvon (85.2 per cent), Cardiganshire (91.1 per cent), Carmarthenshire (84.5 per cent), and Merioneth (89.4 per cent). High proportions could speak only Welsh at this time; in Anglesey, over 67 per cent could speak only Welsh while in Cardiganshire and Merioneth, comparable percentages were 71.3 per cent and 70.8 per cent. These estimates of the prevalence of the Welsh language in 1861 are clearly conservative, for it was only after 1870 with the growth of the public education movement that English was spoken to any degree.[25]

Both in statistical terms and in sociological terms, Welsh language and Nonconformity were mutually supporting. A correlation analysis for 1891 reveals a high correlation between chapel membership as a percentage of the total population and the Welsh-speaking population as a percentage of the total population ($r = .8750$).[26] Sociologically, Welsh was the medium of expression of the chapel, providing a wall between Welsh Nonconformity and those who could speak only English. Evidence given to the Commission on Religion in Wales supports this contention: "Another county witness . . . assented to the suggestion put to him that 'children who speak Welsh and people who speak Welsh are more amenable to the influence of Nonconformity than people who are not' and that it was 'a matter of great importance to have a bond of unity like this linguistic bond.' "[27]

Reciprocally, however, the chapels had been the chief agents in the preservation of the Welsh language as a medium of expression. The growth of Nonconformity in the early nineteenth century had given a great impetus to the use of Welsh in education and persuasion, especially in the Sunday schools which were attended not only by children but also by adults.[28] Evidence given to the Land Commission is quite unambiguous on this point:

It (Nonconformity) was the chief agent in the preservation of the Welsh language.

It is probable that but for the immense impetus given to the study and use of the Welsh language by reading the Welsh Bible and by listening to pulpit oratory that the Welsh language would have more and more tended to die out as the habitual language of the majority of the inhabitants of the whole of Wales.[29]

As far as social values are concerned, two are of political relevance and therefore worthy of note: (1) egalitarianism, (2) enthusiasm for education. The egalitariansim of Welsh rural society stood in clear contrast to the caste distinctions of the English counties.[30] The sources of this egalitarianism or what has been referred to as a "healthy social democracy"[31] were three-fold: first, because of the smallness of the farms, contact between farmer and worker was frequent contrasting with the lack of contact on the large labor farms of Norfolk and Suffolk, where caste was notorious. The easy relationship between the Welsh farmer and his worker found expression in the custom of taking in the farm workers as lodgers. Second, there was a rapid social mobility between the rank of farm worker and the rank of farmer.[32] Third, Welsh rural society was dominated internally by the chapel; the priest had a monopoly of power and was unchallengeable given the importance of religion in the system of social values.

The enthusiasm for education is one more indication of the significance of Nonconformity in rural Welsh life. The Commission on Welsh Land stated that:

The necessity of a trained Nonconformist clergy became at a very early stage evident to the leaders of the movement and theological seminaries and colleges were founded, at first on a small scale and afterwards, according to better methods. And this demand for an educated ministry in turn gave rise to that general and spontaneous demand for education for all classes . . . .[33]

Despite impending changes that were to place rural Wales in the mainstream of British political life, politically relevant goals at this time, however, did not extend to any form of organized political action; rather politically relevant goals were confined at this time to the extension of full civil rights to Nonconformists by Parliamentary lobbying and publicity.effected by the Liberationist society. The social context for more militant political activity was already established, however, the dependent Welsh-speaking Nonconformist farmers forming an organized group quite distinct from the English-speaking, Church of England landlord society. Finally, in economic terms, Welsh rural society was subservient to the Anglicized landlord society. Goods were forwarded both as rent and in kind to the large landowners and to the church of the landowners, the Church of England, in the form of tithe. Political links re-emphasized this subordinate position; not only were the landowners the Conservative Members of Parliament of rural Wales— usually elected unopposed—but, as will be seen, local power also devolved from the landlords in their positions as Justices of the peace, Lord Lieutenant of the county, and so forth.

The Landed Aristocracy. It is more difficult to make viable social generalizations about the landlords who dominated Welsh society at this time. They were a minority and, hence, Census data which do not cross-classify social variables with the occupation of landlord offer a meager basis for inference. Qualitative data allow one to sketch in the general outline of the social system to which they belonged.

Occupationally, the anglicized landlord society consisted of the landlords, their farm managers and other appurtenances of an alien culture in the form of the representatives of the Church of England. The members of this social system belonged to the Church of England and spoke English, thus contrasting with the Welsh-speaking, Nonconformist indigenous inhabitants. The landlords held a monopoly of power in Wales; they represented rural Wales in the House of Commons, albeit on the basis of elections which were usually unopposed by the Welsh tenantry. The allocation of political power in mid-nineteenth-century Wales was a tradition vested in the hands of the great territorial families rather than in the hands of the people. As Morrish has written: "Before 1868, political control had been in the hands of the Anglicized Welsh landlords: Meyrick, and Bulkeley in Anglesey, Lord Penrhyn (Douglas-Pennant), Smith and Lord Newbrough (Wynn) in Caernarvon; the Wynne family in Denbigh, Lord Henmer in Flint; the Wynnes and Prices in Merioneth. . . ."[34] Furthermore, apart from the allocation of power at the national level, the great landlords were also supreme at the local level. In their positions as commanders of the county militia and as the local judiciaries, they dominated rural Wales.[35]

Unequal in political and economic relations, the landlords and their representatives on the one hand and the Welsh tenantry on the other hand were quite antithetical in their social values. Differing in language, religion and economic position from the tenantry, the landlords deepened the rift by withdrawing from local society and offering only a totally different cluster of social values:

Fashioning their culture to the pattern of the English gentry, their whole outlook became thoroughly anglicized and more and more remote from that which was traditionally Welsh. Above all things they maintained that the peasantry should honour the King and abide by the law and seek not in their coming and going to dispute the ruling of the Church in its sphere more than the ruling of the State in its civil spheres.[36]

The failure of the landowners to participate in rural Welsh society created a vacuum which, as noted already, came to be occupied by the Nonconformist ministers.[37]

External Links. While, in terms of dominance relationships, the anglicized landlord society was dominant both economically and politically over the Welsh tenantry, they were, however, subservient to the remainder of British society in the sense that their own power flowed from the authority of the British polity itself—the House of Commons and the House of Lords. Action by the House of Commons in, for example, regulating rentals or altering the basis of the franchise could easily undermine the dominant position of the landlords in Wales. Furthermore, the flows of sentiment which go to make up loyalty were directed towards England. As Table 6–4 below shows, over 50 per cent of the landlords belonged to an English social club, while over 30 per cent had had an English university education; a large propor-

Table 6–4

Some Social Relationships of Welsh Landlords[a]

	All Landowners	Owning Over 10,000 Acres
Attending English public school	48.2%	66.0%
Attending English university	37.5	47.6
Members of English social club	69.6	71.4
Resident in England	19.6	23.8

[a]Based on a sample of fifty-six Welsh landlords from John Bateman, *The Great Landowners of Great Britain and Ireland* (London, 1883)

tion also resided in England. These proportions were greater in the case of landlords owning over 10,000 acres.

Apart from these links expressing the power relationship between the Welsh rural society and its dominant aristocracy, other links of an equally politically relevant nature were also in the making. In particular, concomitant with the general improvement of communications in the nineteenth century, there were growing intellectual links not only with England but also with Ireland. It was from England that the work of the group working for civil rights for Nonconformists—the Liberationist society—spread to Wales. The diffusion of ideas from Ireland via newspapers and pamphlets gathered force after about 1870.[38]

The foregoing description is an ideal type, however, and pays scant attention to geographical variations within rural Wales; in fact, as Figure 6–2 shows, this rural-traditional factor showed wide differences in its significance from place to place. The type of rural society described reached its most ideal form in west and northwest Wales—precisely those counties in which the residual vote has been found to be at a maximum in Figure 6–1. To the southeast and northeast of this zone is a belt in which the magnitude of this factor is decreased and Figure 6–1 shows corresponding declines in the magnitude of residuality. The counties making up this area had lower proportions speaking Welsh, and attending Nonconformist chapel.[39]

THE SOCIAL MILIEUX OF URBAN WALES

The second sociopolitical context which has been isolated is that of urban Wales, an area in which in 1950–1951 the underestimated residual voting behavior was largely for the Labour party. Ninety years earlier, what is now urban Wales was entering the Industrial Revolution.

Occupationally, urban Wales consisted in 1860 of coalmining populations in Glamorganshire and Western Monmouthshire together with certain metallurgical industries and tertiary activity in the coastal towns of Newport, Cardiff and Swansea. Merthyr Tydfil was also noted for its metal-making activities at this time. In the interior, concentration of the male occupied population in mining was high; over 20 per cent of the occupied male population in Glamorgan and Monmouthshire were engaged in mining while in eastern Glamorgan around Merthyr, that figure rose in excess of 40 per cent.

The statistics of churchgoing for 1851 suggest that the county of Glamorgan had a comparatively high proportion of its population as Nonconformists while Monmouthshire had a comparatively low proportion. Even the latter county, however, had a higher proportion in chapel-going populations than did certain rural areas of English-speaking Wales (e.g., Montgomery, Pembrokeshire and Radnorshire). The figures of Nonconformist populations for 1891 confirm the general impression of comparative magnitude suggested by the 1851 figures. Glamorganshire had a higher than average proportion of Nonconformists (38 per cent as compared with the average of 30.2 per cent) while Monmouthshire was much lower (21 per cent). In the coastal towns, the proportions were still lower; only in the case of Swansea did they exceed 20 per cent. By 1891, Monmouthshire and the coastal towns were less Nonconformist than the rural areas of English-speaking Wales.

The earliest data on Welsh-speaking population are available for 1891. The pattern that they present is one of negligible proportions speaking Welsh in Monmouthshire and in the coastal towns of Cardiff and Newport. In Swansea and in the coalfield area, however, proportions speaking Welsh were much higher, rising to 20 per cent for Glamorgan as a whole and 30 per cent in the case of the Merthyr area.

The proportions of Welsh-speaking population for 1891 are approximately matched by the proportions of the 1861 populations born outside Wales. In Cardiff and Newport, the highest proportions in all of Wales—49 per cent and 33 per cent respectively—were found. Proportions were lower in the coalfield area but only in the Merthyr area was the proportion lower than the mean value for Wales.

Even at this early date urban Wales was Liberal in politics. Its representatives were members of the industrial families of South Wales: Sir John Guest of Merthyr, Lewis Weston Dillwyn of Swansea, and the Talbots and Vivians of Margan and Swansea, respectively. The Conservative vote in the area was meager though it was higher in the more anglicized coastal towns than in the coalfield areas.

Such political solidarity is expressive of the value syndrome characteristic of South Wales at this time; this value syndrome cut across class divisions and, in it, three particular elements can be identified. First, South Wales was a stronghold of free-trade sentiment. The large urban centers of the coast were fortresses of classic economic orthodoxy. In Cardiff and Swansea free-trading Liberals were especially strong in the Chambers of Commerce. The South Wales Chamber of Commerce in 1901 competed with the Miners' Federation in their denunciation of the Hicks-Beach export duty on coal as a menace to coal exports.[40]

Second, urban South Wales at this time was characterized by a placidity of industrial relations. Relationships between management and men were characterized by agreement and conciliation; resort to the strike weapon was deprecated by men and master alike. E. W. Evans has described the retarded state of labor union development in the coalfield area at this time:

> The most important characteristic of these District unions, however, was their emphasis upon peaceful settlement of disputes. The Rhondda and Aberdare Associations were specifically devoted to encouraging mutual understanding between employer and workman, and the other district organizations pursued the same policy. They were designed purely for the purpose of defending the workman's just rights and did not countenance any aggressive policy towards the coalowners.[41]

Both these characteristics of the value syndrome are related to the dependence of South Wales on overseas markets for its coal and, to a lesser extent, for its metal industries. After 1850, South Wales underwent a phenomenal industrial and demographic growth, a growth which depended on the maintenance of markets outside of the British Isles.[42] From this followed the concern with the removal of duties which would impede the outward flow of industrial goods and minerals and the inward flow of food products for which the industrial goods and mineral products were being exchanged.

In management-labor relations dependence on foreign markets found expression in the sliding scale. From 1875 to 1900, miners' wages in South Wales were determined by a sliding scale according to which the miner's wage varied with the selling price of coal. It is the awareness of dependency on foreign markets, the general expansion in South Wales at this time, and the introduction of the sliding scale which provided the normative milieu for conciliatory relations between management and labor.

Third, there was a considerable degree of unity in the secondary associations to which man and master belonged. The Nonconformist chapel provided a focus in much of the coalfield area for such association. Thus, many of the later industrialists, especially coalowners and managers, were Welsh Nonconformists who preserved a close relationship with their employees with whom they could combine against the anglicized squires who ruled Welsh society.[43] As Brennan et al., have written: "It is . . . difficult to accept the idea of class conflict and belong to a chapel in which your employer and other middle class people take part. . . ."[44] Support for free-trade Liberalism was a function of concern for overseas trade and lack of civil rights.

Furthermore, Liberalism continued to dominate this mining-industrial area some time after it had ceded to the Labour party in other mining-industrial areas of Great Britain. Morgan has explained it thus: "The basic cause of the continuing ascendancy of Liberalism lay in the unity of outlook which persisted between those professional and mercantile Liberals . . . and the working class mind. They shared the same animosities—the bishop and the squire, the alien church and the dear loaf—and they inherited the same Nonconformist tradition."[45]

In terms of its interrelationships with other areas, the South Wales industrial area was highly dependent upon overseas trade. During the 1861–1891 period world demand for coal and metals, relative to supply, soared. If that demand had slackened, South Wales would clearly have been in a highly vulnerable situation.

Population movements over this period were largely directed into the area rather than away from it. In the fifty years prior to 1911 the population of Glamorgan registered an increase of 235 per cent and the larger proportion of these were young English-speaking men from Wales.[46] A smaller proportion migrated into Glamorgan and Monmouth from England. Immigration on such a scale depended heavily upon the buoyancy of overseas trade.

In common with rural Wales, urban Wales wished to see the Disestablishment of the Church of England and the extension of complete civil rights to Nonconformists. Unlike the rural areas, however, urban Wales manifested a much greater interest in economic goals which were quite independent of chapel concerns; an overriding concern in industrial South Wales at this time was the maintenance of overseas markets and conciliation in labor relations. The greater emphasis upon economic goals may be attributed to three factors: first, Nonconformists were quantitatively less significant in urban than in rural Wales. Second, urban Wales was predominantly Liberal-voting after the franchise reform of 1867 which gave the vote to urban householders; rural Wales had to wait till 1885 before a major part of the population received the vote. The frustration of a discontented people served to heighten the conflict between landlord and tenant. Finally, overseas markets were much more important for the economic well-being of urban Wales than was the case for the rural areas.

Geographical variations in this social system may be discussed in terms of two dimensions. First, there were differences between the coalfield in Glamorgan on the one hand and the coastal towns and the Monmouth coalfield on the other hand. This dimension has already been alluded to in the foregoing discussion; it is highly amenable to statistical verification, showing a higher proportion of Nonconformists, Welsh speaking and Welsh born in the Glamorgan part of the coalfield than elsewhere. Free-trade goals were more important than religious goals in Monmouthshire, Newport, Cardiff and Swansea.

The second dimension is apparent only from an examination of qualitative evidence. Between the eastern half and the western half of the coalfield there existed a marked divergence in the tenor of industrial relations. In the east there was less of the unity between employer and employee which was found in the west. This was expressed in two ways: first, the ironmasters of the east were usually alien in both language and religion from the indigenous Welsh.[47] Williams has stated that:

The ironmasters, many of whom had their origins in English middle class Dissent, became allied through marriage, and association with the gentry, and adopted their Anglicanism. Seldom did Welsh workmen attain to high administrative posts. "In the works," says a Government investigator in 1847, "the Welsh workman never finds his way into the office. He never becomes either clerk or agent. He may become an overseer or contractor, but this does not take him out of the labouring and put him into the administering class."[48]

Second, the eastern part of the coalfield had a history of industrial strife not present in the west. It was in the Ebbw Vale and Merthyr area on the borders of Glamorgan and Monmouthshire that Chartism received its most vociferous expression in the later eighteen thirties.[49] In the western half of the mining area, however, Cooney et al., have suggested that the managers and employers were not so much the Anglican ironmaster type which has just been outlined as characteristic of East Glamorgan and West Monmouthshire.[50] The typical industrialist of the Swansea area was Welsh speaking, Nonconformist and Liberal. This also is the conclusion of a Welsh Nationalist who described conditions in the anthracite area in the northwest of Glamorgan:

> Up to as late as the postwar period the industry was Welsh, not only in its workers—it still remains that—but also in its proprietors, local owners who shared a common tradition and history with their men, who recognized a whole body of customs of ancient standing and whose relation to their men was therefore a human and civilized relation.[51]

Political Change, 1871–1921

THE EMERGENCE OF LIBERALISM IN RURAL WALES

Prior to 1860 the Anglican squirearchy, despite their alien language and religion confronted a politically quiescent tenantry. Beginning just prior to 1860, however, certain factors promoted a gradual heightening of tension and the initial politicization of the Welsh tenantry. After 1870 existing cleavages were aggravated by two factors: first, the emergence of a land issue and, second, the development of political issues surrounding the possibility of the Disestablishment of the Church of England in Wales and a Welsh Nationalist movement. These events are described under the heading of destabilization.

By 1890, political relationships between tenant and landlord were beginning to attain some sort of equilibrium: no longer did the landlord exacerbate the situation by evicting his Liberal-voting tenants and no longer did the tenant strive for greater security of tenure. The redistribution of power within the rural system and the impact of external social and economic factors led to a gradual détente between tenant and landlord and the emergence of the stable Liberal-voting pattern which endured into the years following the First World War. These sequences of events are described under the heading of stabilization.

Destabilization of Tenant-Landlord Relations, 1861–1891. The goals of rural Welsh society and the goals of the anglicized landlord society did not coincide. Whereas the landlords wished to retain the social "status quo," the Welsh tenantry was eager to extend the civil rights of those belonging to the Nonconformist chapels. The equilibrium between needs and power to satisfy those needs became increasingly unstable in the eighteen forties and eighteen fifties.

Among the factors which encouraged the gradual heightening of tension, the following are identifiable. First, Welsh opinion was being rapidly mobilized by an organization pressing for civil rights for Nonconformists—the Liberationist society. The Liberationist society, with its bases in English Nonconformity, underwent a rapid expansion in Wales at this time.[52] By the eighteen fifties, the society had cells in all parts of Wales and in 1868, the nucleus for a coherent political organization in Wales had been formed.

Second, the image of Welsh education was of significance. A Parliamentary Commission of Inquiry into Welsh education in 1847 presented a highly critical picture, pointing out a lack of schools, poor teaching methods and poorer teachers.[53] The report of the alien Commission led to a wave of indignation among a people proud of and zealous for an education so closely bound up with Nonconformity and this exacerbated relations between Nonconformist majorities and Anglican minorities.[54]

Third, this period was characterized by an extension of the Oxford movement to Wales. It aroused a strong reaction in rural Wales as it was regarded as progressing towards the Roman Catholic church: tractarianism—as it was also known—was associated with the extreme Toryism to which Welsh Nonconformists were most opposed. It was probably this issue above all others that led to the unity between the apolitical Methodists and the more overtly political Congregationalists and Baptists.[55]

It was the stimulus of the tractarian issue that eventually provided the trigger action for the destabilization of relationships between landlord and tenant in rural Wales. In 1859 the landowning Wynne family, noted for their tractarian beliefs, put forward one of their representatives as Conservative candidate for Merioneth. He was opposed by the Welsh Nonconformists with a Liberal candidate; such overt opposition to the landowning family was followed by a series of evictions of tenants who had voted for the Liberal candidate. The evictions only served to heighten the intensity of feelings regarding the conflict of goals and the single challenge of 1859 from the Welsh Nonconformists was followed by a series of challenges in 1868. Gaining votes as a result of the extension of the franchise to urban householders in 1867, the Welsh Liberals made great progress in the most Welsh-speaking of the counties, returning Members of Parliament for Carmarthenshire, Cardiganshire, Caernarvon and Merioneth. Further evictions followed, especially in the counties of Caernarvon, Carmarthen and Cardigan, but by that time yet other issues were emerging to strengthen Welsh Nonconformity's identification with the Liberal party.

Between 1868 and 1890, equilibrium between the dominant aristocracy and dependent tenantry of rural Wales underwent further disturbance. Goal conflict during the period was heightened not only by the evictions of tenants and the hurt pride of the landowners, but also by the injection of new issues that partly flowed from this heightened goal conflict and flowed back to reinforce it. These new issues were exacerbated by events in Ireland, in the Antipodes and in the Americas.

Firstly, congruent with the conflicts regarding religion and political expression, a land issue emerged during this period. Four aspects to this land question can be recognized: (1) rising rents—rents were often raised following improvements made by the tenant;[56] (2) insecurity of tenure;[57] (3) a preference exhibited by the landowners for tenants who were Anglican or Conservatives—as against Nonconformists and Liberals—when farms became vacant;[58] (4) the payment of tithe-rent-charge to the Church of England. After 1879, the Welsh land question was severely aggravated by falling prices for food on the world markets due to the extension of cheaply managed farmland in the New World and in Australasia. There are at least two examples of actual aggravation of the issue. First, Vincent suggests that the landlords were slow to reduce the rents of tenants with the onset of depression. Evidence from the Royal Commission on Land in Wales does show that rents decreased less in Wales over this period than in England:

> There seems to be in fact only one conclusion possible, namely, that though the physical and industrial conditions both in Wales and in the northwestern counties of England are practically identical, and though the agricultural depression has been equally felt in both districts, yet rents have in the English counties been reduced more than the extent of their reductions in the principality.[59]

Further, Morgan has suggested a link between the tithe riots which occurred in North Wales after 1886 and the effect of the depression on farming income.[60]

The emergence of a land question led to the foundation of organizations on behalf of both tenant and landlord, thus further intensifying intragroup communication among those most involved in the social conflict. In 1880–1890, Anti-Tithe Leagues were formed in most counties of North Wales and organized resistance against the payment of tithe;[61] such resistance frequently led to physical violence. In 1886 the Welsh Land League was formed with a program of a 50 per cent rent reduction and a land court for rental arbitration.[62] By 1887, the Anti-Tithe Leagues and the Welsh Land League had amalgamated.[63] Similarly, on the part of the landowners, organizations such as the North Wales Property Defense Association were formed.[64]

A second bundle of issues was more directly religious and national in origin. After 1868, the Disestablishment of the Church of England as the Church of Wales became an important policy objective for Welsh Liberals; in the latter two decades of the century this demand developed into a nationalist movement.

Disestablishment symbolized the Nonconformist campaign for social equality. The Liberation movement was early in its support for Disestablishment, basing its arguments on the traditional Liberationist arguments of the unscriptural and unjust nature of any established creed. In a land where the Church of England was identified not only as an alien religion but with economic and political oppression by anglicized landlords, Disestablishment was a radical issue of great political significance.

By the mid-eighteen eighties, however, Disestablishment was argued far less on the traditional grounds set out above and more on grounds akin to nationalism. By 1886, a Young Wales movement—Cymru Fydd—had been formed. The main insistence of this movement was that the Liberal party should pay greater attention to the needs of Wales.[65]

Of prime importance in the emergence, firstly of the Disestablishment issue and secondly of the nationalist movement, was the course of events in Ireland, where the British were increasingly hard pressed by the demands of a people—alien in religion and culture—for Home Rule. Thus, Disestablishment only really emerged as an issue after the success of the Irish Disestablishment Act of 1869.[66] As Morgan has written:

On a wide range of issues, the needs of Wales seemed to find a direct parallel in Ireland. Irish Disestablishment had spurred on the cause of religious equality in Wales. The Welsh Sunday Closing Act had followed upon a similar measure for Ireland. ... Here, too, there seemed to be a similar social structure, a poor struggling peasantry, largely out of sympathy in race and religion with an exploiting landowning class. The success of Parnell's obstruction in the Commons encouraged the Rev. Herber Evans to advocate a national party for Wales also.[67]

Stabilization of Tenant-Landlord Relations: 1891–1921. Having examined destabilization, those factors which tended toward a return to equilibrium will be scrutinized. Certain factors promoted a decrease in the intensity of intragroup communication; intragroup communication was both a cause and a function of the intensity of goal conflict and group identification. The factors may be divided into two groups; first, there were those factors relating to a redistribution of power within the community—these were external factors stemming from action by the British polity. Second, there were changes in the impact of external social and economic events on rural Wales.

Redistribution of power in the rural system took place over this period at both the national and local levels. Primarily, it involved changes in the franchise and changes in the laws regulating the exercise of the franchise. These changes allowed the Welsh tenantry to return Members of Parliament representing views congruent with their own to the House of Commons. Two Reform Acts specified the extent of the redistribution of power. The Reform Act of 1867 gave the county (i.e., rural and small town) vote to nearly all landowners, tenant farmers and middle-class householders, and to the higher income groups among village tradesmen. The borough vote was given to all settled householders. The effect of the new franchise was much more pronounced in the boroughs than in the rural counties; in Merthyr Tydfil, for instance, the Reform Act led to an increase in the electorate of 1000 per cent. The Reform Act of 1885 enfranchised the rural vote on the basis of household suffrage, thereby doing for rural areas what the 1867 Act had failed to do. Further, in 1888 the Local Government Act terminated the ascendancy of the anglicized aristocracy at the local level. By creating democratically elected county councils there ensued the demise of the age-long domination of the landowners as JP's and as self-perpetuating governors of the countryside.[68]

None of these Acts would have seriously undermined the power of the landowners in the rural areas, however, if it had not been for the provisions of the Ballot Act of 1872. By enforcing secrecy of the ballot most of the overt methods which landowners had employed to control the vote of their tenants evaporated. This does not signify that pressure by the landlord was eliminated; ignorance and indifference dictated that loyalty to a landowner would be an important determinant of political behavior in certain areas for a number of years in the future.[69]

The results of these extensions of the vote were twofold. First, in political terms the Liberals were able to arrive at an almost complete ascendancy in rural Wales in 1886; only certain of the more English-speaking areas resisted. The 1867 franchise made the dissenters dominant in nearly all Welsh counties[70]; however, only 65.5 per cent of Wales' Members of Parliament were Liberals at that time; not until 1880 did that figure exceed 85 per cent. Several reasons can be adduced to account for this slow spatial growth of Liberalism; first, the 1867 franchise was by no means so kind to the rural vote as it was to the vote of urban populations. Second, the landed influence remained strong for a long while in counties with a large English-speaking population as in Brecon, Radnor, Pembrokeshire and Denbigh. Even as late as 1914, the Liberal candidate for Radnor could complain that, "Every squire in the county is a rampant Tory and every conceivable influence brought to bear on the voters."[71] It was those counties with a larger English-speaking population which remained most impervious to Liberalism. In 1886, one of Montgomery's two Members of Parliament was a Conservative; the Member for Radnor was a Conservative and one of Denbigh's three Members was also a Conservative, contrasting with the Liberal monopoly in such counties as Anglesey, Cardigan, Merioneth and Carmarthen.

There is a clear correspondence between the Welsh-speaking areas in which Liberalism grew during these years and the distribution of residual voting in Wales. Those rural counties having smaller proportions of Welsh-speaking people and Nonconformists—such counties as Pembrokeshire, Radnor and Brecon—exhibited much slower rates of growth in Liberal voting and are today counties in which the residual vote is much lower than it is in areas to the northwest. The greater hold of the landed aristocracy in the more English-speaking areas may well account for the spatial lag.

Second, in terms of group identification and the intensity of group feeling, the redistribution of political power appears to have led to a détente. In the latter part of the century, the Royal Commission on Land in Wales commented on the Ballot Act of 1872: "In our view, the passing of that Act has undoubtedly tended to remove friction between landlord and tenant in consequence of votes adverse to the opinions of the former being given by the latter."[72]

Social and economic change initiated from outside the rural social system also tended to reduce the monopoly of communication by intragroup communication and hence effect a new social equilibrium. First, the teaching of English in Welsh schools grew rapidly after the Education Act of 1870, thus opening up the possibility of greater contact with those who could speak only English and therefore tending to dilute views based on a Welsh language–Nonconformist syndrome.

Second, issues which had exacerbated the goal conflict declined in significance. Thus, as far as the land question was concerned, the depression was less acute after 1900 as prices for dairy farmers again began to increase. Moreover, the Agricultural Holdings Act of 1900 gave some guarantee of judicial arbitration over tenant compensation. The decline of tension between the two social groups continued over this period; following 1891 no new issues emerged to take their place—agricultural Wales remained agricultural, insulated from the external influences which were leading to a reorientation of political opinion in South Wales at this time. The achievement of disestablishment in 1919 marks the satisfaction of rural society goals but even before then, the redistribution of power towards the end of the nineteenth century had so altered relations between landlord and tenant that the Act of Disestablishment had little practical value. Even by 1906 relations between chapel and church had altered sufficiently for the Commission on Religion in Wales to remark: "There is a considerable body of evidence which shows that outside matters of Divine worship, there is generally no lack of good feeling or cooperation between the Nonconformists and the Church of England. The two systems, as it were, cooperate in a third which belongs exclusively to neither."[73]

In summary, social conflict was occurring between two groups, both of which had, first, a high degree of group identification, and second, a high degree of intragroup communication. The redistribution of power within the community led to a gradual decline in group identification and hence in the degree of intragroup communication. External social and economic events influenced the degree of intragroup communication and hence the degree of group identification. There were spatial lags in this process of adjustment, however, so that the landlords were able to retain power for much longer in those areas where the English-speaking population and the population belonging to the Church of England were larger. Such areas today exhibit lower magnitudes of residual voting behavior.

THE EMERGENCE OF THE LABOUR PARTY IN URBAN WALES, 1891–1921

In urban Wales during the period 1861–1891, there was none of the instability and social ferment so characteristic of rural Wales. This stability can be related to two factors: first, the absence of a power conflict such as was occurring in rural Wales, and, second, the lower intensity of intragroup communication due to the first factor listed above and also to the absence of external economic and social stimuli.

Already by 1868, urban Wales, unlike rural Wales, was Liberal in its politics. In an area where industrialists were as economically powerful as landowners, the landowners had never been able to obtain a monopoly of political power as in rural areas where domination by the landed interest was strong.

Second, there were not those external social and economic stimuli which provoked a high degree of intragroup communication as in the case of rural

Wales. In an area where only about 20 per cent of the occupied male population was in agriculture, the tithe issue or the problem of high rents under the impact of the agricultural depression was of slight moment. Similarly, the great emphasis on economic values reduced the importance of those religious values which so sustained intragroup communication in rural Wales.

Between 1890 and 1920 sharp goal conflicts emerged within the mining community. These conflicts of group aims were associated with the decline of religious-nationalist goals and the elevation of economic goals as a result of the former and of new external influences on the coal industry considered both as a social and as an economic unit. The rise of one set of goals and the demise of the other cluster of objectives were concomitant and tended to reinforce one another in providing a fertile soil for the Labour party.

The Decline of Religious-Nationalist Goals. It has already been observed that language and religion have been closely interwoven in Wales providing each other with mutual support. The sustenance which Welsh nationalism derived from religious fervour has also been remarked upon. Clearly, as Nonconformity declined, so one might expect the incidence of spoken Welsh and the intensity and extensiveness of Welsh nationalist sentiment to decrease.

The decline of religion resulted from the impact of social and economic forces external to the area: first, there were the results of social interaction with England and second, the results of a receipt of immigrants from rural Wales. Interaction with England led to a decline in the incidence of spoken Welsh: the preservation of the Welsh language was essential in so far as attendance at chapels—which usually conducted services in Welsh—was to be maintained. The Welsh-speaking element was also the hard core of support for the local cultural system which was centered on the chapel.[74] The spread of public education after the Education Act of 1870 and the influx of migrants from England tended to lead to a reduction in the proportion speaking Welsh.

The receipt of immigrants from the traditional culture of the rural hinterland did not counteract the tendency towards a more secular society. The new migrants from the rural areas provided social structures less susceptible to chapel influence than in the case of their fathers.[75]

First, new immigrants tended to be young—precisely in the age groups most susceptible to diversion by new forms of recreation and most likely to be speaking English. Their preoccupations contrasted with those of the older miners: "In the life of the old-fashioned collier religion continues to play a large part; his preoccupation with the affairs of his church or chapel, his other-worldliness of spirit cause him to hold aloof from active participation in the work of his lodge or in trade union politics."[76]

Second, the new immigrants contained a majority of men; i.e., the sex group least amenable to chapel going in a time of declining attendance: "Congregations on the whole are smaller and less fervent. The most obvious loss in many places has been in male membership, for women frequently are in a large majority."[77]

Third, the new immigrants were English speaking—a sign that the great growth of public education after 1870 was having its effect upon the distribution of spoken languages.

The Increased Importance of Economic Goals. During this period economic values came to dominate Welsh urban society in much the same way that religious values dominated Welsh rural society. The increased importance of economic goals was due to increased conflict over the division of the regional product between worker and owner. The increased conflict itself stemmed from two sources: first, economic dislocations resulting from the disruption of overseas markets; second, the introduction of ideas of class conflict and more militant workers' demands from England.

In periods of high prices, the sliding scale which regulated wages in the coal industry according to the price of coal was quite acceptable to the worker and, as noted earlier, was an important element of the ideological unity between employer and employee characteristic of the coalfield between 1861 and 1891. After 1880, however, periods of depression coinciding with the falling off in foreign demand for South Wales coal led the men to question the comparative justice of the sliding scale to the worker on the one hand and to the owner on the other hand. Thus, from 1892 to 1899, the industry was in the trough of a severe price slump and there was an actual decline in the number employed in 1892–1893 and 1895–1896.[78] E. W. Evans has commented that "the steady fall in wage rates between November 1891 and June 1893 which the Colliery Workmen's Federation (the coalminers' labor union) could do nothing to check, led to an intensification of the campaign against the sliding scale."[79] This intensification led to a six-month stoppage in 1898 for the abolition of the sliding scale.

Into this rapidly changing environment came ideas of class conflict and notions of more militant worker organization from England. In the area of politics, the conversion of individual miners' lodges to socialism was accomplished by missionaries from other parts of the coalfield or from England.[80] In labor organization the English-founded Miners' Federation of Great Britain came to play an increasingly important role in social change in the area. It came into being in 1889 and aimed at a more aggressive wage policy together with an Eight Hour Day and the replacement of sliding scales by conciliation board agreements; it encouraged opposition to sliding scales. In 1899 the South Wales miners were affiliated to the Miners' Federation of Great Britain as the South Wales Miners' Federation and pledged themselves to abolish the sliding scale when the current agreement expired. Encouragement of the Eight Hour issue led to further bitter contention in South Wales. Only in Lancashire did the miners work a longer day than in South Wales; the Eight Hour Day was therefore bitterly contested.[81] The enactment of the Eight Hour Day Bill in 1909 led to a serious reduction in men's earnings and initiated a series of disputes which dragged on interminably and led ultimately to the men questioning the utility of the conciliation board set up by union and owners.[82]

The Consecutive Decline of Religion and the Increased Importance of Economic Goals. The decline of religion in the life of the South Wales collier and the increasing importance of militant economic conflict in his life were closely interlinked. Increased worker militancy was a reaction to deteriorating economic conditions largely because the chapel was not prepared to offer any alternative. The attitude of the chapels to the social problem was not one which would ensure their survival and salience in the local value system.

Doctrinally, Welsh Nonconformity was a strict form of puritanism which insisted on piety, chapel attendance and integrity of character. It created a concern with the world to come and therefore militated against the use of force or violence in order to improve conditions in the present world. This doctrine received a leaven of self-interest from the leading personnel of the chapel: in the larger urban centers such as Merthyr Tydfil, the "articulate spokesmen of dissent came from the solicitors and shopocracy rather than from the ironworkers and colliers."[83] These facts of doctrine and economic self-interest had two effects: opposition to militant workers' organizations and second an indifference to the social condition of the mining population.

The chapels had maintained unfavorable attitudes toward trade unions throughout the nineteenth century though only the Methodists seem to have made an unequivocal statement of the position. Thus, the Wesleyan Conference of 1833 advised members to play no part in unions and the Calvinistic Methodists who were predominant in South Wales decided as early as 1831 that unionists could neither join nor remain within the organization. The fact that most of the trade unions held their meetings in public houses (taverns) also provoked a general hostility to their cause from the teetotaling chapel-goers.

Congruent with this attitude, the chapels also displayed a general in-difference to the social plight of the miners. Cooney, Pollins and Brennan have written that:

Of the true nature of such problems as unemployment, bad living conditions, a sense among workers of exploitation and oppression and their criticism of an economy which seemed incoherent and unjust, the churches hardly seemed aware. So far as the nineteenth century churches had any philosophy about industrial problems, it was expressed in terms of the betterment of personal relations between employers and workers. This kind of simple morality became increasingly inadequate as the scale of industrial organizations increased.[84]

In such an environment, militant trade unionism and socialism could compete easily with a chapel which opted out of a position on the social problem. The inveighing of the chapel against the materialism and atheism of the new workers' movements[85] did not prevent the withdrawal of younger people from the chapel, especially those from the working class,[86] thus depriving the chapels of a future source of leadership and social class balance.

Political Feedback. Given the destabilizing effects of incipient economic goal conflict certain other events followed and led to an increasing polarization of economic interest within the community. On the one hand, militant workers' organizations challenging the old political and economic leadership of the workers emerged; and on the other hand, the structure of ownership in South Wales showed an increasing degree of concentration. The continued decline of the chapel provided no mediating institution.

In the period after 1900, militant political organizations and industrial labor organizations emerged side by side, stimulating one another to further growth. The membership of the nascent Independent Labour Party, for instance, "includes some of the most intelligent and most active members of the Federal Lodges and these carry the Socialist message into every meeting of their Trade Union . . . there is scarcely a Trades and Labour Council or a Federal Lodge or district meeting in the coalfield today which has not been permeated to a greater or lesser extent with Independent Labour Party doctrine. . . ."[87] In terms of worker militancy, an organization which intensified the activity of the South Wales Miners Federation was the Plebs League. Formed for the purpose of advocating labor-controlled working-class colleges with the class war idea as the underlying principle of their education, they called for direct action instead of constitutional method and in the great Cambrian Strike of 1910–1911 their influence in the workers' union movement became increasingly powerful.

The increasing militancy was especially noticeable among three social groups: the English speaking, the younger men and the chapel-abstaining population. The new propaganda of militancy—the propaganda of the Independent Labour Party or the Miners' Federation of Great Britain was written in English, and hence was most effective in reaching those speaking English rather than those speaking Welsh. As related below, the more militant attitudes took root first in English-speaking Monmouthshire and only later spread to the western areas of the coalfield where Welsh speech was longest preserved.

Spokesmen have been quite unambiguous about the youth of the early twentieth century militants in South Wales. A Government Report of 1917 identified the younger men with socialism and trade unionism—a view which found an echo in a Welsh national magazine: "A very much larger proportion of the young men (than of the old men) have come under Independent Labour Party influence, and it is these who constitute the driving force in the industrial and political Labour movement in the South Wales coalfield."[88] Indeed, the great strikes of 1910 and 1911 were caused largely by the contest for supremacy between younger figures—Stanton, Hartshorn and Winstone— and the aging leadership of the South Wales Miners' Federation: "The younger leaders were Socialists, imbued with Communistic theories concerning the relations of capital and Labour and the older leaders were orthodox trade unionists."[89] The role of chapelgoers in the new militancy, however, was small. Cooney *et al.*, have made it quite clear in their study of South West Wales that the present high age of working class deacons is due to the great defection from the chapel in the opening years of the twentieth century.[90]

Just as the increasing militancy of the miners can be partly perceived as a response to unemployment resulting from the failure of markets overseas, so the amalgamation of mining concerns may be attributed to the same source. By 1918, for instance, three men controlled 40 per cent of the output of the coal industry in South Wales. For two reasons such concentration of ownership enhanced rather than mollified the conflict between worker and owner. First, it led to a decline of that paternalism which had fostered ties of unity; Cooney *et al.*, have remarked on the degree to which the amalgamation of concerns not only in coal but also in tin-plate replaced the paternal pattern of industrial relations by an impersonal and alien organization. Second, the increased strength resulting from concentration of ownership made the employers increasingly reluctant to make concessions.[91]

While the employers and employees drew further apart in their economic attitudes, the chapel failed to fill the void by acting as a mediating influence. The doctrinal character of Nonconformity which made it antagonistic to unionization of labor has already been remarked upon. When militant unionism came into being, its viability as a flourishing institution in the coal-field was challenged; when thousands defected from the chapel, its demise was assured in a downward spiral of declining support.

When faced with the growing conflict between master and man, the chapels failed to offer a positive mediating position. Rather they appear to have been characterized by a lack of social commitment for fear of offending those who had not yet left the chapel. Cooney *et al.*, have remarked upon the deliberate effort by the Nonconformist chapels to avoid involvement in political questions and to avoid conflict between middle class and lower class within the chapel.[92] A second element in the chapel's continued decline was its refusal to conduct services in any language other than Welsh at a time when the use of English was spreading rapidly and the use of Welsh becoming defunct.

Defection from the chapel contained within it the seeds of further decline by depriving itself both of funds and of idealistic leadership. Although one of the continual complaints of the South Wales chapel since that time has been declining funds, leadership has also been a critical issue as Cooney *et al.*, have been at pains to clarify:

> The leadership of the industrial workers passed increasingly to secular organizations. Because the problems with which these organizations were concerned were seen as immediate and dramatic, they attracted to their leadership many who in an earlier generation would have been church leaders. The present relatively high age of working class deacons compared with middle class deacons is, we believe, an indication of the church's failure to hold the allegiance of the working class leaders in the local community.[93]

In summary, the political response to all these factors took the form of a division into two major groups: first, those who espoused a more militant unionism and workers' politics voting Labour. Social changes manifested themselves in the decline of the Liberal vote in the coalfield area and its replacement by a dominantly Labour vote. H. M. Williams has drawn attention to the strong relationship between the decline of the per cent Liberal vote and the coincidental increase of the per cent Labour vote.[94] In 1895, out of the Members of Parliament representing coalfield constituencies, eight were Liberals; in 1922, out of a total of fifteen Members of Parliament representing coalfield constituencies, thirteen were Labour Members. Second, those who remained loyal to the remnants of the traditional chapel culture voted Liberal. The new political role of the coalowners—former Liberals—is difficult to ascertain; the analysis, however, suggests that reaction to the new workers' militancy and the withdrawal of the chapel from social conflict would lead to a revival of Conservative activity under their aegis.

Contemporary Reactions to Sociopolitical Milieux

Despite the growth of survey data banks in University Political Data archives, investigators working at the regional level are likely to experience continuing difficulties in assembling adequate supplementary survey data for cross-locality comparisons; this is particularly so in the United Kingdom where there is no accumulation of national sample survey results from university agencies as in the United States.

For Wales it has been possible to procure some survey data for approximately 1,350 respondents, originally collected by a commercial polling agency.[95] The aims of such commercial houses are not strictly academic and hence the criteria adopted in designing the sample and establishing questions are not the most ideal from our point of view: for example, in this particular case there are insufficient Liberals in the sample to justify inferring from sample to population; further, there are no data at all on the crucial variables of language and religion.[96] This situation is likely to be not at all atypical in ecological analyses of regional politics such as this one and considerable ingenuity will have to be displayed in maximizing the utility of such data. In this particular case the data include the following individual attributes: place of residence (urban or rural), age, sex, trade union membership, objective social class, individual's perception of social class and party preference at the 1959 election. To these variables employed by the polling agency it is possible to add our own contextual variables based on the factor analysis. In the light of the small sample, it seemed advisable to limit ourselves to a dichotomization between urban Wales on the one hand and rural Wales on the other hand; in order to avoid confusion with place of residence categories within sociopolitical contexts these two regional categories will be referred to henceforth as traditional and modern Wales.

Traditional Wales has been defined as those constituencies in the first and second quartiles on Figures 6–2 and 6–3; i.e., traditional Wales consists of the more agricultural areas, the areas in which chapel-going is a more prevalent social activity, in which Welsh is still spoken to a greater extent and in which the Liberal party still claims a good deal of support. Modern Wales, contrariwise, consists of the areas in which employment is predominantly in mining and manufacturing, where the chapel has lost the appeal it once had and where the population is anglicized to a much greater extent. Examination of the relationships between individual characteristics and behavior can be made for different contexts in order to determine the manner in which context and individual characteristics together influence party preference.

In the light of available data resources and the preceding factor analysis and historical analyses, the following hypotheses seem feasible: (1) that social class factors are much more significant in differentiating party preference in modern Wales than in traditional Wales: the extreme class polarization that occurred in the South Wales coalfield in the late nineteenth century and early twentieth century was not replicated in the less modernized areas of Wales. In the latter all social classes were tied together by common religion and/or similar tenurial relations in their antagonism toward the landed aristocracy. (2) As a corollary of the above it will be hypothesized that factors mutually independent of social class are much more significant in differentiating party preference in traditional Wales than in modern Wales. Ideally one would have liked to have incorporated such variables as religion and language into the analysis; however, there is a good deal of evidence (see supra) to suggest that those most prone to retain strong links with the Welsh-speaking Nonconformist culture syndrome have been the female and the aged rather than the male and the younger elements of the population. (3) That in traditional Wales, as befits its nineteenth-century agrarian origins, radicalism is a rural phenomenon rather than an urban feature; in modern Wales no such residential differentiation is expected given the absence of an agrarian issue dominating local politics and given the high proportion of the rural population engaged in mining. Ideally one would have liked to have tested this for the Liberal vote; however, there is a good deal of evidence in the literature of comparative political sociology to suggest that political radicalisms of the day tend to succeed each other, finding fertile soil in the same social structural situation. Goguel, for example, has shown how the high Communist votes experienced in certain parts of rural France—particularly in the Massif Central—occur in exactly the same areas which experienced high degrees of left-wing radical activity in the nineteenth century.[97]

In the tabulations which follow, the dependent variable for given social categories will be the proportion of the voters voting for the Labour party. The procedure undertaken will be to examine the interplay of individual variables and party preference within, firstly, regional contexts, and, secondly, regional contexts together with place of residence.

Regional Context and Social Characteristics. The research strategy here is to examine the relationships between social characteristics and party preference in traditional Wales and modern Wales, respectively, for three social characteristics at a time: (a) sex, age, and subjective evaluation of one's own social class; (b) sex, age and interviewer's evaluation of respondent's social class (i.e., objective social class); (c) trade union membership, age and subjective social class; (d) trade union membership, age and objective social class. The size of the sample prevents one from considering more than four independent variables at any one time (including regional contexts) or from examining such cross-tabulations as sex and trade union membership;

i.e., cross-tabulations in which certain cell entries would be exceedingly small.

It is clear from Table 6–5 and the accompanying measures of partial association[98] that in traditional Wales nonclass factors are much more important in explaining party preferences than in modern Wales; not only does

TABLE 6–5

Percentage Labour Vote by Region, Subjective Social Class, Sex and Age

| | TRADITIONAL WALES | | | | MODERN WALES | | | |
| | LOWER CLASS | | UPPER CLASS | | LOWER CLASS | | UPPER CLASS | |
Age	Male	Female	Male	Female	Male	Female	Male	Female
Young	66.7%	63.6%	50.0%	32.9%	84.7%	68.8%	31.8%	55.8%
	(114)	(110)	(48)	(73)	(111)	(77)	(44)	(52)
Old	69.8%	59.3%	55.1%	22.8%	78.9%	69.9%	27.9%	50.0%
	(146)	(113)	(49)	(92)	(109)	(93)	(61)	(58)

Notes:

Effect of age (traditional Wales) = .015
Effect of age (modern Wales)   = .036

Effect of subjective class (traditional Wales) = .246
Effect of subjective class (modern Wales)   = .342

Effect of sex (traditional Wales) = .157
Effect of sex (modern Wales)   = .053

social class explain a greater degree of the behavioral variance in modern Wales than in traditional Wales, but there are much greater disparities between the political behavior of men and women in the latter area than in the former. Age, however, does not show the anticipated variation in impact; rather it seems to exert little differentiating effect on party preference at all.

Table 6–6 and the associated coefficients of partial association present a broadly similar picture. Again, nonclass factors are much more important in traditional Wales than in modern Wales, women being much less likely to vote for the Labour party than men, holding objective social class constant; age has once more a minimal impact. Note, however, that using objective class as the indicator of social class, one finds a much greater proportion of the variation of the Labour vote associated with social class in modern Wales than in traditional Wales, than was the case with subjective social class. This appears to be the result of a greater congruence between objective social class and subjective social class in modern Wales when compared with traditional Wales. Thus, for modern Wales the association between objective social class and subjective social class as measured by eta[99] is somewhat higher than in traditional Wales: .267 compared with .192. This heightened accuracy in perception of one's own social class is almost certainly an indicator of a much higher degree of class awareness in modern Wales than is the case with traditional Wales.

TABLE 6–6

Percentage Labour Vote by Region, Objective Social Class, Sex and Age

| | TRADITIONAL WALES | | | | MODERN WALES | | | |
| | LOWER CLASS | | UPPER CLASS | | LOWER CLASS | | UPPER CLASS | |
Age	Male	Female	Male	Female	Male	Female	Male	Female
Young	67.0% (101)	57.0% (142)	54.1% (61)	31.7% (41)	88.2% (110)	75.5% (90)	25.0% (44)	35.9% (39)
Old	70.4% (152)	53.8% (156)	51.2% (43)	8.2% (49)	82.6% (109)	68.1% (113)	21.3% (61)	44.7% (38)

Notes:

Effect of age (traditional Wales) = .065
Effect of age (modern Wales)   = .020

Effect of objective class (traditional Wales) = .257
Effect of objective class (modern Wales)   = .469

Effect of sex (traditional Wales) = .230
Effect of sex (modern Wales)   = −.018

TABLE 6–7

Percentage Labour Vote by Region, Subjective Social Class, Trade Union Membership[a] and Age

| | TRADITIONAL WALES | | | | MODERN WALES | | | |
| | LOWER CLASS | | UPPER CLASS | | LOWER CLASS | | UPPER CLASS | |
Age	TU	NTU	TU	NTU	TU	NTU	TU	NTU
Young	81.1% (85)	55.3% (139)	63.6% (22)	34.3% (99)	88.3% (103)	66.6% (84)	57.5% (40)	40.9% (61)
Old	75.2% (85)	60.1% (173)	50.0% (24)	30.7% (117)	71.6% (74)	76.5% (128)	47.3% (38)	36.1% (83)

[a]Whether a respondent belongs to a trade union or not is represented in the body of the table in an abbreviated form: TU or NTU, respectively.

Notes:

Effect of age (traditional Wales) = .045
Effect of age (modern Wales)   = .050

Effect of subjective social class (traditional Wales) = .303
Effect of subjective social class (modern Wales)   = .232

Effect of trade union membership (traditional Wales) = .224
Effect of trade union membership (modern Wales)   = .112

Tables 6–7 and 6–8 again demonstrate the differences between traditional and modern Wales in terms of the degree to which political behavior is a function of social class in the two areas. As when sex was held constant, however, it will be noted that the differences between the two regional contexts are much clearer when examining objective social class than for subjective social class. Moreover, the tabulations also suggest the importance of the trade union in making the individual independent of the milieu in

TABLE 6–8

Percentage Labour Vote by Region, Objective Social Class, Trade Union Membership[a] and Age

| | TRADITIONAL WALES | | | | MODERN WALES | | | |
| | LOWER CLASS | | UPPER CLASS | | LOWER CLASS | | UPPER CLASS | |
Age	TU	NTU	TU	NTU	TU	NTU	TU	NTU
Young	80.7%	51.5%	69.0%	35.6%	89.9%	73.6%	37.9%	21.9%
	(78)	(165)	(29)	(73)	(109)	(91)	(29)	(64)
Old	72.3%	57.5%	53.3%	23.4%	72.4%	76.7%	41.2%	24.6%
	(94)	(214)	(15)	(77)	(76)	(146)	(34)	(65)

[a]Whether a respondent belongs to a trade union or not is represented in the body of the table in an abbreviated form: TU or NTU respectively.

Notes:

Effect of age (traditional Wales) = .076
Effect of age (modern Wales) = .021

Effect of objective social class (traditional Wales) = .202
Effect of objective social class (modern Wales) = .467

Effect of trade union membership (traditional Wales) = .268
Effect of trade union membership (modern Wales) = .111

which he lives by tying him into a national communications network; holding social type constant, the crossregional differences are in general much greater in the case of nonunionists than in the case of unionists.

Regional Context, Urban-Rural Differences and Social Characteristics. A further areally varying context is added if one includes place of residence differences. Due to the small entries appearing in some cells when one controls for residence type, these tabulations are limited to three independent variables as opposed to the tabulations of four independent variables each considered above.

TABLE 6–9

Percentage Labour Vote by Region, Sex and Place of Residence

| | TRADITIONAL WALES | | MODERN WALES | |
Place of Residence	Male	Female	Male	Female
Urban	53.5%	42.1%	64.7%	62.6%
	(99)	(211)	(312)	(225)
Rural	68.2%	52.5%	75.0%	63.6%
	(258)	(177)	(11)	(55)

Notes:

Effect of place of residence (traditional Wales) = −.125
Effect of place of residence (modern Wales) = −.056

Effect of sex (traditional Wales) = .135
Effect of sex (modern Wales) = .067

Tables 6–9, 6–10, 6–11, and 6–12 and their accompanying coefficients of partial association demonstrate the degree to which radicalism in traditional Wales is still—as with nineteenth-century Liberalism—a rural phenomenon. The strikingly consistent magnitude of the coefficients for the effect of place of residence in traditional Wales contrasts with the regularly negligible effect of the urban-rural dichotomy in modern Wales.

TABLE 6–10

Percentage Labour Vote by Region, Age and Place of Residence

| | TRADITIONAL WALES | | MODERN WALES | |
Place of Residence	Young	Old	Young	Old
Urban	49.6% (149)	42.2% (161)	68.0% (250)	60.9% (284)
Rural	60.3% (199)	62.3% (239)	66.6% (30)	64.8% (37)

Notes:

Effect of place of residence (traditional Wales) = −.154
Effect of place of residence (modern Wales)   = −.012

Effect of age (traditional Wales) = .027
Effect of age (modern Wales)   = .044

TABLE 6–11

Percentage Labour Vote by Region, Subjective Social Class and Place of Residence

| | TRADITIONAL WALES | | MODERN WALES | |
Place of Residence	Lower Class	Upper Class	Lower Class	Upper Class
Urban	56.3% (167)	33.5% (143)	76.7% (344)	41.1% (192)
Rural	69.9% (316)	40.3% (119)	75.5% (45)	45.4% (22)

Notes:

Effect of place of residence (traditional Wales) = −.102
Effect of place of residence (modern Wales)   = −.005

Effect of subjective social class (traditional Wales) = .262
Effect of subjective social class (modern Wales)   = .328

Taking each of the Tables in turn, Table 6–9 shows—as with Tables 6–5 and 6–6—that sex differences again emerge as much more important in traditional Wales than in modern Wales in accounting for party preference. Note, however, that despite the fact that rural areas in Wales have higher levels of Labour voting than urban areas when taking sex differences into

TABLE 6–12

Percentage Labour Vote by Region, Objective Social Class and
Place of Residence

Place of Residence	TRADITIONAL WALES		MODERN WALES	
	Lower Class	Upper Class	Lower Class	Upper Class
Urban	52.2% (230)	26.5% (79)	79.2% (371)	29.5% (166)
Rural	65.1% (293)	43.8% (114)	74.5% (51)	36.5% (16)

Notes:

Effect of place of residence (traditional Wales) $= -.150$
Effect of place of residence (modern Wales) $= .010$
Effect of objective social class (traditional Wales) $= .234$
Effect of objective social class (modern Wales) $= .438$

account, the differences between men and women in voting for the Labour party are much greater in rural areas than in urban areas: this suggests that the radicalism of rural areas in traditional Wales is not associated with those social changes leading to a redefinition of sex roles which are found in the urban areas of traditional Wales.[100] Differences in female and male voting behavior between urban and rural areas, however, suggest that there is a diffusion of new sex roles proceeding outward from the urban centers. This diffusion interpretation receives more support when one notes that these differences between male and female voting are much reduced in modern as compared with traditional Wales though the reduction is greater for the urban population than for the rural population.

Table 6–10 also verifies the low effect of age on political behavioral differences between the two regional contexts as noted earlier. Closer examination of Table 6–10, however, suggests the presence in both regional contexts of age differentials in urban areas but not in rural areas; the reasons for such tendencies have yet to be identified.

Tables 6–11 and 6–12 cross-tabulate Labour voting with regional contexts, place of residence and social class: subjective social class in Table 6–11 and objective class in the case of Table 6–12. They confirm the findings of Tables 6–5 and 6–6, respectively, in that they do demonstrate the greater significance of social class in modern as opposed to traditional Wales and also the greater variation manifested in the case of objective social class as opposed to subjective social class.

In summary, the examination of the available survey data resources does allow one to verify certain hypotheses suggested by the contextual analysis. Specifically, at least four conclusions emerge from these cross-tabulations. First, social class is clearly of more significance in explaining political behavior in modern Wales than in traditional Wales; moreover, the higher correlation between subjective and objective social class in modern Wales suggests a higher degree of class consciousness there. Second, nonclass factors, in particular, sex, are more important in traditional as opposed to modern Wales; age, however, seems to have little differentiating effect in either region. Third, trade union membership in traditional Wales appears to provide the individual with a protection against the impact of his immediate environment by integrating him to a greater extent into a national communications network. In modern Wales, the individual is exposed to a milieu in which class differences are far more salient in political discussion; in traditional Wales, however, we have seen that class polarization of politics has been considerably less—trade union membership has provided an important channel for Labour party penetration into that area. Finally, there is a large amount of evidence that in traditional Wales, the Labour party has met with greatest success in the more rural areas—the areas in which political Liberalism made its greatest gains in the nineteenth century.

Summary and Implications

The political meaningfulness of the original regional typology of Wales has been confirmed by the historical analysis and survey data analyses for the respective regions: the antithesis of agricultural, Welsh-speaking, Nonconformist Traditional Wales with its Liberalism on the one hand and mining, English-speaking, non-conconformist modern Wales with its support for the Labour party on the other hand is upheld by parallel distinctions in terms of social structure, political issues and individual reactions to the sociopolitical milieu.

In traditional Wales the long dominant Liberalism derives largely from the cues presented by the Liberal party to a population agitated by religious and economic discrimination on the part of an English-speaking Anglican minority. Though the conflicts within the social structure have long since been stabilized by such legislative acts as the Local Government Act of 1888, the absence of social class issues and the significance of radical roots in the Welsh countryside are still reflected in contemporary survey data.

In modern Wales, on the other hand, nineteenth-century mining and industrial communities tied together by common links and economic dependence on the overseas-oriented coal trade gave way in the latter years of the nineteenth century to a social class cleavage which was vigorously exploited by the Labour party. Although a decline in the fortunes of the coal trade and a failure of the social consciousness of the chapel prepared the ground, it was English immigrant unionists who were the most ardent propagators of left-wing radicalism. Yet while in traditional Wales the trade union is still important in the diffusion of Labour party propaganda, such is no longer the case in modern Wales. There, survey evidence suggests that support for the Labour party is now associated with a high level of class consciousness independent of union membership.

Methodologically, the study has certain implications that are worth pursuing. In particular, this study has attempted to explain cross-locality variations as a function of sociopolitical contexts. The advantages of this approach are several. As Scheuch has pointed out elsewhere,[101] it does obviate the ecological fallacy that has marred so much previous work. Secondly, emphasis on context implies an emphasis on information transmission and therefore on the processes resulting in the many individual electoral decisions, which when aggregated, produce the observed areal pattern of voting. Instead, therefore, of a search for correlates of areal differences, the investigation maximizes the use of available historical data, examines the reactions of individuals to milieux and stresses strategic social locations—such as that of the chapel deacon—which link context to individual behavior.

However, the attempt at such contextual analysis as is exemplified in this paper suggests that if cross-locality studies are to progress, there is a strong need for a formalization of the contextual approach defining its scope, relating it to network models as a whole and indicating some of the problems involved in its application. For example, one needs to define the variety of spatial scales at which information flows, and the impact of spatial structure as well as social structure on the flow of information. Moreover, a great deal of work needs to be done on the contextual significance of certain variables. Does the sex ratio, for example, with its relatively low variability have the same impact on behavior as class structure with its relatively high variability? Furthermore, what is the impact of the areal size of one's observational units on correlation results? It has been shown, for instance, that in the U.S. correlations at the county level are not necessarily paralleled by correlations at the state level.[102] The application of spectral methods to such problems might go a long way toward elucidating the variable scales at which different processes operate.[103]

Substantively, the implication of greatest interest revolves around the resolution of the problem posed by Figure 6–1. That map identified residuals from the regression of the left-wing vote on certain social class variables for England and Wales as a whole. As a result of this regional analysis, one can say that in Wales, at least, the residual areas are areas in which some contextual factors other than social class factors have exercised an influence upon political behavior. The fact that there are such areas gives pause for thought; many political sociologists have made the bland assumption that social class was all-important:

> The simplicity of the British social structure, the high degree of national unity and the two-party system have helped to concentrate attention on the distribution of wealth between classes. British policies are almost wholly innocent of those issues which cross the social lines in other lands—for example, race, nationality, religion, town and country interests, regional interest or the conflict between authoritarian and parliamentarian methods.[104]

The factors which have been adduced to explain the regional anomalies are precisely those which Bonham scorns. In traditional Wales political issues surrounding language and religion provided the basis for Liberal support in the area. In modern Wales, the very high Labour vote relative to social class appears to owe its origin to the very intense social class cleavage of the early nineteenth century building on sporadic regional unemployment, English trade unionism, the failure of the chapel and the tradition of nineteenth-century left-wing radicalism. Certainly the change from Liberal to Labour must have been easier to make than the change from Conservative to Labour. Within Wales, therefore, the impact of class seems to have varied according to the influence of other factors of a regional, religious, personal or historical character.

Robert Alford has found a similar inverse relationship between social class and other factors in a comparative study of nations rather than regions.[105] Using sample survey data, Alford has examined political behavior in four countries—the United Kingdom, Australia, the United States and Canada—and has tried to estimate the degree of class polarization; i.e., the degree to which party preferences are a function of social class. He finds that class polarization is greatest in Britain and least in Canada with Australia and the United States occupying the intermediate positions. In those nations where class polarization is reduced, Alford finds that regional and religious factors are important. In Quebec middle class and lower class have combined to vote for the Liberals; in the U.S. South, middle class and lower class have combined to vote Democratic. In the United Kingdom and Australia, Alford claims, such factors are of little significance and indeed, compared with the other nations, this does seem to be so. The degree of polarization in these four nations seems to be related to other phenomena: the less class polarized systems are those in which labor unionism is less prevalent, in which local personalities have a greater influence upon political behavior, in which political parties are less likely to be organized on a mass basis with branches down to the local level and political competition is more restricted.

Alford has attempted further to infer from these cross-sectional relationships to a sequential model of political change:

Class polarization of the support for national parties seems to be most evident in the countries where a national political identity has replaced political identities centered on regional or religious loyalties. The aspects of modernization mentioned above (industrialization and urbanization) favor the emergence of national political identities and thus favor class polarization of the parties—up to a certain point. These societies . . . may all be moving toward a common level of structurally based class cleavages—cleavages which remain while traditional political identities dwindle in importance.

A national communications system may be a necessary instrument of national integration given a minimum level of industrialization and urbanization. Unless some means of communication exists between regions, no common political action can develop, regardless of common interests or values. Likewise, no true sense of national identity can exist unless there can be regular interchanges of ideas, people and goods between the various regions of a nation. The expansion of national organizations of all kinds, whether business, recreational, trade unions or otherwise, contributes to the communication of ideas and grievances; it creates the possibility of the formation of a national public opinion.[106]

The analysis in this paper has turned up examples to support Alford's thesis—examples that his analysis did not provide. Thus, increasing class militancy in South Wales at the end of the nineteenth century has been traced to English influences and militant centralized unionism replacing the local concensual unions of the coalfield. These are examples of the diffusion of class polarization on a macroscale. On the microscale, the sample survey data suggest diffusion processes from modern Wales to traditional Wales with class consciousness penetrating the rural areas and providing a new basis for preference.

Alford's thesis, therefore. not only obtains across nations; it also obtains within nations giving rise to recurrent spatial configurations of political behavior. Supporting evidence for such assertions can be obtained from outside of England and Wales. Rokkan and Valen, in a recent study of regional contrasts in Norwegian political behavior, find that class polarization is much greater in cities than in rural areas and that interregional political differences are greater for rural areas than for cities, testifying to the comparative strength of barriers to communication:

Urbanization, industrialization and the growth of a nationwide money and market-economy have created new lines of conflict in national politics and have also gradually affected the alignments of leaders and followers in the local communities. Conditions in the peripheral areas have created important barriers, socio-economic as well as geographical, against the spread of partisan politics and have made for persistently low levels of politicization.[107]

Blondel has documented analagous contrasts for a nation at a much earlier state of urbanization and industrialization—Brazil—comparing the peasant who is deferential to the wishes of his patron to the relatively independent and more class conscious industrial worker.[108]

This conclusion suggests that one important task awaiting contextual analysis is the examination and explanation of the diffusion patterns that recurrent spatial structures suggest. If this paper leads to a greater interest in and attention to political diffusion patterns, it will have served a useful function.

ASPECTS OF ELECTORAL BEHAVIOR IN ENGLISH CONSTITUENCIES, 1832–1868[1]

T. J. NOSSITER

PUBLIC opinion in modern Britain is homogeneous and national so that psephologists can assume two facts: that there are certain basic determinants of voting; and that at election time there is a fairly uniform "swing "of voters over most of the country. Class is the fundamental social basis of voting behavior in which there is comparatively little regional or local variation. The merits of local candidates or local issues rarely affect the result more than a few hundred votes.

By contrast the accepted view of the course of nineteenth-century elections at least until the 1870's denies both these contemporary assumptions: there were few basic social determinants along the lines of group membership, and there was little effective national opinion and consequently no "swing" of opinion. Elections, it is argued, were won and lost either through the interplay of the power and influence of competing members of the ruling class or at most through its interaction with local opinion on those local issues which infrequently arose. National opinion was occasionally roused by such exceptional issues as Reform, the Corn Laws, or the Crimea, but for the most part was nonexistent or embryonic. As one contemporary, Bishop Maltby of Durham, put it in 1841, his tenants had little chance of forming "correct judgments" on parliamentary events and so were disposed to lean on the opinions of those who were familiar with the arguments for public measures. This alleged absence of a broad social basis to elections or any effective public opinion is commonly explained by historians in terms of the heterogeneity of post-industrial revolution England, which was initially less rather

A paper prepared for delivery and discussion at the World Congress of the International Political Science Association, Brussels, September 1967.

Notes to this chapter are on pp. 371–372.

than more uniform in character, the limitations of the reformed franchise, and the gross impurities and distortions of the electoral machinery, magnified by the system of voting in public. How far is this view justified? There is certainly much truth in the conventional analysis but both the absence of social dimensions to voting in the face of the random play of influence and corruption, and the weakness of national movements of opinion have been somewhat exaggerated. This paper, therefore, aims firstly to show with statistical evidence some of the social factors operating in the period between the first two reform bills and, secondly, to suggest tentatively that public opinion may well have existed to an extent historians have denied.

Nobody who has read the accounts in newspapers, private letters, and Victorian fiction of election malpractices can fail to acknowledge the role of influence and corruption. In the private papers of the Tyneside radical, Joseph Cowen, for example, there survives a letter from the Berwick agent for the Northern Reform Union reporting in 1859 his sufferings in his shop-keeping business for his beliefs: "the devils," (in this case the whigs) he wrote,

have done me as much harm as possible. Every customer possible is driven off . . . Another notice to quit which must, I believe, be obeyed at May Term . . . I have taken a small shop not one-fourth large enough for me—and at present I am in a prospective fix—nay more I cannot lay in my ordinary stock through the winter in preparation for summer as I see no certainty of securing a place suitable in point of situation and size—some places are let to others, some too narrow entries . . . others are upstairs.[2]

In this notorious constituency one fifth of the voters would not poll without payment,[3] and votes were quite openly bought and sold in the marketplace according to the ordinary laws of supply and demand, although the price never reached the record figure of one hundred and forty pounds per vote once recorded in Norwich. For a poor elector the franchise was an economic asset in such places. As a Durham voter said with simple logic in reply to a sophisticated London barrister's smart question why he took bribes, "Money is a good thing to look at."[4]

Even royal commissions and parliamentary committees revealed extensive bribery and treating but it would be perhaps unwise to assume that a voter necessarily accepted money from a party he would not have supported anyway. Indeed the commonest allegation was not bribery but influence, the use of a superior social or economic status as a power position over the voter.

Three points, however, need to be made in this connection: first the political conventions of the day recognized a line, albeit an unclear one, between legitimate influence and illegitimate. In rural society the mark was often overstepped although even there the shortage of good farming tenants exercised constraints on tyranny but in the towns, and especially the larger ones, there was some meaning to the distinction. The complexity of the social and economic life of towns was a defense for the determined voter who could normally find an excuse for evasion if he so wished by playing off one influence against another. The second point is that "influence" often shades into the pressure of group membership. Some of the so-called pressures of influence which were listed in Dod and alleged in press accounts of elections seem to have been what we would regard as the unexceptionable pressure of identification with a social group. In other words sometimes influence in the nineteenth-century sense was equivalent to group pressures in the twentieth-century one. An extract from a newspaper leader of 1859 makes this confusion of meanings plain. "Canvassing," the article ran,

settles the results of election contests and with few exceptions every man on the register has been found and made note of. Personal influence, private feeling, trade interest, the lawyer, the surgeon, the banker, the minister, the customer are all brought to bear on the man who is unfortunate enough to be a registered elector.[5]

Trade interest, religious allegiance, the views of "influentials" in the modern sense and private feeling all affect the voter at the point of decision making, not merely the power of individuals. As is clear from a close reading of Dod, individual influence was gradually making way after 1832 for group influence. Thirdly, influence was attempting a ready-made excuse for any loser of an election even when none had been exercised in any objectionable way, and it is, therefore, wise to seek more certain proof of its use than mere allegation by interested parties.

Hard-headed contemporaries such as Bonham and Parkes, the conservative and liberal agents whose livelihood depended on the accuracy of their assessment of the situation, believed in public opinion, and were evaluating it at least as early as 1835. "You know," Parkes wrote to Lord Durham about this time,[6] "the driving rate of the currents rushing under the apparently calm surface of society," and reporting on election prospects on another occasion he was confident "Liberal opinions are gaining, not losing in the English towns; as indeed must be the case with such a vast increase of locomotion and such a rapidly progressing diffusion of knowledge."[7] The newspapers, partially freed from the tax on knowledge in the 1830's, both stimulated and reflected this quickening interest in politics, and there was hardly a major town without at least one journal for each party, and in some, organs for tory, whig, and radical. Commercial enterprises, they could not have carried so much political comment if there had been little appetite for it, and it is arguable that the patronage of the press mattered in the boroughs little less than the patronage of individuals.

In sum, while there may not have been any composite public opinion there was, as Professor Gash, the leading authority on the political practices of the period up to 1852, points out,[8] a mass of overlapping and sometimes conflicting opinions radiating out from small circles of "influentials" at the center of militant political and trade unions, chartism, the moderately radical dissenting shopocracy, the complacently liberal professional class and the whig gentry. These circles of opinion are in principle no less mappable than the political ideas of their representatives in parliament, whom Professor Aydelotte has shown can be ranged on ideological scales.[9] Before exploring the social boundaries of opinion in the constituency some information about the sources of data will be discussed. This paper is mainly concerned with the English borough constituencies with additional examples from the English counties. The choice of examples is loosely biased toward the northeast and the northern counties as a whole, but no general statements are made without some attempt having been made to check them against comparable data from other parts of the country for which purpose Dr. Vincent's recent compilation, *Poll Books*, has been invaluable.[10]

The most important part of the British electorate after the Reform Act of 1832, just as was the case before it, was the English boroughs which formed almost one half of the total representation in the house of commons with 323 seats out of 658. This was a disproportionate share of English representation in relation to their population, the 44 per cent of the people living in the towns receiving 69 per cent of the seats at the expense of the counties, an imbalance which was only partially redressed by the rural nature of some of the smaller boroughs and the agricultural element in the urban electorate of even some of the largest towns.

With the exception of the City of London which had four members, the boroughs returned either one or two members to parliament, 51 of the former, and 134 of the latter. Twenty-one of the two-member boroughs had been newly enfranchised in 1832 and the rest dated from earlier times. All of the new creations had by 1852 electorates of more than 1,000 voters, and this figure has been taken as a convenient boundary to mark the "large town" in this paper. In addition 41 of the older parliamentary boroughs fell into the same category of 1,000 voters, and are included in the classification of "large towns." Nine or ten of these are given as notoriously corrupt in Dod's *Electoral Facts* but have been included despite this on the grounds that the line marking degrees of corruption is a very thin one; on the other hand five other "large towns" are listed by Professor Gash in his *Politics in the Age of Peel* as nomination boroughs and these are excluded from normal calculations.[11] The vast majority of nomination boroughs, however, came from the smaller towns. The 51 single-member boroughs were in terms of numbers bound to be much less significant in their contribution to the commons, although many of them were larger than the smaller two-member constituencies. Nineteen of this class were newly enfranchised while 32 were old two-member seats reduced to one in 1832. None of the reduced boroughs had more than 1,000 electors by 1852, but eight of the new constituencies had, although in three, extensive influence prevailed to vitiate the effect of size.

The basic type of constituency was still, therefore, the two-member, which raises the difficult problem for this research of the optional vote. Electors were entitled, although not compelled, to cast two votes and not just one. The only proviso was that they were not allowed to vote twice for the same person; they could, however, if they wished vote for two candidates of the same party, or alternatively they could cast their votes for candidates of opposing parties. This possibility of voting across party lines was a bogey for politicians of the period equal to the fear today of husband and wife canceling each other's vote out by voting for different parties. Such a system had enormous consequences, neglected by historians, for the political system as a whole in arresting the development of party at the local level, tending to promote center politics, and at least arguably assisting minority sections of the major parties to break away, and maintain and increase themselves by alliance with the political "enemy."

These unfamiliar electoral arrangements are seen at their clearest if the standard terminology is adopted, used by some but not all contemporary writers: single, double and split voting. Single votes, often called plumpers, were those cast for only one candidate; double votes were those cast for two candidates of the same party; and split votes were two votes cast for candidates of competing parties. Normally single votes were cast when an elector's own

Table 7–1

Cross-Party Voting in the Six Northern Counties, 1832–1868

	1832	1835	1837	1841	1847	1852	1857	1859	1865	1868
Carlisle	5.93			12.76	9.13	2.25	12.01	4.16	5.19	5.08
Cockermouth				0.88		3.24				
Durham	13.08	17.98	26.49		12.84	10.5				5.6
Sunderland			31.04		54.19	44.87	45.40	15.75	37.00	
Blackburn		50.16		14.39	27.82	24.3			17.54	
Bolton	40.81	51.79	20.58	11.86	8.95	26.69				
Lancaster			13.23	15.36		26.5		83.19	3.03	
Liverpool	9.96	4.83	1.67	1.55						
Manchester	27.5	22.95	8.63							6.81
Oldham			1.75							
Preston							37.67	45.52	65.00	1.34
Wigan	30.66		4.9	0.56						5.25
Berwick	26.64	56.14	19.52	31.48	49.51	31.57	31.11	13.75	11.12	3.82
Newcastle/T.	46.50				8.87	22.43	13.54			
Beverley		20.02	5.56	6.03	13.85	4.95		12.84	9.48	7.89
Bradford	30.17				4.92	10.50		49.25		
Halifax		12.48	4.03	5.55	43.71	10.28	12.70			
Hull	21.85	14.16	4.67	2.55		5.41		17.04	17.45	5.68
Knaresborough	20.77	65.69	30.09	12.99	35.00	15.18	17.92	17.36	17.42	
Leeds	5.89	3.92	2.48	2.33	51.65	2.15	8.99	7.17	4.55	8.89
Pontefract						39.17			21.6	20.55
Ripon	0.61	3.61								
Scarborough	21.04	40.45	33.97	35.69		33.24		5.6	28.12	
Sheffield						14.11	9.36		32.17	22.73
York		10.74	10.53	11.95	7.09	27.31	17.17	6.88	4.12	3.40

party put up only one candidate but they could also be used to register antagonism to a second candidate of his own party, say a radical feuding with a whig or vice versa. The withholding of the second vote did no harm to the elector's first choice but did damage everyone else. Double votes were straight party votes, so that it was the object of every local Tadpole and Taper, Disraeli's lugubrious party agents, to convert these doubles into splits. Splits, in some contemporary usage improperly taken to include what are here called double votes, were votes across party lines, and of key importance for the outcome of elections. Their extent and character are of enormous interest, but unfortunately we can only discover the exact figures in a limited number of cases because not all polls exist in detail—among serious losses are the London constituencies for which not a single example survives from any election between 1832 and 1868—and where they do exist the time involved in extraction may hardly repay the effort.

Bean's invaluable *Parliamentary History of the Six Northern Counties* has an extensive list for the North, which has been supplemented from other sources to give a fairly complete picture of split voting in 25 boroughs in Lancashire, Yorkshire, Cumberland, Westmoreland, Northumberland and Durham.[12] The detailed results are presented in Table 7–1 and summarized below. In addition a less extensive search made for the rest of the country to give some check on the representativeness of the north is also summarized in Table 7–2.

TABLE 7–2

Extent of Split Voting in English Boroughs, 1832–1868

	1832	1835	1837	1841	1847	1852	1857	1859	1865	1868
No. of boroughs in 6 North cos.										
N =	15	14	16	15	12	20	9	11	13	12
Mean (%)	20.8	26.8	13.8	10.7	26.7	19.5	22.4	26.7	16.1	8.1
No. oforoughs in the rest of England										
N =	8	11	11	8	9	11	7	8	9	6
Mean (%)	25.3	18.0	15.1	8.6	26.3	19.3	16.0	18.5	12.5	12.6

Three times in the north—1835, 1847 and 1859—one quarter of the electorate split their votes, and on three other occasions—1832, 1852 and 1857—one fifth polled across party lines. The smallest percentages in the north prior to 1868—in 1837 and 1841—were still as much as 14 per cent and 11 per cent, illustrating the extent of the failure of the party system to mobilize the electorate before 1868; nor is there any clear secular trend in the percentages toward firmer party organization in elections as time passed.

Split voting could, and did, come from four possible sources: competing influences; the appeal of individual candidates; party tactics; or real *political* inclinations. Competing influences, perhaps between a tory landlord and a liberal employer, could drive an elector to split but this form was generally commoner in county divisions than urban ones. Candidate appeal naturally counted in an age when local politics counted more, but it is difficult to envisage reasons why either the role of influence or of the merit of candidates should have varied from election to election in the way in which it did. It seems, therefore, that the major part of the explanation must lie in tactical considerations and the mixed political alignments of the period to which historians have paid insufficient attention.

The history of liberal party quarrels is littered with internecine electoral strife when whigs or radicals attempted to blot out the rival gang by open or secret deals with the tories to split liberal votes upon them. Once this happened, trust was undermined and past sellouts became a perpetual thorn nagging at party unity. The conservatives rarely split in the same way except during the corn law row, but as the minority party in many towns they often tried to exercise a kind of casting vote between the liberal candidates and choose the most acceptable companion for Westminster. The whigs, whose political views were often not basically different from their own were a natural first choice. Overall the detailed calculations suggest that it was the conservative voter who was splitting rather than the liberal, but these are only tendencies.

The final possible explanation of split voting is the possibility that it offered an outlet for distinct political attitudes which were widespread though not fitting into the conventional party mold. Peel, Gladstone, Disraeli and Palmerston were politicians, and the ultras, "dillies," tory-radicals, Peelites, and liberal/conservatives were political groups who immediately spring to mind as outside the normal party system. Contemporaries certainly believed that there was more involved here than mere election tactics. As Gladstone himself wrote about the year following 1846, political differences no longer lay between the parties but within them. He went on to say that "Conservative Liberals" and "Liberal Conservatives" represented distinct classes of people not political opportunists. If this was so who were these split voting electors?

Their greatest incidence seems to have been among the older pre-1832 enfranchisements where party traditions and institutions were less defined in terms of a whig interpretation of history and commoner in the smaller constituencies; but even in the older "large towns" and some new ones there is evidence that the most frequent form of split, the combined whig and tory vote, was mainly recruited from the ranks of the upper and professional classes. For example, in Newcastle at the 1832 election two fifths of all the electors split thus, and among the upper classes as many as 73 per cent among freemen and 54 per cent among ten pound householders.[13] The trades people, craft and retail alike, were less than averagely inclined to split in this way. Again, in the same town in 1835 three fifths of the genteel and professional classes polled whig and tory compared with only 14 per cent of the shopkeepers and 30 per cent of the craftsmen.[14] It is perhaps worth considering whether there might be any continuity with liberal unionism in the 1880's when these voters may conceivably have resigned from the liberal party on the social grounds that the party machine in the large towns had been captured by the lower middle-class shopocracy which they had "betrayed" in the 1830's. Whatever the answer to this question, split voting is an important aspect of nineteenth-century politics which has been neglected by historians writing tidy accounts of the development of party in English politics.

The Reform Act of 1832 abolished a number of ancient franchises and created the additional one of the ten pound householder, who was quickly to become as much a social curiosity as the old 40s. freeholder in the counties. This step was designed to change the structure of the electorate in favor of the supposedly liberal minded and incorruptible middle classes of the towns. Few of the working class could hope to be enfranchised as ten pound house-holders by such a high property qualification when terrace housing might be rented on average from four pounds to eight pounds per year. At the same time the freemen franchise by means of which a substantial number of the working class had received the vote in the past was restricted to the existing voters and their eldest sons. Thus the working-class proportion of the elec-torate declined while the middle-class proportion soared. Perhaps more important, however, was the concentration of the working class in the old free-men boroughs so as virtually to silence the voice of the great new industrial proletariat of the north and midlands while letting the less politically con-scious artisans of the craft era living in the smaller market towns of the south vote in fairly large numbers.

A measure of the social balance of the electorate is offered by the parlia-mentary return of the number of working-class voters in 1865–1866 on the eve of the second reform bill.[15] Only one quarter of the electorate in the English boroughs was defined as working class and in a number of leading industrial centers such as Leeds with 7 per cent the proportion was very low indeed. In 18 single-member constituencies set up in 1832 the average was only 18 per cent and in 32 boroughs reduced to one member in 1832 only 20 per cent. The two-member boroughs were marginally more democratic: nineteen 1832 enfranchisements averaged 24 per cent all of them large towns; another 36 large towns averaged 32 per cent; while the small towns of less than 1,000 electors (in 1852) averaged 24 per cent. The importance of the working class (mainly freemen) for the purposes of corruption is underlined by the fact that in the eight most notoriously venal boroughs the average was as high as 40 per cent. As the return excluded such men as foremen and the like, there may be a slight understatement of the position, but there is no doubt of the broad picture of social exclusiveness and a middle-class elector-ate, particularly in the industrial areas of the north. The freeman elector is well enough known, but what sort of man was the ten pound householder beyond usually being middle class? In 1831 Brougham told the lords what kind of person he expected the ten pound householder in the ordinary middling borough to be: "Occupiers of such houses, in some country towns, fill the station of inferior shopkeepers; in some of the better kind of tradesmen (artisans)—here they are foremen of workshops—there, artisans earning good wages—sometimes, but seldom, labourers in full work; generally speaking they are a class above want, having comfortable houses over their heads, and families, and homes to which they are attached."[15a] But ten pounds was only the minimum qualification and the majority of the newly enfranchised were much better off than this.

From the printed poll books, contemporary directories, and census records, it is easy to find out fairly exactly what the electorates consisted of in different types of towns and where housing had a different value. However, only a

TABLE 7–3

Social Composition of the Borough Electorate in Designated Constituencies Between 1832 and 1866[1]

No. of M.P.s	Period of Enfranchisement	Borough	Date of Election	Gent. & Profess. (%)	Manuf. & Merch.[2] (%)	Retail (%)	Craft (%)	Drink Trade (%)	Farming (%)	Shipping (%)	Others (%)
1	1832	Ashton	1841	14	17	29	17	13	—	—	9
2	Pre-reform	Cambridge	1866	21	—	23	29	2	—	—	14
2	Pre-reform	Durham	1837	19	—	19	51	9	—	—	—
1	1832	Gateshead	1837	19	16	34	17	14	—	—	—
			1852	22	21	32	9	11	—	2	16
1	1832	Huddersfield	1837	5	29	18	11	11	10	7	16
2	Pre-reform	Ipswich	1839	20	5	28	28	7	5	7	—
2	1832	Leeds	1834	12	26	19	13	7	3	—	20
2	Pre-reform	Leicester	1861	9	20	36	20	2	2	—	11
2	Pre-reform	Maidstone	1865	14	11	23	32	6	—	—	14
2	Pre-reform	Newcastle/T	1860	21	8	49	16	5	1	1	—
2	Pre-reform	Nottingham	1832	10	58[3]	8	13	3	16	—	—
2	1832	Oldham	1852	12	20	32	2	18	—	—	16
1	1832	Rochdale	1841	18	24	30	13	15	—	—	—
			1857	18	9	27	21	14	—	—	11
1	1832	South Shields	1852	7	10	37	14	14	—	18	—
2	1832	Sunderland	1845	16	3	29	22	14	—	16	—
			1852[4]	16	?	26	18	9	—	20	—
1	1832	Tynemouth	1852	14	8	30	15	10	—	23	—

[1]Durham, Gateshead, Ipswich, Leicester, Newcastle, Nottingham, S. Shields, Sunderland, and Tynemouth are from my own research; all others are calculated from figures in Dr. Vincent's *Poll Books*. The two sources are not necessarily comparable.
[2]Including textiles.
[3]Including operatives.
[4]Single (Plumper) votes only.

fairly broad accuracy can be achieved which is maximized when the poll books, themselves, state the voter's occupation, as was the case in earlier elections and more often in freemen boroughs, and minimized when they do not, and second-hand, and perhaps out-of-date information in local directories has to be used. Initials, spelling, addresses are all changeable, and one cannot always be sure that the one is not dealing with a father and a son. But as few could have been interested in consciously forging information to confound later historians the rules of statistical probability should cope with the failings of poll books and directories.

Much more problematic is the aggregation of the data into social groups. The early decades of reformed England were still an age of developing status and class awareness—can the older professions and the newer commercial ones of engineers, agents, brokers, and accountants be lumped together as a group? Even more worrying is how far it is right to speak of a "shopocracy," as a number of contemporaries did, made up of retail traders and emerging as a group distinct from the craft tradesmen in which they had their origins. At the margins there were many difficult cases such as the merchant, an avocation fitting for a gentleman but also a status to which a successful shopkeeper might aspire as the summit of his career. Rate books are some help but until we have more demographic and sociological information about nineteenth-century society the exercise must be imperfect. Ultimately the justification for grouping occupations in particular ways must be heuristic.

Contemporaries spoke of professional men, of craftsmen, of shopkeepers, and it seems reasonable to order the data in this way to test for wide patterns of occupational and status politics. On this basis five basic categories have been used in analyzing urban electorates: retail shopkeepers; craft tradesmen; professional, upper and upper middle-class gentlemen, the drink trade, and manufacturing and merchandising; in addition, in those cases where they apply, there are separate groups for farmers and shipping. In Table 7–3, some examples are given of the overall composition of the electorate between 1832 and 1867. From it certain important political inferences may be drawn.

Most striking is the pre-industrial revolution character of the electorate made up mainly of shopkeepers, artisans, gentlemen and professional people rather than capital and labor.[16] In the newer industrial centers, indeed, the manufacturing and merchant classes formed a sizeable proportion of the constituency (as did agriculture in some of the constituencies even in Lancashire, Yorkshire or the northeast). In Sunderland, for example, the largest shipbuilding port in England, and a one industry town, only about one fifth of the electors were immediately connected with shipping. Nottingham was, in this respect, exceptional in so far as nearly three fifths of the electorate worked in lace, hosiery and textiles, which may perhaps help to account for its manifest but unusual corruption. Secondly, and highly significant for the structure of party support, the proportion of retail shopkeepers was very high, the largest single group in all but three out of nineteen sampled cases, and more than one quarter of all votes in fourteen instances. How right Brougham was in his assessment of the ten pound householder. The drink trade was less important in the larger cities than in the smaller towns, about 10 per cent of the

Table 7-4

Extent of Liberal Support Among Occupational Groups in Designated Constituencies, 1832–1866[1]

PERCENTAGE OF LIBERAL VOTE

No. of M.P.s	Period of Enfranchisement	Borough	Date of Election	Upper & Profess. (%)	Manuf. & Merchants Including Textiles[2] (%)	Retail (%)	Craft (%)	Drink (%)	Textiles Where Separated[3] (%)	Farm (%)	Shipping (%)	All (%)
1	1832	Ashton	1841	40	—	61	61	36	54	—	—	54
2	Pre-reform	Cambridge	1866	38	60	60	56	44	—	—	—	49
1	1832	Gateshead	1852	41	37	72	23	20	—	—	—	64
1	1832	Huddersfield	1837	61	70	55	57	41	50	12	—	54
2	Pre-reform	Ipswich	1839	36	60	60	46	54	—	21	58	50
2	1832	Leeds	1834	38	50	53	62	37	61	—	—	51
2	Pre-reform	Liverpool[4]	1832	50	64	48	—	—	—	—	—	45
2	Pre-reform	Maidstone	1865	44	60	55	56	40	—	—	—	52
2	Pre-reform	Newcastle	1832	61	—	75	63	68	—	—	—	65
2	Pre-reform	Newcastle	1835[5]	38	—	86	70	—	—	—	—	?
2	1832	Oldham	1852	44	74	58	—	28	—	29	—	53
1	1832	Rochdale	1841	33	—	67	64	44	61	—	—	54
1	1832	Rochdale	1857	47	—	65	58	19	39	—	—	48
1	1832	South Shields	1852	44	—	83	89	61	—	—	17	63
2	1832	Sunderland	1845	38	—	60	50	48	—	—	24	44
2	1832	Sunderland	1852	66	—	84	84	83	—	—	50	63
1	1832	Tynemouth	1852	61	—	74	28	32	—	—	27	49

[1]Gateshead, Ipswich, Liverpool, Newcastle, S. Shields, Sunderland, and Tynemouth, are drawn from information in Dr. Vincent's *Poll Books*. The two sources are not necessarily comparable,

[2]Where inseparable.

[3]Textiles includes operatives.

[4]These figures are based on a small sample.

[5]These figures are for the 60 per cent of voters doubling or splitting.

electorate on average, reaching its highest proportion in the mill towns of York-shire and Lancashire, and its lowest in the Midlands. Craftsmen, mechanics and artisans were well represented, and some were no doubt in business on their own account, but the semi- and unskilled working class were virtually unrepre-sented in the newer industrial towns, and uncommon in the old. Finally, the genteel and professional classes, having not yet begun their suburban retreat, remained important rarely forming less than 10 per cent of the electorate and sometimes as much as 20 per cent. Two relevant conclusions can be drawn for the general problem: in electorates of this nature there cannot have been many seriously exposed to external pressure to vote against their real inclinations; and as so many were in occupations requiring clerical ability, the vast majority must have been sufficiently educated to have political views of their own.

To what extent did the different social and occupational groups tend to act politically in the same way? Calculations made from research on north-eastern constituencies by the author and from data collected from the more accessible poll book sources of occupational information by Dr. Vincent show (in Table 7–4) percentages of liberal support in a variety of places for five major categories of occupations with the addition of textiles, farming and shipping where they are locally significant.

In widely scattered places the core of liberal support was the shopkeeping class, which with the occasional exception was more liberal than any other group, and much more so than the professional and upper classes. The constancy of this allegiance belies the common belief that their custom exposed them to undue influence. Almost equally strongly liberal was the manufacturing and commercial interest. On the other hand, the upper classes as a whole were generally more a source of conservative than liberal support. The drink interest varied wildly in its politics for the obvious reasons that of all classes the publicans stood to gain most from free-flowing money at election times and that brewing as a localized activity had no particular political flavor at this time. The north east was one among many areas where the trade was frequently whig. Although the evidence for such a conclusion is limited there are hints in the table that political behavior was becoming more homo-geneous between these groups, and a more national opinion emerging by the eve of the second reform bill.

So far the liberal party has been treated as a united organization which it was notoriously not, and it is worth exploring the social distinctions between whigs and radicals along similar lines. The basic division was between the radical shopkeepers and the upper-class whigs, seen perhaps at its clearest in Newcastle in 1835 when 60 per cent of the voters split or doubled among the whig, tory, liberal, and radical candidates[17] (Table 7–5).

Two thirds of the upper classes split for the whig and tory ticket while less than 10 per cent doubled for the liberal and radical. Among the shopocracy the situation was reversed: 55 per cent supported "the left" but only 14 per cent "the right"; while among tradesmen there was no significant bias one way or the other, although possibly there was a trend towards radicalism which was masked by the long-term effects of earlier upper-class purchase of

Table 7-5

*Analysis of the Social Basis of Double and Split
Voting in Newcastle, 1835*

	Upper & Profess. (%)	Retail (%)	Craft (%)
Whig-Tory	62	14	30
Whig-Liberal	31	31	35
Radical-Liberal	7	55	35
Total	100	100	100

freedom for such voters. Twenty-five years later in 1860 there was the same social contrast in the city between the two liberal factions.[18] In a straight fight without tory intervention, the whigs once more proved to be the party of the professional, manufacturing and upper classes, and the radicals the shop-keepers' party (Table 7-6).

Table 7-6

*Analysis of the Occupation Origins of Whig and Radical
Voters in the Newcastle By-Election of 1860*

	Whig (%)	Radical (%)
Upper and Profess.	29	16
Manufacturers	15	2
Shipping	—	2
Retail	30	64
Craft	20	12
Drink	6	4
Total	100	100

In neighboring Gateshead and Sunderland similar situations prevailed in 1837 and 1852.[19] (Tables 7-7 and 7-8).

The full implications of these tables in demonstrating the existence of social determinants to voting can be best appreciated by contrasting them with an illustration from the neighboring county constituency of North Durham, which, although it was highly industrialized and urbanized, showed no such patterns even as 1868. There was very little structural difference between most of the areas yet conservative support varied from as much as 88 per cent to as little as 28 per cent for polling districts numbering hundreds of votes. Over 600 voters from a selection of areas voting liberal and conservative but in other respects alike were traced from the poll book to the local directories and then classified by occupational groups.[20] Table 7-9 shows the percentage support each group gave to the liberal party in politically contrasted areas.

There is little or no sign of any constituency-wide support for either party

TABLE 7-7

Analysis of the Occupation Origins of Whig and Radical
Voters, Gateshead, 1837 and 1852

	1837 ELECTION		1852 ELECTION		
	Whig (%)	Radical (%)	Whig (%)	Radical (%)	Tory (%)
Upper and Profess.	23	12	30	11	19
Manuf. and Merchants	9	21	25	12	22
Retail	25	41	25	47	32
Craft	21	13	11	12	6
Drink	18	12	6	14	14
Other	3	—	3	4	7
Total	99	99	100	100	100

TABLE 7-8

Distribution of Party Support Among Occupational Groups,
Sunderland, 1852

	Upper & Professional (%)	Shipping (%)	Retail (%)	Craft (%)	Drink (%)	All Voters
Whig	40	18	16	25	76	28
Radical	26	32	68	59	7	35
Tory	34	50	16	16	17	37
Total	100	100	100	100	100	100

TABLE 7-9

Percentage of Liberal Support among Occupational Groups in
Predominantly Liberal and Conservative Areas of North Durham, 1868

LIBERAL VOTE IN PER CENT

	Gent.	Prof.	Agric.	Eccles.	Trade	Mnfs.	Coal	Drink	All
Liberal Areas	58	58	62	40	69	89	50	78	72
Conservative Areas	41	6	31	0	31	55	22	10	26

among any but the highest occupational groups. On the contrary the evidence suggests great responsiveness to the political complexion of the immediate neighborhood, and presumably to the influence of leading landed magnates. The lower down the scale a voter's occupation the more likely he was to incline to the politics of the district in which he lived. Because of this tradesmen of all sorts, innkeepers and even the farmers were as classes of voters tory in tory areas and liberal in liberal ones.

The professional classes were themselves not immune from this local influence, and it was only at the level of the gentry, the clergy and the manufacturer, influences in their own right and part of the wider upper-class society, that group political tendencies are discernible: the clergy in a county where many patrons presenting to livings were whig remained steadfastly tory; and the manufacturers obdurately liberal. Thus, in an urban and industrial county like Durham the best guide to county voting behavior was still the pattern of landownership. It is here not in the towns that the traditional view of the role of influence in nineteenth-century elections is more than justified.

Influence was, of course, present as Dod shows[21] in many towns outside the well-known patronage and family boroughs but the difference was that not only was it smaller in scale but more important, it interacted with, not overwhelmed, other social factors to produce the final election result. Quite typical of this process was a by-election in Sunderland in 1845 fought between Hudson, the Railway King, and Colonel Thompson, the prominent radical and Anti-Corn Law Leaguer. Both sides brought massive influence to bear, the conservatives through Hudson's own personal interest and through the shipowners and the liberals through Sir Hedworth, the Lambton family, and Williamson's industrial estate at Monkwearmouth. Cobden's anxious comment on the League's opponent reflected the contest's character: "He (Hudson) would go into the constituency with an *intangible* bribe for every class. . . . His *undetectable* powers of corruption at this moment are greater than the prime minister's.[22] It perhaps even seems a little unfair to condemn a politician for providing jobs for the unemployed; however influence was broadly conceived at this time. Despite this immense influence social factors were still evidently at work in an analysis of the voting of occupational groups and, most interestingly, can be seen interacting with influence proportional to its weight. The whole of the electorate is analyzed by occupation and polling district in Table 7–10.[23]

TABLE 7–10

Analysis of Voting in the Sunderland By-Election of 1845 by Occupation, Polling District, and Influence

Polling District	Prevailing Influence	Upper Classes (%)	Shipping (%)	Retail (%)	Craft (%)	Drink (%)	All (%)
Monkwearmouth	Williamson & Lambton (Lib.)	42	71	29	50	6	51
Bishopwearmouth	None	64	77	36	47	59	56
Sunderland Parish	Shipowners & Hudson (Cons.)	76	100	50	62	58	58
All Sunderland		62	76	40	50	52	56

Reading down the table the major occupational groups show an increase in conservative support as liberal influence decreases and conservative influence grows, but except in the understandable case of the shipping interest, influence never entirely destroys the impact of occupation as a social determinant but merely limits it.

So far the evidence for the social determinants of voting has been confined to the analysis of occupations, but the argument can be taken further by relating voters to indicators of status and income, to age, size of family, and finally to religious affiliation. The source of income and status data are the full census records available in the Public Record Office and the surviving rate books, usually in County Record Offices.[24] For other demographic data the census records alone have been used. Information for these potential determinants has been collected for individuals but for religious affiliation this is rarely feasible within a realistic time span, and the argument has had to rest on correlations between religious distributions and voting data for sub divisions of the whole constituency derived from comparisons of the results of the school board elections of 1871 with the general election of 1868.

The tracing of income, status and demographic data about individuals involves a great deal of research, and so only the one example of Gateshead in 1852 is given to illustrate the probable broad trends (Table 7–11). From the

TABLE 7–11

Age Distribution of Gateshead Voters, 1852 Election, in Five-Year Generations

Age in 1851	Period When Voters Attained Majority	Whig (%)	Radical (%)	Tory (%)
+60	−1812	33	27	40
55–59	1813–17	28	28	44
50–54	1818–22	53	5	42
45–49	1823–27	63	20	17
40–44	1828–32	55	23	22
35–39	1833–37	28	30	42
30–34	1838–42	53	28	19
25–29	1843–47	54	15	31
Less than 25	1848–52			
Distribution of party support in whole sample		45	23	32

point of view of its typicality the use of Gateshead should underestimate rather than overestimate the impact of these social factors for three reasons: firstly, Gateshead was not a "large town" in the sense used in this paper, having an electorate of only 600 voters in 1852; secondly, although a new creation of 1832 there were powerful interests at work in the constituency which had normally been able to return the sitting members unopposed[25]; and thirdly, the sitting whig members had been sufficiently liberal in their voting in parliament as to pass at times for radicals—the influence perhaps of the Lambton's peculiar brand of advanced whiggery.[26] In these circumstances, it is unlikely that Gateshead exaggerates the extent of social determinancy in voting in the 1850's. The only major reservation must be whether a northeast constituency would be representative of the country as a whole. This must be an open question.

The whigs, tories and radicals in Gateshead each brought out a candidate in the 1852 general election.[27] The sitting whig member was returned at the head of the poll with 45 per cent of the votes cast, the tory was second with 32 per cent, and the radical last with 23 per cent. Some interesting findings about the nature of their respective supporters emerges from the detailed comparisons of poll, rate and census records set out in Table 7–12.

TABLE 7–12

Some Demographic Distinctions Between Whig, Radical, and Tory Voters, Gateshead, 1852

	MEAN RATEABLE VALUE			No. of Servants Per Voter	% of Voters Without Servants
	All Voters	Retailers	Drink Trade		
Whig	£50	£25	£50	0.95	24
Radical	£22	£18	£28	0.63	54
Tory	£45	£22	£40	0.88	37

	Mean Age of Voters	Mean Age of Voters Excl. of 60 +	No. of Children per Voter
Whig	43	40	1.9
Radical	44	39	2.6
Tory	46	42	2.2

Whig and tory supporters were not only absolutely more prosperous but also within each band of occupations attracted the better-off. If the rateable value of the house in which the elector lived and the number of his servants are taken as some measure of his income and standing, then whigs and tories lived in substantially better types of housing and employed more servants. Far fewer whigs and tories than radicals had no domestic help at all, and the radicals' "servant problem" was only partly relieved by the use of apprentices from the shop. As the occupational structure of the whig and tory parties in Gateshead was biased toward the more successful upper middle-class levels the difference in income reflected in housing is clearly to some extent a function of this fact but not entirely, as, if the comparison is confined to a specific occupational group, say the shopkeepers, or the publicans, the housing standards of radicals are still inferior to those of whigs and tories at the same level of society. Less certainly, the size of a man's family is some indication of social status, and for men of the same age the radicals again score least by having the largest families. On all the indices the tories, although scoring much better than the radicals, appear not to have been quite as well-off as the whigs.

It had originally been wrongly hypothesized that the mean age of whig, radical and tory voters would vary but, as the tables show, there was little difference even if the extreme cases of over-sixties are excluded from the count. The mean age of the electorate of whatever party was around forty. But this similarity of means hides a far more revealing difference in the age structure. If the voters are arranged into their generations, it can be seen that certain age groups varied a great deal from the overall distribution of party support in the sample. This parallels modern findings of age cohorts preferring one or other party throughout their life and suggests by analogy that we may seek an explanation in the voter's early political experiences. Adopting this assumption, we could expect that voters who began to vote in the period of reform excitement between 1828 and 1832 might prefer the liberals to the tories, and that, conversely, those starting during the revival of the conservative party in the 1830's might incline to the tories. Both these predictions are confirmed.

The fact that tory support was strongest in the older generations and weakest in the middle and younger ones augured ill for them in the longer term. They could expect to lose their most faithful supporters through death without gaining many younger recruits until they could catch the imagination of a new generation. In the short run, therefore, the passing of years could be expected to erode conservative support unless the political climate drastically changed.

The final individual social determinant requiring investigation is religion.[28] Studies of its role in politics have been bedeviled by four unknowns: firstly, membership of a religious denomination does not necessarily imply either particular attitudes or actions in the nineteenth century any more than it does now; secondly, we do not know how far the members of particular denominations had the right to vote even in the most prominent dissenting centers; thirdly, there is no means of discovering how a man evaluated his membership of a religious organization compared with other social groups to which he belonged when it came to voting; finally, where nonconformists occupied important secular positions, we cannot be sure that the adherence of voters was because of denominational affinities or because such men were, say, important employers. An instance of the last problem is the role of the Quakers in Darlington, a town sometimes referred to as the English Philadelphia. Quakerism was an exclusive sect, which even in Darlington numbered only a few hundred souls, so that the political power of the Friends there cannot be seen as so much religious as the familiar secular authority of being the leading employers, bankers and civic dignitaries.

Arguments based on the influence of religion in the major nonconformist towns are not necessarily valid for the average case. The religiosity of the Victorians at large was very much a myth as the 1851 census of church attendance revealed.[29] Estimating the interaction of religion with politics is complicated by the difficulty of finding a satisfactory measure of the strength of church and dissent. The census itself is no help and instead we must use the sparse school board election returns of 1871.

The school board was a board of management elected locally to run the state schools set up by the 1870 education act.[30] The electorate was roughly the same as the new parliamentary franchise of 1867 and, therefore, comparable with the general election of 1868. Normally school board elections were fought along religious lines, and in the first elections in the winter of 1870–1871 the turn out was high. As the poll was taken before the ballot act, the results were declared by polling districts which tally broadly with those of the general election of 1868. Clearly the two elections were not strictly comparable, but together they do shed light on the extent to which religious commitment influenced voting. Three cases are analyzed, Newcastle, not a notable nonconformist town, Leeds and Sunderland, both fairly strong methodist centers.[31]

TABLE 7–13

Religion and Voting, Leeds, 1868 and 1871

Leeds Polling Districts	1868 General Election, Conservative Share of Poll and Rank Order %		1871 School Board Election, Rank Order of Support for Anglican Candidates
Chapel Allerton	55	1	5
Farnley	52	2	1
Kirkstall	48	3	3
Headingley	45	4	2
Kirkgate	45	5	4
Potternewton	41	6	14
Mill Hill	41	7	7
Beeston	40	8	19
Bramley	36	9	11
Armley	32	10	13
North West	32	11	9
South	31	12	15
North	29	13	16
West	29	14	6
North East	28	15	7
East	26	16	17
Holbeck	24	17	12
Burley	23	18	10
Hunslet	21	19	20
Wortley	19	20	17
All Leeds	29		

Leeds is considered first because of the large number of subdivisions used in the declaration of election results. Table 7–13 is arranged to show the similarities between the rank order of the conservative share of the poll at the 1868 general election and of support for anglican candidates in the school board election three years later.

The correlation of conservatism and anglicanism is striking, for the five most anglican districts of Leeds were also the five most conservative, while three out of the five least anglican were among the five most hostile to the conservatives.

Newcastle, according to the 1851 census, was among the least God-fearing and most religiously ill-provided large towns in the country. Only 13 per cent of the population attended a service in the evening, when nonconformists principally worshipped. The polling districts of Newcastle were rather larger than those of Leeds and the comparison is therefore not so fine; however, it can be extended further back to elections before the 1867 reform bill.

Table 7–14 shows the rank order of support for nonconformists in the school board election of 1871, the radical share of the poll in straight fights with the whigs in 1860 and 1865, and the liberal share of the poll against a conservative in 1868. In addition, the percentage increase in the electorate between 1865 and 1868 is shown indirectly to give some measure of the class character of the different wards, indicating the scale of working-class enfranchisement by the second reform bill.

TABLE 7–14

Religion and Voting in Newcastle, 1860, 1865, 1868 and 1871

Newcastle Polling Districts	Increase in Electorate, 1865–68 (%)	1860 Election, Radical Share and Rank Order (%)		1865 Election, Radical Share and Rank Order (%)		1868 Election, Liberal Share and Rank Order (%)		1871 School Board Election, Rank Order
Elswick	308	53	1	50	1	90	1	1
St. Nicholas		50	2					3
Westgate	323	48	3	44	2	88	2	4
Byker		48	3					
St. John	154	46	5	42	3	86	3	2
All Saints	215	43	7	36	4	80	4	5
St. Andrew	146	44	6	31	5	72	5	7
Jesmond		32	8					6

In Newcastle, just as in Leeds, the political rankings are essentially similar to religious differences, and this is true before as well as after the second reform act. This table broadly suggests that, by the 1860's in Newcastle, working-class districts were more likely to be dissenting and radical, and middle-class areas anglican and either whig or tory, although the interpretation of the results of Tyneside is complicated by the fact that a number of the major industrialists were closely allied with the radical dissenting group but not necessarily themselves active and prominent local dissenters.

The Sunderland case is interesting because the 1868 election was here fought between whig and radical not liberal and conservative as in Newcastle and Leeds.[32] The liberal antagonists in Sunderland, although labeled whig and radical, adopted almost identical platforms and there was nothing to choose between them in terms of their local civic virtue. Their only distinguishing feature was that the radical was a nonconformist and the whig an anglican, so that religion had an unusual importance. How far in such circumstances was sectarianism positively correlated with radicalism? Table 7–15 compares the radical majority over the whig by wards in the general election of 1868 with the rank order of support for nonconformists in 1871.

TABLE 7–15

Religion and Voting in Sunderland in 1868 and 1871

Sunderland Polling Districts	1868 General Election, Majority for Nonconformist Radical Over Anglican Whig Candidate (%)	1871 School Board Election, Rank Order of Support for Nonconformist Candidates
Sunderland/East Ward	1	4
St. Michael's	1	5
Deptford/West Ward	7	7
Pallion	8	7
Bridge	9	6
Monkwearmouth	11	1
Bishopwearmouth	15	2
Hendon	20	2

In fact where dissent was strong—in Monkwearmouth, Bishopwearmouth and Hendon—the radical gained much more support, but the converse— that where dissent was weak the radicals would lose—was not true. In Deptford, Pallion and Bridge wards, the industrial suburbs of Sunderland, full of shipyards and factories, membership of work, occupational and trade union groups diluted the effects of religious affiliation. These three examples with their different political histories are confirmation of the importance of religion for the voter before and after the 1867 reform bill. In the longer run the indifference of the working-class voter to institutional christianity rendered religion decreasingly significant as a determinant of voting behavior. But at least until the 1870's religion can be seen in relationship to voting, although it overrode other factors only where dissent or anglicanism was particularly strong. Nor should it be assumed without investigation that religion was a direct and independent force when circles of religious commitment overlapped so often with membership of other social groups. Religion interacted with many other social determinants to produce the final election results.

We have now considered some of the basic social determinants of voting in the constituency. It remains briefly to consider the second problem of to what extent, if at all, there existed a national public opinion. Three methods have been adopted to explore this question, the analysis of the mean conservative vote in English borough constituencies, the measurement of the range of "swing" between elections by means of interquartile ranges and, finally, the investigation of the movement of opinion in the large towns by means of histograms showing the distribution of these major towns along a continuum of conservative support. As this work is still in its early stages the results and the conclusions drawn from them must remain highly tentative. Nevertheless, there are indications of the operation of more than local and adventitious forces at work between 1832 and 1868.

There are two major difficulties, ignoring a host of minor ones, in any calculations at the national level, both of which stem from the two-member system: firstly, and already discussed is the problem of the split votes; secondly, the fact that parties did not put up any consistent number of candidates for the available two seats in two-member boroughs. Sometimes, depending on their assessment of their strength, they would only bring out one candidate, at other times two, and on occasion more might appear from other factions of the party. Even without the added complication of split voting or willful single voting, the effect could be that there appeared to be a massive shift of opinion from one party to another which was entirely fictitious and produced by the putting up of a second candidate where there had previously only been one, so doubling the total votes cast for that party. It might, perhaps, be argued that the decision to contest the second seat would, in view of the deterrent effect of the high cost of elections to a candidate, normally rest on some considerable shift of opinion beforehand, but this is unconvincing. A computer program is in the course of preparation to take some account of the difficulties of the single and double vote system and the results presented below in terms of simple percentages should be treated with caution (Tables 7-18 and 7-19).

The analysis of the mean conservative vote in English one- and two-member constituencies between 1832 and 1880 is shown in Table 7–16.

TABLE 7–16

Mean Conservative Percentage of the Poll in General Elections,
English Boroughs, 1832–1880

	1832	1835	1837	1841	1847	1852	1857	1859	1865	1868	1874	1880
1-Member	48.5	44.2	47.3	47.8	44.3	48.7	43.9	47.6	47.4	47.9	50.2	45.4
2-Member	36.0	43.5	45.7	48.8	44.3	43.3	40.7	43.1	45.3	37.8	46.7	42.7
2-Member "Large Towns"	31.0	38.0	43.6	46.0	39.1	37.3	40.2	37.7	41.6	37.7	47.2	41.8

There is a distinct movement of opinion particularly in the two-member boroughs and "large towns." During the 1830's there was a steady shift towards the tories, culminating in Peel's victory in 1841, but from then until 1857 they lost ground until their position was worse than that of 1835 if not quite so bad as that of 1832. A recovery in 1859 and 1865 was severely jolted in 1868 but resumed in 1874. It is perhaps noteworthy that the conservative share of the poll in 1865 was almost as large as that of 1874, which may suggest a revision of the usual view of the original contribution made by Disraeli's reorganization in the 1870's. Changes in support in the single-member boroughs were both much smaller than in the two-member constituencies and out of step with them. There was no radical swing to the liberals comparable with the two-member boroughs in either 1832 or 1868, and except in 1841 and 1847 the conservatives invariably secured more support in single than in two-member constituencies.

The second way of testing for the existence of a national opinion at this time is to measure the range of swing from constituency to constituency at general elections (Table 7–17). The smaller the range of swing in the English boroughs the more likely there is to be a widespread public opinion. The single-member boroughs have been eliminated together with those cases where changes in the number of candidates between two elections produced freak swings. Even so such comparisons are bound to be unreliable in view of the lack of correspondence between the number of voters and the votes they cast.

TABLE 7–17

Range of Swing and Interquartile Points in English Two-Member Boroughs, 1832–1880

	Mean Swing to Conservatives (%)	Interquartile Range	No. of Cases	POSITION OF INTERQUARTILE POINTS	
				Liberal (%)	Conservative (%)
1832–35	3.8	8.8	69	−1.7	10.5
1835–37	1.1	10.5	84	3.4	7.1
1837–41	1.6	8.0	78	2.3	5.7
1841–47	−2.3	8.2	67	6.6	1.6
1847–52	−0.5	9.0	74	5.2	3.8
1852–57	−1.3	7.4	75	4.3	3.1
1857–59	1.2	11.0	57	2.2	8.8
1859–65	1.1	7.4	62	3.3	4.1
1865–68[1]	−3.8	8.4	59	4.6	3.8
1868–74	4.5	8.8	73	−0.5	9.3
1874–80	−2.0	4.6	79	4.2	0.4

[1]Note the change in size and composition of the electorate in 1867.

Three conclusions can be drawn from this table: firstly, the interquartile range was a large and fairly constant one; secondly, that in 1880 the range fell to almost half of what it had normally been since the first reform bill; and thirdly, that although the range was steady throughout the period, the position of the interquartile points moved to and fro. A further analysis of the large towns on the same basis showed that there was little difference from the general pattern. In every case except 1852–1857 and 1859–1865 half the English two-member constituencies fell outside an 8 per cent range and twice—in 1835–1837 and 1857–1859—outside a 10 per cent range. Suddenly, however, in 1874–1880 a much more "national" opinion emerges, when the interquartile range falls from nearly 9 per cent to less than 5 per cent so that half

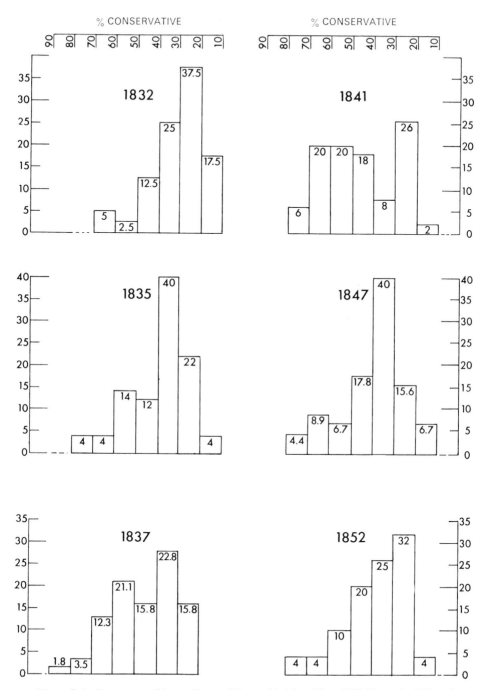

Figure 7–1. Percentage of Large Towns (Those with More Than 1000 Voters in 1852 and Represented by 2 M.P.'s) Showing Deciles of Support for Conservative Party.

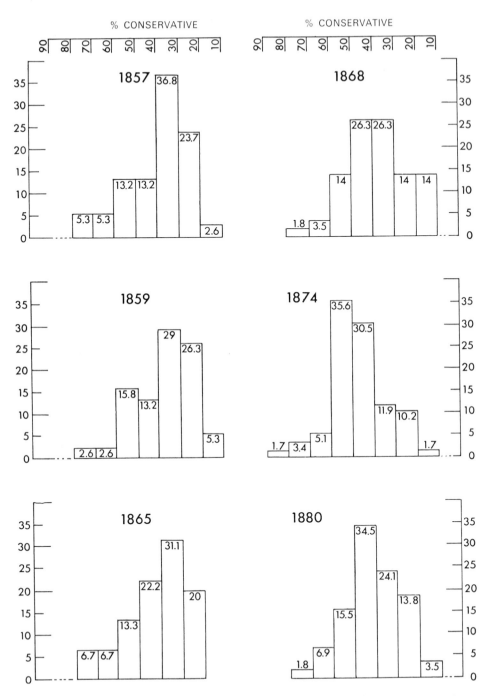

Figure 7–2. Percentage of Large Towns (Those with More Than 1000 Voters in 1852 and Represented by 2 M.P.'s) Showing Deciles of Support for Conservative Party.

the English two-member boroughs were now within a few per cent swing of each other.

How far does this dramatic fall in the interquartile range confirm the traditional view of a national opinion emerging in the 1870's under the combined impact of the second reform bill, the ballot act and the party organization and personalities of Gladstone and Disraeli? Clearly English politics became "nationalized" in a totally new way at this time, and a new balance was struck between the center and the periphery, but it is not altogether justified to interpret the wider range of the period preceding as evidence of the absence of any sort of public opinion before then and only indicative of the effects of local purse and influence. Three reasons for discerning some public opinion between 1832 and 1867 can be suggested. Firstly, the electoral system then worked in a way which magnified the apparent range of swing by the extensive use of split voting and the fluctuations in the number of candidates each party brought out for the contest—after 1868 split voting declined rapidly, and it became normal for the parties to pit two candidates against the opponent's two. Secondly, although the range did not itself vary greatly during this period, the actual interquartile points moved backwards and forwards across the political spectrum. Finally, there is the evidence of changing support for the parties revealed in the accompanying histograms (Figures 7–1 and 7–2) of voting behavior in the large towns from 1832 onwards.

The histograms cover almost half the 135 two-member constituencies and yet show an election-by-election movement of opinion. They are drawn to show what percentage of all contested large towns in a given election fell within each decile of conservative support (ignoring the first and last decile). This reveals distinct movements of the electorate toward the conservatives from 1832 to 1841, away from them from 1847 to 1859, and briefly again to the conservatives in 1865 when the large towns of the north, especially where the proportion of working-class electors was high, became disgruntled with the liberal party.

The extended urban electorate in 1868 inclined to the conservatives, and Gladstone gained a substantial victory in terms of seats. However, the histogram reveals that this was not so entrenched a liberal majority as in the past, as one quarter of the constituencies fell in the 40–50 per cent conservative range, a fact proven in 1874 with the major conservative landslide in the English towns. This setback was only partially offset in 1880, 60 per cent remaining 40 per cent conservative or better. The histograms, it should be noted, do not distinguish between whig and radical, which might reveal further interesting trends.

Each of the three major "parties," conservative, whig and radical had a different social base. The conservative party between the 1830's and the 1860's was the most representative of the electorate as a whole but tended to draw more of its support from the upper classes, certain of the older free trades such as cordwainers and masons, and from shipping; the whigs were very clearly the party of the professional, manufacturing, and upper middle

Table 7–18

Single-Member Boroughs—Conservative Per Cent Vote 1832–1880

	1832	1835	1837	1841	1847	1852	1857	1859	1865	1868	1874	1880
Abingdon	78.11				50.33		45.25	54.15	54.83	43.13	47.42	
Ashton-u-L.		27.63	43.98	45.60						52.36	51.78	46.58
Banbury			29.30				21.17		31.07	33.96	47.08	36.41
Bewdley				49.27	50.31			47.19		55.34	44.51	46.99
Bury			20.05	46.98								
Calne								25.36				18.30
Chatham		52.01		33.86	voided	56.89	51.10	52.23	41.66	47.64	59.97	51.02
Cheltenham			32.04	46.03	voided	52.91	46.52	49.67	50.61	46.19	53.52	49.77
Christchurch				52.49					59.60	47.90	61.70	49.21
Clitheroe	44.13		48.59	49.28	voided	45.83				52.31	52.71	44.55
Droitwich		50.20								56.71	33.75	29.92
Dudley	41.86	56.34	57.12	69.76		63.39		45.52	34.33		44.81	37.47
Eye												53.05
Frome	61.98	43.67	50.82	54.42			22.09	56.89	47.04	45.46	53.54	
Gateshead						31.88				36.59	24.73	21.47
Grimsby	34.73	46.61							45.93		50.94	40.42
Helston			56.14	54.45				55.24	48.32	43.09	47.03	52.27
Horsham		49.40	49.66		voided	48.59	59.66	49.23	50.00	61.66	54.55	
Huddersfield											46.79	39.03
Hythe	46.27		35.88				34.49			29.12	45.15	
Kendal											30.70	32.61
Kidderminster	51.96	38.05	55.77	51.46		38.19	38.42	48.94	51.35	39.23	53.36	45.06
Launceston	51.57	55.08								voided	68.37	56.79
Liskeard		35.96	45.67		40.77			49.38				
Malmesbury			45.89	45.65		48.30			46.42	51.77		66.05
Midhurst										58.87		63.61
Morpeth											14.93	
Northallerton				47.11			49.41	49.64	55.71	50.92	50.46	55.77
Petersfield	44.62	37.50	50.75									
Rochdale	38.92	53.09	48.27			41.48	52.16					
Rye		32.37		29.19	32.10	46.43			48.86	50.69	52.55	49.68
St. Ives											63.48	47.41
Salford	42.11	41.84	49.94	46.83						50.68	50.82	42.90
Shaftesbury		38.44	49.44	47.98	45.24							
South Shields	25.78	31.92				34.58	36.67		37.22			24.87
Thirsk										51.61	50.08	53.98
Tynemouth				41.93			50.82		47.00	39.38		32.94
Wakefield			44.27	52.21	47.77	60.31	52.41	49.81	47.41	49.27	52.65	45.01
Wallingford		55.04	57.40		51.87	50.88	52.46		45.52	55.86	56.82	48.17
Walsall	56.82		48.37	48.30	17.84			43.62			33.84	
Wareham	44.44		47.69	53.02			49.47		46.58	44.07	63.01	47.98
Warrington	46.44	53.24	52.26			52.32				49.66	56.69	45.17
Westbury			49.48		46.71	48.94			voided	51.41	48.96	52.54
Whitby	60.96						66.57		51.96	36.69	46.34	39.47
Whitehaven	54.43									59.34		52.90
Isle of Wight	13.59	41.10	52.86		43.93	53.45	45.52	47.86	47.46	45.24	50.14	49.84
Wilton												
Woodstock									54.58	51.07	58.48	53.11
No. of cases	17	20	25	19	14	16	12	14	22	32	35	38
Mean	48.54	44.19	47.28	47.84	44.25	48.67	43.86	47.61	47.36	47.87	50.15	45.38

Table 7–19

Two-Member Boroughs—Conservative Per Cent Vote, 1832–1880

	(1) 1832	(2) 1835	(3) 1837	(4) 1841	(5) 1847	(6) 1852	(7) 1857	(8) 1859	(9) 1865	(10) 1868	(11) 1874	(12) 1880
Aylesbury	74.22	65.00	73.81	—	66.54	44.89	36.74	67.02	—	35.10	35.86	27.27
Andover	—	35.82	—	30.17	60.43	92.88	67.12	68.99	—	—	—	—
Barnstaple	38.39	43.99	64.53	50.72	67.43	70.77	81.82	19.45	52.90	35.08	45.70	35.83
Bath	—	24.82	53.00	43.78	35.02	32.34	32.88	34.47	—	30.26	49.14	45.94
Bedford	30.80	38.40	68.26	67.56	64.53	41.12	38.45	49.83	34.12	33.04	31.85	26.80
Berwick-on-Tweed	32.15	37.37	68.43	63.25	55.92	38.16	23.83	54.88	42.46	42.17	45.47	43.68
Beverley	31.69	39.21	62.35	65.72	40.28	29.35	33.67	63.04	72.82	56.43	—	—
Birmingham	—	21.31	19.72	30.60	28.62	—	—	15.06	—	26.31	—	32.36
Blackburn	35.63	30.07	44.26	67.08	37.64	26.30	—	38.72	60.11	53.21	51.63	49.04
Bodmin	29.16	60.09	30.37	55.29	55.87	66.57	26.66	34.14	18.54	—	—	—
Bolton	28.81	40.42	34.49	43.23	35.50	28.28	35.03	—	48.66	52.24	50.91	48.66
Boston	27.26	44.00	43.71	65.85	33.41	31.07	—	27.13	41.30	55.37	36.46	52.01
Bridgewater	—	44.33	98.76	53.21	30.88	25.90	24.34	43.50	39.90	47.71	—	—
Bridgenorth	—	72.12	68.21	76.94	73.22	73.94	—	—	67.01	—	—	—
Bridport	26.80	32.86	29.16	29.40	36.98	23.70	14.95	22.37	—	—	—	—
Brighton	—	19.84	28.38	24.43	33.52	30.79	20.54	23.06	27.14	34.85	56.40	74.44
Bristol	29.35	61.82	68.53	67.81	52.64	28.28	—	32.54	—	27.70	47.93	39.38
Buckingham	33.26	—	70.43	—	—	—	31.59	63.40	—	—	—	—
Bury St. Edmunds	31.85	64.79	48.21	53.03	66.67	72.02	65.59	69.57	63.10	35.52	58.96	59.83
Cambridge (Boro)	24.24	32.50	47.00	52.28	23.22	53.53	51.23	52.66	51.19	43.06	50.96	45.32
Cambridge (Univ.)	—	—	—	—	81.63	—	—	—	—	—	—	—
Canterbury	—	31.74	51.05	68.31	71.89	58.11	39.77	—	54.47	72.86	62.04	53.52
Carlisle	11.64	—	—	27.92	33.88	28.78	35.27	31.07	34.13	32.39	43.36	26.38
Chester	—	—	12.83	—	—	—	—	33.82	33.87	32.22	35.60	38.90
Chichester	49.58	44.67	34.28	—	—	—	—	33.10	—	—	—	—
Chippenham	44.69	—	—	75.32	—	—	70.96	—	70.40	—	—	—
Cirencester	—	91.33	—	—	—	67.32	72.95	70.54	75.07	—	—	—
Cockermouth	—	—	—	28.09	34.71	—	—	—	—	—	—	—
Colchester	48.69	—	74.77	—	67.02	74.84	52.69	70.68	63.48	46.44	55.02	48.39
Coventry	18.63	31.12	44.86	25.81	27.76	—	8.74	25.90	51.52	51.28	49.97	48.23
Cricklade	—	—	68.52	—	—	—	70.98	66.23	70.64	60.96	54.03	49.05
Derby	21.15	24.40	37.62	26.14	29.11	31.11	19.91	18.27	31.69	20.49	25.67	14.11
Devizes	19.75	31.43	—	—	—	—	56.64	69.55	55.69	—	—	—
Devonport	—	26.96	—	29.18	28.32	49.56	—	46.60	50.73	47.20	53.86	53.96
Dorchester	—	—	—	—	—	63.05	—	—	59.27	—	—	—
Dover	49.07	68.95	64.78	55.31	62.36	67.65	39.83	54.34	53.17	65.96	57.18	51.98
Durham	31.27	37.66	38.46	—	28.77	31.88	—	—	—	31.30	31.94	30.69
Evesham	22.03	—	68.16	61.32	34.54	42.38	57.82	48.70	53.35	—	—	—
Exeter	26.47	39.26	—	67.01	—	66.09	—	—	—	48.18	53.24	62.83
Finsbury	22.98	25.04	20.05	—	—	—	13.70	—	—	18.58	25.16	28.98
Gloucester	29.03	43.92	35.17	44.31	—	31.97	34.29	27.28	30.84	43.96	49.61	43.41
Grantham	74.14	82.49	70.81	—	—	72.28	66.50	—	72.63	—	33.06	39.93
Greenwich	—	26.63	36.77	27.62	—	30.56	—	10.17	22.58	40.98	51.16	53.15
Guildford	29.17	33.23	73.89	69.79	68.24	28.21	39.58	—	36.18	—	—	—
Halifax	20.79	32.39	23.86	28.78	31.03	32.31	29.66	—	—	38.89	26.24	21.36
Harwich	50.68	83.33	48.62	52.96	54.09	53.37	37.74	50.74	67.50	—	—	—
Hastings	—	32.21	65.11	—	49.83	53.38	—	36.03	47.45	38.38	40.50	34.60
Hereford	24.09	32.32	33.23	23.00	—	24.29	—	—	34.18	47.26	50.78	43.09
Hertford	61.22	67.53	31.19	—	—	42.43	33.75	—	—	—	—	—
Honiton	60.88	71.63	68.84	—	—	62.36	52.44	—	35.09	—	—	—
Hull	27.77	38.71	51.64	51.89	—	43.40	56.90	—	34.00	39.09	45.52	30.75
Huntingdon	61.05	—	—	—	—	—	—	—	—	—	—	—
Ipswich	35.78	51.51	50.13	48.00	54,30	50.44	49.83	58.45	47.07	31.16	54.94	50.09
Knaresborough	16.00	44.82	28.50	76.19	28.50	49.33	75.73	71.14	68.72	—	—	—
Lambeth	—	18.87	25.09	42.17	—	—	—	—	—	19.22	31.85	30.37
Lancaster	—	—	58.78	69.33	64.96	40.39	61.30	50.34	32.20	—	—	—
Leeds	28.54	36.29	31.04	49.54	37.77	32.30	33.34	33.24	35.15	29.09	45.81	34.38
Leicester	28.41	52.60	44.46	—	30.16	19.98	—	24.83	30.21	15.20	27.65	27.49
Leominster	—	—	64.49	—	—	68.60	—	—	75.49	—	—	—
Lewes	—	28.67	47.°5	49.23	28.64	—	—	36.49	44.67	—	—	—
Lichfield	—	—	—	29.55	—	24.53	—	—	33.46	—	—	—
Lincoln	28.01	41.36	52.61	56.62	49.45	42.45	41.18	36.51	30.44	—	36.57	25.12
Liverpool	45.41	51.89	52.36	56.46	71.22	78.85	66.10	—	—	68.21	52.08	56.61
London (City)	14.54	35.93	19.31	50.19	43.57	24.28	—	—	23.25	42.22	55.58	63.77
Ludlow	55.02	71.85	35.81	73.87	65.44	74.72	—	—	76.46	—	—	—

Table 7–19 (continued)

	(1) 1832	(2) 1835	(3) 1837	(4) 1841	(5) 1847	(6) 1852	(7) 1857	(8) 1859	(9) 1865	(10) 1868	(11) 1874	(12) 1880
Lymington	78.79	—	75.51	75.06	62.15	68.27	39.37	62.80	44.50	—	—	—
Lynn Regis	—	79.92	69.78	—	—	75.51	—	—	66.16	70.25	54.56	50.16
Macclesfield	60.63	65.53	35.98	32.26	28.26	28.05	32.60	46.26	34.86	30.37	45.60	46.10
Maidstone	30.34	42.35	71.29	78.09	—	33.21	53.72	49.15	48.56	47.17	47.68	53.13
Maldon	36.46	66.14	67.68	68.74	66.72	75.07	64.18	68.33	69.10	—	—	—
Manchester	16.10	26.31	21.93	44.41	—	42.54	—	20.40	—	39.25	51.00	45.10
Marlborough	77.61	—	—	—	—	—	14.17	—	—	—	—	—
Marlow	—	44.05	—	70.28	72.10	81.63	—	76.15	—	—	—	—
Marylebone	—	—	26.26	43.82	24.45	—	—	10.21	—	12.14	37.57	45.79
Newark	69.89	—	—	76.22	71.15	73.88	—	—	—	28.17	46.48	49.05
Newcastle-u-Lyme	—	—	81.70	66.82	32.42	40.10	55.42	—	41.90	43.81	66.45	37.94
Newcastle-on-Tyne	34.48	22.46	46.38	—	28.29	28.11	26.75	—	—	16.57	31.20	19.21
Newport (I. of W.)	27.15	48.38	47.62	52.65	51.30	45.87	47.30	73.46	63.48	—	—	?
Northampton	47.06	34.93	30.30	29.53	40.11	29.44	28.06	26.39	44.00	32.30	45.79	?
Norwich	52.67	54.29	50.36	—	30.35	41.36	26.73	47.39	43.44	33.74	48.26	44.03
Nottingham	17.05	—	40.47	21.31	34.83	42.98	37.91	27.72	49.32	53.02	47.53	39.10
Oldham	6.41	35.36	26.14	—	33.36	?	—	—	44.42	49.87	50.54	45.52
Oxford (City)	14.33	71.96	65.14	62.71	—	—	—	—	—	18.49	32.27	33.12
Oxford (Univ.)	—	—	—	—	71.68	65.75	—	—	74.88	—	—	—
Penryn & Falmouth	63.41	67.00	32.88	40.99	63.26	72.62	—	40.75	—	53.95	45.93	42.36
Peterborough	—	26.74	28.09	29.90	—	30.04	—	21.43	—	—	17.24	21.00
Plymouth	—	32.16	39.59	25.56	33.12	31.22	21.49	36.00	31.30	26.62	54.23	50.09
Pontefract	—	33.65	—	40.35	30.73	28.74	34.79	31.22	33.78	36.10	62.70	41.22
Poole	—	27.78	45.65	31.82	—	—	37.95	38.05	26.02	—	—	—
Portsmouth	—	26.45	42.92	—	—	—	33.87	51.02	43.13	40.94	56.24	52.39
Preston	31.39	33.67	29.81	43.47	32.85	30.29	35.56	39.36	—	55.32	76.24	68.93
Reading	—	30.04	32.63	58.61	42.57	27.23	—	27.60	23.55	23.11	47.80	30.11
Retford East	28.25	65.26	68.82	—	—	—	—	—	—	—	—	40.64
Ripon	48.86	79.37	—	—	—	40.49	—	—	—	—	—	—
Rochester	35.11	31.87	47.16	51.19	42.48	53.81	—	42.92	20.09	20.28	26.22	49.22
St. Albans	30.64	40.86	38.75	57.66	54.58	dis-franchised	*	*	*	*	*	*
Sandwich	38.98	68.89	46.14	—	30.43	—	24.79	43.52	29.84	27.67	40.25	—
Salisbury	28.97	—	—	67.19	16.43	29.92	—	27.35	27.07	30.39	50.93	46.52
Scarborough	21.17	39.20	35.83	32.19	—	27.85	20.79	4.14	21.56	17.48	32.37	42.67
Sheffield	—	—	—	20.81	12.73	17.60	25.33	—	23.96	12.60	—	32.91
Shoreham	60.61	—	34.48	72.95	—	—	78.68	—	75.89	—	84.74	68.89
Shrewsbury	64.40	71.25	52.34	57.15	34.27	31.72	42.42	—	—	40.95	45.64	45.45
Southampton	41.37	55.62	50.60	53.81	—	42.93	—	—	31.78	52.64	47.77	49.16
Southwark	—	—	18.00	—	—	—	—	—	—	17.29	31.35	45.18
Stafford	—	55.67	51.46	63.47	66.21	25.50	36.81	47.55	28.04	32.87	51.16	45.56
Stamford	76.96	—	—	—	—	—	—	—	—	—	—	—
Stockport	33.13	33.82	34.70	23.73	32.31	28.96	26.04	26.94	30.03	49.68	48.61	47.56
Stoke-on-Trent	27.39	—	58.98	55.66	37.99	30.30	44.29	36.89	35.57	—	26.36	20.91
Stroud	—	—	17.72	25.17	13.75	25.72	—	—	—	26.84	48.33	47.24
Sunderland	19.43	47.18	35.08	—	—	42.08	37.16	35.25	21.89	30.19	23.82	22.52
Taunton	—	—	31.66	37.29	28.66	31.42	33.17	53.51	36.80	31.51	—	51.08
Tavistock	—	—	—	—	—	—	—	—	12.11	—	—	—
Tewkesbury	31.24	33.51	66.90	34.28	—	27.17	43.19	—	71.54	—	—	—
Thetford	—	—	—	—	68.86	—	—	—	—	48.37	—	—
Tiverton	—	8.34	24.03	—	—	—	—	—	31.52	—	31.74	29.35
Totnes	20.62	—	25.64	—	26.32	26.58	35.28	28.91	42.74	—	—	—
Tower Hamlets	—	7.98	—	16.06	—	4.58	—	—	—	21.16	50.31	29.88
Truro	28.41	41.58	29.10	—	—	48.52	—	40.89	—	40.16	59.81	56.06
Warwick	40.83	38.82	33.19	—	46.25	69.09	—	—	66.98	43.24	62.00	60.04
Wells	10.55	—	—	—	—	40.39	—	—	—	—	—	—
Wenlock	—	74.45	—	—	—	—	—	—	—	—	61.87	69.34
Westminster	—	22.26	25.87	33.80	18.44	25.86	—	—	—	29.68	71.53	58.08
Weymouth	46.32	22.83	60.69	50.54	49.77	38.41	25.49	52.87	51.06	39.41	50.32	30.85
Wigan	17.68	45.33	47.11	50.66	—	65.01	64.04	62.37	—	46.39	54.74	51.42
Winchester	19.74	45.93	66.20	63.16	62.03	35.72	37.23	56.31	60.50	39.72	72.51	61.76
Windsor	—	28.07	14.89	30.43	—	44.50	36.11	70.71	45.58	—	—	—
Wolverhampton	23.36	25.62	37.14	—	—	—	—	—	—	—	15.10	19.79
Worcester	—	29.57	—	36.26	35.31	21.76	22.32	—	29.94	33.16	44.98	32.36
Wycombe	27.17	22.70	—	38.30	—	—	—	—	—	⌣	—	—
Yarmouth	31.06	53.20	46.87	34.51	53.58	28.22	44.77	55.16	56.86	—	—	—
York	20.09	40.31	67.42	66.50	—	40.69	37.46	33.51	36.31	37.16	61.51	30.74

classes, the party of 1832 to the extent that it was they who provided the steam for Reform; and the radicals were the "shopocracy" with certain select groups of artisans, tailors, glassworkers and the like, members in some cases of the Unions of 1832, who were "betrayed" in their desire for more than whig reform. Two important occupational groups have been omitted, the drink trade and the craftsmen as a whole. The latter are perhaps not easy to isolate, shading in many instances into the smaller manufacturer and in others into the shopocracy, but it does seem that publicans and craftsmen were reasonably evenly divided between the three parties, perhaps because publicans found an equally satisfactory demand from each at election time and craftsmen because as many had received their freedom at the hands of one political benefactor as another. In particular elections and in particular places, these lines were blurred by fluctuations in influence, corruption, party alignments and the pull of candidates, but during years of confusion about "party" at Westminster, the voters of the wide variety of towns studied here remained remarkably clear in their commitment.

Income, social standing, religion and age cohorts were also shown to be related to voting behavior. In a detailed analysis of the electors of one town in the middle of the period, the more prosperous were shown to prefer the whig and tory parties to the radicals not only overall but even within particular occupational groups. It was clear also that the older generations tended to support the conservatives rather than the liberals in 1852 but that Peel's efforts in the 1830's had succeeded in winning the allegiance of the voters who came to political maturity in those years. Religious affiliation was demonstrated from school board returns to correlate with political behavior even for the extended mass electorate of 1868, although chapel or church was one factor among many interacting to produce the final result.

Such information as has been used in this paper relating to the counties supports the generally accepted view of rural politics as resting on the structure of landownership and not at all on occupational group membership except at the highest social levels.

Finally, some tentative evidence from national voting returns was offered for the existence of public opinion between 1832 and 1868, although the qualitative change in the political mobilization of the English towns in the post-1867 period was clear.

8

REGIONAL CONTRASTS IN NORWEGIAN POLITICS:
A Review of Data from Official Statistics and from Sample Surveys

STEIN ROKKAN and HENRY VALEN

ARKED and persistent differences between East and West, South and North, inland and coast can be documented throughout the history of Norwegian politics. The struggles over national unity in the Middle Ages essentially reflected tensions between three potential centers of political power: Oslo, Bergen and Trondheim. With the establishment of representative government in 1814 contrasts between these different regions soon found expression in the recruitment of opponents to the central bureaucracy and in the alignments within the legislature. With the organization of standardized electoral bookkeeping it soon became possible to study these differences statistically and with the emergence of the nationwide parties after 1879 such statistical comparisons became matters of immediate concern to practical politicians, journalists and scholarly observers. The first straight two-party contest in Norway, the election of 1882, produced a striking contrast between the central constituencies around the national metropolis and the provinces to the South, West and North, and the very first attempt at analysis[1] focused on the theme of the two distinct cultures within the nation: the urban and European at the centre, the rural and national in the provinces. The election

Reprinted from *Cleavages, Ideologies and Party Systems, Contributions to Comparative Political Sociology*, edited by E. Allardt and Y. Littunen (Helsinki: The Westermarck Society) 1964.

Notes to this chapter are on pp. 372–374.

of 1888 gave evidence of yet another line of cleavage and added a further dimension to the analysis: the provincial and rural Left was split on issues of religious orthodoxy and tolerance and marked differences were documented between the upland and inland valleys in the East and the West and the "dark coastal strip" in the South and the West. This split within the provincial Left gave rise to extensive discussions of cultural contrasts within Norway and stimulated the first systematic effort of electoral geography: the analysis of the racial characteristics of the "Liberal" and the "Moderate" parishes by the geologist and geographer Andreas M. Hansen. His work on *Norsk folkepsykologi*, first published in 1898,[2] is indeed a curious document. Fifteen years ahead of André Siegfried's *Tableau politique de la France de l'Ouest* he drew up electoral maps and compared them with corresponding maps for anthropological characteristics such as head form, hair colour and height. His ecological analyses indicated, at least for the South and the West, marked correlations between racial and political characteristics: the orthodox "Moderates" dominated the parishes populated with darker-haired "round-heads," primarily along the coast, while the Liberals, the "pure Left," had their strongholds further inland, in parishes populated in greater proportion by tall, fairerhaired "longheads." What made this effort interesting was not this simple correlation, however, but the attempt to study the decisions at elections in their *broader cultural context*. Andreas Hansen made it quite clear that he did not advocate any *direct* relationships between anthropological characteristics and the distributions of political decisions: to him the anthropological data (from measurements of recruits for the armed forces) served as *indicators of the distinctiveness of each local culture* and his primary concern was to find ways of explaining differences in political outlook through studies of differences in predominant norms and personality characteristics. At this level, however, the evidence he could assemble was scanty and anecdotal and his work left many questions unanswered. *Norsk folkepsykologi* was hardly more than a fragment and did not lead to any further studies at the time, but with all its racial myth-making and all its methodological weaknesses it remains an original and suggestive work of great potential importance in the study of local political variations.

With the introduction of manhood suffrage in 1900 and the enfranchisement of the women in 1913 a wide range of tasks opened up for political statisticians but not a single academic historian, geographer or social scientist took up the challenge. The historian Edvard Bull wrote a remarkable analysis of the political repercussions of rapid industrialization in Norway[3] but this was based on a few cases only and did not give any details of the variations between regions. The elder Bull's work was not followed up at the time and further studies of the politics of industrialization were not carried out until well into the 1950s. The social historian Edvard Bull, a son of the elder pioneer, developed an archive of information on the conditions of workers in the early phase of industrialization and carried out a series of local case studies of workers' voting before and after the extension of the suffrage.[4] But again nothing was done to fit these cases into their national statistical context: the local studies were not followed up through broader analyses of regional variations in political reactions to industrialization.

A brave attempt to fill some of the lacunae in the historical geography of Norwegian elections was made during the 1950s by Gabriel Øidne. Very little of his work has been published but it is clear from his one major article[5] that he concentrated his analyses on local traditions in voting since the 1880s and essentially followed in the footsteps of Andreas Hansen. His primary concern was with the cultural distinctiveness of the West and the differences between the inland and the coastal communes. He assembled a great deal of information on variations in religious involvement and showed through a series of maps the correlations between various measures of religious orthodoxy and the vote.

Within our programme of electoral studies at the University of Bergen and at the Institute for Social Research in Oslo[6] we have in recent years become increasingly concerned to reach some understanding of these regional contrasts in Norwegian politics. In an earlier paper we presented a broad range of data, and some initial analysis, of variations in levels of *electoral mobilization and party membership* and focused quite particularly on contrasts between central and peripheral communities in each region.[7] In this paper we shall present a series of tables for *variations in party strength* between regions and between communities and point to some of the major sources of such variations. It is our intention to carry out such analyses for all elections since 1882 but for the period up to the second World War we have so far only been able to assemble the published statistics and not been in a position to go into any detail community by community. For the elections from 1945 we are much better equipped for detailed analyses: we not only have established an extensive archive of data for each commune but also have access to several sample surveys of the national electorate and of local communities.

Our concern in this paper will be with the *description of differences* among regions. We shall consider only a few variables at a time and we shall only give a couple of examples of the first results of our attempts at multiple regression analysis. We see a number of interesting possibilities of detailed multivariate analysis in the data in our ecological archive and we hope on some future occasion to report further on our efforts to make sense of the variations between the communities of our country and to fit them into a broader theoretical framework.

Phases in the Development of the Norwegian Cleavage System

The history of electoral politics in Norway may schematically be set out as a sequence of successive changes in the structure of cleavages and alignments within the national polity.[8]

We may conveniently distinguish five dimensions of conflict in the system:

first the *territorial* opposition (T) between capital and provinces, between centre and periphery;

secondly the *socio-cultural* (SC) conflict between the academically educated, "Europeanized" officials and patricians in the cities and the increasingly status-conscious and nation-oriented peasants in the rural districts;

thirdly a *religious* opposition (R) between the secularism and tolerant liberalism of the established urban population and the orthodox and fundamentalist Lutheranism of large sections of the rural and recently urbanized population;

fourthly an economic conflict in the *commodity market* (CM) between the buyers and sellers of agricultural and other primary economy products, again essentially a conflict between the urbanized and the persistently rural interest sectors;

and fifthly and finally, an economic conflict in the *labour market* (LM), first between employers and wage-earners and, later, primarily in the larger units of the economy and in the public sector, between employers and salaried employees.

The sequences of phases in the development of electoral alignments can be schematically set out as indicated in Table 8–1.

In the first phase, 1882–1885, the salient cleavages were territorial and socio-cultural: the Left was strongest in the rural areas outside the center and the Right was strongest in the capital and in the cities in the East and in the Trøndelag. The striking difference between Bergen and Kristiania reflects a persistent territorial opposition and to some extent also a difference in the character of the alliances within the local élite: Ulf Torgersen's analysis of the recruitment of electors suggest a markedly lower level of status polarization in Bergen than in the capital.[9]

The Left acceded to power in 1884 but did not survive as a united party for more than four years: it split up into a "Pure" wing of radical nationalists and a "Moderate" wing of spokesmen for traditional religious and moral values. This split cut across the earlier territorial cleavage and produced a temporary alliance between Conservatives at the center and fundamentalists in the periphery. The "Moderates" were concentrated in the South-west: they had their only urban strongholds in the cities of Stavanger and Hauge-sund and they derived most of their support from the coastal communities in that region. The contrasts between these outer districts and the agricultural communities in the inner fjords and valleys were indeed striking and there is much evidence to suggest that the differences between "Moderates" and "Pures" in fact reflected contrasts in community norms and traditional ethical attitudes. It is difficult to assemble reliable data for detailed statistical tests of these differences for this early phase but Øidne's analyses[10] and our own work on the geography of the Christian vote certainly suggest such a relationship between community culture and political alignment.

This three-party system was not destined to last long. The struggle over the union with Sweden and the introduction of manhood suffrage set the stage for a series of changes in the political alignments. The threat of a war with Sweden dampened the opposition between Left and Right and the entry of the

TABLE 8–1

PHASE	CONDITIONING EVENTS	ELECTIONS	MAJOR PARTY ALTERNATIVES	T	SC	R	CM	LM	Other
I	Struggle for parliamentary supremacy	1882–85	Right — Left	X	X				
II	Victory of Left, extension of suffrage	1888–97	Right — Mod. — Left	X	X	X			Foreign policy
III	Manhood suffrage, struggle over Union with Sweden	1900–15	Nat. Lib. — Right — Left — Wk.dem. — Lab.	X	(X)	X)		X	
IV	Industrialization, proportional representation	1918–30	Nat. Lib. — Right — Agr. — Left — Soc.dem. ('19–'27) — Lab. — (CP) ('23—)	X	(X)	X)	X	X	
V	Economic crisis	1933–36	Right Nat. Soc. — Com-monw. — Right — Agr. — Left — Lab. — (CP)	X	X	X	X	X	
VI	World War	1945–57	Right — Agr. — Chr. — Left — Lab. — CP	X	X	X	X	X	Foreign policy
VII	Cold War	1961–	Right — Center — Chr. — Left — Soc.P. — Lab.	X	X	X	X	X	EEC NATO

CLEAVAGE LINES: T, SC, R, CM, LM, Other

workers into national politics changed the character of the cleavage system. Concerted efforts were made to establish a broad "Unionist" front against the emerging working class movement,[11] but the earlier conflicts between the center and the provinces, the urban culture and the rural, were far from resolved and in fact proved markedly more divisive than straight class issues throughout the period up to 1918. The Left was torn over issues of workers' rights and social legislation but the core of the party united in the defense of the rural "counter-culture," the rural language and the rural moral traditions. In the South and the West the earlier split over religious orthodoxy lost in importance and the Left was again the dominant party in the countryside. The concentration on issues of cultural defence set the South and the West distinctly apart from the rest of the country. The growth of industry and the increasing dependence on the money and market economy increased the pressures toward a polarization of politics between the Socialists and the Conservative Right but the social and the cultural conditions for such a polarization varied markedly from region to region and from community to community. To study these variations we have calculated crude "polarization scores" for the rural areas and the cities of each region from 1903 onwards. This analysis suggests that the process of polarization approached its maximum as early as by 1921 in the central region around the capital, took considerably longer in the inland areas of the East, in the Trøndelag and in the North, but never got very far in the South and the West. This is a crucial contrast in the system: most of the tables in our study will in fact serve to describe this contrast in further detail.

In the next phases of our electoral history the working class movement increased its votes almost continuously: there was a setback in 1930 through the mobilization of new waves of women voters but the economic crisis of 1931–1932 shook the system to the core and rallied large masses of new voters to the Labour party. The party came to power in 1935 but was still far from evenly entrenched throughout the territory: even as late as in 1936 its strength in the South and the West was hardly more than half of its strength in the East, the Trøndelag and the North. The party drew its support from a variety of lower-status groups in the nation: not only unionized industrialized workers and public employees, but also agricultural and forestry workers in the East, smallholders and fishermen in the Trøndelag and the North. This broad socio-economic basis gave strength to the party but also set limits to its freedom of action in developing coherent policies: the conflict over the entry into the European Economic Community brought out in the open the cleavages within the party and accentuated the difficulties of within-party aggregation of so many divergent interests (see Tables 8–39 to 8–41 and the comment below).

This steady growth of the Labour party had important repercussions on the alignments of the opposition parties. The old Left was divided over conflicts of interest and ideology along several axes. the urban-rural axis and the liberal-fundamentalist axis. The result was a split into three parties: the Left first shed a purely economic interest party, the Agrarians, in 1918, and then experienced a division over religious issues in the thirties. The Agrarians found their greatest strength in the East Inland and the Trøndelag but also proved remarkably successful in the South/West. The Christians first established themselves in the West and continued the traditions of the Moderates: see the parallels in relative strength presented in Table 8–27. The fundamentalists of the West had been mobilized again and again in the years since the first World War and the ground had been well prepared for an explicitly Christian party: the two referenda on the prohibition of alcohol sales in 1919 and 1926 (see Table 8–27) and the mass campaign against the alleged irreligiosity of the Labour party in 1930 had set the stage for the movement. The party quickly established itself on a par with the other two at the centre of the political spectrum. Gabriel Øidne has established through his electoral cartography a close fit between the strength of the Moderates in the nineties and the strength of the Christian in the fifties and our own statistical checks tend to confirm this for at least two of the Western provinces.

With the establishment of the Christians as a nationwide party in 1945 the Norwegian system reached a temporary equilibrium. For sixteen years to come the voters were generally faced with six alternatives: the *Communists*, strong in 1945, but without importance after 1948, the governing *Labour* party, and four opposition parties, the old *Left* (generally rendered in English as the Liberals), the *Christian People's* party, the *Agrarians*, since 1958 called the *Centre* party, and finally the *Right* (generally translated as the Conservatives). The opposition between the Labour majority and the four non-socialist parties reached a peak in 1949 over issues of detailed price regulation but in the 1950's there was a distinct trend toward de-ideologization and de-politicization.[12] This policy of *rapprochement* came under heavy fire from the neutralist left of the Labour party and in 1961 a splinter party advocating basic changes in foreign policy finally presented itself to the voters: this *Socialist People's* party won two seats in the Storting and reduced the Labour party to a minority position for the first time after the war. The situation in Parliament became highly unstable: the two left Socialists found themselves in the position of arbiters between the 74 Labour and the 74 in the non-socialist opposition. The Labour party decided to stay in power but had to rely on support from the opposition on the right in carrying out its policies. This happened just before the storm broke over the issue of Norwegian entry into the European Economic Community. In this fight, perhaps the bitterest experienced in Norwegian politics since the early thirties, the Labour government and the trade-union movement sided with the Conservatives in advocating entry while the left Socialists and the Agrarians came out strongly against. The Liberals and the Christians were split and the old-established regional contrasts in Norwegian politics again manifested themselves. As we shall see in Tables 8–39 to 8–41 the Southerners and Westerners again stood out as the defenders of the cultural autonomy of the provinces against the encroachments of the center: this time the enemy was not just in Oslo, but, what made it much worse, in the distant bureaucratic centres on the European continent.

The Two Peripheries: The South/West and the North

Our sketchy review of the electoral alternatives and the distributions of votes since 1882 has underscored the persistence of regional differences in political alignments in Norway.

The South and the West have stood out again and again as the regions of the strongest cultural resistance to centralizing and urbanizing forces and have offered the most effective barriers against the spread of polarized class politics.

By contrast the North has stood out as the polarized periphery: economically the most backward of all the regions it has a persistent record of radicalism and was the first to send Labour representatives to the Storting after the introduction of manhood suffrage in 1900.

But these are impressions from comparisons of aggregate figures. How clearly do these contrasts come out in detailed scrutiny community by community? How far do the differences in politics between the regions reflect differences in social structure and in the level of economic growth and how far do they reflect differences in local cultural traditions?

We are not yet in a position to give precise answers to such questions for the early elections, but we have assembled a considerable body of information on variations between communities for close to one hundred years and we shall use the data from this "ecological archive" to throw light on the character of the regional differences in Norwegian politics.

Our punched-card archive[13] currently consists of commune-by-commune data for all local and national elections from 1868 to 1967, census data for 1875 through 1960, educational, agricultural, industrial and fiscal statistics, data from a church attendance count, data on local party organizations and party memberships, data on nominees to lists for the *Storting* elections. So far we have used the data in this archive for descriptive rather than analytical purposes. The bulk of the tables presented in this paper present similarities and differences in distributions on political variables between communal units classified in terms of one, two or three geographical, socio-economic or cultural variables. In the cruder descriptive presentations (*e.g.*, Table 8–13) we have simply aggregated electorates and votes within each group of communes and given percentage distributions for these aggregates: these then express averages weighted for commune size but give no indication of ranges of within-group variation. In some of the tables (*e.g.*, Table 8–14) each commune counts as one unit irrespective of the size of its electorate: this allows statements about the range of variation for given political attributes within each group of communes. This is also the procedure we have used in our attempts to establish multiple regression coefficients for a few of the documented independent variables (Tables 8–20 to 8–26): in these analyses the size of the units has been disregarded.

In the bulk of the analyses the dependent variable is a straight-forward political variable such as turnout or the strength of a given party expressed in per cent. Only in one case so far have we tried out an index based on an assumption about some constant source of support for a given party: this is our "*CP+Lab − Ind.*" score which simply gives the difference, negative or positive between the Socialist strength in the electorate and the proportion of the labour force in manufacturing, mining or construction. This score is based on the crude assumption that 100 per cent of the votes from "industrial" households go to the CP or to Labour. This, of course, constitutes a blatant overestimation of the actual level of class voting: this can easily be seen from the distributions found for each occupational group in a nation-wide survey (Tables 8–18 and 8–19). Nevertheless the score gives a very clear picture of differences between regions and types of communes and has proved of distinct heuristic value in our research. We hope in our future work to develop a scheme of *alternative assumptions about the political preferences of each socio-economic stratum* and to test these assumptions through analyses of commune-by-commune discrepancies between calculated and observed distributions of the vote. Calculations of this type have recently been tried out with some success in France by Joseph Klatzmann, Jacques Desabie and Mattei Dogan[14] and the potentialities of the technique have been ingeniously demonstrated on Swedish data in a recent article by Gösta Carlsson.[15]

Our first set of ecological tables focus on the *residential and the socio-economic structure* of the communes within each of the basic divisions of the country.

A cursory glance at the electoral statistics will show that the political differences between the South/West and the other regions are less pronounced in the *cities* than in the rural districts. Our crude score for Socialist-Conservative polarization gives these differences between the South/West and the other regions for 1957 (Table 8–2):

TABLE 8–2

	Oslofjord	East Inland, Trøndelag	North	South/West
(1) Principal cities	.89	.87	—	.75
(2) Other cities	.87	.83	.84	.68
(3) Rural districts	.83	.83	.82	.56
Diff. (1) — (3)	.06	.04	.02	.19

The differences between the regions are clearly most marked in the countryside. Table 8–13 goes into further detail and shows that the contrasts are most pronounced in the sparsely populated, pre-industrial communes but tend to disappear in the urbanized and industrialized areas. It is in the low-density, low-industry communes, the typical primary-economy communes, we find the most distinctive patterns of regional politics. The crucial difference lies in the balance of strength between the offshoots of the old Left and the working class parties. In the South and the West the three Middle parties are still dominant, in the East and the Trøndelag and even more markedly in the North they have been overshadowed by the Socialists (Table 8–3).

Clearly the Socialist parties have been able to mobilize very important electoral resources in the rural areas of the East and the North but have found conditions much more difficult in the South and West. Where did they find these resources in the East and in the North and why did they fail in the South/West? Our further tables seek to throw light on these questions.

We shall consider in turn three sources of primary-economy strength: the households of actives in *forestry*, the households of *smallholders and farmers* and the households of *fishermen*. Table 8–14 gives rough estimates of the likely contributions of Socialist votes from the forestry sector of the primary economy. In the East and the Trøndelag the Socialist parties appear to derive the bulk of their rural strength from the forestry labor force: the greater the number of actives in forestry in a rural commune the greater the

TABLE 8–3

STRENGTH IN 1957

Least Industrialized Communes in	Socialists	Middle parties (Lib., Chr., Agr.)	Conservatives
South and West	20.6	46.2	6.0
East and Trøndelag	40.0	29.4	6.5
North	36.5	18.7	8.3

number of Socialist votes from non-industrial households. In the South and the West there is a similar trend but there are only a few typical forestry communes in these regions and these add very little to the total electoral resources of the Socialist parties. In the North there is no consistent trend in the data: the very few forestry workers in that region clearly cannot make much of a difference for the Socialist parties.

The table also tells us of differences in residual sources of electoral support for the Socialist parties. In the South and the West the communes with the lowest proportions of actives in forestry appear to give the Socialists very few votes outside the industrial households: indeed in close to half of them the Socialists do not appear to have exhausted their industrial potential.[16] In the East and the Trøndelag the Socialists can count on sizeable support from households in other sectors than industry and forestry and in the North this is in fact the normal situation: we shall explore these further sources of support in later tables.

Why such differences between regions? One line of explanation focuses on *status inequalities* and *class hatred* as crucial variables: the rural communities of the East, the Trøndelag and the North have tended to be much more hierarchized and have offered much stronger incentives to class politics than the equalitarian communities so frequently found in the South and the West.

This hypothesis could be tested in a variety of ways. In our first attempts at analysis we have used *the sizes of holdings* in forestry and agriculture as indicators of socio-economic differentiation within communities. For purposes of description we shall first present simple classifications of all communes by the proportions of large holdings in forestry (Table 8–15) and agriculture (Table 8–16): in the next section we shall present details of an attempt at multiple regression analysis using means and variances as predictors of party strength.

The South and the West stand out as regions of small holdings and of minimal variations in the size of units. As seen from Table 8–15 there are very few forestry communes in these regions. The 35 communes with more than 2.5 per cent of their active population in forestry are practically all in the South: in the West the forestry sector is minimal and the small variations in the numbers of forestry workers appear to be of no political significance. Variations in *agriculture* count much more and the statistics of agricultural censuses offer striking evidence of regional differences in community structure. The agricultural census of 1959[17] gives the regional variations in the size of farm units as shown in Table 8–4.

TABLE 8–4

	Total Holdings over 5 da. in Rural Communes	Mean Size in Decares	Proportion of Units over 100 Decares
East and Trøndelag	108,981	61.01	18.4%
South and West	74,757	35.99	3.4%
North	42,237	30.11	1.7%
The nation	225,975	46.95	8.9%

How would we expect such differences in the structure of the primary economy to be reflected in political behavior? Here it is essential to distinguish between absolute and relative size. In absolute terms we might expect the holders of small units to suffer economic hardship and to be easily swayed by class ideologies. In relative terms, the political weight of the size of the holding will vary with the community context: holders of small units will react one way in situations of direct dependence on large farms and forest estates in their own community, quite another way in communities where their neighbors are all roughly equals. In the South and the West the holdings tend to be very small by the standards of the East but in the majority of communities they are *all* small by such standards and there is therefore very little basis for class resentment and class cleavage in local politics. In the East and the Trøndelag holdings vary much more in size, both within and across localities, and there will be much more pronounced tendencies toward a political polarization of the votes in the primary economy. In the East and the Trøndelag the result is quite clearcut: the Socialist "surplus" is much larger in communes with a number of large forestry units. The explanation seems relatively simple: large forestry units require wage labour and most of the workers will tend to be seasonally employed and eke out their timing through small agricultural holdings of their own. Table 8–16 tends to confirm this interpretation: the Socialist "surplus" is largest in communes with a majority of small farm holdings and much less in communes with a large number of fair-sized farms. Clearly the rural structures most likely to prove polarizing are those made up of marked majorities of smallholders, forestry workers and other seasonal labourers dependent on a few dominant forest owners and large-scale farmers: in such communities age-old antagonisms between the "populace" and the "lords" will almost invariably find political expression in heavy Socialist surpluses.

Class antagonisms also explain the high level of polarization in the *North*. In these provinces the smallholders and the fishermen had for centuries depended for their living on owners of port facilities who bought their produce and controlled their credit. With the extension of the suffrage in 1900 resentments against this system of economic dependence soon found political expression and the Labour party very quickly established itself as a serious contender for power in the far North: the first five Socialists to be elected to the *Storting* all came from the North, four of them from the fisheries districts of Troms and Finnmark, one from the new industrial center at Narvik. In the elections which followed the Socialists spread throughout the Northern provinces and increased their votes almost continuously. By 1927 the two

TABLE 8–5

	1945	1949	1961
	CP	CP	CP + Left Soc.
	Lab.	Lab.	Lab.
All rural districts	.23	.11	.10 (Left Soc. in 5 of 18 provinces)
Nordland	.23	.10	.19 (Left Soc. list)
Troms	.23	.09	.05 (no Left Soc.)
Finnmark	.38	.28	.20 (no Left Soc.)

Socialist parties had reached a clear majority position in the region and after the setback in 1930 continued towards a position of absolute dominance. The split between Communists and Labour was of little importance in the thirties, but in the election just after World War II the CP established itself as a major wing of the working class movement of the North. Its votes fell markedly after the events of 1948, but the party lost much less in the farthest North near the Soviet Union than in the rest of the country (Table 8–5).

We hope to go into details of an analysis of the Communist-Labour ratios in another context:[18] in this paper we shall in most cases concentrate on the total Socialist strength and seek to identify major sources of variation in this total.

In Table 8–17 we have classified all the rural communes by one of our criteria of peripheral status: this is a score which we first developed in an analysis of turnout variations[19] but which has also proved useful in our explorations of regional differences in party support. The political distinctiveness of the North stands out very clearly in this table: the peripheral communes in the East, the South and the West are all markedly less polarized than the central ones, but in the North the periphery differs very little from the other rural communes in the region.

In a further analysis we classified the communes by the proportion of economically active in fisheries and shipping: this was essentially a measure of the coastal vs. inland character of the geography. Again the North stood out as the most polarized region: even in the typical fisheries districts polarization was as high as .79 as against .75 for the East and the Trøndelag and as little as .43 for the South/West. The contrast between the two coastal areas was indeed highly revealing: in the North the Socialists mobilized close to 60 per cent of the votes cast and the Conservatives were strongest among the opposition parties; in the South/West the offshoots of the old Left mobilized close to two-thirds of the valid votes while the Conservatives were the weakest of the non-socialist parties. In both regions the Christian People's party found its surest sources of strength in the coastal communes: these are, as we shall see in later tables, areas of intensive religious activity and as a result more likely to add to the electoral potential of the Christians.

Throughout our work with the ecological data we have been concerned to cross-check out interpretations through parallel analyses of data from cross-sectional sample surveys. The design and size of the samples will not allow as detailed regional breakdowns as in analyses of official statistics, but even the crude classifications possible within a normal-sized nationwide sample will provide useful guidance in interpreting the ecological findings.

In Table 8–18 we have grouped the respondents in our nationwide survey of 1957 into 10 occupational categories and for each of these given the distributions of intended votes in the two principal divisions of the country: the East, the Middle and the North versus the South and the West. As suggested by our ecological analyses the differences between the two divisions proved most pronounced for smallholders and fishermen (44 vs. 13 per cent Socialist), and for workers outside manufacturing industries and construction (61 vs. 45 per cent). Interestingly enough the regional contrasts also proved marked for public employees (40 vs. 5 per cent). This clearly reflects long-term differences in the channels of recruitment of local leadership. The old Left recruited much of its leadership among lower public officials, sheriffs, teachers, newspapermen, and once in power placed increasing numbers of supporters in public employment. The continued dominance of the Middle parties has kept these channels open in the South and the West while the dominance of the Labour party in the other regions has made for substantial changes in the politics of public employees.

Table 8–19 gives further confirmation of our interpretation of the ecological findings: the differences between the South/West and the other regions tend to disappear in the cities and the most urbanized communes but are particularly marked for workers in the least industrialized areas (33 vs. 64 per cent

Socialist) and for farmers and fishermen (9 vs. 32 per cent). The rural communes are much less class polarized in the South/West than elsewhere: the offshoots of the old Left recruit their support from cross-sections of the local citizenry and tend to express territorial and cultural opposition rather than class interests.

The Socio-Economic Bases of Regional Differences: An Attempt at Multivariate Analysis

The close fit between the ecological findings and the nationwide survey data has encouraged us to move further toward detailed multivariate analyses of the variations among rural communities in Norway. Tables 8–20 to 8–26 summarize our findings for two sets of independent variables.

The first set of independent variables are all indicators of *economic modernization*: the level of industrialization as measured by the census of 1950, the level of urbanization as measured by the proportions in "agglomerations" as defined in the same census, and the level of "monetization" as measured by the income per taxpayer in 1957. Table 8–20 gives the zero-order correlation coefficients between each of these indicators and the percentage strength of each of the six parties in 1957. It will be seen that the voting strength of only three of these parties could be predicted with some confidence from these indicators: the votes of the Communists, of the Labour party and of the Conservatives. This is fully in accordance with our general scheme of analyses: the Socialist parties and the Conservatives fit the "economic-functional"axis of our model, the Liberals and the Christians the "territorial-cultural" axis. The correlations for the Liberal party are particularly low: the party rallies support from a variety of sources in the electorate and its strength cannot be predicted from such simple indicators of economic development. The correlations for the Christian People's party are all negative and in several cases markedly so: this party has taken over much of the strength of the old Left in the non-agricultural periphery and represents much more consistently a rejection of the secular values characteristics of urban society. The correlations for the Agrarian party are finally practically all markedly negative: this is the organ of *functional* representation for the fulltime farmers and forest owners but it has very little of the diffuse territorial appeal characteristic of the old Left.

Table 8–21 gives the results of a multiple correlation analysis for the three indicators and presents the "normalized regression coefficients" for the CP, Labour and the Conservatives: this line of analysis is mainly of interest for the three polarized parties.

The analysis indicates that

(a) both the CP and Labour have their strength in industrialized communes, but in the East and the South/West the CP is more dependent on high income averages while Labour is largely independent of variations in monetary income levels;

(b) in the North the level of industrialization adds to the strength of the

Socialist parties, but the income level is in both cases without importance; the CP, however, garners more of its strength in agglomerations, while Labour is almost as strong in the low-density periphery as in the more urbanized areas;

(c) the Conservative party differs markedly in its socio-economic basis from region to region: it is everywhere strongest in the urbanized areas, but the income level is decisive in the East and the Trøndelag only and slightly negatively correlated with its strength in the North.

In the East, the Trøndelag and the South/West the three variables account for a substantial amount of the variance in votes for the parties at the two extremes of the political spectrum, the Socialists and the Conservatives: for these regions we can say with some confidence that economic growth will increase the level of political polarization. In the North the three variables account for much less of the variance for Labour and the Conservatives: in this region the backward periphery is already quite polarized and modernization as such is of less importance for variations in party strength.

Tables 8–22 to 8–26 give the results of an attempt at an analysis of the sources of electoral strength in the primary economy. In this analysis we shall focus upon the three parties which draw their main strength in rural areas: the Agrarians, the Liberals and the Christian People's party. In addition we shall include in the analysis our usual score for Socialist support from sources outside industry.

Tables 8–22 and 8–23 confirm our earlier findings for the sources of non-industrial support for the Socialist parties: forestry and, to a lesser extent, agriculture in the inland areas of the East/Trøndelag and the South/West regions, and fishery in the coastal areas of all regions.

Tables 8–24 to 8–26 demonstrate the importance of the structure of the rural community for the support of the different parties. In the regression analyses a stepwise computer program was used: this gives the regression coefficients only for those of the predictor variables which are found to account for a significant share of the variance in the dependent variable.

Let us first look at our estimates of *Socialist support outside the industrialized sectors* of each community. Using our usual estimation score we find the level of non-industrial Socialist support to be less dependent on the proportion of actives in agriculture than on the proportions in forestry in the inland areas and on the proportions in fishery on the coast. The coefficients for the size of holdings in farming and forestry are smaller and more difficult to interpret. These variables are least important in the East and the Trøndelag. In the South/West the Socialist vote is largest when the *within-community* contrasts in farm size is small. Thus the normalized regression for standard deviation in farm size is −.153 in inland areas and −.128 on the coast. In the North the Socialists are strongest in communities in which the average farm size is low. This pattern is consistent for coastal as well as inland areas.

The findings for the *Agrarians* are the simplest to interpret. The best predictor for the strength of this party is simply the proportion of actives in agriculture. The size of agricultural holdings also counts: the larger the average farm in the community, the better the chances for the Agrarians (cf. the crude breakdown in Table 8–16). The simple explanation is that the larger the farms the more likely the farmers are to depend entirely on joint action to defend prices and to protect the market. In the North, where markets are more local and farms less productive, the Agrarians have not established themselves as firmly in the farming communities: here we find the *size* of farms more important than the *proportions* in farming in the inland areas and practically as important on the coast.

The interpretation of the regression coefficients found for the *Liberals* and the *Christians* is not as straightforward. In the *inland* areas of the East/Trøndelag as well as the South/West the Christians tend to be stronger the more equal the distribution of holdings in the community. But this relationship is restricted to the *forestry* score. For the *Liberals* there is a similar tendency in the East/Trøndelag but this party increases its strength with more equal-sized *farms*. In the South/West, however, the Liberal vote is unaffected by inequalities in the farm size but it gains in strength with increasing inequalities in the size of forest holdings. These findings reflect complex differences in the structure of the primary-economy communities and require much more detailed analysis than we can give them in this context.

The findings for the coastal areas of each region underscore a crucial difference between Liberals and Christians. Our four predictor variables contribute very little to the reduction of the variances in Liberal strength on the coast. By contrast the Christian People's party clearly depends for its strength on the proportion of actives in the *fisheries*: this is indeed an essential factor accounting for the strength of the party in the coastal periphery.

The results reported here stand in need of detailed checking through alternative procedures of computation and analysis. Our measures of mean size and standard deviation are of course heavily intercorrelated (thus for the East/Trøndelag the zero-order correlation between mean and sigma is .87 for farm size and .92 for forestry size) and this reduces the value of our regression equations. We are currently working out an alternative procedure for the description of within-community size distribution using *Lorenz curves* and *Gini indexes.*[20]

In evaluating our findings, it should be noted that the size of the normalized regression coefficients only expresses the *relative* weight of each of the variables included in the matrix for the individual party. Thus the coefficients cannot be used for cross-party comparisons. From Tables 8–22 and 8–24 it will be seen that the zero-order correlations between the structural variables and the party strength tend to be higher for the Agrarian party and for the score for Socialist support outside industry than they are for the Liberal and the Christian People's parties. This difference comes out even clearer when we calculate for each party *how much of the variance in its local strength is accounted for by all our predictor variables:*

TABLE 8–6

| | REDUCTION IN THE VARIANCE OF THE DEPENDENT VARIABLES | | | | | |
| | EAST/TRØNDELAG | | SOUTH/WEST | | NORTH | |
Party or Score	Inland	Coast	Inland	Coast	Inland	Coast
Liberal	9.4%	—	16.0%	8.0%	—	—
Christian	14.1%	13.3%	4.1%	10.5%	3.7%	5.6%
Agrarian	63.7%	77.4%	68.7%	75.1%	50.8%	59.1%
CP+Lab.–Ind.	54.8%	42.7%	50.8%	37.7%	13.1%	43.6%

Our structural variables account for a substantial share of the variances for the Agrarians and for our "non-industrial" Socialists, but markedly less for the Liberals and the Christians. It is, of course, possible that even for the Liberal and the Christian People's party a greater amount of the variance can be accounted for through the addition of further indicators of socio-economic structure and development, but it seems clear from this initial analysis that cultural variables may prove as important in explaining the political basis of these parties: this is the line of analysis we want to explore in our next section.

The Cultural Distinctiveness of the South/West

So far we have focused our analysis on *structural* variables. In simple summary, we have tried to identify the structural conditions for the maintenance of territorial politics in peripheral localities and we have focused our explorations on two sets of community characteristics: the *type of primary economy* predominant in the community and the *size distribution* of the local holdings. Schematically, the findings of our analysis can be set out in a fourfold table (Table 8–7) for the sources of party strength in the primary economy communities:

TABLE 8–7

| | | COMMUNITY STRUCTURE | |
		More Hierarchial	*More Equalitarian*
TYPE OF PRIMARY ECONOMY:	*Inland: agriculture/ forestry*	*East/Trøndelag* Socialist and Agrarians the strongest.	*South and West* Liberals and Agrarians the strongest.
	Coast: fisheries	*North:* Socialists and Conservatives the strongest.	*South / West* Christians the strongest.

The entries in each of the cells represent statistical tendencies, but these are not very marked and there is a great deal of variance still to be accounted for. The socio-economic distinctiveness of the South and the West may explain *some* of the deviations from the average national alignments, but the bulk of the variance can only be explained in *cultural* terms. To determine the weight of such cultural variables is not a simpler matter, however. We have been able to assemble a variety of information on the overall contrasts between the regions and among the provinces within the regions, but to determine the importance of these differences in cultural conditions *locality by a locality* has proved highly problematic. Our findings, therefore, can hardly be more than suggestive of promising lines of further inquiry.

Ever since the emergence of mass politics the South and the West have given greater support than any other regions to three sets of policies:

a. they have been the strongholds of the *rural language movement* against the standard *riksmål* identified with the capital and the urban bourgeoisie,
b. they have offered a fertile soil for *temperance and prohibition movements,* and
c. they have constituted a bulwark for the defence of *Lutheran orthodoxy and pietistic fundamentalism* against the radicalizing and secularizing influences of the cities.

In Table 8–27 we have assembled some evidence from official statistics of the persistence of such differences over time. In their language policies, in their stand on temperance and prohibition, and in their support of distinctly Christian parties, the South and the West have continuously tended to differ from the rest of the country ever since the beginning of competitive national politics.

This does not mean that the two regions have always pulled together on all such questions nor that the localities within each region have all pulled in the same direction. Our crude differentiations by province within each region tell a story of complex variations both over time and across localities. The two provinces of the South have differed considerably: Aust-Agder has been closer to the East in the level of class polarization, but has at the same time been a stronghold of revival movements and dissident free churches and has, since 1949, returned disproportionately high numbers of votes for the Christian People's party; Vest-Agder, by contrast, went heavily Moderate in 1888, but has not proved very fertile soil for the Christians in the elections since 1945. The outer coastal areas of the West were stronger in their fundamentalism than in their rejection of the urban language: the stronghold of the Moderates in 1888, the province of Rogaland, was very slow in introducing *landsmål* in its schools (see the figures for 1910). The *nynorsk* movement is strongest in the least urbanized of the provinces, Sogn og Fjordane, but this is the least fundamentalist of the provinces: it still has the lowest per cent of Christian votes of its Middle party total. The northernmost of the Western provinces, More og Romsdal, was early a stronghold of the teetotalist movement, but gave very few of its votes to the Moderates in 1888: today, however, it has the highest share of Christian votes in the region, but marked divisions have persisted between the fundamentalist south and the more secular north of the province. There is no one-to-one fit between the levels of support for the three sets of policies at any given time: what makes the South/West such a characteristic division of the country is the *parallel* development of three distinct cultural movements, all directed against standards and practices seen to be spreading from the central areas, and the cities. These movements did not always pull together, but their net impact on national politics was unmistakable: they all stood for the defence of the rural values against the centralizing forces triggered off through economic development and the strengthening of governmental agencies.

Gabriel Øidne has drawn up maps for the strength of the Moderates in 1891 and the strength of the Christians in the fifties and found a close correspondence area by area. Our own statistical tests indicate very little influence of the early political traditions in the *fisheries* communes, but some slight impact in the *agricultural* communes: the Christians get a high share of the votes in the coastal districts whatever the strength of the Moderates while in the agricultural communes they tend to be stronger where the Moderates were strong and weaker where they were weak. The differences are particularly striking in the provinces of Rogaland and Hordaland and are only slight in the provinces to the north: in these the Moderates were much weaker and, given the electoral system then in force, this makes it much more difficult to measure their exact local strength. It is possible that our results are artifacts of the method used in comparing party strengths over such long periods, but the crude statistics available for the early period make further checks very difficult. Clearly to pursue these detailed ecological studies of continuities in religious and political traditions it will be essential to assemble commune by commune and period by period information on memberships in religious associations and temperance movements and this will, if at all possible, require a major effort of data collection. So far we have only been able to work with data from a *church attendance count* carried out in 1956[21] and with the official statistics for the language form used in local primary schools. Highly suggestive data have recently been made available on memberships in temperance organizations,[22] but a detailed analysis of these data cannot be published here.

Table 8–28 gives the first results of a secondary analysis of data from a privately organized count of attendance at services under the Lutheran State Church over a period of ten weeks in the spring of 1956. There are a number of difficulties of interpretation and detailed controls are necessary in the analysis. The findings of this first nationwide count of church attendance are nevertheless of great interest. It will be seen that the attendance figures for the peripheral communes are everywhere markedly higher than in the cities and the urbanized rural areas. Considering the differences in the average distance to places of worship this difference is indeed striking. On the other hand it must be realized that in a great many peripheral communes services will be much less frequent than in the densely populated areas and this may of course increase the averages per service. But it is also very likely that infrequent church services will increase the number of laymen's meetings of a religious character: on this point we have no direct data commune by commune, but our survey findings (Tables 8–29 and 8–30) tend to support this interpretation.

Table 8–28 shows a markedly higher level of attendance in the South than in the other regions. The high figures for the cities, towns and suburbs of the South stand in distinct contrast to the figures for the urban sections of the other regions. Interesting enough, the urban areas of the South also register the highest proportions of dissenters from the State Church: the great majority of these are members of "Free Churches" and various sects who have rejected the religious stewardship of the established State Church. If we look further to the rural communes we again find very high attendance figures for the South, but also for the West. By contrast, rural areas nearest to the center of the nation appear to be the most secularized. The rural areas of the Eastern Inland and the Trøndelag show intermediary level of attendance while the figures for the North suggest marked contrasts between types of communities: attendance was relatively low in the centrally located inland communes but markedly higher in the periphery.

Table 8–29 gives data from a nationwide sample survey and confirms the high level of religious participation in the South. In this region, 38 per cent of the adults indicated that they would from time to time attend either a church service or a religious meeting: this compares with 32 per cent for the West, 27 per cent for the North and around 25 per cent for the other regions. The tally between the church attendance count and the survey responses is surprisingly close considering the differences in procedure. The only major discrepancy is found for the West: the survey placed the West with the South as the regions of highest attendance while the count places the West roughly at the same level as the Trøndelag and lower than the North.

Politically church attendance may not be as significant as membership in distinctive religious associations. The Lutheran State Church can count on the formal allegiance of some 95 per cent of all Norwegian citizens. Hardly more than one quarter of them extend their religious activities beyond the conventional attendances at christenings, weddings and funerals. Many of the regular churchgoers, however, will manifest their religious commitments much more directly through memberships in activist bodies of various types: women's club, charitable organizations, societies for the support of missions. Religious life in Norway has ever since 1814 been marked by a polarization between the government-appointed clergymen and the activists in revival movements, mission organizations and "Free Churches." The conflict between the established Church and the fundamentalist organizations paralleled very closely the conflict between the King's officials and the old Left: there was the same rejection of central authority and the same assertion of the values and traditions of rural life against the corruption of the cities. Much has changed since the early conflicts over the control of the

Church, but membership in mission societies is still a telling indicator of religious orientation and as such also politically significant.

Table 8–30 gives a breakdown of a nationwide sample by type of religious membership and again underscores the regional contrasts in religious life. In its cities, the South/West differs very little from the rest of the country, but very striking differences are found for *women in the rural communes*. In the South/West 30 per cent of the women in rural working class households are found to belong to some religious association within the Church: the figure for the other regions is 15 per cent. The difference is also marked for women in smallholders' and farmers' households: 48 per cent vs. 34 per cent. Perhaps more significant are the differences in the support of the orthodox and fundamentalist *"mission societies"*: 23 per cent vs. 10 per cent and 45 per cent vs. 31 per cent. These societies tend to be stronger in all strata of the South and the West and, as we shall see, make up the core of the Christian People's party.

We have not yet been able to carry out a commune-by-commune analysis of the membership strength of the *temperance organizations* and our nationwide survey of 1957 did not cover the variables in this area as thoroughly as required for the present purposes. Fortunately a membership count undertaken for 1960 by Arne Dolven gives us a clear picture of these regional variations and also allows some further differentiations by clusters of communes. The basic findings of this count can be set out as follows.[23]

TABLE 8–8

TOTAL MEMBERSHIPS FOR ALL TEMPERANCE ORGANIZATIONS COVERED

	Mean for Region	Range of Means for Areas (*Handelsområder*) Within each Region	Range of Means for *Handelsdistrikter* (Smallest Data Units)
East	2.03	1.15 — 3.99	0.25 — 6.16
South	7.98	6.79 — 8.85	2.84 — 17.75
West	6.00	2.68 — 8.59	1.85 — 17.34
		(N. Møre) (S. Møre)	
Trøndelag	3.43	3.23 — 3.95	0.95 — 6.81
North	1.86	1.54 — 2.35	0.44 — 4.57

The South and the West again stand out as the strongholds of cultural resistance against the evils of urban life. However, as in the count for church attendance the contrasts in the regional averages are not as significant as the variations at the levels of the locality. Unfortunately we have only recently been able to incorporate these temperance data in our general file of data by commune: When this paper was written data were only available for the 119 "trade districts," not for the 680 rural communes and the 64 urban units in our archive.

We have so far been able to document the cultural distinctiveness of the South and the West on three scores: the frequencies of religious attendance, the number of memberships in religious associations, and the number of memberships in temperance organizations. The contrast in *local language options* is equally marked and readily documented: Table 8–27 gives a straight-forward account of variations among regions and among provinces and could without any difficulty be followed up by detailed tables for ranges of variation at the level of the commune. There are problems about the inter-pretation of such official figures, however. The decisions on the language to be used in the local primary school need not always reflect the wishes and the usages of the majority: such decisions tend to be in the hands of a few articu-late community leaders and quite particularly the local teachers. A check against data from sample surveys of the adult electorate is therefore of great interest. In the nation-wide sample survey we carried out in 1957 we asked each of our sampled citizens which language form he or she used "when writing." The intention was to elicit open answers to a question about actual linguistic usage. Table 8–31 gives a classification of the responses and a breakdown by region, by type of community and by the occupation of the head of the household. The survey suggests that the *nynorsk* counter-language is much weaker in actual usage than in the schools: the official statistics for 1957 indicated that about *one-third* of all *children* in rural schools were taught in *nynorsk* while the survey suggests that only *one-sixth* of the *adults* living in rural community actually use the language. Similar differences have been found in responses to questionnaires administered to recruits to the armed forces. The *nynorsk* movement can no longer stem the flow of communica-tions and conformity pressures from the urban centres, but it can still count on strong and articulate minorities in each community to control local decisions on the choice of·language: this appears to be most plausible interpretation of the discrepancies found in the data.

The breakdown of survey responses gives us a clear picture of the sources of *nynorsk* strength:

TABLE 8–9

	Oslofjord	East Inland/ Trøndelag	North	South/West
Urbanized, Industrialized Areas	Negligible	Negligible	Negligible	*One of every 6th*
Primary-economy areas				
Farm households	*One of every 20th*	*One of every 6th*	Negligible	*Half of the households*
Other ,,	Negligible	Negligible	Negligible	*Half of the households*

It is in fact almost exclusively in the South and the West that we find homogeneous *nynorsk* communities: communities where the entire local culture is marked by the ideology of rural defence and where all adults except a few "strangers" speak and write *nynorsk*. Outside the South and West the primary-economy communities are more likely to be linguistically divided:

the farmers and the teachers brought up in the ideology of rural opposition will stick to *nynorsk* while employees, businessmen and members of the professions may speak a local dialect, but are more likely to be swayed by the pressures of the urban language norms, at least when writing.

How do these differences in cultural characteristics affect the political alignments in the communities and in the regions? We shall first review a set of ecological findings and then proceed to an analysis of survey data. Table 8–32 cross-classifies all the rural communes by region, by level of church attendance and by the language taught in the primary schools and finally adds a straight-forward control for socio-economic structure: the communes have simply been grouped in two on the basis of the proportion of economically active in agriculture. An over-all analysis for the rural communes makes it clear that the *local language* option is politically the most significant of our indicators of cultural distinctiveness:

TABLE 8–10

| | RURAL COMMUNES | | | |
| | LARGELY AGRICULTURAL (35% AND OVER) | | LESS AGRICULTURAL (UNDER 35%) | |
	Middle Party Strength in p.c. of Votes Cast	Polariza-tion Score	Middle Party Strength	Polarization
Bokmål communes				
All	40.5	.78	23.3	.83
Low church attendance (under 9.1%)	38.7	.80	21.3	.84
High (over 14.1%)	41.0	.77	31.4	.77
Mixed communes				
All	47.7	.71	35.5	.72
Low church attendance	42.6	.73	34.3	.73
High	49.1	.72	42.1	.65
Nynorsk communes				
All	58.5	.58	52.2	.54
Low church attendance	57.7	.60	49.3	.56
High	59.8	.57	59.9	.44

The *nynorsk* communities definitely offer the best conditions for the maintenance of Middle party strength: this goes for the typical agricultural communities, where the Agrarians rarely rally less than a quarter of the votes cast, as well as for the other rural communities where the functional politics of the Socialists and the Right contrast much more directly with the cultural politics of the Liberal and the Christians.

The *nynorsk-bokmål* differential is not as pronounced in the typical agricultural communes as in the others: in the one group the contrast in polarization score is .58 to .78, in the other .54 to .83. What is even more interesting is that the church attendance level appears to be without political significance in the typical agricultural communes, while clearly a factor of some weight in the other rural communes: in *nynorsk* communes registering low attendance the polarization score was found to be .56, while in the high attendance communes it was as low as .44.

We know from our earlier tabulations that the two cultural indicators we have used in this analysis have a highly uneven regional distribution. If we control for region, will the pattern of differences disappear or will they also remain *within* each region? This is the question to which Table 8–32 is addressed. Within- region differences do indeed prove much less marked than the between-region differences. If we limit our comparisons to the two cultural extremes, the low attendance *bokmål* communes and the high attendance *nynorsk* communes, we get these patterns of variation:

TABLE 8–11

	LARGELY AGRICULTURAL		LESS AGRICULTURAL	
	Low Attendance, *Bokmål*	High Attendance, *Nynorsk*	Low Attendance, *Bokmål*	High Attendance, *Nynorsk*
East, Trøndelag and North				
Middle party strength	39.5	47.6	21.0	39.6
Christian votes in p.c. of				
− Lib. + Chr. votes	70.3	55.9	55.6	44.4
− Middle party total	28.6	22.9	34.7	25.3
Conservative strength	10.6	5.6	18.0	6.0
Polarization score	.79	.73	.86	.73
South and West				
Middle party strength	57.5	64.9	37.9	61.4
Christian vote in p.c. of				
− Lib. + Chr. votes	42.8	55.4	37.9	57.0
− Middle party total	33.0	30.2	33.1	48.5
Conservative strength	21.3	7.8	15.6	7.4
Polarization score	.49	.50	.65	.43

It will be seen that even the *least* polarized of the groups in the East, Trøndelag, North division has a markedly higher score than the *most* polarized of the groups in the South/West. The within-region differences prove on the whole negligible in the typical agriculture communes. The only exception is for the level of Conservative strength: this highly city-centered party will almost invariably be weaker in *nynorsk* than in *bokmål* communes, but proves relatively independent of the level of church attendance. The language/religion differential is much more marked in the less agricultural communes: among these the differences between the two cultural extremes is indeed highly significant in the South/West. What is particularly important here is that the two factors appear to be of equal importance in reducing polarization (Table 8–12).

We find a similar pattern if we look more specifically at the strength of the Christian People's party. In the East, Trøndelag and the North our two indicators are not of much use as predictors of Christian strength: the party has not made any inroads against the old Left and the Agrarians in the *nynorsk* communities and, at least in the typical agriculture communes, does not even seem to depend specifically on the regular churchgoers for support. The only clearcut findings are for church attendance in the less agricultural communes: in these churchgoing clearly increases the Christian share of the vote. There is a good deal of evidence that the party has recruited a very different clientèle in the eastern, middle and northern provinces than in its original strongholds in the rural West. If we look at the breakdowns for the

TABLE 8–12

CHURCH ATTENDANCE

	Low	High	All	Difference L − H
Bokmål (B)	.65	.60	.64	.05
Mixed	.66	.53	.64	.13
Nynorsk (N)	.56	.43	.51	.13
All	.62	.48	.58	.14
Diff. B − N	.09	.17	.13	

South/West region, we again find a clear difference between the agricultural communes and the others: where the Agrarians are strong, the Christians gain very little from the *nynorsk* speakers and churchgoers, but where the agricultural basis is narrower the total language/church-attendance differential is very marked, not only as measured by the Liberal-Christian balance, but also by the total level of polarization and the Christian share of the Middle party total.

Our tabulations of survey data suggest a similar pattern of variations. Tables 8–33 and 8–34 set out the findings for the nationwide cross-section interviewed in 1957 and show how dependent the Middle parties in general and the Christian People's party in particular are on the widespread clientèle of religious activists. The members of the "Inner Mission" and other orthodox bodies vote heavily for the Christian People's party in all regions of the country: the greater strength of the Christians in the South and the West largely reflects the higher level of memberships of such fundamentalist movements in these regions. There are important differences among socio-economic strata and among types of localities, however, and these require further analysis.

In Table 8–33 we have grouped the survey respondents by the occupation of the head of each household and within each of these groups shown the differences in political allegiance between the avowed members of religious associations and the others. The result for the working class is as expected: the religious activists are less likely to vote with their class and more likely to vote for one of the Middle parties. On this score there is very little difference between the two divisions of the country. The results for the farmers, smallholders and fishermen goes in the same direction but in this sector there is a marked difference between the regions: in the East, Trøndelag and North the religious differential is very marked while in the South/West there is hardly any difference at all. This fits in with the findings of our ecological analysis: in the typical primary-economy communes of the South/West the Middle parties will almost invariably be in control of local politics and no single indicator, whether level of religious activity, memberships in temperance organizations or local language option, is likely to prove of statistical significance in accounting for deviations from this basic pattern. This, however, does not mean that religious membership is without political importance at the individual level: there may be little difference between members and others in the proportions supporting *one* Middle party *or* the other, but there is a marked difference, less so, however, in the South/West than in the rest of the country, in the *Christian People's party's share* of this Middle party vote.

The result for the middle-class stratum is also very clear-cut. In both regions religious activity proves an excellent predictor of the vote: the Socialists are weaker (16 per cent vs. 29 per cent in the East, Trøndelag, North, 8 per cent vs. 16 per cent in the South/West), the Christians are stronger (31 per cent vs. 5 per cent, and 33 per cent vs. 3 per cent) and the Conservatives tend to lose out (20 per cent vs. 37 per cent and 21 per cent vs. 25 per cent) among the members of religious organizations.

Table 8–34 tells essentially the same story, but shows that active participation in services and meetings is a better predictor of political position than nominal membership. In all the urban areas we find markedly heavier support for the Middle parties among the religiously active than among the passive: most of this religious clientèle support the Christian People's party, but the rates for the women are markedly higher than for the men. In the rural communes, the Middle parties prove much stronger among the religiously active than the passive in the East, Middle and North, but not in the South/West: in these regions the Middle parties have achieved a dominant position and do not depend as much on the religiously most active groups in each community. The Christian share of the Middle party total does depend on the level of religious participation, however: in fact even more markedly in the South/West than in the other rural areas.

The nationwide cross-section interviewed in 1957 is too small to allow detailed break-downs for more than one cultural indicator at a time: this is why Tables 8–33 and 8–34 concentrate on religious variables only. Fortunately we have at hand local data for the South/West which allow cross-classifications by all the three cultural indicators discussed in this section: in the local sample surveys carried out in the Stavanger Area in 1957[24] we asked questions not only about *language choice* and *religious activity*, but also about *stand on the temperance issue*. The question asked was very straight forward: "Do you consider yourself a temperance man?[25] In Table 8–35 we have cross-classified the three indicators and controlled for the occupation of the head of the household. The results are indeed striking: within the working-class sample we find the Socialists (CP grouped with Labour) weakest among the religiously active temperance people opting for *nynorsk* (33 per cent) and strongest among the religiously passive *bokmål* people, whether with the temperance movement or not (83 per cent and 72 per cent). These three indicators account for the bulk of the deviations from straight class voting in the Stavanger area. The only party to gain from these deviations are the Christians: at least in the working class their strength appears to be almost exclusively a function of such cultural and moral commitments. The strength of the Liberals is much more difficult to explain: the party has its followers not only in all strata, but also in all the distinct cultural and religious groupings.

This comes out even clearer in the figures for the sample of farmer and middle-class households. The Liberals find sizable support in all the groups distinguished through the cross-classification of the three indicators, while the Christians derive most of their support from the religiously active and the Conservatives hardly gain a single vote in the *nynorsk* circles and only a few among the temperance people. The parties at the two poles of the political spectrum, the Socialists and the Conservatives, are both weak among the religiously active and among the *nynorsk* speakers: they both uphold urban secular values in politics and attempt to keep questions of private morals out of public debate. But the two parties differ very much on the temperance question: the Labour party has always had a strong temperance wing while the Conservatives have upheld the urban traditions of convivial drinking and fought bitter fights with the Middle parties over restrictive alcohol policies.

The data we have at hand do not tell us whether the patterns of variations found in the samples interviewed in the Stavanger area would hold for the other regions of the country. The marginal frequencies for each of the three indicators as well as for the principal parties would be very different in a nationwide sample and the findings for the Liberals and the Chrisitans are likely to prove very different in the East, possibly also in the Trøndelag and the North, from what we find for the South/West: this, at least, is what our ecological analyses suggest. The urbanized wing of the old Left, the present Liberal party (it is still, of course, called the "*Left*," but we translate it by the term "Liberal," in discussing developments since the thirties) stands for different value and policy positions in the two divisions of the country: we shall discuss some evidence of this in the section on the Common Market issue below. The contrast between the radical "Oslo" Liberals of the East and the more moderate Liberals of the South and the West clearly reflects their very different position in community politics. In the South and the West the old Left and its various offshoots have been in power since the 1880's and the more urbanized of the followers of this movement no longer distrust central authority to the extent the party did at the beginning. At the center, by contrast, the old Left lost out to the power-holders in the Labour movement, in farming and in business and, in addition, shed some of its religiously active clientèle to the Christians: the result was a fundamental radicalization and an increasing openness to the ideological claims of alienated opponents of all established power.

Politicization and Polarization: Contrasts Between West and North

We have reviewed a variety of data on socio-economic, cultural and political differences between the different regions of Norway and we have focused our attention on two crucial dimensions of the system: the *territorial-cultural* and the *functional-economic*.

So far we have tried to document variations along these dimensions through analyses of *national* elections, but they are even more salient in the study of variations in *local* elections. The territorial-cultural emphasis will tend to limit party competition within local units and to reduce politics to questions of external representation. The functional-economic emphasis cuts across local geographical units, undermines established local leadership and introduces elements of direct interest conflict into community politics.

In an earlier paper we described the process of *"politicization"* in Norway and mapped the spread of partisan competition from the central, economically advanced areas to the backward areas of the periphery.[26] The rural communes of the West and the North resisted this movement the longest and we shall present here some additional data on the current levels of politicization in these regions.

Tables 8–36 and 8–37 show the differences between coastal and inland and central and peripheral communes in the strength of non-partisan lists and the number of nationally registered parties competing in local elections. The coastal areas of the West stand out as the least politicized, the central inland areas of the North as the most. The overall level of politicization is much lower in the West: the differences between central and peripheral and even between coastal and inland communes are nowhere near as clearcut as in the North. In the West low politicization tends to be a characteristic of all rural communities, in the North it is mainly present in the typical fisheries communes and some peripheral inland areas. Even if we restrict our comparison to such outlying areas we find a characteristic difference: in the West the typical situation is one of no parties or only one party in competition with local lists; in the North there will most frequently be two parties competing with local lists.

This clearly reflects differences in the level of political polarization. Table 8–38 gives details of a comparison of the results of national elections in communes at different levels of politicization. The differences between the South/West and the North are indeed striking. In the South/West the Middle parties have their greatest strength in the least politicized communes. This holds both for inland and coastal communes but the difference between the least politicized and the most politicized communes is much more marked inland than on the coast. The difference for the Socialists is equally striking: they are at their weakest in the least politicized communes and at their strongest where the local elections take the form of straight contests between nationally registered parties. In the North the pattern of variation is quite different: on the coast the Socialists are strong whatever the level of politicization and the Conservatives tend to be the strongest of the opposition parties in the least politicized communes; inland the Socialists are strongest the higher the level of politicization but the Conservatives tend to be strongest in less politicized communes.

Urbanization, industrialization and the growth of a nationwide money and market economy have created new lines of conflict in national politics and have also gradually affected the alignments of leaders and followers in the local communities. Conditions in the peripheral areas have created important barriers, socio-economic as well as geographical, against the spread of partisan politics and have made for persistently low levels of politicization. But in the West the traditions of territorial representation and Middle party dominance have slowed down the process of politicization not only in the coastal areas and the inland periphery but even in highly developed rural communes. In the North, by contrast, the even greater geographical barriers have not held up the process of politicization and polarization. The typical situation in the Northern periphery is not one of Middle party dominance but one of open conflict between the Labour party and a variety of opposition groups, sometimes presenting purely territorial lists, sometimes joint "bourgeois" lists, sometimes straight party lists. The presence of the Labour party, possibly also of the Conservative party, in peripheral politics tends to make competition much more intensive than in the typical Western periphery: we have established in an earlier analysis that in these Northern communes the contestants tend to mobilize more support for their groups in the local than in the national elections.[27] Politics in the Northern periphery is indeed still localized and the choice of party is still largely determined by territorial tensions within each commune rather than by straight economic conflict. The Labour party is without comparison the strongest party in the periphery but the level of cross-local organization is still poor: as we have documented in an earlier paper[28] the numbers of local branches and the levels of membership are very low in these areas but whatever the local organizational strength of the party its list will almost invariably mobilize the greatest number of supporters in the community.

Territorial vs. Functional Strains: The Conflict over Entry into the European Common Market

The overall tendency in Norwegian politics in this century has been toward a reduction of territorial strains and an increase in the importance of purely economic conflicts in the system. In the 1950's the system came close to a stable equilibrium and the territorial contrasts were less salient than in any earlier period since the emergence of mass democracy. This equilibrium was quickly broken when in August, 1961, the political leaders were suddenly forced to decide whether or not to apply for membership in the European Common Market, the EEC. The leaders of the Labour party and the trade-union movement allied themselves with the Conservatives in advocating entry while the Middle parties were either split or entirely against any application for full membership. Violent mass campaigns were staged on both sides during the autumn and the winter and the movements of opinion could to some extent be followed in the results of the regular polls of the Gallup Institute. We were kindly given access to the raw data of some of these polls and have given a few initial results of our analysis in Tables 8–39 to 8–41.

We have compared in these tables the response distributions at the beginning of the public debate in September, 1961, with the corresponding distributions at the peak of the campaign, in February, 1962. It will be seen that in September a majority of the nationwide sample either ignored the issue or were unable to state a position. By February an overwhelming majority knew about the issue and more than two thirds of those who knew of it took a stand. Most of these newly mobilized citizens seem to have decided against entry. No panel studies were carried out, but comparisons of net changes from September to February gives clues to an understanding of this process of mass persuasion.

The campaign against entry was particularly effective among the Middle party voters. Interestingly enough the Liberals and the Christians did not move in the same direction in the urbanized areas and in the sparsely populated countryside. The urban Liberals moved heavily against entry while the Christians in the cities changed very little. By contrast the Christians in the countryside were almost all mobilized against the EEC (there were strong warnings against the danger of Catholic influence inherent in the Treaty of Rome!) while the rural Liberals were much less affected. This illustrates the new alignment brought about by the EEC issue: radicals in the cities joined up with fundamentalist Lutherans in the periphery.

The voters of the South/West again stood out as the defenders of territorial and cultural autonomy. In all except one of the parties the voters from the South/West were more frequently against the EEC in September than the voters from the other regions. The exception, interestingly enough, was the Liberals: they were more frequently for entry in the South/West than in the East. This reflected the position taken by the leading party newspapers: the dominant Liberal newspapers of the West advocated entry while the radical paper in Oslo, *Dagbladet*, came out against. The figures for February confirm these differences: the Liberals were evenly split in the South/West but overwhelmingly against entry in the rest of the country. The old alliance of the 1880's tended to reaffirm itself: the urban radicals aligned themselves with farmers and with religious dissidents in the countryside in their attack on central bureacracy.

The Labour party was seriously split over the EEC issue. The party leadership took a clear stand for entry but was opposed by the smallholders and the fishermen: Table 8–41 shows a clear majority of these against entry in September and a fairly even split in February. Among the workers opposition to entry was strongest in the largest cities and in the sparsely populated areas: a parallel to the situation for the Liberals and the Christians.

The Conservatives, finally, were massively for entry on both occasions. The only group seriously resisting the movement were the self-employed and the employers in the countryside: many of them tended to side with the Agrarians in their fears for the economic consequences of entry. In the case of the Liberals and the Christians, however, the motives for resistance were clearly cultural and ideological rather than economic: they continued an ingrained tradition of opposition to central authority.

The mass mobilization of opinion against membership in the EEC brought about a compromise: the *Storting* decided by a three-fourths majority to apply for membership but stipulated that the people were to be consulted in a referendum before any terms of affiliation were accepted.[29] But history decided otherwise: General de Gaulle called off the campaign on 14 January, 1963, and the issue disappeared from Norwegian politics, at least for some years. Functional-economic cleavages came to the fore again and the old divisions within the bourgeois opposition lost some of their importance: the result was the first serious Cabinet crisis for 28 years.

TABLE 8–13

Socialist–Conservative Polarization in 1957: Contrasts Between Communes at Different Levels of Urbanization and Industrialization

Communes	Density	Industrialization 1950 Census	No. of Comm.	Total Electorate = 100%	CP + Lab.	Lib.	Chr.	Agr.	Cons.	Polarization score[1]
East and Trøndelag	Low	Low: under 23.1%	129	211,262	40.0	4.9	7.6	17.9	6.5	.79
		Medium: 23.2 – 25.7%	90	250,642	43.9	4.7	6.4	14.9	9.3	.83
		High: 35.8%+	36	131,933	50.6	3.6	6.1	9.4	10.6	.86
	High	High	34	232,312	47.7	5.3	6.3	3.6	17.6	.85
	Cities	Low: under 37.1%	7	52,635	46.3	5.1	5.7	1.1	22.6	.86
	+ towns	High: over 37.1%	26	485,575	44.6	5.0	5.0	0.2	28.3	.88
South and West	Low	Low	131	138,199	20.6	12.7	16.4	17.1	6.0	.48
		Medium	85	119,657	23.6	14.0	15.4	14.4	6.2	.50
		High	35	84,524	31.9	11.3	15.5	9.6	6.2	.59
	High	Low	4	7,083	15.9	14.7	16.1	5.7	10.1	.46
		Medium + High	24	120,674	36.3	13.7	10.6	5.0	11.4	.66
	Cities	Low	9	40,513	33.9	17.9	9.6	0.2	17.8	.65
	+ towns	High	11	161,596	40.4	14.2	7.8	0.4	17.8	.73
North	Low	Low	71	108,631	36.5	4.7	7.4	6.6	8.3	.79
		Medium	25	55,665	38.8	5.4	6.4	7.3	8.3	.80
		High	4	22,422	49.4	3.6	6.4	6.2	6.2	.85
	High	Low + Medium	10	20,071	43.8	4.3	5.0	2.1	12.7	.86
		High	3	9,914	57.2	4.3	3.6	0.3	11.8	.90
	Cities	Low	10	38,263	45.9	8.2	4.5	0.3	17.6	.83
	+ towns	High	1	4,805	54.9	4.7	3.4	0.2	10.7	.89

1   $\dfrac{\text{Soc.} + \text{Cons.}}{\text{Soc.} + \text{Left} + \text{Chr.} + \text{Cons.}}$

Table 8–14

*Regional Differences in Socialist Support Outside Industry: By the
Per Cent of Actives in Forestry*

			INDEX CP + LAB. — IND.[1]		
Region	% of actives in forestry[2]	N = 100%	Q_1	Md	Q_3
East and	0—2.1	97	9.0	15.4	24.7
Trøndelag	2.2—7.5	88	10.6	18.9	24.1
	7.6—14.3	51	22.8	26.7	33.1
	14.4+	53	33.—	43.6	58.6
South and	0—0.3	177	−11.6	9.2	9.7
West	0.4—2.1	63	− 3.1	4.1	14.6
	2.2+	35	5.2	13.9	26.8
North	0—0.3	57	29.3	41.1	53.8
	0.4—2.1	47	30.2	38.2	45.1
	2.2+	12	31.3	39.6	53.8

[1] The difference for each commune between the per cent of economically active in mining, manufacturing and construction by the 1950 census and the per cent of the *electorate* voting CP or Labour in 1949.
[2] According to the 1950 census.

Table 8–15

*Regional Differences in Socialist Support Outside Industry: By the
Proportion of Large Forestry Units in Each Commune*

				INDEX CP + LAB. — IND.[1]		
Region	% of Actives in Forestry 1950	% of Units over 1000 da.	N = 100%	Q_1	Md	Q_3
East and	Under 2.1	Under 2.5	53	−8.5	14.0	20.1
Trøndelag		Over 2.5	44	9.9	19.2	27.1
	Over	Under 2.5	22	9.5	15.6	24.9
		2.5—11.8	94	15.4	24.7	32.5
		Over 11.9	76	25.5	33.4	48.2
South and	Under 2.1.	Under 2.5	187	−9.3	1.0	10.0
West		Over 2.5	53	−4.6	2.2	15.4
	Over	Under 2.5	2		12.5	
		Over 2.5	33	5.7	14.3	27.1
North	Under 2.1	Under 2.5	73	35.3	43.5	57.1
		Over 2.5	31	23.2	31.2	40.8
	Over	Under 2.5	4		36.1	
		Over 2.5	8		41.4	

[1] For explanation see Table 8-14.

TABLE 8–16

Party Strength in the Agricultural Communes in 1961: Variations by the Median Size of Farm Units in Each Commune

RURAL COMMUNES WITH 25% OR MORE ACTIVES IN AGRICULTURE IN 1960

Region	Median Size of Farms in da.	No. of Comm.	No. of Votes Cast = 100%	VOTES CAST FOR				
				Soc.[1]	Lib.	Chr.	Agr.	Cons.
Oslofjord	Under 36	4	7,726	61.4	3.2	8.7	19.1	7.6
	36—58	11	16,865	53.2	4.6	11.1	21.2	9.9
	Over 58	18	30,894	43.3	3.2	13.4	27.0	13.1
East Inland/	Under 32	56	97,569	66.2	4.2	3.8	18.1	7.7
Trøndelag	32—47	72	113,670	54.6	5.9	7.6	23.2	8.6
	Over 47	42	48,515	46.2	9.7	8.2	29.9	5.8
South/West	Under 29	62	44,999	32.7	16.0	21.4	20.4	9.5
	29—41	64	51,337	28.8	14.5	21.8	26.4	8.5
	Over 41	47	46,361	25.8	13.5	19.3	31.5	9.9
North	Under 29	24	20,516	55.9	6.9	10.0	12.7	14.5
	29—41	29	19,221	59.0	6.7	8.2	17.2	8.9
	Over 41	6	6,235	54.0	7.2	8.2	21.0	9.6

[1] CP + SP + Labour.

TABLE 8–17

Differences in Party Strength Between Central and Peripheral Areas Within Each Region: Data for 1957

RURAL COMMUNES ONLY

Region	Accessibility[1]	No. of Communes	Electorate 1957 N = 100%	VOTES CAST FOR						Polarization[2]
				CP	Lab	Lib.	Chr.	Agr.	Cons.	
East and	High	97	464,014	2.9	43.4	4.4	6.3	9.0	14.1	0.85
Trøndelag	Medium	163	335,707	3.2	41.0	4.9	6.7	14.9	7.6	0.82
	Low	29	26,428	0.8	32.7	7.2	10.8	14.7	5.1	0.68
South and	High	48	173,204	1.2	30.6	13.8	13.0	7.4	9.7	0.61
West	Medium	193	261,199	0.6	24.2	12.7	15.1	13.7	6.3	0.53
	Low	34	35,734	0.02	17.8	12.7	17.0	18.6	6.1	0.45
North	High	11	19,753	3.1	37.7	4.6	5.0	4.6	11.9	0.85
	Medium	49	122,613	3.9	37.6	4.9	6.6	5.9	8.6	0.81
	Low	56	74,337	2.3	35.3	4.5	7.2	6.6	7.9	0.80

[1] A score for average accessibility originally developed for analyses of electoral turnout and based on (a) the per cent of the 1950 population in "house clusters", (b) the per cent of children of school age taught in central boarding schools within the commune because of distances from their homes, (c) the per cent of school children taught in one-class or two-class schools (because of low density of population).

[2] $\dfrac{CP + Lab. + Cons.}{CP + Lab. + Lib. + Chr. + Cons.}$

Table 8–18

Regional Contrasts in Party Preferences Within Major Occupational Groups: Survey Data for 1957

INTENDED VOTE 1957

	N	CP	Lab.	Lib.	Chr.	Agr.	Cons.	Un-clear	Non-voter
Total cross-section sample	1546	1%	40	6	7	7	14	12	13
East, Middle North	1125	2%	45	3	6	5	15	12	12
South, West	421	x	27%	12	9	12	12	11	17
Primary: all	407	1%	31	6	9	22	7	9	16
EMN	283	1%	41	4	7	17	7	8	15
SW	124	—	9%	13	13	33	6	9	18
Farmers	171	1%	14	10	9	38	9	9	11
EMN	98	1%	19	6	7	37	8	17	20
SW	73	—	7%	15	11	40	10	8	10
Smallholders, fishermen	138	1%	34	4	11	12	7	9	22
EMN	100	2%	42	2	8	8	10	8	20
SW	38	—	13%	8	18	24	0	10	26
Workers	98	1%	56	4	5	6	3	8	17
EMN	85	1%	64	2	5	3	3	8	13
SW	13								
Non-prim. manual: all	644	2%	58	3	4	1	7	10	13
EMN	479	3%	61	3	4	1	7	11	11
SW	165	1%	50	5	7	4	7	7	20
Manufacturing	285	1%	64	3	4	1	4	12	11
EMN	214	2%	65	2	3	1	5	13	9
SW	71	—	58%	7	8	3	0	7	17
Crafts	106	3%	55	2	6	1	8	7	19
EMN	77	3%	60	1	5	0	8	9	14
SW	29	3%	41	3	7	3	10	0	31
Other	253	2%	54	4	4	2	10	11	13
EMN	188	3%	57	4	4	1	9	11	11
SW	65	—	45%	5	5	5	12	11	18
Non-manual: all	464		23%	8	9	1	32	16	11
EMN	336	1%	26	4	9	1	34	15	10
SW	128	—	14%	19	9	3	25	18	12
Self-employed	53	—	21%	2	11	2	24	21	19
EMN	38	—	18%	—	8	3	26	24	21
SW	15								
Salaried, public	130	—	30%	15	12	2	22	14	5
EMN	93	—	40%	10	12	0	20	14	4
SW	37	—	5%	30	14	5	27	14	5
Salaried, private	189	1%	25	5	8	2	33	15	11
EMN	139	1%	27	1	9	1	38	15	7
SW	50	—	20%	14	6	4	20	16	20
Employer	92	—	10%	9	3	0	46	17	15
EMN	66	—	11%	5	5	0	50	12	18
SW	26	—	8%	19	0	0	35	31	8
No occup. (present or past) given	31	—	32%	6	10	0	10	16	26

Note Respondents have been classified by the *occupation of the head* of the household. If the head was no longer economically active, he was classified by his past occupation.

TABLE 8–19

Differences in Class Voting Between Communes of Different Economic Structure Within Two Contrasting Regions: Survey Data for 1957

Occupation of head	Residence	Region	N = 100%	Soc.	Middle Party	Cons.	Unclear-Non-Voter
Worker	City or	SW	77	61	8	9	22
	town	EMN	230	63	7	9	21
	Industrialized	SW	31	45	30	3	22
	rural comm.	EMN	161	65	6	5	24
	(30% or more in ind.)						
	Other rural	SW	70	33	24	4	39
		EMN	173	64	10	4	22
Independent in primary economy	Industrialized rural comm.	SW	25	4	68	8	20
		EMN	40	32.5	30	2.5	35
	(25% or more in ind.)						
	Other rural	SW	86	10	58	6	26
		EMN	158	32	35	11	22
Middle class (salaried, indep. outside primary econ.)	Cities, towns, heavily industrialized rural comm. (40% +)	SW	84	13	25	29	33
		EMN	228	26	11	39	24
	Other rural	SW	44	16	42	18	25
		EMN	.108	29	18	25	28

INTENDED VOTE 1957

TABLE 8–20

Economic Modernization and Party Support: Ecological Correlations Between Three Indices of Economic Development and the Strength of Each Party in 1957

		CORRELATION COEFFICIENTS		
		East and Trøndelag	South and West	North
C.P.	Per cent in manufacturing, mining and construction	.31	.40	.39
	Per cent in agglomerations	.21	.37	.41
	Mean income per taxpayer	.34	.43	.35
Lab.	Per cent in manufacturing, etc.	.48	.56	.38
	Per cent in agglomerations	.32	.39	.29
	Mean income per taxpayer	.45	.41	.38
Lib.	Per cent in manufacturing, etc.	−.12	−.07	.01
	Per cent in agglomerations	−.15	−.05	−.09
	Mean income per taxpayer	−.16	.05	−.01
Chr.	Per cent in manufacturing, etc.	—.17	−.19	−.30
	Per cent in agglomerations	−.15	−.16	−.20
	Mean income per taxpayer	−.24	−.07	−.28
Agr.	Per cent in manufacturing, etc.	−.50	−.35	−.03
	Per cent in agglomerations	.09	−.37	−.34
	Mean income per taxpayer	−.47	−.30	−.06
Cons.	Per cent in manufacturing, etc.	.30	−.04	−.09
	Per cent in agglomerations	.39	.29	−.26
	Mean income per taxpayer	.51	.17	.19

Table 8–21

Economic Modernization and Political Polarizations: Coefficients of Regression of Three Party Strength Variables on Three "Urbanization-Industrialization" Variables

Variables: 1 — the per cent of the electorate voting for the given party in 1957
2 — the proportion of actives in manufacturing and construction
3 — the mean income per taxpayer
4 — the proportion of the population living in agglomerations.

Party	Normalized Regression Coefficients	East and Trøndelag	South and West	North
C.P.	β_{12}	.155	.174	.341
	β_{13}	.280	.240	−.079
	β_{14}	.091	.130	.340
	Multiple R	.352	.470	.495
Lab.	β_{12}	.479	.475	.469
	β_{13}	.022	.046	−.060
	β_{14}	−.010	.101	.134
	Multiple R	.571	.578	.334
Cons.	β_{12}	−.374	−.215	.094
	β_{13}	.665	.097	−.129
	β_{14}	.207	.351	.294
	Multiple R	.554	.507	.237

Table 8–22

Electoral Resources Outside Industry: Correlations Between the Proportions of Actives in Agriculture and Forestry and the Per Cent of the Electorate Voting for Each Party

INLAND[1] RURAL COMMUNES BY REGION

CORRELATION COEFFICIENTS

C.P.	Agriculture	−.42	−.39	−.33
	Forestry	.33	.18	.11
Lab.	Agriculture	−.49	−.59	−.14
	Forestry	.26	.34	.04
C.P.+ Lab. − Ind.[2]	Agriculture	.28	.24	.09
	Forestry	.66	.61	.03
Lib.	Agriculture	.17	−.07	−.02
	Forestry	−.16	−.10	−.09
Chr.	Agriculture	.18	.02	−.02
	Forestry	−.16	—.14	−.20
Agr.	Agriculture	.76	.82	.60
	Forestry	−.01	−.05	.22
Cons.	Agriculture	−.51	−.39	−.06
	Forestry	−.24	.18	−.16

[1] "Inland" communes are here defined as those with 1% or more of their actives in forestry.
[2] See Table 8–14.

TABLE 8–23

*Electoral Resources Outside Industry: Correlations Between the Proportions
of Actives in Agriculture and Fishery and the Per Cent of the
Electorate Voting for Each Party*

COASTAL RURAL COMMUNES BY REGION

		East and Trøndelag	South and West	North
C.P.	Agriculture	−.41	−.32	−.23
	Fishery	−.27	−.04	−.07
Lab.	Agriculture	−.55	−.43	−.20
	Fishery	−.19	−.14	−.07
C.P.+ Lab. − Ind.	Agriculture	.31	.12	−.07
	Fishery	.45	.42	.56
Lib.	Agriculture	−.07	−.12	−.04
	Fishery	.02	.22	−.05
Chr.	Agriculture	.30	−.03	.04
	Fishery	.16	.26	.19
Agr.	Agriculture	.85	.85	.73
	Fishery	−.42	−.52	−.46
Cons.	Agriculture	−.54	−.18	−.16
	Fishery	.04	−.04	−.11

TABLE 8–24

*The Political Relevance of Variations in the Size of Units in Agriculture and
and Forestry: Correlations for the Three Middle Parties and the
"C.P. + Lab. − Ind." Score*

INLAND RURAL COMMUNES BY REGION

INDEPENDENT VARIABLES

Party or Score	Region	Mean Farm Size	Standard Deviation Farm Size	Mean Forest Size	Standard Deviation Forest Size
Lib.	ET	−.06	−.16	−.01	—.08
	SW	−.30	−.17	−.11	−.03
	N	−.05	.02	.06	.01
Chr.	ET	−.04	−.08	−.22	−.30
	SW	.01	.10	−.19	−.22
	N	−.01	.09	−.22	−.22
Agr.	ET	.33	.25	−.05	−.02
	SW	.46	.26	.00	.02
	N	.66	.49	.13	.14
CP+Lab.− Ind.	ET	−.07	−.03	.27	.29
	SW	−.13	−.23	.58	.57
	N	−.25	−.18	−.11	−.07

TABLE 8–25

The Primary Economy Basis of Party Strength: Inland Rural Communes.[1]
*Normalized Coefficients of Regression of Four Party Strength Variables
on Six Agriculture—Forestry Variables*

Party	Predictors	East and Trøndelag	South and West	North
Lib.	(2) Per cent of actives in agriculture	.162	—	—
	(3) Per cent of actives in forestry	−.272	−.370	—
	(4) Mean size of farm units	.191	−.364	—
	(5) Standard deviation of farm units	−.332	—	—
	(6) Mean size of forest units	.153	−.502	—
	(7) Standard deviation forest units	—	.679	—
Chr.	Per cent of actives in agriculture	.180	—	—
	Per cent of actives in forestry	—	—	—
	Mean size of farm units	−.106	—	—
	SD of farm units	—	—	—
	Mean size of forest units	.360	—	−.219
	SD of forest units	−.645	−.215	—
Agr.	Per cent of actives in agriculture	.731	.769	.376
	Per cent of actives in forestry	—	—	—
	Mean size of farm units	.268	.124	.495
	SD of farm units	—	—	—
	Mean size of forest units	—	—	−.196
	SD of forest units	.059	.099	
C.P.+	Per cent of actives in agriculture	.307	.349	.373
Lab.−	Per cent of actives in forestry	.524	.442	—
Ind.	Mean size of farm units	−.144	—	−.470
	SD of farm units	—	−.153	—
	Mean size of forest units	—	.226	—
	SD of forest units	.145	—	—

[1] See the definition used in Table 8–22.

Table 8–26

The Primary Economy Basis of Party Strength: Coastal Rural Communes.[1]
*Normalized Coefficient of Regression of Four Party Strength Variables
and Four Agriculture—Fishery Variables*

Party	Predictors	East and Trøndelag	South and West	North
Lib.	Per cent in agriculture	—	—	—
	Per cent in fishery, etc.	—	.158	—
	Mean farm size	—	−.213	—
	Standard deviation farm size	—	—	—
Chr.	Per cent in agriculture	.394	—	.243
	Per cent in fishery, etc.	.287	.333	.338
	Mean farm size	—	—	—
	SD farm size	—	.230	—
Agr	Per cent in agriculture	.794	.708	.519
	Per cent in fishery, etc.	—	−.104	—
	Mean farm size	.221	.170	.442
	SD farm size	—	—	−.174
C.P.+	Per cent in agriculture	.523	.484	.553
Lab.−	Per cent in fishery, etc.	.622	.625	.740
Ind.	Mean farm size	—	.192	−.246
	SD farm size	—	−.328	—

[1] In this table all communes are included in which the per cent in fishery and shipping was 1 or higher. It should be noticed that there is some overlap between the areas covered in Tables 8-25 and 8-26 since a number of communes have one per cent or more actives both in forestry and in fishery.

TABLE 8-27

Persistent Differences in Language, Values and Politics: Statistics for the Rural Districts of Each Region for

(a) choices of language for children in primary school
(b) membership in teetotalist organizations in 1923
(c) votes in the prohibition referendum in 1926
(d) votes for Moderates and Christians 1888-1961.

Region	Province	LANGUAGE[1] % of School Districts Using Landsmål/Nynorsk		TEMPERANCE		THE "CHRISTIAN" SHARE OF THE OLD LEFT[4] 1888		1945		1961	
		1910	1956/57	Teetotalists[2] per 1000 Adults 1923	Votes for prohibition[3] 1926	Left + Mod.	Mod. in % of L.+Mod.	Middle Parties	Chr.in % of Middle	Middle Parties	Chr.in % of Middle
Oslofjord		0	0	18.4	26.2	45.2	20.3	25.5	43.9	24.0	34.2
East Inl.		13.5	35.7	25.9	35.4	66.0	25.1	27.3	9.8	21.5	24.2
South	Tot.	28.8	48.5	79.4	74.8	68.7	53.0	47.7	—	48.7	34.8
	Aust-Agder	42.8	49.7	41.5	71.0	63.0	45.1	38.7	—	41.4	41.8
	Vest-Agder	18.5	47.5	112.8	79.2	73.4	58.7	56.4	—	54.9	30.4
West	Tot.	47.4	94.0	93.7	76.3	82.2	55.3	57.0	34.1	51.8	38.1
	Rogaland	23.7	85.8	71.6	81.3	84.8	75.4	42.4	29.4	54.2	36.7
	Hordaland	57.7	95.1	72.4	70.9	77.7	61.1	53.2	50.3	46.0	40.3
	Sogn og Fj.	57.8	99.8	104.4	71.4	77.0	55.6	52.1	—	51.5	29.2
	Møre og Romsd.	42.0	93.1	129.9	82.9	90.0	33.4	66.9	44.1	57.4	41.9
Trøndelag		14.2	42.9	82.8	60.8	65.3	11.9	41.2	16.8	36.3	27.7
North		4.4	13.1	33.9	53.2	77.9	20.2	17.4	—	25.5	36.3

[1] For 1910: *NOS* V. 218, Tab. 1, p.3. For 1956—57: *NOS* XI.344, Tab. 14, p.19. The 1910 table gives figures by *district* only while later statistics also indicate the *no. of children* in *nynorsk* schools. The national figures for 1956—57 were 49.0% of the districts, but only 33.5% of the children: the *nynorsk* districts are clearly less densely populated than the others.

[2] *NOS* VII.129, Tab. 29. These statistics were unfortunately discontinued after 1923, cf. *NOS* VII.196, p. 51x.

[3] *NOS* VIII.14, Tab. 29. The distributions for the first referendum in 1919 are of less interest in this context since the votes in the rural districts were so overwhelmingly for prohibition at that time:

Cities and towns			Rural communes		
	For	*Agst.*		*For*	*Agst.*
1919	44.5	55.5	1919	70.1	29.9
1926	30.3	69.7	1926	51.7	48.3

[4] The percentages for the Left, the Moderates/Christians and the Agrarians are calculated on the basis of *valid votes*, not on the basis of the total electorate.

TABLE 8–28

Estimated Proportions of Churchgoers and Dissenters by Region and Type of Commune

Types of communes distinguished:[1]

A: Cities, towns, suburbs
B: Rural, high density
C: Rural, low density, not periph., inland

D: Rural, low density, not periph., coastal
E: Peripheral
E1: Peripheral, largely inland
E2: Peripheral, largely coastal

		Electorate 1957 = 100%	Attendance Count '56: Estimated No. of Churchgoers in % of Electorate[2]	Dissenters[3] in % of Electorate
Oslofjord:	Tot	710,552	*6.0*	*6.6*
A[4]		522,885	3.8	6.7
B		22,261	7.9	6.7
C		98,688	12.3	6.3
D		66,718	12.8	6.6
East Inland:	Tot	434,699	*13.9*	*5.9*
A[5]		95,905	5.5	9.8
B		33,460	9.7	9.3
C		280,825	16.3	4.1
D		10,371	19.0	11.9
E		14,148	29.8	3.6
South:	Tot	117,877	*19.8*	*11.1*
A		41,037	13.5	13.1
B		17,329	11.5	10.7
C		16,815	32.7	12.0
D		31,457	20.4	9.7
E		11,239	34.5	6.5
West:	Tot	553,520	*14.5*	*3.4*
A[6]		218,578	4.6	5.0
B		36,255	12.9	2.6
C		86,477	20.6	1.8
D		169,934	20.2	3.0
E 1		18,336	36.3	1.2
E 2		27,940	25.6	1.2

[1] This classification of communes is based on (a) the standard typology used by the Central Bureau of Statistics for the 1950 census, (b) a score for "peripherality" constructed by the geographer A. Thormodsaeter (for details see S. Rokkan and H. Valen, "The Mobilization of the Periphery", *op. cit.*, p. 117) and (c) the per cent of actives in fishing and shipping. For five of the regions "inland" communes have less than 2.5% in fishing and shipping according to the 1950 census, "coastal" communes more than 2.5%. For the North the cut-point was set at 16.2%.

[2] Church attendance for each commune is here defined as the *total of average attendances* at each of the local places of worship controlled by the State Church. The averages are calculated from counts over ten weeks in the spring of 1956. The measure does not take into account variations in the average distance to places of worship or in the frequency of services and is difficult to interpret without controls of this kind.

[3] Data by commune received from the Central Bureau of Statistics (cf. the data by *parish* in *NOS*. XI.153). The assistance of Dr. Edvard Vogt in the preparation of these data for mechanical processing is gratefully acknowledged.

[4] Attendance data for 4 urban units with a total electorate of 10,769 are missing: they have been excluded from the table.

[5] Data for two urban units (electorate 2093) missing.

[6] Data for one urban unit (849) missing.

TABLE 8–28 (*continued*)

		Electorate 1957 = 100%	Attendance Count '56: Estimated No. of Churchgoers in % of Electorate[2]	Dissenters[3] in % of Electorate
Trøndelag:	Tot	208,236	*14.6*	*2.5*
	A	72,759	6.9	3.5
	B	12,390	14.7	1.1
	C	78,922	18.5	1.3
	D	21,928	18.8	4.0
	E 1	4,128	15.4	0.6
	E 2	18,109	23.4	3.0
North:	Tot	259,771	*17.3*	*4.8*
	A	47,007	5.6	4.5
	B	11,814	20.8	2.3
	C	26,663	10.9	2.4
	D	83,062	16.5	6.0
	E 1	24,503	26.9	3.5
	E 2	66,722	24.8	5.3

TABLE 8–29

Frequencies of Attendance at Church Services and Religious Meetings: Differences Between Six Regions of Norway Found in the 1957 Survey

| | | | | | REPORTED ATTENDANCE 1957 | | | |
Region	Sex of Respondent	N = 100%	(1) Attends Church, Attends Meetings %	(2) Church, Never Meetings	(3) Never Church, Attends Meetings	Total (1)+(2)+(3) Attends One or the Other %	(4) Never Church, Never Meetings	NA
Oslofjord	Tot.	478	6	8	9	24	67	9
	M	220	4	8	8	20	71	9
	W	258	8	9	10	27	64	9
East Inland	Tot.	298	6	12	7	26	69	5
	M	145	2	10	2	14	79	6
	W	153	11	14	12	37	59	4
South	Tot.	97	16	8	13	38	47	14
	M	46	17	7	9	33	52	15
	W	51	16	10	18	43	43	14
West	Tot.	324	10	12	10	32	61	7
	M	172	10	14	8	32	61	7
	W	152	10	10	12	32	61	7
Middle	Tot.	221	6	8	8	22	74	5
	M	112	7	7	3	17	79	5
	W	109	5	9	14	27	69	4
North	Tot.	128	7	9	11	27	72	1
	M	67	9	6	9	24	76	—
	W	61	5	13	13	31	67	2

The question was:
"How many times during the last month have you
a. been to church service?
b. been to religious meetings?
c. listened to a service on the radio?"
The marginal response distributions were:

	Never	Occasionally, Varies	1—3 Times Last Month	Every Sunday	More Frequently	NA, Other
Church	76%	2	16	1.5	0.5	4
Meetings	77%	2	13.5	1.5	1	5
Radio	17%	14	20	30	12	8

233

TABLE 8-30

Membership in Religious Associations: Survey Data for Differences Between Occupational Groups in the Two Contrasting Divisions of the Country

Region	Occupation of Head	Type of Locality	Sex	N = 100%	Member of State Church, No Assoc.	MEMBER OF RELIGIOUS ASSOCIATIONS			
						Mission Societies	Other, in State Church	Dissenter	NA
East Trøndelag, North	Worker	Tot.	M	281	90	4	3	2	1
			W	283	82	7	6	5	1
		Urban	M	111	91	1	3	3	2
			W	119	83	4	7	6	—
		Rural	M	170	88	6	3	2	1
			W	164	81	10	5	4	—
	Smallholder, farmer		M	87	92	5	—	2	—
			W	111	60	31	3	5	—
	Middle class		M	169	88	5	4	4	—
			W	167	81	7	5	5	1
South, West	Worker	Tot.	M	92	91	3	4	1	—
			W	86	74	13	8	5	—
		Urban	M	34	94	—	6	—	—
			W	43	88	2	9	2	—
		Rural	M	58	90	5	3	2	—
			W	43	60	23	7	9	—
	Smallholder, farmer		M	56	82	13	—	5	—
			W	55	45	45	3	5	2
	Middle class		M	69	84	9	1	4	1
			W	59	76	15	4	5	—

TABLE 8–31

Differences in Language Preference Between the Regions: Survey Data for 1957

QUESTION: WHICH LANGUAGE FORM DO YOU PREFER WHEN YOU WRITE?

			N = 100%	Riksmål	Bokmål[1]	Landsmål, Nynorsk	Other Answers[2]
Total Nationwide Sample[3]			*1546*	*65*	*19*	*12*	*4*
Oslofjord	Cities and urbanized areas	Total	364	77	17	—	6
		Working class	191	78	14	—	8
		Farmers, etc.	16	82	—	6	12
		Middle class	157	75	21	—	4
	Other rural	Total	101	67	17	4	12
		Working class	39	62	18	2	18
		Farmers, etc.	38	66	18	5	11
		Middle class	24	80	12	4	4
East Inland/ Trøndelag	Cities and urbanized areas	Total	213	82	14	2	2
		Working class	123	82	15	2	1
		Farmers, etc.	20	70	25	—	5
		Middle class	70	84	10	3	3
	Other rural	Total	293	69	18	10	3
		Working class	86	84	8	3	5
		Farmers, etc.	156	60	23	15	2
		Middle class	51	75	19	4	2
South, West	Cities and urbanized areas	Total	229	56	25	18	1
		Working class	113	60	23	17	—
		Farmers, etc.	23	39	4	57	—
		Middle class	93	56	32	11	1
	Other rural	Total	188	37	9	49	5
		Working class	52	41	13	45	1
		Farmers, etc.	101	36	7	51	6
		Middle class	35	35	11	48	5
North	Cities and urbanized areas	Total	40	68	30	2	—
	Other rural	Total	87	43	54	3	—
		Working class	28	47	50	3	—
		Farmers, etc.	47	43	55	2	—
		Middle class	12	33	59	8	—

[1] Includes 4 respondents stating they preferred "*samnorsk*".
[2] These were: 5 respondents: "a mixture," 6: "both forms," 3: "what I was taught at school," 13: "ordinary language," 36: NA and Refuse.
[3] The total sample of 1546 included 31 respondents for whom no previous or present occupation could be registered. The other 1515 have been grouped by the occupation (present or past) of the head of the household.

Language Form, Church Attendance and Politics: By Region and by the Proportion of Actives in Agriculture

| | | | RURAL COMMUNES ONLY | | | | | CHR. IN % OF | | |
| | | | PER CENT CAST FOR | | | | | | | |
Estimated Church att.	No. of Comm.	No. of Votes Cast 1957 = 100%	Socialists	Middle Parties	Cons.	Polarization Score	Lib.+Chr.	Middle Party Total	All Non-Soc.
East, Trøndelag, North									
35% or less in agriculture									
Bokmål									
All	174	473,588	60.9	21.8	17.3	.85	57.0	35.4	19.7
High	50	66,736	60.3	27.0	12.7	.82	64.1	38.5	26.2
Low	124	406,852	61.0	21.0	18.0	.86	55.6	34.1	18.7
Mixed									
All	44	85,709	58.2	29.8	12.0	.80	54.7	32.0	22.9
High	16	16,351	53.3	34.3	12.4	.74	58.2	38.3	28.1
Low	28	69,358	59.4	28.7	11.9	.81	53.6	30.3	21.4
Nynorsk									
All	7	10,185	61.7	32.6	5.7	.80	49.4	25.3	21.5
High	3	2,436	54.4	39.6	6.0	.73	44.4	25.3	22.0
Low	4	7,749	63.9	30.4	5.7	.82	51.8	25.3	21.4
More than 35% in agriculture									
Bokmål									
All	76	103,352	50.6	39.3	10.1	.79	67.6	27.3	21.7
High	35	33,390	52.1	38.8	9.1	.80	61.8	24.5	19.9
Low	41	69,962	49.9	39.5	10.6	.79	70.3	28.6	22.5
Mixed									
All	53	68,701	49.4	43.5	7.1	.76	58.6	23.8	20.5
High	37	41,664	48.1	45.5	6.4	.76	57.9	21.9	19.2
Low	16	27,037	51.4	40.4	8.2	.77	70.9	29.3	24.0
Nynorsk									
All	51	57,115	49.4	45.6	5.0	.75	50.9	20.7	18.6
High	32	31,782	46.8	47.6	5.6	.73	55.9	22.9	20.5
Low	19	25,333	52.5	43.3	4.2	.77	44.1	17.7	16.1

TABLE 8–32 (continued)

RURAL COMMUNES ONLY

| | | | PER CENT CAST FOR | | | | CHR. IN % OF | | |
Estimated Church att.	No. of Comm.	No. of Votes Cast 1957 = 100%	Socialists	Middle Parties	Cons.	Polarization Score	Lib. + Chr.	Middle Party Total	All Non-Soc.
South, West									
35% or less in agriculture									
Bokmål									
All	24	41,522	45.5	39.9	14.6	.64	40.8	34.6	25.4
High	11	11,842	42.6	45.3	12.1	.60	47.5	37.8	29.8
Low	13	29,680	46.5	37.9	15.6	.65	37.9	33.1	23.4
Mixed									
All	30	83,827	44.5	41.5	14.0	.64	48.9	39.4	29.5
High	9	12,728	37.8	53.4	8.8	.53	61.9	48.6	41.7
Low	21	71,099	45.8	39.3	14.9	.66	45.8	37.1	26.9
Nynorsk									
All	61	93,537	38.3	54.1	7.6	.51	56.6	46.0	40.3
High	30	35,174	31.2	61.4	7.4	.43	57.0	48.5	43.3
Low	31	58,363	42.5	49.7	7.8	.56	56.2	44.1	38.2
More than 35% in agriculture									
Bokmål									
All	9	6,010	22.7	60.1	17.2	.50	41.2	27.9	21.7
High	8	3,815	23.6	61.6	14.8	.50	40.2	25.2	20.3
Low	1	2,195	21.2	57.5	21.3	.49	42.8	33.0	24.1
Mixed									
All	19	17,833	28.3	63.2	8.5	.51	49.4	28.1	24.8
High	14	10,787	29.6	62.9	7.5	.52	46.2	24.9	22.3
Low	5	7,046	26.3	63.6	10.1	.48	53.6	33.0	28.5
Nynorsk									
All	132	103,698	26.6	65.7	7.7	.49	56.7	31.2	27.9
High	95	73,469	27.3	64.9	7.8	.50	55.4	30.2	27.0
Low	37	30,229	25.0	67.7	7.3	.46	59.7	33.5	30.3

237

TABLE 8-33

Party Preference and Religious Membership: Differences Between Members and Others Within Major Occupational Groups in the Two Divisions of the Country

Region	Occupation	Religious Affiliation	N = 100%	INTENDED VOTE 1957 (%)				CHR. IN % OF		
				Socialist	Middle Party	Cons.	Unclear, Uncertain, Non-Voter	Lib. + Chr.	Middle	All Non-Soc.
East, Trøndelag, North	Worker	Member	74	43	19	8	30	79	55	55
		Not member	486	67	6	6	21	45	36	17
	Primary independent (farmer, fisherman)	Member	51	22	55	8	16	85	39	34
		Not member	147	36	27	10	28	40	10	8
	Middle class	Member	49	16	33	20	30	93	62	62
		Not member	285	29	11	37	24	52	47	10
South, West	Worker	Member	30	33	27	7	33	83	63	50
		Not member	148	50	17	6	28	41	29	21
	Primary independent	Member	39	5	67	5	23	67	31	29
		Not member	71	11	56	7	25	38	15	13
	Middle class	Member	24	8	45	21	26	80	73	50
		Not member	103	16	27	25	32	12	11	5

TABLE 8–34

Differences in Party Preference Between High-Frequent and Low-Frequent Participants in Religious Activities: By Region, Type of Locality and Sex

Region	Type of Locality	Frequency of Attendance at Services/Meetings[1]	Sex	N = 100%	INTENDED VOTE 1957[2] Socialist (%)	Middle	Cons.	Lib. + Chr.	CHR. IN % OF Middle	All Non-Soc.
ETN	Cities	Higher	M	21	29	20	24	50	50	29
			W	40	30	20	15	100	100	57
		Lower	M	170	57	5	20	50	38	7
			W	178	44	8	26	42	40	10
	Rural	Higher	M	40	35	38	10	89	66	52
			W	61	33	34	7	88	68	56
		Lower	M	280	54	14	12	50	29	18
			W	261	46	15	10	42	20	12
SW	Cities	Higher	M	21	0	77%	10	64	56	50
			W	21	33	24	19	80	79	44
		Lower	M	75	42	18	20	27	22	11
			W	64	34	17	16	14	12	6
	Rural	Higher	M	25	36	32	8	83	63	50
			W	25	16	36	8	86	67	55
		Lower	M	78	27	39	12	18	8	6
			W	71	17	44	0	30	14	14

[1] The "Higher" attenders are those who stated they went to a church service *or* a religious meeting *at least twice* a month. For questions and marginal response distributions, see Table 8–29.

[2] Percentages do not add up to 100 since the figures for non-voters and uncertains have not been entered in the table.

239

TABLE 8-35

The Three Cultural Indicators and the Vote

Data for the Stavanger area on the impact of language commitment, religious activity and stand on the temperance issue on the vote: by occupation

Language	Religious Activity[1]	Temperance Stand[2]	WORKING CLASS							FARMERS AND MIDDLE CLASS						
			N = 100%	Soc.	Lib.	Chr.	Agr.	Cons.	Other	N = 100%	Soc.	Lib.	Chr.	Agr.	Cons.	Other
Bokmål	High	Yes	175	47%	11	13	1	4	24	106	9%	31	21	9	16	14
		No	76	63%	11	1	0	11	14	77	10%	32	3	12	30	13
	Low	Yes	52	83%	2	0	0	4	11	39	20%	18	10	8	18	26
		No	123	72%	10	1	0	4	13	103	29%	21	1	4	33	11
Nynorsk	High	Yes	46	33%	13	30	11	0	13	63	3%	21	25	38	0	13
		No	12	5	(2)	(1)	(1)	(1)	(2)	19	11%	10	5	53	16	5
	Low	Yes	8	(2)	(1)	0	(4)		(1)	18	0%	28	6	55	0	11
		No	20	50%	10	0	15	5	20	15	20%	13	0	47	7	13

[1] Index based on church attendance, attendance at religious meetings, listening to religious services on the radio, membership in religious associations. The maximum score was 8. In the table, the "low" category scored 0 or 1.

[2] Respondents classified on the basis of responses to the question "Regner De Dem som avholdsmann?" ("Do you consider yourself a temperance man?")

TABLE 8-36

Differences in the Levels of Politicization Between Central and Peripheral, Inland and Coastal Communes at the Elections of 1947, 1951, 1955 and 1959: West and North Only

Levels of politicization distinguished:
- 0 — No nationally registered parties in election
- 1 — Only one such party list
- 2—N — Two or more party lists, also non-party votes
- 2—P — Only party lists.

	No. of comm. '47—'55 =100%	1947				1951				1955				No. of comm. 1959 =100%	1959			
		0	1	2—N	2—P	0	1	2—N	2—P	0	1	2—N	2—P		0	1	2—N	2—P
West																		
Cities, towns, suburbs	16	—	—	38%	62	—	—	19%	81	—	—	6%	94	15	—	—	13	87
Other urbanized	11	—	26%	37	37	—	18%	36	46	—	18%	46	36	11	—	9%	55	36
Non-periphery, inland	47	10%	6	39	45	6%	13	34	47	6%	13	30	51	45	6%	9	36	49
Non-periphery, coast	100	28%	22	31	19	25%	27	34	14	28%	28	38	16	100	25%	18	45	12
Periphery, inland	17	17%	5	48	30	24%	12	29	35	17%	12	23	48	17	23%	—	47	30
Periphery, coast	27	49%	11	18	22	46%	18	18	18	30%	22	18	18	27	24%	24	32	20
North																		
Cities, towns, suburbs	12	—	—	33%	67	—	—	33%	67	—	—	25%	75	12	—	—	33%	67
Other urbanized	4	—	—	25%	75	—	—	75%	25	—	—	75%	25	4	—	—	50%	50
Non-periphery, inland	11	—	9%	27	64	—	—	18%	82	—	18%	18	64	11	—	27%	27	46
Non-periphery, coast	33	9%	9	61	21	3%	6	64	27	3%	15	64	18	33	6%	12	58	24
Periphery, inland	18	22%	17	44	17	11%	17	56	17	6%	11	67	17	18	6%	11	56	28
Periphery, coast	49	8%	18	43	31	12%	18	41	29	16%	10	51	23	49	18%	20	35	27

Note: The communes have been grouped as in Table 8-28.

TABLE 8-37

Nationally Registered Parties in Local Elections: Differences Between Central, and Peripheral, Inland and Coastal Communes at Local Elections 1947-1959: West and North Only

NUMBER OF NATIONALLY REGISTERED PARTIES NOMINATING LISTS

	No. of comm. = 100%	1947			1951			1955			1959		
		Q_1	Md	Q_3	Q_1	Md	Q_3	Q_1	Md	Q_3	Q_1	Md	Q_3
West													
Cities, towns, suburbs	16(15)	4.0	4.5	5.0	3.7	4.4	4.9	3.8	4.4	4.9	3.9	4.5	5.1
Other urbanized	11	0.9	2.5	3.6	1.4	2.8	4.4	1.8	3.3	4.3	2.8	4.1	4.7
Non-periphery, inland	47(45)	1.2	1.8	3.1	1.2	2.2	3.2	1.5	2.7	3.9	2.2	3.5	4.4
Non-periphery, coastal	100	0.0	1.0	2.8	0.0	0.9	2.7	0.0	1.3	2.9	0.0	1.6	3.4
Periphery, inland	17	1.3	1.8	2.9	0.1	1.8	2.9	0.6	2.1	3.0	1.1	2.1	3.0
Periphery, coastal	27(25)	0.0	0.2	2.3	0.6	0.3	1.8	0.0	1.3	2.5	0.1	1.3	3.0
North													
Cities, towns, suburbs	12	3.2	3.5	3.8	3.3	3.6	4.0	3.2	3.8	4.4	3.3	3.8	4.7
Other urbanized	4	3.0	3.0	3.0	3.0	3.0	3.5	3.0	3.5	4.0	3.0	4.0	5.0
Non-periphery, inland	11	1.6	2.4	3.1	1.7	2.3	2.9	1.8	2.5	3.3	0.9	4.5	4.5
Non-periphery, coastal	33	1.3	2.2	2.9	1.5	2.3	3.2	1.6	2.5	3.4	1.8	2.7	4.0
Periphery, inland	18	0.2	1.4	2.3	0.8	2.0	2.6	1.5	2.3	2.8	1.5	2.3	2.8
Periphery, coastal	49	0.9	1.5	2.2	0.7	1.5	2.2	0.1	1.7	2.5	0.3	1.4	2.4

Note: the communes have been grouped as in Table 8-36.
The Ns in parentheses refer to 1959.

242

Table 8–38

Local Politicization and National Party Strength: Comparisons for 1947–49 and 1955–57 for the West and the North.[1] *Low-density Rural Communes Only*

RESULTS FOR SUBSEQUENT NATIONAL ELECTION

PER CENT VOTES FOR

Level of Politicization[2]	Year	Electorate = 100%	Soc.	Lib.	Chr.	Agr.	Cons.	Polarization Score
West								
Inland[3] *1947*	*1949*							
0		6,865	13.6	17.4	24.3	15.0	8.1	.34
1		5,855	18.1	21.8	24.1	12.5	4.6	.33
2—N		51,290	24.8	17.5	9.1	19.8	7.4	.55
2—P		38,676	29.7	14.6	13.7	12.6	6.7	.56
1955	*1957*							
0		4,492	13.6	10.4	13.2	30.6	4.8	.44
1		12,105	18.2	11.3	17.2	25.0	5.9	.46
2—N		32,200	27.0	10.1	13.3	18.9	5.7	.58
2—P		56,016	27.5	9.5	11.5	19.4	6.2	.62
Coast *1947*	*1949*							
0		50,739	15.4	23.3	20.9	7.2	8.0	.35
1		30,458	19.0	20.8	26.3	3.8	5.9	.35
2—N		67,796	24.7	19.0	17.3	5.6	7.5	.47
2—P		38,558	26.5	18.6	17.6	5.5	7.2	.48
1955	*1957*							
0		37,129	14.1	15.9	23.2	11.9	5.1	.33
1		37,398	18.1	14.8	20.1	8.4	6.0	.41
2—N		89,129	24.1	13.5	18.1	8.9	6.5	.49
2—P		30,218	27.9	12.5	14.4	10.1	7.1	.57
North								
Inland[3] *1947*	*1949*							
0		1,314	18.9	19.4	0.8	—	8.7	.58
1		4,123	40.3	12.4	3.3	—	11.9	.78
2—N		2,702	45.7	7.6	4.2	13.2	5.7	.81
2—P		20,280	53.5	6.2	4.3	5.3	5.8	.85

[1] This table serves primarily to establish the regularities in the *direction* of the differences in party strength between communes at different levels of politicization. The actual percentages cannot be compared across the pairs of election years because of changes in the *party alternatives* set for the voters at the national elections. These deviations from straight six-party contests occurred on the two occasions analyzed here:

	1949	1957
West (four province constituencies)	*Chr.* no list in Sogn og Fjordane. *Agr.* no list in Møre og Ro. Joint list *Agr./Cons.* in Rogaland.	*CP* no list in Sogn og Fjordane.
North (three province constituencies)	*Chr.* no list in Finnmark. *Agr.* no list in Troms and Finnmark	*Agr.* no list in Finnmark. Joint list *Lib.–Cons.* in Finnmark.

[2] For notation see Table 8–36.

[3] "Inland" communes: less than 2.5% of the actives in fisheries and shipping by the 1950 census.

Table 8–38 (continued)

RESULTS FOR SUBSEQUENT NATIONAL ELECTION

PER CENT VOTES FOR

Level of Politicization[2]	Year	Electorate = 100%	Soc.	Lib.	Chr.	Agr.	Cons.	Polarization Score
1955	*1957*							
0		734	25.2	8.0	2.5	9.0	17.2	.80
1		4,833	29.9	7.1	4.9	10.5	6.2	.75
2—N		5,339	43.8	3.3	4.0	11.9	8.9	.88
2—P		20,193	50.9	4.0	4.2	8.3	5.3	.87
Coast *1947*	*1949*							
0		10,635	35.0	6.3	6.6	2.4	9.7	.78
1		14,799	42.5	6.7	5.0	2.0	7.6	.81
2—N		97,254	41.1	7.4	5.2	2.2	8.3	.80
2—P		45,559	35.8	8.4	6.6	3.9	9.2	.75
1955	*1957*							
0		10,155	35.3	4.7	8.4	4.1	7.7	.77
1		11,758	38.9	3.7	6.3	6.7	10.2	.83
2—N		110,714	38.7	5.2	9.3	7.1	8.8	.80
2—P		37,224	36.4	6.4	6.6	6.3	8.3	.77

TABLE 8-39

The Mobilization of Opinion Against EEC Entry: Differences Between the Major Regions of Norway in September 1961 and February 1962 (Data from Surveys Carried out by Norsk Gallup)

Party	Region	SEPTEMBER 1961 N= 100%	Not Heard or Read abt. EEC	Heard/Read abt. EEC N=100%	For EEC	Against EEC	DK	FEBRUARY 1962 N= 100%	Not Heard or Read abt. EEC	Heard/Read abt. EEC N=100%	For EEC	Against EEC	DK	INCREASES SEPT.–FEB. (1) in % Stating Preference	(2) in % Against EEC	Difference (1)–(2)
CP+ SP	Tot.	38	16	32	19	78	3	68	7	62	13	81	6	6	9	− 3
Lab.	Tot.	889	35	575	34	17	49	754	17	618	44	27	29	26	13	+13
	E	471	34	313	36	13	52	390	21	306	46	26	28	25	12	+13
	SW	226	44	126	38	29	33	195	11	171	42	30	28	26	11	+15
	TN	192	29	136	26	18	56	169	16	141	45	27	28	29	10	+19
Lib.	Tot.	140	17	116	31	17	52	120	7	110	33	45	22	33	28	+ 5
	ETN	74	20	59	22	17	61	47	9	43	23	58	17	43	39	+ 4
	SW	66	14	57	40	18	42	73	6	67	39	37	24	21	20	+ 1
Chr.	Tot.	106	42	62	23	19	58	139	15	116	25	36	39	28	20	+ 8
	ETN	55	29	39	28	10	62	79	10	69	32	28	40	27	18	+ 9
	SW	51	55	23	13	35	52	60	22	47	15	49	36	28	22	+ 6
Agr.	Tot.	132	17	110	36	22	43	125	11	111	32	49	19	24	26	− 2
	E	41	17	34	44	12	44	57	11	51	35	51	14	31	35	− 4
	SW	51	8	47	32	34	34	39	3	38	18	63	19	18	30	−12
	TN	40	28	29	31	14	55	29	24	22	50	18	32	20	4	+16
Cons.	Tot.	233	21	185	46	12	42	278	6	258	59	17	24	25	7	+18
	E	143	18	117	47	7	46	179	8	164	59	13	28	22	6	+16
	SW	41	20	33	42	27	30	62	5	58	60	28	12	29	5	+24
	TN	49	29	35	46	17	37	37	0	36	56	17	27	11	5	+ 6

245

TABLE 8-40

The Mobilization of Opinion Against the EEC 1961–1962: Differences by Region and Type of Locality

Region	Locality	SEPTEMBER 1961					FEBRUARY 1962						INCREASES SEPT.–FEB.		
		N= 100%	Not Heard/ Read abt. EEC	Heard or Read abt. EEC For	Against	DK	N= 100%	Not Heard/ Read abt. EEC	N= 100%	Heard or Read abt. EEC For	Against	DK	(1) in % Stating Preference	(2) in % Against EEC	Difference (1)–(2)
East	Tot.	1034	29	37	15	48	1040	16	859	39	31	30	22	15	+ 7
	Larger cities	357	26	34	14	52	311	12	270	44	30	26	29	15	+14
	Other cities	103	33	52	12	36	166	11	147	35	29	36	14	18	– 4
	Rural aggl.	200	19	37	18	45	140	33	92	37	40	23	7	12	– 5
	Sparsely pop.	374	37	35	16	49	423	17	350	37	30	33	24	15	+ 9
South and West	Tot.	555	35	36	26	38	605	12	523	33	37	30	22	16	+ 6
	Larger cities	107	33	40	19	41	98	13	84	35	40	25	25	22	+ 3
	Other cities	85	41	62	24	14	86	13	74	46	34	20	19	16	+ 3
	Rural aggl.	111	44	45	37	18	90	4	84	31	35	34	27	13	+14
	Sparsely pop.	252	31	24	25	51	331	13	281	30	38	32	25	16	+ 9
Trondelag and North	Tot.	420	30	32	17	51	405	15	338	40	30	30	26	14	+12
	Larger/other cities	68	22	36	15	49	70	0	70	47	20	33	27	21	+ 6
	Rural aggl.	114	39	43	7	50	96	10	86	45	26	29	33	19	+14
	Sparsely pop.	238	27	26	21	53	239	22	182	35	36	29	25	15	+10

TABLE 8–41

The Mobilization of Opinion Against the EEC 1961–62: Differences by Occupation and/or Type of Locality Within Each Major Party (Data from Norsk Gallup)

Party	Occup. of Head	Locality	SEPTEMBER 1961 Not Heard/Read abt. EEC N= / 100%	SEPTEMBER 1961 Heard/Read abt. EEC N=	For	Against	DK	FEBRUARY 1962 Not Heard/Read abt. EEC N= / 100%	FEBRUARY 1962 Heard/Read abt. EEC N=	For	Against	DK	INCREASES (1) in % Stating Preference	(2) in % Against EEC	Difference (1)-(2)
Lab.	Worker	Cities, — largest	150 / 39	92	32	18	50	94 / 11	84	37	30	33	29	16	+13
		— other	66 / 48	34	41	24	35	87 / 16	72	54	29	17	36	12	+24
		Rural aggl.	179 / 38	111	40	12	48	84 / 14	72	40	18	42	18	8	+10
		Sparsely pop.	274 / 36	175	31	21	48	264 / 26	194	43	30	27	21	9	+12
	Salaried	Urban	46 / 22	36	47	3	50	59 / 7	54	50	28	22	34	24	+10
	Indep. nonagr.	Urban	56 / 27	41	34	19	47	124 / 13	107	44	15	41	12	−1	+13
	Indep. nonagr.	Rural	64 / 28	46	33	9	58	43 / 14	37	43	35	22	37	24	+13
	Farmers, fisherm.	Rural	54 / 26	40	15	30	55	47 / 21	37	46	38	16	33	8	+25
Lib.		Largest cities	34 / 12	30	47	7	46	22 / 9	20	25	55	20	25	44	−19
		Other urb., rural aggl.	40 / 25	30	60	13	28	55 / 18	44	34	36	30	2	20	−18
		Sparsely pop.	66 / 14	56	7	25	68	53 / 9	46	35	50	15	49	24	+25
Chr.		Urban, rural aggl.	40 / 38	25	24	24	52	57 / 16	48	40	37	23	35	16	+19
		Sparsely pop.	66 / 44	37	22	16	62	82 / 15	68	15	35	50	22	21	+1
Agr.	Farmers		99 / 13	86	30	23	47	92 / 8	85	25	53	22	26	29	−3
	Others		33 / 27	24	54	17	29	33 / 21	26	58	35	7	21	16	+5
Cons.	Worker, salaried,	Urban	98 / 18	80	49	8	43	113 / 5	106	65	13	22	27	5	+22
	Indep.	Urban	45 / 33	30	37	17	46	46 / 7	42	60	12	28	31	0	+31
	Worker, salaried	Rural	47 / 13	41	44	10	46	80 / 4	77	55	19	26	24	9	+15
	Indep.	Rural	43 / 21	34	50	24	26	39 / 13	33	45	30	25	7	7	0

THREE

The Party and the Polity

9

AN AUTHORITARIAN REGIME: SPAIN

JUAN J. LINZ

I

TYPES OF POLITICAL SYSTEMS

THIS PAPER attempts to conceptualize some differences between political systems, taking the present Spanish regime as example and point of departure. In the decades since World War II, the distinction elaborated by political scientists between democratic governments and totalitarian societies has proven useful scientifically and even more polemically. The terms democratic and totalitarian have come to be used as dichotomous or at least as a continuum. An effort is made to fit various regimes into one or the other type, often basing the decision on nonscientific criteria. While the classification has been useful, it is increasingly necessary to go beyond it. From the beginning social scientists have felt uneasy about placing countries like Spain, and even Fascist Italy or pre-1945 Japan, into the totalitarian category. The uneasiness has grown as they came to deal with the "progressive" one-party regimes of the underdeveloped areas and the "modernizing" military dictatorships. So for example A. Inkeles remarks on

. . . a mode of analysis which can encompass totalitarian systems as divergent in their concrete institutional structure as the Communist and Nazi systems, which

Reprinted from *Cleavages, Ideologies and Party Systems*, edited by Erik Allardt and Yrjö Littunen (Helsinki: The Westermarck Society, 1964). The research on which this paper is based has been supported by the Committee for Comparative Politics of the Social Science Research Council. I am grateful for the editorial assistance of Candace Rogers. I want to thank the Center for Advanced Study in the Behavioral Sciences for the use of their facilities.

Notes to this chapter are on pp. 374–381.

most closely approximate the ideal type; Fascist Italy, which only imperfectly approximated it; and Franco Spain which only imperfectly fits the model in a few crucial respects.[1]

Even a correspondent like Herbert Matthews, far from friendly to the Spanish regime, writes:

> The power (of Franco) is almost unlimited. This does not make Spain a totalitarian country in either the Communist or the Fascist sense. It is an authoritarian country. The authority is exercised by keeping all parts of the regime weak or in conflict with each other. Order is kept essentially because the Spanish people want it, and through the Army and police. This makes Franco's power supreme when he wants to exercise it. Since, like all modern dictators, he does not allow any single man or group to become strong and threaten his power, there is no alternative to Francisco Franco, at least no visible alternative. As long as his position is not attacked and the nation's affairs function smoothly, he keeps hands off.[2]

Raymond Aron faced the same problem after characterizing the constitutional pluralist regimes and the regimes *de parti monopoliste*, when he wrote about a "third class of regime where there is no single party nor multiple parties, not based on electoral legitimacy nor on revolutionary legitimacy,"[3] giving as examples Portugal, Spain and the first phase of Vichy.

Gabriel Almond, in his important article on comparative political systems, has formulated most clearly some main characteristics of this type of regime which we shall call authoritarian; the term is used by many in this connection, even by spokesmen of such regimes. Almond writes:

> (The totalitarian political structure) is anti-pluralistic in intent and method if not in accomplishment . . . Recent developments in the Soviet Union seem to be directed toward providing some explicit structural bases for policy discussion and conflict . . . But what has so far been attained . . . is far from the structural pluralism which is so typical for authoritarian regimes. If one takes such a system as that of Spain it is evident that religious bodies, organized interests, status groups, bureaucratic agencies, as well as the Falange party are "acknowledged" elements in a pluralistic political structure. Interest conflict is built into the system, and is not merely latent and spasmodic as in the totalitarian pattern.
>
> The structures of the two systems differ in a second significant respect. The totalitarian system tends to be highly mobilized, tense and expansive internally and externally. The authoritarian tends to be more stable, more relaxed, although these are differences in degree.[4]

It could be argued that there is no need for a new type—the authoritarian—since regimes so described are really imperfect forms of either totalitarian or democratic polities, tending ultimately in one or the other direction and close, at least in their ideals, to one or the other pole. Failure to reach the totalitarian stage might be due to administrative inefficiency, economic underdevelopment, or external influences and pressures. In regimes approving in principle a Western "progressive" conception of democracy—like the

Mexican or Turkish leadership after their national revolutions—failure might be attributed to economic backwardness and religious traditionalism. To formulate it as sociologists, we might say that when certain functional prerequisites for a stable democracy are absent, some form of authoritarianism is established, in order—presumably—to prepare the country for it; or in other cases a premature transition to democracy leads to a setback in the form of an authoritarian regime. From another angle, we might say that certain characteristics of the social structure make it impossible for those in power to move toward true totalitarianism without endangering their own position. This hypothesis assumes that those in power are deliberately pursuing a totalitarian social order, which strictly speaking may not be the case even for some stages in a transition which actually results in a totalitarian society.

We prefer for purposes of analysis to reject the idea of a continuum from democracy to totalitarianism and to stress the distinctive nature of authoritarian regimes. Unless we examine the features unique to them, the conditions under which they emerge, the conceptions of power held by those who shape them, regimes which are not clearly either democratic or totalitarian will be treated merely as deviations from these ideal types and will not be studied systematically and comparatively.

Like any ideal type, the notion of the authoritarian regime is an abstraction which underlines certain characteristics and ignores, at least for the time being, the fluidity of reality, differences in degree, and contradictory tendencies present in the real world. In any of the European regimes of the interwar years that we would call authoritarian, Fascist elements played a role and significant minorities were striving for a totalitarian state; the Hungary of Horthy, the colonels' regime in Poland, the Rumanian and Yugoslav royal dictatorships, the Portuguese Estado Novo, the Austrian corporative Dollfuss regime, Vichy, are examples. Today the model of the Soviet Union operates similarly in many underdeveloped areas. Such regimes exist under many formal garments and their lack of an elaborate and consistent ideology makes them particularly susceptible to mimicry.[5]

The external forms of the thirties and forties, the uniforms and ceremonies and terminology, and the appeals of today to democratic or socialist values, are more easily assimilated than the institutional realities they represent. We may be seriously misled if we study such regimes through constitutions, laws, speeches, the writing of unknown and unrewarded "ideologists," without inquiring how these are actually translated into social reality. The laws may say, for example, that everyone has to be a member of certain organizations, but later almost nobody is; the law gives the corporative system a monopoly of interest representation, but a study of businessmen shows that they belong to literally hundreds of autonomous interest groups which existed before the regime came to power; a political indoctrination course is provided for in the universities but it turns out to be a course in labor and welfare institutions, and everyone is allowed to pass.

The utility of treating authoritarian regimes as a distinct type will lie in helping us understand the distinctive ways in which they resolve problems common to all political systems: maintaining control and gaining legitimacy, recruiting elites, articulating interests and aggregating them, making decisions and relating to various institutional spheres like the armed forces, religious bodies, the intelligentsia, the economy, etc. If we can find that they handle such problems differently from both democratic and totalitarian regimes, and furthermore if quite different regimes, classified as authoritarian, handle them in ways that turn out to be similar, the distinction will have been justified. Later we will explore in some detail a few examples along these lines.

Before defining an authoritarian regime, let us refer briefly to the conceptions of democracy and totalitarianism from which we start in our comparative analysis. This is particularly important since many authoritarian systems claim to be "organic," "basic," "selective" or "guided" democracies, or at least to govern for the people, if not in fact to be "people's" democracies. We consider a government democratic if it supplies regular constitutional opportunities for peaceful competition for political power (and not just a share of it) to different groups without excluding any significant sector of the population by force. This definition is based on those of Schumpeter, Aron and Lipset,[6] with the addition of the last qualification to include censitary regimes of the nineteenth century, democracies in which the vote has been denied to some groups, but with real competition for support from a limited electorate. As long as new claimants to suffrage were not suppressed forcibly for more than a limited time, we can consider such regimes democratic.

As Schumpeter has stressed, the element of competition for votes makes the whole gamut of civil liberties necessary, since without them there could be no true free competition; this is the link between classical liberalism and democracy. It could be argued that authoritarian regimes, even preconstitutional monarchies, have or had certain civil liberties, but we would not call them democracies for this reason. To give an example in recent years, legalization of a right to strike—perhaps not under that name—has been discussed in Spain, particularly since de facto strikes are tolerated and government officials participate in the negotiations between workers and employers despite their illegality. Similarly, the courts have assumed quite extensive control over administrative acts through the Law of Administrative Procedure, following the model of continental European administrative law and jurisprudence. Many elements of the Reichstat are not incompatible with an authoritarian state and perhaps not even with a "secularized" totalitarian state. However, full civil liberties, including an unlimited right of association and assembly, for example, inevitably create pressures toward political democracy. In this sense, against a strong tradition in continental political theory, we can say that liberalism and democracy are inseparable.

In defining totalitarianism we also want to limit the term somewhat and reserve it for the unique new forms autocratic government has taken since World War I, without denying that similar tendencies existed in the past. Perhaps Kornhauser's characterization is as good as any other, even if it overstresses somewhat the arbitrary aspects, when he writes:

Totalitarian dictatorship involves total domination, limited neither by received laws or codes (as in traditional authoritarianism) nor even the boundaries of governmental functions (as in classical tyranny), since they obliterate the distinction between State and society. Totalitarianism is limited only by the need to keep large numbers of people in a state of constant activity controlled by the elite.[7]

C. J. Friedrich's well-known definition[8] includes the following five clusters of characteristics: an official ideology, often with chiliastic elements; a single mass party unquestioningly dedicated to the ideology, near complete control of mass media, complete political control of the armed forces, and a system of terroristic police control not directed against demonstrable enemies only. In another version central control and direction of the economy is added. This more descriptive definition provides a clearer yardstick, although in view of recent developments I would not give as much emphasis to the role of the police and terror.[9]

DEFINITION OF AN AUTHORITARIAN REGIME

Authoritarian regimes are political systems with limited, not responsible, political pluralism: without elaborate and guiding ideology (but with distinctive mentalities); without intensive nor extensive political mobilization (except some points in their development); and in which a leader (or occasionally a small group) exercises power within formally ill-defined limits but actually quite predictable ones.

To avoid any confusion we want to make it clear that personal leadership is a frequent characteristic but not a necessary one, since a junta arrangement can exist and the leader's personality might not be the decisive factor. Furthermore, the leader does not need to have charismatic qualities, at least not for large segments of the population nor at all stages of development of the system. In fact he may combine elements of charismatic, legal and traditional authority in varying degrees, often at different points in time—though the charismatic element often tends to be more important than the legal authority, at least for some sectors of the population.

PLURALISM

We speak of regime, rather than government, to indicate the relatively low specificity of the political institutions: they often penetrate the life of the society, preventing, even forcibly, the political expression of certain group interests (as religion in Turkey and Mexico, labor in Spain) or shaping them by interventionist economic policies. But in contrast to some of the analysts of totalitarianism, such as Inkeles, we speak of regimes rather than societies because the distinction between state and society is not obliterated. The pluralistic element is the most distinctive feature of these regimes, but let us emphasize that in contrast to democracies with their almost unlimited pluralism, we deal here with *limited* pluralism. The limitation may be legal or de facto, serious or less so, confined to strictly political groups or extended to interest groups, as long as there remain groups not created by nor dependent on the state which influence the political process one way or another. Some regimes even institutionalize the political participation of a limited number of independently existing groups or institutions, and actually encourage their emergence. To take an example, when Primo de Rivera created his National Assembly he provided for the representation of the church, cultural institutions, the nobility, the army and the business community, as well as the newly created party; at the same time he encouraged the creation of economic interest groups that have been the pressure groups of Spanish business ever since.[10][11] Another example is the institutionalization of a complex pluralism in the officially dominant Partido Revolucionario Institucional of Mexico, that prompts V. Padgett to write: "An 'official' party need not necessarily be an instrument of imposition. It may be a device for bridging the gap between authoritarianism and representative democracy."[12] With such a limited but relatively autonomous pluralism, there is likely to be some competition for power, more or less informal, despite open declarations of monopoly. It is quite characteristic in this respect that the Falange, after entering the Franco coalition, dropped Point 27, which read:

> We shall work to triumph in the struggle with only the forces subject to our discipline. We shall make very few pacts. Only in the final push for the conquest of the state will the command arrange for the necessary collaborations, always provided that our predominance be assured.[13]

This pluralism contrasts with the strong domination, if not the monopoly, imposed by the totalitarian party after conquering power; its penetration, through the process the Nazis called Gleichschaltung (synchronization), of all kinds of groups and organizations; the creation of functional organizations serving as transmission belts and auxiliaries for the party, politicizing even areas remote from politics, like sports and leisure.[14]

Serrano Suñer, the once powerful brother-in-law of Franco, head of the Junta Politica, minister of interior and foreign affairs and master engineer of the decree founding the unified party, writes quite accurately and with awareness of the alternatives, as follows:

> In truth, be it an advantage or disadvantage, it is time to say that in Spain there has never been anything that would really look like a totalitarian state, since for this it seems to be a necessary condition that the single party should exist in strength and be really the sole basis of support for the regime—the only instrument and in a sense the only holder of power . . . the complex of forces participating in the Uprising—the army, traditional elements, parties, etc.—has never disappeared, thanks to a policy of equilibrium and through the persistence of the unified elements without ever fusing and without deciding in favor of a total pre-eminence of the official party.
>
> To give each his due: this regime has not been totalitarian as it has not been democratic or liberal. What it would have been without the world war only God knows. What it will finally be is still to be seen.[15]

The difference between authoritarian and democratic pluralism is that the latter is in principle almost unlimited; it is not only tolerated but legitimate;

and its open participation in the competition for power, through political parties, is institutionalized. In a democracy political forces not only reflect social forces, but represent them and to some extent commit them to the support of government policies once these are arrived at; political forces are dependent on the support of constituencies. The "iron law of oligarchy" may make this relative, but the formal principle is upheld.

In authoritarian regimes the men who come to power reflecting the views of various groups and institutions do not derive their position from the support of these groups alone, but from the trust placed in them by the leader, monarch or "junta," who certainly takes into account their prestige and influence. They have a kind of constituency, we might call it a potential constituency, but this is not solely or even principally the source of their power.

The co-optation of leaders is a constant process by which different sectors or institutions become participants in the system. In the consolidated totalitarian system this process takes place between bureaucracies or organizations that are part of the political structure created by the system, generally dependent on the party or an outgrowth of it; in the authoritarian regime pre-existent or newly emergent elements of the society can be represented by this means. The authoritarian regime may go very far toward suppressing existing groups or institutions inimical to the social order; this process of control may affect others, and the threat of control is always present; but due to a number of circumstances the control process is arrested. The strength of ideological commitments; the size, integration, quality of the group wishing a monopoly of power; the strength and legitimacy of existing institutions, and their international ties; the degree of economic autarchy possible; all are factors which may limit maximum suppression of dissidence. Ultimately the conception of power held by the authoritarian leader may make the decisive difference.

MENTALITY VERSUS IDEOLOGY

Styles of leadership, and different ways of conceiving the relation between state power and society, must be examined if we are to analyze the authoritarian regime in its various forms.

We will purposely use the term mentality rather than "ideology." The German sociologist Theodor Geiger[16] has formulated a useful distinction between *ideologies*, which are systems of thought more or less intellectually elaborated and organized, often in written form, by intellectuals, pseudo-intellectuals, or with their assistance; and *mentalities*, which are ways of thinking and feeling, more emotional than rational, that provide non-codified ways of reacting to situations. Ideologies have a strong utopian element; mentalities are closer to the present or the past. Totalitarian systems have ideologies, a point emphasized by all students of such systems, while authoritarian regimes are based more on distinctive mentalities which are difficult to define. The more traditional an authoritarian regime is, the greater the role of the military and civil servants, the more important "mentalities" become in understanding the system, and the more a focus on ideologies, even those loudly proclaimed by the regime, may be misleading.[17]

It is interesting to note that Naguib, a participant in the creation of such a regime, was aware of a distinction along the same lines when he wrote:

> I shall not enumerate my specific differences with the Council here. It is enough, I think, for me to say that most of them revolved around what Abd Nasser has called the "*philosophy*" of the revolution. Perhaps, since neither of us are philosophers, it would be better to call it the "*psychology*" of the revolution.[18] Emphasis supplied.

The result of Nasser's "philosophy" has been described by Nadav Safran in these terms:

> The young authors of the revolution who have presided over Egypt's destinies for the last eight years came to power with no guiding political philosophy beyond a few generalities, and little in the way of a positive program beyond good intentions. They proceeded to work out philosophy and program in a pragmatic experimental fashion, fighting at the same time against the forces of reaction and counter-revolution and struggling among themselves for predominance in their own councils. The result was many false starts, mistaken courses, abrupt reversals, and a high degree of uncertainty.[19]

The new authoritarian leader's lack of clear ideology is evident when we read excerpts like these from Franco's lengthy manifesto of July 18, 1936:

> The situation of Spain is more critical every day; anarchy reigns in the majority of its farms and villages; authorities appointed by the government preside over, if not encourage, the revolts. Differences between factions of citizens are fought out by guns and machine guns . . . We offer you Justice and equality before the law. Peace and love among the Spaniards. Liberty and fraternity free from license and tyranny. Work for everybody. Social justice without bitterness; an equitable and progressive distribution of wealth without destroying or endangering the Spanish economy . . . The purity of our intentions does not allow us to throttle those conquests which represent a step forward in the socio-political improvement. . . and of the inevitable ship-wreck of some legislative attempts, we will know how to save whatever is compatible with the inner peace of Spain and its desired grandeur, making real in our Fatherland for the first time, and in this order, the trilogy Fraternity, Liberty, and Equality. Spaniards: Viva España! Viva the honest Spanish people![20]

The same lack of novelty in themes and symbols can be seen when Vargas says on October 4, 1930, after a similar but less vehement description of the regime's crisis,

> Sheltered by the support of public opinion, with the prestige given us by the adherence of the Brazilians . . . counting on the sympathy of the armed forces and the collaboration of its best part, strengthened by justice and by arms, we hope that the Nation will reassume possession of its sovereignty, without major opposition

by the reactionaries, to avoid useless loss of lives and goods, hasten the return to normality of the country and the restoration of a regime of peace, harmony and tranquillity, under the sign of the law.[21]

Given the reliance of many authoritarian regimes—those of Salazar, Dollfuss, Franco, even Pétain—on conservative interpretations of Catholic social doctrine, we might ask whether this system of thought is an ideology. Inkeles, writing about the ideological aims of totalitarianism, raises the issue as follows:

Invariably this higher goal involves some mystique, some principle above man, some force that responds to laws of its own and that merely requires the state as an instrument through which it may work out its inner imperatives. The mystique may be the dialectical laws of history and social development for the Marxist, the destiny of the nation and race for the Hitlerian, or the ideal of the true Christian society for Franco.[22]

In some cases this ideology competes and coexists with other ideological currents, but even where it is dominant we would argue that it cannot provide the basis for a totalitarian system because of its heteronomous nature. How can a regime base total power on an ideology whose only legitimate interpreters are ultimately outside its control? Given the distinctiveness of Church and State, the internationalism of the Church and the powers of the Pope, the use of a conservative Catholic ideology in itself limits monolithic tendencies toward totalitarianism. The Franco regime's difficulties in the face of a growing labor movement, church inspired or supported, are due largely to this ideological heteronomy. Shifting and divergent interpretations of the Catholic social doctrine in themselves introduce a strong element of pluralism, where the ultimate doctrinal decision is outside the political realm.[23]

APATHY VERSUS MOBILIZATION

Stabilized authoritarian regimes are characterized by lack of extensive and intensive political mobilization of the population. Membership participation is low in political and para-political organizations and participation in the single party or similar bodies, whether coerced, manipulated or voluntary, is infrequent and limited. The common citizen expresses little enthusiastic support for the regime in elections, referenda, and rallies. Rather than enthusiasm or support, the regime often expects—even from office holders and civil servants—passive acceptance, or at least they refrain from public anti-government activity. Let us stress this depolitization is characteristic of stabilized authoritarian regimes, but would not be necessarily true for their formative stages, particularly since their emergence in a crisis would involve considerable and often very intensive popular participation. We would like to argue that this participation is not likely to be maintained over a long period of time, unless the regime moves into a totalitarian or a more formally democratic direction. However, the degrees of mobilization might be the most useful criteria on which to distinguish subtypes of authoritarian regimes.[24]

On the one side we have those that Raymond Aron[25] has characterized as "regimes without parties" which "require a kind of depolitization of the governed" and others we could call "populistic" in which there is a more continuous effort of mobilization, without reaching the pervasiveness and intensity of the totalitarian model. Recognizing the importance of such a distinction,[26] we would like to suggest that often the difference might be more that of stages in the development of nondemocratic regimes than a substantive difference. It would be to misunderstand contemporary Spain to ignore the high level of participation in party activities, youth groups, political oriented welfare activities—not to mention rallies, parades, etc.—during the years of the Civil War in Nationalistic Spain; and the intensity of involvement, ideological and emotional, of people in all sectors of the population must be stressed.[27] No one can deny that this disappeared during the years after the victory. This was not only because, first, the leadership lacked interest in maintaining it, but also because the social structure of a semideveloped country, and the social, institutional and ideological pluralism, made such levels of participation untenable without either channeling them through organized parties or substituting that pluralism with a hierarchical, disciplined and ideologically committed single party. In the contest of the early forties, the first possibility was excluded and the will to impose a truly totalitarian system, destructive of the coalition character of the forces Franco led to victory, was absent from an army (including its leaders) which had no single well-defined ideology. I would like to leave the question open if in the future some of the more "populistic" one-party regimes in Africa and the Moslem countries will not undergo a similar process, transforming the parties and connected organizations into adjuncts of the state apparatus (the bureaucracy) or/and patronage organizations,[28] with little genuine participation, even of a manipulative type.

However, even admitting that the degree of mobilization may depend on the phase in which the system finds itself, we should not ignore that the leaders of such regimes may opt between regarding political mobilization as desirable or preferring to rule without it. The option may reflect ideological predispositions and influences toward social change or arresting such change, but we should not consider this the only or decisive factor. In fact, we could argue that the choice will depend more on the opportunities offered by the social structure, the political context and the international situation for a mobilization in support of those in power, than on the outlook of the rulers. On the other side, the "outcomes," the capacity to do things, and the power for social change may in part depend on the capacity for sustained mobilization.

Thus on the one side we have regimes coming to power after periods of considerable organized political strife, lack of consensus under democratic governments and aborted revolutions: all these will tend to use apathy to consolidate their power, at least the apathy of those not likely to be won over to their policies. The depolitization in these cases would be one way to reduce the tension in the society and achieve a minimum of re-integration, which otherwise could probably be reached only by totalitarian suppression of the dissidents. Privatization under authoritarian regimes has a certain parallel in the "internal migration" of totalitarianism, but differs in that this privatization is consciously or unconsciously encouraged by those in power. Such apoliticism would bar people from positions of power and influence in a totalitarian system; in some authoritarian regimes it is even valued as an asset, or so it is publicly claimed by persons appointed to high office who state they have never been actively involved in "politics." Referring to this depolitization some cynics have called the three F's—Fatima, football, and fados (folk songs) the arcana imperii of Portugal.

On the other side we have regimes trying to gain control of societies in which the masses have never been mobilized by any political force, particularly if the preceding regime had been one of colonial rule, or a traditional monarchy, or even an oligarchic democracy. These situations are likely to coincide with underdeveloped rather than semideveloped societies, where the underprivileged masses have not given their loyalty to any organized movement, and consequently their manipulation is easy, at least initially. The populistic dictators of Latin America could create a certain mass base among workers that the supporters of Franco, even with socially progressive policies and demagogic appeals, would never have succeeded in creating given the previous history of Spain. The content of the policies might not have been as decisive as the level of political social and economic development of the country. The degree of mobilization under authoritarian rule may not depend as much on the desires of the rulers as on the opportunities for mobilization, shaped by previous history, economic and social development, and even the degree of pluralism and complexity of the society. Last but not least, the international situation of the country, the possibility to use or not to use a xenophobic appeal, rallying people of all classes and degrees of identification with the system, to a national cause might be decisive. Foreign pressure can maintain participation in an authoritarian system as nothing else can. After all, in Spain the last successful manifestations of mass participation were achieved when the United Nations exercised their pressure or under the cry of Spanish Gibraltar.

It would take too long to analyze here all the causes of low mobilization or our doubts about the capacity of such regimes to sustain a significant degree of mobilization for any length of time (without considerable changes in other respects—limitation of pluralism and emphasis on an ideology—in a totalitarian direction), but we may list at least some factors. In the absence of a modern revolutionary ideology, reformism, particularly bureaucratic and technocratic reformism, does not provide a chiliastic vision for action, and the structure of underdeveloped countries does not motivate sustained, regular day-to-day activity. Existent or emergent status differences are another obstacle; for example, the equalitarian Falangist "tu," as distinct from the respectful "Usted" as a form of address, was incompatible with differences in education and style of life, and slowly lost appeal. Pluralistic elements of authoritarian regimes resist mobilization as a threat to their distinct constituencies; so, for example, in Spain the church-controlled secondary education system prevented the creation of an effective, large-scale, youth organization across class lines; the women's organizations of the party had to compete with Catholic Action and the traditional welfare organizations like the Red Cross, and so on. Family loyalties, friendship and other particularistic ties divert time and energy from politically inspired secondary groups. With social and economic change come the growth of private interests and the struggle to improve one's living standard. Only in a society where the government is the principal employer, or controls the economy as through co-operatives, can it offer financial rewards to the citizens who participate, but this does not insure that participation will be political; it may come to resemble participation in interest groups like those characterizing democratic society. Economic development and industrialization seem to be a pre-condition for a lively associational life under any system.[29] Limited literacy and low incomes are such obstacles that only the diversion of considerable resources can assure participation for any length of time.

Undoubtedly such social and structural factors may be overcome if the leadership is really committed to the idea of a mobilized society, as the Communist and, even to a minor extent, the Italian Fascist experiences show. The very different attitude of one typical authoritarian leader is well described in these comments of Macartney writing about a Hungarian political leader in the 20's:

> He did not mean opposition ever to be in a position to seriously challenge his own will. But he did not think it any part of the duty of government to pry into and regiment each detail of the subject's conduct, much less his thoughts. For this he was too large-minded, or too cynical, too little a perfectionist . . .[30]

This contrasts markedly with the activism of totalitarian systems, their many forms of participation: the 99 per cent referenda, and more importantly, the myriad of politically closed activities associated with women's organizations, Komsomol, Kraft durch Freude, factory committees and so on. This widespread participation grows out of democratic ideology, whether of a rationalistic classless society or a classless Volksgemeinschaft. Some of these activities end in resembling those in democratic societies more than the totalitarian rulers wish, with the participants becoming hostile or indifferent to their political aspects, and therefore we may say that both democratic and totalitarian regimes encourage a participative rather than a parochial, or subject, political culture, to use the terms of Almond and Verba.[31] In totalitarian systems membership is either obligatory or necessary for success, in democracies there is generally a free choice among multiple groups.

In authoritarian regimes, intermediate systems are frequent: membership may be obligatory but involve nothing more than paying dues, or strictly voluntary without creating any advantages. Presumably political goals take primacy in totalitarian organizations while specific interests predominate in democratic organizations. In Spain, many voluntary associations linked with the party have been consciously depoliticized, as when the official youth organization discontinued its fascist accoutrements and substituted leadership training guides based on Kurt Lewin's experiments in democratic group climates and sociometry. (Changes in terminology were avoided, however, to avoid hurting old-timers' feelings.) In other cases like the SEU—the official student organization—free elections up to the faculty level have allowed even dissidents from the regime to occupy influential positions, something that certainly was not intended.

The depoliticization of officially created associations has certainly not been unique to Spain; with the "end of ideology," the politicization of interest and leisure groups characteristic of European democratic parties from the turn of the century to World War II has also receded. In fact it could be argued that authoritarianism provided a welcome relief from overpoliticization in democratic societies which had not developed apolitical voluntary associations in proportion to the number of fiercely conflicting political groups. An Italian metal worker in his fifties expressed this when he said of his working class neighborhood in Genoa:

I was born here. Then everyone used to know each other, we used to get together, loved each other. After the war came politics. Now we all hate each other. You are a Communist, I am a Socialist, he is a Demo-Christian. And so we avoid each other as much as possible.[32]

In fact in countries like Spain we find a rapid and accelerated growth[33] of voluntary associations, necessarily not openly political and generally apolitical, in recent years, particularly in areas where their numbers had been smallest. In this sense some of Lavau's observations would also be applicable to the apoliticism of the masses in Spain.[34]

I would suggest that the closer an authoritarian regime is to pursuing either the totalitarian or democratic model, the greater will its efforts be toward some kind of mobilization. So the Spanish regime made greater efforts to organize mass meetings, parades, public ceremonies, in the Fascist-inspired period than today; while it has become more pluralistic, it has become less participative. Since both pluralism and participation characterize democratic polities, we can say that certain political systems are more or less "democratic" depending on which element we focus on; using participation as a criterion, Nazi Germany was relatively democratic; using pluralism, a regime like Horthy's, which was certainly not participative, could be termed relatively democratic.

The content of the policies being pursued, socially progressive or conservative, may have something to do with the degree of mobilization a regime encourages, but the social context in which such programs are enacted may have as much importance. I would not be surprised to find quite different degrees of mobilization even where economic development policies, expansion of education or mass media, and welfare state measures are quite similar. Still, I would agree that without such mobilization the introduction of such measures becomes more difficult and their socially integrative function may not be achieved.

THE AUTHORITARIAN PARTY

According to the legal texts of many authoritarian regimes, their single parties occupy a similarly dominant position: to the totalitarian party monopolizing power, recruiting the elite, transmitting both the aspirations of the people and the directives of the leadership.[35] In fact, however, some regimes that in reality approach the totalitarian model legally have multi-party systems, while in others which are legally single party monopolies, the party plays a comparatively limited role. Therefore it is imperative to examine the authoritarian party in its sociological reality.

First and foremost, the authoritarian party is not a well-organized ideological organization which monopolizes all access to power. As we will see later, a considerable part of the elite has no connection with the party and does not identify with it. Party membership creates few visible advantages and imposes few, if any, duties. Ideological indoctrination is often minimal, the conformity and loyalty required may be slight, and expulsions and purges are not frequent and do not represent an important mechanism of social control. The party is often ideologically and socially heterogeneous. Far from branching out into many functional organizations, in an effort to control the state apparatus and penetrate other spheres of life as the Nazi party did, it is a skeleton organization of second-rate bureaucrats. The party becomes only one more element in the power pluralism; one more group pressing for particular interests, one more channel through which divergent interests try to find access to power; one more recruiting ground for elite members.[36] Since tight discipline lacks widespread ideological legitimacy, various functional groups that might have been transmission belts for the leadership's directives, become apolitical interest groups, or autonomous nuclei where a few activists, even those emerging from the grass roots, may follow independent policies.

The importance of the party has many indicators: the number of high officials that were active in the party before entering the elite; the membership figures; the degree of activity indicated by the party budget: agit-prop activity; the prestige or power accorded to party officials; the presence of party cells or representatives in other institutions; the importance of training centers; the attention paid to party organs and publications; the vigor of ideological polemics within the party factions. By all these criteria the Spanish party has never been too strong and today is obviously weak. A look at the party's provincial headquarters, in contrast to other government offices or the Sindicatos (a functional organization theoretically dependent on the party) should convince anyone of the party's second-rate role in Spain.

The different roles of the authoritarian and totalitarian parties may be explained by differences in their origin. Most single parties in authoritarian countries have been created after accession to power rather than before.[37] They have been created by fusing a variety of groups with different ideological traditions and varying social bases, not by completely subordinating some elements to one dominant force. Where politicians of other groupings, including the minor Fascist parties, have been co-opted, no disciplined, integrated organization emerged. In other cases, when the military dictator has tried to create a patriotic national unity organization, the effort was carried out by officers and bureaucrats, who typically do not have the demagogic skills needed to create a lively organization. They are further hampered because they continue devoting most of their attention to government or army offices, where real power, and not merely the promise of it, lies. The old politicians, rallying to organizations like the Imperial Rule Assistance Association[38] or the ex-CEDA (conservative-demochristian deputies in the Republic) leaders in the Falange, are not able to adopt the new style that a totalitarian party requires. Since the party is not tested in a struggle for power, it attracts more than its share of office seekers and opportunists, few idealists, true believers, real revolutionaries. Since its ideology is not defined, indoctrination of the numerous newcomers, entering en masse, is likely to be scanty, and the facts of life soon disillusion the more utopian. Since the primary staff need is to staff the state apparatus, the premium will be on recruiting professionals and bureaucrats, and not the armed intellectuals or bohemians, the marginal men that give the totalitarian movement its peculiar style.

The prominence of the army or civil service in the regime before the party was created, and the solidarity of these groups against newcomers when it comes to making key appointments, makes the rewards of party activity less appealing than membership in the NSDAP or, later, the SS. In underdeveloped countries the army is particularly important, since it does not like the rise of rivals and will seek to prevent the creation of anything like party militias or workers' guards. Any attempt to build up the party beyond a certain point, particularly after the German experience, is likely to encounter the open opposition of the army, as Peron soon discovered. In Spain the relation between party and army during the 40's was not without tension and the overlap in leadership was used to bridge the gap, but from the beginning a law giving all army officers party membership gave them the opportunity (never exercised) to control the party directly.[39] A comment by Serrano Suñer, former chairman of the Junta Politica of the party, describes the relation between army and political groups in many such regimes:

> In the last analysis the center of gravity, the true support of the regime (despite all the appearances which we foolishly try to exaggerate) was and would continue to be the army; the nationalist army—an army that was not politically defined.[40]

In some regimes the fact that the leader, an army officer, or politician with army support like Salazar, was not the leader of a party before assuming power, makes for an ambivalent and uneasy relation between the preexisting parties now subordinated to his leadership. Their identification with the program and ideology is weak; the leader lacks charismatic appeal for the members; his personal ties with the subgroup leaders are likely to be uneven, even when he succeeds in creating them as Franco has done to a large extent. General Antonescu's relation with the Iron Guard, Pétain's with various nationalistic and fascist political groups, are examples of this. Nasser's difficulties with the Baathists in Syria are another.

FORMS OF SOCIAL CONTROL

Similarities between authoritarian regimes and the totalitarians can perhaps go furthest in the control of mass media, particularly in countries in the process of modernization where the technological and capital requirements for setting up the media make such control very easy. Media may vary greatly in autonomy, even under the same regime, but limited pluralism readily creates some islands of exemption; in Spain, for example, church publications are free from government censorship.

The small size of the elite and the persistence within the regime of ties created prior to it, allow for considerable free communication, unless the regime is willing to use a good deal of coercion. The same may be said of contacts with other countries, particularly by the elite. While the monopoly of mass media may be as great as that in totalitarian societies, the impact of this monopoly is less because it is not enhanced by intensive personal propagandizing through agitators and other informal leaders. Even when the freedom of the press is curtailed, truly totalitarian control is not present if there is freedom of travel and, at least, freedom of conversation. (As long as one does not make more than five copies of one's opinions, one cannot be prosecuted for illegal propaganda in Spain.) It may well be that the excesses of control to which a Stalin or Hitler went are really unnecessary.

Terror and police control figure prominently among the characteristics of totalitarianism listed by Friedrich, Brzezinski, Arendt and others, as they should in view of the recent Hitlerian and Stalinist experiments. However recent tendencies toward "socialist legality" may reduce this; and the need for political justice or terror in democracies during crisis situations, while not comparable in volume, suggests that this may not be a good distinction between various types of political systems. Undoubtedly there are differences in the ways in which coercion is used. Whatever repressive practices a democracy may resort to, they are more a reflection of public opinion than of government policy, and the importance of civil rights for the functioning of the system put serious limits to their extension beyond a crisis situation. In authoritarian regimes the existing legal barriers may be weak (though not to be discounted), but the equilibrium of forces on which limited pluralism is based may be a more serious restraint. While repression of the system's open enemies may go far, dissenters within the coalition, or potential members of it, must be handled with more care. While in totalitarian systems members of the elite have often been punished with great harshness, and the setting of examples in show trials has been frequent, in authoritarian regimes exile, kicking upstairs, retirement to private life are more frequent.

While Arendt[41] could perceive no decrease in terror, in fact an increase, after the totalitarian consolidation of power, we may argue that after the birth-pangs of an authoritarian regime are over it may relax. The absence of full ideological self-righteousness is an important restraint. Another is the presence in the elite of men who have held power under states of law, and are themselves lawyers; or, if military, they share at least the military conception of law: legalism may not inhibit repression of the State's enemies, but it does lead to certain procedural rules, to an emphasis on actions rather than intentions. The importance of the armed forces limits the political autonomy and development of the police apparatus; its concern is with actual rather than merely potential opponents. The less dynamic character of such regimes also tends to make the use of force less necessary. The distinction between society and politics, private and public life, means there is less need for the presence of police in many areas of life; limited party membership means information about citizens is also limited, and consequently so is control. Without a "Blockwart"—the Nazi party representative in each dwelling area—gossip available for control purposes is reduced.

THE POSITION OF THE MILITARY

All political systems face the problem of subordinating the military to political authority, and once military dictators start devoting their energies to political problems, they face the same issue. Methods of controlling the military differ in democracies, totalitarian systems, and authoritarian regimes; the equilibrium established between political and military authority will differ as well. In most authoritarian regimes the limited popular consensus, which made such forms of rule necessary or possible in the first place, means there is more need for potential force; this gives the army a privileged position. Normally military affairs are left to military men and not to civilians. The absence of a mass party, and in some countries of a trustworthy and specialized bureaucracy, often leads to the use of military men in political appointments, patronage positions and the administration. The technical branches provide experts for public service or nationalized industries. Nationalism as a simple ideology, easily shared by all classes, makes for an emphasis on the army as a bearer of national prestige. If the break with the past was made by a military coup, the position of the army is likely to be even more enhanced.

Nevertheless there is a certain ambivalence toward the army in the authoritarian regime. On the one hand it is extolled in terms like these:

The army is the shield of Egypt . . . . It carries the responsibility of a heavy and difficult duty . . . the task represented in its defense of the nation against external foes . . . the defense of the nation against internal exploitation and domination.[42]

On the other hand we find the army presented as essentially apolitical, above parties and classes, hoping to transfer its powers to the "people" once order is re-established and the corruption of the previous regime cleaned out. In the manifestos and speeches of the first period of the regime's rise to power, we find expressions like the following:

Everybody knows that I did not initiate the movement with any political objective. I have never been interested in politics nor did I ever think of representing the supreme power of the nation. If at the head of my comrades I raised the national flag I did it only as a patriot and soldier. One cannot judge that way, because there is no army that struggles alone. Our revolution would have failed from the first moment due to lack of interest on the part of the civilian population, if it had only been a military uprising. (Franco, 1938).[43]

I imagined that the whole nation was on tip toes and prepared for action . . . After July 23rd I was shocked by the reality. The vanguard performed its task; it stormed the wall of the fort of tyranny . . . and stood by expecting the mass formations to arrive . . . It waited and waited. Endless crowds showed up, but how different is the reality from the vision . . . We needed action but found nothing but surrender and idleness. (Nasser).[44]

In such regimes emerging from a military action, the army may enjoy a privileged position and hold on to key positions, but it soon co-opts politicians, civil servants and technicians who increasingly make most decisions.[45] The more a regime becomes consolidated, the fewer purely military men staff the government, except when there are no alternative sources of elites. In this sense it may be misleading to speak of a military dictatorship, even when the head of state is an army man. In fact he is likely to carry out a careful policy of depoliticization and professionalization of the army, while he maintains close ties with the officer corps to hold its loyalty.[46]

The military background of key men in authoritarian regimes, and their usual lack of ideological sophistication, make it particularly important to understand the military mentality in relation to internal politics, to styles of political life, conceptions of authority, ideas about cost versus results, legitimate forms for expressing grievances, and so on.[47] The few studies on the role of the military in politics have only raised the issue; real data are still to be assembled.

AUTHORITARIAN REGIMES AND WEBER'S TYPES OF LEGITIMACY

Due to the prominent role of the leader in authoritarian regimes, there is some temptation to identify them with charismatic rule. However we would like to argue that Max Weber's categories can and should be used independently of the distinction between democracy, authoritarianism, and totalitarianism. Within each of these systems the legitimacy of the ruler, for the population or his staff, can be based on one or another of these types of belief.

Undoubtedly charisma has played an important role for masses and staff under Hitler[48] and Lenin; totalitarian regimes have also made demands on their civil service, based on legal authority; and democratic prime ministers have enjoyed charisma. Authoritarian regimes may also have a charismatic element, since they often come into being during serious crisis situations, and control of the mass media facilitates the creation of an "image" of the unique leader. Genuine belief in charisma is likely to be limited, however, since the man assuming leadership was often unknown before, and to his fellow officers is often a primus inter pares, who owes his position often simply to rank. With notable exceptions—Perón or Nasser—the modern army as a rational institution does not breed the irrational leadership type, full of passion, demagogic, convinced of his mission. He is not likely to have, at least for his fellow officers and collaborators, the same appeal that a Lenin or a Hitler could have for those who initiated with him, as marginal men, the long hard struggle for power.

At the same time limited pluralism and the lack of ideological self-righteousness allow more room for the development of general rules institutionalizing the exercise of power, and there is thus a trend toward the secularization of whatever charisma was acquired during crisis. This transition to legal authority has been emphasized in the case of the Spanish regime by one of its leading political theorists, and is even reflected in legal texts.[49] Staffing the system with officers and civil servants, rather than the "old shirts" of street fighting days, contributes to the growth of legalism.

Authoritarian regimes may come to power as de facto authorities with little legitimacy, and develop some charismatic appeal; but they end in a mixture of legal, charismatic and traditional authority. The low level of mobilization may often mean that large parts of the population remain in the position of subjects, recognizing agents of power without questioning their legitimacy; for them habit and self-interest may be more important, and belief unnecessary for effective control.

TRADITIONAL AND AUTHORITARIAN REGIMES

One question some of our readers may raise is: Aren't many such regimes really only a form of autocratic and conservative rule like we find in pre-constitutional and traditional monarchies? It would be foolish to deny that the distinctions are fluid, that a number of authoritarian regimes have emerged out of such political forms, and that the formal constitutional framework may still be a monarchical one. However, we want to stress that we would not want to include in our concept any political system which would strictly fit under the concept of traditional authority in Weber's sense and where rule is based on historical continuity, impersonal familial or institutionalized charisma or various mixtures of patrimonial or feudal rule ... using these terms in a somewhat technical sense.[50] To make it clear, neither Abyssinia, nor Yemen before the recent revolution, nor Tibet, Afghanistan, nor some of the other political entities along the Himalayan border, fit our concept, to mention contemporary systems. Nor would the prerevolutionary European absolute monarchies of the past. Authoritarian regimes are a likely outcome of the breakdown of such traditional forms of legitimacy. This results from a partial social and political mobilization and a questioning of the traditional principles of legitimacy (largely due to their secularization) by significant segments of the society. Authoritarian systems—even those we might call reactionary—are modernizing in the sense that they represent a discontinuity with tradition, introducing criteria of efficiency and rationality, personal achievement and populistic appeals. It should not be forgotten that the regimes we call royal dictatorships in Southeastern Europe were created by kings with very limited traditional legitimacy and that those kings who supported dictators, as did Alphonse XIII in Spain, Victor Emmanuel III in Italy, and several mideastern monarchs, lost their thrones, giving way to democratic republics or authoritarian regimes without a king. The enormous ambivalences surrounding the legitimacy of the Iranian monarchy[51] that was restored by an authoritarian military leader, Reza Pahlevi, are obvious and certainly would not allow this monarchy to be regarded as a purely traditional regime. The attempts of the present Spanish regime to finds its constitutional and legitimacy form as a traditional monarchy certainly suggest the difficulties encountered when moving from an authoritarian regime to a traditional one. There can be no doubt that many of those who are willing to recognize the claims to legitimate rule of Franco would not transfer their allegiance to a traditional monarchy. In our times authoritarian rule almost inevitably leads to questioning traditional authority, if for no other reason than by making the people aware of the importance of the effective head of the government and its secular character. Authoritarian rule might be an intermediate stage in or after the breakdown of traditional authority, but not the route toward its restoration. To specify further the differences would take us at this time too far from the Spanish case.

This might be the place to stress a very important characteristic of many, if not most, authoritarian regimes: the coexistence in them of different legitimizing formulae.[52] The actual pluralism of such regimes and the lack of effective legitimate institutionalization of that pluralism within a single legitimate political formula allowing competition of the pluralistic elements for power, almost inevitably lead to the coexistence of competing legitimacy formulae. So in the case of Spain the traditionalist monarchy desired by the Carlists, a restoration of the pre-1931 monarchy, some form of Catholic corporativism like the present regime under monarchical (or even republican) form, a more dynamic totalitarian vision along fascist lines, even a transition to a democratic republic under christian democratic leadership, are all different formulas open to the supporters of the regime. These supporters give their support in the hope that the regime will satisfy their aspirations and they withdraw their support in so far as they realize that the regime is not doing so, or unable to do so. If we had more space we could develop some of the parallels with Binder's description of the Iranian situation.

Fortunately for many such systems, the great mass of the population in semi- or underdeveloped societies is not concerned with the legitimizing formulae. Instead the population obeys out of a mixture of habit and self-interest,[53] either characterizing the political culture of passive subjects or the parochial (to use the terminology of Almond and Verba).[54] The confusion concerning the sources of legitimacy inherent in many such regimes contributes much of the confusion and pessimism of those most likely to be politically involved. Because of this often the more privileged and those close to the centers of power may appear more alienated from the regime than they really are (at least for all practical purposes). This can help to explain the relative stability of many such systems despite the freedom with which criticism is expressed. The identification with such regimes may not be found in their political formulas, but in the identification with the basic values of the society, its stratification system, and many nonpolitical institutions, which are their infra-structure.

II

Defining authoritarian regimes as a particular type of political system is only useful if we can show that such regimes handle the invariant problems of any political system in a distinctive way. We have already made passing reference to problems like the control of the armed forces, the problem of loyalty, etc., but it may be useful to focus in more detail on a few examples. One is the recruitment and characteristics of the political elite. Another set of questions can be asked about the conditions under which such regimes are likely to emerge and to be stable. Finally, a third set of problems appears when we consider the dynamics of such regimes: whether they will turn totalitarian or democratic, and under what conditions.[55]

THE AUTHORITARIAN ELITE

Let us start with a very specific problem: who constitutes the top elite in authoritarian regimes?

Limited pluralism makes the authoritarian elite less homogeneous than that of the totalitarian system in ideology and political style, and probably in career patterns and background as well. This does not mean that the personalities will be more forceful or colorful. The lieutenants of the totalitarian leader, who rose with him in the struggle for power, often share the demagogic qualities, the marginality and uniqueness, that frequently characterize him; brilliant intellectuals and journalists appear as ideologists in the totalitarian elite's first generation. In contrast, many in the authoritarian elite are less colorful, brilliant or popular; their military, professional and bureaucratic backgrounds do not breed such qualities.

In a sense both the democratic and totalitarian top elites are composed fundamentally of professional politicians, who live through if not for politics. In the totalitarian first generation, the decisive step was to join the party before it came to power; in most democratic countries there is a slow *cursus honorum* through elected or appointed offices, particularly when the parties are bureaucratized and well organized. The second generation of the totalitarian elite may combine a career in the party apparat with some technical specialization, as reflected in the expression: "he did party work in agriculture." Research on totalitarian leadership has underscored its marginality[56] in terms of regional origin, religious affiliation, social mobility, stable work life and so on. In contrast, a significant part of the authoritarian regime's leadership had already participated actively in the country's political life as parliamentarians, and through seniority in the army, civil service, or academic world would have been assured a respectable position in the society under any regime. Given the nonideological character of much authoritarian politics, the emphasis on respectability and expertise, and the desire to co-opt elements of established society, a number of those assuming power will have little previous involvement in politics. Occasionally, particularly at the second level, we find people who define themselves publicly as apolitical, just experts. The old fighters of the extremist groups which contributed to the crisis of the previous regime, who participated in the takeover, who hoped to take power, may find their claims rejected, and will have to content themselves with secondary positions. In some cases their political style, their ideological commitments, their exclusivism, may lead them to break away and retire to private life. This has been the destiny of many Falangist and extreme Carlist leaders under Franco.

Participation in the single party may not be a requisite for entering the elite, but it can be quite helpful combined with other qualifications: a brilliant academic or civil service career, identification with other groups in the pluralistic system such as religio-political interest groups. Such multiple affiliations give the elite member wider contacts and legitimize him in the eyes of the groups that will find themselves represented through him. Some biographies of members of Franco's cabinet, described later, will illustrate this point.

Since both totalitarian and democratic governments want to mobilize opinion, intellectuals play an important role as journalists and ideologists. Lasswell and Lerner have stressed that skill in the use of symbols is decisive. In Spain the only effective journalist in the cabinet was there as a minister without portfolio immediately after the war; a minister of labor with demagogic abilities held the ministry until 1957. Both came from the fascist wing of the system. The more rightist an authoritarian regime, the less place is there for the nonprofessional, nonacademic intelligentsia. Without careful research it is difficult to know if some authoritarian regimes which are described as progressive owe their image to such men; their policies may actually not differ greatly from others not enjoying the same reputation.

Despite their tendency to elect national heroes, in democracies normally only a minority of nonmilitary posts are occupied by officers, and even the defense ministries are often held by civilians. In totalitarian systems a politically neutralized or indoctrinated army may control its own affairs but few key positions outside that realm are held by military men. Authoritarian regimes that emerge as "commissary dictatorships" (to use Carl Schmitt's expression for those whose intent is to re-establish "order" and then transfer power to the constitutional government) tend to be, initially, exclusively or almost exclusively military: the classical junta. There, a balanced representation of the services, rank, and seniority are more important than personality or political beliefs. If such a regime retains power, shifts are likely to take place, either through reinforcement of a faction like the Free Officers of Egypt or through the co-optation of civilians, as in the regimes of Primo de Rivera, Franco and Perón. These civilians may be professional politicians (as in

Eastern Europe during the interwar years), civil servants or experts (Calvo Sotelo in Spain and Salazar in Portugal entered this way), leaders of interest groups or religious organizations (like Artajo, the lay head of Spanish Catholic Action in 1945), or fascists willing to forgo a state dominated by a single party. Soon the balance of power may shift considerably toward the civilian element, which may even assume leadership as Salazar did, but it is unlikely that the equilibrium between civil and military power will be established at the same level as before. The absence of a relatively large, disciplined, dynamic revolutionary party, or the weakness or death of its leadership, is decisive for the establishment in this period of an authoritarian rather than a totalitarian regime. This was the case in Spain with the death of José Antonio (who probably never would have been a real totalitarian leader in any case) and the weakness and dissension in Falangist leadership described so well by Payne. In Rumania, one of the most authentic and revolutionary fascist parties had to play second fiddle in the regime of Marshal Antonescu after losing its leader Codreanu, finally to be ousted after four months of collaboration. The strength of the party also decides if the men co-opted from other groups will be able to maintain some degree of pluralism.

The persistence of the precrisis social order that goes with limited pluralism and co-optation means that the legal profession, so important in democratic politics and even under traditional rulers, will play a much greater role in authoritarian regimes than in totalitarian systems. The same is true of civil servants. Their presence may contribute to the strange combination of Rechtsstaat and arbitrary power, of slow legalistic procedure and military command style, that characterizes some of these regimes. This preoccupation with procedure ultimately becomes an important factor in the constant expansion of a state of law, with an increase in predictability and opportunities for legal redress of grievances. At the same time it may prevent political problems from being perceived as such, irreducible to administrative problems and not soluble by legislation. Legal procedures are often seen, particularly in the continental legal tradition, as an adequate equivalent of more collective, political expressions of interest conflicts.[57]

STABILITY AND CHANGE: PATTERNS OF ENTRY

The top elite of an authoritarian regime, despite its limited pluralism, is likely to be more limited both numerically and in shades of opinion than the spectrum of government and opposition in democracies. The existence of a loyal opposition, and the greater dispersion of power, facilitates the training and emergence of new leaders. Limited pluralism allows new personalities to emerge in the shadows, but their political experience is often inhibited. This slows down renewal of leadership, and each successive generation is likely to have an even smaller activated constituency than those of the original group. The emphasis on stability and continuity in such regimes, one of their main claims to legitimacy against the previous "unstable" democratic system, also contributes to slow renewal. On the other hand a change in the elite's composition can go on more silently and smoothly than under totalitarianism, where changes in leadership are associated with crisis. Turnover in authoritarian elites can take place without purges, by retiring people to secondary or honorary positions, if not to private life. The following incident illustrates how, even in the case of serious disagreement, a minimum of good manners is maintained within the elite: when two ministers were dropped from the Spanish regime's elite, the official announcement of the dismissal omitted the customary formula "thanking you for services rendered"; but a few days later a "corrected" version, including the phrase, was published.[58]

Venomous hatred of defeated elite members is not always absent, but the lack of ideological clarity, of self-righteousness, contribute to making this infrequent. On the other hand the more pluralistic, open structure of society may help make the loss of power less painful.

While the elite is relatively open, predictable ways of entry are lacking, which frustrates the ambitions of many. Because competition for power is not institutionalized effectively, paths to it are obscure: neither devoted partisan service and ideological conformity, nor a steady career through elected office, is available. Success in nonpolitical spheres, identification with groups like religious associations, particularistic criteria of who knows whom, even accident, may be more important. These processes, which incidentally do not necessarily lead to the selection of incompetent people, exist in all systems, but normally they coexist with more universalistic recruitment criteria. With the increasing complexity of industrial society and increasing emphasis on achievement criteria, universalistic standards are used more and more, but there is no purposive planned cadre training or recruitment through youth organizations, party schools and so on such as the totalitarians employ. When the educational system is class biased, this depolitization of the elite results in less equalitarian recruitment than that afforded by totalitarianism; formally no one is excluded, but in fact educational requirements exclude many. On the other hand authoritarian regimes with their universalistic bureaucratic recruitment, may be more open than conservative or bourgeois parties in a society at the same level of economic development. But as Kornhauser has rightly noted: ease of entry into elites, and ability to exert influence on them, are not the same thing and may not even vary together.[59]

The first generation totalitarian elite, having come to power together in a revolutionary group, are likely to represent the same generation and to be younger than their democratic counterparts. Authoritarian leadership is likely to be more heterogeneous, combining younger elements (who may have sought a more revolutionary regime) with older men co-opted into the system because of their experience or symbolic value. Obviously the age composition of an elite is likely to differ, depending on whether we are dealing with the period immediately after the conquest of power or years later when the revolutionary group has consolidated its position. From a sociological point of view it is the age at which the group first obtained office that matters. A very interesting problem is how each type of regime handles the problem of recruitment and succession. One interesting feature of the Franco regime, not unrelated to its pluralism, has been its ability to bring a significant number of younger men into the elite. This is the more surprising when we recall that the political channels for selection and socialization into politics, youth organizations and the party, are so undeveloped. Though this very fact enhances recruitment of the young, since it makes political careers less of a *cursus honorum*. So in the present cabinet there are two men, one of them playing an important role, who were under 17 when the Civil War ended. The average of the "victory cabinet" (1939) was 46.1 years, but most have tended to be slightly older; the average for all ministers from 1938 through 1957 at the time of assuming office was 50.5. Significantly the average for the Republican ministerial elite was 50.8; in terms of age the Franco regime did not mean a great change, compared to that represented by the younger Perónist cabinets. The average age of the Nazi top hierarchy in 1933 was appreciably younger: 41.9 years, as we would expect in a revolutionary elite. It is only natural that in Spain the Minister Secretary General of the Movement should have, generally, the youngest member (average age 41) while the military ministries where seniority counts have been close to or above the middle fifties.

POLITICAL PLURALISM IN THE ELITE OF THE FRANCO REGIME

I The Cabinet.   Using some data on the top Spanish elite, I hope to illustrate and to some extent support some of the points made above. The most important decision-making body is the cabinet, both as a collective body and as individual members each in his area of competence. While cabinet members are not equally powerful, they all have control of significant sectors of administrative policy making, and have taken strong initiative in legislative processes. It therefore seems legitimate to concentrate on cabinet members from the first appointed in 1938 to the last sworn in the summer of 1962, to explore elite pluralism. The number of persons involved is 67, though the number of incumbencies is higher since many have been holdovers from one government to the next and several have held different ministries at one time or another.

Let us start with the political orientations of these men, their former party affiliations, and the groups they may be said to represent (Table 9–1). Since these identifications, a good index of pluralism, are not announced, and political allegiances are not always stable, this involves certain risks. Nevertheless such classifications are made by participants themselves, as the memoirs of Serrano Suñer reveal.[60] Similarly Arrese describes how, in a cabinet crisis, Falangists asked for and received various portfolios.[61]

Of the total, 39 per cent have been army officers; a number of them can be classified as pro-Falangist, pro-Traditionalist, or pro-monarchico-conservative, but their primary identification probably continues to be the army; in the case of 24 per cent no political tendency could be assigned easily. In order not to overestimate the role of the army, it is important to note that of the 26 military in the cabinet, 15 have held defense ministries. Professionals and civil servants without any particular group affiliations number at least ten, or 15 per cent. The Falange, in the strict sense, has contributed 17 members, or 25 per cent, of whom only eight had no other identification prior to the Civil War. Another four had been members of the CEDA (Gil Robles' center-right Catholic party) or close to demochristian organizations; four could be considered technical with Falangist leanings. The other official part of the fused party, the Traditionalists (heirs of the nineteenth-century dynastic and ideological conflict between the liberals and the legitimist-Catholic-conservatives) held three posts, particularly the ministry of Justice where they could enact the pro-clerical legislation in many

TABLE 9–1

Political Background or Identification of Members of the Spanish Cabinet (1938 to 1962)

	Total	% of
Falange:		
Falange with no previous political background	8	12%
Falange with CEDA background	5	7
Technical with Falangist orientation	4	6
Total Falange	*17*	*25*
Traditionalist	3	4.5
Accion Española and non-traditionalist Monarchist	2	3
Civil figure of the Primo de Rivera Dictatorship	3	4.5
Political Catholicism	3	4.5
Opus Dei	3	4.5
Technical or civil service apolitical	10	15
Military:		
With Falangist leanings	3	4.5
With Traditionalist leanings	1	1.5
With Accion Española or Opus Dei ties	2	3
With CEDA background	2	3
Former office holders under Primo de Rivera	2	3
With no particular identification	16	24
Total Military	*26*	*39*
Total	67	100 %

mixed matters. Three civil figures who were already present in the Primo de Rivera dictatorship (1923–1929) together with two military of that period represent an important element of continuity. The small group of Acción Española, inspired largely by the Action Française of the 1930's, contributes several members, some of whom I have included in other groups with which they were later more closely identified. The CEDA, a party that in the February 1936 election was the second largest in Parliament with 88 of 473 seats, contributes three of its deputies, two of them military and one (Serrano Suñer) turned Falangist. Three other important figures are closely identified with the ACNDP (Accion Catolica Nacional de Propagandistas), a small elite group of political Catholics. From this group came a younger professor who as minister of education followed an interesting policy of liberalization.

Let us take the biography of Martin Artajo as an interesting illustration of the representation process. He was born in 1905; his father was a member of parliament under the monarchy; he studied law, graduating summa cum laude, and was president of the Catholic student federation. At 24 he became a letrado del Consejo de Estado (maître des requêtes). In 1934 he participated in a congress of corporative studies in Vienna. He was a member of the ACNDP and before 1936 was Secretary General of Catholic Action. During the war he was on the staff of the military junta's labor commission and of the Ministry of Labor. He was minister of foreign affairs from 1945 to 1957, and up to 1945 had been president of the board of the Catholic publishing trust. His brother was a CEDA deputy; another brother is a Jesuit.

The following excerpts of a letter from the present Cardinal Primate at the time of his dismissal in 1957 illustrate the sense in which he can be said to represent various Catholic groups:

(Though) I expressed . . . yesterday how praiseworthy (and) effective your action has been in your 12 years as Minister of Foreign Affairs . . . I don't want to leave your letter unanswered . . . in it you recall that in 1945 you asked my advice about accepting the ministry, and without any doubt I thought I should advise your acceptance, which I expected would result in the common good of the Fatherland and of the Church. Thanks be to God, events have confirmed these hopes. (He goes on listing the minister's achievements in international politics, particularly those in the area of relations between Church and state, mentioning for example the Concordat.) Spanish Catholic Action, of whose Technical Committee your Excellency was respected president, has been honored by your period of office in the ministry of Foreign Affairs, proving by your outstanding example that out of it (Catholic Action) there can come respectable and efficient public officials.[62]

Martin Artajo represents the kind of politician we would find in the right wing of the Italian Christian Democrats, and his affiliations for a lifetime have been of this kind. He was in effect the nonelected representative of certain religious groups. In a cabinet with men of quite different background, he was one element of pluralism. His success in public life would have been almost as certain in a democracy with a Christian Democratic party, and I am certain he does not exclude even that possibility.

There are other men whose background is in itself "pluralistic" and whose success is not unrelated to that pluralism. Take the present Minister of Finance. Born in a forlorn provincial village in 1914, he studied law, volunteered in the army and became a captain in shock troops. After the war he became an army lawyer through competitive examinations (his rank is now lieutenant colonel) and again through competition became technical secretary of the Sindicatos (corporative structure). He too is a letrado del Consejo de Estado, with a top mark in the examination. For some time he was on the board of a bank, and close to the Opus Dei, a very special type of religious group. Then from the undersecretariat of Public Works he went to Finance. In his career he has established ties with the army, the corporative structure controlled by the party, a highly prestigeful group in the civil service, and an ideologically conservative but technocratically oriented Catholic elite group.

In recent cabinets other members or sympathizers of the Opus Dei, a

religious secular institute, have played a part; at present at least three ministers and several army men may be so identified.[63]

Occupational Background. A large proportion (42 per cent) have a law
degree, but in the Republic this proportion was even larger: 56 per cent
(Table 9–2). Many of them were in two of the grand corps of the administra-
tion, the Letrados del Consejo de Estado (5) and the Abogados of the
Estado (6), among them some of the most powerful figures of the regime. The
Abogados del Estado contributed one out of 86 cabinet members during the
Republic, while some of the slightly less prestigeful sectors of the civil service

TABLE 9–2

Occupational Background of Cabinet Members of the Spanish
Republic (April 1931 to July 17, 1936) and the Franco Regime
(Multiple occupations are coded if important)

	Republic		Franco Regime	
Legal professions:				
Letrado del Consejo de Estado	1		5	
Abogado del Estado	5		6	
Notario or Registrador de la propiedad	7		1	
Diplomats	3		—	
Ministerio Fiscal	2		—	
Juridico militar (legal staff of the armed forces).	—		4	
Judge and judicial secretary	5		—	
Legal but not public official	25		12	
Total with legal background	*48*	56%	*28*	42%
Academic and teaching:				
University professor	17		8	
Public secondary education	1		1	
Commerce	1		1	
Other higher education	4		—	
Primary school teacher	3		—	
Total	*26*	30%	*10*	13%
Engineering	4		8	
Architecture	2		1	
Total	*6*	7%	*9*	13%
Medicine and other health professions:				
Physician	6			
Pharmacist	1		—	
Veterinarian	1		—	
Total	*8*	9%	—	
Journalism	*21*	25%	*3*	4%
Economics and political science	*1*	1%	*3*	4%
Military:				
Navy in the Navy Ministry	2		4	
Army and Air Force in a defense Ministry	2		11	
Subtotal	*4*	5%	*15*	22%
Navy and military in other ministries	—		11	
Total	*4*	5%	*26*	39%
Business	*1*	1%	*3*	4%
Manual Worker	1	1%	—	
Total	(86)	100%	(67)	100%

contributed more. An interesting datum in support of the multiple affiliations thesis is the number (4) of men coming from the legal service of the armed forces, a dual affiliation that must have furthered their career.

The academic world is represented by 8 (12 per cent) university professors, fewer than in the Republic which had 17, or 20 per cent. But the real change reflecting the lesser importance of the intelligentsia in the regime is the absence, with but two exceptions, of the secondary and primary educational system representatives. In summary the teaching professions contribute 13 per cent while they made up 30 per cent of the cabinet between 1931 and 1936. The health professions that contributed 8 men to the Republican cabinets, reflecting the leftist-laicist orientation of the medical profession in much of Europe, are absent. In contrast, naturally reflecting the more technical tasks of the government, the proportion of engineers and architects has increased from 7 per cent to 13 per cent. One of the greatest changes is the proportion of journalists: almost one fourth of the ministers of the Republic, but only a small minority (3) of those in the present regime would mention this as a major activity.

Military men holding civilian ministries constitute an important group, numbering 11, or 16 per cent; among them were a general secretary of the party, the undersecretary of the presidency, and a naval engineer who had a decisive role in the creation of the INI (Instituto Nacional de Industria), the state-owned industrial complex.

It would be interesting to continue with the analysis of the changes in the top elite, the early pluralism of the Consejo Nacional, the absence from the top elite, years later, of the Student Movement's youthful politicians, the rise of the technicians, etc., but the examples given so far must suffice.

II The Elite in General. The political pluralism indicated by the data on the cabinet extends throughout the entire elite. Arrese, when he was secretary general of the party, presented in 1956 to the party's National Council some proposals for new constitutional laws that were received very critically. He felt compelled to defend himself against those who saw these proposals as an attempt by the party to gain greater strength. He wrote that "since some councillors have alluded to the excessive role of the original group of the Falange and of the JONS in the positions of the State and of the Movement," he would give the backgrounds of all levels of the elite at the time by their political origin before July 18, 1936. He stresses the following figures as the share of the Falange:

2 of 16 cabinet members	12.5%
1 of 17 undersecretaries	6.0
8 of 102 director generals	7.8
18 of 50 provincial governors (who are also heads of the provincial party organizations)	36.0
8 of 50 mayors of provincial capitals	16.0
6 of 50 presidents of provincial chambers	12.0
65 of 151 National councillors of the party	43.0
137 of 575 members of the legislature	24.0

        133 of 738 provincial deputies   18.0
        776 of 9155 mayors   8.4
        2226 of 55,960 municipal councillors   9.0

Arrese continues:

I don't say this to make anyone despair, nor to justify anything, but for the benefit of so many speculators of politics who give as an explanation for not joining the Movement the worn-out excuse that the Falange did not leave a place for their honest desire to collaborate.[64]

In official circles one may hear persons described as "of the regime but not of the Movement", "Falangist but not of the Movement", "Falangist against the Regime", "of the regime but apolitical", and so on through a vast variety of possible combinations which no one would say are meaningless descriptions of political views.

The Dynamics of Authoritarian Regimes.   As a final point, let us turn to the dynamics of authoritarian regimes. It could be argued that they are unstable hybrids, subject to pressures and pulls in the direction of democracy or totalitarianism. Undoubtedly their limited ideological creativity makes them unattractive to those who look for logical consistency, meaning and purpose in political life, for real ideals even at great sacrifice. The intellectuals, the young, those intolerant of ambiguity, soon become disillusioned and turn to the two great political myths of our time, which are represented by the major powers of the world. The unfulfilled promises of authoritarianism may make them more susceptible to totalitarianism, which they believe to be more efficient and idealistic; the immobility of limited pluralism has already disillusioned some of them about the chances of speedy, far reaching reform under pluralism. Ideological elements from revolutionary movements like fascism and marxism are a source of tension when incorporated in such regimes and used as standards against which to measure their performance and their pragmatic, often dull, politics. In other cases instability comes from longstanding ideological commitments to constitutional democracy, to which the regime has had to pay lip-service, as in most of Latin America. The same is true in new countries where authoritarianisms was introduced with the promise of preparing the ground for democracy, as in Turkey after World War I and now in the new states styling themselves "guided", "basic", or "presidentialist" democracies. Another source of tension is felt in countries relying on Catholic organic social theories; shifts in church policy may subject them to pressure. However, one should not overestimate the impact of ideological pulls, and instead pay some attention to the economic and social factors contributing to the stability of such regimes. After all, some of them have lasted several decades, even in the face of considerable hostility.

If we were to accept the interpretation that such regimes lie on a continuum between democracy and totalitarianism, we should find many examples of transitions from authoritarianism to one or the other without serious crises or revolutionary changes. This however does not seem to be the case; even when the transition to some kind of democracy has been done with little bloodshed, the democracy has often been unstable. Evolutionary cases are rare—Atatürk's Turkey and Vargas' Estado Novo come to mind and the process would deserve serious study. An initial commitment to democratic ideals, and self-definition as a preparatory stage for democracy, seem relevant, as the borderline case of Mexico also shows. Transitions to totalitarianism have not been frequent either unless we agree with the German conservatives (as I would not) that Hitler in 1933 was really pursuing an "autoritärer Staat," rather than a Nazi revolution. Another possible case would be Cuba, if we assume that Castro was initially willing to stop at a left-pluralist authoritarian system and not pursue totalitarianism. Perhaps Perónism is the most interesting case of a shift toward a more totalitarian conception from what was originally a military dictatorship. Political sociology should devote increasing attention to such problems of transition from one system to another, in the way that Bracher and his collaborators have offered a model for the breakdown of Weimar democracy and the process of Machtergreifung.

Another question is whether totalitarian regimes, whose transformation into the Western type of democracy no one expects, will look more like some of the present authoritarian regimes if their ideological impetus is weakened, apathy and privatization replace mobilization, and bureaucracies and managers gain increasing independence from the party. Some such tendencies are in sight and undoubtedly the difference between some authoritarian regimes and the Soviet Union today is less than in the Stalinist period. I would even venture to say that a country like Poland seems more authoritarian than totalitarian, but my knowledge of that system is too superficial to document this idea.

A dynamic description of authoritarian regimes should locate factors influencing the development of political and social pluralism and mobilization. It is essential to understand the historical constellations from which such regimes emerge: the breakdown of existing democracy, of a traditional society, or of colonial rule. This limits the alternatives open to the authoritarian ruler, the appeals he may use, the type of legitimacy he can claim, and so on, often independently of his own pragmatic or ideological preferences. But the present cannot be understood only in terms of origins. When these regimes began, their futures were generally very ill-defined. (one has only to read the different manifestos and speeches made in the first days of the Spanish Civil War to get a sense of this indeterminacy) and their relative openness makes for considerable shifts if the regime lasts. In the case of Spain it would be extremely misleading to interpret the present only in terms of the past; particularly the forces at play in the late 30's and early 40's, for the simple reason that a considerable part of the second level elite of today was not yet adult at the time, and close to half of the population was not even in their teens. In some of these regimes the bulk of existing information deals with their takeover phase and interest dwindles afterwards, which makes comparative study difficult.

Some of you may have missed a judgment about these regimes. I think that as a social scientist I should not express one. As an individual I could, but as a social scientist I would suggest that the problem be broken down into many subproblems, examining the positive and negative implications of such regimes from many points of view. A number of cases would be required to give a general idea of their functions and dysfunctions for social change, but even so the observer's final evaluation of them would depend much on his own hierarchy of values.

Authoritarian regimes can be evaluated on a variety of dimensions: their ability to create stable political institutions articulating the conflicting interests of society, especially in countries where the regime came to power because of the heat of ideological and interest conflicts; their capacity to handle the succession problem; their ability to foster rapid economic development, both rural and industrial, compared with democratic and totalitarian societies under comparable conditions and considering the costs, both social and economic. We might examine the social and political consequences of some typical authoritarian labor policies: stability of employment vs. aggressive wage policy; imposed or voluntary company welfare benefits vs. a more general state or municipal policy; great emphasis on social security legislation combined with limited autonomy of labor organizations. Problems like these require cooperation between sociologists and economists, and I feel that today we have no good studies along these lines.

Among the most difficult questions of all is that posed by the leaders of authoritarian regimes, when they say that national unity can only be maintained or achieved by excluding open expression of political cleavages through political parties.[65] It has been expressed as follows:

In face of the fundamental problems, the union, the unity of the country is indispensable. Now, without any doubt, the multiplicity of parties ends creating national disagreement about the great questions. No; democracy has nothing to do with the regime of parliamentary assemblies and the agitation of rival political parties. Democracy consists in searching the will of the people and in serving that will.[66]

We don't want democracy to be a source of cleavages, of childish struggles in the course of which the better part of our energies would be wasted. We want . . . to pursue in peace and in union the work of national construction.

Guinea's political unity has been proved by the referendum, and has been growing stronger ever since. It is not our intention to squander this chance of unity by adopting a system which would only reduce our political strength. What Africa needs is a fundamental revolution. It is not too much to ask that all our strength be mobilized and directed toward a common goal. A political system based on two parties would be a certain check on our revolution. The revolutionary dynamism doesn't need any other stimulant than our needs, our aspirations, and our hopes.[67]

Certainly the activation of cleavages in a society where the basic consensus is shattered—as it was in Spain after the October revolution of 1934—or where it has not developed, as in some of the new nations, creates serious problems. Social scientists would have to know much more about the conditions under which the balance of cleavage and consensus required for democratic politics, can emerge. Studies of the integration of new sectors into the society under different political and social institutions, particularly by Bendix and Guenther Roth[68] suggest how difficult it is to weigh the consequences of following one or another path. A comparative analysis of the aftermath of different authoritarian regimes, for example those of Vargas and Perón, would be most important in exploring how authoritarianism can be combined with the expansion of citizenship which characterizes our time.

Evaluation of each authoritarian regime depends finally on the answer to these questions: could alternative systems work in the societies now under authoritarian rule? What conditions are necessary for these alternative systems, and how could they be created? At what cost? I for one have no definitive answers for Spain.

Bibliographic Note. There is no sociological, or even political science analysis of the institutions and operations of the Franco regime. Most of the literature on contemporary Spain deals with the historical background of the Civil War, the well-known books by: Gerald Brenan, *Spanish Labyrinth* (Cambridge: Cambridge University Press, 1943); Salvador de Madariaga, *Spain. A Modern History* (New York: Praeger Paperbacks, 1958); Hugh Thomas, *The Spanish Civil War* (New York: Harper & Brothers, 1961); Franz Borkenau, *The Spanish Cockpit*; D. C. Cattell, *Communism and the Spanish Civil War* (Berkeley: University of California Press, 1955). None of these works is written with a pro-Franco point of view. For that the reader has to turn to Joaquin Arraras, *Historia de la Cruzada Española* (Madrid, 1940—3, 35 vols.) and his *Historia de la Segunda Republica Española* (Madrid: Editora Nacional, 1956).

For a good general history of modern Spain until the Republic see: Vicens Vives, J. Nadal, R. Ortega, M. Hernandez Sanchez Barba, Vol. IV of the: *Historia Social de España y America* (Barcelona: Editorial Teide, 1959).

A very important book whose analysis of the early stages of the Franco regime is better documented than most sources in English—that focus on the Republican side—is Carlos M. Rama, *La Crisis Española del Siglo* XX (Mexico: Fondo de Cultura Economica, 1960).

The literature on Spain after the civil war, both journalistic and scholarly is largely focused on Spanish foreign policy, but does not add much to the understanding of domestic politics. While, as the title indicates, this is also the focus of: Arthur P. Whitaker, *Spain and the Defense of the West. Ally and Liability* (New York: Praeger Paperbacks, 1962), it contains a lot of material on the basis of the regime, the opposition groups, from the semitolerated ones to the Communists, economic policies, etc. We mentioned already the important work of Stanley Payne, *Falange*, but by focusing on only one element in the system, it can only give an incomplete picture. Ebenstein's study of the Church is also useful. Richard Pattee, *This Is Spain* (Bruce: Milwaukee, 1951) is a presentation from a point of view friendly to Catholic political forces within the Regime, but has no scholarly pretensions. For the basic constitutional texts of the Regime until 1945 see Clark, *op. cit.*, translations in English.

10

MAJORITY RULE AND THE REPRESENTATIVE SYSTEM OF GOVERNMENT

WARREN E. MILLER

REPRESENTATIVE government as a viable set of institutions must provide a balance between popular participation and efficient decision making. The desire and commitment to achieve representation of the ordinary citizen's views in the councils of government must be honored to redeem the high value which democratic philosophy finds in the individual. At the same time, the governing institutions must act, and to act decisions must be made that favor some views and deny others. The operating rule for decision making which dominates the electoral institutions of western democratic nations and which is carried into such domains of rationality as the United States Supreme Court is the simple rule of majority control.

The operating principle of majority rule—so pervasive in the Anglo-American tradition—is criticized by those who seek to extend explicit recognition of minorities through proportional representation as well as by those who resist the intrusion of popular sentiment in affairs they deem more suited

Reprinted from *Cleavages, Ideologies and Party Systems*, edited by Erik Allardt and Yrjö Littunen (Helsinki, The Westermarck Society, 1964). An earlier version of this paper was prepared for delivery at the 1962 Annual Meeting of The American Political Science Association, Washington, D.C., September 5–8, 1962. The research reported here was made possible through grants of the Rockefeller Foundation, the Social Science Research Council, and the Horace H. Rackham School of Graduate Studies of The University of Michigan, whose support is gratefully acknowledged. Although the author bears the responsibility for the interpretations presented in this paper, he is indebted to his collaborator on the major study, Donald E. Stokes, for aid in its preparation. The author is also grateful for the assistance of Ralph Bisco and Gudmund R. Iversen.

Notes to this chapter are on p. 381.

to highly expert, professional ministrations. The former hold that the minority receives too short shrift at the hand of representatives who are the choice of, and beholden to, the majority. The latter see evidence that contemporary problems of government have already passed beyond the ken of an apathetic and ill-informed citizen mass.

Unhappily, arguments over proportional representation, majority rule, or, indeed, over the existence of popular participation in public policy formation have of necessity been carried out largely without benefit of direct evidence. The actual preferences of electoral majorities, or minorities, have been loosely inferred from election campaigns and results. They are also derived from public pronouncements of leaders or deduced from sporadic acts of rank and file members. And yet, few serious students of government are convinced the connection between elections and acts of government is sufficiently close to allow the mere existence of a formal system of government to stand as a test of the empirical premises of the system. Nor will they take official statements of group preferences at face value nor will they use isolated incidents of protest as a sure base for wider generalization. The gross and indirect evidence, subject to so many interpretations, becomes persuasive only when national electoral upheavals, massive social protest movements or widespread civil disobedience demonstrate that some policy views have not been adequately represented. Such evidence, including the resolution of violent disagreements, scarcely tells us all we need to know about the routine operation of a system of representative government. Such evidence is symptomatic of malfunctions within the system, but it is at best a partial base on which to establish a satisfactory understanding of the system, whether in crisis or at rest.

This paper does not aspire to present evidence capable of sustaining or demolishing arguments about the propriety of majority rule nor, indeed, about the utility of representative government. It is concerned with the more modest task of describing some of the phenomena which are an integral part of representative government under majority rule. It is concerned with only a severely limited subset of the many phenomena pertinent to a full analysis of the topic; and these selected aspects of the world of politics and government will be described only as they appeared to us within one country, the United States, at one point of time. If this seems to promise a less than definitive discussion of the topic, it becomes appropriate to suggest there are few topics so fundamental to the theory and practice of democratic government about which we have less evidence to guide our critical speculation and to stimulate new and creative ideas.

I

BACKGROUND AND DESIGN OF THE STUDY

In 1958 the Survey Research Center undertook to collect data which would provide the first direct confrontation between the policy preferences of the electorate and the policy acts of its elected representatives. This study of policy agreement is concerned with the U.S. House of Representatives and the constituencies electing its members. A national sample of congressional districts was selected. Elaborate, systematic interviews were conducted with the major party candidates in each district. Interviews were also taken with a small sample of the electorate in each district. Subsequently, census data and election statistics were assembled for each district, and an intensive analysis of the roll call records of the incumbent Congressmen from the districts was completed. The data collection thus contains a wide range of information including descriptions of the political activities, partisan affiliations, political attitudes, beliefs and perceptions of the constituents; the personal policy preferences, role preferences, campaign activities, perceptions, legislative pressures and other elements important in the legislative life of Congressmen; and aggregated descriptions of the social, economic and political attributes of the districts in which the congressional candidates and our samples of their constituents resided.

In some ways, the entire project was a substantial gamble. Electoral research, done at the Survey Research Center and elsewhere, has documented and illustrated the citizens' virtually abyssmal ignorance of the policy acts of their Congressmen. And again in 1958 we found in response to a series of free answer questions that scarcely three per cent of the voters could identify, in even the most gross terms, a single policy stand taken by their Congressman in any given major policy area. At the other end of the line, the literature on Congress and the legislative process has made dramatically evident the terrible complexity of the legislative act and the relative paucity of information conveyed by the visible product which is the recorded roll call.

Despite these large impressions of the quality of the policy concerns of constituents and Congressmen, the general research objective behind the data collection is the study of conditions under which policy agreement between constituent policy preferences and congressional roll call behavior is maximized and minimized. In its particularized forms this objective includes such questions as: Does the extent of policy agreement vary with the role preference of the Congressman? Does agreement occur less often between the Burkean Congressman and his constituents and more often where the Congressman chooses to be an instructed delegate? Does a Congressman's deference to the administration's policy commitments affect the congruence between his roll call behavior and the policy positions of his constituency? Does policy agreement obtain only with regard to constituency majorities or are the wishes of the minority systematically reflected in the representative's legislative policy positions? Does agreement on policy vary with the competitiveness of the partisan division within the district? Does the intrusion of party—through its role in candidate selection, in facilitating election or in the person of party leadership in the House—have an impact on policy agreement?

Each of these questions, and the many others which were culled from the literature or suggested out of the wisdom and experience of academic experts and professional practitioners, assumed that there was some policy agreement to be observed under a variety of circumstances and conditions. The sceptics, and all of us were more or less sceptical in the early stages of the study, feared that policy agreement between the electoral constituency and its Congressman occurs too seldom and then at too grand a level in modern America to be observed in any study embracing only a limited set of legislative acts located in the decisions of a single Congress. Indeed, there were those who insisted that legislation is so much a function of group representation before Congress as to deny all prospect of discovering policy agreement involving the rank and file constituents. There were even those who said the de facto Burkean behavior of Congressmen preoccupied with resolving group conflicts in the national interest is so well understood that an interest in policy agreement between Congressmen and their mass constituencies can be seen only as a naïve, anachronistic preoccupation of midwestern children of outmoded populist persuasions.

Equally serious was the prospect that the techniques available for measuring policy agreement would be too primitive and crude, ill-adapted to the sensitive task of joining the ephemeral sentiments of public opinion to the intricate acts which define public policy. However, other scholars such as MacRae and Belknap had demonstrated that some of the roll call behavior of Congressmen was amenable to systematic summary. Their work showed that the techniques of Guttman scale analysis could be applied to the roll call record. Such analyses produce a standardized reflection of some part of the orderliness, consistency and predictability which have been implicitly recognized by all students of congressional behavior who maintain that Congress can be understood and known in terms sufficiently general to comprehend more than the single vote.

Exploratory work on the 84th Congress gave further evidence that it is possible to identify roll calls which can be combined to describe variations in Congressmen's positions in support of or opposition to some of the large questions of public policy. Consequently, the intention which has now been realized was to employ the methods of cumulative scale analysis to produce simple rankings of Congressmen on several policy questions. Starting with the complete record of roll calls, embracing amendments, motions to recommit, procedural questions—all decisions pertinent to and including the final decision on a bill, members of the 85th Congress were ranked in terms of their support for federal action promoting social welfare programs, the civil rights of Negroes, and an internationalist foreign policy. Of course, some of the roll calls germane to each topic produced ambiguous information about a Congressman's ultimate policy position on the topic. Where the results of the analysis indicated that a roll call could and did mean different things to different Congressmen, the roll call was not accepted as evidence of relative positions on the policy dimension with which it had originally been associated.

Given the rather stringent technical criteria which must be satsified to allow the inclusion of a vote in the final measurement of policy position, it is well worth noting that an impressive proportion of roll call behavior in the 85th Congress conformed to the tested assumption that Congressmen respond consistently and therefore predictably to vote decisions in terms of single, general guiding principles. There are many departures from such a unitary mode of behavior. And many important acts of Congressmen do not become a matter of public record but are lost in the deliberations of the committee and in the informal negotiations which surround every important roll call. Nevertheless, important legislative questions are often brought to a recorded vote; those votes do provide a basis for distinguishing Congressmen who are more in favor of a policy from those who are less favorably inclined; and the analysis of those votes indicates that many of them are cast in terms of a Congressman's persistent preference for a general policy position under which the questions at issue are subsumed.

On the side of the electorate, the study was designed with some confidence based on past research. Earlier work at the SRC and elsewhere had indicated that a paucity of information about the events of government does not prevent the citizen from responding to questions about public policy with a general policy preference in mind. Although the citizen may be poorly informed about the state of civil rights legislation or about the extent of social welfare activity emanating from Washington, he can and will indicate support or opposition to such policies if asked to do so. And the application of cumulative scale analysis to policy attitudes of the members of the national electorate indicates that their attitudes, as the attitudes and the roll calls of Congressmen and the attitudes of non-incumbent congressional candidates as well, reflect the existence of underlying commitments to general policy positions.

Thus the several attitudes expressed by the individuals in our sample from each constituency fit the tested assumption that each specific attitude can be subsumed under a more general policy preference held by the individual. As a consequence of this phenomenon the attitudes expressed on each of a series of questions about governmental policy can be used to rank the constituents of a district in terms of their relative support for specified governmental policies. By averaging the rankings for a set of individuals an average or mean policy preference for each set of constituents can be estimated. These estimates can be made for any subset of constituents represented in the sample. We may estimate the average position for an entire district or separately for the partisan majority and minority within a district. Only mundane questions of expense and technical questions of sample size limit our ability to extend these estimates to labor union members, to Negroes or to any other subset of individuals within a district, across all of the districts of a region or across districts otherwise located by social, political, economic or psychological boundaries.

It is a matter of no small importance to discover that the individuals in each of the major populations under investigation—the national electorate, the incumbent members of the 85th Congress and the nonincumbent challengers for seats in the 86th Congress—could be ranked according to their relative policy preferences in each of the three policy domains. But for all of the important substantive implications which may be generated from this evidence of order and coherence in policy preferences, the feasibility of the study as originally designed hangs on meaningful correlation between comparable phenomena in two different populations. Most important of all is there any consistent relationship between the policy preferences of constituents and the legislative acts of their representatives? To answer this question, and its corollaries evaluating the circumstances which may enhance or inhibit the relationship, we must turn to a technique which will summarize the many individual pieces of evidence which must be considered.

THE MEASUREMENT OF POLICY AGREEMENT

Policy agreement will be defined as the correlation between the relative positions of *groups* of constituents ranked by their mean attitudinal positions

Case I: *Full Policy Agreement*

CONGRESSMAN'S
ROLL CALL POSITION

DISTRICT'S ATTITUDE POSITION	Pro	Neutral	Con	
Pro	33	0	0	33
Neutral	0	34	0	34
Con	0	0	33	33
	33	34	33	100%

Rank correlation = + 1.0

Case II: *No Policy Agreement*

CONGRESSMAN'S
ROLL CALL POSITION

DISTRICT'S ATTITUDE POSITION	Pro	Neutral	Con	
Pro	11	11	11	33
Neutral	11	12	11	34
Con	11	11	11	33
	33	34	33	100%

Rank correlation = 0.0

Case III: *Full Policy Disagreement*

CONGRESSMAN'S
ROLL CALL POSITION

DISTRICT'S ATTITUDE POSITION	Pro	Neutral	Con	
Pro	0	0	33	33
Neutral	0	34	0	34
Con	33	0	0	33
	33	34	33	100%

Rank correlation = − 1.0

on a policy, and the relative positions of their Congressmen, ranked by their roll call records on the same policy. The limits within which policy agreement must fall are suggested by the following hypothetical examples (Case I, Case II, and Case III). Under the first condition, we find a perfect match between the relative policy positions of constituencies and Congressmen. All of the Congressmen who share a particular roll call record come from all of the districts in which constituents are comparably disposed. Under the second condition there is no relationship, reflecting a total absence of policy agreement. Congressmen with one extreme roll call record (Pro) come from districts that have policy preferences exactly like those districts which elect Congressmen whose records are the polar opposite (Con.). The third condition depicts the logical opposite of the first and finds maximum policy disagreement where Congressmen of one persuasion come from districts which, among all districts, give least support to the position supported by their Congressmen. Although this constitutes a rather perverse pattern where entire districts are concerned, we will note shortly that such relationships do occur, particularly where incumbent Congressmen and their minority opposition in the district are concerned.

The data collected from constituencies and Congressmen in 1958 indicate that a substantially different estimate of policy agreement is associated with each of the three policy domains. In the civil rights area, a correlation of $+.6$ reflects very considerably congruence between constituency preference and congressional performance.[1] On the question of a basic foreign policy posture the policy agreement correlation is $-.1$. This is not so much a reliable indication that Congressmen have a slight tendency to be systematically out of line with constituency preferences as it is an emphatic testimony to the absence of policy agreement. Social welfare questions, more durably a focus for political disagreement but less violently a matter of current concern than were civil rights in 1958, provide the base for policy agreement falling between the other estimates and reaching almost to $+.3$. In no case does policy agreement approach the limiting condition in which variations in the conditions maximizing and minimizing agreement would be irrelevant because perfect agreement (as in Case I) had foreclosed the possibility of variations in agreement. But conversely, only foreign policy presents us with the virtual absence of variation in policy agreement. In both the domestic domains there is enough agreement on policy to permit extensive investigation of the conditions which accentuate or diminish that agreement. And even foreign policy, as an example of the null case (illustrated by Case II), has a very real utility in our search for a better understanding of the operation of our system of representative government.

THE LINKS BETWEEN DISTRICT ATTITUDES AND CONGRESSIONAL ROLL CALLS

In pursuing the explication of observed policy agreement, two modes of linking constituent opinion with congressional roll call behavior may be suggested. There are other possibilities as well, but linkage through the Congressman's personal attitudes and through his perceptions of the constituents' preferences are demonstrably the most important. By virtue of the electoral system, each Congressman must stand before his district for reelection every two years. The electorate may choose to elect as Congressman a person who shares in his personal convictions the dominant policy preferences of the district. If the Congressman is thus representative of the district in the sense of being a typical or modal member of the district, his own policy attitudes will provide a base for roll call behavior which is consonant with the preferences of the district. Roll call decisions based on personal conviction will be an involuntary reflection of district attitudes and policy agreement will have been insured through the selection of a right-minded representative.

It is also quite possible, of course, to elect a man in confidence that he will represent the wishes of the district, whatever his own convictions. If such a man is made to know the desires of his supporters, and if he understands that his tenure in office is contingent on the active promotion of those desires, his continued interest in remaining in favor with the voters may lead to roll call behavior consistent with his perception of the requirements for re-election. Whatever his personal policy preferences, policy agreement with his constituents will result as he strives to match his actions to their demands.

Of course, if the constituency has no interest in the representation of its policy views and chooses to ignore the policy preferences of candidates for election, some element of policy agreement may yet result through the co-incident agreement of policy views or through the candidate's voluntary deference to what he perceives to be the dominant wishes of the constituency. Without the deliberate attempt of constituents to assure attitudinal agreement or without the threat of electoral reprisal to promote conformity, the establish-

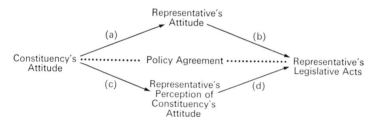

Paradigm for Explication of Policy Agreement

Figure 10–1

ment of policy agreement is an incidental consequence of the electoral process. But with or without conscious intent on the part of those recruiting and electing the Congressman, his attitudinal or perceptual rapport with the district provides the bases on which policy agreement involving his roll call behavior will rest.

A schematic representation of this paradigm is presented in Figure 10–1 below. Each of the two chains connecting constituent attitudes with Congressman's roll call has two links. If either link is broken or even weakened, the chain is no longer an effective connection. Thus, attitudinal agreement between Congressman and constituency, (a), will lead to policy agreement only if the Congressman gives substantial weight, (b), to his own policy preference in making his roll call decision. Or, in the instance of the perceptual chain, diligently voting what is perceived to be the constituent preference, (d), will produce policy agreement only if the perception of constituent policy attitudes is relatively accurate, (c).

Finally, before turning to the examination of representation through majority rule, attention should be drawn to an incidental feature of the paradigm which will be of interest later. In assessing the contribution of each chain to policy agreement, we have computed the correlation between each connecting element (Congressman's attitude and Congressman's perception of constituent attitudes) and the Congressman's roll call position. As a by-product of this computation we have obtained an estimate of the extent to which the Congressman's roll call position is associated with—or determined by—the combination of these two factors. This estimate is in the form of a standard coefficient of multiple correlation.

If this were a study devoted to the explanation of roll call behavior, the roll call end of our paradigm might look something like Figure 10–2. The consequence of an accurate measurement of each of the factors impinging on the roll call decisions, with all of them used in a multiple correlation with a measure of roll call position, would be a coefficient of multiple correlation

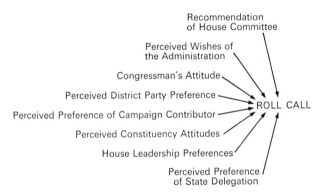

Paradigm for Explication of Roll Call Behavior

Figure 10–2

which would have a value of approximately 1.00. Which is to say, an accurate assessment of all factors relevant to the Congressman's decision would result in a perfect accounting for his behavior—a perfect prediction of that behavior. Inasmuch as the full roster of distinct influences on congressional roll call behavior might well number eighteen or twenty-eight instead of the eight in Figure 10–2 our concern with only two elements and their association with roll call behavior must be properly seen as a concern with a very limited set of factors. If these two elements are found to play a very minor part in the determination of roll call behavior, the study will have supported the charge that policy agreement may be of interest to old-fashioned democratic theorists but of limited importance to those who would develop empirical theory to account for the output of the legislative process.

II

POLITICAL COMPETITION, MAJORITY RULE AND REPRESENTATIVE GOVERNMENT

Whether the symbol is that of the market place of ideas or the arena of political combat, the concept of competition occupies a central place in democratic theory and practice. Competition for political power is the legitimate consequence of individual differences in a society that regards the individual as the supreme political unit and that insists on political equality among individuals. The constitutional guarantees of individual rights take on added meaning when viewed as the guaranteed means by which individuals who constitute a political minority may strive to become a majority. The procedural right of individuals to be heard not only limits the substantive tyranny of the majority but guarantees a base for political competition.

The argument at times runs beyond the simple permissibility of competition and includes a brief for encouraging and sustaining competition by giving the minority a voice beyond the level of the ordinary voter. Thus the case for proportional representation encourages minorities that would be powerless under majority rule to carry their cause to the level of competition among representatives.

In addition to competition treated as a right or an extension of rights, competition may be viewed as salutary for instrumental reasons. Thus, to insure responsive and responsible government there should be a minority capable of providing a real alternative to elected leadership. With ordinary voters free to extend or withhold their favors, the threat of electoral reprisal may enforce the responsibility so essential to representative government. Moreover, if the possibility of overturning an earlier majority is real, the chance for electoral victory may encourage the minority to offer superior leadership alternatives and thereby force an upgrading in the quality of leadership offered to the voters.

The latter perspective is particularly persuasive if one assumes that the complexities of modern life, and the limited competencies of ordinary voters, make of democracy the freedom to choose between alternate candidates and little more. Somewhat more generously it may be assumed that democratic government rises and falls with the quality of the alternatives for leadership presented for electoral approval. It may be further assumed that superior leadership can be produced only if a real chance for victory encourages the most competent of the minority to challenge the incumbency of the majority. Stringent competition breeds a positive cycle of strong contenders for public favor, while the hopeless competition of a single party area relaxes the pressure and allows leadership to sink to the lowest common denominator within both the monolithic majority and the impotent minority.

Competition may be encouraged to maximize the representation of minority interests and insure a superior quality among the alternatives made available to the voters, but at some point deliberation must give way to decision. In the

Anglo-American tradition, majority rule has been adopted as the rule which permits a decision and yet gives maximum representation to equally valued participants. The logic seems impeccable: if everyone is valued equally, 101 voters preferring A are to be favored over 100 preferring B. And yet, majority rule at times promises to confound the objectives of encouraged competition. From A. Lawrence Lowell on, the principal authorities have observed in two party competition the seeds of a politics of moderation. Where the minority does have a real chance, and where the majority is under the constant threat of defeat with a marginal loss of support, it is said the competition is only over control of the middle of the road. Far from resulting in a clean, sharp contest with important alternatives articulated for the voters by the best exponents of contrasting views, balanced competition has produced the politics of tweedledum and tweedledee. In explanation it is suggested that the representative who wins in a close race becomes a prisoner of his narrow margin of victory. The majority loses some of its claim on its champion and the minority gains representation in return. But the competition which was to produce clearcut alternatives and enhance the quality of alternatives presented to the voters has produced a mean product with little attraction to any faction. The calculus of the election thereby demeans the institutions so carefully erected to give voice to the diversity of the society.

III

DATA PERTAINING TO ELECTORAL COMPETITION AND MAJORITY RULE

Data collected in the study of policy agreement call into question most of the broad empirical generalizations just reviewed. Our new found ability to inspect hitherto inaccessible phenomena also results in evidence that unexpectedly illuminates new facets of the topic and at times redefines the nature of the problem we are studying. Illustrative of data which lead one to question some of the established conclusions are the following appraisals of inter-party differences in roll call behavior associated with the relative balance of partisan competition in the congressional district. In Table 10–1 we find evidence apparently indicating that party differences across competitive or marginal districts are indeed blurred in comparison with those which obtain among Congressmen from the safe districts. In each of three policy domains the contrast between policy positions of Democrats and Republicans in Congress is greater among Congressmen from safe districts and lesser among representatives from marginal districts.

Despite the impressive regularity of this evidence, the case for the hypothesis that close electoral competition limits the differences between policy alternatives offered to the voters is not easily made. In only two of the six *intra*-party comparisons (within Republicans in social welfare and within Democrats in foreign policy) is there clear evidence that electoral competition is associated with a more moderate policy position. In two other cases (Democrats in social welfare and Republicans in civil rights) competition tends to be associated with a more extreme roll call position. The remaining comparisons provide no evidence one way or the other—except to deny the expectation that marginal district Congressmen will drive the middle of whatever road has been taken by their colleagues.

Even more pertinent to the basic logic of the hypothesis is the question of intra-district differences in proffered policy alternatives. Within a system of single member districts, roll calls are inherently limited as data relevant to the hypothesis. They permit comparisons only across or among districts while the hypothesis demands inter-district comparisons of intra-district phenomena. In the assessment of party differences in Table 10–1, Democratic Congress-

TABLE 10–1

*Partisan Differences in Roll Call Behavior Associated with Partisanship
Competition in Northern Districts*

	Democratic Congressmen	Republican Congressmen	Difference
Social Welfare:			
Safe Districts*	4.39†	0.69	3 70
Marginal Districts*	4.56	2.40	2.16
Foreign Policy:			
Safe Districts	4.29	1.39	2.90
Marginal Districts	3.83	3.38	0.45
Civil Rights:			
Safe Districts	5.00	2.40	2.60
Marginal Districts	5.00	4.55 .	0.45

* Safe and marginal are defined here and throughout this paper by the Congressmen's own descriptions of their respective districts. In the course of the interview each Congressman was asked: "How about the relative strength of the parties in your district? Over the years has the district been a safe district, a fairly close district, or what?" The answers were categorized according to the following scheme:
1. Safe Democratic
2. Fairly safe, usually Democratic
3. Fairly close, Democrats usually have the edge
4. Fairly close, goes back and forth
5. Fairly close, Republicans usually have the edge
6. Fairly safe, usually Republican
7. Safe Republican
In this paper a safe district is one classified as 1, 2, 6 or 7; all others are defined as marginal districts.
† The scores are the mean rank orders for each set of Congressmen. Because of different bases for scoring each set of roll calls, these data should not be compared *across* policy areas. One cannot deduce from these data that marginal district Democrats were less internationalist (3.83) than they were liberal (4.56), etc.

man A from Congressional District 1 is being compared with Republican A from District 2, where Districts 1 and 2 are both safe districts. Then Democrat B from District 11 is compared with Republican B from 12, where 11 and 12 are marginal or competitive districts. Because the difference between Democrat A and Republican A is greater than the difference between Democrat B and Republican B, the data may be thought to fit the hypothesis that party differences are greater under single party domination of districts and are minimized by tightened electoral competition. But, if Democrat A takes a policy based on what the electoral situation in his district allows or demands, he is taking a position vis-à-vis the position of the Republican candidate and the voters *within his district*—not in response to the position being taken by some Republican Candidate A who is going to be elected in some other district. Similarly, Republican A takes his position in terms of his own district, not in recognition of some remote district that is going to elect a Democrat. In the absence of direct, intra-district comparisons of contending candidates, analyses which are limited to comparisons across districts must rest on the assumption that policy position is determined *only* by a previously defined party line and by deviations from the party line imposed by the necessities of meeting the electoral competition. In the safe districts the party line must prevail; in the marginal districts the party line is modified only to meet the competition.

American legislative politics is, of course, shot through with other sources of influence on a legislator's behavior: regionalism, urbanism or religion, seniority, committee action or leadership role, to mention only a few. The Congressmen's lackadaisical adherence to party line, which the hypothesis of moderation is presumed to explain, is exacerbated by the frequent intrusion of such factors. It is extremely hazardous to assume the roll call position of any subset of Congressmen reflects, above all else, adherence to the party line, or party loyalty modified only by electoral exigencies. The extent of this hazard is suggested by data which are first cousins to the roll call records but which permit both intra- and inter-district comparisons: the personal policy preferences of both incumbent and nonincumbent candidates for Congress as reflected in expressed attitudes toward policy alternatives.

The direct counterpart of the social welfare portion of Table 10–1 describing the attitudinal positions of the incumbents whose roll call positions are described in Table 10–1, is presented in Table 10–2. By the same logic

TABLE 10–2

Partisan Differences in Policy Attitudes on Social Welfare Legislation Associated with Partisan Competition in Northern Districts

	Democratic Congressmen	Republican Congressmen	Difference
Safe Districts	3.14*	0.60	2.54
Marginal	3.74	0.86	2.88

* The scores are means computed on a five point cumulative or Guttman-type scale.

which finds party differences on *roll calls* blurred by intra-district electoral competition, the data of Table 10–2 indicate a sharpening and exaggeration of party differences on policy *attitudes* associated with the same intensification of intra-district contests.

The data which permit a direct examination of intra-district differences in candidate policy preferences are presented in Table 10–3. The top portion of the table describes the more detailed, direct confrontation of groups of opposing candidates; the bottom portion summarizes these data by eliminating the party designation for districts and the incumbency of the candidates. Both portions of the table sharpen the evidence that party differences *within* the district are heightened when electoral competition is keen and reduced under single party domination of congressional electoral politics.

The evidence from Tables 10–2 and 10–3 could still be reconciled with the original hypothesis associating moderation of party differences with intense electoral competition. This would be possible if the roll calls for each group of Congressmen (those from safe and those from marginal districts) were quite differently related to their respective policy attitudes. For example, one might imagine that keen electoral competition produces an intra-party demand, within each party, for a candidate who isn't going to be confused with

TABLE 10–3

Partisan Differences in Policy Attitudes in Social Welfare Legislation Associated with Partisan Competition in Northern Districts

A

	Incumbents	Nonincumbent Candidates	Difference
Democratic Districts			
Safe	3.14*	1.52	1.62
Marginal	3.74	0.90	2.84
Republican Districts			
Safe	0.60	2.62	2.02
Marginal	0.86	3.47	2.61

B

	All Democratic Candidates	All Republican Candidates	Difference
Safe Districts	2.81	0.89	1.92
Marginal Districts	3.62	0.88	2.74

* The scores are means computed on a five point cumulative or Guttman-type scale.

the opposition candidate. Electoral realities then lead the victorious candidate—who must anticipate going back to the voters two years hence—to modify his public position and thereby maximize his chances for re-election. In safe districts there may be no such need for a differentiation between private (personal or intra-party preferences) and public (roll call) policy positions. The elected candidate may be free to vote his views or to deviate from them only to accentuate the uniqueness of his party's views.

Once again, however, the data confound such an extrapolation from the original hypothesis. Congressmen from marginal districts do not exhibit more discrepancy between attitudes and roll calls, nor is there a consistent tendency for them to vote a position relatively more moderate than their expressed attitudes. Congressmen from safe districts do exhibit more discrepancy between attitudes and roll call and the discrepancies minimize party differences as often as they accentuate them. Data pertaining directly to attitude-roll call relationships are even more convincing. We shall shortly examine evidence indicating that the Congressmen from marginal districts are much more likely to translate their own policy preferences directly into roll call behavior than are Congressmen from the safe districts; and we shall note that translation results in much less policy agreement than exists between constituents and Congressmen in one-party districts.

To return the argument to its starting place, the data of Table 10–1 may suggest that electoral competition is associated with greater support for governmental intervention and activism in handling major national problems, but they cannot be taken as reliable evidence that electoral competition promotes the politics of tweedledum and tweedledee. It may be quite true that systems governed by majority rule grapple with alternatives less extreme than those juxtaposed by and within other systems. But the data we have examined here give no support to the notion that *within* a system governed by majority rule there is a comparable variation in clarity of alternatives associated with the first cause of the hypothesis—electoral pressure to acquire majority support at the polls.

For the analysis of other aspects of the problem it is useful to turn to the rather full array of data produced by assembling the various parts of our paradigm for the analysis of policy agreement. The paradigm includes four elements: (1) constituency policy preferences, (2) the policy attitudes of Congressmen, (3) the Congressmen's perceptions of the constituency attitudes, and, finally, (4) the Congressmen's roll call behavior. Each of the relevant relationships associating one element with another is expressed as a statement of correlation in the figures which follow.

The Antecedents of Roll Call Behavior

Although our ultimate interest lies in the explication of policy agreement, a striking indication of the more general importance of congressional attitudes and perceptions of district attitudes is provided by the coefficients of multiple correlation (R) associated with the congressional roll call behaviors. From Figure 10–3a we may conclude that the two elements contribute more than half of the total determination of the social welfare roll call positions. In the realm of social science, in which correlations approaching .5 are considered to be rather magnificent, two predictor correlations approaching .8 are rarely found. In the two multiple correlations of .73 and .77 we are given evidence of an astounding importance for these two elements in their contribution to the general phenomenon of congressional legislative decision-making.

At the same time the comparable pairs of coefficients for civil rights and foreign policy roll calls (.89 and .65 in Figure 10–3b, and .73 and .21 in Figure 10–3c) demonstrate that these two components of the Congressman's internal world must vary in the importance of their contribution to different roll call decisions. In particular, they account for only a minute fraction of the foreign policy decisions made by Congressmen from competitive districts. The immediate explanation of why this should be so is provided by another element of substantial importance to the legislative process. On matters of foreign policy, Congressmen from marginal districts more often than others attached considerable importance to the position advocated by the administration. The reality of that importance may be directly inferred from the fact that, in general, where the administration's wishes influenced the Congressman, that influence contributed a larger part to the total determination of roll call behavior and the other contributing factors—such as the Congressman's own policy preference or his perception of district preferences—played a relatively lesser role. In all three policy domains, roll call behavior was less a function of the two attitudinal and perceptual factors whenever the Congressmen recognized that they had been influenced in their roll calls by their knowledge of the administration's position on bills before the House. For the case in point, the administration's position on foreign policy was much more often seen as important by Congressmen from competitive districts. (This was less often the case in civil rights and much less the case on social welfare.) The Congressmen's own attitudes and their perceptions of constituent attitudes consequently contributed less to their ultimate decisions on the affected roll calls.

Policy Agreement in Competitive Districts

Perhaps the most unexpected of the broad findings contained in Figures 10–3a, 10–3b, and 10–3c is the discovery that neither the minority nor the majority constituents in marginal districts enjoy any positive agreement with the roll call decisions of their Congressmen. From the concept of the electorally produced politics of moderation we might have expected to find marginal minorities relatively well represented, although at the expense of reduced policy agreement for members of the majority. Or, at the extreme of recent theories, the suggestions of Huntington might have been read to imply maximum policy agreement in the marginal districts, at least with the district majorities. Instead, of course, we note the instance of foreign policy where the majority positions in marginal districts are actually systematically opposed by the roll call voting of their Congressmen (policy disagreement of $-.27$ in Figure 10–3c).[2] This clearly confounds any general expectation that sharp electoral competition binds representative and represented more tightly together. The virtually complete absence of policy agreement for the marginal majorities in the other two policy domains ($-.08$ on civil rights, Figure 10–3b, and $+.08$ on social welfare, Figure 10–3a) completes the statement of denial of the expectation.

The minority fares no better under competitive conditions. Their relative advantage over the majority on foreign policy is clearly only relative ($+.05$ to $-.27$, Figure 10–3c), and the more plausible expectation of policy agreement less than that for the majority holds true with a vengeance on social welfare matters. Here the relative absence of policy agreement with the majority, +.08 in Figure 10–3a, stands in sharp contrast with the minority policy *dis*agreement of −.34. The sharp partisan polarization of constituent attitudes in competitive districts results in systematic disagreement between the attitudes of minority constituents and those of the Congressmen from their districts. This attitudinal disagreement is translated into policy disagreement as the Congressmen from marginal districts engage in the very close match between their attitudinal positions and their roll call positions in Congress as reflected in the coefficient of +.75.

Representation Relationships for Majorities and Minorities in Constituencies Divided According to the Congressman's Perception of the Balance of Electoral Competition.

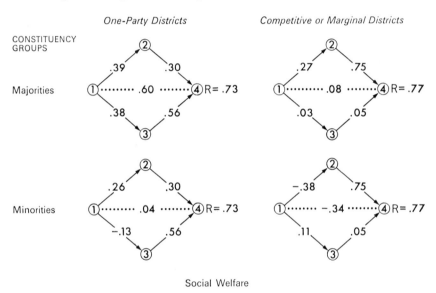

Social Welfare

Figure 10–3a

Key for Figures 10–3a, 10–3b, and 10–3c.

1. Constituency Policy Attitudes
2. Congressmen's Policy Attitudes
3. Congressmen's Perceptions of Constituency Attitudes
4. Roll Call Record

The coefficients given between 1 and 2, 1 and 3, and 1 and 4 are simple or zero-order product-moment correlations. The coefficients between 2 and 4, and 3 and 4, are the normalized regression coefficients from the regression equation in which 4 is predicted from 2 and 3. Hence, these coefficients express the relation of 2 or 3 with 4 as the other predictor is "controlled."

R is the product-moment coefficient of multiple correlation, expressing the combined relation of 2 and 3 with 4. The square of R is the coefficient of multiple determination, expressing the proportion of the variance of 4 that is accounted for by 2 and 3 together.

Representation Relationships for Majorities and Minorities in Constituencies Divided According to the Congressman's Perception of the Balance of Electoral Competition.

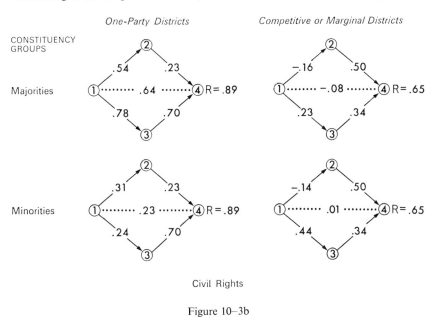

Civil Rights

Figure 10–3b

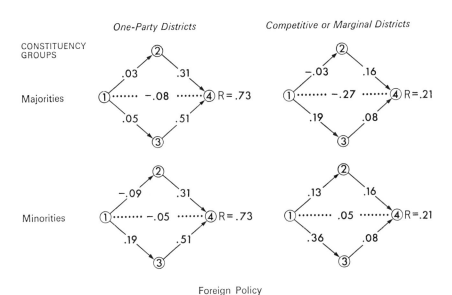

Foreign Policy

Figure 10–3c

In general, policy agreement in competitive districts is thwarted by weak or disrupted links in one or the other of the two chains connecting constituency attitudes and congressional roll calls. In the case of foreign policy the very limited relationships between the Congressman's roll call and his attitudinal and perceptual positions foredooms the development of policy

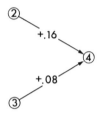

Competitive Districts

Figure 10–4. Foreign Policy, from Figure 10–3c

agreement. With both potential causal chains weakened at the point of contact with the roll call decision, antecedent conditions have no more than academic interest for understanding the absence of policy agreement involving either minority or majority constituents. Nevertheless, for other reasons it is worth noting the perceptions of district attitudes were more or less well aligned with the objects being perceived (coefficients of +.19 and +.36 with majority and minority attitudes, respectively), and that the corresponding attitudinal links between Congressmen and constituents (−.03 and +.19) were visibly weaker than the perceptual links.

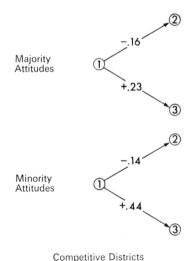

Competitive Districts

Figure 10–5. Civil Rights, from Figure 10–3b

The absence of policy agreement on civil rights matters is clearly a consequence of the presently inexplicable attitudinal disagreement. There seems to be no obvious reason why attitudinal disagreement should prevail in the marginal districts, particularly not in the face of the Congressmen's relatively accurate perceptions of the constituents' preferences. Were it not for that disagreement and the relative dominance of the Congressman's own attitude in his roll call decision, policy agreement would have been produced by way of the perceptual linkage with minority attitudes (①— +.44 →③— +.34 →④) and we might have observed an important instance in which electoral competition was associated with a real advantage in policy agreement for minority constituents.

In the case of social welfare, one of the explanations for the observed data on policy agreement lies beyond the immediate variables of the paradigm. Were it not for the systematic intrusion of some factor dysfunctional for policy agreement, the chain involving the Congressman's enactment of attitudinal agreement (①— +.27 →② — +.75 →④) (Figure 3a) would have produced evidence of a positive relationship between majority policy preferences and the roll call record. The same factor which depressed policy agreement for the majority may have contributed some increment to the negative agreement for the minority. Without such an assist, the less than perfect match between congressional attitude and roll call ($\beta = +.75$) would have resulted in a somewhat more subdued statement of policy disagreement. However, even without the unidentified factor, the attitudinal disagreement with minority constituents would have resulted in clear evidence of policy disagreement (through the chain :①— −.38 →②— +.75 →④). And inasmuch as it may be a factor common to relationships involving both majority and minority constituents, the unknown intruder may bear no essential responsibility for the marked contrast between null policy agreement for the majority and policy disagreement for the minority.

The Attitudinal and Perceptual Antecedents of Roll Call Behavior

Another major surprise which permeates the data of Figures 3 lies in the uniform differences in the strengths of relationships between roll call position and congressional attitudes and perceptions. Generally speaking, one might be impressed with the potential for irresponsibility on the part of Congressmen from safe districts. Secure in their electoral dominance, one might expect their roll call records to reflect their own attitudes more often than what they perceive to be district preferences. Quite independently, one might anticipate that the competitive electoral situation and a political career hanging in delicate balance might well dispose the marginal district Congressman to eschew Burkean self-assessment in favor of a sensitive concern for local district preferences when making his legislative mark. Both expectations are contradicted by the data from all three policy domains. The social welfare data from Figure 10-3a present the sharpest contrast between expectation and reality. It is the marginal district Congressmen who virtually ignore what they think to be district preferences in favor of their personal attitudes on policy questions—and this by a spectacular margin reflected in the coefficients of +.75 and +.05. They can scarcely be following a voting strategy which will disguise their relatively extreme personal preferences noted in Tables 10–2 and 10–3. While representatives from one party districts are not completely self-effacing, they do reflect what they understand to be district sentiment more faithfully than they attempt to enact their own policy predilections. The relative differences between the weights of +.75 and +.05 and between those of +.30 and +.56 are repeated with slightly different magnitudes for civil rights (+.50 to +.34 and +.23 to +.70) and foreign policy (+.16 to +.08 and +.31 to +.51).

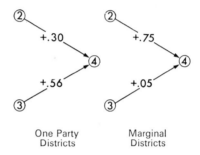

One Party   Marginal
Districts   Districts

Figure 10–6. Social Welfare, from Figure 10–3a

The full explication of these unexpected but unambiguous findings must await a complete understanding of the origins, correlates and implications of electoral competition. But without following this path to its end, a number of persuasive hypotheses may be advanced to account for the otherwise anomalous data. In the first place, Congressmen from one-party districts enjoy a longer tenure in office and have a visibly longer span of time to be made aware of district preferences. This awareness is suggested by the visibly greater accuracy of their perceptions of majority preferences on established questions of domestic policy (+.38 to +.03 on social welfare, for Congressmen from safe and marginal districts, respectively, and +.78 to +.23 on civil rights). Moreover, in response to direct questioning, representatives from marginal districts less often report unqualified confidence in their knowledge of district wishes. A general correlate of a Congressman's lack of confidence in his knowledge of the district's preference is a greater reliance on his own preference in the roll call decision. Coming full circle with these data we find Congressmen from one-party districts more accurate in their perceptions of the districts' wishes, more confident that they know the districts' wishes, and more likely to reflect the perceived wishes in their roll call votes.

Another even more important element of the explanation may lie in something so apparently remote as population mobility which has produced change in the political composition of congressional districts. Congressmen who perceive their districts as undergoing population change appear to be extremely sensitive to these changes. They follow a decision-making pattern in their roll calls which gives much greater relative prominence to their understanding of district preferences than to their personal policy preferences. Congressmen who perceive major changes in district composition are very heavily concentrated in the one-party districts. Once again we may close the circle and reduce our perplexity about the uniformity of the attitude-perception patterns in Figures 10–3a, 10–3b and 10–3c. We may conclude that drastic changes in the composition of the constituency, stimulating the Congressman's concern over constituency sentiment and emphasizing the

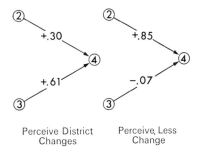

Perceive District   Perceive, Less
Changes   Change

Figure 10–7. Social Welfare, from Figure 10–3a

importance of that sentiment in his legislative acts, have occurred more often or more prominently in one-party districts and have precipitated some of the rather unique patterns of behavior which distinguish Congressmen from one-party districts from those representing competitive districts.

Policy Agreement in One-Party Districts

Rather amazing evidence of policy agreement is associated with both of the domestic policy topics in the one-party districts of the nation. And both in the case of social welfare and civil rights, policy agreement is most clearly a matter of congruence between the policy attitudes of majority constituents and the relative roll call records of their respective Congressmen. Policy agreement with the majority on social welfare produced a coefficient of +.60; on civil rights it was measured at +.64.

To provide a basis for evaluating these two most extreme examples of policy agreement, the following hypothetical and idealized cases have been created. Case A presents a complete policy agreement. Case B presents an idealized version of policy agreement reflected in a correlation of approxi-mately .6. For those readers accustomed to tables of proportions, Case C presents the same idealized display as Case B, but with the entries translated into proportions which total 100 per cent for each column.

The pattern of relative differences between policy agreement statements observed for the majorities and minorities in competitive districts (+.08 and −.34, respectively) is strikingly repeated on social welfare issues in one party districts. The outnumbered minorities in the safe districts fail to have their views reflected in their Congressmen's roll call behaviors, despite a modest attitudinal agreement, because the congressional perceptions of district preferences accord with the majority views but are out of phase with the attitudes of the minorities. By the same token, both chains provide staunch and independently important connections between majority policy preferences and the roll call record. They combine to establish what must be regarded as an extremely high level of policy agreement. In terms of relative

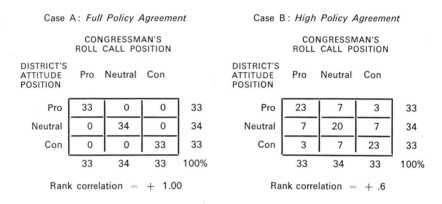

Case A: *Full Policy Agreement*

CONGRESSMAN'S
ROLL CALL POSITION

DISTRICT'S ATTITUDE POSITION	Pro	Neutral	Con	
Pro	33	0	0	33
Neutral	0	34	0	34
Con	0	0	33	33
	33	34	33	100%

Rank correlation = + 1.00

Case B: *High Policy Agreement*

CONGRESSMAN'S
ROLL CALL POSITION

DISTRICT'S ATTITUDE POSITION	Pro	Neutral	Con	
Pro	23	7	3	33
Neutral	7	20	7	34
Con	3	7	23	33
	33	34	33	100%

Rank correlation = + .6

Case C: *High Policy Agreement*

CONGRESSMAN'S
ROLL CALL POSITION

DISTRICT'S ATTITUDE POSITION	Pro	Neutral	Con
Pro	70%	20%	10%
Neutral	20	60	20
Con	10	20	70
	100%	100%	100%

Rank correlation = + .6

importance, however, the perceptual linkage (①→③→④) can be assumed to have contributed considerably more to policy agreement than was contributed by the attitudinal chain (①→②→④).

The even somewhat greater policy agreement involving majority constituents on questions of civil rights for Negroes is also still more strikingly a product of congressional enactment of what is perceived to be the district preference. Congressional deference to constituent opinions accounts for very much more of the total agreement on policy than does involuntary representation through the attitudinal chain.

There is an observable difference between relationships involving majority and minority constituents in civil rights questions in 1958, and yet the larger impression is that of a public issue largely outside the boundaries of partisan competition. The essentially sociocultural nonpartisan quality of the civil

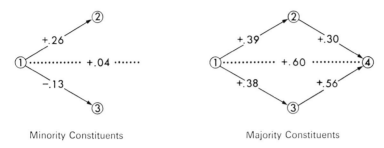

Minority Constituents	Majority Constituents
Figure 10–8. Social Welfare, from Figure 10–3a	Figure 10–9. Social Welfare, from Figure 10–3a

rights issue resulted in a moderate degree of policy agreement extending to minority constituents. As a public issue the civil rights question has been generated largely out of personal contacts or the anticipation of personal contact with the consequences of conflict between cultural norms. With no strong party cues to crystallize opinion on party lines, and with the powerful

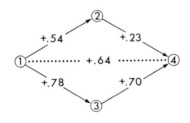

Majority Constituents

Figure 10–10. Civil Rights, from Figure 10–3b

sharing of experience in local social and economic circumstances to unite opinions across party lines, policy positions vary much more among districts and much less within districts than is the case with social welfare. It is clear that the Eisenhower administration was a source of influence in civil rights legislation in the 85th Congress, particularly with Congressmen from the marginal congressional districts across the nation (R = .65). However, such influence did not work to the net advantage of policy agreement either with majority or minority partisans. Much more remarkable is the extent to which roll call behavior by Congressmen from safe districts was a simple product of the two intervening factors present in our paradigm (R = .89). Only a very minor fraction of all roll call votes cast by them on civil rights bills in the 85th Congress need be accounted for by elements other than their own attitudes or their deference to perceived district preferences.

The extreme degree of policy agreement on both social welfare and civil rights questions in safe districts and the very substantial congruence of congressional attitudes and perceptions with the roll call decisions of Congressmen from safe districts suggest another line of inquiry. The two phenomena come together in the safe districts. And yet it is the safe districts that contribute the Congressmen with greatest seniority, occupying the leadership positions within the House. With considerations of seniority and leadership responsibilities in mind, we might have expected safe district Congressmen to vote their convictions while giving short shrift to constituency demands—with re-election being secured by the traditional devices of political leadership in issueless single party areas. Or we might have expected leadership roles to demand enough in the way of flexibility for political negotiation to cut into any preferred consonance which a senior Congressman might wish to maintain with the district which has supported him so faithfully. But instead of presumptive evidence of relatively greater freedom from district policy constraints, or of departures from district rapport necessitated by the responsibilities of leadership, we find Congressmen from safe districts exhibiting the behavior of ambassadors intent upon remaining in favor at home or of barons who learned well the lesson of Runnymede. Of course, it is quite

Safe Districts

Figure 10–11. From Figures 10–3a and 10–3c

possible that all of the limited number of discrepancies in policy agreement in one-party districts are contributed by the handful of Congressmen whose leadership positions are relevant to the policy domain concerned. The logical possibility of this explanation, and others as well, points to one of the avenues along which further investigation must travel.

Both the populist theorist and the exponent of group theory find cause for consternation when foreign policy is the focus of interest in policy agreement. The only measure of policy agreement in this domain which departs significantly from zero is the policy *dis*agreement pertaining to majority constituents in marginal districts. Despite a pattern of determined roll call behavior which is almost indistinguishable from that producing a policy agreement correlation of .6 on social welfare policy, the virtual absence of either attitudinal or perceptual rapport between Congressmen and constituents leaves policy agreement on foreign policy in safe districts a matter of statistical indifference. At the same time, all of the trappings of the legislative process provide an independent accounting for no more than a lesser fraction of foreign policy roll call behavior on the part of Congressmen from safe districts. The absence of policy agreement occurs despite the substantial efforts of safe district Congressmen to enact what they perceive to be the wishes of their constituents. It is the inadequacy of linkage with the district more than their response to nondistrict influences which forestalls ultimate rapport between district attitudes and their roll call performance.

IV

SUMMARY

Four major generalizations supported or suggested by the evidence may be singled out for specific mention.

1. Both the mode and the extent of direct congressional representation of constituent policy preferences vary according to the policy domain. The variability across three major policy questions makes evident the need for a better understanding of the political qualities of policy controversies. In particular we need a fuller specification of the ways in which policy questions are integrated into the representative system. Theoretical speculation has dealt but lightly with the problems inherent in the representation of emerging policy concerns as contrasted with representation of established partisan points of view.

In the study at hand, social welfare best illustrates the well-established policy area. The specifics of the controversy have a very real relevance for large numbers of ordinary voters. The discussion of broad alternatives has been carried on over a considerable period of time. The substantive alternatives have been articulated in terms of partisan political alternatives presented to the voters.

The civil rights of Negroes has re-emerged only in recent years as a popular as well as public issue. The question of race relations has a clear relevance for many people, but the alternative courses of private and public action have not been the subject of popular debate for more than a very limited time. The evolution of alternatives has not been accompanied by a clear specification of partisan differences and the topic has remained ambiguously connected with the partisan alternatives open to the voters.

In the domain of foreign policy, any commitment to a more than sporadic excitement over the largest crisis threatening war has been the monopoly of a very limited number of voters. Despite the objective relevance of foreign policy decisions for the daily life of all, those decisions and the events prompting them remain remote to many people. Understanding of the distant mysteries of foreign policy has not been promoted through the partisan specifications of alternatives. Mr. Eisenhower's great contribution to American political life was to obliterate the isolationist-internationalist dichotomy which had characterized post-war party allegiances. But in making internationalists out of many Republican voters and reviving the possibility of flexibility in America's foreign policy posture, the cues by which policy alternatives are given political implications for the voter were destroyed. In 1958 foreign policy stood as an emerging question for public discussion, so poorly meshed with the existing operations of the representative system as to limit the creation of the links which bind the acts of the representatives into the desires of the represented.

2. There is an important systematic difference between Congressmen from safe and competitive districts in the relative importance of the antecedents associated with their positions on the roll call record. Legislative acts of Congressmen from competitive districts are associated almost exclusively with their own policy preferences rather than with their perceptions of district preferences. The behavior of Congressmen from safe districts reflects a more even balance between the two factors, but their perceptions of constituency policy positions are clearly more highly related to their roll call decisions than are their personal policy attitudes. Although the contrasting patterns suggest the paradox of Burkean Congressmen representing competitive districts and instructed delegates coming from the safe districts, explanations for the differences lie outside explicit considerations of role. Satisfactory interpretations seem more likely to reflect structural aspects of representation affecting the relationship between the representative and the represented.

3. Evenly balanced two-party competition is not necessarily associated with a politics of moderation but it is associated with the reduction if not the total absence of direct representation of constituency policy preferences. The moderation of a Congressman's policy position may be impelled by his sense of vulnerability, but in none of the three cases studied did a meliorating representation of minority preferences result. The variety of explanations needed to account for the lack of policy agreement with either majority or minority constituents suggests that the observed absence of all policy agreement in marginal districts may have been an idiosyncratic result of the particular policies or particular time period studied. The less extreme conclusion that electoral competition reduces policy agreement is more likely to receive confirmation in subsequent research.

4. Majority constituents in safe districts are the most likely to have their policy preferences faithfully reproduced in the legislative behavior of their Congressmen. The absence of policy agreement on the question of internationalism may be more of a commentary on the nature of the issue than on the consequences of majority rule. In both domestic policy domains majority constituents enjoyed greater rapport with their Congressmen than did the minority voters. Both attitudinal agreement and perceptual linkage enhanced policy agreement with the majority. Minority preferences were honored only on the relatively non-partisan question of civil rights and then, most probably, only because of somewhat greater intra-district homogeneity of constituent attitudes. Where there is sufficiently great covariation in the policy attitudes of

majority and minority constituents across congressional districts it becomes impossible for the representatives to reflect policy agreement with their majorities without also providing some match for the preferences of their minorities.

11

THE HEGEMONIC PARTY SYSTEM
IN POLAND

JERZY J. WIATR

E VER Y society has a specific mode of integration and specific institutions which function to maintain the continuity and unity of the entire "social organism." These institutions vary from one society to another and change along with the socio-economic formation. The Marxist model of socio-economic formations constitutes a useful instrument for the analysis of this problem. This model assumes that a given mode of production—a basis for each formation—determines the type of social institutions which in the given political system perform the integrative functions. In the primitive communities, the kin was this institution; in the feudal society, it was the local community based upon the large scale ownership of land; in capitalism, particularly during its classical era, it was the market which performed the basic integrative functions. In the last type of society, integration takes place through spontaneous interaction of individual behaviors regulated primarily by the competitive rules of economy based on private ownership. Clearly, this polycentric model of social integration changed substantially in the course of the process of monopolization and the increasing role of the state—in the course of the transformation of classical capitalism into monopolistic capitalism. However, the basic role of the market as the institution performing the function of social integration is still maintained.

In the socialist society, the market and its spontaneous operations lose their old function although they do not disappear completely. The course of the

Reprinted from *Studies in Polish Political System*, ed. by Jerzy J. Wiatr and Jacek Tarkowski (Warszawa: Ossolineum, 1967), pp. 108–123.

Notes to this chapter are on pp. 381–382.

economic, cultural and other processes is being determined to an increasing extent by the political factor: the authority of the state.[1] This by no means implies that the rulers can undertake their decisions concerning the directions of social processes in an absolute vacuum, free from the pressures of the objective patterns and independent of their will. However, these patterns usually do not appear directly nor in a spontaneous fashion. They constitute the parameters delineating the borders of realism of specific undertakings. Thus, for example, although an unrealistic economic undertaking will be doomed to failure, this failure will become evident only in the course of and as a result of actions leading to the realization of this undertaking. In this fashion, the decision of the respective authorities will become an element of the social process even though it can not be realized. The result of such an undertaking will be a composite of the original design and of the pressures limiting its execution.

None of the large scale socio-economic processes in socialist societies took place as a result of spontaneous interactions of particular individuals. Socialist industrialization, collectivization of agriculture and cultural revolution are a product of determined, consciously made even if without full cognizant of all consequences, decisions. Therefore, contrary to the model of spontaneous interaction of individual behaviors determined by the rules of the market, the socialist societies are characterized by the use of the state authority to direct social processes. In this situation, political institutions acquire a new significance. They are no more an instrument used to defend the economic system from the external and/or internal forces which may threaten its functioning. They become an organic part of the economic system, which could not function without the centers making and executing decisions which determine the direction of large scale social processes taking place in a country.

In this social model, the role of politics becomes central for the life of a society. The role performed by politics in the socialist society corresponds to that performed by the market in the capitalist society: politics constitutes the plane of social integration, determining to a large extent the character and the course of social processes in the "nonpolitical" areas of social life. The political aspect, highly typical for the entire Marxist sociology, becomes necessary when socialist societies are analyzed. For no theoretical explanation of socialist societies will be complete and convincing if the analysis of the political system does not occupy a central place.

In analyzing the problems of power in the socialist society, one should direct attention to the nature of political pluralism characteristic for this system. Political pluralism is understood here as an occurrence in the political life of organized forces legally expressing the interest of differentiated social groups. Thus conceived political pluralism is an expression and a consequence of social pluralism, socio-economic differentiation of the society. Such differentiation is not limited to the division between classes, although as long as these divisions exist they determine the character of social and political pluralism. In turn, as the class divisions become extinguished other aspects of social pluralism become dominant. This process can be observed in Poland as well as in other socialist countries.

In the present phase of the socialist transformation in Poland the evolution of class relations constitutes the basis for the change of political institutions. It would be premature to maintain at the present time that the manifestations of class struggle are already absent in the Polish society. For although the basic exploiting classes have been abolished, the class nature of social conflicts outlives the economic bases of domination and even the existence of the property classes. These conflicts continue to appear basically in the sphere of political attitudes and beliefs. The situation is additionally complicated by the existence of small private business which does not necessarily lead to polarization and generation of class conflicts but potentially constitutes an area of influence of the former privileged classes. Finally, the legally and semi-legally functioning capitalist sector in spite of its economic weakness has some effect on the activeness of antisocialist groups.

Recognizing the existence and the role of class conflicts in the contemporary political life of Poland, one must note at the same time the relative decrease of the sharpness of these conflicts in comparison not only with the first years after the war but also with the period of eight or ten years ago. With reference to the rural areas Bogusław Gałęski described in the following way the advancement of the process of change of class structure:

> The class division among the peasant strata is only of marginal importance when it is formulated in terms of Lenin's categories. The class conflicts based on this categorization cannot be perceived today as the central direction of formation of social forces in the countryside. Although the class division is not a myth . . . , it is unrealistic to associate the future of the rural areas with the class struggle "between the impoverished and the kulaks" and particularly to expect that this class struggle will become the force toward collectivization.[2]

The situation portrayed above is a result of socio-political transformations which made the classical and generally valid formula of Lenin inappropriate for the contemporary Polish conditions. As well as in the countryside, class struggle in the cities, although not yet completely absent, lost its importance in comparison with other problems and other contradictions.

This is the political sense of ongoing socio-political transformation. The deeper this transformation, the weaker is political manifestation of class conflicts. This is also the perspective of the future changes. The relative decrease in importance and scope of class conflicts is expected to be accompanied by such an evolution of the political system which will permit increasingly fuller expression and representation of differentiated interests and aspirations.[3] At the present time the political system is in a manifold way influenced by the class struggle which still takes place within the country and which permeates from the international situation. However, the general trend of the evolution of socialist system is to proceed from the state of dictatorship of the proletariat to an all-national socialist democracy, expressing and realizing the interests of non-antagonistic groups of the socialist society.

Every political system possesses some institutions which can be defined as "constitutive" for this system, i.e., such institutions which by their functioning determine the direction of the entire system. In seeking these institutions, one cannot limit the analysis to the formal structure of the political system.[4] Particularly, the constitutive institutions should not be treated as identical with the highest authorities of the state, since these two concepts may not be the same. A concrete, historical analysis must lead to the identification of those elements of the political system which play a particularly important role in determining the structure of power of the entire system. In Poland, the party system is the constitutive institution.

The basic role of the Polish United Workers' Party in the political system of Poland stems from the fact that this party is the political organization of the working class and other socialist classes and strata. The political power of this party in Poland is an expression of the class rule of the working class. The functions of the party in our political system can be grouped under five categories:

1. The party represents and expresses the socialist ideology underlying the entire political system. It determines the fundamental aims and values which constitute the basis for the functioning of the political and socio-political institutions of our country.

2. Through the activity of its members in the institutions of state and social organizations, the party harmonizes the functioning of these institutions with the basic goals of the system.

3. The party determines the general directives of policy making by the state institutions.

4. The party mobilizes a number of citizens to participate in political decision making at various levels of government.

5. The party recruits and educates cadres of political leaders operating within the party as well as in the institutions of the state.

These principal functions of the party comprise what is commonly called the "directive role of the party." These functions define at the same time the party as the constitutive institution of the political system.[5]

The party itself is in our political system a two-fold institution. One, it is the key center of political power and the political source of decisions directing the society. Two, it represents interests of the working people—not only of the workers but precisely of a broad coalition of the socialist classes and strata which find their place in the party and through the party attempt to realize their interests and demands. This duality of functions generates two divergencies within the party. On the one hand, the long term interests of the entire society are often divergent from the immediate interests of the particular groups within the society. Representing at the same time the interests of particular groups and directing the entire process of socialist transformation, the party is often faced with problems arising from this divergence of interests. On the other hand, the party is the forum of the expression of nonantagonistic classes of interests of various socialist strata of the Polish society. Since the party is not an instrument of political action for only one social class and since it comprises people from various social groups, it is only natural that the party becomes the platform where the divergent interests of the socialist society collide. These divergent interests do not extend to comprise class interests since the antisocialist classes do not find room within the party. As far as class interests are involved, the struggle takes place outside the party, between the party and the antisocialist forces. But those forces which accept the common socialist basis, unified by a common ideology, policy, and intraparty discipline find within the party the room for expression of their demands and claims. In this context, the intraparty democracy gains its full importance: it is the condition for such a resolution of conflicts which harmonizes the interests of workers and their allies rather than leads to open political struggle.

Discussing the role of the Workers' Party in the Polish political system, one should notice that the Polish system differs from the one party system of some other socialist countries. Besides the Polish United Workers' Party, two other parties—the United Peasant Party and Democratic Party—exist in Poland.[6] And while it would be misleading to treat the Polish party system as a multi-party one, it would be equally misleading to perceive the minor parties as insignificant and without any effect on the functioning of the entire system. This point demands a more detailed discussion.

In sociology and political science, the classical division of party system into one-party, two-party, and multi-party systems is the one most often used. This classification, which urgently calls for re-evaluation and revision, is not based on the absolute number of parties in a given country. For instance, the British system is usually called a two-party one, in spite of the fact that smaller political parties exist there in addition to the Conservative and the Labor parties, and the term "one-party systems" is being applied to the systems prevailing in the popular democracies, where other parties and political groups operate in addition to the Communist Party. Thus, the classification schema mentioned above is based not on the number of existing parties, but on the number of parties which *de facto* participate in the struggle for power under the rules of the game as adopted by a given system. In the multi-party system, several political parties, sometimes even more than a dozen, compete for seats in the parliament, and the power is in the hands of more or less unstable coalitions of such parties. In the two-party system the real rivals are only the two principal parties, while the others can only play a marginal role which does not affect the outcome of the struggle for power. Finally, in the one-party system there is within the system no legal competition for power, which is concentrated in the hands of one party operating either alone or in alliance with other parties.

The classification schema is being criticized from various quarters. Its obvious weakness is that it owes its clarity to the subordination of all possible divisions to that resulting from the chances which the various parties have in competing for power. But even when that criterion is adopted, the scheme of triparty division, multi-, two-, and one-party systems is not perfect since it does not take into account the existence of what Maurice Duverger calls the dominant party system. In this terminology, the dominant party occupies an intermediary position between the governing party in a "one-party system" and political parties under two-party and multi-party systems. In this connection he recently wrote:

> *On qualifiait alors de dominant, dans un système pluraliste de partis (multipartisme ou bipartisme), un parti qui présentait les deux caractères suivants: 1° distancer nettement ses rivaux dans l'ensemble d'une période (même s'il arrivait exceptionnellement qu'il soit dépassé à une élection); 2° s'identifier à l'ensemble de la nation: ses doctrines, ses idées, son style, en quelque sorte, coïncidant avec ceux de la période.*[7]

As examples of dominant parties, Duverger quotes the Radical Party during a period under the Third Republic in France, social democratic parties in the Scandinavian countries, the Congress Party in India, etc.

Another criticism of the triple division comes from a Polish theorist, for whom all these systems in which several parties "cooperate" in the wielding of power are multi-party systems. In this sense, he calls the party systems of some people's democracies "multi-party systems based on cooperation."[8]

Thus it seems that the term "one-party system," as it appears in the triparite division schema, deserves closer analysis. What it stands for represents in fact varied constitutional and political forms and stages in historical evolution. An analysis of that usually referred to as the "one-party system" requires examination not only of the number of parties and political groups, but also of some other issues, in particular:

1. The existence or the lack of an actual struggle for power.
2. The existence or the lack of political opposition to the party or parties in power.
3. The existence or the lack of a political differentiation in the form of political parties.
4. The degree of political pluralism expressed by party differentiation and by other forms of political differentiation.
5. The inner nature of the governing party.
6. The social role of the party system and its relation to the principal social forces in a given country.

A comparative analysis of different systems, including those called "one party" systems, should therefore provide information on all those elements which characterize a given party system. But the prerequisite seems to be that the term "one-party system" ought to be replaced by more adequate ones which would better correspond to the real structure of so-called "one-party systems."

In some socialist countries we note an interesting political configuration consisting of the coexistence of several cooperating political parties, one or which, the Communist Party, plays the leading role in the system. The remaining parties share governmental and administrative posts at all levels and participate in policy making, especially in so far as it concerns the groups or strata represented by them; they shape public opinion by their own propaganda machine, but without attempting to undermine the position of the "hegemonic" party. In Poland, this kind of alliance exists between all three political parties (Polish United Workers' Party, United Peasants' Party and Democratic Party) and three political associations of Catholic denomination. Such a system differs essentially from the one-party system *sensu stricto*. Hence it seems proper to suggest the adoption of a different term for it, for instance, the "hegemonic-party system."

The hegemonic-party systems stand midway between the one party systems *sensu stricto* or "mono-party systems" as I should prefer to call them, and the dominant-party systems. Under the monoparty system there is no competition for power within the system, and no acknowledged opposition.

TABLE 11–1

Monocentrism or polycentrism of the system	Polycentrism of the party system				Monocentrism of the party system
Existence or lack of legal opposition	Political opposition exists			No political opposition	
Real competition for power	There is real competition for power		No real competition for power		
Party compositions of the governing majority	Coalition essential	Coalitions are not needed. Governments based on the majority of one party			
	Multi-party system	Two-party system	Dominant-party system	Hegemonic-party system	Mono-party system

In the dominant-party system, a single party secures for itself permanent political leadership, despite the existence of other political parties and groups. All the three systems, i.e., the mono-party, the hegemonic-party and the dominant-party system share the common trait that political leadership is in the hands of a single party which acts as the representative of the entire nation. The evolution of the programs of communists parties, as their power is gaining strength and society is consolidating politically, is characteristic in this respect.

The introduction of the term "the hegemonic-party system" leads to the classification of party systems based on five categories, rather than on three or four. These are multi-party, two-party, dominant-party, hegemonical-party and mono-party systems.

From the point of view of the various aspects of political differentiation, the five party systems described above can be characterized as shown in Table 11–1.

This schema shows the extent to which the various, apparently opposing, party systems share certain common characteristics and the extent to which the degree of opposition between the various types depends on the criteria of differentiation.

In addition to the parties, several other organizations are of political importance. These groups are with increasing frequency treated in the Polish literature as equivalent to interest groups functioning in the political systems of the capitalist countries. The nature and scope of the functioning of these organizations require sociological analysis. Thus far however, little has been done in this direction.[9]

The following organizations seem to be of importance:

1. Socio-occupational organizations, such as the trade unions, Peasant Self-Aid Union, professional associations.

2. Associations and organizations which politically educate and represent some segments of society, such as Socialist Youth Union, Rural Youth Union, Union of Fighters for Freedom and Democracy (a veteran organization), Women's League, etc.

3. Regional organizations.

4. National organizations, such as Byelorussian Socio-Cultural Society, Lithuanian Socio-Cultural Society, Socio-Cultural Society of Germans, Socio-Cultural Society of Jews, etc.

5. Religious organizations, primarily the Catholic Church, and also political associations of religious nature, such as Pax, Znak, etc.

In spite of certain analogies, there is a clear difference in the place and functions of interest groups in Poland and in the capitalist countries.[10] In the latter countries the workers and peasants' organizations utilize their political influence in the society to exert a given pressure on the government. This function is the source of their popular name—"pressure groups." In the socialist system, trade unions and peasant organizations not only represent the interests of their groups vis-à-vis the party and the government but also mobilize the members to the tasks put forth by the party and the government. They function not only as "pressure groups," but also as "mobilizing groups." This dual function of interest groups stems from the new features of the Polish socio-political system and particularly from the role of the party which decisively influences the actions of the socio-occupational organizations as well as the state administration.

This specific institutional structure influences several other features of activity of the interest groups. It should be stressed that the pressures exerted by these groups are not manifested in public controversies but usually assume the form of unpublicized discussions. An important role in these discussions is played not only by the common ideology of the parties, but usually also by commonly accepted principles of current economic policy, for example, concerning the proportions of savings and investment, rate of economic growth, employment and wages, etc.

The organizations belonging to the second type of groups represent, on the one hand, interests of some segments of the society (urban or rural peasants, veterans, etc.) and, on the other hand, they ideologically educate their members into the goals of the party. To treat these organizations simply as an expression of institutional interests and claims of particular groups of the society would be to misunderstand their nature. But it would also be one-sided to perceive these institutions only as an instrument of ideological education by the party.

A particular role is played in Poland by the Catholic organizations, especially by the Church—a formal, hierarchical and centralized organization, of great importance in the life of the society and not without political ambitions. These political ambitions differ from those of the formerly discussed interest groups. The Catholic Church is a perpetually competitive ideological force juxtaposed to the party and the state. Currently, it also constitutes the political opposition. In the situation in which formally there are no Christian parties, the Church performs many of their functions. It has an access to public opinion and vast possibilities for spreading its ideology. Vis-à-vis the state authorities, the Church is attempting to use methods of "pressure from the outside"—through organizing opposition. The Church, one could say, is the only "opposition pressure group."[11]

Of a more complex political nature are such religious organizations as *Pax* or *Znak*. Without surrendering their religious ideology, they accept, in varying degrees, the socialist principles and cooperate with the marxist party, sharing with it the belief that their ideological differences find room within the socialist community.

Particularly important for the political pluralism of the socialist system is the role played by local government. In comparison with the political system of a parliamentary republic, the Polish system of Peoples' Councils means (1) extension of representative systems, (2) geographic decentralization of authority, and (3) multiplication of the number of persons directly participating in government. The first feature consists in forming "local parliaments" in the form of Peoples' Councils at various levels; the second, in giving these councils authority of the state based, however, on local elections and not coming from "above" in the form of nominations; the third characteristic consists in creating organizational forms for the widespread participation of the citizens in the work of the Councils. It is sufficient to say that during each term approximately 300,000 people become councilmen, and another 700,000 cooperate with the Councils through the social organizations to which they belong, such as Committees of the Front for National Unity, Parents' Committees, and various social welfare committees.

It is expected that in the future development of socialist democracy the role of local government will be increasingly greater. The political system of socialism is neither rigidly nor finally formed. Its functioning is changing and will change. The general direction of these changes consists in a combination of political democratization with development of self-governing forms of social life. Contrary to liberal-bourgeois democracy, socialist democracy is based not on rivalry and struggle of various forces but primarily on increasingly broad, direct and indirect, participation of the population in governing. It is in this context that the role of local government, where the citizen can have everyday contact with the functioning of the state, assumes its particular importance.

It seems to us that the above review of the aspects of pluralism in the Polish political system has certain more general implications. The differentiation of each socialist society finds its political expression in some forms of political pluralism, which—and this should be emphasized particularly strongly—is a necessary condition for an effective social control over the system of power and thus a condition for the development of socialist democracy. Such pluralism may occur either in the vertical structure of power (parties, political organizations, national interest groups) or in the horizontal structure (workers' selfgovernment,[12] local government). Historical factors led some socialist countries, for example Yugoslavia, to emphasize the "horizontal" political pluralism; while in other countries, for example Poland, the "vertical" pluralism plays a more important role. What is important, however, is that those systems in their own, pluralistic way open the political channels for the expression of interests of various segments of the population. Each socialist country accumulates specific experiences, but these require common analyses and comparisons. For although the roads of development of socialist democracy are different, such democracy constitutes a historical necessity for the future of socialism.

12

THE TYPOLOGY OF PARTY SYSTEMS— PROPOSALS FOR IMPROVEMENT

GIOVANNI SARTORI

The Number-of-Parties Classification

THERE are some hundred states that display—at least on paper—some kind of party arrangement.[1] The variety of these arrangements is equally impressive. How are we to order the maze? For quite some time party systems have been classified by counting the number of parties—whether one, two or more than two. Recently, however, there has been a mounting wave of dissatisfaction with this approach. LaPalombara and Wiener propose, for the competitive party systems, a four-fold classification which drops altogether the numerical base, precisely "on the assumption that the traditional distinction between two-party and multi-party patterns has not led to sufficiently meaningful insights."[2] This can be readily granted; yet one may be equally dissatisfied with the alternative taxonomies proposed so far.[3]

The trouble with the numerical criterion of classification is that we resort to an accounting system without having counting rules. Paradoxical as this may seem, we are not even able to decide when "two is two," I mean, whether a system is a two-party system. It is hardly surprising, therefore, that the number-of-parties approach gives uninspiring results. But it is surely premature to dismiss a criterion that has yet to be established. I would argue, in fact, that the traditional distinction between one, two and more-than-two party systems is hardly a classification at all—if we require a classification to be derived from

An earlier version of this paper was presented at the Conference of the Committee of Political Sociology in Cambridge, December 1965.

This essay is largely drawn from the chapters 7–12 of my forthcoming volume, *Parties and Party Systems—A Theoretical Framework* (New York: Harper & Row).

Notes to this chapter are on pp. 382–388.

a precisely stated criterion. On the other hand, there are many reasons for exploring first the potentiality of the number of parties base.

For one thing, the number of parties is a highly visible element. It immediately indicates an important feature of political systems, namely, the extent to which power is fragmented or nonfragmented. Intelligent counting can also detect, however roughly, the relative distribution of power among the parties. Furthermore, the tactics of party competition appear to be related to the number of parties, and I will suggest that given numerical thresholds enable us to surmise the more likely patterns of political competition and opposition. These, in turn, have an important bearing on how governmental coalitions are formed and are able to perform. On the other hand, if we reach the conclusion that the number of parties does not really affect the political system, then we should equally conclude that there is no sense in electoral manipulation, i.e., in attempting to impede or to reduce party proliferation.

Clearly, party numbers cannot be taken at their face value, that is, if we resort to counting we should know how to count. However, before entering this discussion a few preliminary remarks are in order. In the first place, there is a difference between saying, e.g., "this system contains two parties," and "this system displays two-party properties," i.e. functions according to the rules of two-partism. For instance, between 1946 and 1966 Austria was a system based on two parties that did not display the functional properties of two-partism. If one distinguishes, as one may, between a classification and a typology,[4] one could say that Austria belonged to the two-party "class" but not to the two-party "type." Conversely, and for the same reason, Australia does not belong to the two-party class, but can be said to belong to the two-party type.

In the second place, the requirement of a number of parties base is not that the entire scheme should be based on a numerical criterion *alone*. Other criteria or dimensions can and should be utilized if our purpose is to establish a *typology* in the strict sense of the notion, i.e., an exhaustive set of concepts that represent "attribute compounds." It will be noted, in fact, that in the typology proposed in this essay, the numerical criterion is supplemented by an ideological criterion. More precisely, I shall argue that the uni-polar systems cannot be meaningfully particularized without accounting for their "ideological intensity"; and I shall equally argue that the pluralistic systems cannot be meaningfully distinguished among themselves unless the number of parties is related to their "ideological distance."

We are confronted, then, with three problems: first, how to count; second, how to count intelligently; third, how to supplement the inadequacies of a purely numerical criterion. In the first respect, we are required to state the rules according to which parties are to be counted or otherwise discounted. In the second respect, we are required to relate the extent of the fragmentation of power to the relative distribution of such power. In a number of instances, the fact that few parties denote low fragmentation whereas many parties indicate high fragmentation is not, per se, very telling. Hence intelligent counting requires us to ask "how many" with an eye on "how strong." In the third respect, we are required to construct a typology which retains those properties that numbers alone cannot detect.

With these considerations in mind, the traditional three-fold scheme is here replaced by a seven-fold taxonomy which distinguishes among the following categories of party polities:

1. one-party
2. hegemonic party
3. predominant party
4. two-party
5. moderate multipartism
6. extreme multipartism
7. atomized

The first three categories result from a breakup of the "one party" lump of the traditional scheme, which brings together the most incongruent varieties of heterogeneous phenomena. Whereas the properly called one-party polities outlaw any other party, the hegemonic systems permit the existence of subordinate parties under the condition that the hegemony of the party in power cannot be challenged. The predominant party systems are, instead, the systems in which the same party happens to win over time, on a competitive basis, the absolute majority of seats. The hegemonic and the predominant systems thus allow for the reclassification of a number of erroneously called one-party systems.

On the other hand, while the traditional two-party category is retained, the traditional multi-party category is again broken down, for I challenge the view that the more-than-two party systems can be dealt with in a single package. If anything, the most important line of division among competitive party systems cuts across the traditional multi-party grouping. The difference between a two- and a three-party system is a relatively minor difference. The major difference is, instead, the difference between limited and moderate pluralism on the one hand, and extreme and polarized pluralism on the other hand. Let me simply say, for the moment, that when the number of relevant parties is "limited"—from three to five—the parties are likely to be "moderate" in their platform and in their competitive tactics; whereas an "extreme" fragmentation—more than five parties—generally reflects and elicits a pattern of immoderate politics in which extremistic appeals largely condition the overall drift of the polity.

Finally, the "atomized" party system is added to the classification to indicate the point at which we no longer need an accurate counting, that is, the threshold beyond which the number of parties—whether ten, twenty or more—makes little difference. This is equally to say that the numerical criterion applies only to the party systems that have entered the stage of structural consolidation.

We are thus led back to the question: How are these numbers counted? In substance, we are required to establish criteria of irrelevance vis-à-vis the smaller parties.

It will not do to say that the irrelevant parties are, in whatever system, the ones that fall below a given threshold of size—for this threshold varies in relation to the relative distribution of power. There is no absolute yardstick for assessing the relevance of size. A party with 10 per cent of seats may count, in substance, far less than a party that only obtains 3 per cent. To simplify the problem, we may leave aside the "electoral party," that is, the strength indicated by the electoral turnout of each party, since it is unnecessary to account for how the votes are translated into seats. However, even the strength of the "parliamentary party," i.e. measured against the percentage of seats, provides by itself a poor indicator unless this indication is related, in turn, to the *governing potential* of each party. What really weighs in the balance is, in fact, the extent to which a party may be required as a coalition partner for one or more of the possible governmental majorities. A party may be electorally weak but have a strong coalition-bargaining potential.[5] Conversely, a party may be electorally strong and yet lack coalition-bargaining power. The caution is that we should account not only for the mathematical possibilities but also for the ideological possibilities of coalition. In other words, "possible majorities" are the ideologically permissible ones.

With this caution in mind the criterion for deciding when a party should, or should not, be counted, is the following: a minor party can be discounted as irrelevant whenever it remains over time superfluous, in the sense that it is *never* needed or put to use for any feasible coalition majority. Conversely, a minor party has to be counted, no matter how small, if it finds itself in a position to determine over time at least one of the possible governmental majorities.

The foregoing rule has a limitation, for it applies only to the parties that are governing oriented and, furthermore, ideologically acceptable to the other coalition partners. This leaves out, or may leave out, some relatively large parties of permanent opposition—such as the anti-system parties. Therefore our "criterion of irrelevance" needs to be supplemented—under special circumstances—by a "criterion of relevance." The question may be reformulated as follows: Which size, or bigness, makes a party relevant regardless of its coalition potential? In Italy or in France one finds, for instance, communist parties that poll as much as 25 per cent of the total vote but whose governmental coalition potential is virtually zero. Yet it would be absurd to discount them. We are thus led to formulate a second accounting rule based on the "power of intimidation," or the blackmail potential,[6] of the opposition oriented parties. Such a subsidiary accounting rule can be formulated as follows: a party is "big enough" to qualify for relevance whenever its existence, or appearance, affects the tactics of party competition, and particularly when it alters the direction of the competition (e.g., by determining a switch from centripetal to centrifugal competition) of one or more of the major, governing oriented parties.

In summary, we can discount the parties that neither have (1) *coalition potential*, or (2) *blackmail potential*. So far with counting. But intelligent counting requires us to establish, in addition, a classification of party systems in which the number of the parties is significantly related to the distribution of power between them. A power configuration can be such that one party "counts more" than all the other parties together. This is notably the case with the predominant party systems; and this is why the primary character-istic retained by the taxonomy is not how many parties—whether only one or more—oppose the predominant party, but the existence of a stabilized situation of predominance. With regard to the predominant party system the relevant indication is, then, that one party holds the absolute majority of seats without being subjected to alternation.

Two-party systems pose no special problem. In this case the power con-figuration is immediately qualified by the numerical criterion: the absolute majority is within reach of two major parties that are, therefore, exposed to alternation. When we come, however, to the area of multi-partism we are again required to read intelligently between the lines. In fact, it is only after having set aside the case of predominance that the numerical criterion comes to characterize a power configuration in which, (1) no party is likely to approach, or at least to maintain, an absolute majority, and (2) the relative strength (or weakness) of the parties can be ranked according to their respective coalition indispensability (or dispensability) and/or (3) their eventual potential of intimidation.

Needless to say, the proposed seven-fold taxonomy of party systems is only a major grid that will be completed along the way with a number of subtypes and possible variations. It should also be stressed that the taxonomy under discussion does not claim worldwide applicability; it applies only to the relatively firmly established and structured party systems, in the sense that the more fluid polities of a number of new states require a special *ad hoc* treat-ment. Finally, let it be noted that, so far, the argument has been deliberately confined to the mileage afforded by a disciplined system of intelligent count-ing.

Predominant Party, Hegemonic Party and Single Party

Perhaps the most grievous lacuna in the literature on parties and party systems can be traced back to the fact that we have never singled out the radically different cases that are melded by the uncritical use of the one-party labeling.

For the sake of convenience, we may begin with a consideration of the predominant party system. It should be clear that my *predominant party* does not coincide with the *dominant party* spoken of by a number of authors. The dominant party category was suggested more or less at the same time by Duverger and Almond. Duverger's examples were the French radicals, the Scandinavian social-democratic parties, and the Indian Congress party.[7] Probably in the wake of Almond's usage, Blanksten mentions a "dominant non-dictatorial party," offering, as clearcut examples of the category, the "solid South" in the United States, Mexico and, as possible additional examples, Uruguay and Paraguay.[8] As these examples suffice to show, the dominant party category resembles a set of Chinese boxes. The Swedish labor party has very little in common with the Indian Congress party; the Mexican Revolutionary People's party (P.R.I.) surely shares nothing with the French radicals; and I do not even believe that the "solid South" and the Mexican system are at all comparable. The fault with the category suggested by Duverger is that it fails to separate the predominant and the hegemonic arrangements—and this is why I propose to drop the "dominant" party labeling.

A *predominant* party system is a system in which other parties not only are permitted to exist, but do exist as legitimate—if not necessarily effective—competitors of the predominant party. The minor parties are truly independent antagonists of the predominant party, and all parties have an equal start. Therefore, the predominant party system actually is a plural party system in which rotation does not occur in fact. It simply happens that the same party manages to win, over time, an *absolute majority* of seats (not necessarily of votes) in parliament. The relative majority is not a sufficient condition of "predominance," as far as the qualification of the party system is concerned. That is to say, no constitutional impediment, and no conspicuous unfair play or ballot stuffing, accounts for the fact that the same party remains in power election after election.[9] Its predominance basically stems from the fact that it is consistently supported by a winning majority of the voters. Therefore, a predominant party can, at any moment, cease to be predominant. Indeed there are instances in which a predominant party system has been regularly offset by a turnover.[10] Notable examples of this type of system are a number of state legislatures in the United States (which are erroneously called "one party" states), Japan,[11] India,[12] and Uruguay.[13] In such systems, political opposition does exist, and the predominant party has to compete for power.

Although a predominant party can assert itself either within the framework of a two-party format (as in the United States) or within the framework of a highly fragmented pattern (as is particularly the case with the Congress party in India), nonetheless, for the purpose of establishing a continuum, one may consider the predominant party system as the variant of two-partism in which no alternation in power occurs (*de facto*) for a considerable length of time.[14] Granted that the predominant party system can also be a variant of a multi-party system, it is useful to stress that a situation of predominance can be a normal outcome of two-partism.[15]

The predominant party system can thus be defined as the type of party pluralism in which no alternation in office occurs over time, even though alternation is not ruled out and the political system provides all the opportunities of open and effective dissent, i.e., for opposing the predominance of the ruling party.

The case of the *hegemonic party*[16] is entirely different. In this instance, there is neither a formal nor a *de facto* competition for power. Other parties are permitted to exist, but as satellite parties, for they are not permitted to compete with the hegemonic party in antagonistic terms and on an equal basis. Not only does alternation not occur in fact; it *cannot* occur as the possibility of a rotation in power is not even envisaged. The implication is that the hegemonic party will remain in power whether it is liked or not. While the predominant party still operates under the conditions that make for a responsible government and cannot disregard the rule of antici-pated reactions—as Friedrich would have it—no real sanction commits the hegemonic party to responsiveness. Whatever its policy, its domination cannot be challenged. In short, whereas the predominant party belongs to the plural-istic-competitive systems, the hegemonic party does not,

Wiatr applies the "hegemonical party" labeling to present-day Poland, which is indeed a fitting example. In his own description, the Polish non-communist parties (namely, the United Peasant's party, the Democratic party, plus three political associations of Catholic denomination) "share governmental and administrative posts at all levels . . . they shape public opinion . . . but without attempting to undermine the position of the hege-monical party."[17] Clearly, not only alternation but any sort of effective competition are ruled out.[18] Therefore, I cannot follow another Polish author, Zakrzewski, when this pattern is presented as a "multiparty system based on cooperation."[19] This is, to say the least, a euphemistic way of putting it. As the actual working of the Polish system well shows, a hegemonic party system is definitely not a multiparty system but is, at best, a *two-level system* in which one party tolerates and discretionally allocates a fraction of its power to subordinate political groups. We shall return shortly to the reasons for the establishment of such a system in its possible varieties. What-ever those reasons, the fact remains that the hegemonic party formula affords the appearance but not the substance of competitive politics, for it does not allow open contestation and effective dissent.

Once the predominant party and the hegemonic party are extracted from the heap, we are left with the real *one-party* polities, that is, the political systems that do not permit the existence of any other party. There are many varieties of the one-party pattern, but all belong to a family whose peculiar feature is to veto—both *de jure* and *de facto*—any kind of party pluralism.

At this end of the spectrum the numerical criterion is clearly useless; one is just one, and there is little that can be added. How are we to qualify, then, the various types and subtypes of the one-party polities? We usually say that the single party can be more or less oppressive, more or less pervasive, more or less intolerant. This is tantamount to saying that the one-party polities pose a problem of intensity of repression, in the broad meaning of the term. And it is precisely on the basis of an order of decreasing intensity of repression, or coercion, that the three following patterns can be meaningfully singled out:

1. one-party totalitarian
2. one-party authoritarian
3. one-party pragmatic.

The very fact that the third subtype is called one-party pragmatic shows that I follow LaPalombara and Wiener in utilizing, as a second dimension, the "ideology-pragmatism" continuum[20]—with two amendments, however; one of substance and the other of terminology. I do not quite understand, as a matter of fact, why LaPalombara and Wiener apply the ideological criterion to the competitive systems but not to the noncompetitive systems. My first amendment is, then, to apply the ideology-pragmatism dimension to the entire spectrum. Consequently the terminological amendment is to say "one-party pragmatic" instead of "one-party pluralistic."[21] The label one-party pragmatic is preferable also for reasons of clarity. Quite aside from the fact that "pluralism" should not be abused and that wishful thinking does not need to be encouraged, the point is that the hegemonic party polities could also be called, with better reason, one-party pluralistic.

It should be understood, in the first place, that the distinction between pragmatic and ideological parties is meant to replace, and hopefully to improve upon, the distinction between "nondoctrinal" and "doctrine based" parties.[22] Any party, at a certain point, may respond to the needs of a particular situation, or to the challenge of its competitors, by providing itself with a "doctrine." If used alone, doctrine-based and nondoctrinaire point to a superficial, or too superficial, layer of differentiation; whereas the opposition between ideology and pragmatism refers us, ultimately, to a *mentality*, that is, to a deep-rooted source of differentiation.

However, whenever the problem merely is to qualify the uni-polar polities, the "ideological mentality" may be kept in the background. It will be sufficient to retain the meaning in which ideology signifies a typically doctrinaire, principled and dogmatic approach eventually associated with "hot politics," i.e., with a highly passionate and emotive involvement in politics. Again, for the sake of avoiding unnecessary complication, I will not commit myself to a definition of "pragmatism" and will simply say that this term signifies "feeble ideology" and, in this relative sense, "nonideology." Differently put, I am more concerned with the ideological than with the pragmatic end of the continuum. I shall speak, in fact, of an "ideology variable" *tout court*. Finally, it should be clear that ideology is taken, in turn, as an indicator of the repressive or extractive capabilities of a political system. Indeed, mobilizational and highly extractive polities require "ideological heating," whereas a pragmatic mentality and/or feeble ideological affect is conducive, at most, to control systems.

If the one-party polities can be divided into three major subtypes, the hegemonic party polities also display different extractive and repressive capabilities and are liable to particularization along similar lines. Of course there can be no "totalitarian" hegemonic party—this would be a *contradictio in adiecto*—but there can be a more or less "authoritarian" kind of hegemonic party. Under the assumption that the more authoritarian variety is likely to be, at the same time, the more ideological variety, the subtypes may be indicated as follows:

1. ideological hegemonic party
2. pragmatic hegemonic party.[23]

Out of the two subtypes, the one that has materialized more definitely is the ideological hegemonic party. Poland belongs, in fact, to this variety. In this case the peripheral parties are truly "satellite parties," and the question is to what extent the satellite parties really have a share in basic decision making. To share an office does not necessarily mean that the power is also shared. Even if the satellite parties are given administrative and governmental positions, they are not participants *optimo jure*, of equal right, and it seems clear that their inferiority status vis-à-vis the hegemonic party is bound to affect heavily, indeed very heavily, their chances of independent behavior. My own feeling is that even if one leaves aside the instances in which satellite parties are merely a camouflage (e.g., Eastern Germany), at its very best the Polish type of hegemonic party arrangement can produce a simulated pluralism, a simulated "party market," so to speak.

Why simulate a party market? One possible answer is that this is not only a psychological outlet and a safety valve of the political system designed to placate opposition, but also a means of providing the dominant elite with a flow of information or, at any rate, with more information than the one party is generally able to gather.[24] In this sense the hegemonic party formula still allows, somehow, for "expression." The difference is that expression is *more* than information. In the first case demands are being communicated that require some degree of satisfaction, whereas in the second case the communication amounts to a mere report.[25] Even assuming, therefore, that the information is not highly inadequate and distorted, the political system does not provide any mechanism for carrying it over into the machinery of government; whatever the information, the hegemonic party can enforce its own will.

Despite these reservations, the case of the hegemonic party deserves to be kept separate from the case of the one party in the strict sense. Even in its ideological and authoritarian patterning, the hegemonic "two-level" arrangement attempts to deal with the other groups with an absorptive rather than with a purely negative or destructive approach. In this sense even a "simulated" party market may come to play an important role.

Furthermore, and especially, we must not lose sight of the other possibility: the pragmatic variety of the hegemonic party. It is true that the pragmatic hegemonic party is still a somewhat phantomlike occurrence. For instance, whereas the difference between USSR and Poland is definite, no hard and fast distinction can be drawn between the pragmatic one party and the pragmatic hegemonic party. Portugal and Paraguay belong more to the former category, whereas Mexico appears to be moving in the latter direction; but these attributions are open to question. Yet, if we are to keep an eye on future developments, the pragmatic variety of the hegemonic party is a distinct possibility, both as a result of an ulterior loosening up of the one-party pragmatic polities, or as one of the possible outcomes in some of the new states. Moreover, we need a pigeonhole for the fake predominant party systems, that is, for the predominant party that *de facto* impedes an effective competition. In this case, it cannot be assumed that the predominant party would remain predominant if the "formal" permission of party competition were to be applied. Therefore, if the system lacks an ideology which legitimizes the subordination of the other parties, it can be reclassified fittingly as a hegemonic polity of the pragmatic variety.

Two-Party Systems

Two-party systems are by far the better-known type. This is because it is a relatively simple system, because the countries that practice two-partism are important countries, and because they represent a paradigmatic case. Even so, we are immediately blocked by the simple question: How many two-party systems are there in existence? The reply varies, awaiting for a decision on how the parties should be counted. According to Banks and Textor, eleven of the 115 countries covered by their survey fall under the two-party rubric.[26] But the figure is surely exaggerated, for it includes a country such as Colombia that can hardly be considered a party system at all.[27] Among the more democratic nations, six countries, namely, England, the United States, Australia, New Zealand, Canada and Austria, are generally considered two-party, or quasi-two-party systems. However, not only can the Austrian pattern hardly be considered an established one, but a strict standard would consider Canada[28] and Australia[29] anomalous and dubious cases.

As noted earlier, we have here two distinct problems that we generally attempt to solve in one blow. One is to decide when a country belongs to the two-party "class," and this depends on the accounting system. For the sake of clarity in this case I shall speak of *format*. The other problem is to decide whether we have a two-party "type" of system. Again for the sake of clarity, with reference to the properties of the system I shall speak of two-party *mechanics*.

The first question is: When is it that a third party, or even third parties, should be discounted? According to our first criterion of irrelevance—the coalition criterion—the reply is straightforward. We have a two-party format whenever the existence of third parties does not prevent the two major parties from governing alone, i.e., whenever coalitions are unnecessary.

The argument is more complex, however, as soon as we pass on to ask: Which are the properties that qualify the two-party type of system? Granted that the major characteristic of two-partism is that one party governs alone, we must immediately add: alone, but not indefinitely. For if it is always the same party that remains in office election after election, the system should be reclassfied as a predominant party system. This is the same as saying that alternation in power is the distinguishing mark of the mechanics of two-partism. One may also say that "two" differs from "three" whenever third parties do not affect, in the long run and at the national level, the alternation in power of the two major parties. However, neither the "alternation" nor the "governing alone" clauses are rigidly applicable.

Alternation should be loosely understood as implying the *expectation* rather than the actual occurrence of governmental turnover. Alternation only means, then, that the margins between the two major parties are close enough, or that there is some credibility in the expectation that the party in opposition has a chance to oust the governing party. It is only under this loose formulation, in fact, that the United States can be considered, at the federal level, a two-party system. On the other hand, the alternation clause implies that Austria was not a two-party type of system until 1966.[30] On similar grounds, we must be unexacting also with regard to the requirement that *both* parties should be in a position to win for themselves an absolute majority, and hence to govern alone. In fact, it is only by conceding that the clause may apply only to *one* of the major parties (not to both) that Australia definitely qualifies for inclusion.

The lenient conditions for a system that functions according to the rules of two-partism would thus be following: (1) two parties are in a position to compete for the absolute majority of seats; (2) at least one of the two parties actually succeeds in winning a sufficient majority; (3) this party is willing to govern alone; (4) alternation or rotation in power remains a credible expectation.

Now it becomes clear why almost each author can produce a different list of the existing two-party countries. With reference to the two-party format, the requirement of alternation in power is immaterial. Hence, one can include in the list also the predominant party systems in which the opposition is represented by only one party (e.g., Uruguay). For the same reason, it is irrelevant whether a party that could govern alone chooses not to do so (e.g., Austria qualifies for inclusion since 1946). On the other hand, Australia should and Canada might be excluded.

If we refer instead to the mechanics of two-partism, we see that the essential properties of two-partism can be adjusted also to a three-party format. Hence, if we agree that the requirement of one-party government may apply to only one of the parties, Australia re-enters; and if one-party government need not be a majority government, Canada equally passes the test (and testifies to the importance of the "conventions" of the British constitution).

The distinction between format and mechanics affords also a ranking of two-party systems, according to whether they satisfy both or only one of the aforesaid criteria. For instance, England and New Zealand are "perfect" two-party systems in that they display—in spite of their third parties—both the format and the full set of properties of two-partism. The United States is a far less perfect instance, for the format is there, but the alternation in power is dubious (unless we account for the federal structure and consider the distribution of Republican and Democratic majorities in the various states).

Then there are the countries that abide by the mechanics of two-partism but not by its format. And I would definitely rank last those countries which display a two-party size, but not the properties of two-partism. Indeed, this latter group can be admitted only as a member of the two-party "class," hardly as a member of the two-party "type."[31]

The fact that two-party systems are rare could support the view that they are "difficult"; but the emphasis is generally on the view that two-party systems represent a paradigmatic case, i.e., an "optimal" solution. The claim generally is that two-party systems obtain beneficial returns for the polity as a whole. More precisely, two-party systems always "work," whereas the more the parties the more we find "less-working" solutions and, ultimately, non-viable systems. The claim is not unwarranted, but cannot be warranted by pointing to the countries in which two-partism happens to work. Indeed, these countries are so few that one may well argue that all the more-than-two party systems are such precisely because the two-party solution either did not endure or would prove to be unworkable. The retort could be, then, that two-partism generally fails, or would fail if attempted.

We are thus referred to the question: Under what conditions does a two-party system work as predicted by the model? The model predicts that in a two-party system the parties will compete centripetally, soft-pedaling cleavages and playing the game of politics with "moderation."[32] This happens, however, because "centripetal competition" is rewarding. Why is it rewarding? Presumably because the floating voters themselves are moderates, i.e., located between the two parties, somewhere around the center of the spectrum of opinions. If the major group of floating voters were "unidentified" extremists, i.e., extremists prepared to switch from an extreme left to an extreme right, and vice versa, centripetal competition would no longer be rewarding. In short, two-partism "works" when the spread of opinion is small and its distribution is single peaked.

This is not to say that two-partism presupposes consensus, for it is equally true that the centripetal mechanics of two-partism creates consensus. This is to say, then, that there is a significant relation between the number of parties on the one hand, and the "space" or spread of interparty competition on the other hand. If this space of competition is called *ideological distance*, the rule of thumb could be the following: the smaller the ideological spread of opinion, the smoother the functioning of two-partism; whereas the greater the ideological distance, the more a two-party format is dysfunctional. It is not true, then, that two-party systems always work. Rather, these systems represent an optimal solution only when they work, that is, whenever they presuppose and/or produce a highly consensual political society characterized by a minimal ideological spread. Hence, whenever a two-party format does not function as required by the model, the model predicts that the parties will become more-than-two, i.e. that we shall obtain another type of party system.

A number of authors speak of one-and-a-half, and of two-and-a-half party systems. Those labels are either superfluous or positively misleading. A one-and-a-half party system is a predominant system within a two-party format; and a two-and-a-half party system indicates two-party mechanics within a three-party format. If so, England is definitely a two-party system, for the revival of the Liberal party does not detract from the fact that the third party does not affect in the least the two-party mechanics of the system. Likewise, it is improper to speak of Western Germany as a two-and-a-half party system, for the Bonn Republic has been, so far, a three-party system with so little inclination for two-partism as to prefer a "grand coalition" to a sufficient coalition.[33]

Limited and Moderate Pluralism

Some preliminary clarifications are in order with respect to the entire group of the more-than-two party systems. Having reference to the structural configuration of party competition I shall speak—regardless of the number of parties—of *bipolar* and *multipolar* systems. In the first case, the political system operates according to a dualistic alignment of the government-opposition kind. In the second case, instead, the political system pivots on three poles (at least), and its structural mechanics no longer displays a dualistic configuration.

The major distinction remains, however, the distinction between the classification and the typology. When I say *limited* and *extreme* pluralism, I indicate "classes" detected by the numerical criterion. When speaking, instead, of *moderate* and *polarized* pluralism, I indicate "types," that is, the properties displayed respectively by the two systems. In other terms, and in line with our previous usage, the labels "limited" and "extreme" pluralism apply to a *format* and point to a smaller or greater degree of party fragmentation. The labels "moderate" and "polarized" pluralism apply, instead, to the *mechanics* of these systems.

As in the case of two-partism, the number of parties points to a set of functional properties, i.e., the format and the mechanics appear to be linked. However, just like a two-party format may not produce a two-party type of mechanics, we can equally expect to find a situation of limited pluralism displaying "immoderate" properties, or a situation of extreme pluralism which is "nonpolarized." The reason for this is very simple: a numerical criterion detects fragmentation; but fragmentation is not necessarily the same as, or caused by, "ideological distance."

In practice, there is no problem whenever the format of the "class" and the properties of the "type" coincide. For instance, as long as a two-party system works, we can safely assume that the ideological distance is small. Likewise, whenever a system of extreme pluralism is "nonworking," we can safely surmise that the spread of opinion covers a maximum of ideological distance. The problem arises only when there is a discrepancy between the number of parties (fragmentation) and the mechanics that one would expect on such a basis. But we shall see that this problem is not difficult to come by.

Thus far we have established that limited pluralism begins with more-than-two parties. Where does it end? It appears that five is the critical threshold. That is to say, the "class" of limited pluralism generally contains from three to five parties. It should be stressed that these numbers indicate the "relevant" parties. Thus, according to my accounting system the German Federal Republic and Belgium are three-party sized systems, Sweden and Denmark are four-five party systems, while Norway and especially the Netherlands and Switzerland are borderline cases.[34] They are borderline cases, to be sure, in terms of format; which is not the same as saying that the Netherlands and Switzerland are difficult to locate with reference to their properties.

The question turns, then, on the properties of moderate pluralism, that is, on the mechanics of the *type*. With respect to the properties of two-partism, the major distinguishing trait of moderate pluralism is coalition government: no party can govern alone unless it is willing (and permitted) to form a minority government, i.e., to govern without a pre-established majority. Thus the formula of moderate pluralism is not alternative government, but rather "alternative coalitions." In most other respects, however, the mechanics of moderate pluralism tends to resemble and to imitate the mechanics of two-partism. In particular, the structure of moderate pluralism remains "bipolar." Instead of only two parties, we generally find bipolar alignments of alternative coalitions. But this difference does not detract from the fact that competition remains centripetal, and thereby from the fact that the mechanics of moderate pluralism is still conducive to "moderate politics."

Although the distinguishing characteristics of moderate pluralism are not impressive vis-à-vis the two-party type, they come out very neatly vis-à-vis the case of extreme pluralism. Awaiting a treatment of the latter case, let us mention the following two distinctive marks: moderate pluralism *lacks* relevant antisystem parties (e.g., communist and/or fascist parties), and hence *lacks* bilateral oppositions. Putting it the other way around, in a system of moderate pluralism all the parties (counted according to my accounting rules) are "governing oriented," that is, available for cabinet coalitions—the property that Val Larvin calls *Allgemein-koalitions-fähigkeit*. Hence, all the nongoverning parties can coalesce qua oppositions, and this means that the opposition will be "unilateral"—all on one side, either on the left or on the right.

We shall see later how many consequences follow. For the moment it is important to note that these two features represent handy "control indicators" for the purpose of checking whether growing fragmentation does correspond, roughly, to growing ideological distance. Reverting to a previous point, whenever the question is whether the numerical base does detect the properties of the type, one can swiftly check by ascertaining whether or not a more-than-two party system contains antisystem parties and bilateral oppositions. If the system does not, we are definitely confronted with a case of moderate pluralism. As we know, on the sheer basis of a numerical criterion the Netherlands and Switzerland represent a borderline "class." But the absence of antisystem parties immediately shows that the two countries in question definitely belong to the "type" of moderate pluralism. The fragmentation is relatively high, but our control indicators issue the warning that we are confronted with a fragmented party system which is not caused by ideological distance.

The point may be generalized and restated by saying that we now have at our disposal the indicators for "ideological distance." In fact, if the number of parties grows, and yet all the parties still belong to the "same world"—i.e.

accept the legitimacy of the political system and abide by its rules—then it is clear that the fragmentation of the system cannot be attributed to ideological incompatibility. In this case—which is the case of the Netherlands and Switzerland—the fragmentation is related to a multi-dimensional configuration: a poli-ethnic and/or a multi-confessional society.

Granted that we may be confronted with instances of nonideological fragmentation, whenever the number of parties exceeds the critical threshold and we do find antisystem parties and bilateral oppositions, then it is clear that we have ideological fragmentation, i.e., that more-than-five parties do reflect the amount of ideological distance that makes a bipolar mechanics impossible. It is expedient to assume, therefore, that we may proceed on the basis of the numerical criterion with the caution that control indicators are available for the borderline cases.

Extreme and Polarized Pluralism

While the case of the bipolar systems—two-partism and moderate multi-partism—only requires underpinning, the case of extreme pluralism confronts us with a class whose distinctiveness has escaped attention. There are two reasons for this. One is the use of "dualistic blinders," that is, the tendency to explain any and all party systems by extrapolating from the two-party model. These dualistic blinders have been proposed by Duverger as an almost "natural law" of politics: "A duality of parties does not always exist, but almost always there is a duality of tendencies. . . . This is equivalent to saying that the center does not exist in politics: there may well be a Center party, but there is no center tendency. . . . There are no true centers, only superimposed dualisms."[35]

The second reason is, obviously, that the case of extreme pluralism can hardly be singled out unless we know how parties are to be counted. However, as soon as we establish an accounting system we can neatly sort out from the heap of "poly-partism" two distinct patterns.

As we have seen, countries such as the German Federal Republic, Belgium, Sweden, Denmark, represent instances of limited pluralism. Conversely, in present-day Italy, during the French Fourth Republic and in Weimar Germany there have consistently been six to seven relevant parties—in spite of a number of splits and reunifications. These countries definitely display, then, a more-than-five format. Hence, according to my accounting system, they belong to another "class": extreme pluralism.

Let it be recalled that these attributions result from two criteria of relevance/irrelevance, that is, discarding the parties that lack "coalition use," and re-introducing the parties whose "power of intimidation" affects the tactics of interparty competition. Admittedly, my counting rules may still leave us to argue whether a small, marginal party should be counted or not, and may still confront the classification with some troublesome borderline cases. However, since we have "control indicators" for checking whether the format of the class does coincide with the properties of the type, the taxonomy is not affected by minor accounting discrepancies. There is no magic in the number five as such—just as there is no magic in the number two. These numbers indicate turning points, thereby allowing for a margin of flexibility. This is why I deliberately speak of more-than-five, to signify that the threshold is "around five," not necessarily and precisely "at five."[36]

To say that the *class*—extreme pluralism—has escaped recognition, is equally to say that the *type*—polarized pluralism—has escaped recognition. It will be necessary, therefore, to begin with a somewhat detailed description. For the sake of convenience, I will illustrate first the features of polarized pluralism that have been presented, thus far, as "control indicators." It should also be noted that I deliberately avoid, for the time being, the term "properties," to which I shall revert when assessing the importance of the various traits.

1. The first distinctive feature of the type under consideration resides—as we know—in the presence of *antisystem parties*. Polarized pluralism is characterized, one may also say, by an antisystem opposition—generally of the communist or of the fascist variety. By saying "antisystem," I mean that this kind of opposition would not change—if it could—the government but the *system* of government. An antisystem opposition abides by another belief system, by a belief system that does not share the values of the political order within which it operates. Antisystem parties represent, then, a totally "other" ideology—and this is why they indicate a maximum of ideological distance.

It should be clear, therefore, that variations of tactics and strategy are immaterial to my definition. In particular, I have never equated antisystem with "outside the system."[37] An antisystem party may play the game from within no less than from without, by "smiling infiltration" no less than by conspicuous obstruction.[38] The fact that the major Western communist parties are currently playing their game within the system and according to some (not all) of its rules, does not detract from the fact that wherever a Communist party has seized governmental power, a system of constitutional democracy has never survived.[39] Hence, awaiting for an instance in which a communist government will submit to a free electoral verdict resulting from pluralistic competition, whatever we mean by saying that Western communism is becoming more and more "integrated" does not mean that Communist parties can be reclassified as being "prosystem."[40]

2. The second distinctive feature of polarized pluralism resides—as we know—in the existence of *bilateral oppositions*. When the opposition is unilateral, i.e., located on one side of the government, no matter how many parties oppose it they can join forces and propose themselves as an alternative government. In the polarized polities we find, instead, two oppositions which are mutually exclusive: they cannot join forces. In fact, the two opposing groups are more likely to agree with the government than among themselves—each opposition is closer, if anything, to the governing parties than to one another. The system has two oppositions, then, in the sense that they are "counter-oppositions" which fight one another even more than the government.

The foregoing characteristics are the most visible ones, and already suffice to identify the type. If there are more than five parties, if the system displays bilateral counter-oppositions (in the plural) which include parties that oppose the very political system, then this type of multi-partism is definitely far removed from the type of multi-partism characterized by a unilateral opposition, by the absence of relevant antisystem parties, and hence by a bipolar mechanism of competition between governing-oriented parties. Actually, these distinguishing traits are so easily detectable that it is astonishing that they should have escaped attention—indeed a proof of the extent to which we have been victims of a dualistic blinding. A number of additional characteristics are less visible, though not less important, and can be explained as consequences or ramifications—though it should be clear that we are analyzing a syndrome.

3. If one wonders how we pass from unilateral to bilateral oppositions one is immediately alerted to the third feature: the systems of polarized pluralism are *center-based*. We have two counter-oppositions precisely because they are divided by the existence of center-located parties. This is also to say that the existence of bilateral oppositions is not only an indicator of ideological distance, it is equally an indicator of a center-based system.

The systems of polarized pluralism are characterized, then, by the center placement of a party (Italy), or of a group of parties (France, Weimar). Granted that a unified and a fragmented center make a difference, all the cases of extreme multi-partism have a fundamental trait in common: the metrical center of the system is occupied. This implies that we are no longer confronted with bipolar interactions of the left-right kind, but at the very least with triangular interactions. The system is multipolar in that it is based on at least three pillars: left, center and right. While the mechanics of moderate pluralism is bipolar precisely because the system is not center-based, the mechanics of polarized pluralism is multipolar and cannot be explained, therefore, by a dualistic model.

It is important to stress that when one speaks of a center-based system, one is concerned only with a center positioning, *not* with center doctrines, ideologies and opinions—whatever these may be.[41] However, the physical occupation of the center is, in and by itself, no small thing, for it implies that the central area of the political system is *out of competition*. In other terms, the very existence of a center party (or parties) discourages "centrality," the centripetal drives of the political system. And the centripetal drives are precisely the moderating drives that keep the system together. This is why this type of system is center-fleeing, or centrifugal, and thereby conducive to immoderate or extremist politics.

4. If a political system obtains antisystem, bilateral oppositions and discourages—with its center-based multipolar structure—centripetal competition, these traits add up to saying that we have a polarized system. *Polarization* can thus be considered a fourth, synthetic characteristic and defined as a state of the system resulting from strong ideological distance. The polarizing input can be mainly at the left end (Italy), at the right end

(Weimar in the thirties), or at both ends (France).[42] The fact remains that in all cases the spectrum of political opinion is highly polarized: its lateral poles are literally "two poles apart," and the distance between them covers the maximum conceivable spread of opinion.[43] This is tantamount to saying that "consensus" is low, that cleavages are very deep, and that the legitimacy of the political system is widely questioned.

To be sure, the system is center-based precisely because it is polarized. Otherwise there would neither be a central area large enough to provide space for occupancy, nor would a center placement be rewarding—for the center parties capitalize on the fear of extremism. However, it should not escape our attention that we are confronted with a circularity. In the long run a center positioning is not only a consequence but also a cause of polarization, for the very fact that the central area is occupied feeds the system with center-fleeing drives and discourages centripetal competition.

5. The fifth feature of polarized pluralism has already been touched upon. It is the likely prevalence of the *centrifugal drives* over the centripetal attraction. The characteristic trend of the system is the enfeeblement of the center, a persistent loss of votes to one of the extreme ends (or even to both). Perhaps at a certain moment the hemorrhage can be stopped; still, the centrifugal strains appear to counteract successfully any decisive reversal of the trend. When the Weimar Republic and the French Fourth Republic were confronted with decisive crises, the political system was ready to fall apart—which it did. Italy still holds itself together, but from 1946 to 1968 the Italian Communist party has grown from 19 per cent to over 25 per cent of the total vote, while the neo-fascist, right-wing polarization at the other end of the spectrum has more or less maintained its position. So far, after more than twenty years and despite growing prosperity, the Italian political system is still characterized by center-fleeing rather than by centripetal competition.

6. The sixth feature of polarized pluralism is its congenital ideological patterning. This is more than the ideological distance of which we have spoken so far. We revert here to a more substantive meaning of ideology. As noted earlier, the notion of ideology may also signify a highly emotive involvement in politics and/or a mentality, a *forma mentis*. With reference to the unipolar polities the emphasis was on "ideological heating." But with respect to the pluralistic systems the emphasis should be laid on the "mentality," i.e., on ideology understood as a way of perceiving and conceiving politics, and defined, therefore, as a distinctly doctrinaire, principled and dogmatic way of focusing political issues. In this sense, ideology springs from the very roots of a culture (not merely of the political culture), and typically reflects the mentality of rationalism as opposed to the empirical and pragmatic mentality.[44] This is not to say that given a rationalistic culture ideologism necessarily follows. I simply mean that a rationalistic culture is the most favorable soil for the cultivation of ideological politics, whereas an empirical culture makes it difficult for an ideological approach to strike roots.

Be that as it may, in a multi-party system parties of "true believers" stand side by side with parties of "cool believers," i.e., the ideological temperature of each party can be very different. The common characteristic is, rather, that all the parties fight one another with ideological arguments and vie one another with an ideological mentality. The congenital ideological patterning of the polarized polities should not be confused, therefore, with "ideological fever." The temperature of politics may cool down, but a lessening of ideological passion does not transform, per se, an ideological mentality into a pragmatic mentality.

Of course a polity is ideological because the society is ideologized. Even Voltaire's immortal doctor Pangloss would have known that. However, if we are to enter a post Panglossian age of political sociology, due attention should be paid to the fact that the very fragmentation of the party system maintains and upholds the ideological patterning of the society. Objective socio-economic cleavages may no longer justify ideological compartmentalization, and yet denominational, Marxist and nationalistic parties are able to maintain their appeal and to shape the society according to their ideological creeds. When a party system becomes established—by-passing the stage of atomization—parties become built-ins, they become the "natural" system of channelment of the political society. And when there are several built-in, established parties, the system acquires a vested interest in fostering an ideological type of canalization—for two reasons at least. One is that in a situation of extreme pluralism most parties are relatively small groups whose survival is best assured if their followers are indoctrinated as "believers"; and a law of contagion easily explains why the largest party, or parties, follow suit.[45] The other reason is that if so many parties are to be perceived and justified in their distinctiveness, they cannot afford a pragmatic lack of distinctiveness.

7. The seventh feature of polarized pluralism is the emergence of *irresponsible oppositions*. This feature is closely related to the peculiar mechanics of governmental turnover of the center-based polities. On the one hand, the center party (or leading party of the center) is not exposed to alternation: being the very backbone of any possible governmental majority, its destiny is to govern indefinitely. On the other hand, the extreme parties, the parties that oppose the system, are excluded almost by definition from alternation in office—they are not destined to govern. We no longer find, therefore, "alternative coalitions" in which some parties alternate and other parties merely change partners. The mechanics of polarized pluralism is radically different from the mechanics of moderate pluralism. In the latter case *all* the relevant parties are governing oriented and may have access to government. In the case of polarized pluralism we have, instead, a *peripheral turnover* limited to the center-left and center-right parties; for the antisystem parties do not really expect to become governmental parties, even if they wish to.

Peripheral and restricted access to government helps to explain, then, why polarized pluralism lacks a significant responsible opposition and is characterized both by a semiresponsible and a purely irresponsible opposition. An opposition is likely to behave responsibly if it expects that it may have to "respond," that is, to give execution to what it has promised. Conversely, an opposition is likely to be the less responsible the less it expects to govern. Now, in the polarized polities the turnover of the possible allies of the center leading party is mostly imposed by coalition arithmetics. Furthermore, the center-left and center-right parties are likely to share only a peripheral governmental responsibility. Finally, governmental instability and shifting coalitions obscure the very perception of who is responsible for what.[46]

On all these counts, even the governing-oriented parties of the system are not motivated to play the role of a responsible opposition; they can afford to be "semiresponsible." And the antisystem parties are, if anything, motivated to be "irresponsible"; they are a permanent opposition, refusing to be identified with the political system, whose promises are not expected to fall due. Hence, polarized pluralism is characterized by semiresponsible opposition with reference to the parties located at the periphery of the center, and by irresponsible opposition with reference to the extreme parties which oppose the system.[47] And the role played by an irresponsible opposition leads us to the final characteristic.[48]

8. The conclusive feature of polarized pluralism is the extent to which the polity displays a pattern that I call *politics of outbidding*, or of overpromising, which is very different from what is usually called competitive politics. The notion of competitive politics comes from economics, and when we have recourse to analogies we should see to it that the analogy does not get lost along the way. Economic competition is made possible by two conditions: first, that the market escapes monopolistic control; second, and no less important, that the goods are what they are said to be. In the field of economics, this latter condition is satisfied by legal control. If fraud were not punished and if producers could easily get away with selling something for something else—glass for diamonds, any pill for medicine, paper for leather, and so forth—a competitive market would immediately founder.

Similar conditions apply to political competition. Competitive politics is conditioned not only by the presence of more than one party, but also by a minimum of fair competition below which a political market can hardly perform as a competitive market. Admittedly, in politics we must be less exacting, and clearly political fraud is both harder to detect and to control than economic fraud. Yet the distinction between responsible and irresponsible opposition allows us to draw an equivalent distinction between fair and unfair political competition.

If a party can always offer more for less, and can lightheartedly promise heaven on earth without ever having to "respond" for what it promises, this behavior surely falls below any standard of fair competition. In the polarized polities not only does one find such parties, but they are indeed major parties. Therefore, outbidding and overpromising tend to become *the* rule of the game; and I submit that under these conditions "competitive politics" is both an inconvenient choice of vocabulary and a misunderstanding of the facts. Actually the political game is played in terms of unfair competition according to a rule of overpromising, of incessant escalation.

We may now simplify the argument by reducing the somewhat complex pattern described above to a manageable set of properties. The question is:

Which are the properties that qualify the mechanics of polarized pluralism? I would retain the following three: (1) multipolarity, (2) centrifugal competition, (3) immoderate or extremist politics. In contradistinction to moderate pluralism one may equally say that a system of polarized pluralism is *non*bipolar, *non*centripetal and *non*moderate.

A tentative explanation of the etiology of extreme and polarized pluralism would be out of order in this context.[49] The point was to show that the traditional multi-party category grievously muddled two radically different cases, and that the more-than-two party systems cannot be lumped together in a single package. It is fair to ask, nonetheless, what are the chances of survival of the polarized polities. Surely, this variety of multi-partism is an unhealthy state of affairs for a body politic. A political system characterized by centrifugal drives, irresponsible opposition and unfair competition is hardly a viable system. Immoderate and ideological politics is either conducive to sheer paralysis, or to a disorderly sequence of unrealistic and sweeping reforms that are not followed by beneficial returns. This does not necessarily imply that the polarized polities are doomed to failure and to self-destruction, even though they are hardly in a position to cope with explosive or exogenous crises.

The chances of survival of the polarized polities brings us to reconsider the antisystem parties. The question is whether the system will manage to survive long enough to absorb such parties into the existing political order. The evidence, however, is far too thin to warrant predictions on this score.[50] The historian will inevitably discover that in the long run "revolutionary parties" lose their original impetus and accommodate themselves to the regimes that they have been unable to overthrow. But the political scientist may well have to discover that the "long run" was too long for the living actors—and for the political system. Roughly it took half a century for the Marxist socialists to "integrate"—and their integration has not been without losses (to the communist parties). Meanwhile, while the socialists were hesitating, democracy collapsed in Italy, Germany and Spain. Moreover, the problem of absorbing communism seems different enough and the solution more difficult to come by.[51] If we are reminded of the conditions of the working classes during the nineteenth century and the early decades of the twentieth century, revolutionary socialism was indeed a "politics of despair." But present day communist parties in France, Italy, or even Finland hardly reflect conditions of despair—by comparison, they reflect welfare. On the other hand, socialism was and has remained a fairly spontaneous movement with an antiapparat attitude, whereas communism enters the arena as a powerfully regimented movement firmly entrenched through a formidable organizational network. We should neither expect, therefore, that communism can be cured with prosperity (if anything prosperity feeds revolt more than softness in the younger generation), nor underscore the organizational difference. All in all the analogy on the basis of which we predict that communist parties will follow the evolution of the socialist parties, disregards some crucial differences; and I would conclude, more cautiously, that what remains to be seen is precisely whether the polarized systems will be able to outlive the antisystem parties, i.e., whether it is the system or the antisystem that is able to survive longer.

A final caution is in order. As with the case of two-partism—which is generally illustrated with reference to the "pure" English model—the case of polarized pluralism has been illustrated here with reference to the three relatively "pure" cases which represent the full range of possibilities afforded by the type. This procedure affords a number of advantages provided that we are alerted to the fact that concrete systems are often "impure" and tend to depart, therefore, from the "prototype." On the one hand this implies that it is very unlikely that any concrete system will display with equal salience *all* the features reported in my account. On the other hand, the implication is that the concrete systems covered by the "type" are more numerous than the cases utilized for establishing the "prototype."

It would be unreasonable to object, therefore, that one cannot construct a type merely on the evidence afforded by Weimar Germany, France and Italy (since World War Two).[52] Had it not been for its brief span of life, the Spanish Republic would qualify for the first place in our list. Likewise, one could argue that only the lack of sufficient international autonomy and/or overriding external threats keep Finland and Israel from displaying all the properties of polarized pluralism.[53] More significantly, the first South American country having attained the structural consolidation of its party system, Chile, already falls within the category. And this last example suggests that the predictive potentiality of the type should not be underestimated vis-à-vis a number of Latin American countries. In general, extreme and polarized pluralism represents one of the possible outcomes for all the polities which are still in the phase of "party atomism"; this may even turn out to be the most likely outcome for the new States—if they are able to pursue the path of democracy—whenever their quasi-party systems will enter a less volatile stage. Finally, the category alerts us to fatal mistakes of political engineering. I submit, for instance, that India owes a great deal to its single-member district system, for any switch to proportional representation would immediately produce a system of polarized pluralism. It is nice to welcome India's passage from "monopoly to competition";[54] but it is more important to realize what may follow if we fail to distinguish between moderate and extreme multi-partism.

A Scheme for Analysis

There are, admittedly, some difficulties with my scheme. With reference to the distinction between limited and extreme pluralism, Arend Lijphart puts forward the suggestion that "the most objective and straightforward way of comparing the numbers and sizes of political parties in different systems is to examine the cumulative percentages of party strengths in descending order of party size." The method is tested against five countries—Italy, Switzerland, Netherlands, Denmark and Norway—and on the basis of the resulting table,

Lijphart concludes that it is "impossible . . . to make a clear distinction, based on the number and size of parties, between Italy and the other four countries."[55] It would be sufficient to reply that my distinction follows from my counting rules; if these rules are disregarded it goes without saying that no distinction follows. However, since the method suggested by Lijphart will surely please computer "numerologists," it deserves to be discussed on its own merits.

The question is whether the cumulative percentage method leads anywhere in terms of theoretical significance. Having reference to the rank ordering one may wonder, for instance, whether it is suggestive of the likely coalition majorities. In this respect the table presented by Lijphart would suggest that only Switzerland needs a three-party coalition, while Italy, the Netherlands, Denmark and Norway have a largely sufficient majority with two-party government. It so happens that if the parties in question are identified this is very seldom the case.

For instance, the Italian cumulative percentage of the two major parties is 63.5; but these two parties happen to be the Christian Democrats and the Italian Communist party. If applied to the Weimar Republic, the suggestion would have been that at some point in time the Nazis and the Communists could have governed together. In the case of the French Fourth Republic the suggestion would have been that no government could exclude the Communist party, which was invariably the strongest single party. Reverting to the instances cited by Lijphart, in Norway the first two parties are the Socialist (43.1) and the Conservative (21.1), indeed the two mutually exclusive poles of the system. Clearly, the rank ordering obtained with the cumulative percentage method is entirely blind both to ideological incompatibilities and to ideological affinities. It equally fails to appreciate the difference between a minor party with a strong coalition bargaining potential, and a relatively large party that counts for nothing. The point may be generalized as follows: this method gives us no clue about whatever relevance any party might have.

One may ask another question, namely, whether the cumulative percentage method does help in establishing significant thresholds. Once more the reply is negative. If we were to decide, for instance, that the parties obtaining 75 per cent of the total vote are the parties that really matter, in the table of Lijphart, Italy, Switzerland and Norway would become three-party systems, with respectively 77, 74 and 74 per cent. As a matter of fact, the table in question does not even help us to decide which parties can be discounted. We are left to go on counting up to the very end, that is, until we find a party that obtains one seat. All in all, if there are difficulties with my method, no improvement results from the method that Lijphart considers "objective and straightforward." It is nice to let computers do the work for us, but the output will leave us more confused than we already are.

Turning to the real difficulty, the crucial question is; to what extent is the numerical criterion a reliable and sufficient indicator? In other terms, How strong is the coincidence between the *format* of the class and the *mechanics* of the type?

The very fact that I have consistently drawn a distinction between classification and typology goes to show that I am fully aware of the problem. As I have pointed out all along, a two-party format may not display two-party properties, limited pluralism may not be moderate, and, conversely, extreme pluralism may not be polarized. In fact, the class will correspond to the type only under this condition: that the number of parties (fragmentation) varies in accord with a left-right spread of opinion (ideological distance).

Another way of expressing dissatisfaction with my scheme is to note that the numerical indicator is largely insensitive to the existence of socio-political tensions. Canada and Belgium are the obvious cases in point. Here we have a limited fragmentation in terms of the number of parties, and yet far more strains than, e.g., in Switzerland or in the Netherlands. However, if we remember that identical political structures may be superimposed upon entirely different social structures, it is only obvious that the resulting tensions will be at variance. The point is, rather, whether a bipolar or a multipolar structure helps to lessen societal tensions. My argument is that a bipolar system is less exposed and less conducive to polarization, whereas a multipolar system is likely to reinforce and to aggravate polarization. But it is clear enough that if the polarization of a bipolar system sustains a persistent centrifugal trend, then the polity will not remain, in the long run, bipolar. Conversely, a multipolar polity may revert to a bipolar configuration as a result of ongoing depolarization.

Reverting to the initial query, namely, how strong is the coincidence between the number of parties and the mechanical properties of the system, the issue can be settled by ascertaining how frequently the classification and the typology do in fact correspond. But the case for holding on to a numerical indicator is stronger if the numerical classification can be backed by a rationale. My conjecture is, in fact, that a set of mechanical consequences are likely to be engendered by the very number of parties. For instance, if the parties are two immoderate politics is seldom rewarding and appears suicidal for the system, whereas the very way in which more than five parties interact helps to explain a centrifugal pattern of competition. In short, my conjecture is that low or high numbers do contain *mechanical predispositions*.

The conjecture is apparently challenged by the existence of a type of stable democracy that Lijphart labels "consociational," whose essential characteristic is "overarching cooperation at the elite level with the deliberate aim of counteracting disintegrative tendencies in the system."[56] The point is that a consociational type of "grand coalition" arrangement applies to any format. However, as Lijphart himself emphasizes, all the requisite conditions for consociational democracy "have to do with elite attitudes and behavior . . ."[57] In the final analysis, consociational democracy turns out to be a system entirely created by, and dependent on, elite counter-action; such a system exists to the extent that highly responsible and skillful elites decide to swim

TABLE 12–1
Scheme of Analysis

Indicator: Number of parties	Variables: (1) Fragmentation (2) Ideology	Classification	Typology	Major Properties	Alternative Possibilities
1 party	{ No fragmentation / Ideological intensity	One-party	One-party totalitarian	Monopoly	
		Hegemonic party	Hegemonic ideological	Diminishing coercive and extractive capabilities	
			One-party authoritarian		
			One-party pragmatic		
			Hegemonic pragmatic	→	
2 parties	Low fragmentation	Two-party (format)	Two-party (mechanics)	Alternative government / Moderate politics	Two-party polarized
3–5 parties	[Ideological distance] ←→	Limited pluralism	Moderate pluralism	Bipolar coalitions / Centripetal competition	Limited but polarized pluralism
more than 5	High fragmentation	Extreme pluralism	Polarized pluralism	Multipolarity / Centrifugal competition	Extreme but moderate pluralism
1 predominant	Low or high fragmentation	Whatever format	Predominant party system	Unsuccessful competition	Turnover: end of predominance

against the current. If so, it would be highly misleading to draw from Lijphart for predictive purposes;[58] but his argument is very helpful in explaining apparent exceptions.

For instance, Lijphart explains nicely the Austrian case, that is, how a two-party format may not only survive but perform in spite of the *Lagermentalität*, of strong compartmentalization. I am equally pleased with his demonstration concerning the Netherlands and Switzerland, for it adds up to reinforcing my suggestion that more than five parties do represent a critical point. It is precisely because these countries approximate a danger point that they have recourse to consociational practices. Hence, the major reason for their moderate multipartism is that the Swiss and Dutch leadership are determined to counteract the disintegrative predispositions of high fragmentation. Finally, I wholeheartedly agree with Lijphart's emphasis on the crucial role of leadership. But if we are not alerted to the predispositions inherent in growing party fragmentation, not only are we unable to appreciate the extraordinary merits of consociational leadership, we may also incur the error of predicting regularities on the basis of exceptions.[59] In fact, it would be very misleading to say that the Netherlands and Switzerland prove that high fragmentation is irrelevant to the stability and performance of a democracy. The correct argument is, instead, that these two systems "work," notwithstanding the handicap of their fragmentation, thanks to an exceptional leadership and for reasons that cannot be easily repeated elsewhere.

On balance, it seems to me that the numerical indicator and classification perform decently throughout the intricacies of the real world. Granted that we may need the help of control indicators, these are equally based on elemental information. My conclusion is, then, that the numerical classification of party systems recommends itself on three counts: because it is analytical enough, because it does provide insights, and because it is easy to construct. In particular, the insightful simplicity of the numerical classification recommends itself for cross-national worldwide surveys, that is, when we are forced to rely not only on highly visible information, but also on data that can be easily updated.

But let us assume, for the sake of argument, that the number of parties is an irrelevant variable. Even so, the respective properties of two-partism, moderate pluralism, and polarized pluralism remain as they are. In other terms, if one denies that the format affects the mechanics, one may simply disregard the first three columns of the overall scheme presented in Table 12–1, and begin with the fourth column, i.e., with the typology. This leaves us to solve the problems of comparative politics, but no harm follows as long as a scholar deals with single-nation studies, or as long as his comparative perspective is confined to the few countries that he manages to know in depth. Be that as it may, let us turn to Table 12–1, which summarizes the overall discussion.

In reading the table a few reminders and comments are in order. The second column should be understood to mean that the area of monopartism (no fragmentation) varies along a continuum of "intensity of ideology";

whereas the area of poly-partism varies along two distinct, though not un-related, dimensions: the extent of fragmentation and the extent of the spread of opinion (ideological distance). Since the numerical indicator only detects fragmentation, it is no wonder that the *classification* cannot indicate, by itself, whether a political system "works." But the third column accounts also for the ideological spread (via control indicators such as the existence of antisystem parties), and therefore the *typology* does convey indications concerning the working or nonworking predispositions of the political system.

The scheme allows, in the last column, for deviant cases, or alternative possibilities. These deviations represent, very simply, the lack of correspond-ence between the format of the class and the properties of the type. Thus exceptions are not explained away; rather, they lend themselves to the construction of a residual "mixed typology." Whether we should speak of deviant cases or of an alternative typology is a matter of empirical fact. In the table I say "alternative possibilities" under the assumption that the deviations from the major typology are unfrequent. But the substance would not change if the findings did show that the mixes are frequent.

Finally, let it be noted that the predominant party system has been placed at the end of the table because, on the basis of a numerical criterion, this type can be located at different points. Since the predominant party category rep-resents a typically concentrated distribution in which one party overwhelms all the other parties, a numerical indicator can only establish that the type belongs to the area of pluralism.

In summing up, it is fair to say that not only the explanatory power of the scheme is satisfactory, but also that its predictive potential is promising. On the one hand, the scheme satisfies the logical requirement of any taxonomy; its categories are jointly exhaustive and mutually exclusive. On the other hand, the scheme goes a long way toward satisfying the empirical requirement of being exhaustive "as a matter of empirical fact."[60] If classifications are divided into "artificial" and "natural,"[61] and if a classification is all the more natural "the more it aids in the discovery of empirical relationships," the more it "enables us to make the maximum number of prophesies and deductions," and the more it is an all-purpose rather than a single-purpose classification, if so, then the taxonomy under consideration also qualifies as being "natural."[62]

We may now turn to a more simple and manageable scheme. A first simplification follows from the assumption that in most cases the format of the class and the properties of the type coincide. Under this assumption I speak of "taxonomy" and of "categories" (thereby implying that I no longer distinguish between the classification and the typology), and propose the following abridged labels: (1) two-partism, (2) moderate multipartism, (3) extreme multi-partism.

By saying *two-partism* I signify both the format and the mechanics. Like-wise, *moderate multi-partism* replaces the more cumbersome label "limited and moderate pluralism"; and *extreme multi-partism* replaces the equally cumbersome label "extreme and polarized pluralism." The terminological device is simply to revert, at the synthetic stage of the argument, to the suffix "partism." Incidentally, all these stipulations have been consistently adopted throughout the essay.[63] The simplified taxonomy is recapitulated in Table 12–2.

It is apparent that additional qualifications have been injected into Table 12–2.[64] To begin with, I cannot accept the suggestion conveyed by much of the current literature that if a one party polity becomes loose enough, it approaches party pluralism; and that, vice versa, if no alternation occurs within a two-party system, then it approaches a one-party arrangement. This argument owes its plausibility to a classification that fails to distinguish between the cases of monopartism and predominance. The table indicates, therefore, that the so-called "continuum" of party systems is in fact "discontinuous": at one point there are no rules of transformation from one pattern into another, for the passage from monocentrism to pluralism, and vice versa, requires the very breakdown of the political system.[65]

This basic discontinuity can be highlighted in various ways. At the top of the table "party-State systems" are contrasted with "party systems" to signify that the one-party and the hegemonic party arrangements lack subsystem autonomy and are not, therefore, a "party system" in the sense in which the systemic properties result from parties (in the plural) interacting among themselves.[66]

Another way of pinpointing the difference is suggested at the low end of the table where the area of "monocentrism" (a somewhat more accurate label than mono-partism) is characterized by a repressive, or coercive, potential, while the area of "pluralism" (or of poly-partism) is characterized in terms of expressive capability. To be sure, repression does not consist of sheer physical force; it should be understood, rather, as indicating high mobilizational and extractive capabilities obtained via "mass manipulation." Conversely, the more a political system allows for expression, the more it allows for "mass pressure" exerted from below.

Looking at the table, it should be understood that the placing of the categories in an order of decreasing intensity of repression on the left side, and of increasing intensity of expression on the right side, is a very loose approximation. I only wish to convey the idea that a one-party structure of the pragmatic variety is less repressive, or less intolerant, than a hegemonic party structure of the ideological variety. On the other hand, I do not especially wish to argue that extreme pluralism is more expressive than moderate pluralism. Although the broad lines are roughly represented, the details are, as is inevitable, misrepresented.

The warning applies equally to the placement of party atomism, which is not meant to convey the suggestion that this situation corresponds by definition to a high degree of expressive capability. Atomized multi-partism amounts to a situation in which parties are "labels," loose coalitions of notables which often change at each election and tend to dissolve from one election to another. Because this pattern represents the phase of development of party system that precedes its structural consolidation, I have placed

T ABLE 12–2
Taxonomy of Party Polities

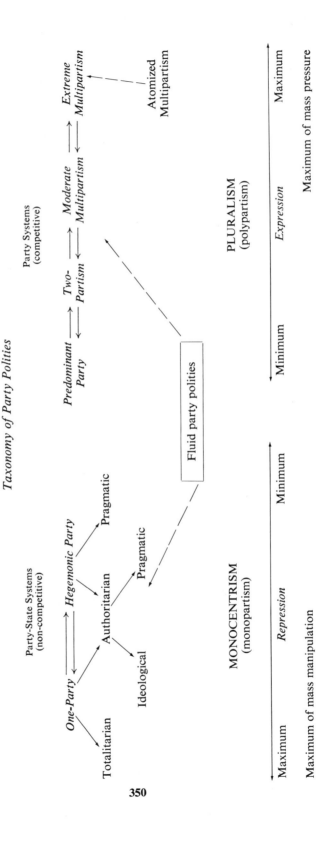

atomized multi-partism below extreme multi-partism to suggest that anacronistic prolonged survivals of party atomism are especially conducive to extreme and polarized pluralism.

It should also be understood that by dividing the *continuum* into two halves, I do not imply in the least that on the one side we only have repression, and on the other we only have expression. Of course not. "Repression" can be defined as a situation in which coercive means of government *prevail* all along the continuum. Conversely "expression" denotes a situation in which pressures from below *prevail* all along the continuum over coercion from above. Obviously, any situation of repression includes some expression, and conversely any situation of expression includes some repression: in fact, I am pointing to a basic discontinuity of the *same continuum*. On the other hand, the continuities are indicated by the various two-way horizontal arrows, which signify that within each area—monopartism or poly-partism—the transitions from one system to another occur with no alteration of the rules of the game. For instance, the transformation of a predominant party system into a two-party or multi-party pattern, and vice versa, is left to the voters' choice.[67] Likewise, the passage from the one-party to the hegemonic party pattern, and vice versa, can occur smoothly, as a mere matter of "letting go" or of "tightening" (whatever the formal rules of the game), on account of the highly discretionary nature of the power systems in question.

Finally, the table carries the indication "fluid party polities." This is also to underline that the taxonomy deliberately excludes all the new states whose political processes are highly diffuse, that is, the formless polities that find themselves in a highly volatile and provisional stage of growth. The exclusion is deliberate for a number of reasons, and implies the following caution: that we should not—for the very fact that we classify—attribute a definite "form" to a state of formlessness. The category is boxed, then, to mean that the fluid polities are included in the table only as a residual category. It should also be clear that the positioning of the category is not meant to suggest that the volatile polities bridge the discontinuity of the continuum, but that their future consolidation will lead them in either one of the two camps.

According to the presentation of Table 12–2 the major categories are seven. However, when the subtypes are included, the taxonomy consists of ten categories: (1) one-party totalitarian, (2) one-party authoritarian, (3) one-party pragmatic, (4) hegemonic-ideological, (5) hegemonic-pragmatic, (6) predominant party, (7) two-partism, (8) moderate multi-partism, (9) extreme multi-partism, and (10) atomized party system.

It is apparent that the taxonomy can be simplified further. Table 12–3 indicates, accordingly, a set of successive aggregations which are largely self-explanatory.

Table 12–3 sets aside the predominant party by considering this system a possible outcome of any type of pluralism. Likewise the atomized systems can be considered a likely predecessor of extreme multi-partism. We are thus left with five major categories, and these can be aggregated, in turn, into three groups, namely, unipolar, bipolar and multipolar systems. Incidentally,

TABLE 12–3

Aggregations

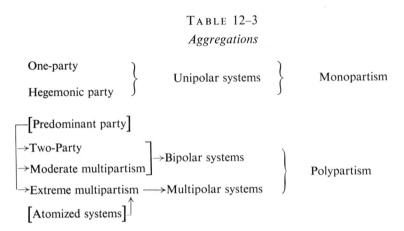

I would recommend these latter labels for their straightforward precision. Finally, let it be noted that if the bipolar systems comprise two-partism and moderate multi-partism, the major division is the one between moderate and extreme multi-partism.

NOTES

PREFACE

1. S. Rokkan, ed. *Approaches to the Study of Political Participation* (Bergen: The Michelsen Institute, 1962), also available as a separate issue of *Acta Sociologica*, vol. VI, no. 1–2.

2. E. Allardt and Y. Littunen, eds. *Cleavages, Ideologies and Party Systems* (Helsinki: Westermarck Society, 1964).

3. S. Rokkan *et al. Citizens, Elections, Parties* (Oslo: The Norwegian Universities Press, and New York: D. McKay, 1969).

4. S. M. Lipset and S. Rokkan, eds. *Party Systems and Voter Alignments* (New York: The Free Press, 1967).

International Cooperation in Political Sociology

1. This is the suggestive term used by Gabriel Almond and Sidney Verba in their discussion of the data basis of comparative research; see *The Civic Culture* (Princeton: Univ. of Princeton Press, 1963), Ch. 2. For a broader discussion across several disciplines see S. Rokkan, "Comparative Cross-National Research: The Context of Current Efforts" in R. L. Merritt and S. Rokkan, eds., *Comparing Nations* (New Haven: Yale University Press, 1966).

2. For further details see S. M. Miller, "Comparative social mobility." *Current Sociology*, 9(1) 1961: 1–89 and D. V. Glass and R. König, eds., *Soziale Schichtung und soziale Mobilität* (Cologne: Westdeutscher Verlag, 1961).

3. See S. Rokkan, ed., *Approaches to the Study of Political Participation* (Bergen: Chr. Michelsen Inst., 1962), 171 pp. (also *Acta Sociol.* 6(1–2), 1962). Some of the papers of the Seminar have since been rewritten for publication in the present volume. Others will appear in S. Rokkan, *Citizens, Elections, Parties* (Oslo: Norw. Univ. Press, 1969). One of the major papers presented at the Seminar was incorporated in S. M. Lipset, *The First New Nation* (New York: Basic Books, 1963). For a report on the deliberations of the Seminar, see S. Rokkan and S. Høyer, *Int. Soc. Sci. Journal*, 14(2), 1962: 351–363.

4. Vol. III (Louvain, I.S.A., 1964).

5. S. M. Lipset and S. Rokkan, eds., *Party Systems and Voter Alignments* (New York: The Free Press, 1967).

6. The final section of the paper by Rokkan and Valen on "Regional Contrasts in Norwegian Politics" does, however, deal with data on reactions to supranational developments: it presents an analysis of survey data on reactions among the Norwegian voters during the conflict over the decision on entry into the EEC.

7. *Int. Soc. Sci. J.*, 16(4), 1964.

8. See the papers by Rokkan, Allardt, Eisenstadt and Marsh in *Transactions of the Sixth World Congress of Sociology*, vol. I (Louvain, I.S.A., 1967).

9. Linz's important paper on Spanish party systems was later printed in *Party Systems and Voter Alignments*, op. cit.

10. Subsequently published in V. Capecchi *et al.*, *Il Comportamento Elettorale in Italia* (Bologna: Mulino, 1968).

11. Berlin, Institut für politische Wissenschaft, Babelstr. 14, 1968, XII, 489 pp. DM 9.

12. See the special issue on "Armed Forces and Society" of the *European Journal of Sociology*, vol. VI, Aug. 1965, and the forthcoming volumes by J. van Doorn, ed., *Armed Forces and Society* (The Hague: Mouton, 1969), and *Military Professionals and Military Regimes* (The Hague: Mouton, 1969).

13. See T. Clark, ed., *Community Structure and Decision-Making* (San Francisco: Chandler, 1968).

14. Some of the papers of the Bergen conference as well as a number of other reports and notes on comparative developmental analysis will be published under Committee auspices in 1969: S. Rokkan, *Citizens, Elections, Parties, op. cit.* A volume based on the Berlin Conference has also been published; see footnote 11.

15. See the report by Stein Rokkan on the ISSC Conference at La Napoule in June 1962, in *Soc. Sci. Info.*, 1(3), 1963:

31–38 and the later reports presented in S. Rokkan, ed., *Data Archives for the Social Sciences* (Paris: Mouton, 1966).

16. See R. L. Merritt and S. Rokkan, eds., *Comparing Nations* (New Haven: Yale University Press, 1966).

17. See particularly S. Rokkan, "Electoral Mobilization, Party Competition and National Integration" in J. LaPalombara and M. Weiner, eds., *Political Parties and Political Development* (Princeton: Princeton University Press, 1966), and M. Dogan and S. Rokkan, eds., *Quantitative Ecological Analysis in the Social Sciences* (Cambridge: M.I.T. Press, 1969).

Chapter 1
Political Cleavages in "Developed" and "Emerging" Polities

1. I have discussed different definitions of democracy and the factors related to varying political systems in detail elsewhere in my writings and do not want to repeat these here. See S. M. Lipset, *Political Man* (Garden City: Doubleday, 1960), pp. 45–96; and *The First New Nation* (New York: Basic Books, 1963), pp. 207–317.

2. M. Ostrogorski, *Democracy and the Organization of Political Parties* II: The United States (Garden City: Anchor Books, 1964), pp. 173, 223–224, 305–306.

3. Maurice Duverger, *Political Parties* (London: Methuen, 1954), pp. xxiii–xxxvii; Max Weber, *Essays in Sociology* (New York: Oxford University Press, 1946), pp. 100–115.

4. In 1861, Napoleon III advised the Prussian government to introduce universal suffrage "by means of which the conservative rural population could outvote the Liberals in the cities." F. Meinecke, *Weltbürgertum und Nationalstaat* (Munich: G. R. Oldenbourg, 1922), pp. 517–518; F. Naumann, *Die politischen Parteien* (Berlin-Schönberg: Buchverlag der Hilfe, 1910), pp. 16–17.

5. Weber, *op. cit.*, pp. 103–104; Guenther Roth, *The Social Democrats in Imperial Germany* (Totowa: The Bedminster Press, 1963), pp. 252–254.

6. Duverger, *op. cit.*, p. 46.

7. Theodore Geiger, *Die soziale Schichtung des deutschen Volkes* (Stuttgart: Ferdinand Enke, 1932), p. 79.

8. See Robert Michels," Die deutschen Sozialdemokratie I. Parteimitgliedschaft und soziale Zusammensetzung", *Archiv für Sozialwissenschaft und Sozialpolitik*, 26 (1906), pp. 512–513; Robert Michels, *Socialismus und Fascismus* I (Karlsruhe:

G. Braun, 1925), pp. 78–79; Robert Lowie, *Toward Understanding Germany* (Chicago: University of Chicago Press, 1954), p. 138.

9. There was, of course, adult male suffrage in the federal parliament, but the three-chamber voting system of Prussia, which discriminated heavily against the workers, served to prevent the large Socialist bloc in the federal Parliament from having much influence, and this meant that the struggle for political democracy had still to be waged. "The federal constitution, as written by Bismarck, had made the federal government practically an appendix of the Prussian cabinet." See Carl Landauer, *European Socialism* (Berkeley: University of California Press, 1959), pp. 366–368.

10. Theodore Schieder, *The State and Society in Our Times* (London: Thomas Nelson and Sons, 1962), p. 121.

11. S. M. Lipset, *Political Man, op. cit.*, p. 149.

12. Joseph Schumpeter, *Capitalism, Socialism and Democracy* (New York: Harper Torchbooks, 1962), pp. 134–139.

13. Mario Einaudi, "Social Realities" and the Study of Political Parties (unpublished paper).

14. See the various articles by David Landes: "French Entrepreneurship and Industrial Growth in the XIXth Century," *Journal of Economic History*, 9 (1949), pp. 49–61; "French Business and the Business Man: A Social and Cultural Analysis" in Edward M. Earle, ed., *Modern France* (Princeton: Princeton University Press, 1951), pp. 334–353; and "Observations on France: Economy, Society and Polity," *World Politics*, 9 (1957), pp. 329–350.

15. "Sluggish economic growth may

generate the deepest and longest lasting protest by reason of the society's inability to provide well-being and social justice to match social aspirations and by reason of the economic elite's failure to inspire confidence," Val Lorwin, "Working Class Politics and Economic Development in Western Europe," *American Historical Review*, 63 (1958), p. 350.

16. See Bruce H. Millen, *The Political Role of Labor in Developing Countries* (Washington: The Brookings Institution, 1963), pp. 38–39; Lorwin, *op. cit.*, pp. 345–346.

17. S. M. Lipset, "The Changing Class Structure and Contemporary European Politics," *Daedalus*, 93 (1964), pp. 271–303.

18. Summary of the main thesis of Edvard Bull, "Die Entwicklung der Arbeiterbewegung in den drei skandinavischen Ländern," *Archiv für die Geschichte der Sozialismus und der Arbeiterbewegung*, 10 (1922) in Stein Rokkan and Henry Valen, "Parties, Elections and Political Behaviour in the Northern Countries: A Review of Recent Research," in Otto Stammer, ed., *Politische Forschung* (Köln: Westdeutscher Verlag, 1960), p. 110; see also pp. 107–108. The specific empirical results of Bull's analysis are presented in some detail in Walter Galenson, "Scandinavia," in Galenson, ed., *Comparative Labor Movements* (New York: Prentice-Hall, 1952), esp. pp. 105–120. I have dealt with this material in *Political Man, op. cit.*, pp. 68–71. A detailed discussion of the relationship between the pace of industrialization and politics may be found in my article, "Socialism-Left and Right-East and West," *Confluence*, 7 (Summer 1958), pp. 173–192.

19. Lorwin, *op. cit.*, p. 350; Lipset, *Political Man, op. cit.*, pp. 70–71; Mancun Olson Jr., "Rapid Growth as a Destabilizing Force", *The Journal of Economic History*, 23 (1963), pp. 529–552.

20. Friedrich Engels, "Letter to Karl Kautsky," Nov. 8, 1884, in Karl Marx and Friedrich Engels, *Correspondence 1846–1895* (New York: International Publishers, 1946), p. 422.

21. "Belgian socialism from the start has been one of the most moderate labor movements." Felix E. Oppenheim, "Belgium: Party Cleavage and Compromise," in S. Neumann, ed., *Modern Political Parties*

(Chicago: University of Chicago Press, 1956), p. 162.

22. Lorwin, *op. cit.*, p. 348.

23. Landauer, *op. cit.*, p. 479.

24. See Harry Laidler, *Socialism in Thought and Action* (New York: The Macmillan Co., 1927), pp. 447–450, 489–490; Franz Borkenau, *World Communism* (Ann Arbor: Ann Arbor Paperback, 1962), pp. 104–106; Heikki Waris, "Finland," in Arnold Rose, ed., *The Institutions of Advanced Societies* (Minneapolis: University of Minnesota Press, 1958), pp. 211–214; for a summary of studies of Finnish political behavior in recent years see Pertti Pesonen, "Studies on Finnish Political Behavior," in Austin Ranney, ed., *Essays on the Behavioral Study of Politics* (Urbana: University of Illinois Press, 1962), pp. 217–234; for a statistical analysis of the way in which the Swedish domination of class position and prestige was overcome see Karl Deutsch, *Nationalism and Social Communication* (New York: John Wiley, 1953), pp. 104–107.

25. See S. M. Lipset, "The Changing Class Structure . . .," *op. cit.*, pp. 271–303.

26. See S. M. Lipset, *The First New Nation, op. cit.*, pp. 286–317.

27. These statements are documented in detail in S. M. Lipset, *Political Man, op. cit.* and I will not reiterate the references here.

28. See Robert R. Alford, *Party and Society. The Anglo-American Democracies* (Chicago: Rand McNally, 1963).

29. The special failing of democracy in Africa clearly deserves some attention. To some considerable extent it would seem to have some relationship to the fact of tribalism. The African states are not societies or nations, they are for the most part heterogeneous collections of linguistically and culturally distinct tribes or smaller nations, without a common language. Before becoming democratic polities they must first become polities. See René Servoise, "Whither Black Africa?," in Bertrand de Jouvenal, ed., *Futuribles* (Geneva: Droz, 1963), esp. pp. 264–267.

30. S. M. Lipset, *Political Man, op. cit.*, pp. 48–67; James S. Coleman, "The Political Systems of the Developing Areas," *op. cit.*, pp. 538–544; Everett Hagen, "A Framework for Analyzing Economic and Political

Change," in Robert Asher, ed., *Development of Emerging Countries* (Washington: Brookings Institute, 1962), pp. 1–8; and Charles Wolf, Jr., *The Political Effects of Economic Programs* (Santa Monica, The Rand Corporation, RM–3901–ISA, February 1964), pp. 19–33.

31. See Karl Deutsch, "Social Mobilization and Political Development," *American Political Science Review*, 55 (1961), pp. 493–514.

32. Kalman H. Silvert, "Some Propositions on Chile," *American Universities Field Staff Reports Service*, West Coast South America Series, 11 (1) 1964, p. 10.

33. Gino Germani, "Social Change and Intergroup Conflicts," Dittoed, 1963, (translated by I. L. Horowitz), p. 15. See also Gino Germani, *Politica y Sociedad en una Epoca de Transición* (Buenos Aires: Editorial Paidos, 1962).

34. There is an extensive theoretical literature attempting to differentiate the conditions of polities in underdeveloped nations from those in the developed countries. As yet, however, such writings have led to few research studies designed to test out the propositions in them. See for example, George Kahin, Guy Pauker, and Lucien Pye, "Comparative Politics in Non-Western Countries," *American Political Science Review*, 49 (1955), pp. 1022–1041; Gabriel Almond, "Comparative Political Systems," *Journal of Politics*, 18 (1956), pp. 391–409; Dankwart Rustow, "New Horizons for Comparative Politics," *World Politics*, 9 (1957), pp. 530–549; Lucien Pye, "The Non-Western Political Process," *The Journal of Politics*, 20 (1958), pp. 469–486; Gabriel Almond, "Introduction: A Functional Approach to Comparative Politics," in Almond and Coleman, eds., *op. cit.*, pp. 3–64; James S. Coleman, "Conclusion: The Political Systems of the Developing Areas," in *Ibid*, pp. 532–576; John H. Kautsky, "An Essay on the Politics of Development," in Kautsky, ed., *Political Change in Underdeveloped Countries* (New York: John Wiley, 1962), pp. 3–119; Edward Shils, "Political Development in the New States," *Comparative Studies in Society and History*, 2 (1960), pp. 265–292, 379–411; Zbigniew Brzezinski, "The Politics of Underdevelopment," *World Politics*, 9 (1956), pp. 55–75; Edward Shils, "On the

Comparative Study of New States," in Clifford Geertz, ed., *Old Societies and New States* (New York: The Free Press, 1963), pp. 1–26; Kalman Silvert and Frank Bonilla, "Definitions, Propositions, and Hypotheses Concerning Modernism, Class and National Integration," in Kalman Silvert, ed., *Expectant Peoples* (New York: Random House, 1963), pp. 439–450; S. N. Eisenstadt, *Essays on Sociological Aspects of Political and Economic Development* (The Hague: Mouton, 1961), pp. 9–53.

35. Although much has been written on these nations, there is little knowledge in depth about them. For example, George Blanksten reports as of 1960 that "only one Latin American political party has been the subject of a full-scale monographic study." See "The Politics of Latin America," in Almond and Coleman, eds., *op. cit.*, p. 479.

36. Donald M. Dozer, *Latin America: An Interpretive History* (New York: McGraw-Hill, 1962), pp. 369–414, and *passim*; George N. Blanksten, *op. cit.*, pp. 481–487; H. Davis, ed., *Government and Politics in Latin America* (New York: Ronald Press, 1958); John J. Johnson, *Political Change in Latin America* (Stanford: Stanford University Press, 1958).

37. Moisés Poblete Troncoso and Ben G. Burnett, *The Rise of the Latin American Labor Movement* (New York: Bookman Associates, 1960).

38. As Shils has pointed out, in the socially less differentiated underdeveloped states the concept of intellectual is broader than in the more advanced countries. It includes "all persons with an *advanced modern education* and the intellectual concerns and skills ordinarily associated with it . . . [T]he intellectuals are those persons who have become modern not by immersing themselves in the ways of modern commerce or administration, but by being exposed to the set course of modern intellectual culture in a college or university," *op. cit.*, pp. 198–199; for a discussion of students as intellectuals and their politics see pp. 203–205.

39. That Castro's initial following was largely based on young, well-educated middle-class Cubans has been documented by Theodore Draper. He points out that of Castro's 18 cabinet members in 1960,

everyone was a university graduate, that they were of middle or upper-class background, and professionals or intellectuals occupationally. Theodore Draper, *Castro's Revolution, Myths and Realities* (New York: Praeger, 1962), pp. 42–43. Draper also points out that the list of Cuban defenders of Castroism who were interviewed by C. Wright Mills in his effort to present the authentic voice of the Cuban Revolution for his book *Listen Yankee* did not include a single worker or peasant. "Without exception, his informants were middle-class intellectuals and professionals," p. 21.

40. Harry Benda includes military officers in the category of the "westernized intellectuals" in the emerging nations, pointing out that they "were often the first group to receive western training," and consequently became a force for modernization, which often brought them "fairly close to the socialism so prevalent among non-western intelligentsias in general." "Non-Western Intelligentsias as Political Elites," in John H. Kautsky, ed., *op. cit.*, pp. 239–244; John J. Johnson, ed., *The Role of the Military in Underdeveloped Countries* (Princeton: Princeton University Press, 1962); Morroe Berger, *Military Elite and Social Change* (Princeton: Princeton University Center of International Studies, 1960); Sydney N. Fisher, ed., *The Military in the Middle East* (Columbus: Ohio State University Press, 1963); Edwin Lieuwen, *Arms and Politics in Latin America* (New York: Praeger, 1960); Lucien Pye, "Armies in the Process of Political Modernization," *European Journal of Sociology*, 2 (1961), pp. 82–92.

41. Morris Janowitz, *The Military in the Political Development of New States* (Chicago: University Press, 1964). For a specification of the sharply different political roles, which may be played by the military in unstable polities, see Gino Germani and Kalman Silvert, "Politics, Social Structure and Military Intervention in Latin America," European Journal of Sociology, 2 (1961), pp. 62–81.

42. The appeal of left-wing ideologies to the intellectuals and other sections of the university-trained intelligentsia in the underdeveloped nations has been analyzed in some detail. See Morris Watnick, "The Appeal of Communism to the Peoples of Underdeveloped Areas," in R. Bendix and S. M. Lipset, eds., *Class, Status and Power* (Glencoe: The Free Press, 1953), pp. 651–662; Hugh Seton-Watson, "Twentieth Century Revolutions," *The Political Quarterly*, 22 (1951), pp. 251–265; John H. Kautsky, *op. cit.*, pp. 44–49, 106–113; Edward Shils, "The Intellectual Between Tradition and Modernity: The Indian Situation," *Comparative Studies in Society and History*, Supplement I, (1961), pp. 94–108. Perhaps the most comprehensive treatment of the subject is Edward Shils, "The Intellectuals in the Political Development of the New States," in John H. Kautsky, ed., *op. cit.*, pp. 195–234.

43. See Glaucio Ary Dillon Soares, "The Politics of Uneven Development: The Case of Brazil," S. M. Lipset and Stein Rokkan, eds. *Party Systems and Voter Alignments: Cross-National Perspectives* (New York: The Free Press, 1967), pp. 467–496.

44. "A ... factor that contributed to the fears of the ruling class was that 'bolshevization' was believed to be penetrating the sons of prominent men, the intelligentsia and the university students who formed the true *elite* of Imperial Japan or who would do so in the future ..." [A Home Ministry Police Report stated:] "'After the Great Earthquake [1923] graduates from colleges and high schools, the so-called educated class, were most susceptible to the baptism of bolshevist thought ...' A situation in which the organization of the workers and farmers was so slight as to present no problem, but in which the *elite* and educated class had become 'bolshevized,' is completely abnormal according to the laws of Marxism ... [W]hat gave the rulers of Imperial Japan nightmares until the last was the 'bolshevization' of the State from within rather than revolution from below." Masao Maruyama, *Thought and Behaviour in Modern Japanese Politics* (London: Oxford University Press, 1963), p. 77.

45. A recent study based on interviews with a sample of 3,000 Japanese men reports that the most radical segment are "the employed professional specialists. They are more in favor of denuclearized neutrality than laborers or blue-collar workers. They lend as much support to political strikes called by labor unions as

do the laborers themselves. Most of the white-collar stratum favors and gives support to the socialist parties." Research Society on Japanese Social Structure, "Special Traits of White-Collar Workers in Large Urban Areas," *Journal of Social and Political Ideas in Japan,* 1 (August 1963), p. 78. A 1958 national sample reported heavy socialist support among professionals and managerial groups. See Z. Suetuna, H. Aoyama, C. Hyashi, and K. Matusita, "A Study of Japanese National Character, Part II," *Annals of the Institute of Statistical Mathematics* (Tokyo), Supplement II, (1961), p. 54; see also Joji Watanuki, "White-Collar Workers and the Pattern of Politics in Present-Day Japan," in S. M. Lipset and Stein Rokkan, eds., *op. cit.*; Robert A. Scalapino and Junnosuke Masumi, *Parties and Politics in Contemporary Japan* (Berkeley: University of California Press, 1962), p. 177; Douglas Mendel, *The Japanese People and Foreign Policy* (Berkeley: University of California Press, 1961), pp. 44–45, 47. A comprehensive report on many Japanese opinion surveys is Allan Cole and Naomichi Nakanishi, *Japanese Opinion Polls with Socio-Political Significance 1947–1957,* Vol. 1, *Political Support and Preference* (Medford: Fletcher School of Law and Diplomacy, Tufts University, 1960), *passim.*

46. See Kalman Silvert, *The Conflict Society: Reaction and Revolution in Latin America* (New Orleans: The Hauser Press, 1961), p. 166; T. B. Bottomore, *Elites and Society* (London: C. A. Watts, 1964), pp. 86–104. An analysis of data collected from a sample of Indian students in 1951 by the Bureau of Social Science Research indicates that over 40 per cent backed the Communist or Praha Socialist parties, both of which were quite weak among the general electorate. In some Latin American countries, such as Panama, El Salvador, Peru, Venezuela, and Brazil, Communists and pro-Castro groups are dominant in elections to the student councils. John Scott reports that "a number of important university campuses including those in Caracas, Michoacán, Lima, Santiago are virtually run by Communists." *How Much Progress?* (New York: Time Inc., 1963), pp. 123–125. In North Africa, also, university students are disproportionately to

the left of the dominant politics. See Clement Moore and Arlie R. Hochschild, "Student Unions in North African Politics," *Daedalus* 97 (Winter 1968) pp. 24–50.

47. The pattern of inappropriate career choice and educated unemployment is discussed in Justus M. van der Kroef, "Asian Education and Unemployment: The Continuing Crisis," *Comparative Education Review,* 7 (1963), pp. 173–180; see also Joseph Fischer, "The University Student in South and Southeast Asia," *Minerva,* 2 (1963), pp. 39–53; on the low economic rewards for Indian university graduates see Edward Shils, "The Intellectual Between Tradition and Modernity," *op. cit.,* pp. 29–41.

48. Kautsky, *op. cit.,* pp. 46–47.

49. Watanuki, *op. cit.*

50. "Definitions, Propositions, and Hypotheses Concerning Modernism, Class, and National Integration," Silvert, ed., *op. cit.,* p. 443.

51. In Japan, it is clear that even if university students, and young professionals, business executives, and the large majority of the intellectuals back the Socialists, Japanese business, both small and large, supports the conservative Liberal-Democrats. Almost all of the vast sums contributed for campaign purposes by Japanese business go to the latter, while the trade-unions are the financial backers of the socialist parties. See James R. Soukup, "Comparative Political Finance: Japan," *Journal of Politics,* 25 (1963), pp. 737–756.

52. Maurice Zeitlin, *Revolutionary Politics and the Cuban Working Class* (Princeton: Princeton University Press, 1967).

53. These continuities are discussed in S. M. Lipset and Mildred Schwartz, "The Politics of Professionals," in H. N. Vollmer and D. L. Mills, eds., *Professionalization* (Englewood Cliffs, N.J.: Prentice-Hall, 1966), pp. 299–310.

54. Uganda provides an interesting special case of the continuity of traditional mechanisms of authority. Uganda contains a large African monarchy, Buganda, which remained politically autonomous and united under its hereditary monarchy during British rule. Consequently, as Apter has pointed out, Buganda was one of the few large native African states whose popula-

tion retained that "extraordinary devotion to the king whose hierarchical authority represents what Weber calls hereditary charisma." See David Apter, *The Political Kingdom in Uganda* (Princeton: Princeton University Press, 1961), p. 457.

55. The weakness of political conservatism in new nations does not mean, of course, that traditional attitudes with respect to other aspects of behavior are also weak. An excellent Indian study points out in detail that the same peasants who vote for modernizing, and even radical, politicians are often strongly attached to the old ways of their village life and resist innovation in agricultural practices. See Kusum Nair, *Blossoms in the Dust* (New York: Praeger, 1962). The distinction between traditional and modern attitudes may be made analytically, but in practice individuals and groups will vary considerably in the extent to which they hold attitudes which are seemingly incongruous. See on this Kalman H. Silvert, "National Values, Development, and Leaders and Followers," *International Social Science Journal*, 15 (1963), pp. 560–570.

56. S. M. Lipset, *The First New Nation, op. cit.*, pp. 78–79, see also pp. 74–90 for a discussion of factors which weaken potential strength of conservative parties in new states.

57. See Soares, *op. cit.*, for an analysis of the way in which illiteracy, "apathy, religion and traditional values . . . immunize and sterilize the peasants [of impoverished north-east Brazil] against class organization and the germ of ideological rebellion." Analyses of voting choices in Chile through use of survey data reveal that degree of adherence to Catholicism is the principle correlate of vote decision. See Ruth Ann Pitts, *Political Socialization and Political Change in Santiago de Chile* (M.A. Thesis in Sociology, Univ. of Calif., 1963); Brunhilde Velez, *Women's Political Behavior in Chile* (M.A. Thesis in Sociology, Univ. of Calif., 1964).

58. As David Apter has pointed out, the elites of rapidly developing societies require a political myth which will bind to them the masses suffering the dislocations of industrialization and modernization. What religious belief did for the western countries, he argues, "political religion" must do for

the currently emerging nations. See "Political Religion in the New Nations," in Geertz, ed., *op. cit.*, pp. 57–104. The English sociologist T. B. Bottomore has also suggested that "Marxism . . . is the Calvinism of the twentieth century industrial revolutions," *op. cit.*, p. 94.

59. This does not mean that I believe that it can not be developed. I would agree here with the programmatic statement made by Edward Shils for the Committee for the Comparative Study of New Nations in which he asserts, concerning efforts to deal with the politics of all nations: "Our task in this regard is to find the categories within which the unique may be described, and in which its differences with respect to other situations may be presented in a way that raises scientifically significant problems. Orderly comparison is one necessary step in the process of systematic explanation . . ." "On the Comparative Study of the New States," *op. cit.*, p. 15. This article is an excellent statement of the problems and ambitions of comparative political sociology as derivative from Max Weber.

60. Guy Hunter points out that in West Africa, socialism as advocated by the governing elite "includes above all the devotion to central planning of the use of resources, both human and material, for the common good. The West African press, both English and French, and the speeches of leaders hammer home again and again this planning theme, often opposed to the selfishness of the profit motive. . . ."

"There is, however, little or no emphasis on the moral aspects of socialism, the gap between rich and poor. In Tropical Africa as a whole exactly the reverse process is at present in full swing; the salaries and perquisites of the ruling group and of the whole professional and educated class are at or near the old expatriate level . . . Despite constant inquiry, we could find little evidence of 'socialist' thinking in this moral sense, save among a few of the younger intellectuals in Lagos and Accra . . ." *The New Societies of Tropical Africa* (London: Oxford University Press, 1962), pp. 288–289.

61. A related discussion on the same point may be found in Adam Ulam, *The*

Unfinished Revolution (New York: Random House, 1960), passim.

62. Evidence that the economically underprivileged do not share the views of the "socialist elite" concerning income differences comes from Communist Poland. An opinion survey inquiring into the proper level of differences in income for various occupations reported "that there is a strong correlation between the incomes of people and their views concerning a maximum scale of income differences ... The poll shows that factory workers, technicians, and certain groups of the intelligentsia with low salaries (teachers, post office workers, social service officials, etc.) are in favor of egalitarianism. On the other hand, an unfavorable attitude prevails among people of whom many have possibilities of high incomes." At the extremes, 54 per cent of the workers favored "relatively equal incomes" as contrasted with 20 per cent of the executives. Fifty-five per cent of the latter were strongly against narrowing the income gap, as compared with 8 per cent of the manual workers. But it should be noted that both the egalitarian-oriented less-privileged respondents and the more well-to-do defenders of inequality justified their opinions by "traditional slogans of the left." See S. M. Lipset, *Political Man, op. cit.*, pp. 224, 228–229, for references.

Chapter 2

Types of Protest and Alienation

1. See, e.g., James S. Davis, "Structural Balance, Mechanical Solidarity and Interpersonal Relations," *The American Journal of Sociology*, LXVII (1963), pp. 444–462.

2. See S. M. Lipset, "Political Sociology," in R. K. Merton, L. Broom, and L. S. Cottrell, Jr., *Sociology Today* (New York: Basic Books, 1959), p. 112.

3. S. M. Lipset, "Party Systems and the Representation of Social Groups," *The European Journal of Sociology* I (1960), pp. 1–38.

4. L. Festinger, "A Theory of Social Comparison Processes," *Human Relations* 7 (1954), pp. 117–140.

5. See Herman Turk, "Social Cohesion Through Variant Values: Evidence from Medical Role Relations," *The American Sociological Review* 29 (1963), pp. 28–37.

6. G. C. Homans, *Social Behavior: Its Elementary Forms* (New York: Harcourt, Brace & World, 1961).

7. E. Durkheim, *The Division of Labor in Society*, translated by George Simpson (New York: The Free Press, 1960).

8. It has been indicated by Veronica Stolte Heiskanen, *Social Structure, Family Patterns and Interpersonal Influence* (Helsinki: Transactions of the Westermarck Society, XIV, 1967), p. 17, that pressure toward uniformity always has to be specified according to the substantive system under investigation.

9. Ulf Himmelstrand, "Conflict, Conflict Resolution and Nation-Building in the Transition from Tribal 'Mechanical' Solidarities to the 'Organic' Solidarity of Modern (or Future) Multi-Tribal Societies," Paper presented at the Sixth World Congress of Sociology, Evian, 1966.

10. Very perceptive views on the nature of the Communist protest in the Finnish society have been presented by Ulf Torgerson, "Samfunnsstruktur og politiska legitimitetskriser," *Tidskrift for samfunnsforskning* 8 (1967), pp. 65–77.

11. The data referred to in this paper are presented in E. Allardt, "Patterns of Class Conflict and Working Class Consciousness in Finland," in E. Allardt and Y. Littunen, eds., *Cleavages, Ideologies and Party Systems* (Helsinki: The Westermarck Society, 1964), pp. 97–131.

12. Erik Allardt and Olavi Riihinen, "Files for Aggregate Data by Territorial Units in Finland," in S. Rokkan, ed., *Data Archives for Social Sciences* (Paris: Mouton, 1966).

13. The data are presented in E. Allardt, *op. cit.*, pp. 97–131.

14. Yrjö Littunen, "Aktiivisuus ja radikalismi," with an English Summary: "Activity and Radicalism," *Politiikka*, A Quarterly Published by the Finnish Political Science Association, 2 (1960) 4, pp. 182–183.

15. See especially William Kornhauser, *The Politics of Mass Society* (New York: The Free Press, 1959).

16. See, e.g., T. B. Bottomore and M. Rubel, eds., *Karl Marx: Selected Writings in Sociology and Social Philosophy* (London: Watts, 1956), pp. 178–202.

17. The observations are more fully reported in E. Allardt, "Reactions to Social and Political Change in a Developing Society," in K. Ishwaran, ed., *Politics and Social Change* (Leiden: Brill, 1966), pp. 1–10.

18. P. Worsley, *The Trumpet Shall Sound* (London: MacGibbon & Kee, 1957), pp. 183-192.

19. R. F. Maher, *New Men of Papua: A Study in Culture Change* (Madison, Wis.: University of Wisconsin Press, 1960).

20. Melvin Seeman, "On the Meaning of Alienation," *American Sociological Review*, 24 (1959), pp. 783–791.

21. Neil J. Smelser, *Theory of Collective Behavior* (New York: The Free Press, 1963), pp. 23–34.

22. Robert K. Merton, *Social Theory and Social Structure* (New York: The Free Press, 1957), p. 140.

CHAPTER 3

Depoliticization and Political Involvement

1. Seymour M. Lipset, *Political Man. The Social Bases of Politics* (New York: Doubleday, 1960), p. 406.

2. Unfortunately, the only satisfactory account of significant aspects of ideology and politics in Sweden over the last forty years is available only in Swedish: Leif Lewin, *Planhushållningsdebatten* (Stockholm: Almqvist & Wiksell, 1966). This is a detailed and learned summary and explication of political themes vindicated and policies advocated in the Swedish debate about social and economic planning from the Twenties and up into the Sixties.

3. Edward Shils, "The End of Ideology?" *Encounter*, 5 (November 1955). See also Daniel Bell, *The End of Ideology* (New York: The Free Press, 1960).

4. Herbert Tingsten, "Stability and Vitality in Swedish Democracy," *The Political Quarterly*, 2 (1955), pp. 140–151.

5. See, for instance, Kurt Samuelsson, *Är ideologierna döda?*, Stockholm, Aldus/Bonniers, 1966, and for an authoritative view of a leading politician, Tage Erlander, *Tingsten har fel—ideologierna lever*, LO pressavdelningen, Serie IV, Dagspressen, N:r 34, April 20, 1966. Outside Sweden one finds a critical analysis of the end-of-ideology literature in Joseph LaPalombara, "Decline of Ideology: A Dissent and an Interpretation," *American Political Science Review*, LX, 1966, pp. 5–18.

6. This can be considered a more explicit and detailed version of the kind of working definition of ideology suggested by Zbigniew Brzezinski: An ideology "is essentially an action program suitable for mass consumption, derived from certain doctrinal assumptions about the general nature of the dynamics of social reality, and combining some assertions about the inadequacies of the past and/or present with some explicit guides to action for improving the situation and some notions of the desired eventual state of affairs." See Z. Brzezinski, *Ideology and Power in Soviet Politics*, New York, Frederick A. Praeger, 1967 (rev. ed.), p. 5. Brzezinski's definition seems too restrictive, however, in that it makes no allowance for more loosely structured relationships between the various components of a given ideology. Furthermore we wish to take issue with the requirement that ideologies be "suitable for mass consumption." Esoteric ideologies for elite consumption are not unknown in politics.

7. See for instance, Georg H. von Wright, *Norm and Action*, London, Humanities Press, 1963, and by the same author, *Logic of Preference*, Edinburgh, Edinburgh Univ. Press, 1963, and R. P. Abelson and M. J. Rosenberg, "Symbolic Psycho-logic: A Model of Attitudinal Cognition," *Behavioral Science*, 1958, 3, pp. 1–13.

8. Herbert Tingsten, *op. cit.*, p. 145.

9. When ideologies are considered mainly rationalizations of "hidden forces" this often results in the belief that ideologies essentially are irrational products of a "false consciousness." This is much too rash conclusion. Cf. Reinhard Bendix,

"Industrialization, Ideologies and Social Structure," *American Sociological Review*, 1959, vol. 24, pp. 618–628. Rationalizations can take the form of uninformed autistic thinking but may also consist of attempts to reconstruct, in reasonable accordance with rules of logic and verification, the values and factual assumptions motivating a set of originally intuitive and spontaneous lines of action. Even if one can be rather certain that no political ideology ever will attain the level of logical consistency and empirical relevance acceptable to most philosophers of ethics and science, this does not justify a refusal to see the differences of degree which still differentiate ideologies in these respects.

10. The following simple indexes only serve to illustrate the way some of the variables substructed under the concept of "depoliticization" might be quantified and measured.

Ideological saliency $= \Sigma I \, / \, \Sigma (I+T)$

Separation of functions of ideology and practical politics $= 1 - \Sigma (I \, \& \, T) \, / \, \Sigma I$

where T stands for references to factual, technical and economic issues of politics, and I stands for references to values prominent in political ideologies, and (I & T) stands for the joint and integrated appearance of these two types of references in one and the same context. Empirical values of I and T can be estimated through content analysis of political platforms, programs, editorials and debates. For a beginning along these lines of content analysis, see Svennik Höyer, "Political Commitment and Audience Coverage: a content analysis of Norwegian newspapers," Bergen, Norway, *International Unesco Seminar, Christian Michelsen Institute*, 1961, Document no. CMI/SEM61/P/3 (mimeogr.). In collaboration with Bo Ohlström, the present writer has made an attempt to apply similar indices in a content analysis of moral of "ideological," factual and technical arguments in the Swedish newspaper debate about the utility of acquiring nuclear weapons to the Swedish armed forces. See Bo Ohlström, "Information and Propaganda. A Content Analysis of Editorials in Four Swedish Daily Newspapers," *Journal of Peace Research*, 1966, Vol. 3, pp. 75–88, particularly pp. 77 and 82. Another study is under way in collaboration with Alpheus Manghezi of the University of Ibadan, exploring the degree of contextual separation of references to ideologically prominent values on the one hand, and to technical and factual arguments on the other, with regard to certain controversial issues facing Nigerian newspaper editorialists between 1959 and 1965.

11. The concept of *property space* has been developed in several papers by Paul F. Lazarsfeld and Allen H. Barton. A summary of principles and illustrations of the application of this concept has been made by Allen H. Barton in Paul F. Lazarsfeld and Morris Rosenberg (editors), *The Language of Social Research*, New York, The Free Press, 1955, pp. 40–53.

12. In the Soviet Union where ideological consensus no doubt is much more evident than in Western democracies there nevertheless seems to be also a high degree of ideological saliency and a considerable impact of ideology in practical politics. At the same time, however, there are many symptoms of a separation of functions of ideology and practical politics. The tendency mentioned by Tingsten to retain ideological symbols and emblems as honorifics that are useful in political ritual seems to obtain additional momentum in the Soviet bloc by the fact that ideological faithfulness probably is one of the most important sources of legitimate power and unity in a totalitarian system where other sources of legitimacy are less available. (See Zbigniew Brzezinski, *The Soviet Bloc—Unity and Conflict*, Cambridge, Mass., Harvard University Press, 1960. *See also* the same author's "Communist Ideology and International Affairs," *The Journal of Conflict Resolution*, 1960, vol. 4, pp. 266–290). The partly disconnected state of affairs which results when ideology is used to establish the legitimacy of political power can be illustrated by cases where a certain point of view is heavily criticized in one context for being "revisionist" or not in accordance with the great Marxist-Leninist tradition while at the same time being taken as a quite reasonable standpoint in the context of specific political actions. See Zbigniew Brzezinski, "A Book the Russians Would Like to Forget," *The Reporter*, December 22, 1960, pp. 28–30.

13. Leif Lewin, *op. cit.*

14. See Robert K. Merton, Leonard Broom and Leonard S. Cottrell, Jr., eds., *Sociology Today. Problems and Prospects*, New York, Basic Books, Inc., 1959, p. 6, note 4.

15. One of the main reasons for using the term *pragmatic* function rather than the term *instrumental* function in discussing the use of ideology is my desire to avoid the connotation of instrumental or means behavior. From our following discussion it can be seen that a pragmatic use of ideology may imply a specification of ends as well as a specification of means. For instance, when pragmatically exploring possible alternative political decisions, 'and possible consequences, one might discover both some very desirable consequences of which one had no clear notion in advance and some very undesirable, unintended consequences. As a result, one may feel compelled to modify or specify the political goals toward which one is striving. Compare the distinction between the *means-ends* scheme and the scheme of *alternatives and consequences* made by Herbert Simon, *Administrative Behavior*, Second Edition, New York, Macmillan, 1959, pp. 64–70.

16. The brand of functionalism utilized in our discussion is the one set forth by Robert K. Merton, in *Social Theory and Social Structure*, rev. ed., New York, The Free Press, 1957, Ch. I. Thus far only manifest functions of ideology have been alluded to. In our suggestive definitions of pragmatic and expressive functions of ideology we only talk of *intended and recognized* consequences, that is of manifest functions. Later on some arguments will be made which imply the existence of latent functions and dysfunctions.

17. Here is another reason for using the term *pragmatic* function of ideology rather than the term *instrumental* function. We have just recognized that on the level of political parties an expressive function of a given ideology may imply the use of this ideology as an *instrument* for the purpose of molding the loyalties of certain groups of people. If on this level of analysis the term "instrumental" had been used instead of the term "pragmatic" in our discussion about the functions of ideology, confusion would have been inevitable.

18. Cf. the discussion of various defini-

tions of rationality in Herbert Simon, *op. cit.*, pp. 75–77.

19. For a discussion of symbolic "reassurance" see Murray Edelman, *The Symbolic Uses of Politics* (Urbana: University of Illinois Press, 1964). Full of insights and stark illustrations is Thurman Arnold's classical discussion of related problems in *The Symbols of Government* (New Haven: Yale University Press, 1935), and *The Folklore of Capitalism* (New Haven: Yale University Press, 1937—reprinted as paperback with a new preface, 1964). See also Torgny Segerstedt, *Symbolmiljö, mening och attityd* (Symbolic Environment, Meaning and Attitude) Uppsala: Lundequistska, 1956, p. 12.

20. In the Barnard-Simon theory of organizational equilibrium the concept of *organizational solvency* has been suggested. See H. A. Simon, D. M. Smithburg, and V. A. Thompson, *Public Administration*, New York, Knopf, 1950, pp. 381–82. Our concept "political effectiveness" of a party may be conceived as a special case of organizational solvency.

21. Cf. Torgny T. Segerstedt and Agne Lundquist, *Människan i industrisambället*, del II (Man in Industrialized Society, Part II), Stockholm, Studieförbundet Näringsliv och Samhälle, 1955, p. 336.

22. For such a situation of "quasi-permanent" opposition occupied by a Social-Democratic Party, see Guenter Roth, *Social Democrats in Imperial Germany*, Totowa, N.J., Bedminster Press, 1963.

23. What is called here a dissociative shifting of gears from a practical to an expressive concern etc. can be understood as a special case of phase-movement in a Parsonian four-dimensional action space, the Liberal Party as a whole being conceived as moving through different phases in that space in a rather wide orbit with a periodicity corresponding to the period between elections. See Talcott Parsons, Robert F. Bales and Edward A. Shils, *Working Papers in the Theory of Action*, New York, The Free Press, 1953, Ch. III and Ch. V. Within that same conceptual framework one might hypothesize that the Social Democratic Party in Sweden has tended to solve the four problems of the action space in a different way, that is through a role-differentiation which implies

a set of short-term, non-synchronized phase movements in the peculiar orbits of each individual role-set more than by a pronounced phase-movement of the party as a whole.

24. Cf. Sigvard Rubenowitz, *Emotional Flexibility-Rigidity as a Comprehensive Dimension of Mind*, Stockholm, Almqvist & Wiksell, 1963, pp. 98–115, 186–191.

25. Probably these structural conditions are most likely to be found in certain totalitarian political or religious systems. But even in constitutional democracies one can occasionally find these structural conditions—for instance *within* some political parties, and with regard to certain threatened, controversial or marginal issues and values.

26. See for instance Gardner Lindzey (editor), *Handbook of Social Psychology*, Vol. II, Cambridge, Mass., Addison-Wesley, 1954, Chapter 30.

27. Concepts like *affinity, goodness-of-fit, congruence, interpersonal balance*, etc., are abundant in the literature about personality, social roles, and interpersonal relations. See, for instance, Fritz Heider, *The Psychology of Interpersonal Relations*, New York, John Wiley & Sons, 1958, or George G. Stern, Morris I. Stein and Benjamin S. Bloom, *Methods in Personality Assessment*, New York, The Free Press, 1956. In a paper on "Role-Playing Specification, Personality and Performance", Edgar F. Borgatta shows that goodness-of-fit of role and personality is of crucial importance to the productivity and enjoyment of the actors (*Sociometry*, 1961, Vol. 24, pp. 218–232). The present writer has adopted the affinity of goodness-of-fit hypothesis for explaining part of the variation of political involvement (Ulf Himmelstrand, *Social Pressures, Attitudes and Democratic Processes*, Stockholm, Almqvist & Wiksell, 1960, Section 2.5.3.2.).

28. Ulf Himmelstrand, *Social Pressures, Attitudes and Democratic Processes*, Stockholm, Almqvist & Wiksell, 1960, pp. 188–192, 259, 325 f. and 339 f.

29. The hypothesis proposed by Elihu Katz, Paul Lazarsfeld and others about a two-step flow of communication in political campaigns can be interpreted as saying that on the whole there is a consecutive ordering of the two communication channels

just mentioned—the mass media and the word-of-mouth. Politically more active people expose themselves to the mass media and then pass the political message along to other less exposed people by word-of-mouth (Elihu Katz and Paul F. Lazarsfeld, *Personal Influence: The Part Played by People in the Flow of Mass Communication*, New York, The Free Press, 1955). Ithiel de Sola Pool has remarked, however, that the direct impact of mass media on people probably is increasing because of television, and the impact of opinion-leaders declining (Eugene Burdick and Arthur J. Brodbeck, editors, *American Voting Behavior*, New York, The Free Press, 1959, Chapter 13). The results of a comprehensive survey made by the Swedish Broadcasting Corporation (published by Rune Sjödén in 1962) gives substantial support to Pool's conclusion. A very large part of the public is reached directly by political appeals in TV and not only indirectly through the relay link provided by opinion leaders. See also Sveriges Officiella Statistik, *Riksdagsmannavalen åren 1959–1960, II* (The Elections to the Riksdag During the Years 1959–1960), Stockholm, Statistiska Centralbyrån, 1961, which contains several pages of descriptive data about TV exposure in the 1960 election.

30. It should be pointed out, perhaps, that on the level of the mass electorate the expressive and the pragmatic type of concern with politics necessarily manifest themselves in ways slightly different from what is characteristic on the level of formal and informal party leadership. This is because the types of political information and gratification available to the man in the street is different from what is available on the level of political parties. Cf. Ulf Himmelstrand, *Social Pressures, Attitudes and Democratic Processes*, Stockholm, Almqvist & Wiksell, 1960, pp. 263–269, where, however, the term "instrumental" is used instead of the term "pragmatic."

31. *Ibid.*, pp. 93 ff, and 280 f.

32. *Ibid.*, p. 95–99.

33. Cf. Karl Pribram, *Conflicting Patterns of Thought*, Washington D.C., Public Affairs Press, 1949.

34. The distinction made between the *social* type of motivation which is required to sustain political involvement among

"expressive ideologists", and the *individual-istic* type of motivation sufficient or nearly sufficient to keep "pragmatic ideologists" and "pure pragmatists" involved in politics is similar to a distinction made by Lipset, Trow, and Coleman (cf. *Union Democracy*, New York, The Free Press, 1956, pp. 98–102). They distinguished two processes: Conservative union members were dependent on social relations developed in the non-political occupational community in order to get activated politically, while liberals were motivated directly by their values to participate in union politics. Also compare the different behavioral consequences of "identification" and "internalization" as analyzed in Herbert C. Kelman, "Compliance, Identification, and Internalization. Three Processes of Attitude Change," in *The Journal of Conflict Resolution*, 2 (1958), pp. 51–60.

35. Ulf Himmelstrand, *op. cit.*, pp. 47–49, 76–87, and 263 ff. A slight change in terminology has been made in the present paper. In my book the variable is called "Independence of Affective Loadings of Symbolic Activity."

36. *Ibid.*, pp. 126 ff, 162 ff, and 193. More recently a factor analysis of 32 items assumed to relate to the KEY-variable (then still called the *L*-variable) was undertaken by S. Rubenowitz (*op. cit.*, pp. 98–119, and 181). The main factor was identified as the KEY-factor. Items showing high scalabilities in earlier KEY-scales (=*L*-scales) constructed by the present author all turned up with high factor loadings in the KEY-factor identified in Rubenowitz's factor study.

37. Ulf Himmelstrand, *op. cit.*, pp. 152–154, and 300.

38. *Ibid.*, pp. 341–344. As a matter of fact I have used the difference between the proportions of *high*-KEY and *low*-KEY subjects as an indicator of dominant environmental ideological style, in order

to make finer discriminations possible.

39. *Ibid.*, pp. 353 ff.

40. The technique used here to study the joint effects of individual and environmental variables has been systematically explored in a paper by James A. Davis, Joe L. Spaeth, and Carolyn Huson, "A Technique for Analyzing the Effects of Group Composition," in *American Sociological Review*, 26 (1961), pp. 215–225.

41. C. E. Osgood, G. J. Suci, and P. H. Tannenbaum, *The Measurement of Meaning*, Urbana, Ill., Univ. of Illinois Press, 1957, p. 74.

42. The distinction between "mass-society" and "pluralist society" is here understood as in William Kornhauser, *The Politics of Mass Society*, New York, The Free Press, 1959. In his contribution to the present volume Erik Allardt has suggested an interesting connection between mass societies and an expressive political style, and between pluralist societies and a more pragmatic political orientation.

43. Ulf Himmelstrand, *op. cit.*, pp. 188 f.

44. *Ibid.*, pp. 51 f., and 264–267. See also Erik Allardt "Community Activity, Leisure Use and Social Structure," *Acta Sociologica* 6(1962) pp. 73–76 and Yrjö Littunen, "Aktiivisuus ja Radikalismi' (Activity and Radicalism) in *Politiikka*, 2 (1960), pp. 151–186. With an English summary on pp. 185 f.

45. Gabriel A. Almond and James S. Coleman (editors), *The Politics of the Developing Areas*, Princeton, N.J., Princeton Univ. Press, 1960, pp. 20–25. Almond characterizes the culturally mixed character of political systems in terms of Parsons's pattern variables.

46. In collaboration with Jan Lindhagen the present author has carried out a panel study to illuminate certain aspects of the "phase movement" presumably taking place between elections in the Swedish electorate. A first report of results is expected in 1969.

CHAPTER 4

The Trend Toward Political Consensus: The Case of Norway

1. E.g., Seymour Martin Lipset, *Political Man*. Garden City, N.Y., Doubleday, 1960, especially chapter XIII.

2. E. g., Daniel Bell, *The End of Ideology: On the Exhaustion of Political Ideas in the Fifties*. New York, The Free Press, 1960.

3. See Stein Rokkan, *Sammenlignende politisk sosiologi*. Bergen, Chr. Michelsens Institutt, 1958.

4. See Otto Kirchheimer, "The Waning of Opposition in Parliamentary Regimes." *Social Research* 24, 1957: 127–156.

5. *Stortingstidende* 13 Oct. 1960, p. 123.

6. Sjur Lindebraekke, *Tillit og tillits-politikk*. Kragerø, Naper 1953, pp. 11–12.

7. *Stortingstidende* 14 Oct. 1960, p. 204.

8. *Studentene fra 1935*. Oslo, 1960.

9. A content analysis of the subject matter of the articles of the journal mentioned for the years 1946, 1950, 1954 and 1958 shows that the proportion of articles dealing with a social, economic, political or military subject had declined from 47 per cent in 1946 to 30 per cent in 1958, while the proportion of articles dealing with literary, religious, psychological or philosophical subjects increased from 40 per cent to 53 per cent in the course of the same period.

10. Edward Shils, *The Torment of Secrecy*. New York, Free Press, 1956, part IV. It is in itself a remarkable fact that so many of the criticisms of present-day political consensus are couched in terms of "system needs." It is very common to find arguments to the effect that a certain amount of conflict is necessary if democracy is to prevail, that there really should be more issues (without any specification) and that there should be higher political interest among people (without mentioning issues). This tendency is highly reminiscent of the character of much contemporary American political debate, where "ideology" has become something of a *Schimpfwort*, rather regardless of the substantive content of the ideological position.

11. S. Rokkan and H. Valen, "The Mobilization of the Periphery: Data on Turnout, Party Membership and Candidate

Recruitment in Norway," *Acta Sociologica* 6(1962) pp. 111-158.

12. This was written before the national election of 11 September, 1961. At this election the Labour party lost votes for the first time after the War. This was primarily due to the emergence of the left-wing *Socialist People's Party*. The results were as follows:

	Total Votes	Per Cent of Votes Cast
1957: Labour	865675	48.3%
1961: Labour	860526	46.8%
Socialist People's	43996	2.4%
Total	904522	49.2%

13. The figures for 1957 are given in Rokkan and Valen, *op. cit.*

14. In the analysis of the radicalization of the Norwegian labour movement, all writers are relying, directly or indirectly on the work of the Norwegian historian Edvard Bull, who was the first to speculate on the conditions making for this development. But they often omit a factor of a more political character, studiously emphasized by Bull: in Norway there were few ties between the Liberal and the working-class movements since parliamentary government had been established already in 1884, without the support of the working class, while in Sweden and Denmark a Liberal-Labour alliance had to fight together against the establishment to gain full political rights. This politically necessary alliance probably did as much as the purely social-structural conditions to "domesticate" the workers in Denmark and Sweden and thus added to the contrast with "radical" Norway. The importance of an electoral system that gave the Labour party a considerable under-representation in parliament is another "political" factor, that should not be forgotten in the concern with social-structural explanations.

CHAPTER 5

Aggregate Election Data and British Party Alignments, 1885–1910

1. Recent published work is discussed in D. E. Butler and James Cornford, "Britain" in *International Guide to Electoral Statistics*, Vol. 1, *National Elections in Western Europe*, ed. Stein Rokkan and Jean Meyriat (forthcoming). Exceptions to this general remark are two articles: J. P. D. Dunbabin, "Parliamentary Elections in Great Britain, 1868–1900. A Psephological Note," *English Historical Review*, Vol. LXXXI, No. 318, Jan. 1966, pp. 82–99; and Trevor Lloyd, "Uncontested seats in British General

Elections, 1852–1920," *The Historical Journal*, VIII, 2 (1965), pp. 260–265. Most of the work on particular general elections remains unpublished at the present time.

2. W. Dean Burnham, "The Changing Shape of the American Political Universe," *A.P.S.R.*, LIX: i (1965).

3. This analysis includes all constituencies in England, Scotland and Wales with the exception of the University seats. The Regions are composed as follows:

1. Scotland.
2. North: Northumberland, Cumberland, Westmorland, Durham.
3. Yorkshire.
4. Lancashire and Cheshire.
5. Midlands: Derbyshire, Nottinghamshire, Lincolnshire, Staffordshire, Warwickshire, Northants, Leicestershire, Rutland.
6. West: Shropshire, Herefordshire, Worcestershire, Gloucestershire.
7. Wales including Monmouth.
8. South: Berkshire, Buckinghamshire, Oxfordshire, Wiltshire, Hampshire, Isle of Wight.
9. South-West: Dorset, Somerset, Devon, Cornwall.
10. East: Bedfordshire, Huntingdonshire, Cambridgeshire, Norfolk, Suffolk, extra-Metropolitan Essex.
11. Home Counties: Middlesex, Surrey, Kent, Sussex, Hertfordshire, Metropolitan Essex.
12. London.

4. For the difficulties created by the complex voting qualifications and system of registration, see Neal Blewett, "The Franchise in the United Kingdom, 1885–1918," *Past and Present*, No. 32, Dec. 1965, pp. 27–56.

5. James Cornford, "The Adoption of Mass Organization by the British Conservative Party" in E. Allardt and Y. Littunen, *Cleavages, Ideologies and Party Systems*, Helsinki, 1964. Table IV, p. 422.

6. The twenty-three two-member constituencies present a host of problems for comparative purposes which I have not solved; even calculating party percentages of the vote involves doubtful assumptions, and for most purposes I have had to ignore them. This is an important qualification to any conclusions contained in this paper, as they represent as important bloc of seats in some areas, e.g., Lancashire and the main cities in several counties. They hold particular promise, however, for the analysis of the relations between Liberal and Labour voting.

7. Trevor Lloyd, "Uncontested seats in British General Elections, 1852–1910," *op. cit.* Table 3, p. 263 and p. 265.

8. The resurrection of the Liberals has been well described in A. K. Russell, *The General Election of 1906*, unpublished D.Phil. thesis, Oxford, 1962.

9. Blewett, *op. cit.*, pp. 30–43.

10. Henry Pelling, *The Origins of the Labour Party, 1880–1900*, London, 1954; and Frank Bealey and Henry Pelling, *Labour and Politics, 1900–1906*, London, 1956.

11. Paul Thompson, "Liberals, Radicals and Labour in London, 1880–1900," *Past and Present*, No. 27, April 1964, pp. 73–101.

12. R. G. Gregory, *The Miners in Politics in England and Wales, 1906–1914*. Unpublished D.Phil. thesis, Oxford, 1963, gives an excellent analysis of this process.

CHAPTER 6

Geography, Social Contexts, and Voting Behavior in Wales, 1861–1951

1. Stein Rokkan, "Electoral Mobilization, Party Competition and National Integration," in LaPalombara and Weiner (eds.), *Political Parties and Political Development* (Princeton: Princeton University Press, 1966), p. 265.

2. See, for example, (i) John Bonham, *The Middle Class Vote* (London: Faber and Faber, 1954). (ii) David E. Butler and Richard Rose, *The British General Election of 1959* (London: Macmillan, 1960).

3. As examples, see (i) A. H. Birch, *Small-Town Politics* (Oxford: Oxford University Press, 1959). (ii) R. S. Milne and

H. C. Mackenzie, *Straight Fight* (Hansard Society for Parliamentary Government, 1954).

4. James Cornford, "The Transformation of Conservatism in the Late Nineteenth Century," *Victorian Studies*, Vol. 7 (1963), pp. 35–66.

5. J. M. Lee, *Social Leaders and Public Persons: A Study of Country Government in Cheshire since 1888* (Oxford: Clarendon Press, 1963).

6. See, for example, André Siegfried, *Tableau Politique de la France de l'Ouest sous la Troisième République* (Paris: Librairie Armand Colin, 1913).

7. Jean Blondel, *Voters, Parties and Leaders: The Social Fabric of British Politics* (Harmondsworth: Penguin Books, 1963), p. 64.

8. Kevin R. Cox, "Regional Anomalies in the Voting Behavior of the Population of England and Wales: 1921–1951" (unpublished Ph.D. dissertation, Department of Geography, University of Illinois, 1967).

9. James S. Coleman, "Relational Analysis: The Study of Social Organization with Survey Methods," *Human Organization*, Vol. 17 (1958–59), pp. 28–36.

10. Hayward Alker, *Mathematics and Politics* (New York: Macmillan, 1965), p. 103.

11. R. Smet and H. Evalenko, *Les Élections Belges* (Brussels: Institut de Sociologie Solvay, 1956).

12. Only in the less urbanized sections of European Russia was rioting related to aspects of the agrarian structure: in the more urbanized areas, ease of access to alternative employment in the cities provided a supplementary source of income to overcome deprivation induced by an inequitable land tenure system. See Kevin R. Cox and George J. Demko, "Agrarian Structure and Peasant Discontent in the Russian Revolution of 1905," *East Lakes Geographer*, No. 3 (1967).

13. Hayward Alker, Statistical Non-additivity in International Relations Theory (Mimeo.), p. 9.

14. Hanan C. Selvin and Warren O. Hagstrom, "The Empirical Classification of Formal Groups," *American Sociological Review*, Vol. 28 (1963), pp. 399–411.

15. An example of the first approach is provided by Cox in his study of suburban voting behavior in the London metropolitan area. See Kevin R. Cox, "Suburbia and Voting Behavior in the London Metropolitan Area," *Annals of the Association of American Geographers*, Vol. 58, No. 1 (March, 1968), pp. 111–127.

16. This is the approach adopted by Allardt in his ecological studies of Finnish Communism; see Erik Allardt, "Patterns of Class Conflict and Working Class Consciousness in Finnish Politics," in Erik Allardt and Yrjö Littunen (eds.), *Cleavages, Ideologies and Party Systems* (Helsinki: Westermarck Society, 1964), pp. 91–131.

17. Cox (1967).

18. A comprehensive text on most of the factor analytical methods in common usage is: Harry Harman, *Modern Factor Analysis* (Chicago: University of Chicago Press, 1960).

19. Great Britain, Parliamentary Papers, Cmd. 8221, Cmd. 8222, 1896, "Report and Appendices of the Royal Commission on Land in Wales and Monmouthshire," p. 148.

20. K. O. Morgan, *Wales in British Politics: 1868–1922* (Cardiff: University of Wales Press, 1963), p. 9.

21. Great Britain, Parliamentary Papers, "Report and Appendices of the Royal Commission on Land in Wales and Monmouthshire," p. 148.

22. A. D. Rees, *Life in a Welsh Countryside* (Cardiff: University of Wales Press, 1950), p. 112.

23. Morgan, p. 13.

24. J. E. Vincent, *The Land Question in North Wales* (London: Longmans, 1896).

25. Morgan, p. 8.

26. The association was quite obvious to contemporary observers: "If we ask what proportion of those who habitually attend or connect themselves with any place of worship are Nonconformists or Church people, there can be no doubt that the former class is in a very large majority, especially in the agricultural districts in which the use of the Welsh language predominates." Great Britain, Parliamentary Papers, "Report and Appendices of the Royal Commission on Land in Wales and Monmouthshire," p. 98.

27. Great Britain, Parliamentary Papers, Cmd. 5432, 1910, "Report of the Royal Commission Appointed in Inquire into the

Church and Other Religious Bodies in Wales," p. 97.

28. Morgan, p. 8.

29. Great Britain, Parliamentary Papers, "Report and Appendices of the Royal Commission on Land in Wales and Monmouthshire," p. 103.

30. For example, Morgan's comment: "There was not that distinction between Welsh farmers and the cottagers that exists in the large farm English counties." Morgan, p. 214.

31. A. W. Ashby, "Some Characteristics of Welsh Farming," *Welsh Outlook*, XX (1933), p. 294.

32. *Ibid.*

33. Great Britain, Parliamentary Papers, "Report and Appendices of the Royal Commission on Land in Wales and Monmouthshire," p. 103.

34. D. J. Morrish, "A Geographical Study of the Results of British Parliamentary Elections from 1868 to 1910" (unpublished M.Sc. thesis, University of Exeter, 1955), p. 114.

35. Morgan, pp. 4–5.

36. R. A. Roberts, *Welsh Home-Spun: Studies of Rural Wales* (Newtown: 1930).

37. As A. D. Rees wrote about the landowner: "They had become strangers in their own land and their ignorance of Welsh life made it difficult for them to play an active part in it. However well disposed they may have been, they could be little more than patrons of a culture which existed apart from them and which was moved by forces from outside their world." Rees, p. 154.

38. The Church of England was disestablished in Ireland in 1869; after this date, many Welshmen came to perceive numerous parallels between the repression of an alien culture in Ireland and their own relationship to the anglicized landowners.

39. The rural constituencies for 1951 falling into this category were Pembrokeshire, Brecon, Radnor, West Flint, Denbigh and Conway.

40. Morgan, p. 214.

41. E. W. Evans, *The Miners of South Wales* (Cardiff: University of Wales Press, 1961), p. 137.

42. Brinley Thomas, "The Migration of Labour into the Glamorgan Coalfield, 1861–1911," *Economica*, X (November, 1930), pp. 275–294.

43. Morgan, pp. 10–11.

44. T. Brennan, E. W. Cooney and H. Pollins, *Social Change in South West Wales* (London: Watts, 1954), p. 150.

45. Morgan, p. 254.

46. Brinley Thomas.

47. David Williams, *A History of Modern Wales* (London: 1950), p. 246.

48. *Ibid.*

49. *Ibid.*, p. 237.

50. Brennan, Cooney and Pollins, p. 20.

51. J. E. Daniel, *Welsh Nationalism: What It Stands For* (London: 1937).

52. Morgan, p. 17.

53. Williams, p. 255.

54. Williams, p. 257.

55. Doctrinally, the Methodists had tended to see the life of this world as a wilderness and to direct their thoughts toward "the world to come." Baptists and Congregationalists, on the other hand, had a tradition of activity in social and political reform. In the earlier years of the nineteenth century, the Methodists had supported the Church of England in its traditional concern for the preservation of social stability and constitutional loyalty. Methodists shared with other Nonconformists, however, a violent detestation of Roman Catholicism and it was felt that the Oxford movement was progressing toward Roman Catholicism. See Williams, p. 259.

56. See, for example, Vincent, p. 141; and Williams, p. 259.

57. Vincent, p. 141.

58. *Ibid.*

59. Great Britain, Parliamentary Papers, "Report and Appendices of the Royal Commission on Land in Wales and Monmouthshire," p. 470.

60. Morgan, pp. 84–85.

61. Vincent, p. 8.

62. Morgan, p. 58.

63. Morgan, pp. 84–85.

64. Morgan, p. 58.

65. Williams, p. 281.

66. Williams, p. 270.

67. Morgan, p. 69.

68. Morgan, pp. 106–107.

69. Morgan, p. 245.

70. H. J. Hanham, *Elections and Party Management: Politics in the Time of*

Disraeli and Gladstone (London: Longmans, 1959), pp. 170–179.

71. Morgan, p. 245.

72. Great Britain, Parliamentary Papers, "Report and Appendices of the Royal Commission on Land in Wales and Monmouthshire," p. 273.

73. Great Britain, Parliamentary Papers, "Report of the Royal Commission Appointed to Inquire into the Church and Other Religious Bodies in Wales," p. 74.

74. Brennan, Cooney and Pollins, pp. 98–99.

75. C. R. Williams, "The Welsh Religious Revival of 1904–5," *British Journal of Sociology*, III (September, 1952), p. 242.

76. Great Britain, Parliamentary Papers, Cmd. 8668, 1917, "Report of the Commissioners Appointed to Inquire into Industrial Unrest No. 7 Division: Report of the Commissioners for Wales including Monmouthshire."

77. B. B. Thomas, *Welsh Outlook*, XX, p. 328.

78. The fall off in demand was often indirect. Decline in foreign orders for tin plate caused by the McKinley tariff in the U.S.A. in 1891 led to a decline in the demand for coal. See Morgan, p. 215.

79. Evans, p. 145.

80. Brennan, Cooney and Pollins, p. 27.

81. Evans, p. 190.

82. *Ibid.*

83. Morgan, p. 13.

84. Breenan, Cooney and Pollins, p. 140.

85. Morgan, p. 211.

86. Brennan, Cooney and Pollins, p. 152.

87. Observer, *Welsh Outlook*, III, p. 248.

88. Observer, p. 247.

89. Morgan, p. 159.

90. Brennan, Cooney and Pollins, p. 154.

91. Evans, p. 190.

92. Brennan, Cooney and Pollins, p. 139.

93. *Ibid.*, p. 140.

94. H. M. Williams, "The Geographical Distribution of Political Opinion in the County of Glamorgan for Parliamentary Elections, 1820–1950" (unpublished M.A. thesis, University of Wales, 1952).

95. The survey data used in this paper are data collected during the eighteen months from January 1960 to June 1961 by Gallup Poll (United Kingdom) and refer to the 1959 General Election vote of respondents as cross-classified with certain other social characteristics. Grateful thanks are extended to Gallup Poll for allowing me to make use of these data.

96. Converse has provided an excellent critique of the data collected by commercial agencies. See Philip E. Converse, "The Availability and Quality of Sample Survey Data in Archives within the United States," in Richard Merritt and Stein Rokkan (eds.), *Comparing Nations* (New Haven: Yale University Press, 1966).

97. Francois Goguel, *Géographie des Elections Françaises* (Paris, 1951).

98. In specifying the degree to which an independent variable statistically accounts for variation in the dependent variable, recourse has been made to a measure of partial association elaborated by Coleman. Given data on the proportions of social groups voting in a given direction, Coleman's method consists of computing the mean percentage difference between all groups characterized by the independent variable under study and all groups not so characterized. Thus, in establishing the impact of urban residence on voting, one would subtract the proportions for all groups residing in rural areas from the proportions for all groups residing in urban areas and divide by half the number of groups involved. The procedure is elaborated in considerable detail in: James S. Coleman, *Introduction to Mathematical Sociology* (New York: The Free Press, 1964), pp. 189–240.

99. An exposition of this measure of association is provided by Hayward Alker, *Mathematics and Politics* (New York, Macmillan, 1965), p. 59.

100. For evidence regarding the spatial diffusion of sex roles in Norway, see Stein Rokkan and Henry Valen, "The Mobilization of the Periphery," *Acta Sociologica*, Vol. 6 (fasc. 1–2), pp. 111–158.

101. Erwin K. Scheuch, "Cross-National Comparisons Using Aggregate Data: Some Substantive and Methodological Problems," in Richard Merritt and Stein Rokkan (ed.), *Comparing Nations* (New Haven: Yale University Press, 1966).

102. H. H. McCarty, J. C. Hook and D. Knos, *The Measurement of Association in Industrial Geography*, State University of Iowa, Department of Geography, Report Number One, p. 16.

103. See, for instance, John M. Rayner, "Correlation between Surfaces by Spectral Methods," (Mimeo., Department of Geography, Ohio State University, 1967).

104. John Bonham, *The Middle Class Vote* (London: Faber and Faber, 1954), pp. 194–195.

105. Robert R. Alford, *Party and Society* (Chicago: Rand McNally, 1963).

106. Alford, p. 310.

107. Stein Rokkan and Henry Valen, "Regional Contrasts in Norwegian Politics," in Erik Allardt and Yrjö Littunen (eds.), *Cleavages, Ideologies and Party Systems* (Helsinki: Westermarck Society, 1964).

108. Jean Blondel, "Structures Politiques et Comportement Électoral dans l'État de Paraiba," *Revue Française de Science Politique*, Vol. 5 (April-June, 1955). pp. 315–344.

CHAPTER 7
Aspects of Electoral Behavior in English Constituencies, 1832–1868

1. I should like to acknowledge the kind help of Dr. Jay Blumler of the Television Research Centre, Leeds University, in the drafting of this paper, and Dr. A. P. M. Coxon, of the Department of Social Studies, Leeds University in computer programming; and in many ways of Mr. M. G. Brock, of Wolfson College, Oxford. Among important references relating to nineteenth-century election studies are N. Gash, *Politics in the Age of Peel* (1953), and *Reaction and Reconstruction in English Politics, 1832–52* (1965); H. J. Hanham, *Elections and Party Management* (1959); Dr. J. R. Vincent, *Polls Books* (1967); C. O'Leary, *The Elimination of Corrupt Practices in British Elections* (1962); J. P. Dunbabin, "Parliamentary Elections in Great Britain, 1868–1900," *Eng. Hist. Rev.*, January 1966; N. Blewett, "Franchise in the United Kingdom, 1885–1918," *Past and Present*, no. 32, 1966; J. Cornford, "Transformation of Conservatism in the Late Nineteenth Century," *Victorian Studies*, vii, (1963); D. C. Moore, "The Other Face of Reform," *Victorian Studies*, v (1961).

2. Mathison to Reed, 25 Nov. 1859, C.1588, Cowen Papers, Newcastle Public Library.

3. Mathison to Reed, Mss. Account Berwick Elections, 1832–59. Cowen Papers, C.763.

4. Parl. Papers 1852-3 (588) xii, Durham City Petition, Select Committee, p. 89, QQ. 30 16–18.

5. *Newcastle Chronicle*, 7 April 1859.

6. Parkes to Lord Durham, 21 July 1835, Lambton Papers.

7. Parkes to Lord Durham, 24 August 1837, Lambton Papers.

8. N. Gash, *Politics, op. cit.*, xiii–xiv.

9. W. Aydelotte, "Voting Patterns in the British House of Commons in the 1840's," *Comparative Studies in History and Society*, v (1962–63).

10. Dr. Vincent's categories are not always consistent.

11. N. Gash, *Politics, op. cit.*, Appendix D.

12. W. W. Bean, *Parliamentary Representation of Six Northern Counties* (Hull, 1890).

13. Newcastle Poll Book, 1832.

14. Newcastle Poll Book, 1835.

15. Parl. Papers, 1866. Borough Electors (Working Classes) Return, lvii, 47, 243.

15a. *Hansard*, viii, 239, quoted by N. Gash, *Politics, op. cit.*, 100.

16. Vincent, *op. cit.*, 20.

17. Newcastle Poll Book, 1835.

18. Newcastle Poll Book, 1860.

19. Gateshead Poll Book, 1837; Sunderland Poll 1852 (in *Sunderland Herald*, 9 July 1852).

20. Note that the county classification is not directly comparable with the urban categories.

21. Dod, *Electoral Facts* (1853).

22. Cobden to Wilson, 24 July 1845, See McCord and Wood, "Sunderland Election of 1845." *Durham Univ. Jnl.*, lii, n.s. 21 (1959).

23. *Ibid.*

24. The Gateshead rate book is in the Gateshead Public Library.

25. Mainly the Strathmore family of

Gibside. The Dowager Countess of Strathmore was married for the second time to William Hutt who became M.P. for Gateshead in consequence. The Ellisons were also influential.

26. See the interesting Parkes-Lambton correspondence in the Lambton Papers.

27. Gateshead Poll Book, 1852.

28. K. S. Inglis, *The English Churches and the Working Classes* 1880–1900 (D. Phil., Oxford, 1956).

K. E. Inglis, "Patterns of Religious Worship in 1851," *Jnl. Ecc. Hist.*, 11 (1960).

29. *Ibid.*

30. I am indebted for advice on the school boards to Mrs. Gill Sutherland of Newnham College, Cambridge.

31. *Sunderland Times* 14, 17 Jan. 1871. *Newcastle Daily Chronicle*, 13 Jan. 1871.

32. *Reform League Papers*, Bishopsgate Institute, London. Election Agents' Reports, Sunderland.

CHAPTER 8

Regional Contrasts in Norwegian Politics

1. Lars A. Havstad, "Stortingsvalgene i 1882," *Nyt Tidsskr.* 1, 1882, pp. 587–595. "De politiske partiers fordeling i Norge," *Nyt Tidsskr.* 2, 1883, pp. 490–502. "Adressene til ministeriet Selmer," *ibid.*, pp. 595–606.

2. Originally issued in the periodical *Ringeren*, later as a book by Jacob Dybwads Forlag, Kristiania 1899, new edition by Det Norrøne Forlag, Oslo 1934, and again in 1943, then clearly with the support of the National Socialist authorities.

3. "Die Entwicklung der Arbeiterbewegung in den drei skadinavischen Ländern," *Arch. f. Gesch. des Sozialismus* 10, 1922, pp. 329–361.

4. *Arbeidermiljø under det industrielle gjennombrudd* (Oslo: The University Press, 1958).

5. "Litt om motsetninga mellom Austlandet og Vestlandet," *Syn og Segn* 63 (3) 1957, pp. 97–114.

6. Set out in S. Rokkan and H. Valen, "Parties, elections and political behaviour in the Northern countries," pp. 120–126, in O. Stammer, *ed.*, *Politische Forschung*, Cologne, Westdeutscher Verlag, 1960, cf. S. Rokkan, "Political Research in Norway 1960–65," *Scandinavian Political Studies*, Vol. I, 1966, pp. 266–280.

7. S. Rokkan and H. Valen, "The mobilization of the periphery," pp. 111–159, in S. Rokkan, *ed.*, *Approaches to the Study of Political Participation*, Bergen, The Chr. Michelsen Institute, 1962, to be reprinted in S. Rokkan, *Citizens, Elections, Parties* (Oslo: Norwegian Universities Press, 1969).

8. For a more extensive analysis of the cleavages underlying the development of electoral alignments in Norway and for fuller statistical documentation, see S. Rokkan, "Geography, religion and social class: cross-cutting cleavages in Norwegian politics," in S. M. Lipset and S. Rokkan, *Party Systems and Voter Alignments* (New York: Free Press, 1967). For detailed information on the organizational structures and the political functions of the parties, see Henry Valen and Daniel Katz, *Political Parties in Norway: a Community Study* (Oslo: Universitetsforlaget, 1964, paperback ed. 1967).

9. "Sosiale klasser, politiske partier og politisk representasjon i norske bysamfunn, I: 1885–1897," *Tss. for Samfunnsforskn.* 2 (3) 1961, pp. 162–181.

10. *op. cit.*

11. For a detailed account of the early Unionist efforts, see Rolf Danielsen, "Samlingspartiet og unionen," *Hist. tss* 41 (4) 1962, pp. 202–320.

12. This trend has been documented in detail through content analyses of newspaper editorials by Svennik Høyer: his report will appear in *Scandinavian Political Studies*, vol. 4, 1969.

13. For further information see S. Rokkan and H. Valen, "An Archive for Statistical Studies of Within-Nation Differences," in R. L. Merritt and S. Rokkan, *eds.*, *Comparing Nations* (New Haven: Yale University Press, 1966); and also, S. Rokkan and F. Aarebrot, *Soc. Sci. Info.* 8 (1) 1969, pp. 77-84.

14. For examples of calculation procedures see J. Klatzmann, "Comportement électoral et classe sociale,", pp. 254–285 in

M. Duverger, F. Goguel and J. Touchard, eds., *Les élections de 2 janvier 1956*, Paris, Colin, 1957, and "Géographie électorale de l'agriculture française," pp. 39–67 in J. Fauvet and H. Mendras, eds., *Les paysans et la politique*, Paris, Colin, 1958; J. Desabie, "Le référendum—essai d'étude statistique," *J. Soc. Stat. Paris* 100 (7–9) 1959, pp. 166–180. For a general discussion of the logic of inferences from ecological variations, see L. Goodman, "Some alternatives to ecological correlation," *Am. J. Sociol.* 64, 1959, pp. 610–625; R. Boudon, "Propriétés individuelles et propriétés collectives: un problème d'analyse écologique," *R. Française de Sociol.* 4 (3) 1963, pp. 275–299 and the chapters by Hayward Alker, Erik Allardt and Tapani Valkonen in M. Dogan and S. Rokkan, eds., *Qualitative Ecological Analysis in the Social Sciences* (Cambridge: M.I.T. Press, 1969).

15. G. Carlsson, "Partiförskjutningar som tillväxtprocesser," *Statsvet. ts.* 66 (2–3) 1963, pp. 172–213. This follows up a series of regression analyses of results by province carried out by C.-G. Jansson, *Mandat-tilldelning och regional röstfördelning* (Stockholm: Idun, 1961). The originality of Carlsson's contribution is essentially this: he derives from a number of nation-wide surveys a series of alternative assumptions about the Socialist strength within each of six occupational groups, calculates for each alternative the expected aggregate vote for each province over a long series of elections and finally analyses changes over time and differences between regions in the discrepancies between observed and expected shares of the votes. He uses this technique to show that, on every one of the plausible assumptions about vote distributions by class, less than one third of the increase in the Social Democrat vote from 1911 to 1940 could be due to changes in the occupational composition of electorate: the rest of the increase must be due to increases in the party's share of the votes within each class. Such long-term analyses are considerably easier in Sweden than in other countries: the official electoral statistics for several decades gave details of the class composition of the electorate. We plan to try out a similar historical analysis for Norway, but this will be much more laborious given the greater difficulties

of collating census data and electoral statistics for continuous units.

16. In an unpublished monograph written within our program, Erling Saeter has shown for the Southern and Western communes that the Socialists have had the greatest difficulties in mobilizing their industrial potential in areas with high proportions of small industrial units and with high proportions of women in the industrial labour force.

17. Nos XII 79, *Jordbruksteljinga i Norge* 20, *juni* 1959, Vol. I, 1961, Table 1. In our calculations farms under 5 da. (151, 301 out of a total of 377,277) have been excluded. The few holdings within the boundaries of cities and towns have also been left out.

18. For a cursory review of information on the politics of Finnmark province see Nils Ørvik, *Europe's Northern Cap and the Soviet Union*, Cambridge, Mass., Harvard University, Center for International Affairs, Occasional Papers in International Affairs No. 6, 1963.

19. S. Rokkan and H. Valen, "The mobilization of the periphery," *op. cit.*, p. 116.

20. See specifically H. Alker and B. Russett, "On measuring inequality," in R. L. Merritt & S. Rokkan, eds., *Comparing Nations* (New Haven, Yale University Press, 1966).

21. First report published by G. Spilling, "Resultater av kirketelling og opinions-undersøkelse," *Kirke og kultur* 62, 1957, pp. 385–399. The raw data of the count were kindly lent us for transfer to punched cards by *Norsk Menighetsinstitutt*, Oslo.

22. A. Dolven, "Norsk avholdsrørsle," *No. tss. om alkoholspm.* 15 (4) 1963, pp. 185–228.

23. Recalculated from Dolven, *op. cit.* The classification in this count of regions does not tally completely with the classification used elsewhere in this article, but this does not affect the basic patterns of differences. Henry Valen will shortly publish a set of detailed tables for teetotalist attitudes and political choice.

24. For detailed reports on these surveys see Valen et Katz, *op. cit.*, Ch. 6 and Appendix A.

25. A detailed secondary analysis of the answers to this question has been carried

out by S. Brun-Gulbrandsen and J. G. Wallace, "Regner De Dem som avholdsmann?" *No. Tss. om alkoholspm.* 15 (3) 1963, pp. 129–155.

26. S. Rokkan and H. Valen, "The Mobilization of the Periphery," *op. cit.*

27. S. Rokkan and H. Valen, *op. cit.*, pp. 123–124.

28. *Op. cit.*, pp. 133–134.

29. See S. Rokkan and S. Høyer, *Samfunnsvitenskapelige undersøkelser om-*

kring den kommende folkeavstemning om Norges inntreden i EEC, Bergen, The Chr. Michelsen Institute, Nov. 1962, 29 pp., mimeo. This was a plan for a series of investigations of aspects of the proposed referendum. For further details on the 1963 crisis, see S. Rokkan, "Norway: Numerical Democracy and Corporate Pluralism," in R. A. Dahl, ed., *Political Oppositions in Western Democracies* (New Haven: Yale University Press, 1967).

CHAPTER 9

An Authoritarian Regime: Spain

1. Alex Inkeles, "Totalitarianism and Ideology," pp. 87–108 in Carl J. Friedrich, ed., *Totalitarianism* (Cambridge: Harvard University Press, 1954), p. 89.

2. Herbert L. Matthews, *The Yoke and the Arrows: A Report on Spain* (New York: George Braziller, Inc., 1957), p. 100.

3. Raymond Aron, Sociologie des Sociétés Industrielles. Esquisse d'une théorie des régimes politiques (Paris: Le Centre de Documentation Universitaire, "Les Cours de la Sorbonne," Sociologie, 1958), pp. 50–51.

4. Gabriel A. Almond, "Comparative Political Systems," *The Journal of Politics*, Vol. 18 (1956), reprinted in H. Eulau, et al., ed., *Political Behavior* (Glencoe, Ill.: Free Press, 1956), pp. 35–42, p. 40. Another formulation of the distinction between totalitarianism and authoritarianism developed independently of ours, but coinciding with it, can be found in an unpublished paper by L. A. Coser, *Totalitarianism, Authoritarianism and the Theory of Conflict. Developmental Models for the New Nations.*

5. To avoid any misunderstanding let it be said that this "mimicry" or "imitation," while not all the reality, is quite real in its consequences. Particularly so since it provides for some participants a concept of legitimacy which does not respond to reality and thereby creates sources of alienation among those initially attracted by the new system.

6. Joseph Schumpeter, *Capitalism, Socialism and Democracy* (New York: Harper & Brothers, 1947), pp. 232–302, esp. 269; Raymond Aron, *op. cit.*, p. 38; Seymour

M. Lipset, *Political Man* (Garden City, New York: Doubleday & Co. Inc., 1960), Chap. II, Economic Development and Democracy, p. 46.

7. William Kornhauser, *The Politics of Mass Society* (New York: The Free Press, 1959), p. 123.

8. There is no point in referring in detail to the extensive literature on totalitarianism since the works of C. J. Friedrich and Z. K. Brzezinski, Sigmund Newmann, Franz Neumann, Emil Ledere, H. Arendt, Barrington Moore, Jr., Adam B. Ulam, Raymond I. Bauer and Alex Inkeles, are well known. A recent review of the problem with references to the non-American literature can be found in the articles by Otto Stammer, G. Schulz, and Peter Christian Ludz, in *Soziale Welt*, Vol. 12, No. 2, 1961, pp. 97–145; Karl D. Bracher, *Die Auflösung der Weimarer Republik* (Stuttgart: Ring-Verlag, 1957); and K. D. Bracher, Wolfgang Sauer, Gerhard Schulz, *Die Nationalsozialistische Machtergreifung* (Köln: Westdeutscher Verlag, 1960) both sponsored by the Berlin Institut für Politische Wissenschaft, incorporate much of recent German scholarship on the breakdown of democracy and the establishment of Nazi totalitarianism. These monumental works should be used to supplement—and in my opinion modify—much of the dated but classic *Behemoth* of Franz Neumann.

9. Friedrich's definition was formulated in "The Nature of Totalitarianism," Symposium on Totalitarianism (*op. cit.*), pp. 52–53, and then expanded and slightly modified in C. J. Friedrich and Z. K. Brzezinski, *Totalitarian Dictatorship and*

Autocracy (Cambridge, Mass.: Harvard University Press, 1956), pp. 9–10.

10. There is no satisfactory study in Spanish or any other language of the Primo de Rivera Dictatorship. Dillwyn F. Ratcliff's *Prelude to Franco* (New York: Las Americas Publishing Co., 1957) is totally insufficient, even when it gives some useful information and translates some documents. The most important partisan source in favor is José Pemartin, *Los valores historicos en la dictadura española* (Madrid: Publicaciones de la Junta de Propaganda Patriotica y Ciudadana, 1929) and the collected writings of Miguel Primo de Rivera himself, *El Pensamiento de Primo de Rivera*, J. M. Peman, ed., Madrid, 1929.

11. A work on the economic policy of that time by Jose Velarde Fuentes is in preparation. For a list of the interest groups created during this period see Roman Perpiña, *De Estructura Economica y Economia Hispana* (Madrid: Rialp, 1952), pp. 317–320.

The interventions of the Dictator in the corporative chamber he created, often in answer to questions from the floor vividly illustrate the pluralism and autonomy of social forces during that dictatorship. See *Intervenciones en la Asamblea Nacional del General Primo de Rivera* (Madrid, 1930). The comparison with the Cortes of the present regime shows the range of pluralism vs. concentration of power in such systems.

12. L. Vincent Padgett, "Mexico's One-Party System: A Re-Evaluation," *APSR*, Vol. 51, No. 4 (December 1957); reprinted in Roy C. Macridis and Bernard E. Brown, *Comparative Politics* (Homewood, Ill.: The Dorsey Press, 1961), pp. 193–197, see p. 197.

13. Point 27 of the Program of Falange Española, quoted in David Jato, *La Rebelion de los Estudiantes* (Madrid: CIDS, 1953), p. 262. For the English translation see the extremely valuable collection of activities of the regime in various spheres, by Clyde L. Clark, *The Evolution of the Franco Regime*, in 3 vols. (Washington D.C., n.d.), pp. 611–12.

14. The Nazi idea of Gleichschaltung is described by Franz Neumann in *Behemoth* (New York: Octagon Books, 1963, reprint of the 1944 edition), pp. 51–55. Much of the work of Bracher, et al., *Die Nationalsozialistische Machtergreifung, op. cit.*, is a carefully documented analysis of how this idea was carried out in the most diverse fields.

15. Ramon Serrano Suner, *Entre Hendaya y Gibraltar* (*Noticia y reflexion, frente a una leyenda sobre nuestra politica en dos guerras*) (Madrid: Ediciones y Publicaciones Españolas S.A., 1947). This is one of the most interesting books on the politics under the Franco regime by a key participant, pp. 38–39.

16. Theodor Geiger, *Die soziale Schichtung des deutschen Volkes* (Stuttgart: Ferdinand Enke Verlag, 1932), pp. 77–79. As he says with a very graphic German expression: "mentality is *subjektiver Geist* (even when collective), ideology is *objektiver Geist*. Mentality is intellectual attitude, ideology is intellectual content. Mentality is psychic predisposition, ideology is reflection, self-interpretation, mentality is previous, ideology later, mentality is formless, fluctuating—ideology however is firmly formed. Ideology is a concept of the sociology of culture, mentality is a concept of the study of social character." And so on.

17. The recent work by Morris Janowitz, *The Military in the Political Development of New Nations* (Chicago: The University of Chicago Press, 1964) shows the difficulty of defining the ideology of the military (often the creators of such regimes) except in some very general terms: nationalism, a certain xenophobia, often anti-communal sentiments, some puritanic tendencies, a proclivity for governmental intervention as an organizational form without much ideological justification and an "antipolitics" outlook (particularly divisive party politics and the mixture of making interest cleavages manifest and afterwards bargaining over them so typical of democratic politics). This "ideology" is so closely related to their professional training, experience and role, and so little related to any intellectual elaboration, that we would prefer to call it a "mentality." As Janowitz himself writes: "The 'mentality' of the military officer seems to be a mixture of half-developed but strongly held ideology and a deep sense of pragmatic professionalism." (p. 67).

18. General Naguib quoted by Daniel Lerner, *The Passing of Traditional Society* (Glencoe, Ill.: The Free Press, n.d.), pp. 242–243.

19. Nadav Safran, *Egypt in Search of Political Community* (1961), p. 253, quoted by Georg Kirk, "The Role of the Military in Society and Government: Egypt," in Sidney Nettleton Fisher, ed., *The Military in the Middle East* (Columbus, Ohio: Ohio State University Press, 1963), p. 84.

20. As quoted in Gernando de Valdesoto, *Francisco Franco* (Madrid: Afrodisio Aguado, S.A. 1943), pp. 115–117. A very similar reference to the liberal values that were not realized can be found in Francisco Franco, *Palabras del Caudillo* (19 abril 1937–31 dicimbre 1938) (Ediciones FE, 1939), p. 287 (dated 1938).

21. Getulio Vargas, *Nova Politica de Brasil, De Alianca Liberal as realizacoes do primeiro ano de governo* 1930–1931 (Rio Janeiro: Livraria Jose Olympio, 1938), p. 63, from a speech on October 4, 1930.

22. Alex Inkeles, "The Totalitarian Mystique: Some Impressions of the Dynamics of Totalitarian Society," *op. cit.*, p. 91.

23. On the relations between Church and State and the different tendencies within Spanish Catholicism see William Ebenstein, *Church and State in Franco Spain* (Center of International Studies, Princeton University, 1960).

24. Immanuel Wallerstein, *Africa. The Politics of Independence* (New York: Vintage Books, 1961), pp. 96–97. Refers to the differences in mobilization in the different single-party systems in Africa, which "at least in theory" are mass parties. In theory the Spanish single-party is also a mass party and in recent years José Luis de Arrese has spoken of the need to revitalize the party and even initiated—when he was Secretary General—attempts in that direction. See his collection of writings: *Hacio una Meta Institucional* (Madrid: Ediciones del Movimiento, n.d.), pp. 113–126.

25. Raymond Aron, *op. cit.*, p. 50.

26. The notion of "populist" regimes has been used by Morroe Berger, *The Arab World Today* (Garden City, New York: Doubleday & Co. 1962), pp. 418–423, and in some interpretations of Latin-American dictatorships to distinguish regimes like Vargas' Estado Novo and Peron's Justicialismo from more old-fashioned military dictatorships.

27. This pattern of passive support rather than mobilization has also been noted by Dionisio Ridruejo, *Escrito en España* (Buenos Aires: Losada, S. A., 1962), when he writes: "... the creation of a political desert has gone much further than it went initially: the destruction of specific political forces of the people and the loss of authenticity or increasing neutralization of those that the (civil) war brought about with its enthusiastic and ambivalent pressures toward an emergency politization. ... Spaniards have been shrunk to their private life without other interests or horizons. This fits the wishes of the groups socially threatened by the popularization of the state and the tastes of the traditional class, attached to its old habits (of passivity).

This makes our case in its superficial style closer to the longing for conformity of certain free societies than to the asceticism of imposed obedience in other societies of absolute regimes. [He means totalitarian systems.] In these, in fact, there is no depolitization in the sense of the reduction of the citizens to the sphere of private life as a consequence of the monopoly of public functions in the hands of an all powerful minority. The monopoly exists, but the intense effort of the minority has been precisely to deprive private life of autonomy and scope and to promote a maximum identification of man and citizen, or to say it in another way infuse to all activities—in occasion even to the most intimate ones—a public dimension. That alternative is something far from pleasant, but it is something different and even the opposite to conformism and, obviously, to the pseudoconformity of which we were speaking."

This work also gives the reader some feeling for the "participatory phase" of the Regime under the influence of Fascist ideas and for how the transition to a more apathetic but more pluralistic political climate took place.

This text of an acute and exiled critic of the regime who, himself, participated in his youthful days in the effort of mobilization under a fascist sign as propaganda chief confirm, independently, our analysis.

His book, written as the title suggests as a critic of the regime who had lived the regime "from the inside", is one of the most useful sources if a reader wants to get a feel for the social forces, institutions, political mentalities supporting the regime, and for its evolution since the days of the civil war. It is a work in the best tradition of the political essay by an active politician. To understand today's Spain, this book is more useful than many by friends of the regime and than most of those written by its enemies.

28. See the data on the role of the Mexican PRI at the local level in a forthcoming paper by Linda Mirin and Arthur Stinchcombe on "The Political Mobilization of Mexican Peasants".

29. My research on voluntary associations in Spain shows that the number of all kinds of associations varies directly with per capita income or industrialization, and less so with education. So in the five provinces with highest per capita income, the number of associations was 53.8 per 100,000 in the capital and 46.1 in the rest of the province, in the five of lowest income, respectively 35.9 and 11.4. Even the number of amateur soccer—the national sport—players is highest in industrial regions like Catalonia (3.0 per thousand) and Vizcaya (2.8) and lowest in the economically underdeveloped areas: Extremadura (0.4), and Andalucia (0.9). This relation—with some interesting variations—holds in general even for Catholic Action, and when political traditions are held constant, for the women's branch of the Falange.

30. C. A. Macartney, *October Fifteenth. A History of Modern Hungary, 1929–1945* (Edinburgh at the University Press, 1957), pp. 37–38. See also pp. 49–60 for the excellent characterization of Horthy, who is certainly a good example of one type of authoritarian leadership. The whole book is useful for understanding the ambivalences and contradictory tendencies in such regimes.

31. I use these terms in the sense they have been introduced by G. Almond and S. Verba in *The Civic Culture. Political Attitudes and Democracy in Five Nations* (Princeton: Princeton University Press, 1963).

32. From the study by the Italian socio-logist Luciano Cavalli, *Quartiere operaio*, pp. 25–64, as quoted by Joseph A. Raffaele, *Labor Leadership in Italy and Denmark* (Madison: The University of Wisconsin Press, 1962), p. 44.

33. Data from a study on voluntary associations in Spain, based on a breakdown by province and date of founding of 8,329 associations registered until 1960. In provinces with a number of associations above the national average, 50 per cent had been founded since 1950, while in a sample of those below the national average it was 73 per cent, 50 per cent of them between 1955–56.

34. Georges Lavau, "Les aspects socio-culturels de la dépolitisation" in *La Dépolitisation, Mythe ou Réalité?* ed. by G. Vedel, *Cahiers de la Fondation Nationale des Sciences Politiques*, No. 120 (Paris: Armand Colin, 1962), pp. 167–206.

35. On the creation of the unified party, the Falange Espanola Tradicionalista y de las Juntas de Ofensiva Nacional Sindicalista, see Serrano Suñer, *op. cit.*, pp. 19–39 and Stanley G. Payne, *Falange. A History of Spanish Fascism* (Stanford: Stanford University Press, 1961) Chaps. 13 and 14, pp. 148–198. Payne's book is an indispensable source on the history of the Falange and its place in the regime.

36. Vide infra the data on the presence of the party in the elite. A report by de Arresse, in *Hacia una . . ., op. cit.*, on the attitude of the Falange toward municipal elections, October, 1948, presents the problem of the Falange Movement in these revealing terms:

"In presenting our candidates should we remember that we are a National Movement and include in our lists all those who, at least in theory [an ironic remark], always in theory, are on our side or remember how precarious the collaboration of people who have called themselves our sympathizers has been, and present only men who are unconditionally ours." (p. 61).

Later he notes how others could show dissidence with the regime while the Falangists were not allowed to do so, during years when the Falange was worn out, as he puts it, with the exercise of powers it was granted fully only when the time came to allocate the blame.

37. For a description of the slowness and

false starts in the creation of the Vaterland Front of Dollfuss, see Gordon Brook Shepherd, *Dollfuss* (London: Macmillan & Co. Ltd., 1961), pp. 103–109, who writes:

"Though Dollfuss had given the Front a flying start as a propaganda movement, its origins as a political organization were pitiful. For weeks after the Chancellor had issued his first nationwide appeals for membership no adequate apparatus existed to deal with the response. It was like a publisher advertising a book which he has neither printed nor bound."

Shepherd goes on to describe the bickering and negotiations with the various elements that were to be integrated into the party, to "remain," in terms of membership "basically the old Christian-Socialist camp dressed up in new ornately patriotic garb."

Janowitz, *op. cit.*, also comments on the difficulties found by the military in the creation of mass political organizations, see pp. 84–93. The difficulties of creating the National Union in Egypt have been commented on by most observers. Georg Kirk, "The Role of the Military in Society and Government: Egypt" in *The Military in the Middle East*, ed. by Sydney Nettleton Fisher (Columbus: Ohio State University Press, 1963) quotes a not unsympathetic researcher:

"When I was in the U.A.R. in 1960 I had the impression that no one took the National Union very seriously; certainly hardly anyone could give a clear description of its complex structure of committees and councils, although they were set out with detailed diagrams in many official leaflets and endlessly written up in the press, with the aim of popularizing the new system."

P. J. Vatiokis, *The Egyptian Army in Politics. Pattern for New States* (Bloomington: Indiana University Press, 1961) in the Chapter 5 dealing with the National Union Scheme is not much more explicit and does not present data that would allow a comparison of rates of mobilization. Macartney, *op. cit.*, contains numerous descriptions of such dominant, official parties created or reorganized from the top. For an extreme case see Chapter VIII, "Apolitical Politics," on the Union Patriotica of Primo de Rivera, in Ratcliff, *Prelude to Franco, op. cit.*, pp.

57–63. See also Pemartin, *Los Valores, op. cit.*, pp. 623–647.

38. On the Imperial Rule Assistance Association, see Robert A. Scalapino, *Democracy and the Party Movement in Prewar Japan* (Berkeley: University of California Press, 1953), pp. 388–389.

39. On the Army and Falange, see Payne, *Falange* (*op. cit.*) passim., and particularly pp. 207–208 on the maintenance of the monopoly of armed force by the army and the non-emergence of any militia type of units (like the SS or even the Milizia in Italy).

40. Serrano Suñer, *op. cit.*, p. 128.

41. H. Arendt in *Origins of Totalitarianism* (New York, 1951), pp. 387 ff. Her analysis may be contrasted with this summary by Herbert Matthews:

"The picture of Franco Spain that is firmly believed by the exiles is distorted and in many respects false. They picture a totalitarian police state that simply does not exist. They have no idea of the degree of tolerance that Franco permits so long as his position and the security of his regime is not threatened," *The Yoke and the Arrows, op. cit.*, p. 184, see also pp. 178, 183.

42. Nasser, as quoted by Vaitiokis, *op. cit.*, p. 239.

43. Franco, Chapter of a book, reproduced in the "Corriere della Sera" (December 4, 1938), p. 286 of *Palabras del Caudillo: 19 abril 1937—31.12.1938* (Ediciones FE, 1938).

44. Nasser, quoted by Daniel Lerner, *The Passing of Traditional Society, op. cit.*, pp. 246–247.

45. The alternative outcomes of this ambivalence: to turn over quickly power to the old politicians or to hold on to power without giving it any real political content, are well analyzed in Jose Antonio Primo de Rivera (the founder of the Falangist party and son of the Dictator) in his "Carta a un militar español," pp. 649–651, *Obras Completas* (Madrid: Ediciones de la Vicesecretaria de Educacion Popular, 1945), ed. and collected by Agustin del Rio Cisneros and Enrique Conde Gargollo.

46. A good indicator are the weekly lists of officers received by Franco that are as long as those of civilian officials and personalities.

47. In an interview with a leading industrialist and banker after probing about the influence that men of his prestige and influence in the business community could exercise if they acted united and presented their points of view I received the following comment: "As a Spaniard you should know better, you know very well that in the army collective remonstrances are never tolerated, only individual protests. So we go each separately through different ways, after agreeing, but never collectively."

48. On charisma and totalitarianism, see Franz Neumann, *Behemoth* (*op. cit.*), pp. 83–97.

On Weber's use of the types of legitimacy see Winckelmann, *Legitimität und Legalität in Max Weber's Herrschaftssoziologie* (Tübingen: J. C. B. Mohr [Paul Siebeck], 1952). The compatibility of the types of legitimacy with different types of political systems, particularly the coexistence of different types of legitimacy in democracy, is discussed by Wolfgang J. Mommsen in *Max Weber und die deutsche Politik 1890–1920* (Tübingen: J. C. B. Mohr [Paul Siebeck] 1959), Chaps. IX, X.

49. See Francisco Javier Conde, *Contribución a la doctrina del Candillaje* and *Representación Política y Regimen Español. Ensayo Político* (Madrid: Ediciones de la Subsecretaria de Educación Popular, 1945), mainly pp. 105–149.

50. We conceive traditional authority in the sense defined by Weber in his *Wirtschaft und Gesellschaft*. For a summary of this part of his work, only partly translated, see Reinhard Bendix, *Max Weber: An Intellectual Portrait* (Garden City, New York: Doubleday & Co., 1962), pp. 329–384. While we want to stress the conceptual difference between authoritarian regimes and traditional rule, we also want to suggest that they sometimes have elements in common and that the students of such regimes could gain many insights from Weber's analysis of patrimonial rule and bureaucracy as those of totalitarianism have gained from his thinking about charisma.

51. See Leonard Binder, *Iran: Political Development in a Changing Society* (Berkeley: University of California Press, 1962), pp. 58–89 and *passim*.

52. Binder, *op. cit.*, has emphasized the

coexistence of different legitimizing formulae and the consequences of this phenomenon, particularly in terms of increased alienation. See pp. 15, 20 and 59–63.

53. Many readers of Weber's analysis of legitimacy forget that in the initial paragraphs introducing the topic he notes that: "In everyday routine life these relationships, like others, are governed by custom and in addition, material calculation of advantage," his point however is that these elements and purely affectual or ideal motives of solidarity are not sufficient bases of domination, particularly in crisis situations, the ones that interest him and political scientists most. He also stresses that obedience by an administrative staff based only on such motives would represent an unstable situation. He does not intend to dismiss their importance, particularly in normal everyday life, nor their importance for the behavior of the mass of the population compared to the staff of the ruler. We feel that it would be as erroneous to ignore the elements of habit and self-interest particularly of the mass of the population as to ignore the role of legitimacy beliefs for rulers and staff in a political system. In this sense a concern with apathetic support and inactive alienation in dealing with political cultures is perfectly compatible with an interest in the problem of legitimacy beliefs. The relevant texts are in *Wirtschaft und Gesellschaft* Kap. III, p. 122, (Tübingen: J. C. B. Mohr [Paul Siebeck] 1956), the new J. Winckelmann edition; and in *The Theory of Social and Economic Organization*, translated by A. M. Henderson and T. Parsons (Glencoe, Ill.: Free Press, 1947), pp. 324–325.

54. *Op. cit.*

55. Political sociology has centered its attention on the relationship between social structure and political institutions, but with important exceptions has tended to neglect the analysis of how different political systems handle the "invariant problems" and, even more so, the dynamics of political change. While the three aspects are closely interrelated they cannot be reduced to the relationship of society and political institutions. In this paper we have consciously attempted to focus on the organizational aspects and the political process without seeing them fundamentally as reflections

of social bases. In a study of specific authoritarian systems and even more their emergence, evolution and breakdown, we would have to give more attention to the interaction between social bases and the political structure; or, to put it graphically, to add to a Weberian approach a more Marxist one.

56. On this marginality see mainly Daniel Lerner, *The Nazi Elite* (Hoover Institute Studies, Stanford: Stanford University Press, 1951), pp. 84–90.

57. The typical political mentality—ideology—of the bureaucrats see Karl Mannheim, *Ideology and Utopia* (New York: Harvest Books, 1936), pp. 118–119.

58. See Clark, *op. cit.*, Vol. I, p. 289, in the case of José Larraz and Pedro Gamero del Castillo ministers of finance and without portfolio, at the time of the change of government on May 19, 1941, while the dismissal of other officials contained the phrase.

59. W. Kornhauser, *The Politics of Mass Society, op. cit.*, p. 52.

60. Serrano Suñer, *op. cit.*, pp. 60–64, 123–125.

61. Personal interview, materials of which were incorporated into chapter 16 of Payne's *Falange, op. cit.*

62. From an exchange published in the *Boletin del ACNDP*, 1–15 april, pp. 607–608.

63. On the Opus Dei, in Spanish politics see Ebenstein, *op. cit.*, passim. However there is no good study of this new religious organization, its structure, membership, ideology, and much of what is written is undocumented. For the Opus position see Julian Herranz, "Opus Dei," in *The Homiletic and Pastoral Review*, January, 1962, with a bibliography of articles and official statements.

64. Arrese, "Nacia un meta," *op. cit.* pp. 212–213.

65. Social scientists raise similar questions, so Immanuel Wallerstein in, *Africa. The Politics of Independence, op. cit.*, writes: "The choice has not been between one-party and multiparty states; it has been between one-party states and either anarchy or military regimes or various combinations of the two." (p. 96), and: "At present many Africans cannot determine the limits of opposition, do not understand the distinction between opposition and secession. This is what the African leaders mean when they argue that 'our oppositions are not constructive.' It is not that they tend to be destructive of the government in power; this is the purpose of an opposition. It is that they tend to destroy the state in the process of trying to depose the acting government.

"This is particularly true because, in almost every African country the opposition takes the form of a claim to regionalism—a demand for at least decentralization in a unitary state, federalism in a decentralized state, confederation in a federation, total dissolution in a confederation. Regionalism is understandable because ethnic loyalties can usually find expression in geographic terms. Inevitably, some regions will be richer (less poor) than others, and if the ethnic claim to power combines with relative wealth, the case for secession is strong. . . . But every African nation, large or small, federal or unitary, has its Katanga. Once the logic of secession is admitted, there is no end except in anarchy. And so every African government knows that its first problem is how to hold the country together when it is threatened by wide disintegration." (p. 98) and we could continue quoting.

I would surmise that Franco, or the supporters of the Yugoslav-Serbian authoritarian regimes, would fully agree with these arguments. And in the case of Spain one cannot deny a certain legitimacy to the argument if one considers the behavior of large part of the Socialist party in the opposition during the October days of 1934, or that of Companys, the head of the Generalitat of Catalonia during those days, or the activities of the Basque nationalists, or those of the extreme Right opposition to the Republic . . . The distinction between opposition to the government, the regime and even the state, was certainly not clear to many Spaniards. (I am sure that Wallerstein would not agree with my application of his conclusions, but then I would suggest that those writing on authoritarian, single-party regimes, the role of the army as modernizer, etc., in underdeveloped areas, would specify further, how in the long-run, such regimes will evolve differently from those in the semideveloped regions of the West.)

66. From the declarations of Franco to the correspondent of *Le Figaro* on June 12, 1958, *ABC* (Madrid) June 13, 1958. The text quoted was important enough to deserve the headlines of the newspaper. Similar statements could be found throughout the political statements of Caudillo.

67. These quotations are respectively from Camille Alliali, Secretary General of POIC—Ivory Coast—and Sekou Toure—Guinea—quoted by Szymon Chodak, in a paper on "The Societal Functions of Party Systems in Sub-Saharan Africa," in E. Allardt and Y. Littunen, *Cleavages, Ideologies and Party Systems*, pp. 256–280.

68. Reinhard Bendix, "Social Stratification and the Political Community," *European Journal of Sociology*, Vol. 1, No. 2, 1960, pp. 3–32; "The Lower Classes and the Democratic Revolution," *Industrial Relations*, Vol. 1, No. 1, October 1961, pp. 91–116; and the chapter by R. Bendix and Stein Rokkan, "The Extension of Citizenship to the Lower Classes" in R. Bendix, *Nation-Building and Citizenship* (New York: Wiley, 1964). His study: *Work and Authority in Industry* (New York: John Wiley & Sons, Inc., 1956) is also relevant. See also the study by Guenther Roth, *The Social Democrats in Imperial Germany. A Study of Working-Class Isolation and National Integration* (Totowa: N. J., Bedminster Press, 1963). These studies as well as the comparative research on labor movements, like those of Galenson, should be taken into account before such ideas of unity, rather than painful integration by conflict, are accepted.

CHAPTER 10
Majority Rule and the Representative System of Government

1. See page 306 for an illustration of a data array associated with a product-moment correlation of +.6.

2. This scarcely need be interpreted as perversity on the part of the Congressman —Republican majorities that are slightly less than internationalist represented by Congressmen who followed Eisenhower's internationalism or Democratic majorities favoring internationalist policies but represented by Democrats resisting Eisenhower's leadership could account for the negative statement of policy agreement.

CHAPTER 11
The Hegemonic Party System in Poland

1. O. Lange, *Ekonomia polityczna. Zagadnienia ogolne* [Political Economics, General Problems], Warszawa, 1963, pp. 166–167.

2. B. Gałęski, *Chłopi i zawód rolnika* [Peasants and the Occupation of Farming], Warszawa, 1963, p. 150.

3. J. J. Wiatr, "L'avenir des institutions politiques dans un régime socialiste," *Bulletin SEDEIS-Futuribles*, No. 102, 1965.

4. S. Ehrlich, ed., *Studia z teorii prawa* [Studies in the Theory of Law], Warszawa, 1965.

5. J. J. Wiatr, "One Party Systems: The Concept and Issue for Comparative Studies," in E. Allardt and Y. Littunen, eds., *Cleavages, Ideologies, and Party Systems*, Helsinki, 1964.

6. C. Wycech, "Rodowód i działalność Zjednoczonego Stronnictwa Ludowego," [Genealogy and Activities of the United Peasants' Party], *Kultura i Społeczeństwo*, No. 3, 1964. The author provides interesting figures illustrating the growth of the Peasants' Party. In 1937, it had 152,000 members. In 1950, 194,000 members. In 1963 it had over 316,000 members. In comparison, in 1963 the Polish United Workers' Party had 1,397,000 members while the Democratic Party had approximately 57,000 members.

7. M. Duverger, "Sociologie des partis politiques," in G. Gurvitch (ed.), *Traité de Sociologie*, vol. 2, Paris, 1960, p. 44.

8. W. Zakrzewski, "W sprawie klasy-

fikacji systemów partyjnych" [On the Classification of the Party Systems], *Studia Socjologiczno-Polityczne*, No. 10, 1961. Other objections to the tripartite scheme of classification of party systems are also raised here.

9. First empirical works are, however, beginning to appear. See for example, W. Narojek, "Organizacja w układzie miasta" [Organizations in a City Setting], *Studia Socjologiczno-Polityczne*, No. 17, 1964 and W. Adamski, "Koncepcja 'grup interesu' w środowisku wiejskim" [The Concept of "Interest Groups" in a Rural Setting], *Studia Socjologiczno-Polityczne*, No. 19, 1965.

10. S. Ehrlich, *Grupy nacisku w strukturze politycznej kapitalizmu* [Pressure Groups in the Political Structure of Capitalism], Warszawa, 1963, and W. Wesołowski, *Studia z socjologii klas i warstw społecznych* [Studies in the Sociology of Social Classes and Social Strata], Warszawa, 1962, chap. 3.

11. In present-day Poland the Roman Catholic Church is beyond doubt the strongest and the best organized pressure group. It directly intervened in politics only once, during the election campaign to the Sejm in 1957, when its appeal that the whole electorate should go to the polls was interpreted as support for the political course represented by Władysław Gomułka, but the indirect influence which the Church has on the political attitude of a part of the society may not be ignored. The situation is complicated by the fact that there are in Poland three rival Roman Catholic political groups, which formally are not political parties, but which publish political journals and take part in the election by putting candidates on the joint government lists.

12. M. Jarosz, "Samorząd robotniczy jako element struktury społecznej przedsiębiorstwa" [Workers Self-Government as an Element of the Social Structure of an Enterprise], *Kultura i Społeczeństwo*, No. 2, 1965, and M. Hirszowicz, W. Morawski, and J. Feliks, "Warunki działania rad robotniczych" [Conditions of Activity of Workers Councils], *Studia Socjologiczno-Polityczne*, No. 16, 1964.

CHAPTER 12

The Typology of Party Systems—Proposals for Improvement

1. The International Comparative Political Parties Project covers about 90 countries and 250 political parties, a figure that includes only those sponsoring organizations which pass the 5 per cent threshold of seats. Cf. Kenneth Janda, "Retrieving Information for a Comparative Study of Political Parties," in W. J. Crotty, ed., *Approaches to the Study of Party Organization* (Boston: Allyn and Bacon, 1967), Appendix B.

2. *Political Parties and Political Development* (Princeton: Princeton University Press, 1966), p. 34. The four types proposed by LaPalombara and Wiener are: (1) hegemonic-ideological, (2) hegemonic pragmatic, (3) turnover-ideological, (4) turnover pragmatic (p. 36).

3. Cf. especially the classification of Gabriel Almond in *The Politics of the Developing Areas* (Princeton: Princeton University Press, 1960), esp. pp. 40–43, and its latest revision in collaboration with G. Bingham Powell, *Comparative Politics, A Developmental Approach* (Boston: Little, Brown, 1966), pp. 217, 259–298.

4. See P. F. Lazarsfeld, Allen H. Barton, "Qualitative Measurement in the Social Sciences," in D. Lerner, H. D. Lasswell, eds., *The Policy Sciences* (Stanford: Stanford University Press, 1951), p. 169: "by 'type' one means a specific attribute compound." The requirement of a classification mereiy is, instead, that the categories be defined by a single criterion. Whenever it is unnecessary to distinguish the classification from the typology, I shall use the term taxonomy.

5. This is usually the case with the parties located around the central area of the political system, i.e., the minor center-left and center-right parties. A limiting case would be the Italian Republican party (PRI), a party with an average return—

over a period of twenty years—of less than 2 per cent, which despite its micro-size has provided a majority for a number of governmental coalitions.

6. See the "blackmail party" of Anthony Downs, *An Economic Theory of Democracy* (New York: Harper and Row, 1957), pp. 131–132.

7. Maurice Duverger, "La Sociologie des Partis Politiques," in G. Gurvitch, ed., *Traité de Sociologie* (Paris: Presses Universitaires, 1960), vol. II, p. 44. Almond (*op. cit.*, pp. 40–42) specifies "dominant non-authoritarian," but provides no examples.

8. In Almond and Coleman, eds., *The Politics of the Developing Areas*, *op. cit.*, p. 480. Coleman, same volume, also finds "dominant" parties in India, Turkey and Mexico, plus Algeria, Nyasaland, Ghana, Tunisia, Malaya and Mali.

9. The text implies that the recourse to some tricky devices does not matter as long as it can be reasonably assumed that in a situation of fair competition the predominant party would equally reach the absolute majority.

10. This is notably the case of twelve States in the U.S. that Avery Leiserson calls "two-party cyclically competitive" (*Parties and Politics*, New York, Knopf, 1958), pp. 167–170. Whether certain party systems are to be classified under the "predominant" or the "cyclically competitive" labeling is largely a matter of convenience and of record. E.g., Norway's overall record is cyclically competitive, but during the period 1945–1965 Norway was a predominant party system (while, *pace* Duverger, Sweden never was).

11. Cf., among others, R. A. Scalapino, J. Masumi, *Parties and Politics in Contemporary Japan* (Berkeley: University of California Press, 1962). Japan is a predominant party system since the 1955 merger of the two conservative parties into the Liberal-Democratic party, which obtains almost two thirds of the seats in the Diet.

12. W. H. Morris-Jones follows the label of Duverger, but makes the point that "domination" rules out alternation, not competition ("Dominance and Dissent," in *Government and Opposition*, IV, July–September 1966, pp. 451–466). Therefore Morris-Jones is actually making reference

to what I call "predominance." In general, see W. H. Morris-Jones, *Government and Politics in India* (London: Hutchinson University Library, 1964); and the forthcoming book of Myron Weiner, *Party Building in a New Nation: The Indian National Congress*.

13. Uruguay can be considered an extreme case of predominance, for the "Colorado" party was victorious over the "Blanco" from 1868 to 1959. On the other hand, one may well wonder whether the real units are the *lemas* (parties) or instead the *sublemas*. In the latter case Uruguay represents a two-party disguise of a multi-factional reality.

14. The positioning is also justified by the limiting case of the "solitary" party, as R. Girod calls it in Allardt and Littunen, eds., *Cleavages, Ideologies and Party Systems* (Helsinki: The Westermarck Society, 1964), pp. 137–138. Girod applies the notion to a Swiss canton, but it could apply also to those States in the American South in which the Republicans do not even bother to contest elections, Surely, "solitary party" is less misleading than "one-party." A solitary party pattern could be defined a situation in which the opposition happens to fall below the threshold of rewarding contestation, i.e., to be at a subcompetitive level.

15. Moreover, each party of a two-party system can be viewed as an alliance at the national level of constituency parties which, in their safe constituencies, happen to be "predominant." In other terms, a predominant party pattern is—at the constituency level—a frequent outcome of a plurality single-member district system.

16. I draw the label (with a small correction) from Jerzy J. Wiatr, in *Cleavages, Ideologies and Party Systems*, *op. cit.*, pp. 283–284. I cannot accept, on the other hand, the conceptualization of LaPalombara and Wiener in *Political Parties and Political Development*, *op. cit.*, p. 35, which is far too broad.

17. *Cleavages, Ideologies and Party Systems*, *op. cit.*, p. 283.

18. The electoral arrangements amply testify to this conclusion. "Under the hegemonical-party systems, the existing parties and groups form a joint list. ... The leading role of one party eliminates

political rivalry between the various parties. ... An agreement as to the distribution of parliamentary seats, or seats in local government bodies, is concluded before the elections" (J. Wiatr, *loc. cit.*, p. 287). Additional insights can be drawn from the analysis of the Polish elections of 1957 by Zbigniew Pelezynski in D. E. Butler, et al., *Elections Abroad* (London: Macmillan, 1959), pp. 119–179. See also J. Wiatr, ed., *Studies in Polish Political System* (Ossolineum: The Polish Academy of Sciences Press, 1967), pp. 108–139.

19. The quotation is drawn from Wiatr, *loc. cit.*, p. 282.

20. *Political Parties and Political Development, op. cit.*, esp. p. 36. See *supra* note 2.

21. This is only a terminological amendment, since the definition remains as it was: a "quasi-authoritarian political system dominated by a single party which is pluralistic in organization, pragmatic in outlook and absorptive rather than ruthlessly destructive in its relationships to other groups," (*Political Parties and Political Development*, pp. 38–39).

22. E.g., Neil A. McDonald, *The Study of Political Parties* (New York: Random House, 1955), pp. 31–32.

23. One may equally distinguish, to be sure, among (1) authoritarian and (2) pragmatic-hegemonic systems. In the case of military rule, for instance, a high degree of authoritarianism with little ideological backing is a conceivable pattern.

24. I would actually limit to this instance Neumann's generalization that in a dictatorial system the party "serves ... as a necessary listening post." (In S. Neumann, ed., *Modern Political Parties*, Chicago: University of Chicago Press, 1956, p. 398.) Both the Italian Fascist party and the Nazi party were highly inefficient listening posts, for the dictator was told only what he wanted to hear; the case was not very different with Stalin.

25. It should be clear that my "information" is narrower than Lasswell's "intelligence phase" (H. D. Lasswell, *The Decision Process*, University of Maryland, 1956), for it applies only to a realistic flow of information.

26. *A Cross Polity Survey* (Cambridge: MIT Press, 1963).

27. The Colombian constitution of 1958 establishes that only two parties are permitted and that the seats will be allotted on an equal basis to the Conservatives and the Liberals, whatever the returns may be. The Colombian formula testifies to the fertility of man's imagination and thereby highlights the inevitable shortcomings of any logical scheme of classification. In substance it amounts to an electoral system which requires the incumbents to fight for their election.

28. Canada is currently anomalous on two counts: (1) the cyclical revival and persistence of two minor parties (the CCF/NPD, plus the Social Credit Party) which have at time prevented either of the two major parties (the Conservative and Liberal Party) from obtaining an absolute majority in the House of Commons, and, consequently (2) single-party minority governments. In particular, since 1921 third parties have kept either of the major parties from a legislative majority in six of the first thirteen parliaments, and in recent years only the 1958 landslide enabled the Conservatives to govern with a solid majority. The literature is extensive. See especially Leon D. Epstein, "A Comparative Study of Canadian Parties," APSR, March 1964, pp. 46–59; G. A. Kelly, "Biculturalism and Party System in Belgium and Canada," in *Public Policy* (Cambridge: Harvard University Press, vol. XVI, 1967), pp. 316–357; Hugh G. Thornburn, ed., *Party Politics in Canada* (Scarborough: Prentice-Hall, Canada, 1967) *passim.*, and particularly the chapter by James Meisel, "Recent Changes in Canadian Parties," which predicts a multi-party evolution of the Canadian system.

29. Australia is a dubious case in that only the Labour party is in a position to govern alone; the alternative, and the alternation in office, requires a coalition among the Liberal party and the (minor) Country party. At the constituency level, however, the latter two parties operate on the basis of a permanent electoral agreement and do not present candidates against each other. For a general overview, see L. C. Webb, "The Australian Party System," in *The Australian Political Party System* (Sydney: Angus and Robertson, 1954); and J. D. B. Miller, *Australian Government and Politics* (London: Duckworth, 1964).

30. For the previous twenty years the Socialist and Catholic Austrian parties adopted a "proporz" system of governmental coalition. Therefore Arend Lijphart rightly considers Austria a classic instance of "consociational" system (*infra*, notes 55, 56, 57). It should be noted, however, that each of the two major Austrian parties just fall short of the absolute majority. It is hardly surprising, therefore, that their choice was to govern together (until 1966) with a 95 per cent majority, rather than alone with almost no majority. A lucid analysis is F. C. Engelmann, "Austria: The Pooling of Opposition," in R. A. Dahl, ed., *Political Oppositions in Western Democracies* (New Haven: Yale University Press, 1966), pp. 260–283.

31. We would be confronted, otherwise, with the paradox that Austria qualifies since 1946 as the "purest" two-party system, since two parties obtain roughly 95 per cent of the seats with a system of proportional representation. Note, in contrast with Austria, that in New Zealand the third party (the Social Credit party) obtains a 7–9 per cent of the total vote with a plurality system.

32. See Anthony Downs, *op. cit.*, chap. 8. My argument is based, however, on a revision of the Downsian model. Cf. G. Sartori, "Modelli Spaziali di Competizione tra Partiti," in *Rassegna Italiana di Sociologia*, 1, Gennaio-Marzo, 1965, pp. 7–29.

33. In general, for a valuable discussion of those aspects of two-partism which exceed the limits of a taxonomical analysis see: Leslie Lipson, *The Democratic Civilization* (New York: Oxford University Press, 1964), chap. 11; and Leon D. Epstein, *Political Parties in Western Democracies* (London: Pall Mall Press, New York: Praeger, 1967), chap. 3 and *passim*.

34. For the Scandinavian area in general a recent summary overview is Nils Andrén, *Government and Politics in the Nordic Countries* (Stockholm: Almqvist and Wiksell, 1964). The chapters of Stein Rokkan on Norway and of N. Stjernqvist on Sweden, in R. A. Dahl, ed., *Political Oppositions in Western Democracies*, *op. cit.*, are very illuminating. The best on the Netherlands is—in the same volume—the brilliant chapter of Hans Daalder, "Opposition in a Segmented Society." On Switzer-

land see esp.: R. Girod, "Geography of the Swiss Party System," in *Cleavages, Ideologies and Party Systems, op. cit.*, pp. 132–161; and, in general, George A. Codding, *The Federal Government of Switzerland* (Boston: Houghton Mifflin, 1961).

35. Maurice Duverger, *Les Partis Politiques* (Paris: Colin, 2nd ed., 1954), p. 245, and, *passim*, pp. 239–246, 251, 261–265. The idea of a "natural dualism" was theorized in 1926 by Herbert Sultan. For a devastating criticism of Duverger's "eminently superstitious impression that phenomena occur in pairs," see Aaron B. Wildavsky, "A Methodological Critique of Duverger's Political Parties," *The Journal of Politics*, 1959, pp. 303–318.

36. Arend Lijphart notes with reference to my earlier essay "European Political Parties, The Case of Polarized Pluralism" (in *Political Parties and Political Development, op. cit.*, pp. 137–176) that "Sartori does not consistently draw the line between moderate and extreme multiparty systems at the same point" ("Typologies of Democratic Systems," *Comparative Political Studies*, No. I, 1968), p. 16, Lijphart is quite right. When drafting the chapter of the LaPalombara and Wiener volume, I was not clear-headed as to how the parties should be counted, and this explains my oscillations. It should be clear, therefore, that my present views place the dividing line not between four and five, but between five and six parties.

37. This is Sidney Tarrow's quick reading: "Sartori concludes that the PCI is outside the system altogether" ("Political Dualism and Italian Communism," APSR, I, 1967, p. 40). Since Tarrow builds his case on the argument that the Italian Communist party is not a "devotee or combat party," let it also be clear that nothing of the sort is implied by my notion of antisystem party.

38. Needless to say, if a party is actually dedicated to revolutionary preparation and activities, then it should be called a revolutionary party. Such a party is surely antisystem, but the obverse is not true: an antisystem party need not be, in actual practice, revolutionary.

39. From time to time Communist parties have entered short-lived "popular

front" coalitions, and currently participate in a coalition government in Finland. But they have never been given a controlling position (such as the Ministry of Interior, or the Defence Department), that is, they have never obtained, in Italy and France, a "power seizure" platform. In Finland the communists obtained the Ministry of Interior in 1948 and the country did not follow the Czechoslovak path only because the Finnish President alerted the Army.

40. In this vein Sidney Tarrow (*loc. cit.*, pp. 40–41) goes as far as to conclude that "the symbiotic stability of the Italian political system . . . depends precisely upon the existence of a Communist party like the PCI," and that the PCI should be credited with the merit of having "forced a conservative government upon a path of reform." In my opinion conclusions of the sort can be warranted only on the basis of the "mental experiment" recommended by Max Weber, i.e., by asking, "What would have been possible otherwise?" Thus Tarrow simply ignores the extent to which the "anticipated veto" of the PCI either provides a magnificent alibi, or paralyses whatever attempt at constructive reform. Furthermore, Tarrow argues the case as if no Socialist party existed, and triumphantly neglecting the political system, i.e., the structural stalemate produced by a Communist-Catholic either-or.

41. Duverger's thesis that "the center never exists in politics" (*op. cit.*) confuses the various aspects of the problem, and should be reversed: a center "tendency" always exists; what may not exist is a center party.

42. For a visual representation and some details see my chapter in *Political Parties and Political Development, op. cit.*, pp. 154–155.

43. It should be noted that this definition of "polarization" contradicts Duverger's usage. While I hold that a political system may be bipolar and not polarized, Duverger actually identifies polarization with bipolarity (e.g., *Les Partis Politiques, op. cit.*, p. 279).

44. For the distinction between the rationalistic and the pragmatic mentality, see G. Sartori, *Democratic Theory* (New York: Praeger, 1965), chap. XI; and "Politics, Ideology and Belief Systems," APSR, June 1969.

45. This contagion affects even the parties that would benefit, theoretically, from "catch-all" tactics, as Kirchheimer would have said. Thus LaPalombara has correctly noted that the Italian Catholic party, the DC, has acquired over the years a more ideological platform than it displayed under the leadership of Mr. De Gasperi. See "Decline of Ideology: A Dissent and Interpretation," APSR, 1, March 1966, pp. 15–16.

46. The thesis that the "obscurities" of coalition governments "dissipate civic interest," as Merriam put it, is usually referred to multi-partism in general. The text suggests that this is the case with extreme multi-partism, far less with moderate multi-partism.

47. It is not true, therefore, that anti-system parties may abide by *all* the rules of the game. In this respect at least, they surely do not.

48. On the subject of opposition, I wish to acknowledge my debt to the landmark volume *Political Oppositions in Western Democracies, op. cit.*, and particularly to the concluding chapters of R. A. Dahl, pp. 332–401. See also, in general, the English quarterly *Government and Opposition*.

49. For an attempt in this direction see G. Sartori, "Political Development and Political Engineering," in *Public Policy* (Cambridge, Mass.: Harvard University Press, vol. XVII, 1968), esp. pp. 288–297 .

50. Much of this evidence is based, in fact, on verbal behavior. In particular, many American observers obtain the feeling that Western communists are becoming "integrated" from interviewing. It would be nice to have Russian or, better, Chinese interviewers coming over, and to have their reports as well.

51. This is to cast doubts on the more recent evolution of Duverger's thought, to be found, e.g., in his *Introduction à la Politique* (Paris: Gallimard, 1964): "The Socialists that were revolutionaries in 1900, began to integrate in the regime in 1920. But they admitted this only after 1945 . . . Communist parties are evolving in the same direction in France and Italy" (pp. 266–268). Granted that we should distinguish between the words and the deeds, we should also distinguish, I suggest, between

the scientific and the persuasive discourses. Wishful thinking is essential to the latter, but does not belong to the former.

52. Out of the three countries, the French Fourth Republic is already a less "pure" case, for the right-wing pole of the system was represented by a protest attitude more than by outright opposition to the system: the Poujade vote, as well as the various reincarnations of the Gaullist stand, expressed "feeble loyalty" rather than straight "refusal."

53. The case of Israel is particularly interesting vis-à-vis the predictive potentialities of the model, for the observers did not expect the sudden reinforcement of the Herut party, i.e., of an extreme right-wing polarization, in reaction to the extreme left wing Mapam party (indeed an extremist party in the fifties). The suggestion conveyed by the example is that extreme pluralism "feeds back" powerful reactions all the way from one pole to its counter-pole.

54. See W. H. Morris-Jones, "From Monopoly to Competition," in *The Asian Review*, I, November 1967, pp. 1–12. This is not to criticize the article but to stress the misleading nature of the labels in current usage, for India is not a case of monopoly but of "predominance," and thereby already a competitive system; while competition may not be a cure if it becomes outbidding.

55. "Typologies of Democratic Systems," *loc. cit.*, pp. 33, 34.

56. *Ibid.*, p. 21.

57. *Ibid.*, p. 24. The behavioral attributes required from consociational elites are nothing less than the following: (1) ability to recognize the dangers inherent in a fragmented system, (2) commitment to system maintenance, (3) ability to transcend cultural cleavages at the elite level, (4) ability to forge appropriate solutions for the demands of the subcultures (pp. 22–23).

58. For instance, nothing in Lijphart's argument would have predicted, or can explain, why Western Germany has entered a consociational experiment.

59. Lijphart's conclusion that "there is no empirical relationship between the number of parties in the system and its stability" (p. 35) testifies, I submit, to this error.

60. See Carl G. Hempel, *Fundamentals of Concept Formation in Empirical Science* (Chicago: The University of Chicago Press, 1952), p. 51.

61. *Ibid.*, pp. 52–54.

62. See Arend Lijphart, *loc. cit.*, p. 7, and *contra* 46–47 p. 35.

63. See the initial scheme, *supra*, sect. 2.

64. These additional qualifications are drawn from my forthcoming volume, *Parties and Party System—A Theoretical Framework*, *op. cit.*, and are summarized, hereinafter, in an outrageously abridged form, for which I must beg from the reader more than ordinary tolerance.

65. Two countries are generally cited to prove the contrary, Mexico and Turkey. But Mexico bears false witness, since it is a hegemonic party system that has yet to cross the border. As for Turkey's transition to democracy in 1945–1946, one should not forget that Inonu's switch to a democratic constitution was a vital requirement for a small country that badly needed protection against the USSR. Actually a "spontaneous" passing to party pluralism occurred in 1930; and Ataturk swiftly reverted to the single party. This precedent gives ground to the suspicion that Inonu might well have followed Ataturk's example (when he was ousted by Menderes) had it not been for external pressure and the economic aid that was involved. This is not to deny the sincerity of the democratic goals of the Republican People's Party, but only to explain why Turkey is not a really "convincing" example. See *contra* Kemal H. Karpart, *Turkey's Politics: The Transition to a Multiparty System* (Princeton: Princeton University Press, 1959). Subsequent events—the hanging of Menderes and military intervention—add weight to the suspicion that low international autonomy rather than the achievement of democratic viability explain Turkey's present-day stand.

66. This is also to meet the point made by Leslie Lipson and others that "a party is, by definition, a part of the whole. As such, it signifies the existence of other parts, i.e., a coexistence of parties. To speak of a one-party system, therefore, is to employ a contradiction of terms." (*The Democratic Civilization*, *op. cit.*, p. 311.) See also Sigmund Neumann in *Modern*

Political Parties, op. cit., p. 395: "A one-party system is a contradiction in itself."

67. The text implies that the positioning, in Table 12-3, of the predominant party system abides by the logic of establishing a continuum, without detracting, therefore, from the fact that a situation of predominance is unrelated to the format.

Index

Abadan, Nermin, 11
Aberdare Association, 136
Abrams, Mark, 4, 7, 10
Abrams, Philip, 9
Abyssinia (Ethiopia), 41, 269
Acción Democrática (Venezuela), 37
Act of Disestablishment (1919), 143
Acta Sociologica, 80
Afghanistan, 269
Africa, 6, 31, 35, 37-38, 42, 260
Aggregate election data, British
  electorate growth, 115
  Labour Party, 109, 115-16
  regional party variation, 107-13
  voter turnout, 113-14
Agrarian Party
  Finnish, 51
  Norwegian, 95-96, 101-2, 195-96,
    203-6, 212, 214, 220
Agricultural Holdings Act (1900), 143
Akiwowo, A., 11
Alford, Robert, 6, 12, 158-59
Alienation
  forms of (*table*), 62
  types of, 60-61
Alker, Hayward, 118
Allardt, Erik, 3, 6-9, 12, 18
Almond, Gabriel, 90, 252, 262, 270, 326
Alphonse XIII, 270
Anarchism, working class, 28
Anarcho-syndicalism, 29-30, 37

Anomic alienation, 62
Anti-Revolutionary Party (Dutch), 34
Anti-system parties, 325, 337-38, 342
Anti-Tithe Leagues, 140
Antonescu, Ion, 266, 273
Antonio, José, 273
Apathy, mobilization versus, 259-64
Aprismo (Peru), 37
Arendt, Hannah, 266
Argentina, 35, 37
Aron, Raymond, 3, 5-8, 252, 254, 260
Arrese (Falange leader), 275, 279-80
Artajo, Martin, 273, 276-77
Asia, 31
  political parties in, 35, 37, 38
Atatürk, Kemal, 281
Atomized party system, 324, 349, 351
Australia, 158, 323, 331-32
Australian New Guinea, 57-60
Austria, 13, 34, 94, 97, 323, 331-32, 347
Austria-Hungary, 26
Authoritarian party, characteristics of,
  264-66
Authoritarian regimes
  apathy in, 259-64
  definition of, 255
  distinguishing characteristics of, 252-55
  dynamics of, 280-83
  elite members of, 271-74
  legitimacy of, 268-69
  mentality versus ideology in, 257-59

Authoritarian regimes (*cont.*)
  pluralism in, 255-57
  military in, 267
  party in, 264-66
  social control in
    media, 266
    terror, 266-67
  traditional regimes and, 269-71
Aydelotte, W., 162
Azumi, Koya, 11

Backwoods Communism (Finland),
    50-53, 55, 57
Ballot Act (Britain: 1872), 141, 142
Banks, Arthur, 331
Bean, W. W., 165
Bekombo, A., 6
Belgium, 35, 119, 346
  class tensions in, 26, 30-31
  limited pluralism in, 334, 336
Belknap, George, 287
Bell, Daniel, 6
Bendix, Reinhard, 5-6, 10, 283
Bernard, Stéphane, 10
Bernstein, Eduard, 27
Betancourt, Rómulo, 37
Binder, Leonard, 270
Bipolar party systems, 351
Bismarck, Otto von, 40
Blankstein, George, 5, 326
Blondel, Jean, 10, 118
Bolivia, 35, 37
Bolshevik Party, 43
Bonham, John, 157, 162
Bonilla, Frank, 39
Brazil, 35, 37, 159
Brennan, T., 136, 146
Britain, *see* Great Britain
Brougham, Henry Peter, 167, 169
Brzezinski, Z. K., 266
Bull, Edvard, 191
Bull, Edvard, Jr., 30, 191

Burke, Edmund, 97
Burma, 36, 38
Burnham, W. Dean, 107
Busia, K., 6

Cambrian Strike (1910-11), 147
Canada, 158, 331-32, 346
Canton, Dario, 11
Capecchi, Vittorio, 13
Capitalism, 38, 95, 312
Carlists, 270, 272
Carlsson, Gösta, 198
Castro, Fidel, 37, 40, 281
Catholic Party (Dutch), 345
Catlin, G. E. C., 6
Center Party, *see* Agrarian Party—
    Norwegian
Ceylon, 36
Chartism, 138, 162
Chile, 35, 37, 343
Chr. Michelsen Institute (Bergen,
    Norway), 3-4
Christian Democratic Party, 34
  Italian, 277
  in Latin America, 37
Christian People's Party (Norway),
    96, 101, 196, 201, 203-8, 210,
    212, 214-16, 219-20
Church of England, 132-33, 137, 138,
    140, 143
Clark, Terry, 18
Cleavages, political
  developed polities and, 24-35, 42
    Norway, 192-218
  emerging polities, 37-42
Codreanu, Corneliu Zelea-, 273
Cohesion, uniformity and, 45-46
Coleman, James S., 118
Colliery Workmen's Federation, 145
Colombia, 35, 331
Comintern, 102-3

Committee on Political Sociology of
the International Sociological
Association, 3-20
activities of, 4-5, 19-20
founding members of (*table*), 3-4
restructuring of, 17-18
Committee on Stratification and Mobility
of the International Sociological
Association, 3-5, 9
Committee on Urban Sociology of the
International Sociological
Association, 14
Common Market, Norway and,
195-96, 216, 218-20
Communist Party, 316-17, 337
British, Wales and, 118, 121
Finnish, 31, 34, 49-53, 55-57, 60
French, 29-30, 150
German, 27-28
Italian, 34, 339
in Latin America, 37
Norwegian, 96, 101, 196, 198,
201, 203-4, 216
Competitive congressional districts,
constituent/representative policy
agreement in, 299-303
Congress Party (India), 37, 317, 326-27
Congressional roll call behavior
antecedents of, 298-99, 303-5
constituent opinion and, 290-92
inter-party differences in, 294-95
intra-district differences in, 295-98
Consensus, political, 93, 102, 104
Conservative Party, 24-25, 34, 37
British, 108, 110, 112, 116, 166,
171-72, 174, 176-77, 179-82,
185, 189, 316
Wales and, 118, 121, 135, 139-40,
142, 149
Norwegian, 95-97, 100-2, 196, 202-4,
213, 215-16, 218-19, 345
Conservative Youth (Norway), 101

Contextual analysis, 118-19, 157
Converse, Philip, 12
Cooney, E. W., 138, 146-48
Cornblit, Oscar, 11
Cornford, James, 9, 117
Counter-pressures, depoliticization and,
80
Cowen, Joseph, 161
Cross-pressures, depoliticization and, 80
Cuba, 5, 281
Cumulative scale analysis, 287
Cymru Fydd (Wales), 140

Dagbladet (Norway), 219
Dagens Nyheter (Sweden), 65
Dampierre, Eric de, 5
Daudt, Hans, 12
De Gaulle, Charles, 22
Democratic Party (Poland), 316, 318,
328
Democratic political systems
distinguishing characteristics of, 251-54
legitimacy of, 268
military in, 267
participation in, 262-63
pluralism in, 255-257
Denmark, 30
limited pluralism and, 334, 336, 343,
345
Depoliticization, 64
electorate involvement and
Norwegian, 93-94, 98-102
Swedish, 78-90
ideology and, core values of, 68
meanings of, 65, 69-72
Norway and, 94-104
Sweden and, 64-65, 69-70, 78-92
types of, 71-72
Deprivation
diffuse, 55, 61
institutionalized relative, 54
Desabie, Jacques, 198

Diederich, Nils, 12
Dillwyn, Lewis Weston, 135
Disraeli, Benjamin, 40, 164, 166, 181, 185
DiTella, Torcuato, 6
Dittberner, M., 12
Division of labor, 45, 60
    definition of, 46
    organic solidarity and, 47, 54
Dod, C. R. P., 162-63, 174
Dogan, Mattei, 3, 7, 11, 12, 18, 198
Dollfuss, Engelbert, 259
Dolven, Arne, 210
Dominant party system, 317-19, 326-27
Durham, John George Lambton, 1st Earl
    of, 162, 174, 175
Durkheim, Emile, 9, 47-48
Duverger, Maurice, 9, 317, 326-27, 336

Ebbighausen, R., 11
Ecological analysis
    quantitative, 120
    voting behavior and, 117
        Norwegian, 198-203
        Welsh, 118, 149
Education Act (1870), 142, 144
Egypt, 38, 272
Eight Hour Day Bill (1909), 145
Einaudi, Mario, 28
Eisenhower, Dwight D., 309
Eisenstadt, Shmuel N., 3, 5, 6, 17
Electoral competition, majority rule and,
    294-98
Electoral Facts, 163
"End of ideology, the," 64, 93, 263; *see
    also* Depoliticization
Engels, Friedrich, 1, 30, 43
"Entideologizierung," 93; *see also*
    Depoliticization
Ethiopia (Abyssinia), 41, 269
Eulau, Heinz, 7
Europe, 25, 26, 30
    Marxism in, 42-43

European Economic Community (EEC),
    see Common Market
Evalenko, H., 119
Evans, E. W., 136, 145
Evans, Rev. Herber, 141
Expressive ideology, 72-74, 77-78
Extreme multipartism, 324, 348, 351-52
Extreme pluralism, 334, 336-37, 340, 343,
    346, 348-49, 351

Factor analysis, 50, 68, 119, 149-50
    principal axis, 121
Falange, 252, 256, 265, 272-73, 275-76,
    279-80
Fascism, 37, 252-53, 262-63, 265, 337
Festinger, L., 45-47, 53
Figueres, José, 37
Fijalkowski, Jürgen, 12
Finland, 127, 342-43
    communism in
        backwoods, 49-53, 55-57
        class tensions and, 31
        industrial, 50-53, 55-57, 60
        political cleavages and, 34
Finnish National Commission, 8
France, 1, 7, 12, 150, 343
    class tensions in, 26, 28-32
    political party structure in, 34-35, 40,
        325, 336, 338-39
Franco, Francisco, 252, 256, 258-59, 261,
    266, 268, 270, 272, 274-75
    elitist regime of, political pluralism in,
        275
French Revolution (1789), 34
Friedrich, C. J., 255, 266, 328

Galeski, Boguslaw, 314
Gallup Institute polls, 219
Gash, N., 162, 163
Geiger, Theodor, 257
Geographical distribution, voting behavior
    and, Welsh, 124, 127

German Federal Republic, *see* Germany
Germani, Gino, 3, 6, 11, 18, 36
Germany, 1, 13, 29, 102, 342
  class tensions in, 26-28, 31
  limited pluralism in, 333-34, 336
  political party cleavage in, 34, 35
Gini indexes, 205
Girod, Roger, 4
Gladstone, William E., 116, 166, 185
Goguel, François, 150
Gould, Julius, 7
Great Britain, 1, 9, 12, 117
  class tensions in, 24, 26-28, 30-31
  political parties in
    Communist, 118, 121
    Conservative, 108, 110, 112, 116,
      118, 121, 135, 139-40, 142, 149,
      158, 316
    electorate growth and, 115
    Labour, 26, 33, 95, 109, 115-16, 118,
      124, 127, 134, 136, 143-44,
      147-51, 155-58, 316
    Liberal, 108-13, 115-16, 118, 121,
      127, 135, 137-43, 148-50, 156, 158
    voter turnout and, 113-14
  regional political variation in, 107-9,
    149
    fluctuations in, 109-11
    Home Rule and, 111-13
    Welsh, 117-18, 121, 124, 132-34, 144
  two-party system in, 331-33
  voting practices in, 160-63
    age difference and, 176-77
    class aspects of, 166-76
    national public opinion and, 160,
      180-89
    religion and, 177-80
    split, 163-66, 181
Gruner, Erich, 11
Guest, Sir John, 135
Guttman scales, 85-86, 89
  analysis of, 287

Hagstrom, Warren O., 119
Hamilton, Richard, 12
Hansen, Andreas M., 191, 192
Haya de la Torre, Víctor Raúl, 37
Hegemonic party system, 317-19, 324,
  327-28, 349, 351
  Polish, 315-16, 318, 328, 330
  types of, 329-31
Henmer, Lord, 133
Herzog, Dietrich, 11, 12, 18
Hitler, Adolf, 266, 268-69, 281
Hochfeld, Julian, 3
Homans, G. C., 46
Home Rule, Irish, 111-13, 141
Horizontal pluralism, 321
Horthy, Nicholas, 253, 263
House of Representatives (U.S.),
  constituent/representative policy
  agreement in, 285-311
Howard, Perry, 5
Hungary, 253
Huntington, Samuel P., 299

Ideology
  consensus and, 65, 69, 78
  definition of, 65-69
  diverse styles of, 77-78
  functions of, 72-78
    expressive, 72-74, 77, 78
    instrumental, 77
    pragmatic, 72-74
    Swedish party, 75-77
  impact of, 70-71
  legitimacy and, 77
  manifest, saliency of, 70-71
  mentality versus, 257-59
  politics and, separation of, 70-71
  saliency of, 79, 81, 82
India, 327, 343
  political cleavage in, 36, 41
Indonesia, 38, 41

Industrial Communism (Finland), 50-53, 55-57, 60
Industrial Revolution, 43, 134
Influence, political, 94
Inkeles, A., 251, 255, 259
Institut für politische Wissenschaft (Berlin), 11, 13
Institute for Social Research (Oslo), 192
Instrumental ideology, 77
International Conference on Comparative Political Sociology
First, 7-9
Second, 9-10
Third, 10, 11-13
International Congress of Political Science, 4
International Guide to Electoral Statistics, 19
International Political Science Association, 9
International Social Science Council, 17, 19
International Sociological Association (ISA), 3, 11
Research Committees of, 3-4, 9
officers of (*table*), 13
restructuring of, 13-18
Iran, 41
Ireland, 134, 139, 141
Irish Disestablishment Act (1869), 141
Irish Home Rule, 111-13, 141
ISA, *see* International Sociological Association
Israel, 36, 343
Italy, 7, 13, 251-52, 270, 342-343, 345
class tensions in, 26, 28-29
political party structure in, 34-35, 40, 325, 336, 338-39

Jana Sangh Party (India), 41
Janowitz, Morris, 3-4, 6, 11, 17, 38

Japan, 36, 38, 41, 251, 327
Junta Politica, 256, 265

Kabu, Tommy, 59
Kaiser (author), 121
Kautsky, John, 39
Kennedy, John F., 73
KEY-scales, 85-89
Kirchheimer, Otto, 97
Klatzmann, Joseph, 198
Kornhauser, William, 5, 254, 274

L-scales, 85
Labour Party
British, 26, 33, 95, 109, 115-16, 316
Wales and, 118, 121, 124, 127, 134, 136, 143-144, 147-51, 155-58
Norwegian, 94-95, 97, 99-102, 195-98, 201, 203-4, 216, 218
Labour Representation Committee (Britain), 115
Labour Youth Organization (Norway), 100-1
Lambton, John George, 1st Earl of Durham, 162, 174, 175
Landauer, Carl, 30
LaPalombara, Joseph, 322, 328-29
Lasswell, Harold D., 272
Latent structure analysis, 68
Latin America, 6, 261, 280
political cleavage in, 35, 37-38, 41-42
Lavau, Georges, 263
Lebanon, 36
Lee, J. M., 117
Left Party, *see* Liberal Party—Norwegian
Legitimacy
concept of, 46
conflicts in, 53, 60
governmental, 252, 268-69
traditional, 269-70
ideology and, 77
Lenin, V. I., 268-69, 314

Lerner, Daniel, 5, 272
Lewin, Kurt, 263
Lewin, Leif, 72
Liberal Party, 24, 33-35, 37
  British, 109-13, 115-16, 162, 166,
    171-72, 174-77, 179-80, 182, 185,
    189
    Wales and, 118, 121, 127, 135,
      137-43, 148-50, 156, 158
    Norwegian, 96, 101, 191, 196, 198,
      203-6, 212, 214, 216, 219-20
    Swedish, 75-76
Liberationist society, 134, 139
Libertas (Norway), 95
Liepelt, Klaus, 11, 13
Lijphart, Arend, 343, 345-47
Limited pluralism, 255-57, 269, 271, 273,
  334, 336, 343, 346, 348
Linz, Juan, 3, 5-7, 9, 11-12
Lipset, Seymour Martin, 3-4, 6, 8-11, 14,
  17, 64, 254
Littunen, Yrjö, 8
Lloyd, Trevor, 109
Local Government Act (1888), 141, 156
Lorenz curves, 205
Lorwin, Val, 30
Louis Phillipe, 28
Lowell, A. Lawrence, 294
Ludz, Peter Christian, 12
Lukic, R., 4
Lutheran State Church (Norway), 208-10
Luxembourg, 35
Luxemburg, Rosa, 43

Macartney, C. A., 262
MacDonald, (James) Ramsay, 116
McKenzie, Robert T., 4-5, 7, 10
MacRae, Duncan, 287
Makler, Harry M., 11
Malaysia, 36, 41
Maltby of Durham, Bishop, 160
Manifest ideology, saliency of, 70-71

Marginal voters, 94
Marshall, T. H., 5
Martov, Julian, 43
Marvick, Dwaine, 6, 11
Marx, Karl, 1, 43, 54, 66-67
Marxism, 42-43, 57, 60, 66-67
Mass mobilization, electoral, 98-102
Matthews, Herbert, 252
Mayntz, Renate, 7
Meaninglessness, alienation and, 62
Mechanical solidarity, 47, 54
Media, authoritarian social control and,
  266
Merton, Robert K., 63
Mexico, 5-6, 35, 38, 255, 281, 326, 330
Meyer, Armin, 12
Michels, Robert, 1, 9
Miners' Federation of Great Britain, 116,
  145, 147
Minnesota Multiphasic Personality
  Inventory, 85
M.N.R., 37
Mobilization, apathy versus, 259-64
Moderate multipartism, 324, 348, 351-52
Moderate Party, Norwegian, 196
Moderate pluralism, 334-36, 348-49
Monopolistic capitalism, 312
Morgan, K. O., 136, 140-41
Morrish, D. J., 133
Multi-party system, 316-17, 319, 322
Multipolar system, 351

Naguib, Mohammed, 258
Nasser, Gamal Abdel, 258, 266, 268-69
National Liberation Movement (Costa
  Rica), 37
National Science Foundation, 11
Nationalization, Norway and, 95, 97
Nazis, 27-28, 251, 263-64, 267, 275
Netherlands, 12, 35, 334-36, 343, 345-47
Nettl, Peter, 10
Neumann, F. L., 9

New Guinea, Australian, 57-60
New Zealand, 331-32
Nigeria, 35
Nonconformists, Welsh, 121, 124, 127,
129, 131-40, 142-43, 146, 148,
150, 156
Northern Reform Union, 161
Norway, 9, 13, 30, 334, 336, 343, 345
Common Market and, 195-96, 216,
218-20
depoliticization in, 94-104
political parties in
Agrarian, 95-96, 101-2, 195-96,
203-6, 212, 214, 220
Christian People's, 96, 101, 196, 201,
203-8, 210, 212, 214-16, 219-20
Communist, 96, 101, 196, 198, 201,
203-4, 216
Conservative, 95-97, 100-2, 196,
202-4, 213, 215-16, 218-19
Labour, 94-95, 97, 99-102, 195-98,
201, 203-4, 216, 218
Liberal, 96, 101, 191, 196, 198,
203-6, 212, 214, 216, 219-20
Socialist People's, 196
regional political differences in
cultural distinctiveness and, 206-8
historical development of, 192-96
language dictinctiveness and, 211-12
peripheries of, 197-203
polarization of, 217-18
religious distinctiveness and, 208-10
socio-economic bases of, 203-6
temperance and, 210-11
Nuclear weapons, 95
Nuffield Foundation, 10
election studies of, 107

Øidne, Gabriel, 192, 193, 196, 208
One-party congressional districts,
constituent/representative policy
agreement in, 305-9

One-party system, 316-19, 324, 328, 349,
351
types of, 328-29
Organic solidarity, 47, 54, 60
Osgood, Charles, 88
Ostrogorski, M., 1, 9, 24-25
Oxford movement, 139

Padgett, V., 256
Pakistan, 38, 41
Paliau, 59-60
Palmerston, Lord (Henry John Temple),
166
Paraguay, 327, 330
Parkes (liberal agent), 162
*Parliamentary History of the Six Northern
Counties,* 165
Parnell, Charles Stewart, 141
Parsons, Talcott, 10, 72
Partido Revolucional Institutional
(Mexico), 256, 327
Party systems, 316-19
numerical classification of, 347
criteria of, 322-26
taxonomy of *(table),* 350
seven-fold, 324
ten-fold, 351
three-fold, 351
*Party Systems, Party Organizations
and the Politics of New Masses,*
13
Party Systems and Voter Alignments,
7, 10, 12
Payne, Stanley, 273
Peel, Sir Robert, 166, 181, 189
Peoples' Councils (Poland), 320
Perón, Juan, 37, 265, 272, 283
Peru, 35, 37
Pétain, Henri Phillipe, 259, 266
Pizzorno, Alessandro, 7
Plebs League, 147

Pluralism
  extreme, 334, 336, 340, 343, 346,
    348-49, 351
  horizontal, 321
  limited, 334, 336, 343, 346, 348
  moderate, 334-36, 348-49
  polarized, 334, 336-43, 348, 351
  political, 252, 259, 263, 270, 313, 320,
    330
    Franco regime and, 275-80
    limited, 255-57, 269, 271, 273
  social, 313-14
  vertical, 321
Poland, 7, 253, 281
  Catholic Church in, 320
  class conflict in, 314
  hegemonic party system in, 315-16,
    318, 328, 330
  interest groups in, 319-20
  Peoples' Councils in, 320
  political pluralism in, 313-14, 320-21
Polarized pluralism. 334, 336-37, 342-43,
    348, 351
  properties of, 337-42
Policy agreement,
        constituent/representative
  competitive districts and, 299-303
  congressional roll calls and, 290-92
  measurement of, 289-90
  one-party districts and, 305-9
  representative government and,
    285-89
  summary of, 309-11
Polish United Workers' Party, 315-16,
    318
Political cleavages
  developed polities and, 24-35
    Norway, 192-218
  emerging polities and, 37-42
Political competition, 341
  majority rule and, 293-94

Political sociology, 19
  comparative
    contemporary methodology in,
      2, 4, 20
    development of, 1-2
Poll Books, 163
Pollins, H., 146
Portugal, 252, 261, 330
Powerlessness, alienation and, 60
Pragmatic ideology, 72-74
Predominant party system, 324, 326-27,
    351
Primo de Rivera, Miguel, 256, 272, 276
Przyworski, Adam, 10
Public opinion, voting practice and,
    British, 160, 180-89
Pye, Lucian, 5

Reference groups, 53-55, 61
Reform Act of 1832, 163, 166
Reform Act of 1867, 141
Reform Act of 1885, 141
Representative government
  majority rule in, 284-85
    electoral competition and, 294-98
    political competition and, 293-94
  policy agreement in,
        constituent/representative, 285-89
Reza Shah Pahlevi, 270
Rhondda Association, 136
Right Party, *see* Conservative Party—
    Norwegian
Robles, Gil, 276
Rokkan, Stein, 3, 5, 7-8, 10, 12, 17-18,
    99, 159
Rose, Richard, 10, 12, 17
Roth, Günther, 10, 283
Royal Commission on Land in Wales,
    129, 131-32, 140, 142
Russia, 31, 43, 119, 127, 201, 252-53,
    281, 330
Safran, Nadav, 258

Salazar, Antonio de Oliveira, 259, 265, 272

Saliency, ideological, 79, 81, 82
  manifest, 70-71

Samtiden (Norway), 97

Särlvik, Bo, 13

Sartori, Giovanni, 3, 10, 12

Scheuch, Edwin, 5, 10, 12, 157

Schmitt, Carl, 272

Schumpeter, Joseph, 28, 254

Scotland, 108, 112, 116

Scott, Robert, 6

Seeman, Melvin, 61

Segal, David, 11

Self-alienation, 162

Selvin, Hanan C., 119

Shell, Kurt, 9

Shteynberg, V. A., 5

Siegfried, André, 117, 191

Silver, Allan, 5

Situational alienation, 62

Smelser, Neil, 61-62

Smelt, R., 119

Social change, attitudes toward, 57-60

Social control, forms of, 266-67

Social Democratic Party, 34
  Finnish, 49, 51
  German, 27
  nationalist, 37
  Swedish, 75-77, 91-92

Social pluralism, 313-14

Socialism, 44, 342
  Japanese, 38
  Norwegian, 95, 97
  in underdeveloped countries, 38, 42-43
  Welsh, 146

Socialist Party
  Dutch, 345
  in Europe, 24-25
  Finnish, 31, 34
  German, 27

Italian, 29, 34
  in Latin America, 37
  Norwegian, 345
  in Scandinavia, 95

Socialist People's Party (Norway), 196

Solidarity, 47, 54, 58, 60
  social, 45-47

Sotelo, Calvo, 273

South Africa, 113

Soviet Union, *see* Russia

Spain, 28, 251-52, 254, 342
  apathy in, 260-63
  authoritarian elite of, 272-75
    political pluralism in, 275-80
  authoritarian party in, 264-66
  ideology versus mentality in, 258-59
  legitimacy in, 269
  military in, 268
  pluralism in, 255-56
  social control in, 266
  traditional monarchy form in, 270

Split voting, 163-66, 181

Stalin, Joseph V., 266

Stammer, Otto, 3, 7-8, 11, 13

State capitalism, 95

Suñer, Serrano, 256, 265, 275

Survey Research Center
    (Ann Arbor, Mich.), 285-86, 288

Sutton, Francis X., 6

Sweden, 13, 74, 81, 334, 336
  class tensions in, 26, 30
  depoliticization in, 64-65, 69-70, 89-92
  party ideologies in, functions of, 75-76

Switzerland, 334-36, 343, 345-47

Szymon, Chodak, 11

Tenant/landlord relations, Welsh
  destabilization of, 138-41
  stabilization of, 141-43

Terror, totalitarian social control and, 266-67

Textor, Robert, 331
Thailand, 41
Tibet, 269
Tingsten, Herbert, 65, 68, 70
Tocqueville, Alexis de, 1
Torgersen, Ulf, 9, 11, 193
Tories, *see* Conservative Party—British
Totalitarian political systems
  authoritarian regime versus, 251-55
  elite of, 271-74
  ideology and, 257
  legitimacy of, 268
  military in, 267
  mobilization in, 259-63
  party in, 264-65
  pluralism and, 255-56
  social control in, 266-67
Touraine, Alain, 7
Tractarianism, 139
Trade-unionism, 26-27, 29, 32, 76,
  146-47
Traditional political regimes, 269-71
Treaty of Rome, 219
Turkey, 36-37, 41, 255, 280-81
Two-party system, 316-17, 319, 322, 324,
  331-34, 348, 351-52

Uganda, 35
Ulam, Adam, 7
Uncertainty, alienation and, 60
UNESCO, 8, 15, 17, 19
Uniformity, social
  mechanical solidarity and, 47, 54
  pressure toward, 45-46, 61
  types of, 49
Unipolar systems, 351
United Nations, 18, 36, 261
United Peasant Party (Poland), 316,
  318, 328

United States, 1, 44, 74, 107, 149, 158
  class tensions in, 25-26
  policy agreement in,
    constituent/representative,
    284-311
  two-party system in, 326-27, 331-32
Uprootedness, alienation and, 60-61
Uruguay, 35, 327, 332

Valen, Henry, 10, 13, 99, 159
Vargas, Getulio, 37, 258, 281, 283
Venezuela, 35, 37
Verba, Sidney, 80, 262, 270
Vertical pluralism, 321
Vichy government, 252-53
Victor Emmanuel III, 270
Vincent, J. E., 131, 140, 163, 171
Voter mobilization, Norwegian, 98-102

Wales, 108, 111, 116
  Northwest, 124, 127, 140
  rural, 127-29, 149
    landed aristocracy of, 132-34
    Liberalism in, 138-43
    tenantry of, 129-32, 133
  socio-political milieux of, 120-27
    contemporary reactions to, 149-56
  South, 118, 124, 127, 135-37, 143,
    145, 147-48, 150
  urban
    industrial relations in, 134-38
    Labour Party in, 143-49
  voting behavior in
    Britain and, 117-18, 121, 124,
    132-34, 144
    methodology and, 118-20
Watanuki, Joji, 39
Weber, Max, 1, 25, 268-69
Weimar Republic, 27, 28, 336, 338-39,
  343

Welsh Land League, 140
Welsh Sunday Closing Act, 141
Wesleyan Conference of 1833, 146
West Germany, *see* Germany
Whigs, *see* Liberal Party—British
Waitr, Jerzy, 3, 6, 7, 10
Wiener, Myron, 322, 328-29
Wildenmann, Rudolf, 12
Williams, David, 137
Williams, H. M., 148
World Congress of Political Science,
   Seventh, 9

World Congress of Sociology
   Fourth, 3
   Fifth, 5-7
   Sixth, 10-11, 14, 17
   Seventh, 17

Yemen, 269
Young Conservatives (Norway), 101
Yugoslavia, 321

Zakrzewski, W., 328
Zamoshkin, Y. A., 5